ANIMATED TV SPECIALS

the complete directory to
the first twenty-five
years, 1962-1987

George W. Woolery

The Scarecrow Press, Inc.
Metuchen, N.J., & London
1989

ALSO BY GEORGE W. WOOLERY:

Children's Television: The First Thirty-Five Years, 1946-1981.
   Part I: Animated Cartoon Series (1983)

Children's Television: The First Thirty-Five Years, 1946-1981.
   Part II: Live, Film, and Tape Series (1985)

British Library Cataloguing-in-Publication data available

Library of Congress Cataloging-in-Publication Data

Woolery, George W., 1931-
   Animated TV specials.

      Includes indexes.
      1. Television specials--Dictionaries. 2. Animated films--Dictionaries.
   3. Television broadcasting of animated films--Dictionaries. I. Title.
   PN1992.8.S64W66 1989   016.79145'3   89-5856
   ISBN 0-8108-2198-2

For my mother,
Leotia Pearl Sutton Woolery

And in memory of
Daws Butler, Les Goldman, Mary Matthews-Grow,
Bernard "Bernie" Gruver, Bill Scott,
Jack Silver, and Ken C. T. Snyder

CONTENTS

ACKNOWLEDGMENTS

For their valuable research assistance: Jim Fanning, who delved into materials in the Walt Disney Archives, Burbank, California; Sandra Archer, who provided reviews from the Margaret Herrick Library, Motion Picture Academy of Arts and Sciences, Beverly Hills, California, and the reference staffs of the Orange, California, Main and Taft Branch Libraries.

For their assistance in providing information and materials at the networks: Mike Schum, ABC Audience Information; Squire Rushnell, ABC, Vice President, Long Range Planning and Children's Programs; Elaine Kule, Linda Steiner, ABC Children's Programs; Cheri Nicklaus, ABC Press Information; Judy Price, CBS, Vice President, Children's Programs; Kevin McDonald, Mike Alexander, CBS Press Information; Nancy Delaney, CBS Program Information; Dorothy Austin, Rob Maynor, Bud Tennerani, NBC Press Information; Betty Jane Reed, NBC Program Analysis; Janet Ellingson, PBS Press Information, Los Angeles; and Victoria Pearson, HBO.

For the recollections and materials from the producers: William H. Stevens, Jr., Atkinson Film-Arts; Denise Ferguson, Ross Bagdasarian Productions; Joseph Cates, Karen Perlito, Cates Films; Dawnald Henderson, Children's Television Workshop; John Cosgrove, Carmel Wilson, Cosgrove-Hall Productions; Shamus Culhane, Shamus Culhane Motion Picture Enterprises; Carol Corwin, Anne Lieberman, DIC Enterprises; David R. Smith, Walt Disney Archives; Marian Effinger, Walt Disney Television; Bill Hutten, Tony Love, Encore Enterprises; Phil Roman, Film Roman; Pamela Vincent, Filmation Studios; Herb Klynn, Format Productions; Linda Rosenbaum, Hanna-Barbera Productions; Gerald Tripp, Hinton Animation; Faith Hubley, Hubley Studios; Chuck Jones, Linda Jones Clough, Chuck Jones Enterprises; Margaret Loesch, Dorie Wells, Marvel Productions; Lee Mendelson, Glenn Mendelson, Kristy Mendelson, Lee Mendelson Productions; Bill Melendez, Steve Melendez, Evert Brown, Bill Melendez Productions; Lee Mishkin, Lee Mishkin Animation; Donna Evans, Fred Wolf, Trudi Takamatsu, Murakami-Wolf-Swenson Films; Patrick Loubert, Linda Ekdahl, Deborah Patz, Nelvana Limited; Russell F. Harms, Mary Ann Barothy, Perennial Pictures; Adrian Woolery, Playhouse Pictures; Robert L. Rosen, Angela Owens, RLR Associates; Arthur Rankin, Jr., Heather Winters, Adrienne Davis, Rankin/Bass Productions; Lou Reda, Lou Reda Productions; Rick Reinert, Pauline

Weber, Rick Reinert Productions; Lynne Batchelor, Ruby/Spears Enterprises; Don Bluth, Cindy Ankney, Sullivan Studios; Carole Weitzman, Mary Lou Phipps-Winfrey, Sunbow Productions; Sarah Baisley, Mark Hoffmeier, Leslie Allery, Stephen Corn, Taft Entertainment; Thomas Mayfield, Ted E. Bear Productions; Eric Frankel, Dana Gallo, Warner Bros. Television; Lena Tabori, Welcome Productions.

For the helping hand of the distributors: Berle Adams, Berle Adams Company; Kim Breda, Blair Entertainment; John Claster, Claster TV Productions; Alan Press, Columbia Pictures Television; Diane Ripandelli, Coral International Television; Rosie Lynn Dahdouh, Crawley's International; Frederick L. Gilson, Gretchen Bonsall, Gilson International; Owen S. Simon, Marilyn Martin, Group W Productions; Richard Furth, Harmony Gold Productions; Janet Meyer, International Lutheran Layman's League; Teri Schaffer, KingWorld; Beth Mulnick, LBS Communications; Michele Obeji, Lorimar Home Video; Jeff Pryor, Lorimar-Telepictures (Lorimar Television Syndication); Linda Langergaard, Luther Church in America; Gerri Paré, MCA Television; Marvin Grieve, MG/Perin; Coleen Malone Villegas, MGM-UA Television Syndication; Daniel Mulholland, Muller Media; Diane Barkoe, Brenda Cherpitel, SFM Entertainment; Liz McDermott, Donna Benjamin, Scholastic, Inc.; Martha Strauss, Douglas Parker, Susanne Ritt, D. L. Taffner; John Garofolo, Twentieth Century-Fox Television; Henry Saperstein, Patty Saperstein, UPA Productions of America; Betsy Vorce, Louis Brewster, Lisa Merians, Viacom Enterprises; John Riggio, Worldvision Enterprises; W. P. Donnelly, Wrightwood Entertainment.

For the cooperation of the creative agencies and marketing organizations: Mary Barela, Applause; Claudia Boynton, Evergreen Marketing; Charles Shutt, King Features Entertainment; Zoann Merryfield, Hallmark Properties; Paul Pressler, David Gillies, Marketing and Design Group (MAD), General Mills; Jim Davis, Kim Campbell, Paws, Inc.; Charles Schulz, Charles M. Schulz Creative Associates; Patricia Hafer, Selchow & Righter; Jack Thinnes, Jorjene Ream, Sive Associates; Harvey Levin, Julie Garn, Those Characters From Cleveland (American Greetings); Lee Ann Brodsky, Lee Mendelson, George Pipal, United Media; Tom Drape, Sherrill Wringler, Universal Licensing.

And Steve Binder, John Cawley, Mike Colicchio, Mark Evanier, June Foray, Arnold Friedman, Cathy Guisewite, Mark Kausler, Bill Littlejohn, Dennis Lynch, Romeo Muller, James Parten, Charles Swenson, Tom Wilson, and Rudy Zamora.

_____ PREFACE _____

This is an encyclopedic listing of all the special animated television
presentations aired on the various networks or syndicated extensively
in the United States, from the first in 1962 through the 1986-1987
season. The entries include both daytime and prime-time programs.
Both animated cartoon and stop-motion animated puppet films are
documented with basic information to provide a historical profile.

Not included, generally, are those programs identified initially
with the theatrical movie genre, animated films first exhibited in
domestic theaters and later televised as part of a regular series or
as a "special movie presentation," such as Dumbo, Charlotte's Web,
and Snoopy Come Home. Also omitted are animated-cartoon programs
scheduled as part of a regular series, like the cartoon hours seen
on the weekly Walt Disney series or on Saturday mornings, unless
they were rebroadcast as specials.

Several made-for-TV animated movies, however, will be found
among the entries as well as theatrical animated short subjects later
reedited for special programming, such as the Bugs Bunny specials
and the Walt Disney cartoons and featurettes like Winnie the Pooh.
Several series' episodes described as a "special animated presentation" are included, such as Happily Ever After on PBS's Wonder-
works and Family Dog on NBC's Amazing Stories. A few hosted
animated-film anthologies, previews and illustrated films animated by
camera movement which were televised as specials also are documented.
Programs that used or integrated both animation and live-action are
included if the animation was predominant, at least 60 percent of the
film.

This is the first book to trace the history, growth and development of animated films broadcast as special television programming
in the United States through descriptive profiles. They contain a
wealth of features, and valuable cross-references are included to
assist identification. A standard format was created to arrange the
information in each profile in an orderly manner, as follows:

BROADCAST HISTORY

Includes the date each film program premiered, with identification

of the network and the day(s) and the time(s) it was aired, followed
by the date(s) of the repeat broadcast(s). For syndicated (SYN)
programs and cable-TV (CTV) presentations, reference is made to
the date or first year(s) it was aired, plus multi-option and/or repeats, unless otherwise indicated. AM or PM always refers to Eastern
Standard Time unless otherwise noted as Central (CST) or Pacific
(PST) Standard Time. In all cases multiple sponsorship is implied,
with various advertisers participating on a non-exclusive basis, unless the confirmed major sponsor(s) are listed.

PRODUCTION CREDITS

Includes the Executive Producer(s), Producer(s), Director(s),
Writer(s) and credits for Music and Lyrics as appropriate. The
production company, studios or supplier are all located in the U.S.
unless a foreign origin is noted. They are followed by the length
of the television program, given in minutes only if the running
time was longer than a thirty-minute program. If serialized, the
number of parts follow. All productions were presented in color
unless black-and-white (B&W) is indicated. The Distributor listed
is the last known of record, followed by the inclusive or hypenated
year(s). Reference is made to known Record Album(s) and Home
Video cassettes.

NARRATORS, HOSTS AND PRINCIPAL
CHARACTERS AND VOICES

Includes the narrators, hosts, special guest stars and the
major characters and known voices as applicable. Some supporting
characters and voice imitations are covered in the description. The
live-action Cast, Announcer and Vocalists appear as appropriate.

DESCRIPTION

Includes a brief summary of the content and sometimes the
background of the main characters. Pro-social themes and educational goals are mentioned when appropriate. Comments also note
the origins, reference to other related films, landmark films, historical and anecdotal background. Song titles from the musical films
are documented. Television Academy and Motion Picture Academy
awards are indicated. Also included are references to other major
films based on the characters and post-1981 and prior series described in Children's Television: The First Thirty-Five Years,
1946-1981, Part I, Animated Cartoon Series (Scarecrow, 1983) or
Part II, Live, Film, and Tape Series (Scarecrow, 1985), followed by
the page number(s).

SOURCES

For the Broadcast History the scheduling information is based on the program logs of the New York, Chicago and Los Angeles editions of TV Guide, cross-checked against the respective ABC, CBS and NBC Program Information department files and in some cases the TV logs of The New York Times, Los Angeles Times and the Orange County, California Register.

The production and voice credits, content and other data were drawn from the files of producers, networks and syndicators, press releases, promotion kits, TV Guide, reviews in newspapers, Variety, Daily Variety, The Hollywood Reporter and other periodicals. Extensive use was made of the author's personal collection of off-air and other video cassette recordings.

Some of the research for this project began at the Annenberg School of Communications, University of Southern California, Los Angeles, California, as an outgrowth of academic and professional interest. The book also benefited by suggestions from Tim Brooks, vice president for program research at NBC and co-author of The Complete Directory to Prime Time Network TV Shows (Ballantine, 3rd ed., 1985). A list of persons who shared in supplying information for this volume is contained in the acknowledgments.

The purpose of this reference book is to document and describe the animated films televised as "special" programs in the United States. Additionally, it was created to provide an accurate and substantive summary of their use as scheduled network and syndicated programming and their availability for home video entertainment. The author welcomes comments.

George W. Woolery
P.O. Box 3804
Orange, California 92665

INTRODUCTION

Television has changed the focus and form of the animated film, and one of the best examples is the animated special presentations. Relegated principally to the theater as short cartoons and movies during the first half of this century, animated films today are profoundly more pervasive as a part of the video medium. Not only has animation been adapted for periodic specials, but for television commercials, weekly series, weekday strip-series, mini-series, weekend morning blocks, brief inserts, program titles and promos, network and station logos, made-for-TV movies, music videos and home video cassettes. To an unprecendented extent, television claims and controls the king-sized share of animated film production and determines the art form's destiny.

Considering the short history of the animated video film, an astonishing amount of footage has been produced for television. By themselves, the 348 daytime and prime-time film series which have been documented in Children's Television: The First Thirty-Five Years, 1946-1981, Part I, Animated Cartoon Series (Scarecrow, 1983) represent an amazing panoply of artwork. Since 1981-1982, there has been a steady addition of new network Saturday-morning cartoon shows and extraordinary expansion in the production of new half-hour, 65-episode, weekday strip-series placed in syndication on local stations which has dramatically changed off-network children's programming. Yet, whether they were made for the networks, syndication or cable TV, the animated TV specials have contributed to television programming in a more dynamic fashion.

Prime-time animated TV specials have enjoyed extraordinary prestige among the video animated-film forms. Since 1965, they have been distinguished by annual Television Academy awards not granted to animated series with any regularity until the 1980s. They also have enjoyed exceptional audience exposure, far and above that of the Saturday and weekday series. In testimony to their enduring popularity, dozens of animated specials in first-run and repeats continue to delight millions of TV viewers each season. Despite their aesthetics or whether they employ limited or more fully articulated movements--as by themselves beauty and fluidity of motion can not guarantee a successful, entertaining or popular film--animated specials continue to flourish. Limited only by the wispy fancies of the creative mind, the art of breathing life into an inanimate form literally remains boundless.

xiii

This book documents the first 25 years of animated TV specials, from the first animated prime-time hour program in 1962 through the 1986-1987 season. Containing 434 individual film titles, it is the first book to single out this particular video genre and provides data not compiled in other directories on television programming. A definitive review of each film's broadcast history, credits and content has remained unrealized until this survey was accomplished. While the summaries may rekindle some fond memories, the purpose of this retrospective is not purely nostalgic, for many of the films are still seen as network repeats, dozens of others are aired regularly in syndicated reruns on local stations and more than two-thirds have been released on home video cassettes.

Historically, the animated TV special evolved from the TV spectacular, initially popularized as a 90-minute program, a NBC innovation in the early 1950s to which the web remained dedicated for many years before the other networks became active on a comparable scale. Later, the word "spectacular" was dropped for the less flamboyant term, "special." Created as an attractive single program and inserted into a regular network or station schedule as a preemption of regularly scheduled episodic programming, it gained importance when the rising cost of producing weekly series brought a steady decline in the number of first-run episodes a network bought each year.

Since the late 1960s, there has been increased use of such "one-shot" programs, with each network committed to presenting 70 or more specials each season. About 20 percent were animated specials in first run or repeats, although CBS often has exceeded the average and is by far the leading network to underwrite and broadcast the animated special program. The use of specials has allowed some advertisers to continue sponsorship when the cost of a weekly series became prohibitive for a single advertiser, to provide a kickoff event for special promotions, to target specific demographic groups and to provide prestige programming of their own selection. And it has permitted programmers to try out new ideas and formats. In the 1970s, the special fanned out into other areas, the daytime schedule and even weekly and monthly programs and special films made for syndication. By expanding the range of program fare, overall, the special presentation has improved the quality of television.

From a programming standpoint, it did not take long to recognize that an appealing special could provide higher ratings than the average episodic series fare. For example, Christmas specials traditionally have produced 20-plus ratings and high 30's shares, drawing larger audiences than the regularly scheduled programs which they replaced for a night, even though many were repeated year after year. And because they could help elevate a network's overall viewership rating, many of the enticing new animated specials and repeats have been broadcast during the "sweeps-rating" months of November, February and May.

With only a single, very brief middle commercial for Coca-Cola, One Hour in Wonderland (December 25, 1950), a Christmas show aired on NBC at 4:00-5:00 PM, was the first special program with cartoon elements, the forerunner of the "one-shot" animated TV special. Produced by Walt Disney Productions, it was hosted by Edgar Bergen with his dummies Charley McCarthy and Mortimer Snerd and by Walt Disney himself with music by his studio aggregation, the Firehouse Five Plus Two. The cost of the program, Disney's first made-for-TV, reportedly ran into six figures.

Taking place at the Disney Studios' Christmas party, the program was about half live-action and was pegged on the Magic Mirror on the Wall, voiced by Hans Conreid, that could make any wish come true. Naturally, everyone in the studio wished to see one of their favorite Disney films. Opening with "The Happy Song" from Snow White (1937), the show featured a brief scene with the Seven Dwarfs and used film clips of Mickey Mouse and Pluto, Donald Duck, Br'er Rabbit being chased in a carnival hall of mirrors from Song of the South (1946), and presented a preview excerpt of the Mad Hatter tea party from Alice in Wonderland (1951). In his review, Jack Gould of The New York Times wrote: "After several years of video puppets, it is heady wine for a television viewer suddenly to partake of the imaginative fantasy and entrancing humor which are the stamp of Mr. Disney's genius."

A sequel, The Walt Disney Christmas Show (December 25, 1951), aired on CBS at 3:00-4:00 PM and previewed scenes from Peter Pan (1952). Conreid repeated his role as the Magic Mirror, Bobby Driscoll was seen as Peter Pan and Kathy Beaumont as Wendy, who played hostess for the studio Christmas party. The Magic Mirror presented scenes from Snow White in ten different languages and one from Bambi (1942) in Hindustani. A small hand mirror, voiced by Bill Thompson, provided additional Disney animated-cartoon clips.

While they cannot be classified as "specials" in the pure definition of the term, the animated episodes seen on the weekly series presented by Walt Disney also preceeded the idea. These hour-long thematic shows, which began in prime-time on Disneyland (ABC, 1954-1958), recycled cartoons from the Disney library, adding new wraparound and tie-in footage and serving to popularize the studios' cartoon characters and animated movies. Aired under such titles as "A Pictorial Salute to Mickey Mouse" (October 27, 1954), "The Goofy Success Story" (December 7, 1955) and "A Day in the Life of Donald Duck" (February 1, 1956), their vanguard contribution to the "one-shot" concept can not be dismissed. Indeed, some of the programs were reedited and broadcast as special presentations later, particularly on NBC, such as On Vacation With Mickey Mouse and Friends (April 11, 1979), Happy Birthday, Donald Duck (April 4, 1979) and This Is Your Life, Donald Duck (February 22, 1980), and the Disney cartoons recycled for such new NBC programs as Disney's DTV Valentine (February 14, 1986) and Down and Out With Donald Duck (March 25, 1987).

Added impetus for the animated TV special arrived in the early 1960s, when audiences were introduced to eleven cartoon series broadcast in prime time on the three networks. The only big hit was The Flintstones (ABC, 1960-1966), the first and last regular cartoon series to invade the evening viewing hours successfully. Only four lasted more than one season, and of the total, three were placed in syndication and eight rescheduled on Saturday mornings. While most of these nighttime programs were short-lived, their ripple effects continue unabated. Since 1966, there has not been a cartoon series scheduled during a regular season after 7:30 PM on network television. Instead, programmers have preferred to dole out the prime-time animated film in small doses as a periodic special, usually telecast during the earliest prime-time hours, which affords a large juvenile audience.

With very few exceptions, among them the CBS programs The 2000 Year Old Man (January 11, 1975), Emmy award-winner Carlton, Your Doorman (May 21, 1980), The Romance of Betty Boop (March 20, 1985), and Emmy award-winner Cathy (May 15, 1987) and NBC's A Doonesbury Special (November 27, 1977) and The Coneheads (October 14, 1983), animated specials have been primarily juvenile-oriented, although adults do watch and enjoy them. Often promoted as family fare, the vast majority of the programs adhere to holiday themes, subjects drawn from juvenile literature or are centered around children's playthings, using popular TV-cartoon, comic-book, comic-strip and children's book and toy characters. An endless parade of comic cartoon characters and androgynous talking animals have helped save Christmas, New Year's and even Halloween. Seldom has the animated special presented an original story with new, unfamiliar characters.

Even though most of the films are largely formulaic and something less than pure "adult fare," there is no basis to denigrate the importance or validity of the prime-time animated programs. Not only do they provide an entertaining respite from interminable hours of live-action programming, but they deliver a viable younger market for specialized sponsors. To produce a half-hour prime-time thematic program that is somewhat unique and artistically attractive is challenging and laborious. The task requires the talents of highly skilled and veteran artists, complemented by an experienced production staff and in some cases, since the mid-1970s, supplemented by foreign studios for economic reasons. The time required, usually six to eight months, the artistic effort and the money involved are substantially greater than that expended for the average episode of a network Saturday morning or syndicated series. And producers of the genre regularly turn out some of the finest animated film seen on television--or, for its length, anywhere.

Commissioned by Timex and aired on NBC in color, UPA's dim-sighted cartoon star appeared in Mr. Magoo's Christmas Carol (December 18, 1962), the first made-for-TV animated-cartoon special.

It was also the first animated TV musical, an hour-long adaptation
of Charles Dickens' perennial holiday classic with a fine score by
Jule Styne and Bob Merrill, and a professional cast including Jim
Backus voicing Magoo in the role of Scrooge. Although there had
been prior cartoon musicals, this was television's avant-garde, an
impressive debut and thoroughly entertaining. Historically, it was
the pioneer, the beginning of an animated-cartoon genre for prime-
time programming, and its favorable reception encouraged the development of other characters and properties for such "one-shot" treatment.

Coinciding with the increased penetration of home color sets
and the conversion to full prime-time color schedules on NBC and CBS
in Fall 1965 (ABC would follow in 1966) and the spiraling growth of
half-hour color-cartoon programming on Saturday mornings by 1965-
1966, some very popular newspaper comic-strip characters provided
the dynamic breakthrough for the genre. A year previously, producer Lee Mendelson formed an association with Charles Schulz and
animation-producer Bill Melendez to bring the Peanuts clan to television in an entertainment format after their appearance in a TV-
commercial series for Ford. They made a pilot, but the biggest
names in television wanted no part of it. For more than a year, one
of the hottest cartoon properties languished until John Allen at McCann-
Erickson Advertising, seeking a holiday show for Coca-Cola, thought
the Peanuts folks would do just fine.

Normally a much longer task, but rushed to completion in three
months from a one-page premise, the result was A Charlie Brown
Christmas (December 9, 1965) aired on CBS. Kept very simple with
nothing fancy or "cartoony," it was considered an inked disaster at
a preview for network executives, who underestimated its potential.
A whopping surprise, the show turned out to be one of the highest-
rated animated specials of all time, capturing nearly half of all the
sets turned on in 1965, a 47 audience share, and racking up a 57
share for the repeat broadcast, December 11, 1966, a 51 in 1967,
and 54 in 1969. A highly acclaimed presentation, it received excel-
lent reviews and thousands of appreciative letters. The first animated
special to receive an Emmy award, it also received the first Peabody
award for an animated program, described as "... a little gem of a
show that faithfully and sensitively introduced to television the Peanuts collection of newsprint characters...." It was the first and only
animated-cartoon special to receive such prestigious dual honors.

A Yuletide classic, aired on CBS every year since its debut,
A Charlie Brown Christmas is the longest-running animated-cartoon
special extant. In several ways it broke with the traditional TV
special format: the Peanuts special was a half-hour show instead of
the then customary hour-long program; the cast was voiced by real
children, amateurs with absolutely no professional experience; and
it used an off-beat jazz score by Vince Guaraldi which introduced his
acclaimed "Linus and Lucy Theme" and included a one-minute segment

with Linus quoting from the Bible. In the wake of its unprecedented reception and ratings, the film instigated 27 Charlie Brown thematic specials on CBS through 1986-1987, three anniversary tributes and two compilations of short films, and the hour-long animated adaptation of the musical You're a Good Man, Charlie Brown (November 6, 1985).

These half-hour shows comprise the longest-running series of animated specials on television, spanning more than 22 years. No less than seventeen Charlie Brown shows have been nominated for an Emmy award. Three others were honored with Emmy awards: You're a Good Sport, Charlie Brown (October 28, 1975), Life Is a Circus, Charlie Brown (October 24, 1980) and Charles Schulz as writer for A Charlie Brown Thanksgiving (November 20, 1973). Also, an Emmy award was received for Happy Anniversary, Charlie Brown (January 9, 1976) for the best documentary. And the Schulz-Mendelson-Melendez Memorial Day tribute, What Have We Learned, Charlie Brown? (May 30, 1983), earned the trio their second Peabody award.

The half-hour cartoon special began to appear regularly in 1966 when a second series, featuring the characters from children's book author Theodor Seuss Geisel, debuted on CBS with Dr. Seuss' How the Grinch Stole Christmas (December 18, 1966). Produced by Chuck Jones and Ted Geisel and aired annually on the network since its premiere, the enduring holiday show, along with their second special, Dr. Seuss' Horton Hears a Who (March 19, 1970), garnered a Peabody award for the Dr. Seuss series. Subsequently produced by Geisel with David H. DePatie and Friz Freleng and later with Marvel Productions, the nine films that have been aired have included the popular Dr. Suess' The Cat In The Hat (March 10, 1971); Dr. Seuss' The Lorax (February 14, 1972); the first film not adapted from the books, Dr. Seuss' The Hoober-Bloob Highway (February 19, 1975); and the Emmy award-winners on ABC, Dr. Seuss' Halloween Is Grinch Night (October 29, 1977) and Dr. Seuss' The Grinch Grinches the Cat In the Hat (May 20, 1982).

The first black cast of cartoon characters seen in prime time arrived on NBC in Bill Cosby's Hey, Hey, Hey--It's Fat Albert (November 12, 1969), the first of five Fat Albert specials produced by Filmation (the last three were shown on CBS as holiday special programs). Adapting their theatrical featurettes for the 30-minute format, Disney studios presented the first of three NBC specials starring Pooh Bear in Winnie the Pooh and the Honey Tree (March 10, 1970). The fourth, Winnie the Pooh and a Day for Eeyore (April 6, 1986), produced on contract by Rick Reinert, premiered on the Disney channel on cable TV. Chuck Jones introduced the first of his three ABC specials starring Chester Cricket with A Cricket in Times Square (April 24, 1973) and his CBS trilogy from The Jungle Book with Rikki-Tikki-Tavi (January 9, 1975).

After the remarkable ratings success of a weekly five-program, half-hour Bugs Bunny prime-time series on CBS (April-June, 1976), using films reedited from the network's Saturday morning show, Chuck Jones also launched the most popular of the Warner Bros. cartoon stars in prime-time "one-shots." His made-for-TV Carnival of the Animals (November 22, 1976), with Michael Tilson Thomas conducting, was the first of fourteen CBS Bugs Bunny thematic specials. Jones also produced two other original programs, A Connecticut Rabbit in King Arthur's Court (February 23, 1978) and Bugs Bunny's Bustin' Out All Over (April 21, 1980) and teamed with Friz Freleng on a fourth, Bugs Bunny's Looney Christmas Tales (November 27, 1979). The others were reedited from previously exhibited theatrical cartoons, most programmed initially on the daytime schedule. Among them, The Bugs Bunny Mystery Special (October 15, 1980) was rebroadcast at 9:30-10:00 AM, Saturday, December 5, 1981, opening a new time-period line-up of the network's weekly children's series.

Other network series of half-hour prime-time specials have included a youthful Flip Wilson and his friends in the films from De-Patie-Freleng Enterprises featuring Clerow Wilson (NBC), the second to feature black characters in prime time; the Mendelson-Melendez specials with Babar, the Little Elephant (NBC); Shamus Culhane's trilogy featuring Noah's Animals (ABC); Thomas Mayfield's two films featuring Ted E. Bear (NBC/CBS); Cullen-Kasden Productions' three films with The Family Circus (NBC); the RLR Associates' and Murakami-Wolf-Swenson Films' trilogy presenting Puff, the Magic Dragon (CBS); Chuck Jones' two films with Raggedy Ann and Andy (CBS); Cates Productions' five specials with The Berenstain Bears (NBC); the Warner Bros. and Freleng's and Jones' films headlining Daffy Duck (NBC); and more recently the orange tubby-tabby, star of two specials from Mendelson-Melendez and four from producer Phil Roman on CBS, beginning with Here Comes Garfield (October 25, 1982) and including the Emmy award-winners Garfield on the Town (October 28, 1983), Garfield in the Rough (October 26, 1984) and Garfield's Halloween Adventure (October 30, 1985).

Spin-offs and rebroadcasts from the daytime children's schedule have provided a distinct group of network half-hour and hour prime-time specials. Active in the production of "one-shots" since their ABC musical spoof Alice In Wonderland (March 30, 1966), William Hanna and Joseph Barbera have been a major provider of such special series. A Flintstone Christmas (December 7, 1977) was the first of seven NBC thematic specials using characters from their caveman comedy. Presenting episodes from their hit Saturday morning series, The Smurfs (November 29, 1981) was the first of six films on NBC featuring the little blue folks, the others in original programs. Also from Hanna-Barbera, The Popeye Show (September 13, 1978) used CBS Saturday episodes and was followed by an original Valentine's Day show; Casper's Halloween (October 30, 1979) on NBC was followed by a Christmas show; and The Pac-Man Halloween Special (October 30, 1982), compiled from the ABC Saturday episodes, also had an original Christmas sequel. ABC's Pink Panther in "A Pink Christmas" (December 7, 1978) was the first of three spin-offs featuring the title character from DePatie-Freleng-Mirsch and NBC's A Chipmunk Christmas (December 14, 1981) was the first in a spin-off trilogy from Bagdasarian Productions and Ruby-Spears Enterprises. It's an Adventure, Charlie Brown (May 16, 1983) utilized six episodes created for the CBS Saturday morning series.

In another prime-time format, which inaugurated the "preview" special, Hanna-Barbera's hour-long show, The World of Secret Squirrel and Atom Ant (September 12, 1965), introduced two programs which were aired on the NBC Saturday morning children's schedule in 1965-1966. Similar previews followed on the other networks: Rankin-Bass's The King Kong Show (September 6, 1966), with two half-hour ABC episodes starring the great ape, and Filmation's 30-minute show on CBS, Archie and His New Friends (September 14, 1969), which introduced the series' new character, Sabrina, the Teenage Witch. In the 1970s and 1980s, the concept expanded from a preview of a single new series to a sneak peek at the network's entire children's line-up, hosted by popular prime-time stars. In a new approach, four episodes of Kissyfur (NBC, 1986-1987) were aired as prime-time specials by the network to promote its new Saturday morning series.

Joining a unique group in TV annals, comprised of just a few nationally televised programs, Winnie the Pooh and Tigger Too (November 28, 1975) and The Tiny Tree (December 14, 1975), both of which debuted on NBC, were aired on all three networks in prime time, the only animated specials to belong to that exclusive coterie.

The hour-long NBC animated-cartoon special, Return to Oz (February 9, 1964), marked the first entry associated with Arthur Rankin, Jr. and Jules Bass, another prolific pair of TV-special producers who went on to present a string of network "one-shots," including the perennial cartoon classics on CBS, Frosty the Snowman (December 7, 1969) and 'Twas the Night Before Christmas (December 8, 1974). Rankin-Bass became noted for their use of well-known properties, many adapted from popular songs, and the casting of film-star celebrities as narrators and voices for many of the characters.

Rankin-Bass pioneered the laborious stop-motion animated puppet film for "one-shots," a technique they called Animagic, used for seventeen of their prime-time specials. Narrated by James Cagney, the first was The Ballad of Smokey the Bear (November 24, 1964), an hour-long NBC Thanksgiving musical presentation based on the U.S. Forest Service's fire-prevention symbol. Using their Animagic technique, Rankin-Bass produced some of the most popular of the network holiday programs, including Santa Claus Is Comin' to Town (December 14, 1970) and its sequel The Easter Bunny Is Comin' to Town (April 6, 1977), both on ABC and narrated by Fred Astaire;

Here Comes Peter Cottontail (April 4, 1971) and The Emperor's New Clothes (February 21, 1972), both on ABC and narrated by Danny Kaye; The Little Drummer Boy (December 19, 1968) and The Little Drummer Boy, Book II (December 13, 1976), both narrated by Greer Garson and aired consecutively on NBC annually through Christmas 1980.

The most popular animated-puppet film of them all, Rudolph, the Red-Nosed Reindeer (December 6, 1964), produced by Rankin-Bass, is also the longest-running animated TV special of them all, holding the all-time record through 1986. The hour-long film has been aired annually since its premiere on NBC and on CBS since 1972. Narrated by Burl Ives, it was based on a 1939 story by Robert L. May which was adapted to music by Johnny Marks in 1949 and popularized by Gene Autry's recording. The song and the Rudolph character fostered two sequels seen on ABC, Rudolph's Shiny New Year (December 10, 1976), narrated by Red Skelton, and Rudolph and Frosty (November 25, 1979), narrated by Mickey Rooney, the first and only 90-minute animated-puppet special broadcast thus far.

Also pioneering in the longer format, the first made-for-TV animated-cartoon movie aired in prime time was The Point (February 2, 1971), an ABC 90-minute musical fable poking fun at conformity. Produced by Murakami-Wolf Films, it was the only animated special to introduce an original hit song, "Me and My Arrow" by Harry Nilsson, who supplied the concept and the score. John and Faith Hubley's 90-minute CBS special presentation, Everybody Rides the Carousel (September 10, 1976), described the evolution and end of the human life-cycle. And Rankin-Bass provided the acclaimed Peabody award-winning made-for-TV, 90-minute animated-movie adaptation of J.R.R. Tolkien's The Hobbit (November 27, 1977) on NBC.

The first made-for-TV two-hour animated special presentation, The Lion, the Witch and the Wardrobe (April 1 & 2, 1979), an Emmy award-winner from the Children's Television Workshop and Bill Melendez Productions, was serialized on CBS in two-parts on consecutive evenings. A sequel to The Hobbit, Rankin-Bass's The Return of the King (May 11, 1980) on NBC was the first two-hour made-for-TV animated movie. It was followed by Hanna-Barbera's syndicated two-hour movie, Yogi's First Christmas (November 22, 1980), Filmation's two-hour NBC special movie presentation, Flash Gordon--The Greatest Adventure of Them All (August 21, 1982) and the Rankin-Bass two-hour ABC films, The Flight of Dragons (August 3, 1986), The Wind in the Willows (July 5, 1987) and their two-hour film, ThunderCats Ho! (SYN, 1986).

Gene Kelly and Hanna-Barbera brought the first combined live-action and animated special to television on NBC, the Emmy award-winning Jack and the Beanstalk (February 26, 1967). Kelly reacted and sang with cartoon characters in an hour-long tuneful version of the classic fairy tale. Wraparound live-action segments were used for NBC's 30-minute Goldilocks (March 31, 1970), with Mary Frances Crosby seen in the title role and Bing Crosby with the rest of his family voicing the bears. Bill Cosby appeared on CBS as the title character spinning the animated tales on Aesop's Fables (October 31, 1971), a "host technique" used subsequently in various formats for several animated specials, including Cosby again in a hot-air balloon as a raconteur for Filmation's Journey Back to Oz (December 5, 1976) on ABC.

On the daytime schedule, NBC Children's Theatre (NBC, 1963-1973) used the live-action and animated technique to present a basic lesson in biology in All About Me (January 13, 1973), an hour-long microscopic trip inside the human body. For the ABC Afterschool Specials (ABC, 1972-   ), DePatie-Freleng and Herb Klynn produced two 60-minute combination films with similar themes, The Incredible, Indelible, Magical, Physical, Mystery Trip (February 7, 1973) and a sequel, The Magical Mystery Trip Through Little Red's Head (May 15, 1974). The CBS Library Specials (CBS, 1979-1982), aired periodically on the daytime schedule and based on juvenile books recommended by the Library of Congress, used the combined-technique for three hour-long programs from Bosustow Entertainment, beginning with The Incredible Book Escape (June 3, 1980).

Tales of Washington Irving (November 1, 1970) inaugurated a series of hour-long cartoon specials on CBS. It was the pioneer network animated-daytime special and the first of 24 films produced for the sponsor, Kenner Products division of General Mills, through Sive Associates. Broadcast between 1970 and 1983, usually around the Thanksgiving and Christmas holidays to promote Kenner's annual new toy lines, the concept was created and supervised by Jack Thinnes of Sive. The films aired under the umbrella title Famous Classic Tales, although initially for a time as Family Classics Theater, which was dropped when it was learned it was the copyrighted title of another prior series. Drawn from classic stories, fifteen specials were produced by Air Programs International, Sydney, Australia, and nine provided by Hanna-Barbera Productions.

The second film of Famous Classic Tales was the only 90-minute entry, A Connecticut Yankee in King Arthur's Court (November 28, 1970), which premiered on Thanksgiving Day, the first made-for-TV animated movie produced for a network daytime schedule. The CBS series included such API titles as The Legend of Robin Hood (November 14, 1971), The Prince and the Pauper (November 26, 1972) and Hanna-Barbera's first film for the series, The Count of Monte Cristo (September 23, 1973) and Davy Crockett on the Mississippi (November 20, 1976). Generally, the programs were aired twice on CBS before they were placed in syndication. An exception was A Christmas Carol (December 13, 1970), which was broadcast by the network annually through 1983. Some subsequent films, such as The Legend of Hiawatha (November 24, 1983), were later acquired by Kenner and aired subsequently under the umbrella title Kenner Family Classics.

The original API films were sold in 1983 to distributor D. L. Taffner and syndicated as "Animated Classics for Children," and the Hanna-Barbera films were placed in syndication by Worldvision Enterprises.

Offering a half-hour elementary lesson in geology with a trip through the layers of the Earth, the pioneer network Saturday morning animated-cartoon special was John and Faith Hubley's Dig (April 8, 1972), aired on CBS at 12:00-12:30 PM, preempting a rerun of The Monkees (...CBS, 1969-1972...). In the Fall, Hanna-Barbera's 1972-1973 Emmy award-winner, Last of the Curlews (October 4, 1972) marked the premiere of the inaugural season of the ABC Afterschool Specials. An hour-long film with an ecology theme, it concerned the plight of the Eskimo Curlew and the bird's fight for survival against the elements and man, the hunter. The studio followed it with an afterschool adaptation of Cyrano (March 6, 1974). Telecast on NBC Special Treat (NBC, 1975-1985) were several hour-long animated-cartoon films, It's a Brand New World (March 8, 1977), Treasure Island (April 29, 1980) and Oliver Twist (April 14, 1981).

An enduring series of new cartoon specials have been broadcast periodically on Saturday mornings on the ABC Weekend Specials (ABC, 1977-   ), an anthology of both live-action and animated programs drawn from popular children's books and novels. An animated classic from Joseph Ruby and Ken Spears about a puppy who searched doggedly for a boy of his own, The Puppy Who Wanted a Boy (May 6, 1978) prompted three sequels. Other "one-shots" included Weep No More, My Lady (February 10, 1979), The Incredible Detectives (November 17, 1979), Bunnicula, the Vampire Rabbit (January 9, 1982), Bad Cat (April 14, 1984), The Bollo Caper (February 2, 1985), The Velveteen Rabbit (April 20, 1985), and two films from Rick Reinert featuring ABC's tap-dancing cat who extolled the virtues of reading books, initially Cap'n O.G. Readmore's Jack and the Beanstalk (October 12, 1985).

Adapting the prime-time format which serialized best-selling novels and books, successfully pioneered by Roots (ABC, 1976), the ABC Weekend Specials is particularly noteworthy for introducing films in two and three parts on consecutive Saturday mornings. The Ruby-Spears' production The Horse That Played Centerfield (February 24 & March 3, 1979) launched the two-part concept which has included their studios' The Trouble With Miss Switch (February 16 & 23, 1980) and its sequel, Miss Switch to the Rescue (January 16 & 23, 1982); and Southern Star Productions' The Amazing Bunjee Venture (March 24 & 31, 1984) and its sequel, The Return of Bunjee (April 6 & 13, 1985). The three-part specials began with Ruby-Spears' Scruffy (October 4, 11 & 18, 1980) and was followed by Southern Star's The Secret World of Og (April 30, May 7 & 14, 1983) and DIC Enterprises' Liberty and the Littles (October 18 & 25, November 1, 1986).

The syndicated animated TV special emerged as early as 1965, when the first of two thematic religious series was placed in distribution.

Based on the Davey and Goliath (SYN, 1962-   ) stop-motion animated
puppet programs underwritten by the Lutheran Church in America,
Art and Ruth Clokey produced six half-hour holiday specials, beginning with Christmas Lost and Found (SYN, 1965-   ), using camera
techniques developed in their popular series Gumby (NBC, 1957/
SYN, 1965-   ). As well, the International Lutheran Laymen's
League sponsored four half-hour animated-cartoon programs featuring Benji and his dog Waldo, beginning with Christmas Is (SYN,
1970-   ).

In the 1980s, the syndicated animated TV special, along with
five-part mini-series and 65-episode weekday strip-series, made
strong inroads in non-network children's television. In particular,
the toy companies became a major factor in such programming when
their research indicated that network Saturday morning programs
were not the best way to build sales for new toys and playthings.
To introduce their new lines, the manufacturers turned to syndicated
specials broadcast in 100 to 150 major markets throughout the United
States in the early evening or during daytime hours on a specific
date or week, sometimes within a "window" which required the film
to be aired between two inclusive dates. Most of the specials were
offered on a barter basis with a primary advertiser who provided two
or three commercials on the program.

Enterprising sponsors developed several series of cartoon
specials for such syndicated programming, beginning with The World
of Strawberry Shortcake (March 28, 1980), the first of six specials
featuring the little moppet and her pastry friends created by Those
Characters From Cleveland (TCFC), an American Greetings company,
with the Marketing and Design (MAD) division of General Mills for
Kenner-Parker Toys. Others soon followed: The Care Bears (April
1983) from MAD and TCFC; My Little Pony (April 1984) from Sunbow
Productions for Hasbro Industries; Rose-Petal Place (May 1984) and
Rainbow Brite (June 1984) from Hallmark Properties; and The Blinkins
(Fall 1986) from MCA-TV and LJN Toys.

As well, there have been a number of syndicated "one-shots,"
among them The Special Magic of Herself the Elf (1983), The Charmkins (1983), Peter and the Magic Egg (1983), The Glo-Friends Save
Christmas (1985), Poochie (1985), Pound Puppies (1985), Star Fairies
(1985) and The Adventures of the Scrabble People in "A Pumpkin
Full of Nonsense" (1985).

Developed as "special" programming, several syndicated packages have been circulated by distributors to local stations, such as
LBS Communications' "LBS Children's Theatre" (SYN, 1983-1985),
an eclectic package with some foreign films, and mainly off-network
specials, like the Reader's Digest presentations from Gerald Potterton Productions; D. L. Taffner's "Animated Classics for Children"
(SYN, 1983-   ), with off-network films from API; Telepictures
popular "Animated Holiday Specials" (SYN, 1985-1987), principally

with off-network films from Rankin-Bass; "The Charles Dickens' Classics" (SYN, 1985-   ), produced by Burbank Films, Sydney, Australia, and distributed by Twentieth-Century Fox Television; and "Family Classics" (SYN, 1986-   ), an eclectic package from Viacom Enterprises with 20 films produced by Rankin-Bass during their formative years.

A recent development has been the syndication of first-run animated TV specials for the prime-time access period, 7:30-8:00 PM, and on weekend afternoons. Viacom Enterprises pioneered in this category with A Cosmic Christmas (SYN, December 7, 1977) from Nelvana Limited, Toronto, Canada, the first of six holiday films including The Devil and Daniel Mouse (SYN, 1978), Romie-0 and Julie-8 (SYN, 1979) and Intergalactic Thanksgiving (SYN, 1979). The number one rated syndicated animated special in 1980, The Christmas Raccoons (SYN, 1980), was the first of three "Raccoons" cartoons from Evergreen Productions, Canada. Also, Atkinson Film-Arts, Ottawa, Canada, produced a series of holiday and other "Cartoon Classics," beginning with The Little Brown Burro (SYN, December 13, 1978), including Rumpelstiltskin (SYN, 1985) and Babar and Father Christmas (CTV, 1986). Encore Enterprises launched the first of four "Rusty and Buttons" specials with The Christmas Tree Train (SYN, 1983), and Perennial Pictures the first in its "Mirthworm" series with A Merry Mirthworm Christmas (CTV, 1984). The CBS O&O stations entered this field with Christmas Every Day (SYN, 1986).

In a July 18, 1987, proclamation commemorating the 50th anniversary of animated feature films, President Ronald Reagan hailed Walt Disney's Snow White and the Seven Dwarfs as a milestone in America's artistic history. The President praised such films for their magic, lasting vitality, fundamental values and as an art form whose achievements since 1937 "have mirrored the artistic development of American culture." Yet, since 1962, the prime-time animated film specials, some seen by greater audiences than Snow White in all its releases (55 million viewers watched a 1969 repeat broadcast of A Charlie Brown Christmas) constitute an even greater impact on the art form. Television is our mirror and reflects our culture more pervasively and persuasively than any other twentieth-century medium.

ABBREVIATIONS

ABC	Capital Cities/ABC (American Broadcasting Company)
API	Air Programs International, Sydney, Australia
BBC	British Broadcasting Corporation
BV	Buena Vista Distribution Company (Walt Disney)
CBC	Canadian Broadcasting Corporation
CBS	Columbia Broadcasting System/CBS, Inc.
CCF	Cinema Center Films (division of CBS)
CPB	Corporation for Public Broadcasting
CRC	Société radio de la Canada (French language television)
CTV	Cable Television
CTV	Canadian Independent Television
CTW	Children's Television Workshop
DIC	DIC Enterprises, Inc. (U.S. division of DIC Audio-visuel, Paris, subsidiary of CLT/RTL European entertainment conglomerate)
DIS	Disney Channel (CTV)
HBO	Home Box Office (CTV)
ITV	Independent Television Network, England
LBS	Lexington Broadcasting Service
MAD	Marketing and Design Group, General Mills
MGM	Metro-Goldwyn-Mayer (Turner Entertainment)
MGM/UA	Metro-Goldwyn-Mayer/United Artists
MTM	MTM (Mary Tyler Moore) Productions
NBC	National Broadcasting Company (division of General Electric)
NG	National General (film distributor)
NIK	Nickolodeon (CTV)
NTA	National Telefilm Associates (Republic Pictures)
O&O	Owned and Operated Network Stations
PAR	Paramount Pictures Corporation
PBS	Public Broadcasting System
R&D	Research and Development
RAI	Radiotelevisione Italiana (Italian TV network)
SHO	Showtime (CTV)
SYN	Syndicated (programs supplied to local stations)
TECO	The Taft Entertainment Company (parent of Hanna-Barbera Productions; Hanna-Barbera Productions, Australia [Southern-Star Productions]; Ruby-Spears Enterprises; Worldvision Enterprises)

TCF	Twentieth Century-Fox Films
TCFC	Those Characters from Cleveland (division of American Greetings)
TCF-TV	Twentieth Century-Fox Television
TMS	TMS Entertainment (division of Tokyo Movie Shinsha, Tokyo, Japan)
UA	United Artists
UPA	UPA Productions of America/UPA Pictures
USA	USA Entertainment Network (CTV)
WB	Warner Bros. Films
WB-TV	Warner Bros. Television
WD	Walt Disney Company/Television

ANIMATED TV SPECIALS

ADVENTURES OF ENERGY, THE

Broadcast History
    Premiere: 1983-1984
    SYN/local station option
Producer: Jean Chalopin
Director: Jean Louis Besson
Company: DIC Audiovisuel, Paris, France
Distributor: LBS Communications ("LBS Children's Theatre")/1983-
    1985

The Adventures of Energy examined the ways in which man harnessed
energy throughout the ages in a dramatic and scientific illustration
of the subject.
    The special was one of 20 half-hour films in an eclectic pack-
age of animated special programming syndicated under the umbrella
title "LBS Children's Theatre," usually broadcast weekly and on
holidays between 1983-1985.

ADVENTURES OF HUCKLEBERRY FINN, THE

Broadcast History
    Premiere: November 23, 1984
    CBS/KENNER FAMILY CLASSICS, Friday 10:00-11:00 AM
    Sponsor: Kenner Products (Toy Group, General Mills)
Producer: John Erichsen
Director: Paul McAdam
Writer: John Palmer
Music: Richard Bowden
Company: John Erichsen in association with Triple Seven Concepts/
    60 minutes
Home Video: Children's Treasures (Embassy)

The Adventures of Huckleberry Finn was adapted from Mark Twain's
1884 novel about a homeless, carefree rebel rafting down the Mississippi with his friend Jim, a runaway slave. It was one of a new
series launched in 1983 for Kenner Toys.

ADVENTURES OF SINBAD, THE

Broadcast History

3

Premiere: November 23, 1979
CBS/FAMOUS CLASSIC TALES, Friday 9:00-10:00 AM
Sponsor: Kenner Products (Toy Group, General Mills)
CBS/Repeat: November 27, 1980
SYN/Repeats: 1981 +
Producer: Walter J. Hucker
Director: Richard Slapczynski
Writer: Kimmer Ringwald
Music: Richard Bowden
Company: Air Programs International, Sydney, Australia/60 minutes
Distributor: D. L. Taffner ("Animated Classics for Children")/1983-
Home Video: Classics for Kids (MGM/UA)

Voices
    Peter Corbett, Barbara Frawley, Ron Haddrick, Philip Hinton,
    Bevan Wilson

The Adventures of Sinbad took place in the world of the Arabian
Nights, where an adventurous young sailor volunteered to recover
Baghdad's magic lantern and its genie from the wicked Old Man of
the Sea, who purloined it. Hoping to win the riches that would allow
him to wed the city's beautiful princess, Sinbad's quest proved to
be a dangerous one. Not only was he up against the wiles of the
Old Man, aided by the powers of the captive genie, but the sailor
faced dragons, giant birds, prehistoric creatures, a cyclops, pirates
and a rampaging elephant before reaching his goal, the Old Man's
secret island.
    This was the last of 15 specials from API, Australia, produced
through Sive Associates for Kenner Products which, with Parker
Brothers, formed the "Toy Group" (nee "Fun Group") of General
Mills. Under the umbrella title Famous Classic Tales, 24 specials
(including 9 from Hanna-Barbera Productions) were aired on CBS
between 1970 and 1983, beginning with the Tales of Washington Irving [q.v.], usually during Thanksgiving week and prior to Christmas. Jack Thinnes created the concept and supervised the productions for Sive, which also syndicated the films after their network
run until they were sold in 1982-1983 to D. L. Taffner. Some later
programs were broadcast under the title Kenner Family Classics,
several provided by other producers in association with Triple Seven
Concepts for the Toy Group, General Mills.

ADVENTURES OF THE GET ALONG GANG, THE

Broadcast History
    Premiere: 1984
    SYN/local station option (KTLA, Los Angeles, June 2, 1984, Satur-
        day 7:30-8:00 PM PST)
    Sponsor: Tomy Toys
    SYN/Repeats: September 3, 1984 +
Executive Producers: Jane Startz, Ray Peterson

THE ADVENTURES OF THE GET ALONG GANG. © 1984, American Greetings Corporation. Produced by Nelvana Limited, Toronto, Canada. Courtesy of Scholastic Productions and Those Characters from Cleveland.

Producers: Michael Hirsh, Patrick Loubert, Clive A. Smith
Associate Producer: Craig Virden
Directors: Raymond Jafelice, Bill Speers
Writer: Peter Sauder
Music & Lyrics/Theme: Walt Woodward
Music: Peter Jermyn, John Meldrum
Company: Scholastic Productions in association with Those Characters From Cleveland and Nelvana Limited, Toronto, Canada
Distributor: Scholastic Productions/1984-
Home Video: Lorimar Home Video #208 (nee Karl-Lorimar)

Principal Characters and Voices

Montgomery Moose	Charles Haid
Dotty Dog	Mara Hobel
Zipper Cat	Jim Henshaw
Bingo Beaver	Marla Lukofsky
Portia Porcupine	Gloria Figura
Woolma Lamb	Julie Cohen
Catchum Crocodile	Dan Hennessey
Leland Lizard	Dave Thomas
Officer Growler	Mark Gordon
Mr. Hoofnagel	Wayne Robson
The Announcer	Bruce Pirrie

Vocalist: John Sebastian

The Adventures of the Get Along Gang featured six young animal friends, Montgomery, Dotty, Zipper, Bingo, Portia and Woolma, demonstrating the value of honesty, friendship and cooperation during their annual scavenger hunt. Mr. Hoofnagel, owner of the Ice Cream Emporium and Sweet Shop, offered to name a new ice cream after the winner, who also received all the milkshakes he or she could drink. Gathered at their clubhouse, a Caboose car parked on a railroad siding, the members prepared for the big event as the unsavoury Catchum Crocodile and Leland Lizard also planned on winning first prize, willing to cheat to do it. Their bragging about how they would win annoyed the gang, especially Bingo Beaver, who was so incensed he bet Catchum the gang's clubhouse on the outcome. Unknown to the gang, however, Catchum had already assured his win by sneaking another item worth 2,000 points on the list made up by Officer Growler, a Lacertilia Squamata, which happened to mean lizard (and Catchum's pal Leland was you-know-what). On the day of the hunt, the gang discovered Catchum's trick and it soon became apparent they would not only lose the contest, but their clubhouse as well. Even when they put all their items together they could not beat Catchum's total score. Having only one chance to win, the gang entered the local Grand Prix Auto Race and won the Grand Prize Cup and with it topped Catchum's score to win the Scavenger Hunt. In the process they learned a valuable lesson about teamwork and sharing. Song/Theme: "The Get Along Gang" (Sebastian).

The special was a TV pilot based on the characters created by Those Characters From Cleveland, an American Greetings company, licensed as a doll and toy line. The film was included in the Saturday morning series, The Get Along Gang (CBS, 1984-1986), which was later syndicated by LBS Communications as part of the 90-minute weekend daytime package Kideo TV (SYN, 1986-).

ADVENTURES OF THE SCRABBLE PEOPLE IN "A PUMPKIN FULL OF NONSENSE," THE

Broadcast History
    Premiere: October 31, 1985
    SYN/local station option
Producer: Alvaro Arce
Directors: Alvaro Arce, Jaime Diaz
Writer: George Atkins
Music: Miguel Pizzaro
Lyrics: Alvaro Claudio Arce, Ada Lobos
Company: Arce Productions with Jaime Diaz Studios, Buenos Aires, Argentina
Distributor: ARP Films/1985-
Home Video: Children's Video Library (Vestron)

Principal Characters and Voices

Tad/Terry	Brianne Sidall
Sir Scrabble	Kevin Slattery
Rot	Bob Singer
Muddler	George Atkins
Lexa	Melissa Freeman
Rotunda	Kathy Hart Freeman

The Adventures of the Scrabble People in "A Pumpkin Full of Nonsense" opened in a magical pumpkin patch where a Halloween visit by Mr. Scrabble and the boy Tad and the girl Terry began the tale. Tumbling to the bottom of a gigantic pumpkin where the town of Nonsense was located, they learned of the unhappiness of the Scrabble People, because the letters were scrambled or missing on their signs and there was no school as the subjects were forbidden to learn how to read or spell. The ruler of Nonsense was the Muddler, (Baron of Bad Guys, Count of Confusion, Earl of Errors and King of Chaos), aided by his lackey Rot and an army of Scramblers, flying-monkey-like creatures, who insured his autocratic ways by prohibiting knowledge among his people. For intending to teach the alphabet to the townspeople, his Nastiness imprisoned the heroic Sir Scrabble, which pleased his fat daughter Rotunda, who wanted him for her husband. Aided by the fugitive schoolteacher Lexa, who was the only one able to read and write, Sir Scrabble was finally released. In the end it was goodness over wickedness, learning over ignorance, which spelled an end to the Muddler, thanks to the learning skills of his young companions, who turned the Land of Nonsense into the Land of Makesense. Songs: "Scrabble People March," "This is the City of Nonsense" (Muddler), "Together We'll Dream for a While" (Rotunda).

Designed to infuse such pro-social concepts as the importance and fun of reading and development of academic skills, the special was underwritten by Selchow & Righter, manufacturer of Scrabble and the Scrabble People playsets of pre-school learning toys.

AESOP'S FABLES

Broadcast History
    Premiere: October 31, 1971
    CBS/Sunday 7:30-8:00 PM
    CBS/Repeat: December 23, 1974
Executive Producer: Lee Rich
Producers: Louis Scheimer, Norman Prescott
Directors: Hal Sutherland, Bob Chenault
Writer/Lyrics: Earl Hamner
Music: Richard Delvy, Dave Roberts
Company: Lorimar Productions in association with Filmation
Home Video: Lorimar Home Video #127 (nee Karl-Lorimar)

Cast

Aesop	Bill Cosby
Joey	Keith Hamilton
Marta	Jerelyn Fields

Principal Characters and Voices

Tortoise	John Byner
Hare	Larry Storch
Eagle	Roger C. Carmel
Lady Eagle	Jane Webb
Donkey	John Erwin
Owl	Dal McKennon

Aesop's Fables presented two tales attributed to the venerable Phrygian, portrayed by Bill Cosby replete with sandals and toga in this live-action and animated special. Cosby spun the moralistic fables about the tortoise that wanted to fly and the tortoise's race with the hare to Joey and Marta, a pair of lost children he encountered while on a journey through an enchanted forest. Plucking on a lyre, he also talked through two musical poems about the tortoise's feats.

ALICE IN WONDERLAND (or "What's a Nice Kid Like You Doing in a Place Like This?")

Broadcast History
    Premiere: March 30, 1966
    ABC/Wednesday 8:00-9:00 PM
    ABC/Repeat: November 19, 1967
    SYN/Repeats: 1976 +
Executive Producers: William Hanna, Joseph Barbera
Producer/Director: Alex Lovy
Writer: Bill Dana
Music/Songs & Lyrics: Lee Adams, Charles Strouse
Music: Hoyt Curtin
Company: Hanna-Barbera Productions/60 minutes
Distributor: Worldvision Enterprises/1979-

Principal Characters and Voices

Alice	Janet Waldo
	Doris Drew Allen (singing)
Cheshire Cat	Sammy Davis, Jr.
White Knight	Bill Dana
Queen of Hearts	Zsa Zsa Gabor
White Rabbit	Howard Morris
Hedda Hatter	Hedda Hopper
Mad Hatter	Harvey Korman
Alice's Father/Humphrey Dumpty	Allan Melvin
King of Hearts/March Hare	Daws Butler
Dormouse/Fluff (Alice's dog)	Don Messick
Caterpillar	Alan Reed/Mel Blanc

Alice in Wonderland spoofed Lewis Carroll's classic tale and characters in an original musical story about the adventures of Alice and
her dog Fluff in Wonderland. The film also added some new cast
members, such as Hedda Hatter, the female counterpart of the Mad
Hatter, and the alter-ego voices of The Flintstones' Fred and Barney, inseparately tied together as one very long talking caterpillar
with heads on each end. And there were some amusing variations
on the familiar characters; Humphrey Dumpty was so named because
he sounded like Humphrey Bogart, and Bill Dana wrote himself into
the role of the White Knight, complete with his Jose Jimenez voice.
Described by Dana as a fantasy, "a musical comedy, not an adaptation of Lewis Carroll's book," the treatment placed Alice in an ultra-
modern setting. Songs included: "Life's A Game" (White Rabbit,
Alice), "What's a Nice Kid Like You Doing in a Place Like This?"
(Cheshire Cat), "They'll Never Split Us Apart" (Caterpillar), "I'm
Home" (Alice).
　　The special was the seventh film treatment of Lewis Carroll's
characters since Alice first fell down the rabbit-hole in 1865, and
the second animated adaptation following Walt Disney's 1951 movie
version. The first was a silent live-action film made in 1910 by the
Edison Company.

ALICE IN WONDERLAND

Broadcast History
　　Premiere: February 11, 1973
　　SYN/FESTIVAL OF FAMILY CLASSICS, WABC, New York, Sunday
　　　7:00-7:30 PM
　　SYN/Repeats: 1973 +
Producers/Directors: Arthur Rankin, Jr., Jules Bass
Associate Producer: Mary Alice Dwyer
Writer: Sandy Glass
Music: Maury Laws, Jules Bass
Company: Rankin-Bass Productions
Distributor: Viacom Enterprises ("Family Classics")/1986-
Home Video: Prism

Alice in Wonderland followed the blonde, pig-tailed tot's visit to be-
wildering Wonderland where she encountered a host of strange characters, including the blue Caterpillar, Mad Hatter, March Hare, Cheshire
Cat, the Dormouse, who looked and sounded like a punch-drunk
fighter and the Red Queen, who used a flamingo for a croquet mallet.
Modeled on Tenniel's illustrations, the amusing and peculiar cast
were drawn from the classic Alice in Wonderland (1865) by Lewis
Carroll, the pseudonym of English writer, Rev. Charles Lutwidge Dodg-
son (1832-1898).

ALICE'S ADVENTURES IN WONDERLAND

Broadcast History
    Premiere: 1983-1984
    SYN/local station option
Director/Writer (English): Fred Laderman
Company: Greatest Tales
Distributor: LBS Communications ("LBS Children's Theatre)/1983-
    1985

Alice's Adventures in Wonderland were abbreviated for this half-hour
imported adaptation. Bored with the heat on a summer's day, Alice
slipped into dreamland where she noticed a white rabbit carrying a
watch who was noticably upset at being late. Her fascination with
the curious March Hare drew her down into a topsy-turvy whimsical
world of Wonderland where she went through mysterious changes in
size. There she joined a zany tea party with the Mad Hatter, who
told riddles with no answers, a deadly game of croquet with the Queen
of Hearts, who only wanted to cut off her head, and other madcap
escapades. The special was reedited from a foreign film.

ALL ABOUT ME

Broadcast History
    Premiere: January 13, 1973
    NBC/NBC CHILDREN'S THEATRE, Saturday 1:00-2:00 PM
Executive Producer: George Heinemann
Producer: C. C. Ryder
Director: Bill Ackerman
Writers: Willie Ito, Ric Gonzalez, Bill Ackerman, Cal Howards, Roy
    Freeman
Music & Lyrics: C. C. Ryder
Lyrics/"Skin Song": Roy Freeman
Company: Animated Cartoon Productions/60 minutes

Principal Characters and Voices
Colonel Corpuscle   Sterling Holloway
Scott   Peter Halton

All About Me was a primer in biology, exploring the human body
through an amusing musical fantasy for children eight to fourteen.
The story centered around Scott, a little boy who fell asleep while
in class and dreamt he took a tour of his own body to learn how it
functioned. Escorted by Colonel Corpuscle, who thought Scott was
a germ, the boy was lectured while witnessing the various organs
and biological functions. Songs: "All About Me," "Heart Song,"
"The Medulla Do," "Feet Are Neat," "Skin Song" (Holloway).
    The microscopic premise, used previously for the movie Fantas-
tic Voyage (TCF, 1966) and its spin-off Saturday morning animated
series (ABC, 1968-1970) and others, was also adapted for two ABC

specials, The Incredible, Indelible, Magical, Physical Mystery Trip
[q.v.], whose storyline was somewhat similar, and its sequel The
Magical Mystery Trip Through Little Red's Head [q.v.].

ALL NEW ADVENTURE OF DISNEY'S SPORT GOOFY, AN

Broadcast History
     Premiere: May 27, 1987
     NBC/Wednesday 8:00-9:00 PM
Producer: John Klawitter
Associate Producer: Lynn-Jensen Klawitter
Director: Matt O'Callaghan
Writers: Tad Stones, Michael Giaimo, Joe Ranft
Music & Lyrics/Theme: Dale Gonyea
Music: John Debney
Company: Happy Feets Productions for Walt Disney Television/60
     minutes

Narrator: Stan Freberg

Sportscaster: Chick Hearn

Principal Characters and Voices ("Soccermania")
Goofy   Tony Pope
Scrooge McDuck/Beagle Boys/
     Gyro/Gearless   Will Ryan
Huey/Dewey/Louie   Russi Taylor
Beagle Boy #1   Jack Angel
Museum Curator   Phil Proctor

An All New Adventure of Disney's Sport Goofy premiered an original
featurette starring the popular Disney canine and included additional
scenes from his previously exhibited cartoons narrated by Stan Freberg. Chick Hearn, the Los Angeles Lakers' sports announcer, provided the "play-by-play" off-camera coverage for the new 20-minute
short, Sport Goofy in Soccermania, the first original Goofy cartoon
since 1965. It focused on Donald Duck's nephews, Huey, Dewey
and Louie, who coerced their stingy Uncle Scrooge McDuck into
sponsoring their soccer team of misfits, the Greenbacks, and mistakenly providing a valuable trophy. When word got around the
cup was worth a million dollars, the Beagle Boys bullied their way
into the competition. Determined to retain the trophy, Scrooge Mc-
Duck drafted Goofy to manage the team. But the unscrupulous
Beagle Boys kidnapped Goofy before the big game. All seemed lost
as the Beagle Boys plied their dirty tricks and the Greenbacks were
down 10-zip until Goofy escaped and returned at the half to lead the
team to a comeback one-point victory, reminding everyone, "If you
play fair and work together as a team, anyone can be Number 1."
Using clips from his prior cartoons, Goofy was featured in several
prior syndicated specials titled Sport Goofy [q.v.] and Walt Disney's

Mickey, Donald and Sport Goofy Show, [q.v.]. Song/Theme: "You Can Always Be Number 1."

AMAZING BUNJEE VENTURE, THE

Broadcast History
    Premiere: March 24 & 31, 1984
    ABC/ABC WEEKEND SPECIALS, Saturday 12:00-12:30 PM
    ABC/Repeats: September 15 & 22, 1984; January 18 & 25, 1986;
        September 12 & 19, 1987
Executive Producer: Doug Paterson
Producer: Steve Lumley
Director: Don MacKinnon
Writer: Malcolm Marmorstein
Music: Don Randi
Company: Hanna-Barbera Productions, Sydney, Australia, (Southern
    Star Productions)/60 minutes, 2 parts

Narrator: Michael Rye

Principal Characters and Voices
Bunjee/Willy/Pterodactyl/
    Tyrannosaur   Frank Welker
Karen Winsborrow/Baby #2   Nancy Cartwright
Andy Winsborrow   Robbie Lee
Mr. Winsborrow/Milkman   Michael Rye
Mrs. Winsborrow/Baby #1   Linda Gary
Waxer/Drasto   John Stephenson

The Amazing Bunjee Venture was a science fiction story about two
youngsters who, via a time machine, met Bunjee, an elephant-like
talking creature with a round body, orange hair, suction feet and
an inflatable trunk that allowed him to fly. After they accidentally
activated their father's newest invention, Karen and Andy Winsborrow magically appeared in the year 100 million B.C., had a surprise encounter in the jungle with a predatory pterodactyl and were
rescued by Bunjee, who helped them return home and unwittingly
traveled with them. The Winsborrow family adopted Bunjee, who
faced unusual problems; the substitution of chicken for pterodactyl
eggs in his diet made him nauseous, he had difficulty sleeping in a
bed and was a curiosity of enormous scientific and monetary value.
When he found Bunjee devouring his eggs, Willy, the neighborhood
supermarket man, enlisted a nutty veterinarian who helped him capture the creature. Determining he was for real, Willy and the vét
were consumed by thoughts of commercial exploitation when Bunjee,
who declared he belonged to no one, broke free. During the ensuing
chase, Bunjee rescued Willy from certain death after a fall, prompting him to confess his ill-treatment of Bunjee and recognize the fact
that Bunjee had feelings just like everyone else. Back at the Winsborrow home, Bunjee, while still complaining about his reaction to

© 1984 Hanna-Barbera Australia

THE AMAZING BUNJEE VENTURE. ©1984, Hanna-Barbera Productions, Inc. Courtesy of TECO and Capital Citiex/ABC.

chicken eggs, unexpectedly laid two of his own. When two little Bunjees were born, he decided to return home so they could grow up on pterodactyl eggs. Given the Winsborrows' time machine so that Bunjee and his offspring could visit them at any time, the creature returned to his prehistoric land. Lamenting he did not have a picture of Bunjee to show his friends, Andy was convinced by his family that after their recent experience, the fewer people who knew about Bunjee, the better. The two-part special was adapted from the book by Stan McMurty and prompted a sequel, The Return of Bunjee [q.v.].

ANIMALYMPICS: WINTER GAMES

Broadcast History
    Premiere: February 1, 1980
    NBC/Friday 8:00-8:30 PM
    NBC/Repeat: July 4, 1982
Producers: Steven Lisberger, Donald Kushner
Director: Steven Lisberger
Writers: Steven Lisberger, Michael Fremer
Music: Graham Gouldman
Company: Lisberger Productions
Record Album: A&M 4810

Principal Characters and Voices
Barbara Warblers/Brenda Springer   Gilda Radner
Keen Hacksaw   Harry Shearer
Rugs Turkell   Billy Crystal
Henry Hummel/others   Michael Fremer

Animalympics lampooned sports announcers and events of the first Animalia Winter Games. Four reporters, Henry Hummel, Rugs Terkel, Keen Hacksaw and Barbara Warbles, handled the coverage for the Z.O.O. network ("We bring out the beast in sports"), interviewed various sports experts and provided the thread of continuity for the vignettes. For instance, there was Kurt Wuffer, a hot-dogging dachshund skiing in a realistically rendered slalom race, who while practicing became lost in the mountains and discovered "Dog-ra-la," a secret winter paradise. The participants also included a figure-skating prima donna Ostrich and teams of ice hockey-playing bulls and bears. Several events were built around songs in the score. Sort of a mixture of Hanna-Barbera's Laff-a-Lympics (ABC, 1977-1978/1980/1986) and the Disney shorts in which Goofy demonstrated various sports, there were occasional funny visuals, such as a score-board full of jokes. Songs included: "We've Made It to the Top."
    A sequel covering the Summer Games was not aired by the network after the United States boycotted the 1980 Moscow Olympic Games. Later, the two films were spliced together and with some added scenes released as the movie Animalympics (Lisberger, 1983).

ARABIAN NIGHTS, THE

Broadcast History
    Premiere: February 4, 1973
    SYN/FESTIVAL OF FAMILY CLASSICS, WABC, New York, Sunday
        7:00-7:30 PM
    SYN/Repeats: 1973 +
Producers/Directors: Arthur Rankin, Jr., Jules Bass
Associate Producer: Mary Alice Dwyer
Writer: Fred Halliday
Music: Maury Laws, Jules Bass
Company: Rankin-Bass Productions
Distributor: Viacom Enterprises ("Family Classics")/1986-
Home Video: Prism

The Arabian Nights conjured up genies, gems, flying carpets, assorted sheiks and Aladdin's famed lamp in a fantasy about a daring
teenager, Pindar. He set out to win the hand of his love, Fatha,
from her uncle Omar, the Thief of Baghdad, by undertaking dangerous missions to obtain a treasure guarded by the powerful Great
Genie and the magic slippers of the Cruel Caliph. Pindar also had
the loyal support of the ruby-eating Gagulpha bird and eventually
won his bride.

ARCHIE AND HIS NEW FRIENDS

Broadcast History
    Premiere: September 14, 1969
    CBS/Sunday 7:30-8:00 PM
Producers: Louis Scheimer, Norman Prescott
Director: Hal Sutherland
Music/Songs & Lyrics: Jeff Barry
Music: George Blais, Jeff Michael
Company: Filmation

Principal Characters and Voices
Archie Andrews   Dal McKennon
Reggie Mantle/Moose   John Erwin
Jughead Jones   Howard Morris
Veronica Lodge/Betty Cooper/
    Sabrina   Jane Webb

Archie and His New Friends introduced a new character to prime-
time viewers, Sabrina the Teenage Witch, who made her debut September 13, 1969, on the Saturday morning series The Archie Comedy
Hour with Sabrina, the Teenage Witch (CBS, 1969-1970). A new
girl in the neighborhood, Sabrina was snubbed by Veronica and
Betty but befriended by Archie when she enrolled at Riverdale High
School. Later, in a fiercely competitive race for the student-body
presidency, Reggie was up to all his nasty tricks in an attempt to

defeat the more popular Archie, but continually thwarted through the magic of apprentice witch Sabrina, who struggled to conceal her mystical powers from her friends and appear as a normal teenager. Songs: "Get On the Line," "You've Got to Have an Image."

The special was a spin-off from the popular Saturday morning series, The Archies (CBS, 1968-1976/NBC, 1977-1978), based on the comic feature that debuted in Pep Comics #2 (December 1941) drawn by Bob Montana and attributed to publisher John L. Goldwater. Although it aired one day after the premiere of the new series, in effect it was a prime-time preview of the Saturday show, the pioneer on CBS. The sixteen-year-old sorceress was inspired largely by Samantha Stephens on Bewitched (ABC, 1964-1973) and also appeared in her own spin-off series, Sabrina and the Groovie Goolies (CBS, 1970-1971) and Sabrina, the Teenage Witch (CBS, 1971-1974/NBC, 1977-1978), described in Children's Television, Part I, (Scarecrow, 1983), pp. 20-23, 245-247. The characters were revived as junior high school students for the Saturday series, The New Archies (NBC, 1987-   ).

ARCHIE, SUGAR SUGAR, JINGLE JANGLE SHOW, THE

Broadcast History
    Premiere: March 22, 1970
    CBS/Sunday 7:30-8:00 PM
Producers: Louis Scheimer, Norman Prescott
Director: Hal Sutherland
Music/Songs & Lyrics: Jeff Barry
Music: George Blais, Jeff Michael
Company: Filmation
Record Album: Colendar KES 101

Principal Characters and Voices

Archie Andrews	Dal McKennon
Reggie Mantle/Moose	John Erwin
Jughead Jones	Howard Morris
Veronica Lodge/Betty Cooper/	
Sabrina	Jane Webb

The Archie, Sugar Sugar, Jingle Jangle Show used selected scenes from the Saturday morning series The Archies (CBS, 1968-1976/NBC 1977-1978), featuring the same Riverdale High School characters plus Sabrina, the Teenage Witch, as the bubblegum rock group "The Archies." Similar to music videos and utilizing pulsating psychedelic artwork, the special presented four popular songs introduced on the daytime series, tied together by brief gag vignettes. The actual music was performed by "The Archies," a professional rock group utilized for recording the musical portions in the series and other performances. Songs: "Sugar Sugar" (their number-one hit record in 1969); "Jingle Jangle" and "Who's My Baby" (two best sellers); "You've Got to Have an Image."

AROUND THE WORLD IN 80 DAYS

Broadcast History
Premiere: November 12 & 19, 1972
SYN/FESTIVAL OF FAMILY CLASSICS, WABC, New York, Sunday
7:00-7:30 PM
SYN/Repeats: 1973 +
Producers/Directors: Arthur Rankin, Jr., Jules Bass
Associate Producer: Mary Alice Dwyer
Writer: Leonard Starr
Music: Maury Laws, Jules Bass
Company: Rankin-Bass Productions/60 minutes, 2 parts
Distributor: Viacom Enterprises ("Family Classics")/1986-
Home Video: Prism

Around the World in 80 Days was a faithful two-part adaptation of
Jules Verne's tale set in 1872 about Phileas Fogg, who hoped his
wager and his trip around the globe with his valet Passepartout
would bring him and his beloved Belinda together despite her uncle's
attempts to subvert his plans through the hindering schemes of the
detective Fix.

B.C.: A SPECIAL CHRISTMAS

Broadcast History
Premiere: c1971
SYN/local station option
Executive Producer: Gordon Arnold
Producer: Vladimir Goetzelman
Director: Jim Miko
Writer: Johnny Hart
Music: Sam Dari
Company: Cinera Productions, Ltd., in association with Hardlake
Animated Pictures and Field Enterprises
Home Video: Embassy Home Entertainment (with B.C.: THE FIRST
THANKSGIVING)

Principal Characters and Voices
Peter	Bob Elliott
Wiley	Ray Goulding
Fat Broad	Barbara Hamilton
Cute Chick	Melleny Brown
Thor	Henry Ramer
Clumsy	Keith Hampshire
Curls	John Stocker
B.C.	(non-speaking)
Santa Claus	(non-speaking)

B.C.: A Special Christmas brought Santa unexpectedly to cave-
land, ruining a scam by the imaginative Peter and his friend Wiley,
the bearded one-legged poet. Conceived as a sting by which the

caveman could exploit the community and make a bundle selling trees and gift rocks, they created a mythical gift-giver in whose name it would be carried out, "Santa Claus." Selecting December 26th, a day they named X-mas, when everyone gave gifts in his name, Peter and Wiley prepared a bogus relic, a stone-tablet which related the legend to give their con credence. When Wiley complained their fiction was stretching credibility, Peter told him, "If they buy the fat dude in the red suit, they gotta go for the flying reindeer." The pair set about gathering trees and gift-wrapping rocks, but Wiley was dubious, "What if the people want to select special gifts for one another?" "That's just tough," replied Peter, "they're all gonna get rocks." "Gee," said Wiley, "you're all heart!" On Christmas day the scheme backfired when everyone received a real gift from Santa-- Thor a wheel, Clumsy a sundial, Fat Broad some pink boots, Cute Chick a necklace--in the real spirit of good will and love. "That old rascal really crossed us up," said Peter, "We created a myth that came true." The title character, B.C., was seen only briefly.

The film was based on John Hart's daily newspaper comic B.C. (February 17, 1958), which was followed by a Sunday version (October 19, 1958) for Publishers-Hall Syndicate. It was first made into a short cartoon for Curiosity Shop (ABC, 1971-1973), described in Children's Television, Part II, (Scarecrow, 1985), pp. 133-135.

B.C.: THE FIRST THANKSGIVING

Broadcast History
    Premiere: November 19, 1973
    NBC/Monday 8:00-8:30 PM
    Sponsor: General Mills
    SYN/Repeats 1975 + ; 1983-1985 ("LBS Children's Theatre")
Executive Producers: Abe Levitow, David Hanson
Director: Abe Levitow
Writers: John Hart, Jack Caprio
Music: Mario Darpino
Company: Levitow-Hanson Films in association with Field Enterprises
Distributor: MG-Perin/1986-
Home Video: Children's Treasury #1388/Embassy (with B.C.:
    A SPECIAL CHRISTMAS)

Principal Characters and Voices

B.C.	(non-speaking)
Clumsy	Daws Butler
Turkey/Peter/Thor	Don Messick
Grog/Wiley	Bob Holt
Fat Broad/Cute Chick	Joanie Sommers

B.C.: The First Thanksgiving put John Hart's prehistoric comic-strip clan in hot water while trying to stalk a sly gobbler. After the gullible B.C. was erroneously credited with the invention of fire, Fat Broad decided to heat up a vat of rock soup she was preparing

B.C.: THE FIRST THANKSGIVING. © 1973, Field Enterprises, Inc.
Produced by Levitow-Hanson Films. Courtesy of MG/Perin.

for dinner. Since "there's only one way to flavor rock soup and
that's with a dead turkey," she sent the weird assortment of cave-
men, B.C., Wiley, Peter, Thor and Grog, out on a cross country
chase for the bird, complicated by the fact that nobody knew what
a turkey looked like. A zany feathered fowl who could sing like
Barbara Streisand, the turkey himself joined in the chase, and in
the confusion a dinosaur drank the soup and put out the fire. At
the end of the day, when they all gathered around to give thanks
for their dinner of rocks, the one who had the most to be thankful
for was the lucky bird.

BABAR AND FATHER CHRISTMAS

Broadcast History
    Premiere: December 1986
    HBO/December 5, 1986, Friday 6:00-6:30 AM, 4:30-5:00 PM
    HBO/Repeats: multiple option, December 9-24, 1986
    CBC/December 15, 1986, Monday 7:30-8:00 PM
    CRC/BABAR ET LE PERE NOEL, December 25, 1986, Thursday
       12:00-12:30 PM
    SYN/Repeats: 1986 + (22 countries)
Executive Producer: Merilyn Read
Producer: Alison Clayton

BABAR AND FATHER CHRISTMAS. © 1986, MTR Ottawa Productions, Ltd. Produced by Atkinson Film-Arts, Ottawa, Canada. Courtesy of Crawley Films Limited.

Director: Gerry Capelle
Writers: Laurent de Brunhoff, Merilyn Read, Gerry Capelle
Music: Gary Morton
Company: Atkinson Film-Arts, Ottawa, Canada with MTR Ottawa
   Productions in association with the CBC
Distributor: Crawleys International/1986-
Home Video: Hi-Tops Video (nee Media Home Entertainment)

<u>Narrator</u>: Laurent de Brunhoff

<u>Principal Characters and Voices</u>

Babar	Jim Bradford
Celeste	Louise Villeneuve
Arthur	Kemp Edwards
Zephir/Mice/Lazzaro/Podular	Rick Jones
Retaxes/Father Christmas	Les Lye
Pom	Amie Charlebois
Flora	Courtney Caroll
Alexander	Kai Engstad
Professor	Noel Council
Secretary/Elf #1	Bridgitte Robinson
Elderberry/Elf #2/Boatman	Derek Diorio
Gendarme	Roch Lafortune

Babar and Father Christmas took place far away from man's country, in the town of Celesteville in Elephant Land, ruled by the wise and gentle King Babar and his Queen Celeste. Father Christmas had never visited this kingdom, so with great anticipation, the little elephants, Pom, Flora and Alexander, their cousin Arthur and their friend Zephir the monkey decided to write to the kind old gentleman who brought toys to little children. When there was no reply, Babar set out in search of Father Christmas, sidetracked and delayed along the way by Retaxes the Rhinocerous, his archenemy who stopped at nothing to find Father Christmas to foil his effort. Despite all his nasty schemes, Babar was successful, and the youngsters of Elephant Land enjoyed their first true Christmas with presents. Gemini Award (1987), Best Animated Program, Canadian television.

This third Babar special was based on the last book by Jean de Brunhoff, published in 1940. His son, Laurent de Brunhoff, current author of the Babar books, with more than 30 in the series, served as story consultant and narrator.

BABAR COMES TO AMERICA

Broadcast History
    Premiere: September 7, 1971
    NBC/Tuesday 7:30-8:00 PM
    Sponsors: Healthtex; Burger Chef (1975-1976)
    NBC/Repeat: February 27, 1972
    SYN/Repeats: 1975 +
Executive Producer: Lee Mendelson
Producers: Lee Mendelson, Bill Melendez
Directors: Bill Melendez, Ed Levitt
Writer: Laurent de Brunhoff
Music: John Scott Trotter
Lyrics: Tom Adair
Company: Lee Mendelson-Bill Melendez Productions in association
    with Laurent de Brunhoff and with the cooperation of Random
    House
Distributor: Lee Mendelson Productions/1986-
Home Video: Children's Video Library (Vestron)

Narrator: Peter Ustinov

Vocalists: (The Celesteville Singers)
    Sue Allen, B. J. Baker, Bill Lee, Lulie Jean Norman, Bob Tebow

Barbar Comes To America featured the travels of the slightly paunchy King of Elephant Land and his entourage. Invited to visit America and Hollywood, Babar and Celeste, his Queen, set out by their official hot air balloon while his star-struck cousin Artur and the elder Cornelius boarded an ocean liner. After surviving a terrible storm, a crash on a deserted island and an encounter with a whale that marooned them on a reef, Babar and Celeste were rescued by the ship carrying Artur and Cornelius to New York. Bored with the Big Apple and meandering sightseeing, Washington, D.C., where they dined at the White House, and New Orleans and their trip up the Mississippi on a riverboat, the prank-playing Artur turned up missing when they toured a Michigan automobile factory. Searching along the way for his cousin, Babar and the others arrived in San Francisco and helicoptered to Los Angeles, where they attended a party thrown by a famous Hollywood producer. He dropped the word about a new star they would see in his next picture, none other than Artur, and since he needed three more elephants, Babar, Celeste and Cornelius were also offered roles in the movie. Songs: "Long Live Babar," "The Babar Waltz," "Take a Balloon," "It's a Lovely Day in New York."

The script was adapted from French post-impressionist painter Jean de Brunoff's popular children's picture-books, Travels of Babar and Babar Comes to America, by his son Laurent de Brunhoff, who continued to author the Babar series beginning in 1946.

BABAR, THE LITTLE ELEPHANT see STORY OF BABAR, THE
LITTLE ELEPHANT, THE

BAD CAT

Broadcast History
      Premiere: April 14, 1984
      ABC/ABC WEEKEND SPECIALS, Saturday 12:00-12:30 PM
      ABC/Repeats: September 29, 1984; October 26, 1985
Executive Producers: Joseph Ruby, Ken Spears
Associate Producer: Larry Huber
Director: Charles A. Nichols
Writers: Mark Evanier, Sharman Di Vono
Music: Dean Elliott
Company: Ruby-Spears Enterprises

Principal Characters and Voices

Bad Cat	Bart Braverman
Gordon	Hal Smith
Neddy	Tress MacNeille
Vernon Turner	Bobby Ellerbee
Jim Harrison	Alan Young
Steve Harrison	Steve Spears
Pam Harrison	Amy Tunik
Champ	Frank Welker
Dierdra	Judy Strangis
Dimples	Didi Conn
Riff	Jon Bauman
Mouser	Marvin Kaplan

Bad Cat followed the adventures of a rambunctious teenage feline with

an undeserved reputation as a troublemaker, who had to struggle
for acceptance when his owners, the Harrison family, moved to a
new neighborhood. With his parents, Gordon and Neddy, Bad Cat
was released in his new environs, but not before son Steve put a
new collar around his neck with the name and address of the family's
grocery store. Sizing up the new arrivals in the neighborhood,
Riff, a big tough bully cat, was watching with his girlfriend Dierdre
and local gang members Mouser, Champ and Vernon Turner, when
Bad Cat took off his collar, intending to retrieve it later. Fur flew
after Bad Cat's first encounter with Riff, which led to animosity
when he not only beat him in a rigged mouse-catching contest but
also walked Dierdre home. To get even, Riff and the gang wrecked
the park recreation center and left Bad Cat's collar at the scene.
The police assumed he was responsible. No one, not even his parents, believed his explanation, but Riff's foul frame-up cost him his
popularity when most of his gang pledged their allegiance to Bad
Cat, including Dierdre. To regain his dominance, Riff challenged
Bad Cat to the supreme test, "The Feline Challenge," a dangerous
race through streets and alleys, promising to 'fess up' if he lost,
but if he won Bad Cat had to leave. With Mouser, Riff managed to
sidetrack Bad Cat and was winning the race until he became trapped
accidentally in a locked car careening downhill. Hearing his cries,
Bad Cat unselfishly rescued his nemesis. Grateful for his life, Riff,
who learned about acceptance and fair play the hard way, willingly
admitted to the vandalism and cleared Bad Cat's name. In the
special, adapted from the book by David Vincent, the cats, although
they lived among humans, spoke only to each other.

BALLAD OF PAUL BUNYAN, THE

Broadcast History
    Premiere: January 7, 1973
    SYN/FESTIVAL OF FAMILY CLASSICS, WABC, New York, Sunday
      7:00-7:30 PM
    SYN/Repeats: 1973 +
Producers/Directors: Arthur Rankin, Jr., Jules Bass
Associate Producer: Mary Alice Dwyer
Music: Maury Laws, Jules Bass
Company: Rankin-Bass Productions
Distributor: Viacom Enterprises ("Family Classics")/1986-
Home Video: Prism (with JOHNNY APPLESEED)

The Ballad of Paul Bunyan evoked the image of the legendary giant
lumberjack and his magic axe, narrated by the grizzled oldtimer for
a little girl and boy as he plucked at his banjo. He told how the
infant Paul was found afloat in his crib by lumberjacks Crosscut
Kelly and Stump Watson, who struggled to clothe and feed him as
he grew into a skyscraper giant capable of challenging the hated
tyrannical lumber boss, Panhandle Pete. Inevitably, Panhandle and
Paul headed for a showdown, determined in three contests of skill
and strength with each winning one event, climaxed by a hole-digging

contest. Headed for certain defeat after Panhandle's men stole his magic axe, when the lumber boss returned it because he could not make it work, Paul went on to best his boastful opponent by digging a hole so large it later became Niagara Falls.

BALLAD OF SMOKEY THE BEAR, THE

Broadcast History
Premiere: November 24, 1966
NBC/Thursday 7:30-8:30 PM
Sponsor: General Electric
NBC/Repeats: May 5, 1968; May 4, 1969
SYN/Repeats: 1980 +
Producers: Arthur Rankin, Jr., Jules Bass
Director: Takeo Nakamura
Writer: Joseph Schrank
Music & Lyrics: Johnny Marks
Company: Rankin-Bass Productions in association with Videocraft International/60 minutes
Distributor: Viacom Enterprises/1986-

Narrator
Big Bear   James Cagney

Principal Characters and Voices
Smokey   Barry Pearl
Turtle   William Marine
Beaver   Herbert Duncan
Mrs. Beaver   Rose Marie Jun
Fox   George Petrie
Mama   Bryna Raeburn

The Ballad of Smokey the Bear related how the carefree but unhappy and timid little cub overcame his fears and became a legend as the symbol of the U.S. Forest Service fire-prevention campaign. Narrated by James Cagney as Smokey's brother, Big Bear, the tuneful Thanksgiving special flashbacked to Smokey's younger years, playing in the forest with his friends Turtle, the Beavers, Fox and Smokey's girlfriend Delilah. When the serenity of the woodland was shattered by a forest fire in which Smokey suffered burned paws, singed fur and loss of his mother, the sad day left a depressed and withdrawn bear who became frightened just by the thought of fire and smoke. One day, a grown-up Smokey discovered an escaped gorilla carelessly starting small brush fires, polluting the streams and uprooting newly planted seedlings. When Big Bear's plans to entrap the ape went awry, Smokey finally found the courage to capture him and dispatch him back to the zoo. With everything well and peaceful in the woodland, a brave new Smokey, wearing his ranger hat and toting his spade, became a reminder to all to keep the forest green. Songs: "Ballad of Smokey the Bear" (Cagney and chorus), "Tell It To a Turtle," "Delilah," "Don't Wait," "All Together," "Curiosity," "Anyone Can Move a Mountain." The film used stop-motion animated puppets (Animagic), accomplished in Japan, the first of the genre to be televised as a primetime special. Smokey the Bear was the first cartoon character (symbol) protected by an Act of Congress and began his TV appearances in 1950 in public service films. The special preceded the Saturday morning animated-cartoon series, The Smokey Bear Show (ABC, 1969-1971), described with his origins in Children's Television, Part I, (Scarecrow, 1983), pp. 261-263.

BANJO, THE WOODPILE CAT

Broadcast History
  Premiere: May 1, 1982
  ABC/Saturday 8:00-8:30 PM
  ABC/Repeat: August 7, 1983
  HBO/Repeats: multiple option, 1984-1985
Producers: Don Bluth, John Pomeroy, Gary Goldman
Director: Don Bluth
Music/Songs & Lyrics: Don Bluth
Music: Robert F. Brunner
Company: Banjo Productions in association with Don Bluth Productions
Home Video: Children's Video Library (Vestron)

Narrator: Beah Richards

Principal Characters and Voices
Banjo   Spanky Marcus
Crazy Legs   Scatman Crothers
Zazu   Beah Richards
Papa Cat/Freeman   Jerry Harper
Mama Cat/Cleo   Georgette Rampone
Jean   Ann E. Beesley
Emily   Robin Muir
Farmer/Warehouseman   Ken Samson

Announcer: Mark Elliott

Vocalists: (The Cat Sisters)
  Sue Allen, Sally Stevens, Jackie Ward

Banjo, the Woodpile Cat starred a mischievous kitten who hitched a ride on a passing farm truck, forsaking the comfort of his country home for the promise of good times. After falling into trouble once too often, the spunky runaway, with the voice and mind of a rebellious 11-year-old, ended up far away in the big city, confronted by a series of new horrors. In a driving thunderstorm, Banjo, cold and wet, encountered roaring cars and a street-wise hep cat, the

BANJO, THE WOODPILE CAT. © 1979, Banjo Productions. Courtesy of Banjo Productions.

fun-loving Crazy Legs, who befriended the lost little adventurer and tried to get him on a truck home. After failing in that attempt, the alley cat introduced Banjo to his lady friend, Zazu, lead singer of the swinging Cat Sisters, Cleo, Marina and Zazu, who was quick to compassionately cheer the bewildered, homesick small pussycat. A nightclub sequence and a terrorizing chase by a pack of big-toothed, slathering wild dogs also punctuated Banjo's big city adventures, and after a tortuous trek he finally arrived home in the happy ending. Songs: "He Couldn't Be Good" (Crothers), "Off to the City" (Banjo theme), "The Rain Song," "Boogie Baby" (Cat Sisters), "I'll Stick with You."

An unusual devoted effort in classic animation with fully articulated movements, the film was produced over a period of seven years in the garage of Don Bluth while he was working at Disney Studios. Bluth and dozens of his artist friends worked on the project, and during continual reworking a number of sequences were dropped and the final cut further trimmed for a half-hour special. Only those who accomplished substantial work or were on the final crew received screen credit. The home video cassette featured additional minutes of material not previously broadcast.

BE MY VALENTINE, CHARLIE BROWN

Broadcast History
Premiere: January 28, 1975
CBS/Tuesday 8:00-8:30 PM
Sponsors: Kellogg's, Dolly Madison; Peter Paul Cadbury, Nabisco
CBS/Repeats: February 10, 1976; February 14, 1977; February 9, 1979; February 11, 1983; February 11, 1984; February 14, 1987
Executive Producer: Lee Mendelson
Producer: Bill Melendez
Director: Phil Roman
Writer/Creator: Charles M. Schulz
Music: Vince Guaraldi, John Scott Trotter
Company: Lee Mendelson-Bill Melendez Productions in association with Charles M. Schulz Creative Associates and United Feature Syndicate
Home Video: Hi-Tops Video (nee Media Home Entertainment)

Principal Characters and Voices

Charlie Brown	Duncan Watson
Linus Van Pelt	Stephen Shea
Lucy Van Pelt	Melanie Kohn
Schroeder	Greg Felton
Violet	Linda Ercoli
Sally Brown	Lynn Mortensen

Be My Valentine, Charlie Brown found hearts fluttering at Birchwood School where the Peanuts clan was getting ready for Cupid's holiday. Romance was in the air, and Linus had brought a huge box of candy for his homeroom teacher. Believing that the candy was for her, Sally reciprocated with a homemade card for Linus. Snoopy created a special homemade heart for his friend Woodstock, who likewise presented one to his favorite beagle. Lucy, meanwhile, demanded some affection from Schroeder: "Originally, Valentine's Day was set aside as a lovers' festival. Oh, Schroeder, isn't that romantic?" But Schroeder only had love for his music and in a tantrum Lucy destroyed his toy piano. Waiting, and waiting, and waiting for his cards to arrive at the mailbox, in frustration Charlie kicked the pole and hurt his toe. "I think I could spend my whole life here and still never get a valentine," he muttered. And at the school Valentine's Day party, the expectant tyke brought his briefcase in which to tote all his cards but was the only member of the class not to receive one. "Who would waste a valentine on stupid ol' Charlie Brown?" said heartless Lucy. Feeling guilty about the shabby treatment Charlie received, Violet gave him a recycled card the next day over Schroeder's protests. Charlie happily accepted it. "I guess I let Schroeder down," he told Linus, "but it was my first valentine, you know."

The special created great sympathy for Charlie Brown and elicited an unprecedented national response. Viewers by the hundreds sent Valentine cards to poor ol' Charlie everytime it aired.

BEAR WHO SLEPT THROUGH CHRISTMAS, THE

Broadcast History
  Premiere: December 17, 1973
  NBC/Monday 8:00-8:30 PM
  Sponsor: Florists Telegraphic Delivery Service (FTD)
  NBC/Repeats: December 16, 1974; December 25, 1977; December
    19, 1978; December 23, 1980
  CBS/Repeat: December 15, 1979
  SYN/Repeats: 1981 +
Executive Producer: Norman Sedawie
Producer: David H. DePatie, Friz Freleng
Directors: Hawley Pratt, Gerry Chiniquy
Writers: Larry Spiegel, John Barrett
Music & Lyrics: Doug Goodwin
Company: Sed-bar Productions in association with DePatie-Freleng
  Enterprises
Distributor: WesternWorld Television/1986-
Home Video: Family Home Entertainment

Narrator: Casey Kasem

Principal Characters and Voices
Ted E. Bear   Tommy Smothers
Patti Bear   Barbara Feldon
Professor Werner Von Bear   Arte Johnson
Santa Claus   Robert Holt
Weather Bear   Kelly Lange
Honey Bear   Michael Bell

Other Voices
  Casey Kasem, Caryn Paperny

The Bear Who Slept Through Christmas concerned the awakening of
Theodore Edward Bear, who had never experienced the Yuletide
because he was always in hibernation. As the bears employed at
the Organic Honeyworks prepared to stop work for the winter, Ted
E. Bear wanted to find out more about what he learned of while at
Grizzly University, the annual event called Christmas. It was supposed to be a wonderful time, all the lights, the music and a big
human in a red suit. Ted had tried before, but like all bears fell
soundly asleep through the winter. But this time he decided one
evening to set out to find Christmas in the big city. The hustle
and bustle made Ted a little nervous and he soon found himself
locked in a toy store on Christmas Eve with all the unsold toys.
With Christmas only a few hours away, he was afraid he would not
witness what he had waited so long to see. With the help of the
toys, Ted escaped from the store and encountered the jolly man in
the red suit to find the meaning of Christmas as a present in a little
girl's arms. The film was based on a story by John Barrett.

BEAUTY AND THE BEAST

Broadcast History
    Premiere: November 25, 1983
    CBS/KENNER FAMILY CLASSICS, Friday 3:00-4:00 PM
    Sponsor: Kenner Products (Toy Group, General Mills)
    CBS/Repeat: November 22, 1984
    Executive Producers: Joseph Ruby, Ken Spears
    Associate Producer: Larry Huber
    Director: Rudy Larriva
    Writers: Steve Gerber, Martin Pasko
    Music: Dean Elliott, Paul DeKorte
    Company: Ruby-Spears Enterprises in association with TCG Products
    /60 minutes
    Home Video: Family Home Entertainment

Narrator: Paul Kirby

Principal Characters and Voices
Beauty/Jacqueline/Queen/
    Old Crone   Janet Waldo
Beast/Prince   Robert Ridgely
Erwina/Stately Lady/Messenger
    Boy   Linda Gary
Merchant/Sailor/Male Voice   Stacy Keach, Jr.
Rene/Cockatoo   Alan Young
Gerard   Paul Kirby

Beauty and the Beast was a rather literal adaptation of Madame Le-
prince de Beaumont's classic fairytale about an ugly beast who lived
in a magnificent palace in the forest, restored to a handsome prince
by a kiss from the beautiful girl he loved, in spite of the efforts of
her selfish and greedy family.

BERENSTAIN BEARS' CHRISTMAS TREE, THE

Broadcast History
    Premiere: December 3, 1979
    NBC/Monday 8:00-8:30 PM
    Sponsor: Kellogg's
    NBC/Repeat: December 15, 1980
    HBO/Repeats: multiple option, 1985-1986
    Executive Producers: Joseph and Gilbert Cates
    Producer: Buzz Potamkin
    Director: Mordicai Gerstein
    Writers/Creators: Stan and Jan Berenstain
    Music: Elliot Lawrence
    Lyrics: Stan Berenstain
    Company: Cates Brothers Company in association with Perpetual
        Motion Pictures
    Home Video: Children's Treasures (Embassy Home Entertainment)

Narrator: Ron McLarty

Principal Characters and Voices

Papa Bear	Ron McLarty
Mama Bear	Pat Lysinger
Brother Bear	Jonathan Lewis
Sister Bear	Gabriela Glatzer

The Berenstain Bears' Christmas Tree told how the search for the perfect Christmas tree led to an understanding of the real meaning of the holiday for the jolly ursine family. The musical tale found overbearing Papa ignoring Mama Bear's advice to buy a tree as he set out to find one of his own in Bear Valley. As the narrator pointed out, in his attempt to find the ideal tree for the Bear's home, there was something important he was forgetting--"Christmas was for giving! It wasn't for getting!" During his search, Papa encountered the forest animals and birds who made their homes in the trees he coveted, creatures faced with eviction from their shelter in the cold winter snow. Through them and Sister and Brother, his children, Papa had a change of heart in a warm display of understanding and sharing of the Christmas spirit with the forest folk. Songs: "The Bears' Christmas" (opening chorale), "The Christmas Tree," "The Christmas Star."

This was the first animated film starring the tot-oriented Bear family, based on the familiar characters in more than two dozen picture-books by Stan and Jan Berenstain, considered one of the top children's book properties in the United States with 45-million copies published. The property was also adapted for a Saturday morning series, The Berenstain Bears (CBS, 1985-   ).

BERENSTAIN BEARS' EASTER SURPRISE, THE

Broadcast History
    Premiere: April 14, 1981
    NBC/Saturday 8:30-9:00 PM
    Sponsor: Kellogg's
    NBC/Repeats: April 6, 1982; April 20, 1984
    HBO/Repeats: multiple option, 1986-1987
Executive Producer: Joseph Cates
Producers: Buzz Potamkin, Hal Hoffer
Directors: Mordicai Gerstein, Al Kouzel
Writers/Creators: Stan and Jan Berenstain
Music: Elliot Lawrence
Lyrics: Stan Berenstain
Company: Joseph Cates Productions in association with Perpetual
    Motion Pictures
Home Video: Children's Treasures (Embassy Home Entertainment)

Narrator: Ron McLarty

Principal Characters and Voices

Papa Bear	Ron McLarty
Mama Bear	Pat Lysinger
Brother Bear	Knowl Johnson
Sister Bear	Gabriela Glatzer
Boss Bunny	Bob McFadden

The Berenstain Bears' Easter Surprise was another special for small fry featuring the cuddly critters from Bear Country, imparting a lesson about the meaning of the holiday. Easter was approaching, but Bear Valley was still blanketed in snow and showed no sign of seasonal change. Papa Bear set out to find the Easter Hare, Boss Bunny, to find out why Spring had not arrived and discovered the egg-deliverer had gone on strike and threatened to quit, causing Bear Country to be stuck in Winter. Papa Bear tried to pinch hit for the rabbit's annual visit by constructing his own Easter Egg machine, but flopped. Meantime, his son, Brother Bear, was overly concerned that the absence of Easter might do away with the surprise promised by his parents. Not to worry, though, as the Boss Bunny was finally convinced to hippety-hop down the trail again, and the youngest member of the Bear family was exposed to the significance of the springtime renewal. Song/Theme: "Who Cares About Easter?"

BERENSTAIN BEARS' LITTLEST LEAGUER, THE

Broadcast History
Premiere: May 6, 1983
NBC/Friday 8:00-8:30 PM
Sponsor: Kellogg's
NBC/Repeat: THE BERENSTAIN BEARS PLAY BALL, May 20, 1984
HBO/Repeats: multiple option, 1986-1987
Executive Producer: Joseph Cates
Producer: Buzz Potamkin
Director: Al Kouzel
Writers/Creators: Stan and Jan Berenstain
Music: Elliot Lawrence
Lyrics: Stan Berenstain
Company: Joseph Cates Productions in association with Buzzco Productions
Home Video: Children's Treasures (Embassy Home Entertainment #8006)

Narrator: Ron McLarty

Principal Characters and Voices

Papa Bear	Ron McLarty
Mama Bear	Pat Lysinger
Brother Bear	Knowl Johnson
Sister Bear	Gabriela Glatzer

The Berenstain Bears' Littlest Leaguer had another little moral inter-woven into the scenario, especially as it affected Papa Bear, when Little League fever hit Bear Country. Papa Bear thought it was his son who was destined to "play ball," but it was his daughter who seemed more motivated to become "a Ron Grizzly or Tug McBear." He had visions of big headlines, big contracts and big bucks while he dreamt of making his son, and later his daughter, diamond stars. Along the way, Papa Bear forgot that baseball was supposed to be fun for the youngsters, even for such a surprisingly super duper talent as Sister Bear. Mama kept her perspective as Papa Bear's ambitions for his children resulted in another very valuable lesson. Songs: "Baseball Is...," "I Want It All" (Sister), "Come to Our Pickup Baseball Game" (Brother).

BERENSTAIN BEARS MEET BIG PAW, THE

Broacast History
    Premiere: November 20, 1980
    NBC/Thursday 8:30-9:00 PM
    Sponsor: Kellogg's
    NBC/Repeat: November 24, 1981
    HBO/Repeats: multiple option, 1985-1986
Executive Producer: Joseph Cates
Producer: Buzz Potamkin
Directors: Mordicai Gerstein, Al Kouzel
Writers/Creators: Stan and Jan Berenstain
Music: Elliot Lawrence
Lyrics: Stan Berenstain
Company: Joseph Cates Productions in association with Perpetual
    Motion Pictures
Home Video: Children's Treasures (Embassy Home Entertainment
    #8003)

Narrator: Ron McLarty

Principal Characters and Voices
Papa Bear   Ron McLarty
Mama Bear   Pat Lysinger
Brother Bear   Jonathan Lewis
Sister Bear   Gabriela Glatzer
Big Paw/Announcer   Bob Kaliban

The Berenstain Bears Meet Big Paw delivered another little homily in prime time, this time centered around the true meaning of Thanks-giving. The holiday was near at hand, but so was Big Paw, a monster who, as legend had it, intended to "gobble up" the bruins in Bear Country to punish them for their selfish behavior. Through the actions of Sister and Brother Bear, who were saved from disaster by that monster of monsters, the Bear family learned that some leg-ends were not to be believed as the children showed Mama and Papa Bear the way to understand strangers, whatever their size.

BERENSTAIN BEARS PLAY BALL, THE   see   BERENSTAIN BEARS'
LITTLEST LEAGUER, THE

BERENSTAIN BEARS' VALENTINE SPECIAL, THE

Broadcast History
   Premiere: February 13, 1982
   NBC/Saturday 8:00-8:30 PM
   Sponsor: Kellogg's
   NBC/Repeat: February 12, 1983
   HBO/Repeats: multiple option, 1986-1987
Executive Producer: Joseph Cates
Producer: Buzz Potamkin
Associate Producer: Jere Jacob
Directors: Mordicai Gerstein, Al Kouzel
Writers/Creators: Jan Berenstain, Stan Berenstain
Music: Elliot Lawrence
Lyrics: Stan Berenstain
Company: Joseph Cates Productions in association with Perpetual
   Motion Pictures
Home Video: Children's Treasures (Embassy Home Entertainment
   #8002)

Narrator: Ron McLarty

Principal Characters and Voices
Papa Bear   Ron McLarty
Mama Bear   Pat Lysinger
Brother Bear   Knowl Johnson
Sister Bear   Gabriela Glatzer
Bearcaster/others   Jerry Sroka

The Berenstain Bears' Valentine Special was a pleasant musical romp
through Bear Country with Jan and Stan Berenstain's cute critters,
who spoke mostly in rhyme. Brother Bear, a star ice-hockey forward, tried his best to keep his mind on the forthcoming Valentine's
Day Hockey Game, but a succession of mushy valentines--"Down with
mush, all that gush!"--from "guess who" played hob with his concentration. The whole Bear family was preoccupied with the holiday.
Believing there was more to life than a hockey puck, Sister Bear
played Cupid and found the "14th is more to my style, there's something more worthwhile." In his usual blue overalls, Papa Bear tried
to create a truly grand valentine for Mama Bear: "I won't settle
for the merely sentimental, it must be something monumental." And
Mama, in her white polka-dot blue hat, brought some warm, wise,
common sense to the goings-on. The big game at hand, the Bear
Country Cousins were aligned against the Bear Town Bullies, a hard-
hitting team with a tough goalie, and won, 2 to 1. In a twist at the
close, Brother Bear fantasized his secret admirer was Charlene Bear,
the only "10" at the Bear School, but it was none other than the

Bullies' goalie who, when unmasked, was a she named Honey Bear that admired Brother Bear's hockey prowess. Songs: "A Young Bear's Fancy," "Love Is," "Down With Mush."

BESTEST PRESENT, THE   see   FOR BETTER OR FOR WORSE: THE BESTEST PRESENT

BETTY BOOP   see   ROMANCE OF BETTY BOOP, THE

BLACK ARROW, THE

Broadcast History
    Premiere: December 2, 1973
    CBS/FAMOUS CLASSIC TALES, Sunday 5:00-6:00 PM
    Sponsor: Kenner Products (Toy Group, General Mills)
    CBS/Repeat: September 22, 1974
    SYN/Repeats: 1975 +
Executive Producer: Walter J. Hucker
Directors: Leif Gram, Jean Tych
Writer: John Palmer
Music: John Sangster
Company: Air Programs International, Sydney, Australia/60 minutes
Distributor: D. L. Taffner ("Animated Classics for Children")/
    1985-
Home Video: Classics for Kids (MGM/UA)

Voices
    Alistair Duncan, Jeannie Drynan, Tim Elliott, Barbara Frawley, Ron Haddrick, John Llewellyn, Owen Weingott

The Black Arrow was a literal animated version of the Robert Louis Stevenson historical romance set in the time of the War of the Roses between the Houses of Lancaster and York. It followed the adventures of Squire Dick Shelton, the orphaned young heir to the Tunstall Estate coveted by his guardian Sir Daniel Brackley, who joined the mysterious Brotherhood of the Black Arrow, a band of forest outlaws.

BLACK BEAUTY

Broadcast History
    Premiere: October 28, 1978
    CBS/FAMOUS CLASSIC TALES, Saturday 1:00-2:00 PM
    Sponsor: Kenner Products (Toy Group, General Mills)
    CBS/Repeats: November 11, 1979; KENNER FAMILY CLASSICS, November 6, 1983
    SYN/Repeats: November 9, 1980 +
Executive Producers: William Hanna, Joseph Barbera

Producer: Neil Balnaves
Director: Chris Cuddington
Writer: Kimmer Ringwald
Music: Australian Screen Music
Company: Hanna-Barbera Productions, Sydney, Australia, (Southern
    Star Productions)/60 minutes
Distributor: Worldvision Enterprises/1980-
Home Video: Worldvision

Narrator: Alan Young

Voices
    David Comfort, Cathleen Cordell, Alan Dinehart, Mike Evans,
    David Gregory, Colin Hamilton, Laurie Main, Patricia Sigris,
    Barbara Stevens, Alan Young, Cam Young

Black Beauty was brought to life in an adaptation of the 1877 eponymous children's novel by Anna Sewell, set in the countryside of
England. As a colt, Beauty raced happily through the meadow with
his mother, Duchess. The ebony horse was sleek as a panther and
fleet as a deer. With a blazing white star on his forehead and a
single white hoof, he was a stand out among the other colts and
looked like a great champion. Carefully raised and considerately
treated until injured by Reuben, a vicious groom, Beauty was sold
to various masters at whose hands he experienced starvation, cruelty
and the death of his friend, the mare Ginger. One step ahead of
the slaughterhouse, he was nursed back to health by a friendly
coachman, Jerry Barker, and eventually sold at the Horse Fair to
Joe Green, once a young stable boy who nearly caused his death.
Purchased for Green's young son, Black Beauty was returned to the
meadow in which he grew up, where happily he spent the rest of
his days.

BLINKINS, THE

Broadcast History
    Premiere: Spring 1986
    SYN/local station option
    Sponsor: LJN Toys
    SYN/Repeats: January 1987 +
Executive Producer: Yutaka Fugioka
Supervising Producer: Harvey Harrison
Producers: Charles Swenson, Sachiko Tsuneda
Directors: Osamu Dezaki, Sunao Katabuchi
Writer: Charles Swenson
Music: Dick Eastman, Bobby Hart
Company: MCA Television in association with Tokyo Movie Shinsha,
    Tokyo, Japan
Distributor: MCA Television/1986-

Principal Characters and Voices

Mr. Benjamin	Burgess Meredith
Grog the Frog	Paul Williams
Blink	Missy Gold
Shady	Tracey Gold
Baby Twinkle	Brandy Gold
Flashy	Sagan Lewis
Sparkle	Carrie Swenson
Flicker/Pettiford	Louise Chamis
Slime	Chris Latta

Announcer: Henry Gibson

The Blinkins featured five female fairy-like flitters, tiny bug-like beings who lit up and glowed in rainbow hues, chosen to perform in the annual Flower of Spring Ceremony. Deep in the wood, spunky lavender Blink, dependable tan Sparkle, shy yellow Flicker, glamorous pink Flashy and selfish peach Shady were instructed by Mr. Benjamin the Owl, the guardian of their tree-top home, Twilight Treehouse, how they had to fly over the Flower so that the first ray of Spring sunshine passed through their wings. Baby Twinkle was the blue toddler of Blinkin Land and Pettiford the Ladybug a friend who often carted the Blinkins about on her back. Their archenemy was Slime, a monster who lived at the bottom of the swamp and hated light, Spring and the Blinkins. His toady was Grog the Frog, who was bullied into capturing the Blinkins. Through a ruse involving the vain Shady, Grog was able to encase them all in a large glass jar which sank into the swamp water where, at the bottom of the muck, Slime awaited. Then Blink began to beat her wings and glow, and the others joined in and the light became more intense. An enraged Slime threw the jar up into the air whereupon the Blinkins finally freed themselves. As the first ray of Spring sunshine broke through Winter's clouds, the Blinkins spotted it, chased it and interlocked their wings, focusing the beam on the Flower, to save Spring for another year. Songs: "Blinkins' Theme," "Together," "Rainy Day Blues."

The special was based on the characters from the LJN doll and toy line, licensed by the Merchandising Corporation of America.

BLINKINS AND THE BEAR, THE

Broadcast History
 Premiere: September 1986
 SYN/local station option (KCOP, Los Angeles, September 7, 1986,
  Sunday 7:30-8:00 AM PST)
 Sponsor: LJN Toys
SYN/Repeats: January 1987 +
Executive Producer: Yutaka Fugioka
Supervising Producer: Harvey Harrison
Producers: Charles Swenson, Sachiko Tsuneda

Directors: Osamu Dezaki, Sunao Katabuchi
Writer: Charles Swenson
Music: Dick Eastman, Bobby Hart
Company: MCA Television in association with Tokyo Movie Shinsha,
 Tokyo, Japan
Distributor: MCA Television/1986-

Principal Characters and Voices
Blink	Noelle North
Flash	Daryl Wood
Sparkle	Carrie Swenson
Flicker/Baby Twinkle	Louise Chamis
Shady	Jennifer Darling
Mr. Benjamin	Burgess Meredith
Sneed	Chris Latta
Grog	Hamilton Camp

Announcer: Alan Young

The Blinkins and the Bear introduced a new nemesis for the cast of
Tinkerbell-like creatures who glowed and sparkled in rainbow hues.
At school the Blinkins were taught by Mr. Benjamin the Owl that
they must take part in the fall harvest to provide food supplies for
the coming winter. So off they flew, gathering baskets of nuts and
berries, singing and happy in their work until the precious stores
were threatened by the greedy demands of Grog the Frog and Sneed
the Bear. Flying into Sneed's face to tell him how arrogant and awful he was, the spunky Blink was swatted unconscious and the villianous pair carted off some food, planning to return for more that
night. When Blink recovered, they flew off to see Mr. Ben and together they concocted a plan to rescue their foodstuffs and teach
the nasty pair a lesson. Using a rag doll and long cape, Mr. Ben
and the Blinkins created a giant Queen Blinkin with Flicker as her
voice. When Sneed and Grog returned that night they were confronted by the Queen's powers, thanks to the behind-the-scenes
machinations of the Blinkins and some magic from Mr. Ben, who made
Grog disappear in a powder flash. Threatened with the same fate,
Sneed promised to make amends, not to take advantage of those
smaller than himself and behave like a good bear. Then the bear
trotted off to his cave for his winter nap. Songs: "Blinkins' Theme,"
"Autumn Souvenir," "Working Overtime."
 The film was joined together with The Blinkins and the Blizzard [q.v.] and distributed as an hour-long Blinkins special in January 1987.

BLINKINS AND THE BLIZZARD, THE

Broadcast History
 Premiere: Christmastime 1986
 SYN/local station option

Sponsor: LJN Toys
Executive Producer: Yutaka Fugioka
Supervising Producer: Harvey Harrison
Producers: Charles Swenson, Sachiko Tsuneda
Directors: Osamu Dezaki, Sunao Katabuchi
Writer: Charles Swenson
Music: Dick Eastman, Bobby Hart
Company: MCA Television in association with Tokyo Movie Shinsha, Tokyo, Japan
Distributor: MCA Television / 1986-

Principal Characters and Voices

Blink	Noelle North
Flashy	Daryl Wood
Sparkle	Carrie Swenson
Flicker/Baby Twinkle	Louise Chamis
Shady	Jennifer Darling
Mr. Benjamin	Burgess Meredith
Sneed	Chris Latta
Grog	Hamilton Camp

Announcer: Alan Young

The Blinkins and the Blizzard presented the cute female fairy-like
creatures in another tale involving Grog the Frog and Sneed the
Bear. Searching for her lost doll, a little girl became lost in the
wood and during the ensuing snowstorm was guided to a cozy cave
by the glowing Blinkins, unaware it was Sneed's winter den, while
they flew off to consult Mr. Benjamin. Watching the goings-on and
knowing the Blinkins would return, Grog rigged a net across the
entrance to ensnare them. Upon their return the Blinkins flew into
Grog's net, and, frightened by an aroused Sneed, the little girl ran
into it also. Finding the net, Sneed thanked the stupified Grog and
carted his bundle of "bear food" back into the cave, where he pondered whom to snack on first. Quickly, Blink borrowed a piece of
Flashy's jewelry and boldly volunteered, attracting the bear's attention while she began spinning the jewel in front of him. With the
bear hypnotized, the Blinkins and the girl were soon freed and
Blink commanded the sleeping Sneed to roll over, trapping Grog
under his paw. Fleeing the cave, Blink and the others led the girl
home through the blizzard with their glowing tail-lights. Later, the
little girl's lost doll appeared with a note, "With love, the Blinkins."
Songs: "Blinkins' Theme," "Like Magic," "Hold On."

BLONDIE & DAGWOOD

Broadcast History
Premiere: May 15, 1987
CBS/Friday 8:00-8:30 PM

BLONDIE & DAGWOOD, © 1987, King Features Entertainment, Inc. /
King Features Syndicate, Inc. Courtesy of King Features Entertainment.

Executive Producers: Margaret Loesch, Bruce Palsner, Lee Gunther
Producer/Director: Mike Joens
Supervising Producer/Story Editor: Hank Saroyan
Writers: Bob Smith, Barry O'Brien
Music: Rob Walsh
Company: Marvel Productions with King Features Entertainment in
   association with Toei Animation, Tokyo, Japan

Principal Characters and Voices
Blondie Bumstead   Loni Anderson
Dagwood Bumstead   Frank Welker
Alexander Bumstead   Ike Eisenmann

Cookie Bumstead	Ellen Gerstell
Julius Dithers	Alan Oppenheimer
Cora Dithers/Mrs. Hannon	Russi Taylor
Tootsie Woodley	Laurel Page
Mr. Beasley/Herb Woodley	Jack Angel
Daisy (Bumstead's dog)	Pat Fraley

Blondie & Dagwood updated the couple that first appeared in Depression-era comic pages, the happily married subjects of one of the best-read comic strips of all time. Placed in a contemporary setting, the cast included Blondie, the enduring housewife, and her bumbling spouse Dagwood Bumstead, their teenagers Alexander and Cookie, Dagwood's irascible boss Julius Dithers and his henpecking wife Cora, the mailman Mr. Beasley, neighbors Herb and Tootsie Woodley and Daisy, the family dog. This time, when the quintessential middle-class husband and father Dagwood was finally fired from his managerial position after years of threats from Mr. Dithers, the family was thrown into chaos. Taking charge in her usual competent and practical manner, Blondie decided to go to work to support the family while Dagwood ineptly took over the domestic matters. It all climaxed at a surprise dinner party Blondie threw for Mr. Dithers who, through the prodding of his wife Cora, grumpily rehired Dagwood with an increase in salary. The next morning, Dagwood and Blondie flattened Mr. Beasley, the mailman, in their joint rush to catch the bus enroute to work.

The special was the first animated TV adaptation of the newspaper strip Blondie (September 15, 1930), created for King Features Syndicate by Murat B. "Chic" Young and since 1973 written by his son Dean Young and illustrated currently by Stan Drake. It is carried by more than 2,000 newspapers worldwide. The pair were married in the strip on February 17, 1933, and Alexander, initially called Baby Dumpling, was born in 1934, and their daughter, Cookie, appeared in 1941. The property inspired 28 movies between 1938 and 1951 and two TV situation comedies titled Blondie (NBC, 1957/CBS, 1968-1969).

BOLLO CAPER, THE

Broadcast History
    Premiere: February 2, 1985
    ABC/ABC WEEKEND SPECIALS, Saturday 11:00-11:30 AM
    ABC/Repeats: November 16, 1985; August 16, 1986; November
        29, 1986; July 11, 1987
Producer: Rick Reinert
Directors: Rick Reinert, Dave Bennett
Writer: Malcolm Marmorstein
Music: Steve Zuckerman
Company: Rick Reinert Productions

Principal Characters and Voices
Bollo   Michael Bell

THE BOLLO CAPER. © 1985, Rick Reinert Productions, Inc. Courtesy of Capital Cities/ABC.

Nefertiti/Lulu La Looche/ Lioness/Eleanor the Elephant	Ilene Latter
Clamper Carstair/Lion/Iceberg/ Emperor	Hal Smith
Snag Carstair/Chestnut/Monkey #1	Will Ryan
Felix the Furrier/Monkey #2/ President	Pete Renaday

The Bollo Caper told about a golden leopard who learned that he had to go to Congress to save his own skin and his species. Bollo and his beloved Nefertiti were the last pair of golden leopards in the world and possessed the most beautiful skins in Africa. They soon found themselves stalked by trappers Snag and Clamper Carstair, on assignment for Felix the Furrier in New York City, who was commissioned to find a fantastic fur coat for his movie-star client, Lulu La Looche. Bollo led them away from Nefertiti, but in the process was trapped and tranquilized. Awakening in a crate aboard a cargo plane headed for New York, he managed to escape once it had landed, eluding the waiting Felix and Lulu. A major chase ensued throughout the Big Apple, and along the way the Bronx Zoo animals and a police horse aided his flight. Finally he learned that the only way he could escape a deadly fate was to get Congress to amend the Endangered Species Act to include the Golden Leopard. Hitching a ride to Washington, D.C., on a circus train, Bollo was aided by Eleanor the elephant, who drafted the proposed measure. With Felix, Lulu, Snag and Clamper in hot pursuit, Bollo was chased from the Congress building before he could present his bill and trapped on the White House grounds, where he fell into the arms of a visiting dignitary from Africa. Thus the bill came to the attention of the President. Returned to Africa, Bollo and Nefertiti settled in a protected preserve where they raised a family. Based on a story by columnist Art Buchwald, the special carried some naturalist's statements and a serio-comic plea for the preservation of wildlife.

BUGS BUNNY: ALL-AMERICAN HERO

Broadcast History
    Premiere: May 4, 1981
    CBS/Monday 8:00-8:30 PM
    CBS/Repeats: March 10, 1982; April 16, 1983; May 26, 1984;
        May 10, 1985; January 7, 1986 (partially preempted); June 18,
        1987
Executive Producer: Hal Geer
Producer: Friz Freleng
Directors: Friz Freleng, David Detiege
Writers: Friz Freleng, John Dunn, David Detiege
Music: Carl Stalling, Milt Franklin, Bill Lava
Company: Warner Bros. Television

Principal Characters and Voices
Bugs Bunny/Yosemite Sam/
    Tweety Pie/Sylvester   Mel Blanc
Clyde   Jane Foray

Bugs Bunny: All-American Hero rearranged some past events when his little nephew Clyde asked for help in preparing for an American History test. Assisted in his yarn-spinning by Yosemite Sam, Tweety Pie and Sylvester, Uncle Bugs suddenly became a super-patriot relating his version of the nation's glorious past, such as the "drafting" of George Washington into the Colonial Army and the creation of the first flag, excerpted from the cartoon Yankee Doodle Bugs (August 28, 1954). Other highlights were a clash between Yankee Bugs and Rebel Colonel Sam, during which Bugs took refuge in a southern mansion and disguised himself as Scarlett O'Hara; the Southern armies dispatching Tweety Pie as a carrier-canary through Yankee lines and into the claws of salivating Sylvester; Bugs as a flying ace fighting an aerial duel with Sam Van Spam during the First World War; and Honest Sam running against Bugs for Mayor in a hot political contest and getting carried away with his baby-kissing campaign.

BUGS BUNNY EASTER SPECIAL, THE

Broadcast History
    Premiere: April 7, 1977
    CBS/Thursday 8:00-9:00 PM
    CBS/Repeats: March 18, 1978; April 13, 1979; April 2, 1980;
        April 14, 1984; March 30, 1985
Executive Producer: Hal Geer
Producers: David H. DePatie, Friz Freleng
Supervising Director: Friz Freleng
Directors: Robert McKimson, Gerry Chiniquy, Chuck Jones
Company: DePatie-Freleng Enterprises for Warner Bros. Television/
    60 minutes

Principal Characters and Voices
Bugs Bunny/Daffy Duck/Sylvester/
    Pepe Le Pew/Foghorn Leghorn/
    Yosemite Sam   Mel Blanc
Granny   June Foray

The Bugs Bunny Easter Special attempted to solve a holiday crisis
of sorts when Bugs aided a desperate Granny to find a substitute
for the Easter Bunny, who was bedridden with a cold. Granny had
hoped that Bugs would be the Easter stand-in, but Bugs, busy movie
star that he was, had prior commitments and instead offered his help
in finding someone else. Daffy Duck was the most eager applicant,
but despite his fervent attempts and Granny's fear that the Easter
eggs would not be delivered, she couldn't quite see him in the role.
So Bugs and Granny then auditioned a full roster of other hopefuls,
including Sylvester, Pepe Le Pew, Foghorn Leghorn and Yosemite
Sam, through segments from ten classic animated Warner Bros. shorts.
    The film was the second of fourteen prime-time thematic spe-
cials in the Bugs Bunny series, following the inaugural program
Carnival of the Animals [q.v.].

BUGS BUNNY IN KING ARTHUR'S COURT see CONNECTICUT
    RABBIT IN KING ARTHUR'S COURT, A

BUGS BUNNY IN SPACE

Broadcast History
    Premiere: September 6, 1977
    CBS/Tuesday 8:00-8:30 PM
    CBS/Repeat: April 18, 1978
Executive Producer: Hal Geer
Directors: Chuck Jones, Friz Freleng
Music: Carl Stalling, Milt Franklin, Bill Lava
Company: Warner Bros. Television

Principal Characters and Voices
Bugs Bunny/Daffy Duck/Porky
Pig/Martian (Commander X-2)   Mel Blanc

Bugs Bunny in Space provided an answer to the pressing question,
"What's up, Doc?" in outer space. The "what" turned out to be an
odd little Martian who gave the cheeky rabbit nothing but trouble
as they swapped visits to each other's home planets. Looking for
a typical Earthman to bring back on his flying saucer, the Martian
somehow decided that Bugs was the perfect specimen. Later, Bugs
seized the upper hand, landing on Mars in his rocket to lay claim
to the planet in the name of Earth. The Martian returned the favor
by coming back to Earth, this time to destroy it because it blocked
his view of Venus. With his sidekick, space cadet Porky Pig, Daffy
Duck contributed to the madcap antics by appearing as fearless
spaceman Duck Dodgers in the Twenty-Fourth-and-a-half Century
(July 25, 1953), one of the more redeeming cartoons, involved with
the Martian (Commander X-2) during a search for the rare Aludium
Q-36 on Planet "X". All scenes were selected from previously exhibited productions.

BUGS BUNNY/LOONEY TUNES ALL-STAR 50TH ANNIVERSARY

Broadcast History
    Premiere: January 14, 1986
    CBS/Tuesday 8:00-9:00 PM
    CBS/Repeat: THE BUGS BUNNY/LOONEY TUNES JUBILEE, July
        24, 1987
Executive Producer: Lorne Michaels
Producer: Mary Salter
Associate Producer: Juli Pari
Director: Gary Weis
Director/TV Animation: Chuck Jones
Writers: Tom Gammill, Max Pross, Greg Ford
Music: Hal Willner
Company: Broadway Video in association with Warner Bros. Televi-
    sion/60 minutes

Guest Stars
    Eve Arden, Candice Bergen, Mel Blanc, David Bowie, George
    Burns, Chevy Chase, Cher, Kirk Douglas, Friz Freleng, Jeff
    Goldblum, Jeremy Irons, Chuck Jones, Quincy Jones, Penny Mar-
    shall, Steve Martin, Bill Murray, Mike Nichols, Geraldine Page,
    Molly Ringwald, Danny Thomas, Billy Dee Williams, Chuck Yeager

Principal Characters and Voices
Bugs Bunny/Daffy Duck/ Porky Pig/
    Elmer Fudd/Speedy Gonzales/
    Foghorn Leghorn/Pepe Le Pew/
    Petunia Pig/Yosemite Sam/
    Sylvester/Tweety/Others   Mel Blanc

Road Runner/Wile E. Coyote   (non-speaking)

Bugs Bunny/Looney Tunes All-Star 50th Anniversary was an hour-long special highlighting Warner Bros. half-century contribution to animated art. The Tinseltown testimonial mixed on-screen glories with off-screen "roasts" from celebrities in cameo roles. For instance, David Bowie noted, "A lot of things that I do are picked up from Bugs." And Chevy Chase observed, "Porky (Pig) doesn't get many jobs now." Most of the hour, however, was devoted to clips from dozens of captioned cartoons. Candice Bergen recalled fond memories of Porky Pig, Steve Martin revealed how many of Hollywood's super-stars have stolen routines from Bugs Bunny, and Bill Murray provided clues that Daffy Duck may have been Warner Bros.' actual true genius. It opened with scenes from the 1985 Museum of Modern Art exhibition gala honoring Warner Bros. cartoon art during the studio's Golden Jubilee Anniversary in 1985-1986. Directors Friz Freleng and Chuck Jones shared some real stories behind some of their moments in cartoon history along with voice impersonator Mel Blanc.

Warner Bros. opened its first cartoon studio in 1929, known as "Termite Terrace," and released the first short in 1930. But it was not until 1935 that Porky Pig emerged as its first real star, followed by Daffy Duck in 1937 and Bugs Bunny in 1940. The "was-cally wabbit" was the second cartoon character, following Mickey Mouse, honored with a star on Hollywood Boulevard's Walk of Fame (December 21, 1985). Bugs has appeared on television for more than 30 years, twice as long as his theater appearances. The special was a CBS "Read More About It" book project in conjunction with The Library of Congress.

BUGS BUNNY MOTHER'S DAY SPECIAL, THE

Broadcast History
Premiere: May 12, 1979
CBS/Saturday 8:30-9:00 PM
Sponsor: McDonald's
CBS/Repeats: May 12, 1984; May 10, 1985; May 8, 1987
Executive Producer: Hal Geer
Directors: Jim Davis, Art Davis, Friz Freleng, Bob McKimson
Writers: Dave Detiege, Jim Davis, John Dunn, Warren Foster, Hal
    Geer, Carl Kohler
Music: Milt Franklyn, Harper MacKay, Carl Stalling
Company: Warner Bros. Television

Principal Characters and Voices
Bugs Bunny/Daffy Duck/
    Foghorn Leghorn/Stork   Mel Blanc
Granny/Daisy Duck/Mama Gorilla   June Foray

The Bugs Bunny Mother's Day Special featured a pixilated stork with an unorthodox delivery service. Bugs and Granny met the blundering bird in the park, and when the conversation turned to Mother's Day, the stork butted in to brag about his particular contributions to the holiday. But if delivering babies had been left entirely to this off-course stork, there never would have been a Mother's Day to celebrate. In a series of flashbacks, he lingered with each proud parent for a congratulatory toast until he tippled himself tipsy, mixed up an egg intended for the Daffy Ducks with one meant for a family of crocodiles and managed to make a napping Foghorn Leghorn the puzzled parent of an outsized ostrich. Bugs recalled he too was misdelivered by the bird, not once but twice; first to a kangaroo and then to a gorilla. Only his Bugsian blarney saved him, by a hare, from disaster. And when the stork made a second attempt at delivery to the very wary Daffy, the unwanted egg ended up accidentally again in a home for spinster ducks where the newborn found itself with 40 admiring mothers.

BUGS BUNNY MYSTERY SPECIAL, THE

Broadcast History
Premiere: October 15, 1980
CBS/Wednesday 8:00-8:30 PM
CBS/Repeats: December 5, 1981 (Saturday, 9:30-10:00 AM); March 8, 1983; March 10, 1984; September 14, 1984; June 5, 1987
Executive Producer: Hal Geer
Associate Producer: Jean MacCurdy
Directors: Friz Freleng, Chuck Jones, Gerry Chiniquy
Writers: Jack Enyart, Hal Geer
Music: Harper MacKay
Company: Warner Bros. Television

Principal Characters and Voices
Bugs Bunny/Porky Pig/Elmer Fudd/
   Yosemite Sam/Wile E. Coyote/
   Tweety Pie/Sylvester   Mel Blanc

The Bugs Bunny Mystery Special put Bugs within a hare's breadth of being dubbed Public Rabbit Number One when a series of mistaken identities involved him in a mini-crime spree. Porky Pig opened the show with an Alfred Hitchcock impression, then the whodunit began when Bugs stopped by the bank to withdraw a carrot from his safe deposit box just as a daring daylight robbery was committed by a mysterious Tall Dark Stranger. The villain escaped, but Bugs was arrested by vigilant Special Agent Elmer Fudd and wound up on the rockpile at Sing Song Prison, under the watchful eye of Guard Yosemite Sam. Determined to free himself from injustice, the raucous rabbit made life so miserable for his jailer that Sam threw him out. Heading for the desert and a new life, Bugs ran afoul of his old nemesis, Wile E. Coyote, who was determined to apprehend the fugitive and claim an offered reward. Aware that he still was, in Fudd's words, a "wanted wabbit," Bugs hopped a train that happened to carry Agent Fudd, the Tall Dark Stranger and, in the baggage car, Tweety Pie and Sylvester--the latter, as always, bent upon dispatching the former. After giving Fudd the slip, the harassed hare was accused of kidnapping when Tweety turned up missing. By this time, Bugs was bugged with bum raps and set out to track down the culprit, the Tall Dark Stranger (Porky Pig), with the pursuit involving a hare-raising plane ride, a police chase and a real by-the-fingernails cliffhanger. The special featured previously exhibited cartoons.

On December 5, 1981, The Bugs Bunny Mystery Special launched a new CBS Saturday-morning schedule change for six series and was repeated at 9:30-10:00 AM, replacing The Bugs Bunny/Road Runner Show, which returned the following week in a new timeslot. It was the only Bugs Bunny special seen on the daytime schedule, described in Children's Television, Part I, (Scarecrow, 1983), pp. 51-55.

BUGS BUNNY THANKSGIVING DIET, THE

Broadcast History
    Premiere: November 15, 1979
    CBS/Thursday 8:00-8:30 PM
    Sponsor: Kenner Products
    CBS/Repeats: November 10, 1981; November 12, 1983; November
        20, 1984; November 26, 1985
Executive Producer: Hal Geer
Directors: Hal Geer, David Detiege, Friz Freleng, Chuck Jones, Bob
    McKimson
Writers: John Dunn, Jack Enyart, Warren Foster, Michael Maltese,
    Tedd Pierce
Music: Carl Stalling, Milt Franklin, Bill Lava
Company: Warner Bros. Television

Principal Characters and Voices
Bugs Bunny/Porky Pig/Sylvester/
    Yosemite Sam/Tweety Pie/
    Tasmanian Devil   Mel Blanc
Millicent   June Foray

The Bugs Bunny Thanksgiving Diet offered prescriptions for avoiding holiday gluttony, when Bugs hung out his shingle and dispensed advice, and carrots, to his friends. Dr. Bunny's special brand of medical expertise benefited Porky Pig, Sylvester and Millicent, who fretted about putting on pounds, when Bugs called on the assistance of such friends and adversaries as Yosemite Sam, the Road Runner, Tweety Pie and the Tasmanian Devil to illustrate his theories via animated sequences from previously exhibited cartoons. His biggest problem turned out to be Millicent, the overweight, amorous Slobbovian rabbit whose gastronomic gorging he attributed to an emotional problem. Using the lonesome life of the Coyote (Forlornus Miserablus) as an example, Bugs prescribed love, but backed off from his diagnosis when Millicent found that prescription uncomfortably close at hand. Bugs also tried to help Sylvester consider culinary alternatives to Tweety Pie in an excerpt from the Oscar-winner Birds Anonymous (August 10, 1957), but the obsessed feline finally failed in typically frustrating fashion.

BUGS BUNNY'S BUSTIN' OUT ALL OVER

Broadcast History
    Premiere: May 21, 1980
    CBS/Wednesday 8:00-8:30 PM
    CBS/Repeats: March 20, 1981; May 5, 1984; April 6, 1985; June
      5, 1987
Executive Producer: Hal Geer
Producer/Writer: Chuck Jones
Directors: Chuck Jones, Phil Monroe
Music: Dean Elliott
Company: Chuck Jones Enterprises in association with Warner Bros.
    Television

Principal Characters and Voices
Bugs Bunny/Elmer Fudd/Marvin
    the Martian/Abominable
    Snowman   Mel Blanc
Road Runner/Wile E. Coyote   (non-speaking)

Bugs Bunny's Bustin' Out All Over presented three new cartoons from Chuck Jones. Springtime arrived and stirred the birds, the bees and Bugs' memory when a crowd of young rabbits rushed by, celebrating the end of the school year. He remembered his own childhood where a mischievous infant Elmer Fudd was on the prowl with his popgun, waiting for the opening of "wabbit season." Young Elmer fell off a cliff only to be pushed out of the way by Wile E. Coyote holding a sign which read, "Make way for somebody who really knows how to fall." In the second episode, Bugs was chatting with the blooming flowers and budding trees, welcoming spring, when a carrot on a string caught his attention and the indefatigable rabbit found himself the captive of Marvin the Martian, who took Bugs back to Mars to be a companion for the Abominable Snowman. In the last cartoon, Wile E. Coyote achieved the impossible, finally catching the Road Runner after a 30-year chase, while shrunk to worm size and grasping the now giant bird's leg. Turning to the audience, Wile held up some signs reading, "You've always wanted me to catch him. Now what do I do?"

BUGS BUNNY'S HOWL-OWEEN SPECIAL

Broadcast History
    Premiere: October 26, 1977

CBS/Wednesday 8:00-8:30 PM
Sponsors: Hershey Foods, Parker Brothers
CBS/Repeats: October 25, 1978; October 31, 1979; October 29,
   1980; October 27, 1981
Executive Producer: Hal Geer
Directors: Robert McKimson, Chuck Jones, Friz Freleng, Abe Levi-
   tow, Maurice Noble, Dave Detiege
Writers: Cliff Roberts, Tedd Pierce, Warren Foster, Michael Maltese,
   John Dunn
Music: Carl Stalling, Milt Franklin, Bill Lava
Company: Warner Bros. Television

Principal Characters and Voices
Bugs Bunny/Daffy Duck/Porky Pig/
   Speedy Gonzales/Sylvester/
   Tweety Pie   Mel Blanc
Witch Hazel   June Foray

Bugs Bunny's Howl-oween Special began with a trick-or-treat visit
when the indefatigable rabbit made his holiday rounds disguised as
a witch. Arriving at Witch Hazel's door, she took him for the real
thing, a witchly intruder on her home turf, and planned to eliminate
him with one of her special brews. Wisely, Bugs decided to take
refreshment elsewhere, but not so wisely, he made Dr. Jekyll's
house his next stop. In the adventures that ensued, Witch Hazel
and Bugs tried to best each other as number-one Halloween spooks
and involved a number of innocent bystanders in the fiendish frenzy.
Before the night was out, Tweety Pie and Daffy Duck were turned
into monsters, Speedy Gonzales became Witch Hazel's double, and
Porky Pig and Sylvester had a tough time fending off the hare-
raising haunts. The special combined excerpts from previous exhibited cartoons with new animation.

BUGS BUNNY'S LOONEY CHRISTMAS TALES

Broadcast History
   Premiere: November 27, 1979
   CBS/Tuesday 8:00-8:30 PM
   Sponsor: McDonald's
   CBS/Repeats: December 13, 1980; November 27, 1981; December
      6, 1982; December 4, 1984
Executive Producer: Hal Geer
Producers: David H. DePatie, Friz Freleng (Bugs Bunny portions);
   Chuck Jones (Road Runner portion)
Directors: Friz Freleng, Chuck Jones, Bill Perez, David Detiege,
   Art Vitello, Tony Benedict
Writers: Friz Freleng, John Dunn, Chuck Jones, Tony Benedict
Music: Dean Elliott
Company: DePatie-Freleng Enterprises with Chuck Jones Enterprises
   and Warner Bros. Television

Principal Characters and Voices
Bugs Bunny/Porky Pig/Yosemite
    Sam/Tweety Pie   Mel Blanc
Clyde   June Foray
Road Runner/Wile E. Coyote   (non-speaking)

Bugs Bunny's Looney Christmas Tales featured three new cartoons, including Bugs and his band of carolers in their own version of Charles Dickens' A Christmas Carol and the Tasmanian Devil as an unlikely Santa Claus. After Bob Cratchit (Porky Pig) was fired from his lowly job on Christmas Eve by his nasty boss Ebenezer Scrooge (Yosemite Sam), the forlorn Cratchit was befriended by the sympathetic Bugs Bunny. Trudging their way through the snow, Cratchit insisted that the rabbit join him and Tiny Tim (Tweety Pie) for their meager holiday supper. Touched by Cratchit's humble generosity, Bugs, in his own inimitable way, concocted a scheme to enlighten the miserly Scrooge. After the light finally dawned on Sam Scrooge, the ever-industrious Wile E. Coyote realized a flicker of hope in the news that Road Runners hate the snow. Worried about his own Christmas dinner, Wile determined to freeze the Road Runner into submission and on to his plate with a snow-making machine. But the patent was still pending on the Acme device, and the Coyote was left to his own self-inflicted fate as the elusive Road Runner managed to beep-beep his way through the sleet and snow. Through a complicated series of events, Santa Claus (Tasmanian Devil) dropped down the chimney on Bugs and his wide-eyed nephew Clyde. Unfortunately, the youngster's traditional Christmas Eve offering of milk and cookies did not even make a dent in Santa's voracious appetite.

BUGS BUNNY'S MAD WORLD OF TELEVISION

Broadcast History
    Premiere: January 11, 1982
    CBS/Monday 8:30-9:00 PM
    CBS/Repeats: April 2, 1983; September 14, 1983; July 28, 1984;
        September 6, 1985
Executive Producer/Producer: Hal Geer
Directors: Friz Freleng, Chuck Jones, Robert McKimson, David
    Detiege
Writers: David Detiege, John Dunn, Jack Enyart, Warren Foster,
    Hal Geer, Michael Joens, Chuck Jones, Michael Maltese, Tedd
    Pierce
Music: Carl Stalling, Milt Franklin, Bill Lava
Company: Warner Bros. Television

Principal Characters and Voices
Bugs Bunny/Yosemite Sam/Tweety
    Pie/Porky Pig/Pepe Le Pew   Mel Blanc

BUGS BUNNY'S MAD WORLD OF TELEVISION. © 1982, Warner Bros.,
Inc. Courtesy of Warner Bros. Television.

Bugs Bunny's Mad World of Television tuned in to the video scene
with a disgruntled Board of Directors at QTTV launching a search
for a new president. Bugs' background as a dancer, comedian and
all-around performer made him the perfect candidate and a shoe-in
for the position. But being in charge of entertainment for QTTV
was a heavy responsibility. First, Bugs pondered over a new Tweety
Pie pilot film. Then he contacted Pepe Le Pew to star in a TV
special. And, throughout it all, he had to contend with the antics
of Yosemite Sam, who plotted to overthrow him as head of the station. The special was compiled from previously exhibited cartoons.

BUGS BUNNY'S VALENTINE

Broadcast History
    Premiere: February 14, 1979
    CBS/Wednesday 8:00-8:30 PM
    CBS/Repeats: February 13, 1980; February 4, 1981; February
        2, 1982; February 11, 1984; February 11, 1986
Executive Producer: Hal Geer
Directors: Hal Geer, Jim Davis, Friz Freleng, Chuck Jones, Robert
    McKimson
Writers: Warren Foster, Hal Geer, Michael Maltese, Sid Marcus,
    Tedd Pierce

Music: Harper McKay, Carl Stalling, Milt Franklyn
Company: Warner Bros. Television

Principal Characters and Voices
Bugs Bunny/Yosemite Sam/Daffy
  Duck/ Pepe Le Pew/Forghorn
  Leghorn/Elmer Fudd (Cupid)   Mel Blanc

Bugs Bunny's Valentine featured Elmer Fudd in a new role as Cupid.
Already smitten with romance, Bugs encountered a bediapered Fudd
busily shooting his Valentine's Day arrows. Always quick with a
comment, Bugs put down the chubby cherub's efforts, insisting that
nature alone provided enough love without further stings from Cupid's bowmanship. To show off his potent love-instilling powers,
Elmer fired one of his heady arrows at the garrulous Bugs, and the
usually sensible carrot-muncher suddenly found himself head over
heels in love with an electric rabbit at the dog track, a truly shock-
ing experience for the would-be Lothario. Never one to concede
defeat, Bugs matched his own skills as a matchmaker with Cupid's.
In the competition that followed, Daffy Duck, Yosemite Sam, Pepe
Le Pew and Foghorn Leghorn found themselves victims in hapless
and ridiculous romantic escapades from their previously exhibited
cartoons, as the meddling pair played out a game of Can You Top
This?

BUNNICULA, THE VAMPIRE RABBIT

Broadcast History
    Premiere: January 9, 1982
    ABC/ABC WEEKEND SPECIALS, Saturday 12:00-12:30 PM
    ABC/Repeats: April 17, 1982; October 9, 1982; October 29, 1983
Executive Producers: Joseph Ruby, Ken Spears
Director: Charles A. Nichols
Writer: Mark Evanier
Music: Dean Elliott, Paul DeKorte
Company: Ruby-Spears Enterprises
Home Video: Worldvision

Principal Characters and Voices
Harold/Roy   Jack Carter
Chester/Stockboy/Hank   Howard Morris
Toby Monroe   Pat Peterson
Pete Monroe   Josh Milrad
Mr. Monroe/Storekeeper   Alan Young
Mrs. Monroe/Gertie/Alice   Janet Waldo
Boss/Andy   Allan Dinehart

Bunnicula, the Vampire Rabbit depicted the effects of a strange
bunny on the Monroe household, as told by an intelligent mutt,
Harold, the family's dog. The smalltown family included Mr. Monroe,

a scientist at the Worldco Food Processing plant, his wife and two boys, 8-year-old Toby and 10-year-old Pete. Chester, the family cat, was an avid reader of books and helped Harold look out for the family. A series of incidents at the plant, one in which a rope was chewed through holding a vat that narrowly missed the boss thanks to Mr. Monroe, forced its closure, putting nearly all the townspeople out of work. That day, in an adjoining field, the boys found a shoe box with a sleeping rabbit inside and took him home. An attached note in some Slavic language contained the name Bunnicula. Then began a series of puzzling incidents: during a full moon, the bunny disappeared and a perplexed storekeeper noted his tomatoes drained of juice, and Mrs. Monroe began to find all her vegetables de-juiced and those in the neighbors' gardens as well. Suspicious, Chester read up on Dracula and tried to convince Harold that the bunny was a vampire. Following Bunnicula one night after he rose from his box and made for the gardens, Harold, Chester and the neighbors were convinced of his guilt. In a furious chase, the bunny headed for the plant, where Harold and Chester wound up in a locked closet as Bunnicula bared his fangs and flew about, cornering a pack of wolves in a vat. Blaming the events on the wolves, the town and household returned to normal when the plant reopened. Mrs. Monroe discovered that the boys had not been feeding their new pet, who probably was sneaking out for food. Regretful, Harold and Chester were placated, and the cute little bunny returned again to his box. For an instant he bared his vampire-like fangs, then fell asleep with a smile on his lips. The special was adapted from the book, Bunnicula, a Rabbit-Tale of Mystery (Atheneum, 1979) by Deborah and James Howe, illustrated by Alan Daniel.

CABBAGE PATCH KIDS' FIRST CHRISTMAS, THE

Broadcast History
    Premiere: December 7, 1984
    ABC/Friday 8:00-8:30 PM
    ABC/Repeat: December 13, 1985
Executive Producers: Joseph Ruby, Ken Spears
Associate Producer: Michael Hack
Director: Charles A. Nichols
Writer: Woody Kling
Music & Lyrics/Theme: Joe Raposo
Music: Paul DeKorte
Company: Ruby-Spears Enterprises in association with Heywood Kling Productions

Principal Characters and Voices
Otis Lee   Scott Menville
Dawson Glenn   Josh Rodine
Cannon Lee   David Mendenhall
Sybil Sadie   Phenina Segal

Rachel "Ramie" Marie	Ebony Smith
Tyler Bo	Vaughn Jelks
Paula Louise	Ann Marie McEvoy
Jenny	Gini Holtzman
Colonel Casey	Hal Smith
Xavier Roberts	Sparky Marcus
Lavender Bertha	Tress MacNeille
Cabbage Jack/Gus	Arthur Burghardt
Beau Weasel/Fingers	Neil Ross
Baby Dowd	(non-speaking)

The Cabbage Patch Kids' First Christmas converted the 1984 gift-sensation dolls to cartoon characters who left their cozy home in the cabbage patch to journey to a big city in search of the "Christmas Spirit." Leaving behind Xavier and Baby Dowd in the care of the stork, Colonel Casey, the kids Otis Lee, Sybil Sadie, Tyler Bo, Rachel "Ramie" Marie, Dawson Glenn, Cannon Lee and Paula Louise overcame a plot hatched by Cabbage Jack, Beau Weasel and Lavender Bertha to use them to mine gold through a small tunnel. In town, the seven kids were helped across a busy street by the Clarks, a childless couple, and retrieved Mr. Clark's dropped wallet only to be pursued by the watching thieves, Fingers and Gus. Crawling through a window of the Children's Home, they discovered Jenny, a lonely orphan despondent over being "different," considered unadoptable because of her crippled leg. Hoping the Clarks might adopt the girl, they persuaded Jenny to join them in returning the wallet but again had to escape the pursuing Jack, Weasel and Bertha, and upon entering the Clarks' hotel were grabbed by the thieves. Scurrying away as the police arrived, they spotted the Clarks as runaway Jenny was taken into custody. The kids returned Mr. Clark's wallet and found him overjoyed at the prospect of adopting Jenny. And since Cabbage Patch Kid Paula was almost her twin, the Clarks decided to adopt her too. Returning to their Cabbage Patch with mixed emotions, the kids sat with Casey the stork who had brought the latest baby, as Xavier underscored the moral--that the Spirit of Christmas was a feeling experienced when making someone else happy, as they did for Paula and Jenny. And by demonstrating that everyone was special because everyone was different, the kids spread a message of their own. Song/Theme: "Cabbage Patch Kids."

The special was inspired by the Coleco doll line created by Xavier Roberts and licensed by his Appalachian Artwork.

CAP'N O. G. READMORE MEETS DR. JEKYLL AND MR. HYDE

Broadcast History
    Premiere: September 13, 1986
    ABC/ABC WEEKEND SPECIALS, Saturday 12:00-12:30 PM
    ABC/Repeat: August 8, 1987
Producer: Rick Reinert

CAP'N O. G. READMORE MEETS DR. JEKYLL AND MR. HYDE.
© 1986, Capital Cities/ABC, Inc. Courtesy of Capital Cities/ABC.

Director: Dave Bennett
Writer: Malcolm Marmorstein
Music: Steve Zuckerman
Company: ABC Entertainment Productions in association with Rick
   Reinert Productions

Principal Characters and Voices
Cap'n O. G. Readmore/Vendor/
   M.C.   Neil Ross
Wordsy/Ol' Tome Cat/Poole/
   Robert Louis Stevenson   Stanley Jones
Kitty Literature/Olivia
   Heathpote   Ilene Latter
Lickety Page/Calypso LaRose   Lucille Bliss
Edward Hyde/Newcommon   Hal Smith

Cap'n O. G. Readmore Meets Dr. Jekyll and Mr. Hyde was the second special to star the bright, lively and articulate cat who extolled
the virtues of books and reading on ABC. As was their habit, Cap'n
O. G. and his friends, Kitty Literature, Ol' Tome Cat, Wordsy and
Lickety Page, were holding their Friday Night Book Club meeting
in an alley next to the public library. The rainy, eerie night inspired the group to select the Robert Louis Stevenson classic, The
Strange Case of Dr. Jekyll and Mr. Hyde (1886). When the book
was opened, Wordsy was kidnapped into the story and Cap'n O. G.
followed in an effort to rescue him. In a humorous treatment of
the story, Cap'n O. G. discovered that Wordsy was now calling himself Dr. Henry Jekyll and was about to experiment with a potion to
change from his boring lifestyle to the happy, wild and fun-loving
Edward Hyde. Incorporated into his topsy-turvy adventures in London were the club's other members in various cameo roles, conclud-
ing with the Cap'n and Wordsy's return to the alley when help arrived from a very unexpected source, Robert Louis Stevenson himself, who wrote them out of his story.
    Designed by Rick Reinert, the Cap'n O. G. Readmore character
made his debut in the 1983-1984 season on ABC in Saturday morning
animated inserts and in puppet form in 1985-1986 as a host for the
ABC Weekend Specials, described in Children's Television, Part II,
(Scarecrow, 1985), pp. 7-9.

CAP'N O. G. READMORE'S JACK AND THE BEANSTALK

Broadcast History
    Premiere: October 12, 1985
    ABC/ABC WEEKEND SPECIALS, Saturday 12:00-12:30 PM
    ABC/Repeat: October 4, 1986
Producer: Rick Reinert
Director: Dave Bennett
Writer: Malcolm Marmorstein
Music: Steve Zuckerman

Company: ABC Entertainment Productions in association with Rick Reinert Productions

Principal Characters and Voices

Cap'n O. G. Readmore	Neil Ross
Lickety Page/Jack's Mother/ Hen	Lucille Bliss
Ol' Tome Cat/Jack	Stanley Jones
Kitty Literature/Giant's Wife/ Harp	Ilene Latter
Wordsy/Humpty Dumpty	Will Ryan
Giant/Little Old Man	Hal Smith

Cap'n O. G. Readmore's Jack and the Beanstalk introduced in an animated special the articulate tap-dancing feline, designed by Rick Reinert, originally developed by ABC in cooperation with the Library of Congress to promote and encourage reading. In an alley next to the public library, Cap'n O. G. and his friends, Kitty Literature, Ol' Tome Cat, Wordsy, Lickety Page and Dog-Eared were holding their Friday Night Book Club meeting when the topic turned to the silly behavior of characters in fairy tales. As Cap'n O. G. began to agree, suddenly the bookshelves parted and the Cap'n was confronted by all his favorite fairy tale characters, including Jack from "Jack in the Beanstalk." When he was asked to give an example, Cap'n O. G. pointed out he wouldn't make the same mistakes, such as selling a cow for just a handful of beans. Jack challenged the Cap'n to take his place in the story and improve on his conduct. Zapped into the fairytale, the Cap'n's inept and humorous attempts to fix the plot were the crux of the tale. Returning to the book club, the Cap'n underscored that when he read a book he became the character and that anyone can do that too.

CARE BEARS BATTLE THE FREEZE MACHINE, THE

Broadcast History
    Premiere: Spring 1984
    SYN/local station option (KTLA, Los Angeles, April 6, 1984, Friday 7:30-8:00 PM PST)
    Sponsor: Kenner Products (Toy Group, General Mills)
    SYN/Repeats: October 19, 1984 +
Executive Producers: Bernard Loomis, Carole MacGillvray
Producers: William H. Stevens, Jr., Hugh Campbell
Directors: Paul Schibli, Pino Van Lamsweerde
Writer: Peter Sauder
Music/Songs & Lyrics: Bob Chimbel, Merry Chimbel
Music: Gary Morton
Company: MAD Productions in association with Those Characters From Cleveland and Atkinson Film-Arts, Ottawa, Canada
Distributor: LBS Communications/1984-
Home Video: Family Home Entertainment F371

Voices
Dominic Bradford, Bob Dermer, Abby Hagyard, Rick Jones, Les
Lye, Anna MacCormack, Brodie Osome, Noreen Young

The Care Bears Battle the Freeze Machine called upon the fuzzy
wuzzies to foil Professor Coldheart's fiendish plot to use his new
invention on the local children. It featured the ten bears introduced
in the first special, plus two baby bears, Hugs and Tugs. When
Lumpy and the gang made young Paul the brunt of their cruel jokes,
the whiz kid swore he would get even with them. Watching over
the situation, the Care Bears decided that what Paul needed was a
lesson in making friends and headed down to Earth from Care-a-Lot
in their Cloud Mobiles to help him out. But Professor Coldheart
had his eye on Paul as well and promised the boy his vengeance in
return for some engineering help in fixing his latest diabolical device,
the Freeze Machine. What Paul did not know was that Coldheart and
his lackey Frostbite planned to use the chilly contraption to per-
manently freeze all the children in town. Coldheart demonstrated
its power on Tugs and Hugs, whom he had captured. The Care
Bears raced against time to stop Coldheart's plan but were too late
as the town's children were frozen in their tracks. But by putting
their fuzzy heads together with Paul, they came up with a plan to
use their Care Bear Stare, projected through the machine, to thaw
out Hugs and Tugs plus all the frozen children and teach Coldheart
a lesson. Of course Paul learned a lesson too: making friends was
more fun than freezing them. Songs: "I Want To Be a Care Bear,"
"Give a Little Love," "We're Going to Put the Freeze on Feelings,"
"Making Friends."

CARE BEARS IN THE LAND WITHOUT FEELINGS, THE

Broadcast History
Premiere: Spring 1983
SYN/local station option (KTLA, Los Angeles, April 22, 1983,
Friday 7:30-8:00 PM PST)
Sponsors: Kenner Products, American Greetings
SYN/Repeats: October 26, 1983; October 12, 1984 +
Executive Producers: Bernard Loomis, Carole MacGillvray
Producers: William H. Stevens, Jr., Hugh Campbell
Director: Pino Van Lamsweerde
Writer: Ken Sobel
Music/Songs & Lyrics: Robert Chimbel
Music: Hagood Hardy
Company: MAD Productions in association with Those Characters
From Cleveland and Atkinson Film-Arts, Ottawa, Canada
Distributor: LBS Communications/1983-
Home Video: Family Home Entertainment F357

Voices
Andrea Blake, Justin Cammy, Abby Hagyard, Rick Jones, Les
Lye, Anna MacCormack, Kathy MacLennan

THE CARE BEARS IN THE LAND WITHOUT FEELINGS. © 1984, American Greetings Corporation. Courtesy of Those Characters From Cleveland and Crawley Films Limited.

The Care Bears in the Land Without Feelings introduced the original ten cute teddies with their respective symbols emblazoned on their tummies, which they often used in novel ways. There was Tenderheart Bear with a heart on his paunch; Good Luck Bear with his four-leaf clover on his belly; Funshine Bear, with a smiling sun on his tum; Birthday Bear with a birthday cupcake and candle; Friend Bear with two smiling daisies; Grumpy Bear with a blue raincloud; Cheer Bear with a colorful rainbow; Bedtime Bear with a crescent moon and a star; Love-a-Lot Bear with two intertwined hearts; and Wish Bear sporting a shooting star on his midriff. Living far above the clouds in Care-a-Lot, they commuted to earth in Cloud Mobiles to adventures about friendship, loving, sharing and caring. When young Kevin ran away from home because he didn't care anymore, the Care Bears were quickly on the scene. Following a path from the park to the Land Without Feelings, Kevin fell into the clutches of Professor Coldheart, who turned the boy into one of his slave creatures. With Kevin's friend Donna, the Care Bears set out for Coldheart Castle to rescue the boy but were confronted by a series of obstacles which thinned their numbers, and only Tenderheart got through. However, Wish Bear wished the others to the Castle, where together they used the powers of their Care Bears Stare to free Kevin and turn the Land Without Feelings into one of love and friendship. Songs: "The Care Bears Can," "They Call Me Professor Coldheart," "Everyone Has Feelings."

    Both Care Bears specials have gone platinum in home video

sales, and by 1986 they were among the top five best-selling children's cassettes. Aimed at girls aged 3 to 13, the Care Bears were created in 1981 by Those Characters From Cleveland, the R&D subsidiary of American Greetings, and turned into toys by the Marketing and Design service (MAD) of General Mills. New characters have been added over the years. By March 1985 there were approximately 400 items in the Care Bears line, a licensing phenomenon. The property has been adapted also for a syndicated half-hour, four-part mini-series; a Saturday morning series called The Care Bears Family (ABC, 1986-); and the animated movies, The Care Bear Movie (Goldwyn, 1985), The Care Bears Movie II: A New Generation (COL, 1986), and The Care Bears' Adventure in Wonderland (COL, 1987).

CARLTON YOUR DOORMAN

Broadcast History
    Premiere: May 21, 1980
    CBS/Wednesday 8:00-8:30 PM
    SYN/Repeats: 1984 +

CARLTON YOUR DOORMAN. © 1980, MTM Productions, Inc. Courtesy of Gilson International.

Producers: Lorenzo Music, Barton Dean
Directors: Charles Swenson, Fred Wolf
Writers/Creators: Lorenzo Music, Barton Dean
Music: Stephen Cohn
Company: MTM Productions in association with Murakami-Wolf-
Swenson Films
Distributor: Gilson International/1985-

Principal Characters and Voices

Carlton	Lorenzo Music
Charles Shaftman	Jack Somack
Mrs. Shaftman	Lucille Meredith
Carlton's Mother	Lurene Tuttle
Darlene	Kay Cole
Mr. Gleanson/Fat Man	Paul Lichtman
Dog Catcher	Alan Barzman
Parrot	Bob Arbogast
Pop	Charles Woolf
D.J. (voice only)	Roy West

Carlton Your Doorman brought to two-dimensional life the never-seen
character voiced by Lorenzo Music on the TV sitcom Rhoda (CBS,
1974-1978). Carlton, it seems, was a tall, wispy creature with long,
lank blond hair and a drooping mustache to match, whose mother
spent her days as a New York City bagwoman, rifling through trash
cans. A misfit who sought to better himself and his place in society,
Carlton was enmeshed in a scheme to find a replacement for the dog
Punkin, the pet of Mrs. Shaftman, the apartment owner's wife, a
snarling little beast that died while in his care. In this adult film,
not created for children, when Carlton encountered a shapely jogger,
he ran alongside her saying, "Why waste all this heavy breathing
jogging?" and Mrs. Shaftman invited him to join her in the shower
with, "Come on in, the water's fine." The special was based on the
character created by James L. Brooks, Allan Burns, David Davis
and Lorenzo Music. Television Academy Emmy award (1979-1980),
Outstanding Animated Program.

CARNIVAL OF THE ANIMALS

Broadcast History
    Premiere: November 22, 1976
    CBS/Monday 8:30-9:00 PM
    Sponsors: Kellogg's, Pampers
    CBS/Repeat: July 12, 1979
Producer/Director/Writer: Chuck Jones
Director/Animation: Herbert Klynn
Director/Live Action: Gerry Woolery
Music: Dean Elliott
Music/Director: Michael Tilson Thomas
Music/Pianists: Zita Carno (Bugs), Kathryn Ando (Daffy)

Company: Chuck Jones Enterprises in association with Warner Bros.
Television

Principal Characters and Voices
Bugs Bunny/Daffy Duck/Porky
   Pig   Mel Blanc

Carnival of the Animals, the zoological fantasy by Camille Saint-
Saens (1835-1921), was the basis for this musical half hour. Bugs
Bunny and Daffy Duck, resplendent in tailcoats, high stiff collars
and bristling black ties, performed on twin grand pianos with the
orchestra conducted by Michael Tilson Thomas and, in their own
particular styles, spouted Ogden Nash verses set to the music. A
nice, sometimes frantic but nonviolent bit of animation, the stylish
graphic sequences featured lions, hens and roosters, tortoises,
elephants, kangaroos, fish, the Cuckoo, the swan and other birds
and creatures from the fourteen movements of the score.
    An original cartoon from Chuck Jones and the first of 14 thema-
tic Bugs Bunny specials, the film complemented the second longest-
running syndicated cartoon series (SYN, 1956-), following Popeye
[q.v.] and the long-running Saturday morning series starring Bugs
Bunny (ABC, 1960-1968/1973-1975/1985- ; CBS, 1971-1973/1968-
1985) described in Children's Television, Part I, pp. 51-55. A compilation of ten shorts (1940-1948) were released as the movie Bugs
Bunny Superstar (UA, 1975). Jones also directed The Bugs Bunny/
Road Runner Movie (WB, 1979). Two other compilations, The Looney,
Looney, Looney Bugs Bunny Movie (WB, 1981) and Bugs Bunny's 3rd
Movie: 1001 Rabbit Tales (WB, 1983) were directed by Friz Freleng

CASPER'S FIRST CHRISTMAS

Broadcast History
   Premiere: December 18, 1979
   NBC/Tuesday 8:00-8:30 PM
   NBC/Repeats: December 5, 1980; December 14, 1981
Executive Producers: William Hanna, Joseph Barbera
Producer: Alex Lovy
Director: Carl Urbano
Writer: Bob Ogle
Music: Hoyt Curtin, Paul DeKorte
Company: Hanna-Barbera Productions
Home Video: Worldvision

Principal Characters and Voices

Casper	Julie McWhirter
Hairy Scary/Doggie Daddy	John Stephenson
Quick Draw McGraw/Snagglepuss/	
Augie Doggie/Huckleberry	
Hound/Yogi Bear	Daws Butler
Boo Boo	Don Messick
Santa Claus	Hal Smith

Casper's First Christmas paired the friendly little ghost and his big wacky buddy, Hairy Scary, living in a condemned old house that was to be torn down as soon as the winter snow melted. Since it was Christmas Eve, Casper had planned to await a visit from Santa Claus. Although he had never seen the jolly gent, he had heard all about him and how friends gathered to express friendship on the holiday eve. But Hairy wanted no part of Christmas or Santa Claus and furthermore told Casper that ghosts do not have any friends. Planning to locate a new house they could haunt, Hairy and Casper set out in the falling snow. Meanwhile, after Yogi Bear, Boo Boo, Huckleberry Hound, Snagglepuss, Quick Draw McGraw, Augie Doggie and Doggie Daddy lost their way to the mountain lodge where they planned to celebrate Christmas Eve, they decided instead to relocate at the old house. When Casper and Hairy discovered their unexpected guests, Casper was delighted but the furious Hairy set about scaring the socks off the group and messed up their Christmas decorations. A note Casper left in a stocking for Santa, containing a poignant plea to help save Hairy's house, caused his friend's change of heart, and the pair joined with their new friends for a Merry Christmas and a visit from Santa Claus. Songs: "Comin' Up Christmas," "Much Ado About Christmas," "Casper's Christmas Wish."

The special was based on the character created by Joe Oriolo with Sy Reit for Famous Studios, debuting in The Friendly Ghost (May 5, 1946), purchased in 1958 and owned and copyrighted by Harvey Cartoons. With the new Hairy Scary, the polite poltergeist was revived for the Saturday morning series Casper and the Angels (NBC, 1979-1980), described in Children's Television, Part I, (Scarecrow, 1983), pp. 65-67.

CASPER'S HALLOWEEN
("He Ain't Scary, He's Our Brother")

Broadcast History
   Premiere: October 30, 1979
   NBC/Tuesday 8:00-8:30 PM
   NBC/Repeat: November 1, 1981
Executive Producers: William Hanna, Joseph Barbera
Producer: Alex Lovy
Directors: Carl Urbano, Geoffrey Collins
Writers: Larz Bourne, Bob Ogle
Music: Hoyt Curtin, Paul DeKorte
Company: Hanna-Barbera Productions
Home Video: Worldvision

Principal Characters and Voices

Casper	Julie McWhirter
Hairy Scary/Butler/Rural Man	John Stephenson
Mr. Duncan/Skull	Hal Smith
J.R.	Diane McCannon
Winifred the Witch/Third lady	Marilyn Schreffler
Black Cat/Nice Man/Dog	Frank Welker

Lovella/Bejewelled Dowager/
    Rural Lady   Ginny Tyler
Gervais/Carmelita/Nice Lady   Lucille Bliss
Screech   Michael Sheehan
Dirk   Greg Alter

Casper's Halloween opened on a gloomy haunted house with a bright, cluttered boy's room, home of the friendly ghost who wanted to be out trick-or-treating like the rest of the children. Donning a baseball cap and mask, Casper set off with his empty goodies' sack. Downstairs, Hairy Scary and his ethereal friends, Skull, Winifred and Lovella, excitedly planned some nasty tricks for their favorite night, pegging costumed children as fall-guys. Trying to trick-or-treat, Casper was continually hampered by Hairy and his spirits who frightened the residents and played some mean pranks on the Inner City Orphanage children, too poor to have more than a simple mask and paper sack. Encountering the disappointed orphans, Casper revealed himself as a real ghost, promised to protect them from Hairy's pranks and was accepted as a real boy by the youngsters. The orphans were accused of so much trouble, however, they were ordered back to the orphanage by Mr. Duncan without any candy. When Casper rebuffed Hairy, his big buddy decided to set things right. With Hairy's help, the orphans costumed themselves as ghosts and frightened the dickens out of his gang, coated by Dirk with syrup and dusted by Hairy with flour, unbeknownst to Casper, who had returned home. Dressed in colorful costumes and with bags of candy supplied by Hairy's earlier victim, a sympathetic bejeweled dowager, the orphans appeared at Casper's door with a Casper costume for him. All was forgiven when Hairy led the children and Casper back out to go trick-or-treating anew. Songs: "Halloween Song," "Tonight's the Night," "He Ain't Scary, He's My Brother."

CASTLE

Broadcast History
    Premiere: October 5, 1983
    PBS/KCET, Los Angeles, Wednesday 10:00-11:00 PM PST
    PBS/Repeats: multiple, 1984 +
Producers: Sarah Bullen, David Macaulay
Company: A Unicorn Projects Production presented on PBS by WTVS, Detroit, by T.V. Cartoons, London, England/60 minutes

Hosts: Sarah Bullen, David Macaulay

Castle blended animation and live-action to describe the construction of a thirteenth-century Welsh Castle, mixed with scenes and tours of ancient fortresses located in Wales. The hour-long film painted a vivid picture of life in medieval England and examined the planning, building, habitation and the siege and defense of a fictional fortress. The program was based on the book by David Macaulay.

CAT IN THE HAT, THE   see   DR. SEUSS' THE CAT IN THE HAT

CATHY

Broadcast History
    Premiere: May 15, 1987
    CBS/Friday 8:30-9:00 PM
Executive Producer: Lee Mendelson
Producer: Bill Melendez
Director: Evert Brown
Writer/Creator: Cathy Guisewite
Music: James Lee Stanley, Jimmy Haskell
Company: Lee Mendelson-Bill Melendez Productions in association
    with the Universal Press Syndicate and Bill Melendez Productions,
    London, England.

Principal Characters and Voices
Cathy   Kathleen Wilhoite
Irving   Robert F. Paulsen

CATHY. © 1987, Universal Press Syndicate. Courtesy of Cathy
Guisewite and Universal Licensing.

Andrea	Allison Argo
Mom (Anne)	Shirley Mitchell
Dad (Bill)	William L. Guisewite
Charlene	Emily Levine
Mr. Pinkley	Gregg Berger
Brenda	Desiree Goyette
M.C.	Robert Towers

Cathy, the wide-eyed, long-haired comic-strip character, made her animated debut in this adult special, which comically played on the upswing in her career versus the downswing in her personal life. "I never quit dreaming that I'd dance off into the sunset with a handsome man in a tuxedo. I just added to the dream that when I did it, I'd be the president of a major conglomerate." That's how the irrepressible young careerist representative of everywoman summed up her search for happiness while moving up the corporate ladder and coping with food, parents, failed romances and cravings for chocolate. Agonizing over securing an escort for the Employee of the Year Awards Banquet, for which she was nominated, Cathy intended to share the evening with her longtime boyfriend, Irving, who was seeing another woman. As the banquet neared, Mom pushed Cathy's guilt buttons and she reluctantly renewed her quest for Mr. Right, prodded by her chum Andrea. "Where's your spirit of romance?" Andrea asked. "Where's that naive, juvenile sense of hope?" So off they went with Cathy blazing a trail through the yuppie world of coed aerobics classes, singles mixers and sushi bars in a dauntless effort to find a date, while offering some whimsical perceptions and insights into society and the human condition. Television Academy Emmy award (1986-1987), Outstanding Animation Program.

The film was written and illustrated by Cathy Guisewite, creator of Cathy, which was inspired by a series of drawings in her letters to her parents. The daily strip debuted in 1976 and appears in more than 500 newspapers for Universal Press Syndicate. Her father, William L. Guisewite, voiced her dad.

CHARLIE BROWN CELEBRATION, A

Broadcast History
    Premiere: May 24, 1982
    CBS/Monday 8:00-9:00 PM
    CBS/Repeat: February 18, 1984
Producers: Lee Mendelson, Bill Melendez
Director: Bill Melendez
Writer/Creator: Charles M. Schulz
Music: Ed Bogas, Judy Munsen
Company: Lee Mendelson-Bill Melendez Productions in association
    with Charles M. Schulz Creative Associates and United Feature
    Syndicate/60 minutes

Host: Charles Schulz

Principal Characters and Voices

Charlie Brown	Michael Mandy
Lucy Van Pelt	Kristen Fullerton
Linus Van Pelt	Earl "Rocky" Reilly
Sally Brown	Cindi Reilly
Schroeder	Christopher Donohoe
Peppermint Patty	Brent Hauer
Marcie	Shannon Cohn
Polly/Truffles	Casey Carlson
Snoopy	Bill Melendez

Announcer: John Hiestand

A Charlie Brown Celebration departed from the usual half-hour format and presented a series of short films based on continuing themes from the Peanuts comic strips. Varying in length from one minute to nine minutes, they were similar to the way the newspaper strips run from several days to several weeks and included some of the favorites of Charles Schulz, who appeared as the host. The lively blend of 11 vignettes included school days, kite flying, baseball, Beethoven, summer camp and more. Back in school after summer vacation, Sally could not relax and was afraid she was failing art ("I'll bet Picasso couldn't draw a cow's leg when he was in first grade"), Linus reflected on the learning process ("As the years go by, you learn what sells"), Peppermint Patty received an "F" on her paper ("I've learned never to badmouth a President in a history test"), and Schroeder wondered why he had to explain a poem ("Studying poetry spoils the poems"). Charlie Brown, of course, had his worries--he studied the wrong chapter ("I'm doomed!"). And while a field trip became an outdoor diversion for some classmates, Sally had her doubts ("I know why they brought us here. Our school is overcrowded"). In other shorts, Lucy competed with the piano for Schroeder's attention ("If he was so great, how come the schools don't close on Beethoven's birthday?") and a "woozy" Charlie--convinced that he was at death's door--was forced to leave the pitcher's mound for the hospital, which elicited a promise from Lucy ("If you get well, I'll never pull the football away again!"). She didn't after he was well, but good ol' Charlie still missed the ball and kicked her in the hand ("Next time you go to the hospital, stay there!"). The special was followed by another hour-long anthology, It's an Adventure, Charlie Brown [q.v.].

CHARLIE BROWN CHRISTMAS, A

Broadcast History

Premiere: December 9, 1965
CBS/Thursday 8:00-8:30 PM
Sponsor: Coca-Cola; McDonald's, Peter Paul Cadbury, Nabisco
CBS/Repeats: December 11, 1966; December 10, 1967; December 8, 1968; December 7, 1969; December 5, 1970; December 7,

A CHARLIE BROWN CHRISTMAS. © 1965, United Feature Syndicate, Inc. Courtesy of Charles M. Schulz Creative Associates and United Media.

1971; December 12, 1972; December 6, 1973; December 17, 1974; December 15, 1975; December 18, 1976; December 12, 1977; December 18, 1978; December 10, 1979; December 9, 1980; December 10, 1981; December 6, 1982; December 12, 1983; December 5, 1984; December 4, 1985; December 12, 1986
Executive Producer: Lee Mendelson
Producers: Lee Mendelson, Bill Melendez
Director: Bill Melendez
Writer/Creator: Charles M. Schulz
Music: Vince Guaraldi, John Scott Trotter
Company: Lee Mendelson-Bill Melendez Productions in association with Charles M. Schulz Creative Associates and United Feature Syndicate
Record Albums: Fantasy 8431; Western Publishing
Home Video: Hi-Tops Video (nee Media Home Entertainment)

Principal Characters and Voices

Charlie Brown	Peter Robbins
Lucy Van Pelt	Tracy Stratford
Linus Van Pelt	Christopher Shea
Schroeder	Chris Doran
Peppermint Patty	Sally Dryer

Sally Brown   Kathy Steinberg
Freida   Ann Altieri

A Charlie Brown Christmas became a yuletide classic following its premiere in 1965. Christmas was coming, the other members of the Peanuts clan were looking forward to the fun they would have and the presents they would get, but Charlie Brown was depressed and upset. "You are the only person I know who can take a wonderful season like Christmas and turn it into a problem," said Linus. Next day Charlie decided to visit Lucy's psychiatric booth and she diagnosed his depression as a lack of involvement, suggesting he direct the church play. Enroute to the auditorium, Charlie found Snoopy decorating the doghouse for a display contest and Sally asked him to write Santa Claus to send her money, "preferably tens and twenties." Deciding a Christmas tree would brighten the set, Charlie ignored the glitzy trees for a small scraggly pine, which disgusted Lucy: "Can't you even tell a good tree from a poor tree?" Looking at the sad little tree on the piano, Charlie wondered if there wasn't someone who knew what Christmas was all about. "I can tell you," said Linus, and alone on the stage he gave a soliloquy: "...For, behold, I bring you good tidings of great joy, which shall be to all people. For unto you is born this day in the city of David a Saviour, which is Christ the Lord. And this shall be a sign unto you...." Walking home in the star-filled night Charlie repeated the verse and understood. "I won't let all this commercialism spoil my Christmas," he said, "I'll take this little tree home and decorate it." Next day when Charlie put a blue ornament on the tree, it drooped to the ground, "Augh! I've killed it," he said sadly, "Everything I touch gets ruined!" While he was gone, Linus tenderly put his blanket around the tree, and then as everyone began to hang ornaments on it, the fuller and more beautiful it became. "Charlie Brown is a blockhead, but he did get a nice tree," recanted Lucy. And Charlie Brown wished "A Merry Christmas to All." Television Academy Emmy award (1965-1966), Outstanding Children's Program; George Foster Peabody award (1965).

The program was the first of the Peanuts' specials, the longest-running special series seen on television, spanning more than 22 years. A highly acclaimed presentation, the film is the longest-running animated-cartoon special in TV history, having been repeated every year since its inception. Not only did the show prompt the greatest number of sequels built around the same characters, it was followed by the Saturday morning series The Charlie Brown and Snoopy Show (CBS, 1983-1986) and four animated movies: A Boy Named Charlie Brown (CCF, 1969), Snoopy Come Home (CCF, 1972), Race for Your Life, Charlie Brown (PAR, 1977) and Bon Voyage, Charlie Brown (PAR, 1980). The series' first hour-long animated and live-action film, It's the Girl in the Red Truck, Charlie Brown, has been scheduled for a CBS special Presentation in 1988.

A CHARLIE BROWN THANKSGIVING. © 1973, United Feature Syndicate, Inc. Courtesy of Charles M. Schulz Creative Associates and United Media.

CHARLIE BROWN THANKSGIVING, A

Broadcast History
    Premiere: November 20, 1973
    CBS/Tuesday 8:00-8:30 PM
    Sponsor: Interstate Brands
    CBS/Repeats: November 21, 1974; November 22, 1975; November
        22, 1976; November 21, 1977; November 15, 1978; November
        19, 1979; November 25, 1980; November 23, 1981; November
        20, 1984; November 26, 1985; November 25, 1986
Executive Producer: Lee Mendelson
Producers: Lee Mendelson, Bill Melendez
Directors: Bill Melendez, Phil Roman
Writer/Creator: Charles M. Schulz
Music: Vince Guaraldi, John Scott Trotter
Company: Lee Mendelson-Bill Melendez Productions in association
    with Charles M. Schulz Creative Associates and United Feature
    Syndicate
Home Video: Kartes Video Communications

Principal Characters and Voices

Charlie Brown	Todd Barbee
Linus Van Pelt	Stephen Shea
Snoopy	Bill Melendez
Peppermint Patty	Christopher DeFaria
Lucy Van Pelt	Robin Kohn
Sally Brown	Hilary Momberger
Marcie	Jimmy Ahrens
Franklin	Robin Reed

A Charlie Brown Thanksgiving provided another occasion for the little loser to find himself in a mess. "I don't know why it is, Sally, but holidays always depress me," he said. "Do you realize that Thanksgiving is here again?" "Good grief!" said Sally, "and I haven't even finished eating my Halloween candy." The intellectual Linus did not share the same concerns. "Thanksgiving is a very important holiday," he reminded the pair, "Ours was the first country in the world to make a national holiday to give thanks." Resigned to going with his family to his grandmother's annual meal, Charlie did not know what to do when Peppermint Patty, Marcie and Franklin invited themselves to his house for Thanksgiving dinner. "How do I always get into these things?" said the hapless host. Then Linus came up with a plan to have two dinners, the first for just the clan, but all Charlie could make was "cold cereal and maybe toast." So they enlisted the aid of Snoopy, who turned in his Pilgrim's outfit for a chef's cap, to dish up a meal aided by Woodstock. Linus was called upon to say grace, attributed to Elder William Brewster, a minister at the first Thanksgiving feast in 1621: "We thank God for our homes and our food and our safety in a new land. We thank God for the opportunity to create a new world for freedom and justice. Amen." As Snoopy served up dinner, Patty was outraged. "A piece of toast! A pretzel stick? Ice Cream! Popcorn! Where's the turkey, Chuck?" Charlie was crestfallen. "I ruined everyone's Thanksgiving," he told Marcie. The misunderstanding was resolved in the spirit of Thanksgiving--everyone was invited to the home of Charlie's grandmother for dinner. Back at the beagle's doghouse, Snoopy and Woodstock celebrated with a roast turkey and broke its wishbone together in a display of their friendship. Song/Theme: "Little Birdie" (Guaraldi). Television Academy Emmy award (1973-1974), writer Charles M. Schulz for Outstanding Individual Achievement in Children's Programming.

CHARLIE BROWN'S ALL-STARS

Broadcast History

> Premiere: June 6, 1966
> CBS/Wednesday 8:30-9:00 PM
> Sponsor: Coca-Cola
> CBS/Repeats: April 10, 1967; April 6, 1968; April 13, 1969; April 12, 1970; April 3, 1982

Executive Producer: Lee Mendelson
Producers: Lee Mendelson, Bill Melendez
Director: Bill Melendez
Writer/Creator: Charles M. Schulz
Music: Vince Guaraldi, John Scott Trotter
Company: Lee Mendelson-Bill Melendez Productions in association
    with Charles M. Schulz Creative Associates and United Feature
    Syndicate
Record Albums: Disneyland 2602; 3702 (with book); 402 (single);
    Western Publishing
Home Video: Hi-Tops Video (nee Media Home Entertainment)

Principal Characters and Voices

Charlie Brown	Peter Robbins
Linus Van Pelt	Christopher Shea
Lucy Van Pelt	Sally Dryer
Schroeder	Glenn Mendelson
Frieda	Ann Altieri
Pig Pen	Jeff Ornstein

Charlie Brown's All-Stars was a timely salute to the Peanuts perennial pastime. After playing 999 games the team had yet to score a
win, but even worse their pitcher-manager had given up 3,000 hits
to the opposition. "Do us a favor, Charlie Brown," said Lucy before the next game, "don't show up!" In their last game, he threw
a ball over catcher Schroeder's head, dropped a fly ball in the last
inning, and lost by a score of 123 to 0. "This team will never amount
to anything!" screamed Lucy when she quit. Even his faithful dog
and shortstop Snoopy turned in his cap. Understandably upset, his
team, five boys, three girls and a dog, had lost interest and pursued other sports, surfboarding and skating. Discouraged, Charlie's
hopes were raised when Linus brought him word that Mr. Hennessy,
owner of the hardware store, offered to sponsor his team in a real
league. "Oh boy! ... Real uniforms!" he shouted, "... just the
thing to bring the team together again." But when he learned that
no girls or dogs would be allowed, his dream shattered. Linus told
the gang about how he refused to sacrifice his friends for Hennessy's
new uniforms. With Snoopy's tailoring, Lucy and the team made
Charlie a special manager's uniform--out of Linus's blanket. Rained
out the next day, when Linus went out to the ballfield, there stood
a forlorn Charlie on the pitcher's mound. Noticing the new uniform,
Linus reached over with one hand, took hold of one shirttail, and
put his other thumb in his mouth.

CHARMKINS, THE

Broadcast History
    Premiere: 1983
        SYN/local station option (KTLA, Los Angeles, June 6, 1983, Mon-
        day 7:30-8:00 PM PST)

Sponsors: Hasbro Industries, Kellogg's
SYN/Repeats: 1983 +
Executive Producers: Joe Bacal, David H. DePatie, Tom Griffin
Producer: Bob Richardson
Directors: Gerry Chiniquy, John Gibbs, Nelson Shin, Art Vitello
Writer: George Arthur Bloom
Music: Tommy Goodman
Lyrics: Barry Harman
Company: Sunbow Productions in association with Marvel Productions
Distributor: Claster TV Productions/1983-
Home Video: Family Home Entertainment

Principal Characters and Voices

Dragonweed	Ben Vereen
Brown-Eyed Susan	Aileen Quinn
Poison Ivy	Sally Struthers
Skunkweed	Ivy Austin
Willie Winkle	Martin Biersbach
Bramble Brother #2	Bob Kaliban
Lady Slipper	Lynne Lambert
Bramble Brother #1/ Briar-	
patch/Crocus	Chris Murney
Thorny	Gary Yudman
Popcorn	Peter Waldren
Blossom	Freddi Webber
Announcer	Patience Jarvis/Tina Capland
Little Tulip (baby sister)	
Buttercup (the dog)	

Vocalists
Helen Leonhart, Jamie Murphy, Helen Miles

The Charmkins focused on the fairy tale adventures of Lady Slipper and her friends in Charm World. It was Festival Day and the Charmkins were celebrating. But in gloomy Thistle Down, Dragonweed, the King of the Weeds, and his not-so-merry band, Briar Patch, Thorny, Skunkweed and the Bramble Brothers, were spying on the goings-on through a telescope. The beautiful dancer Lady Slipper, who "floats like a butterfly," had tickled Dragonweed's fancy and he wanted her to dance just for him. Kidnapping Lady Slipper and whisking her off to Thistle Down, Dragonweed warned her Charmkins' pursuers to stay away if they ever wanted to see her again and imprisoned Lady Slipper in a cage, giving her an ultimatum to dance or else. Bravely continuing their search, Brown-Eyed Susan, her brother Willie Winkle, their baby sister Little Tulip, Buttercup the Dog, Popcorn "Poppy" the Cat and Crocus the Parrot ran into the itchy witch of the Woodlands, Poison Ivy, who changed them into funny and unusual objects, like a teapot and umbrella, to illustrate the benefits of disguise. Later, in Thistle Down, Dragonweed captured all the Charmkins except Susan and Crocus, who in turn defeated the evil weed king and his henchmen in a mud ball fight, freed

Lady Slipper and their friends and made a hair-breadth escape via
lily pads back to Charm World, where they were welcomed home as
heroines. The special was based on the doll line created by Hasbro
Industries. Songs: "Charmkins Theme," "Year in the Gloomy
Swamp," "Imagine Me at My Worst," "Subterfugious Hocus-Pocus,"
"Pretty Lucky," "Nothing Is Impossible," "You Can Find a Rainbow
Anywhere."

CHIPMUNK CHRISTMAS, A

Broadcast History
    Premiere: December 14, 1981
    NBC/Monday 8:30-9:00 PM
    Sponsor: McDonald's, 7-Up (1986)
    NBC/Repeats: December 13, 1982; December 9, 1983; December
        5, 1986
Producers: Ross Bagdasarian, Jr., Janice Karman
Director: Phil Monroe
Writers: Ross Bagdasarian, Jr., Janice Karman, Hal Mason
Music: Chris Caswell
Company: Bagdasarian Productions

Principal Characters and Voices
Alvin/Simon/David Seville   Ross Bagdasarian
Theodore   Janice Karman

A Chipmunk Christmas brought home the Yuletide spirit to the mischievous Alvin when he tried to help Tommy Waterford, a seriously
ill boy. Set to play a solo in Carnegie Hall on Christmas Eve, Alvin
went shopping and noticed a pennyless little girl who thought a
harmonica would make a fine gift for the poor and disconsolate boy.
Visiting Tommy, Alvin gave him his own prized harmonica. After
buoying the lad's spirits with his present, Alvin, Simon and Theodore set about raising money to buy another in time for the concert.
They set up a booth charging children a few cents to be photographed
with Santa Claus, actually Alvin disguised in the gent's costume, but
collected only a few dollars. Alvin's dreams of making more money
disgusted an unaware David, who thought him selfish. He ordered
them all to think again about the true meaning of the holiday spirit.
When Tommy's mother called, a surprised David learned that Alvin's
harmonica had worked wonders for the sick boy. Meanwhile, the
Chipmunks chipped in, and aided by a mysterous lady (Mrs. Santa
Claus), Alvin was able to buy a deluxe Golden Echo and with his
brothers caught a hansom cab and arrived just in time for his solo.
Meeting Alvin backstage, a recovered Tommy accompanied the Chip-
munks on his harmonica as they sang "Deck the Halls." Songs:
"Chipmunk Jingle Bells," "Silent Night," "We Wish You a Merry
Christmas," "Sleigh Ride," "Deck the Halls," "Christmas Is."
    The special was the first based on the characters seen in the
revived Saturday morning series, Alvin and the Chipmunks (NBC,

1983-), which added the Chipettes. Originally, the falsetto sing-ing-trio were introduced in the prime-time series, The Alvin Show (CBS, 1961-1965), described in Children's Television, Part I (Scare-crow, 1983), pp. 14-15. Not only have the Chipmunks been familiar TV characters for 26 years in network and syndicated shows, they have been Grammy-winning, platinum-album-selling pop-music stars and have sold more than 35 million records. Their TV and marketing exposure elicited an animated movie, The Chipmunk Ad-venture (Goldwyn, 1987). And the 65-episode off-network series has been scheduled for syndication in Fall 1988 by Lorimar Syndica-tion.

CHIPMUNK REUNION, A

Broadcast History
    Premiere: April 13, 1985
    NBC/Saturday 8:30-9:00 PM
    NBC/Repeat: December 22, 1985
Executive Producers: Joseph Ruby, Ken Spears
Producers: Ross Bagdasarian, Janice Karman
Associate Producer: Larry Huber
Director: Charles A. Nichols
Writers: Janice Karman, Ross Bagdasarian, Cliff Ruby, Elana Lesser
Music: Dean Elliott, Paul DeKorte
Company: Bagdasarian Productions in association with Ruby-Spears
    Enterprises

Principal Characters and Voices
Alvin/Simon/David   Ross Bagdasarian
Theodore/Brittany/ Jeanette/
    Elenore   Janice Karman
Vinnie   June Foray

A Chipmunk Reunion explored the sensitive subject of adoption and why children seek their natural parents. Alvin, Theodore and Simon set off on an adventurous search for their real mother, prompted by their desire to know their birthdates, which even Dave, their adop-tive father, did not know. Braving torrential rains and wild animals in the uninviting forest, they located their mother Vinnie, who years before had to leave her babies on a stranger's doorstep to ensure their survival in a blizzard. All doubt about Vinnie's love for her children was dispelled when she heroically threw and injured herself in the path of a boar threatening the Chipmunks' lives. Nursing her back to health, the Chipmunks were surprised one morning to find her gone. But when they looked for her, they found that Vinnie and the other forest animals had arranged a surprise birth-day party for them. When Dave and his search party of Chipettes--Brittany, Jeanette and Elenore--arrived, he sadly assumed they wanted to stay with their mother. Bewildered, the Chipmunks as-sured him that he was the only parent they had known and, although they loved their mother and promised to visit her often, they wanted to return with him. Once home, Alvin and his brothers realized how fortunate they were to have loving parents and how foolish they were to think they were not like other families.

CHIPMUNK'S VALENTINE SPECIAL   see   I LOVE THE CHIPMUNKS, VALENTINE SPECIAL

CHRISTMAS CAROL, A

Broadcast History
  Premiere: December 13, 1970
  CBS/FAMOUS CLASSIC TALES, Sunday 5:00-6:00 PM
  Sponsor: Kenner Products (Toy Group, General Mills)
  CBS/Repeats: December 12, 1971; December 10, 1972; December 8, 1973; December 14, 1974; December 13, 1975; December 18, 1976; December 10, 1977; November 26, 1978; November 25, 1979; November 28, 1980; December 6, 1981; November 28, 1982; December 4, 1983
  SYN/Repeats: 1984 +
Producer: Walter J. Hucker
Director: Zoran Janjic
Writer: Michael Robinson
Music: Richard Bowden
Company: Air Programs International, Sydney, Australia/60 minutes
Distributor: D. L. Taffner ("Animated Classics for Children")/ 1985-
Home Video: Classics for Kids (MGM/UA)

Voices
  C. Duncan, Ron Haddrick, John Llewellyn, T. Mangan, Bruce Montague, Brenda Senders

Vocalists
  T. Kaff, C. Bowden

A Christmas Carol was an hour-long version of Charles Dickens' classic tale of miserly businessman Ebenezer Scrooge, who scoffed at the joys of the Christmas season until he was visited by spirits who convinced him otherwise.
     It was one of 15 specials produced for Kenner by API through Sive Associates. One of the longest-running special presentations seen on any network, the film aired for 13 consecutive years on CBS, often on the daytime schedule.

CHRISTMAS CAROL, A

Broadcast History
  Premiere: December 21, 1971

TINY TIM and BOB CRATCHIT

A CHRISTMAS CAROL. © 1971, Richard Williams Productions, Ltd. Courtesy of Worldvision Enterprises.

ABC/Tuesday 7:30-8:00 PM
Sponsor: Foundation for Full Service Banks
ABC/Repeats: December 15, 1972; December 14, 1973; December 7, 1974
SYN/Repeats: 1976 +
Executive Producer: Chuck Jones
Producer/Director: Richard Williams
Writer: Charles Dickens
Music: Tristram Cary
Company: Richard Williams Productions, London, England
Distributor: Worldvision Enterprises/1979-
Home Video: In Release

Narrator: Sir Michael Redgrave

Principal Characters and Voices

Ebenezer Scrooge	Alastair Sim
Marley's Ghost	Sir Michael Hordern
Bob Cratchit	Melvin Hayes
Mrs. Cratchit	Joan Sims
Ragpicker/Fezziwig	Paul Whitsun-Jones
Scrooge's Nephew/Charity Man	David Tate
Ghost of Christmas Past	Diana Quick
Ghost of Christmas Present	Felix Felton
Ghost of Christmas Yet to Come	Annie West
Mrs. Dilber	Mary Ellen Ray
Tiny Tim	Alexander Williams

A Christmas Carol faithfully recaptured the style and flavor of the classic holiday tale set in Victorian London. On Christmas Eve, the miser Scrooge, who turned his back on his needy clerk, Bob Cratchit and his family, received a visit from the ghost of Marley, his partner in business, and beheld a series of visions including his own death and resultant derision unless he mended his ways. As a result he awoke on Christmas morning a reformed man and aided Cratchit's crippled son, Tiny Tim, who ended the story with his much-quoted "God bless us, every one!" Motion Picture Academy Oscar award (1972), Best Animated Short Subject.

The late Alistair Sim voiced Scrooge, recreating his role in the 1951 live-action feature directed by Brian Desmond-Hurst. A particularly artful and highly imaginative rendition of the 1843 Charles Dickens' story, the design was based on nineteenth-century engravings of London and the John Leech illustrations in the first edition of the work. The script was also true to the original: a line intimating that Christmas was everywhere was animated as a fifteen-second sequence in which Scrooge and the Ghost of Christmas Present flew all over the world. The most impressive of all the animated versions, glowing with vitality, it was a remarkable achievement in television programming and was also exhibited in theaters.

CHRISTMAS CAROL, A

Broadcast History
    Premiere: 1984
    SYN/local station option (KCOP, Los Angeles, November 23 & 25,
        Friday & Sunday, 12:00-1:30 PM PST)
    SYN/Repeats: 1985 +
Executive Producers: Tom Stacey, George Stephenson
Producer: Eddy Graham
Director: Jean Tych
Writer: Alex Buzo
Music: Neil Thurgate, Bill Burton
Company: Burbank Films, Sydney, Australia (1982)/90 minutes
Distributor: Twentieth-Century Fox Television ("Charles Dickens
    Classics")/1984-
Home Video: Dickens' Classics (Vestron)

Voices
    Ron Haddrick, Philip Hinton, Sean Hinton, Barbara Frawley,
    Robin Stewart, Liz Horne, Bill Conn, Derani Scarr, Anne Hardy

A Christmas Carol was a 90-minute adaptation of the story by Charles
Dickens about a cold-hearted miser who learned the value of compassion through a series of ghostly adventures on Christmas eve.

CHRISTMAS COMES TO PAC-LAND

Broadcast History
    Premiere: December 16, 1982
    ABC/Thursday 8:00-8:30 PM
    ABC/Repeat: December 8, 1983
Executive Producers: William Hanna, Joseph Barbera
Producer: Kay Wright
Director: Ray Patterson
Writer: Jeffrey Scott
Music: Hoyt Curtin, Paul DeKorte
Company: Hanna-Barbera Productions

Principal Characters and Voices

Character	Voice
Pac-Man	Marty Ingels
Mrs. Pac	Barbara Minkus
Pac-Baby	Russi Taylor
Chomp Chomp/Morris/Reindeer	Frank Welker
Sour Puss/Santa	Peter Cullen
Blinky & Pinky Monsters/O'Pac	Chuck McCann
Sue Monster	Susan Silo
Clyde Monster	Neilson Ross
Inky Monster	Barry Gordon

Christmas Comes to Pac-Land featured the popular stars of video arcade games and Saturday morning cartoons, who discovered Christmas when Santa Claus developed sleigh trouble and crash-landed in Pac-Land. Encountering Santa and his reindeer after a wild toboggan chase by the ghost monsters, the Pac family brought him home, where the kindly, bewhiskered gent explained to them the meaning of Christmas and his important mission each year. With his broken sleigh and exhausted reindeer, Santa was afraid he could never make his rounds. Promising to help him save Christmas, Pac-Man and Chomp Chomp set off to find his lost bag of toys, while Morris and O'Pac began repairing his sleigh and Mrs. Pac tended to the reindeer. Bushwhacked by the Ghosts during his search, Pac-Man was left in a weakened state with no power pellets. Struggling to return home, he arrived just in time to promise Santa to help get his sled airborne and led him to the Power Forest. Arriving on the scene to make trouble, the Ghosts were finally placated when Pac-Man explained the emergency of Santa's mission to the children of the world and pleaded with them to open their hearts instead of their mouths. Feeding on power pellets, the reindeer became Pac-energized and with the sleigh jetted off to make Santa's deliveries. Returning home, the Pac family found a Christmas tree loaded with presents, some for the greedy little Ghosts, as all enjoyed their first Pac-Land Christmas

The special was built around the characters from Atari's Pac-Man video game and developed by Hanna-Barbera for the Saturday morning series Pac-Man (ABC, 1982-1984).

CHRISTMAS EVERY DAY

Broadcast History
    Premiere: 1986
    SYN/local station option (KCBS, Los Angeles, December 13, 1986,
        Saturday 7:30-8:00 PM PST)
    Sponsor: Tonka Toys
    SYN/Repeats: 1987 +
Producers: Thea Flaum, Dick Orkin
Associate Producer: Loretta Petersohn
Directors/Animation: Ed Newmann, Monica Kendall
Writers: Dick Orkin, Christine Coyle, Peter Steltzer, Marla Frumkin
Music: George Daugherty
Company: CBS Television Productions in association with Orkin-
    Flaum Productions and Calabash Productions
Distributor: Syndicast Services/1986-

Principal Characters and Voices

Tilly/Cissy	Stacy Q. Michaels
Ned/Butcher/Policeman	Brian Cummings
Helen/Franny/Will	Miriam Flynn
Christmas Fairy	Edie McClurg
Grace/Lucy	Marla Frumkin
George/Pete	Dick Orkin

Christmas Every Day began when little Lucy wished for the holiday to last forever and her father told her a story about a girl, Tilly, who wished for the very same thing and had it come true. In a hundred-year flashback to a Victorian time, Tilly's father brought home a crystal castle ornament for the family tree and told his children it was magical, containing a Christmas fairy with the power to grant special wishes. On Christmas Eve Tilly summoned the fairy, who appeared and reluctantly granted her wish to let every day be Christmas. The next day was just like the day before, from the same gifts to the same Christmas dinner. As the never-ending Yule continued, the household became fed up and the townspeople confused and angry as they coped with depleted forests, raggedy Christmas trees, $5,000 turkeys and mounting piles of presents. The Easter Bunny had reindeer antlers, Halloween trick-or-treaters wore Santa costumes and people went hoarse by July from the endless singing of Christmas carols. The townsfolk decided it was the worst thing that had ever happened. Meanwhile, Tilly had to deal with more than 300 puppies, an endless array of dolls, a birthday that was Christmas and the knowledge that she was responsible for the turmoil. After unsuccessfully trying to run away, she realized after a full year the Christmas fairy was due the next day and she wished for just a normal day to follow. When she woke up there were celebrations all over the country, everyone forgave Tilly and the fairy left it Christmas every year. As Lucy's father pointed out, Lucy and Tilly learned a valuable lesson--to be careful what they wished, it just might come true. The special was based on a short story by William Dean Howells.

CHRISTMAS IS

Broadcast History
 Premiere: November 7, 1970
 SYN/local station option (WNEW, New York, December 20, 1970,
  Sunday 8:00-8:30 PM)
 SYN/Repeats: 1971 +
 Sponsors: Holiday Inns, McDonald's, J. C. Penney, BankAmeri-
  card, Crest, Sears, Burger Chef, Rexall
Executive Producer: Dr. Martin J. Neeb, Jr.
Producer: Rev. Ardon D. Albrecht
Director: Leonard Gray
Director/Animation: Dorse Lanpher
Writer: Don Hall
Music: Jimmy Haskell
Company: Screen Images for Lutheran Television
Distributor: International Lutheran Layman's League/1985-

Principal Characters and Voices
Benji	Richard Susceno
Innkeeper	Hans Conreid
Waldo/Joseph	Don Messick
Mary	Colleen Collins

Other Voices
    June Foray, Jerry Hausner, Vic Perrin

Christmas Is concentrated on the religious meaning of the Christian
holiday through the activities of young Benji and his shaggy dog,
Waldo. Unhappy with his role as "second" shepherd in the school's
annual Christmas play, the pair were transported through a flight
of fantasy back to the world of the Nativity. There Benji and Waldo
witnessed the birth of Christ. Songs: "Christmas Is!" "What Is
Christmas?" "O Little Town of Bethlehem," "Adoration."
    The film was the first of four specials starring Benji and Waldo,
underwritten by the International Lutheran Layman's League.

CHRISTMAS LOST AND FOUND

Broadcast History
    Premiere: 1965
    SYN/local station option
Producers: Art Clokey, Ruth Clokey
Directors: Art Clokey, Raymond Peck
Writer: Nancy Moore
Music: John Seely, Patricia Beck
Company: Clokey Productions for the Lutheran Church in America
Distributor: Department of Telecommunications, Lutheran Church in
    America/1985-

Principal Characters and Voices
Davey Hanson/Sally Hanson/   Norma McMillan/
    Mary Hanson   Nancy Wible
Goliath/John Hanson   Hal Smith

Christmas Lost and Found explored the deeper Christian meaning of
the holiday through the experiences of Davey Hanson. Although he
busied himself with all the usual preparations, he was not embued
with the spirit of the Yuletide. He could see, smell, taste and hear
Christmas, but could not find the Christmas spirit. Proud of his
role as one of the three kings in a Christmas program, Davey com-
pulsively gave up the role to a lonely country boy on the night of
the pageant and began to understand. The real meaning of Christmas had been right in front of him all the time--in the symbolism of
the crêche displayed in the front window of his home.
    The first of six specials sponsored by the Lutheran Church
in America, the film featured the stop-motion animated puppets originally introduced in the series Davey and Goliath (SYN, 1962-),
described in Children's Television, Part II, (Scarecrow, 1985), pp.
140-141.

CHRISTMAS MESSENGER, THE

Broadcast History
   Premiere: 1975
   SYN/local station option
   Executive Producer: Gerald Potterton
   Producers: Murray Shostak, Stan Schwartz
   Director/Writer: Peter Sander
   Music: Jeff Wayne
   Company: A Reader's Digest Presentation produced by Shostak and
      Schwartz with Gerald Potterton Productions, Montreal, Canada
   Distributor: LBS Communications ("LBS Children's Theatre)/1983-
      1985
   Home Video: In Release

Narrator: Richard Chamberlain

The Christmas Messenger was laced with the rich melodies of Christmas
carols. The story was related by a boy who remembered a snowy
Christmas eve when a friendly stranger stopped briefly in his country village. Fascinated with the singing of some carollers, the boy
joined him and as they listened to the lyrical music, animated sequences portrayed the tales of Christmas folklore. Then he learned
the stranger's true identity and came to understand his message to
the world. Songs: "We Three Kings," "I Saw Three Ships," "A
Band of Children," "Deck the Halls," "Good King Wenceslaus."

CHRISTMAS RACCOONS, THE

Broadcast History
   Premiere: December 1980
   SYN/local station option (WCBS, New York, December 3, 1980,
      Wednesday 7:30-8:00 PM)
   Sponsors: GAF Corporation, Bristol Myers; General Foods, War-
      ner Lambert, LJN Toys, Procter & Gamble, Wrigley, Tonka
      Toys, Sunkist
   CBC/December 17, 1980, Wednesday 8:00-8:30 PM
   CBC/Repeats: 1981-1983
   SYN/Repeats: 1981 +
   Executive Producer: Sheldon Wiseman
   Producer/Creator: Kevin Gillis
   Directors: Kevin Gillis, Paul Schibli
   Writer: Juliet Packer
   Music: Kevin Gillis, Jon Stroll
   Company: Gillis-Wiseman Productions in association with Atkinson
      Film-Arts, Ottawa, Canada
   Distributor: Crawleys International/1986-
   Record Albums: Polygram/Starland Records
   Home Video: Embassy Home Entertainment

Narrator: Rich Little

Principal Characters and Voices

Dan	Rupert Holmes
Julie	Tammy Bourne
Tommy	Hadley Kay
Schaeffer	Carl Banas
Ralph	Bobby Dermer
Melissa	Rita Coolidge
Bert	Len Carlson
Cyril Sneer	Michael Magee
Cedric Sneer	Fred Little

Vocalists
    Rita Coolidge, Rupert Holmes

The Christmas Raccoons was structured around an environmental
motif in the Evergreen Forest, "a ways northward, shortly beyond
the horizon," in a two-day period before Christmas. Eight-year-
old Julie and 9-year-old Tommy learned from Dan, their forest-
ranger father, that the trees in their vicinity were disappearing.
Tucked in bed, the youngsters and their wooly sheepdog Schaeffer
entered a snowy, frosty land on a lakeshore in the north woods
where "everything is so real you'd never guess you were dreaming."
In the Raccoon Dominion, Ralph and Melissa and their houseguest
Bert Raccoon had heard about the tree problem but were not ter-
ribly concerned. "At least we live in a safe neighborhood," said
Melissa, the wife of the Ralph Nader of Raccoonland. Little did she
realize that lurking nearby was the scheming Cyril Sneer, who
closely resembled a pink aardvark, a notorious lumber profiteer who
loved but two things: money and chainsaws. A triumph of nasty
greed, the cackling Sneer was out to destroy all the trees in the
forest. When his sniveling son Cedric, a recent college graduate
never found without his pocket calculator, suggested that honesty
may be the best policy, Cyril shouted, "Honest? Who makes big
bucks being honest?" In the course of his crazed plan, he cut down
the Raccoondominium home of the Raccoons. Eventually defeated by
the furry masked critters, with the help of the children and Schaeffer, Cyril agreed to replant seedlings when it was pointed out that
there was money in reforesting. Songs: "Lost Angeles," "Lake
Freeze" (Coolidge), "Shake the Sun," "Perfect Tree" (Holmes).
    The film was also broadcast on the BBC and ITV in England
and was the number one U.S. syndicated animated special and children's show in 1980. It spurred two sequels, The Raccoons and
the Lost Star [q.v.] and The Raccoons on Ice [q.v.]. The overall
success of the Raccoons specials prompted more programs, which
comprise a 13-episode series produced under the aegis of Evergreen
Raccoon Productions, Ottawa, Canada, and aired on CBC, Disney
Channel, BBC and others. A line of dolls, toys and novelties were
licensed by Evergreen Marketing. The music sequences from the
three specials were compiled for a home video cassette, Raccoons:
Let's Dance (Embassy Home Entertainment).

CHRISTMAS STORY, A

Broadcast History
  Premiere: 1972
  SYN/local station option (KCOP, Los Angeles, December 9, 1972,
    Saturday 8:30-9:00 PM PST)
  SYN/Repeats: 1973 +
Executive Producers: William Hanna, Joseph Barbera
Associate Producer: Alex Lovy
Director: Charles A. Nichols
Writers: Ken Spears, Joe Ruby
Music/Songs & Lyrics: Denby Williams, Joseph Roland
Music: Hoyt Curtin
Company: Hanna-Barbera Productions
Distributor: Worldvision Enterprises/1979-

Principal Characters and Voices
Mother/Girl   Janet Waldo
Timmy/Boy   Walter Tetley
Dad/Squirrel   Don Messick
Goober/Sleezer/Runto   Paul Winchell
Gumdrop/Second Dog   Daws Butler
Santa/Fatcat   Hal Smith
Polecat/Postman/First Dog   John Stephenson

Vocalists
  Paul DeKorte, Randy Kemner, Stephen McAndrew, Susie McCune,
  Judi Richards

A Christmas Story involved a little boy, Timmy, his huge dog, Goober,
and a kind-hearted mouse, Gumdrop, on Christmas Eve, and a letter
with a special request for Santa, gone astray. Accidentally, Timmy's
letter had slipped behind a table, where it was discovered by Gumdrop who vowed to deliver it so the boy would not be disappointed
on Christmas morning. Together with his pal Goober, Gumdrop began their midnight quest, peering into toy shops, wandering through
parks and climbing onto roofs, but though they could hear his sleigh-
bells in the darkness, they failed to find the jolly gentleman. As
well, both managed to escape the evening's perils when four felines,
Sleezer, Polecat, Runto and Fatcat nearly made a dinner of Gumdrop
and locked Goober inside a mail truck. Finally, spotting Santa de-
scending a chimney, Gumdrop folded the letter into a glider and
sailed it towards his sleigh, but it went over the roof and into the
snow. Saddened at their failure, the pair returned home with the
soggy note, and with it still clasped in Gumdrop's arms, they fell
asleep. Awakened Christmas morning by the happy shouts of Timmy,
Gumdrop found the opened letter on his chest. Joining Timmy at
the window, Goober and Gumdrop stared at Timmy's special request
come true, "Peace on Earth" spelled out in the sky by the magical
glow of Santa's sleigh, as they heard him shout through the mist,
"Merry Christmas to all, and to all a good night." Songs: "Christmas

Story" (Theme), "Hope," "Where Do You Love?" "Which One Is the Real Santa Claus?"

CHRISTMAS TREE, A

<u>Broadcast History</u>
Premiere: December 17, 1972
SYN/FESTIVAL OF FAMILY CLASSICS, WABC, New York, Sunday
   7:00-7:30 PM
SYN/Repeats: 1973 +
Producers/Directors: Arthur Rankin, Jr., Jules Bass
Associate Producer: Mary Alice Dwyer
Writer: Ken Donnelly
Music: Maury Laws, Jules Bass
Company: Rankin-Bass Productions
Distributor: Viacom Enterprises ("Family Classics")/1986-
Home Video: Prism (with PUSS 'N' BOOTS)

A Christmas Tree was a musical adaptation of the Charles Dickens' fantasy in which the author made a Christmas Eve visit to the home of his young friends, Peter and Mary, and spun tales of his boyhood Christmases. The children became participants in the scenes he described and as the Christmas tree grew to reach the sky the Pied Piper materialized with news that Horatio the Giant had stolen the essence of Christmas. Climbing up the tree, the children learned the essence had been stolen, in turn, by Mantu, the evil magician. Carried by the star atop the tree, the youngsters set out for Mantu's castle, outwitted the trolls who guarded the candy-striped Gaddy-wine River, gave the snow-breathing Dragon of Ochibar a fatal hot-foot, and finally turned Mantu's magic icicle against the sorcerer. So doing, they recovered the wonderful feeling that is the essence of Christmas.

The children's special was adapted from one of six Yuletide stories written by Dickens, among them <u>The Cricket on the Hearth</u> [q.v.] and his classic <u>A Christmas Carol</u> [q.v.].

CHRISTMAS TREE TRAIN, THE

<u>Broadcast History</u>
Premiere: 1983
SYN/local station option (KTLA, Los Angeles, December 24, 1983,
   Saturday, 2:30-3:00 PM PST)
Sponsor: Tonka Toys (1986)
SYN/Repeats: 1984 +
Producers/Directors: Bill Hutten, Tony Love
Writer: John Bradford
Music: Larry Fotine
Company: Encore Enterprises
Distributor: Muller Media/1986-

THE CHRISTMAS TREE TRAIN. © 1983, Encore Enterprises, Inc.
Courtesy Encore Enterprises and Muller Media, Inc.

Principal Characters and Voices

Rusty/Rosie	Kathy Ritter
Buttons	Barbara Goodson
Ranger Jones	Bill Boyett
Abner/Santa Claus	Alvy Moore
George	Bill Ratner
Bridgett	Morgan Lofting

The Christmas Tree Train transported the bear cub Buttons and the
young fox Rusty to the big city for the holidays. Buttons and
Rusty played among the evergreens where the lumberjacks cut the
Christmas trees and accidently were locked in a loaded car as the
train began its journey. Abner and Bridgett Bear and George and
Rosie Fox, the youngster's parents, were worried about the disappearance and sought help from the Forest Ranger Jones, who began
a search. Avoiding several situations that would have resulted in
their capture, the cubs took up shelter in the city in a winter
wonderland park, little realizing the setting was actually a display
in a department store window. At the unveiling the next day, when
the crowd gathered in front of the window, Rusty and Buttons tried
every trick they knew to blend in with the environment. Frantically
searching for the pair, Jonesy and their parents spotted them during
the televised arrival of Santa Claus at the store, and there was a

happy reunion at Jonesy's cabin when Santa delivered them via his sleigh. Songs: "Christmas Tree Train," "It's Snowing, It's Snowing."

CHUCKLEWOOD EASTER, A

Broadcast History
    Premiere: 1987
    SYN/local station option (KCBS, Los Angeles, April 18, 1987, Saturday 12:00-12:30 PM PST)
    SYN/Repeats: 1988 +
Producers/Directors: Bill Hutten, Tony Love
Writer: John Bates
Music: Larry Fotine
Company: Encore Enterprises
Distributor: Muller Media/1987-

Principal Characters and Voices
Rusty/Bluebell	Mona Marshall
Buttons	Barbara Goodson
Abner	Alvy Moore
George/Easter Bunny	Robert Axelrod
Bridgett	Oceana Mars
Skipper	Dan Roth
Ranger Jones	Bill Boyett

A Chucklewood Easter continued the adventures of the bear cub Buttons and the young fox Rusty, busy honing their egg-decorating skills using eggs innocently borrowed from various nests in Chucklewood park. Planning to return the eggs that afternoon, the youngsters lost track of time and when darkness fell decided to return them the next day. That night, the curious pair followed a long procession of rabbits to their burrow deep in the forest. Disguising themselves in kind, they entered the hole which led them to the Easter Bunny's factory where panic ensued when they lost their bunny outfits. Pandemonium ensued at the park also, when several stupified animals found their eggs missing. Attempting to solve the problem, Ranger Jones and the youngsters' parents, Abner and Bridgett Bear and George and Rosie Fox, tried to replace the mixed-up eggs. Meantime, the rabbits put Rusty and Buttons on trial for discovering and violating the Easter Bunny's secret home. All was resolved at the big Easter picnic in Chucklewood park, and upon returning to their cave Buttons and Rusty found two Easter baskets left for them with a note from the Easter Bunny.

CINDERELLA

Broadcast History
    Premiere: September 17, 1972

SYN/FESTIVAL OF FAMILY CLASSICS, WABC, New York, Sunday
7:00-7:30 PM
SYN/Repeats: 1973 +
Producers/Directors: Arthur Rankin, Jr., Jules Bass
Associate Producer: Mary Alice Dwyer
Writer: William J. Keenan
Music: Maury Laws, Jules Bass
Company: Rankin-Bass Productions
Distributor: Viacom Enterprises ("Family Classics")/1986-
Home Video: Prism

Cinderella rendered a comic version of the timeless fairytale for
children about the household drudge, befriended by only a bevy of
birds and mice, tormented by her cruel stepmother and her nasty,
nagging daughters. Then, along came an absent-minded fairy godmother, who had misplaced her wand, temporarily, but finally succeeded in transforming the destitute ward's rags into a beautiful
gown in which she attended the king's ball and met the handsome,
and available, Prince Charming. Losing her slipper, she was tracked
down by a bumbling knight who had difficulty staying on his horse,
reintroduced to the prince and after their wedding lived happily
ever after.

CITY THAT FORGOT ABOUT CHRISTMAS, THE

Broadcast History
    Premiere: 1974
    SYN/local station option (WABC, New York, December 22, 1974,
        Sunday 2:00-2:30 PM)
    SYN/Repeats: 1975 +
Executive Producer: Dr. Martin J. Neeb, Jr.
Producer: Rev. Ardon D. Albrecht
Director: Leonard Gray
Director/Animation: Dorse A. Lanpher
Writer: Don Hinchey
Music: Jimmy Haskell
Company: Screen Images for Lutheran Television
Distributor: International Lutheran Layman's League/1985-

Narrator
Benji's Grandfather   Sebastian Cabot

Principal Characters and Voices
Benji   David Kelly
Matthew (wood carver)   Sebastian Cabot
Wicked Mayor   Charles Nelson Reilly
Henchman   Louis Nye
Waldo (Benji's dog)
Others   June Foray
                             Vic Perrin

THE CITY THAT FORGOT ABOUT CHRISTMAS. © 1974, International
Lutheran Layman's League. Courtesy of the International Lutheran
Layman's League.

The City That Forgot About Christmas, about a visitor who changed
the lives of its citizens, unfolded as a story told by Benji's grandfather. Losing his patience over the frustrations of the pre-Christ-
mas preparations, Benji exclaimed, "Sometimes I wish there wasn't
any Christmas!" Hearing of the boy's outburst, at their next meeting his grandfather related to Benji and his friend Martin the tale
of a loveless city where nobody helped their neighbors. It was an
awful town, where the children put rocks instead of coins in a blind
beggar's cup. Then one day a stranger named Matthew came to
town. He had a smile and kind word for everyone, including the
despicable Mayor, who had no regard for making things better.
Surprised and dismayed that nobody in the town could remember
Christmas, Matthew told the children the story of Jesus as he carved
a live-sized crèche for the coming holiday. His enthusiasm and
spirit were infectious, and soon the whole town began preparing for
the celebration and love was reborn among the townspeople. The
foul Mayor reacted to the change by hatching a wicked plot with his
henchman to sidetrack Christmas. As Christmas Eve dawned, the
town's expectations turned to anger as someone had stolen the figure
of the baby Jesus from the crèche. The reprehensible deed changed

the lives of the citizens, and in the end the spirit of Christmas prevailed, underscoring the Christian meaning of the holiday. Songs: "You Can't Stop Christmas," "Chip, Chip Away."

CLEROW WILSON AND THE MIRACLE OF P.S. 14

Broadcast History
  Premiere: November 12, 1972
  NBC/Sunday 7:30-8:00 PM
  Sponsor: Ideal Toys
  NBC/Repeat: November 19, 1973
Producers: David H. DePatie, Friz Freleng
Director: Corny Cole
Writers: Art Baer, Ben Joelson
Music: Dean Elliott
Company: DePatie-Freleng Enterprises in association with Clerow
  Productions and NBC
Home Video: In Release

Principal Characters and Voices
Clerow/Geraldine Jones/Herbie/
  Reverend LeRoy/The Devil   Flip Wilson
Freddie   Richard Wyatt, Jr.
Miss Davis   Vivian Bonnett
Little David   Kenney Ball
Robert Jackson   Phillip Brown
Dickie Porter   Larry Oliver

Clerow Wilson and the Miracle of P.S. 14 told it like it was, when comedian-actor Flip Wilson (Clerow Wilson was his given name) was a sassy 9-year-old. The New Jersey school he attended was strong on vitality and energy, but so poor that the band could not afford new uniforms. How Flip led Miss Davis' class in trying to raise money for them was the subject of this warm recollection. Humor tempered the deprivation of his childhood, turning each obstacle into an adventure, and was unconcious training for his later life. He became the first black performer to achieve major popularity as host of his own variety hour, The Flip Wilson Show (NBC, 1970-1974), which became a big hit. Introduced on that show, his comic characters--Geraldine Jones, Reverend LeRoy, Herbie and the Devil--were seen in animated cameo roles for the first time in this program. The special prompted a sequel, Clerow Wilson's Great Escape [q.v.].

CLEROW WILSON'S GREAT ESCAPE

Broadcast History
  Premiere: April 3, 1974
  NBC/Wednesday 8:00-8:30 PM
  Sponsors: Burger King, Armstrong, Gillette
  NBC/Repeat: December 16, 1974

Executive Producers: David H. DePatie, Friz Freleng
Director: Corny Cole
Writers: Ben Joelson, Art Baer, Flip Wilson
Music: Dean Elliott
Company: DePatie-Freleng Enterprises in association with Clerow
    Productions and NBC
Home Video: In Release

Principal Characters and Voices
Clerow/Geraldine Jones/Ralph/
    Reverend LeRoy/Herbie/The
    Devil   Flip Wilson
Ralph (the invisible dog)

Clerow Wilson's Great Escape presented a funny, poignant remem-
brance of Flip Wilson's childhood life in a Black ghetto in Jersey
City, New Jersey. In this second special based on recollections from
his youth, Wilson's close-knit family was locked in dire poverty when
a social worker found them living three to a room. She broke up
the family, sending Flip to a foster home where he found himself in
a "sweatshop." His new parents seemed like the world's nicest people until the social worker left and their true nastiness surfaced.
Fortunately, the social worker finally believed Flip's tales of abuse
and managed to reunite him with his own family in a housing project.
Many of his stock characterizations seen on The Flip Wilson Show
(NBC, 1970-1974) were portrayed in animated cameo roles, including
Herbie, the Good Time Ice Cream Man, Reverend LeRoy of the Church
of What's Happening Now and Geraldine Jones, a sassy swinger. He
also had an invisible dog, Ralph, and a favorite exclamation: "The
Devil made me do it!" The special was based on an original story
by Wilson.

COMPUTERS ARE PEOPLE, TOO!

Broadcast History
    Premiere: May 22, 1982
    SYN/local station option
Producer: Michael Bonifer
Director: Denis Sanders
Writers: Michael Bonifer, L. G. Weaver
Music: Don Kuramoto
Company: Walt Disney Television/60 minutes
Distributor: SFM Entertainment/1985-

Host: Elaine Joyce

Voices: (Computers)
    Billy Bowles, Joe Campanella, Nancy Kulp

Computers Are People, Too! portrayed host Elaine Joyce as a skeptical entertainer who guided viewers through a visual wonderland, insisting the much ballyhooed computer prove it could do all it was supposed to do. Taking a look at how and why artists, composers and dancers used computers to create new works, the film spotlighted the unique, colorful graphic images achieved through computer technology to prove that "anything that can be imagined can be real." Demonstrated were artists painting never-before-seen pictures directly on computer screens, young musicians teamed with computer programmers to write original music and Michael Iceberg with his unique Iceberg Machine, a computer-generated keyboard that enabled him to simulate a single instrument or a complete symphony orchestra. The program also visited a summer camp where children took time out from traditional activities to learn hands-on computer technology and examined computerized video games with several new concepts. Tieing in with the theme, the film featured a preview of Disney's movie Tron (BV, July 4, 1982), which utilized computer-generated animation.

Syndicated to more than 150 stations, the program used computer-animated film clips from Panasonic Plane (Robert Able and Associates), Caveman (Computer Image), Refractions (Robert Conley and Cranston-Csuri), Times Square (Digital Effects), Sunstone (Ed Emschweiller, New York Institute of Technology), The Juggler (Information International), Electronic Man (Magi) and Carla's Island.

CONEHEADS, THE

Broadcast History
    Premiere: October 14, 1983
    NBC/Friday 8:30-9:00 PM
    NBC/Repeat: NBC LATE NIGHT MOVIE, March 18, 1984
    SYN/Repeats: 1985 +
    Sponsor: Lego Toys (1985)
Executive Producer: Lorne Michaels
Producers/Directors: Arthur Rankin, Jr., Jules Bass
Writers: Al Franken, Tom Davis
Music: Bernard Hoffer
Company: Rankin-Bass Productions in association with Broadway
    Video
Distributor: Lorimar Syndication ("Animated Holiday Specials")/1985–

Principal Characters and Voices
Beldar   Dan Aykroyd
Prymaat   Jane Curtin
Connie   Laraine Newman

Other Voices
    Cynthia Adler, Tom Davis, Robert McFadden

The Coneheads featured the family that first came to national attention in comedy sketches on NBC's Saturday Night Live (NBC, 1975-),

THE CONEHEADS. © 1983, Rankin/Bass Productions, Inc. Courtesy of Rankin/Bass Productions and Lorimar Syndication.

reborn as an animated adult cartoon special. Remulak was the home planet of the people known as "The Coneheads." An alien couple, Beldar and Prymaat, were sent to planet Earth on a mission for the High Master of Remulak: "to seize the tiny planet inhabited by inferior beings who call themselves humans" as a slave labor force and establish a minor protoid refueling station for a massive fleet of Starcruisers. Finding this task somewhat more complicated than expected, the Coneheads were plunged into an assortment of adventures as years passed; they helped a TV repairman fix his Japanese sets, drank some beer for the first time and gave birth to a baby daughter, Connie. Trying to carry out the orders of their chief, they made plans for the arrival of a Starcruiser and United Nations ambassador by moving 20 miles from the U.N., but because of cutbacks in the Remulak space program no spaceship could arrive for some time. So they settled in on earth, aided by their neighbors, Barry and Carol, and observed the strange customs of the humans, including the activities of their teenager Connie, who went on a date to a rock concert with Ronnie and engaged in her first bout of necking. Life with the Earthlings was just beginning. The Coneheads were created by Dan Aykroyd, Tom Davis and Lorne Michaels.

CONNECTICUT RABBIT IN KING ARTHUR'S COURT, A

Broadcast History
    Premiere: February 23, 1978
    CBS/Thursday 8:30-9:00 PM
    CBS/Repeat: November 22, 1978
    CBS/Repeats: BUGS BUNNY IN KING ARTHUR'S COURT, November 17, 1979; August 19, 1981; March 10, 1982
Producer/Director/Writer: Chuck Jones
Music: Dean Elliott
Company: Chuck Jones Enterprises for Warner Bros. Television

Principal Characters and Voices
Connecticut Rabbit (Bugs Bunny)/
    King Arthur (Daffy Duck)/
    Merlin (Yosemite Sam)/
    Varlet (Porky Pig)/ Sir Elmer
    of Fudd (Elmer Fudd)   Mel Blanc

A Connecticut Rabbit in King Arthur's Court had Bugs taking a short cut recommended by Ray Bradbury to the Georgia Peanut Festival, when he popped up in the midst of Camelot, or thereabouts. Vowing never to ask Bradbury for directions again, Bugs emerged from his underground passageway only to be hoisted suddenly in the air on the lance-tip of Sir Elmer of Fudd, who mistook Bugs for the fire-breathing dragon for whom he had been searching to fulfill his knight-errant errand of ridding Camelot of pesky dragons. Trussed and ready for roasting, Bugs remembered it was an historic eclipse date and pulled the blackout bit, threatening to block out the sun if not released forthwith. With King Arthur looking on, he did just that and when the king offered half his kingdom to restore the sun, Bugs did, also forthwith. Not particularly wanting to settle down in that century, Bugs instead opted for the rental of a real fire-breathing dragon ("each ton of brimstone will get you about three million dragonpower," he figured) to turn machinery for the Bugs Bunny Iron Works and Armor Factory. While the dragon huffed and puffed power into Bugs' enterprises, Sir Elmer dropped by on one of his forays and disabled the critter and therewith Bugs' empire. What ensued was the duel of that or any century between Sir Elmer, the challenger, and Bugs, still suspected of being a dragon in disguise. In the midst of the fray, Bugs sighted "a great carrot-slicer," the sword Excalibur stuck in a stone. Pulling it out, true to legend he became King of England, forthwith. Loosely based on the Mark Twain classic and "plagiarized" by Chuck Jones, the film was the fifth special starring Bugs Bunny [q.v.].

CONNECTICUT YANKEE IN KING ARTHUR'S COURT, A

Broadcast History
    Premiere: November 26, 1970

A CONNECTICUT YANKEE IN KING ARTHUR'S COURT. © 1983,
D. L. Taffner/Limited. Courtesy of D. L. Taffner/Limited.

CBS/FAMOUS CLASSIC TALES, Thursday 12:00-1:30 PM
CBS/Repeats: November 25, 1971; November 23, 1972 (in New
    York on WPIX)
Sponsor: Kenner Products (Toy Group, General Mills)
SYN/Repeats: 1973 +
Executive Producer: Walter J. Hucker
Director: Zoran Janjic
Writer: Michael Robinson
Music: Richard Bowden
Company: Air Programs International, Sydney, Australia/90 minutes
Distributor: D. L. Taffner ("Animated Classics for Children")/1985-
Home Video: Classics for Kids (MGM/UA)

Principal Character and Voice
Connecticut Yankee   Orson Bean

Other Voices
   Ron Haddrick, Barbara Llewellyn, John Llewellyn, L. Ostrich, Brenda Senders

A Connecticut Yankee in King Arthur's Court was based loosely on Mark Twain's story about the ingenious Yankee. Medieval chivalry blended with nineteenth-century technology as the hero used his knowledge of modern inventions and some old-fashioned shrewdness in a battle of wits with Merlin the Magician and King Arthur's knights. Woven into the familiar tale were such recent accoutrements as the telephone, a cigarette lighter, motorbikes, a revolver and a huge electro-magnet which pulled the armor-clad knights to the ground so they could be blown away with compressed air and powerful jets of water during the final confrontation with the Yankee, leading an army of 50,000. However, one knight managed to stab the Yankee, who slowly drifted toward death thinking of Sandy, the maiden he had recently married. At the end, the Yankee awoke in a modern American hospital wondering, "Could it have been just a dream?"
   Initially telecast on Thanksgiving day, the film was the pioneer animated made-for-TV movie aired on the daytime schedule and the second produced by API for the Kenner division of General Mills through Sive Associates.

COSMIC CHRISTMAS, A

Broadcast History
   Premiere: December 6, 1977
   CBC/Tuesday 7:30-8:00 PM
   SYN/local station option (KABC, Los Angeles, December 24, 1977, Saturday 7:30-8:00 PM PST)
   SYN/Repeats: 1978 +
Executive Producer: Jeffrey Kirsch
Producers: Michael Hirsh, Patrick Loubert
Director: Clive Smith
Writers: Patrick Loubert, Ida Nelson Fruet, Laura Paull, Martin Lavut, Ken Sobol
Music/Songs & Lyrics: Sylvia Tyson
Music: Sylvia Tyson, Ed Roth
Company: Nelvana Limited, Toronto, Canada, in association with the CBC
Distributor: Viacom Enterprises/1977-
Record Album: Nelvana Records NEL 7801
Home Video: Warner Home Video #4006 ("Nelvanamation")

Principal Characters and Voices

Peter	Joey Davidson
Dad/Plutox/Santa Joe	Martin Lavut
Lexicon	Richard Davidson
Amalthor	Duncan Regehr
Mom	Patricia Moffat

Grandma	Jane Mallett
Police Chief Snerk	Marvin Goldhar
Marvin	Greg Rogers
The Mayor	Chris Wiggins
Townies	Nick Nichols
	Marion Waldman

A Cosmic Christmas concerned three beings from outer space, and their pet mascot, who landed on the planet Earth with a specific mission: to discover the significance of an unusually bright star that appeared in that proximity 2,000 years ago. Realizing it was the Star of Bethlehem, young Peter and his pet goose Lucy led the aliens on a tour through Peter's town to find the meaning of Christmas. It was just another small town, just another Christmas, but the visitors' 2,000-year search found much that the holiday had become but was never meant to be: the commercialism, the selfishness in the town and among the townspeople. Following their series of adventures, chases and near-tragedies, interspersed with music and merriment, the lives and hearts of the townfolk were changed, thanks to the aliens, as the spirit of the holiday came shining through. Mission accomplished, the trio and their mascot boarded their space ship for the long trip home. Songs: "The Way That Christmas Used to Be," "Why Don't They Look to the Stars?"

COUNT OF MONTE CRISTO, THE

Broadcast History
    Premiere: September 23, 1973
    CBS/FAMOUS CLASSIC TALES, Sunday 5:00-6:00 PM
    CBS/Repeat: December 7, 1974
    Sponsor: Kenner Products (Toy Group, General Mills)
    SYN/Repeats: 1975 +
Producers/Directors: William Hanna, Joseph Barbera
Associate Producer: Zoran Janjic
Director: Peter Luschwitz
Writer: Draper Lewis
Music: Bill Young, William Hanna, Joseph Barbera, Hoyt Curtin
Company: Hanna-Barbera Productions, Sydney, Australia/60 minutes
Distributor: Worldvision Enterprises/1982-
Home Video: Worldvision

Voices
    Elizabeth Crosby, Tim Elliott, Barbara Frawley, Ron Haddrick, Richard Meikle

The Count of Monte Cristo was a faithful adaptation from the nineteenth-century novel by Dumas père and the only one of his stories to be placed in modern times. Edmond Dantès, a young sailor aboard the Pharaon owned by Monsieur Morrell, was unjustly accused of helping the exiled Napoleon on Elba in 1815. Victim of a plot by

the envious seaman Danglers and Ferdinand, the jilted lover of
Dantès' proposed bride, Mercedes, Dantès was arrested and imprisoned
in the Chateau d'If, near Marseille. After fifteen years he finally
escaped by taking the place of his dead companion, the Abbé Faria.
Tied in a sack and thrown into the sea, he cut himself free and was
pulled into a boat by the fisherman Jacopo. They set sail to the Isle
of Monte Cristo and dug up the fabulous treasures in the cavern of
which the dying Faria had told. With his newly acquired wealth
and a new name, the Count of Monte Cristo, Dantès began his planned
revenge, to destroy his enemies and reward his friends.

The film was the first of nine specials produced for Kenner
by Hanna-Barbera Productions, through Sive Associates, which later
syndicated the programs for General Mills through 1981-1982.

CRICKET IN TIMES SQUARE, THE

Broadcast History
    Premiere: April 24, 1973
    ABC/Tuesday 8:00-8:30 PM
    ABC/Repeat: November 9, 1974
    SYN/Repeats: 1979 +
Producer/Director/Writer: Chuck Jones
Associate Producers: Joseph Aidlin, John Allen
Music: Dean Elliott
Music/Violinist: Israel Baker
Company: Chuck Jones Enterprises
Distributor: Berle Adams/1986-
Home Video: Family Home Entertainment

Principal Characters and Voices
Chester C. Cricket/Harry the
    Cat/Father/Music Teacher   Les Tremayne
Tucker the Mouse   Mel Blanc
Mother   June Foray
Mario Bellini   Kerry MacLane

The Cricket in Times Square was a modern fantasy about a cat, a
mouse, a boy and a cricket who spent one summer in the Big Apple
and helped revive a failing newsstand. Chester the Cricket hopped
on a liverwurst sandwich in Connecticut and became trapped in a
picnic basket. Winding up in New York City, the tiny creature was
lucky enough to find three really good friends, the boy Mario Bellini,
whose parents ran the newsstand in the subway station at Times
Square, and two small denizens of the place, a fast-talking Broadway
mouse, Tucker, and his pal, Harry the Cat. Since Mario's father
believed crickets were good luck, he let Mario keep Chester as a
pet. Tucker and Harry became friends with Chester and explained
to the homesick cricket that the newsstand was going broke. One
day Tucker and Harry discovered that Chester had a unique talent
performing beautiful music by rubbing his wings together, which

THE CRICKET IN TIMES SQUARE. © 1973, Chuck Jones Enterprises.
Courtesy of Chuck Jones Enterprises.

sounded like a violin aria, and he could play any melody just by
hearing it once. Quickly, they taught Chester a wide repetoire.
Soon, his haunting music attracted crowds of people, making him a
New York celebrity and the Bellini family newsstand a thriving business. But an autumn leaf drifting down into the subway station
reminded Chester how much he missed the Connecticut countryside
and in a touching good-bye, the entire city paused to hear Chester's
heartfelt farewell performance. The special was based on the eponymous book (Farrar, Strauss, 1960) by George Selden, illustrated by
Garth Williams, and spawned two sequels: A Very Merry Cricket
[q.v.] and Yankee Doodle Cricket [q.v.].

CRICKET ON THE HEARTH, THE

Broadcast History
    Premiere: December 18, 1967
    NBC/THE DANNY THOMAS HOUR, Monday 9:00-10:00 PM
    Sponsor: Burger Chef
    NBC/Repeat: November 25, 1971
    SYN/Repeats: 1978 +

Executive Producer: Danny Thomas
Producers: Arthur Rankin, Jr., Jules Bass
Writer: Romeo Muller
Music: Maury Laws
Lyrics: Jules Bass
Company: Rankin-Bass Productions in association with Videocraft
International/60 minutes
Distributor: Viacom Enterprises/1986-
Record Album: RCA LSC 1140, RCA LSO 1140 (stereo)
Home Video: MGM/UA

Principal Characters and Voices

Cricket Crockett	Roddy McDowall
Caleb Plummer	Danny Thomas
Bertha	Marlo Thomas
Edward	Ed Ames
Tackleton	Hans Conreid
Moll	Abbe Lane
Uriah/Sea Captain	Paul Frees

Cricket on the Hearth was a musical adaptation of the 1845 Christmas fantasy by Charles Dickens about a poor toymaker named Caleb Plummer, his troubled daughter Bertha and a helpful Cricket Crockett in London during holiday time. Cricket became a regular member of the Plummer household after he arrived on Christmas morning. There was a party going on for Bertha's fiancé Edward, who was leaving for duty with the Royal Navy. But Cricket soon became witness to sadness and tragedy, including Bertha's blindness after she learned that her fiancé had been lost at sea and her father's impoverishment at the hands of the skinflint Tackleton. Cricket hopped to the rescue of the bankrupt Caleb, and when Edward surfaced alive and well, he brought lightness out of darkness for Bertha, and happiness returned to the Plummer household. Containing several appealing original songs, the special featured the singing of Danny Thomas' daughter, Marlo, on film for the first time. Songs: "Cricket on the Hearth," "Through My Eyes," "The First Christmas" (Thomas & The Norman Luboff Choir), "Don't Give Your Love Away" (Ames), "Smiles Go With Tears," "That Was Yesterday" (Marlo), "Fish 'n' Chips" (Lane), "Parade of the Toys."

CURIOUS GEORGE

Broadcast History
    Premiere: 1983-1984
    SYN/local station option
Producer: Lafferty, Harwood & Partners
Director: Alan J. Shalleck
Music: Paul Baillargeon, Dean Morgan
Lyrics: Frank Gehrecke
Company: Lafferty, Harwood & Partners in association with Milktrain Productions

Distributor: LBS Communications ("LBS Children's Theatre")/1873-1985
Home Video: Sony

Narrator: Jack Duffy

Curious George starred an inquisitive little monkey who managed to get into trouble as a result of his unbounding curiosity. He was brought from Africa to the big city by his friend, the Man in the Yellow Hat. Together they took off in the Little Blue Car, motoring to minor misadventures from which his friend was always able to rescue him. The special consisted of several short cartoons in a half-hour format and was packaged with others under the umbrella title "LBS Children's Theatre."

The character, known as Zozo in Great Britain, was introduced in the U.S. in Curious George (Houghton Mifflin, 1941) and a subsequent series of children's books by English author and illustrator, Margret and H. A. Rey. Atkinson Film-arts, Ottawa, Canada, produced a four-minute, 104-episode series, Curious George (SYN, 1981-   ), which aired on cable TV.

CYRANO

Broadcast History
    Premiere: March 6, 1974
    ABC/ABC AFTERSCHOOL SPECIALS, Wednesday 4:30-5:30 PM
    ABC/Repeat: April 9, 1975
    SYN/Repeats: 1979 +
Executive Producers: William Hanna, Joseph Barbera
Producer: Iwao Takamoto
Director: Charles A. Nichols
Writer: Harvey Bullock
Music: Hoyt Curtin, Paul DeKorte
Company: Hanna-Barbera Productions/60 minutes
Distributor: Worldvision Enterprises/1979-
Home Video: Worldvision

Principal Characters and Voices
Cyrano de Bergerac	José Ferrer
Roxanne	Joan Van Ark
Ragueneau	Kurt Kasznar
Comte de Guiche	Martyn Green
Christian de Neuvillette	Victor Garber
Duenna	Jane Connell
First Cadet/de Brigny	Alan Oppenheimer
Richelieu	John Stephenson

Cyrano was a literal adaptation of Edmond Rostand's romantic play, Cyrano De Bergerac (1897). The heroic comedy was built around a French folk hero, the famed seventeenth-century long-nosed poet-swordsman who fought injustice while helping his friend win the beautiful Roxanne, whom he himself loved. Cyrano's keen wit and lyrical poetry offset the pathos of the drama, with José Ferrer voicing the character he played in countless stage presentations and the movie Cyrano De Bergerac (UA, 1950), for which he received an Oscar.

DAFFY DUCK'S EASTER SHOW

Broadcast History
    Premiere: April 1, 1980
    NBC/Tuesday 8:00-8:30 PM
    NBC/Repeats: April 14, 1981; April 6, 1982
    CBS/Repeats: April 16, 1984; April 6, 1985
Executive Producer: Hal Geer
Producer: Lee Gunther
Director: Friz Freleng
Writers: Tony Benedict, John Dunn, Friz Freleng

DAFFY DUCK'S EASTER SHOW. © 1980, Warner Bros., Inc. Courtesy of Warner Bros. Television.

Music: Dean Elliott
Company: DePatie-Freleng Enterprises for Warner Bros. Television

Principal Characters and Voices
Daffy Duck/Sylvester/Speedy
    Gonzalez   Mel Blanc

Daffy Duck's Easter Show presented three new cartoon adventures
tied into the holiday theme, starring the mischievous mallard. Daffy
and Sylvester tried to outfox each other to get the golden egg laid
by Prissy the Hen in "Yolks on You." Employed as a guard at a
factory where chocolate Easter bunnies were made in "The Chocolate
Chase," Daffy confounded Speedy Gonzalez who was hired by a group
of mice to find the chocolate holiday treats for some poor children.
In "Daffy Goes North," the irrepressible Duck opted to hitchhike
rather than fly, but quickly learned that thumbing a ride in the
springtime was not the way to go.
    Apart from his cartoons seen on The Bugs Bunny Show and
in syndication, the madcap mallard starred in his own Saturday morning series, The Daffy and Speedy Show (NBC, 1981-1982; CBS,
1982), described in Children's Television, Part I, (Scarecrow, 1983),
pp. 76-77. He also was starred in the feature, Daffy Duck's Movie:
Fantastic Island (WB, 1983).

DAFFY DUCK'S THANKS-FOR-GIVING SPECIAL

Broadcast History
    Premiere: November 20, 1980
    NBC/Thursday 8:00-8:30 PM
    NBC/Repeat: November 24, 1981
    CBS/Repeat: November 12, 1983
Executive Producer: Hal Geer
Producer/Director: Chuck Jones
Writers: Chuck Jones, Michael Maltese
Music: Dean Elliott
Company: Chuck Jones Enterprises for Warner Bros. Television

Principal Characters and Voices
Daffy Duck/Porky Pig   Mel Blanc

Daffy Duck's Thanks-for-giving Special gave a characteristic twist
to the meaning of the occasion, when the garrulous, extroverted
bird hatched a holiday tribute to applaud him for all the joy he had
given the world in his long career. Hoping to bolster his campaign,
the web-footed comic tried to convince the studio to back a sequel
to his cartoon classic, Duck Dodgers in the 24 1/2 Century (July
25, 1953). When the producer wanted none of that idea, Daffy pointed
to all his "great films of the past." Excerpts ensued from such classics as Robin Hood Daffy (March 8, 1958), in which he cut a flamboyant figure as the Knave of Sherwood Forest; Dripalong Daffy

(November 17, 1951), in which he appeared as a freelance hero of the Old West; and His Bitter Half (May 20, 1950), in which Daffy was married off briefly to a volatile spouse with an obnoxious son, Wentworth, a mynah bird. Finally giving in, the producer allowed Daffy to star in The Return of Duck Dodgers in the 24 1/2 Century, a cartoon produced by Chuck Jones as a companion short for Star Wars (TCF, 1977), with Daffy as a fearless space hero who, with his loyal cadet Porky Pig, undertook a critical mission in the cosmos, surviving a close encounter with Marvin the Martian while trying to save the Earth from destruction.

DANIEL BOONE

Broadcast History
    Premiere: November 27, 1981
    CBS/FAMOUS CLASSIC TALES, Friday 9:00-10:00 AM
    Sponsor: Kenner Products (Toy Group, General Mills)
    CBS/Repeat: November 25, 1982
    SYN/Repeats: 1983 +
Executive Producers: William Hanna, Joseph Barbera
Associate Producers: Doug Paterson, Chris Cuddington
Director: Geoff Collins
Writer: Kimmer Ringwald
Music: Australian Screen Music
Company: Hanna-Barbera Productions, Sydney, Australia (Southern
    Star Productions)/60 minutes
Distributor: Worldvision Enterprises/1983-
Home Video: Worldvision

Principal Characters and Voices

Daniel Boone	Richard Crenna
Rebecca	Janet Waldo
Daniel Boone (age 14)/Running Fox	Bill Callaway
Henry Miller/First Settler/ Mr. Harding	Mike Bell
Stearns/Assemblyman/Squire Boone	John Stephenson
Sarah/James/Quiet Dove	Joan Gerber
Washington/Col. Morgan/ Second Settler	Joe Baker
White Top/Painter/Floor Leader	Vic Perrin
Blackfish/Business Man/Indian Dragging Canoe	Barney Phillips
Girty/Oconostata/Finley	Michael Rye

Daniel Boone traced some of the exploits of the eighteenth-century wilderness scout, hunter, tracker, explorer, Indian fighter and crackshot. At age 86 in 1820, Boone reflected on his life for a book about his exciting escapades, as told to a Mr. Harding. Impatient with the writer and his silly painter for creating a much younger, robust portrait of the now white-haired frontiersman, Boone beseeched Harding to tell his story exactly as it happened without flowery descriptions and praise. To begin with, he informed the gent, Boone never wore a coonskin cap and only did his fighting and killing when there was no alternative. In the flashbacks, Boone reminisced on his life as a mischievous boy on his father's farm in North Carolina and winning a shooting contest at the County Fair; his meeting with George Washington; his marriage to Rebecca; the exploration of Kentucky, killing a bear bare-handed and escaping from the Indian White Hat; the establishment of Boonesborough Fort; the loss of his son and his own capture by the British army; his days as hostage of the Shawnee Indians and adoption by the tribe; and his election as an Assemblyman in the new Congress. Reminding Harding that he never sought immortality as a legend, Boone set off on his final journey to join his Indian father in the sky.

DAVID COPPERFIELD

Broadcast History
    Premiere: October 2, 1984
    HBO/Tuesday 6:30-8:00 AM; 4:30-6:00 PM
    HBO/Repeats: multiple option, 1984-1985
    SYN/Repeats: 1985 +
Executive Producers: Tom Stacey, George Stephenson
Producer: Eddy Graham
Director: Ian MacKenzie
Writer: Alex Buzo
Music: Richard Bowden, John Stuart
Company: Burbank Films, Sydney, Australia/90 minutes
Distributor: Twentieth-Century Fox Television ("Charles Dickens Classics")/1984-

Voices
    Ross Higgins, Phillip Hinton, Robyn Moore, Judy Nunn, Moya O'Sullivan, Robin Steward, John Stone

David Copperfield was adapted from the 1850 novel by Charles Dickens. One of the most beloved books in English literature, it concerned a half-orphaned boy who, as an adult, eventually found happiness and success as a writer. Partly autobiographical and Dickens' own favorite among his novels, the story began with David's birth, related his sad experiences as a youth, his school days, and his struggles in London to make a living and involved many characters and minor plots.

DAVY CROCKETT ON THE MISSISSIPPI

Broadcast History
    Premiere: November 20, 1976

DAVY CROCKETT ON THE MISSISSIPPI. © 1976, Hanna-Barbera
Productions, Inc. Courtesy of Hanna-Barbera Productions and TECO.

CBS/FAMOUS CLASSIC TALES, Saturday 1:00-2:00 PM
Sponsor: Kenner Products (Toy Group, General Mills)
CBS/Repeats: October 22, 1977; November 2, 1980; November
   26, 1982
SYN/Repeats: 1978 +
Executive Producers: William Hanna, Joseph Barbera
Associate Producer: Alex Lovy
Producer: Iwao Takamoto
Director: Charles A. Nichols
Writer: Sid Morse
Music/"Davy Crockett Theme": Gairden Cooke, Hoyt Curtin
Company: Hanna-Barbera Productions/60 minutes
Distributor: Worldvision Enterprises/1986-
Home Video: Worldvision

Principal Characters and Voices

Davy Crockett	Ned Wilson
Matt Henry	Randy Gray
Honeysuckle/Pete/The Settler	Mike Bell
Mike Fink/Flatboat Sailor	Ron Feinberg
Running Wolf/Jake	Kip Niven
Settler's Wife/Amanda/Susie	Pat Parris
Sloan/Andrew Jackson/	
Blacksmith	John Stephenson

Davy Crockett on the Mississippi interwove large doses of fiction
with some fact in a depiction of the "b'ar" hunting Tennessee fron-
tiersman, who was provided with a talking pet bruin, Honeysuckle.
The tale, set against a frontier American background, opened with
Davy and Honeysuckle on a peace mission to the Indians for the
President of the United States, when they encountered Matt Henry,
an orphaned 10-year-old on his way to Ankaloola to live with his
Uncle Clarence Henry. Accompanying the boy in the wild country,
Davy hailed a keelboat going down river and made the acquaintance
of Mike Fink, the famous "King of the Keelboats." Downstream they
were accosted by Running Wolf, son of Davy's friend Grey Eagle,
a Shawnee chieftan, who the frontiersman hoped to powwow with
later. Parting with Fink in Ankaloola, Davy and Matt discovered
Clarence had moved, and they set out for Natchez. Along the way
they rescued a settler family from a roaring flood with the aid of
Honeysuckle and crossed paths with General Andrew Jackson. Learning Clarence was not in New Orleans, they tried to locate Mike Fink's
boat, which was in the hands of three river pirates, Sloan and his
two sons Pete and Jake. Buying their own boat, Davy and Matt
rescued Fink, clinging to a log, and pursued the pirates through
turbulent rapids and a thunderstorm. Aided by the fortuitous appearance of Running Wolf and his braves, Davy routed the gang.
Leaving Fink to take Matt on to New Orleans, Davy left with Running
Wolf to meet Grey Eagle to discuss his presidential peace mission.

DECK THE HALLS WITH WACKY WALLS

Broadcast History
    Premiere: December 11, 1983
    NBC/Sunday 7:30-8:00 PM
Producer: Buzz Potamkin
Directors: Candy Kugel, Al Kouzel, Vincent Cafarelli
Writer: Mark Evanier
Music: Elliot Lawrence
Lyrics: Amy Lawrence
Company: NBC Entertainment Productions in association with Buzzco
    Productions

Principal Characters and Voices

Wacky	Daws Butler
Big Blue	Peter Cullen
Springette	Tress MacNeille
Stickum	Marvin Kaplan
Crazylegs	Howard Morris
Bouncing Baby Boo	Frank Welker
Darryl	Scott Menville

Other Voices
    Sharman Di Vono, Cheri Eichen, Bill Scott

Deck the Halls With Wacky Walls put six multi-hued, adhesive and amorphous aliens on Earth, where they became accustomed to some of the Yuletide traditions. Wacky, Big Blue, Springette, Stickum, Crazylegs and Bouncing Baby Boo were on a mission from their far distant planet Kling Kling to determine the meaning of Christmas. Along the way, the strangers encountered a humanoid tyke, a brat named Darryl, who was also searching for the meaning of the holiday. Through their adventures, somewhat akin to the plot of Dickens' A Christmas Carol, Darryl's insolence and selfishness turned to humility and goodwill as all learned the true, non-commercialized meaning of Christmas.

The film was based on the Wacky Wallwalker toys first imported from Japan in 1982 by Tradex, owned by U.S. entrepreneur Ken Hakuta, who sold more than 200 million of the octopus-like crawlers with suction cups enabling them to cling and climb down walls. Several commercials for the toys were aired immediately adjacent to the program.

DENNIS THE MENACE: MAYDAY FOR MOTHER

Broadcast History
    Premiere: May 8, 1981
    NBC/Friday 8:00-8:30 PM
    NBC/Repeat: May 6, 1983
Executive Producers: David H. DePatie, Friz Freleng
Directors: Bob Richardson, David Detiege, Cullen Houghtaling, Art Leonardi, Nelson Shin, Art Vitello
Writer/Creator: Hank Ketcham
Music: Joe Raposo, Eric Rodgers
Company: DePatie-Freleng Enterprises in association with Mirisch Films
Home Video: MGM-UA Home Video

Principal Characters and Voices

Dennis Mitchell	Joey Nagy
Alice Mitchell	Kathy Garver
Henry Mitchell	Bob Holt
George Wilson	Larry D. Mann
Martha Wilson	Elizabeth Kerr
Margaret	Nicole Eggert
Ruff (Dennis' dog)	

Other Voices
    James Hackett, Herbert Rudley, Seth Wagerman, Nancy Wible

Dennis the Menace: Mayday for Mother transplanted the infant terrible from the comic pages to the video screen, marking his primetime animated debut. An original story by cartoonist-creator Hank Ketcham, the holiday plot found Dennis struggling to overcome various setbacks to make a special gift for Mother's Day. Finally he hit upon the idea of making breakfast for his mom by using ingredients whose letters started with m-o-t-h-e-r. Also, he hatched an idea to make his childless neighbor, Martha Wilson, an honorary mom for the neighborhood. With his dog Ruff at his side, Dennis blundered into trouble as usual with Mr. Wilson, annoyed over the boy's antics but eventually melting. Dad Henry was his easy-going self and Alice Mitchell infinitely patient, almost, while Margaret endured and little Joey turned up briefly for a vote on Mrs. Wilson.

Ketcham's own son, Dennis Lloyd Ketcham, was the inspiration for the mischievous tot, who first appeared for the Hall Syndicate as a daily single-panel newspaper cartoon on March 12, 1951, with a Sunday feature a year later. It became so popular the very title became a household phrase. Following the successful live-action series, Dennis the Menace (CBS, 1959-1963/NBC, 1963-1965), the first animated cartoon was created for Curiosity Shop (ABC, 1971-1973), described in Children's Television, Part II, (Scarecrow, 1985), pp. 146-148. The half-hour, 65-episode weekday strip-series, Dennis the Menace (SYN, 1986-), was produced by DIC Enterprises and distributed by DFS Program Exchange.

DEVIL AND DANIEL MOUSE, THE

Broadcast History
    Premiere: October 22, 1978
    CBC/Sunday 7:30-8:00 PM
    SYN/local station option (KABC, Los Angeles, October 26, 1978,
        Thursday 7:30-8:00 PM PST)
    SYN/Repeats: 1979 +
Executive Producer: Jeffery Kirsch
Producers: Patrick Loubert, Michael Hirsh
Director: Clive A. Smith
Writers: Patrick Loubert, Ken Sobol
Music/Songs & Lyrics: John Sebastian, Valerie Carter
Music: Patricia Cullen
Company: Nelvana Limited, Toronto, Canada, in association with
    the CBC
Distributor: Viacom Enterprises/1978-
Record Album: Nelvana Records NEL 7802
Home Video: Warner Home Video #4006 ("Nelvanamation")

Principal Characters and Voices
Daniel Mouse   Jim Henshaw
                                    John Sebastian (singing)
Jan   Annabelle Kershaw
                                    Laurel Runn (singing)
B. L. Zebub (The Devil)   Chris Wiggins
Weez Weasel/Pawnbroker   Martin Lavut
Rock Emcee   John Sebastian
Interviewer   Dianne Lawrence

THE DEVIL AND DANIEL MOUSE. © 1978, Nelvana Limited. Courtesy of Nelvana Limited and Viacom Enterprises.

The Devil and Daniel Mouse conjured up the old arch-fiend in a rock-and-roll parable about fame and its price. Jan and Daniel Mouse, a folk-singing team, lost their jobs when the manager of a local club decided to follow the current trend and reopen as a disco. Striking out on her own, Jan inadvertently signed a contract with B. L. Zebub, selling her soul to the Devil to become a rock sensation. Not one to worry about details, B. L. delegated the job of making Jan a rock star to his comic sidekick, Weez Weasel. While managing to keep them apart and putting off Dan's attempts at reconciliation, the Weez transformed Jan into the number one singer in the country. Then, on the night of her greatest triumph, old B. L. appeared to claim her in fullfillment of the pact. Given until midnight to say goodbye to her friends, her fame fleeting quickly, Jan, at her wits end, finally met up with Dan, who came to her aid. All that stood between Jan the the Devil-monster was a trick played by Dan, affirming the power of music to soothe and transform villainy: "A song in the heart beats the Devil every time." The special was loosely based on The Devil and Daniel Webster by Stephen Vincent Benet. Songs: "Look Where the Music Can Take You," "I've Got a Song to Sing," "Can You Help Me Find My Song?"

DIG. © 1972, The Hubley Studios, Inc. Courtesy of The Hubley Studio.

DIG

Broadcast History
    Premiere: April 8, 1972
    CBS/Saturday 12:00-12:30 PM
    Sponsor: General Foods
    CBS/Repeat: May 5, 1973
    SYN/Repeats: 1980 +
Producers: John Hubley, Faith Hubley
Director: John Hubley
Music: Quincy Jones
Lyrics: John Hubley, Faith Hubley, Quincy Jones
Company: The Hubley Studio
Distributor: Fox-Lorber Associates/1980-

Principal Characters and Voices

Adam	Ray Hubley
Mother	Maureen Stapleton
Rocco	Jack Warden
Fossil Pillar	Morris Carnovsky
First Rock	Phil Leeds
Bones (Adam's dog)	

<u>Vocalists</u>
    Harry "Sweets" Edison, Don Elliott, Ruth Price

<u>Dig</u> took a fantasy trip through the layers of the earth and millions of years of history. An entertaining look at basic geology targeted for children aged 6 to 11, the didatic musical explained such phenomena as earthquakes, volcanoes and the formation of different kinds of rock. Adam and his dog Bones took a wondrous bike ride under the earth's crust where they met Rocco, a "show biz" rock who could talk and liked to travel. He gave them a guided tour through the different geological eras of time, noting the various strata such as Igneous, Sedimentary and Metamorphic. Going back three billion years, they met such characters as the Earl of Limestone and Pre-Cambrian Rock. The special was intended to spark a child's interest in the scientific structure of our planet. Initially, the program preempted repeats of <u>The Monkees</u> (...CBS/1969-1972...) on the network's Saturday morning schedule. Songs: "Rocco's Song" (Warden); "Aunt Sadie's Song" (Elliott); "Uncle Iggy's Song" (Edison); "Cousin Meta's Song" (Price).

DISNEY CHRISTMAS GIFT, A

<u>Broadcast History</u>
    Premiere: December 20, 1983
    CBS/Tuesday 8:00-9:00 PM
    SYN/Repeats: 1986 +
Producers (TV): Frank Brandt, Dennis Landa, Ed Ropolo, Tad
    Stones, V. Renee Toensing
Music/Song & Lyrics: Sammy Cahn, Sammy Fain
Company: Walt Disney Television/60 minutes
Distributor: Buena Vista Television Syndication/1986-
Home Video: Walt Disney Home Video

<u>Characters and Voices Credited</u>
Peter Pan   Bobby Driscoll
Fairy Godmother   Verna Felton
Cinderella   Ilene Woods

A <u>Disney Christmas Gift</u> compiled selected scenes from the studio's movies and from several cartoon shorts to recapture an hour of Disney animation with a Yuletide theme. Featured were the reckless escapades of Mr. Thaddeus Toad from <u>Ichabod and Mr. Toad</u> (1949); an old-fashioned look at a quaint turn-of-the-century sleigh ride and ice-skating in "Once Upon a Wintertime" from <u>Melody Time</u> (1948); Wendy, John and Michael flying off to Never-Neverland with their newfound friend from <u>Peter Pan</u> (1952); Donald Duck avoiding his responsibilities as a department store gift-wrapper from <u>The Clock Watcher</u> (1944); Bambi and Thumper testing the ice on a frozen-over pond from <u>Bambi</u> (1942); the investigative mice, Bianca and Bernard, setting off on to search for their kidnapped friend, Penny, from <u>The</u>

Rescuers (1977); and Disney's animated version of the classic poem, "The Night Before Christmas" (1933). Featured was a first-time glimpse at a sequence from Mickey's Christmas Carol [q.v.]. Song/Theme: "You Can Fly" (Peter Pan).

DISNEY'S ALL-STAR MOTHER'S DAY ALBUM

Broadcast History
    Premiere: May 9, 1984
    CBS/Wednesday 8:00-9:00 PM
Producers (TV): Craig Murray, Robert L. Quinn
Music: John O'Kennedy
Company: Walt Disney Television/60 minutes

Characters and Voices Credited
Fairy Godmother   Verna Felton
Cinderella   Ilene Woods

Disney's All-Star Mother's Day Album took a look at motherhood in a compilation of scenes from the studio's movies and some rarely-seen short cartoons. They included Wendy singing to her brothers in Peter Pan (1952); Mrs. Jumbo on a rampage after the other circus elephants made fun of her infant's oversized ears from Dumbo (1941); a brief scene from The Jungle Book (1967); the young buck's mother escorting her son on his first walk from Bambi (1942); and the fairy godmother casting her musical spell in Cinderella (1947). Familiar Disney cartoon characters were spotlighted, including Dale the chipmunk masquerading as a baby chick in Chicken in the Rough (1950); the dilemma of Mickey Mouse and a fun-loving seal in his bathtub from Mickey and the Seal (1948); Goofy bumbling through household chores in a series of mishaps from Father's Day Off (1952); Pluto's efforts to aid a baby robin to fly in Pluto's Fledgling (1947); Donald Duck mistaken for a newly-hatched chick in Contrary Condor (1944); and an erring stork that delivered a lion cub to a childless ewe from Lambert, the Sheepish Lion (1951). Songs: "Your Mother and Mine" (Wendy, Peter Pan), "Bibbidi-Bobbidi-Boo" (Fairy Godmother, Cinderella).

DISNEY'S ALL-STAR VALENTINE PARTY

Broadcast History
    Premiere: February 14, 1984
    CBS/Tuesday 8:00-9:00 PM
Producers (TV): Dennis Landa, V. Renee Toensing, Fausto Sanchez
Music/Song & Lyrics: Michael Silversher, Patty Silversher
Music-Video: Jymm Magon
Company: Walt Disney Television/60 minutes

Narrator: Rick Dees

Disney's All-Star Valentine Party recylced some of the studio's cartoons starring Mickey Mouse, Donald Duck and Pluto along with
scenes from two Disney movies. It opened with Mickey's Rival
(1936), depicting the rivalry between Mickey and Minnie's old flame
Mortimer, who antagonized a bull, leaving Mickey to save Minnie
from the furious animal. In The Brave Little Tailor (1938), Mickey
captured a diabolical giant terrorizing his village and won the hand
of Princess Minnie. Pluto heroically saved Dinah from drowning, in
Pluto's Heart Throb (1949), while the brutish bulldog Butch stood
sheepishly by, afraid of the water. Donald Duck's plan to win back
his reluctant girlfriend Daisy backfired in Donald's Double Trouble
(1946); his rascally nephews, Huey, Dewey and Louie temporarily
thwarted his romance with Daisy until he jitterbugged wildly around
the room in Mr. Duck Steps Out (1940); and his attempts to improve
his self-control ended when he insulted Daisy's hat and the two
erupted in a tantrum in Cured Duck (1945). The program included
melodious scenes from Snow White and the Seven Dwarfs (1937) and
a poignant sequence on falling in love from Bambi (1942). Song/
Theme: "Mickey, She's Got a Crush on You."

DISNEY'S DTV "DOGGONE" VALENTINE

Broadcast History
    Premiere: February 13, 1987
    NBC/Friday 8:00-9:00 PM
    Sponsors: Kal Kan Pet Food, Worlds of Wonder, Peter Paul Cad-
        bury, Levis
Executive Producer/Director: Andrew Solt
Producers: Jim Milio, Susan F. Walker
Associate Producer: Greg Vines
Writers: Jim Milio, Andrew Solt, Susan F. Walker
Music: John Debney
Company: Andrew Solt Productions in association with Walt Disney
    Television/60 minutes

Principal Characters and Voices

Mickey Mouse	Wayne Allwine
Minnie Mouse/Dalmatian Puppy	Russi Taylor
Professor Ludwig von Drake	Albert Ash
Jiminy Cricket	Eddie Carroll
Goofy	Bill Farmer
Pongo	Will Ryan
Dalmatian Puppies	Lisa St. James
Radio Announcer	Maurice La Marche

Announcer: J. J. Jackson

Vocalists/Musicians
    Paul Anka, Bee Gees, the Flamingos, Olivia Newton-John, Kenny
    Rogers, the Soul Survivors, the Stray Cats, George Thorogood,

John Travolta, Wham!, Deniece Williams, Maurice Williams, "Weird" Al Yankovic

Disney's DTV "Doggone" Valentine was a music-video saluting man's best friend, featuring clips from the studio's cartoons and animated movies hosted by Mickey Mouse, Minnie Mouse, Professor Ludwig von Drake, Jiminy Cricket and Goofy. Pluto, Goofy and other Disney canine characters romped to "Wake Me Up Before You Go-Go," the 1984 hit by British rock group Wham!; "Workin' for a Livin' " by Huey Lewis; "I Only Have Eyes for You" by Olivia Newton-John; scenes of Mickey and Pluto set to "Let's Hear It for the Boy" by Deniece Williams; scenes from Lady and the Tramp (1955) set to Lionel Richie's "Lady" by Kenny Rogers, "Staying Alive" by the Bee Gees and "The Siamese Cat Song" by Si and Am; clips from 101 Dalmatians (1960) set to "Puppy Love" by Paul Anka and Goofy driving on the freeway to "Expressway to Your Heart" by the Soul Survivors; plus others.

DISNEY'S DTV ROMANCIN'   see   DISNEY'S DTV VALENTINE

DISNEY'S DTV VALENTINE

Broadcast History
    Premiere: February 14, 1986
    NBC/Friday 8:00-9:00 PM
    NBC/Repeat: DISNEY'S DTV ROMANCIN', September 7, 1986
Producers (TV): Andrew Solt, Phillip Savernick
Co-Producers: Mark Hufnail, Harry Arends
Director: Andrew Solt
Writers: Jim Milio, Phillip Savernick, Andrew Solt, Susan T. Walker
Music: John Debney
Company: Andrew Solt Productions in association with Walt Disney
    Television/60 minutes

Principal Characters and Voices
Mickey Mouse   Les Perkins
Donald Duck   Tony Anselmo
Jiminy Cricket   Eddie Carroll
Professor Ludwig von Drake   Paul Frees
Gruffi (Gummi Bear)   Corey Burton
Goofy/Pongo (father Dalmatian)   Will Ryan
Chip/Dale/Female Voice   Judith Searle
Dalmatian Puppies #1 & #2   Lisa St. James
Princess Aura   Mary Costa
Prince Philip   Bill Shirley

Announcer: Paul Frees

Vocalists/Musicians
The Contours, Eurythmics, Whitney Houston, Elton John, Huey Lewis & The News, Madonna, Elvis Presley, Lionel Richie, Stevie Wonder

Disney's DTV Valentine was a lighthearted look at love and Valentine's Day as hosts Mickey Mouse, Donald Duck, Jiminy Cricket and Professor Ludwig von Drake introduced "DTV" videos, clips from Disney cartoons cut to classic rock-and-roll music. Also included were the cartoons Donald's Double Trouble (1946) and Mickey's Rival (1936) along with sequences from the Disney movies 101 Dalmatians (1961), Lady and the Tramp (1955) and The Sword In The Stone (1963). The "DTV" stands for Disney Television, the studio's answer to MTV. Songs: "The Shoop Shoop Song (It's In His Kiss)," "I Just Called to Say I Love You," "Dress You Up," "Rock This Town," "Hello," "Hey, Mickey," "Don't Go Breakin' My Heart," "Teddy Bear," "There Must Be an Angel," "Heart of Rock 'n' Roll," "Do You Love Me?"

DISNEY'S FLUPPY DOGS

Broadcast History
Premiere: November 27, 1986
ABC/Thursday 8:00-9:00 PM
ABC/Repeat: THE SUNDAY DISNEY MOVIE, August 30, 1987
Producer/Director: Fred Wolf
Associate Producer: Tom Ruzicka
Writer: Haskell Barkin
Music: Shirley Walker
Company: Walt Disney Television Animation with TMS (Tokyo Movie Shinsha, Japan) Entertainment/60 minutes

Principal Characters and Voices

Jaimie Bingham	Carl Stevens
Bink/Tippi	Susan Blu
Stanley	Marshall Efron
Mrs. Bingham	Cloyce Morrow
Ozzie	Lorenzo Music
Claire	Jessica Pennington
Wagstaff	Michael Rye
Haimish/Attendant/Dink	Hal Smith

Disney's Fluppy Dogs involved 10-year-old Jaimie and his snobbish teenage neighbor Claire, when five magically talking, walking Fluppy Dogs entered their lives from another universe. Stanley, Ozzie, Tippi, Bink and Dink left their distant home in search of adventure with a magic key that unlocked interdimensional doorways. One of the doorways led into a supermarket and a series of frantic encounters with "humans," people who had never seen or heard of the Fluppys, except one. Forced to conceal their magical identity by pretending to be normal dogs, the Fluppys were soon incarcerated in the city pound. When Stanley was adopted by Jaimie, the boy discovered that his new pet not only talked but wanted to rescue his friends and return to his own universe. Unfortunately, the town eccentric, Wagstaff, a collector of exotic animals, recognized the magical Fluppys and vowed to add them to his collection at any cost. Soon Jaimie and Claire were caught up in a series of devious plots, chases and adventures as they aided the Fluppys to escape Wagstaff's clutches and return home before their enchanted key lost its interdimensional powers. The film was the first prime-time animated special produced by Walt Disney Television Animation.

DISNEY'S HALLOWEEN TREAT

Broadcast History
    Premiere: October 30, 1982
    CBS/WALT DISNEY, Saturday 8:00-9:00 PM
    CBS/Repeat: CBS SPECIAL PRESENTATION, October 29, 1983
    Executive Producer: William Robert Yates
    Producers (TV): Ed Ropolo, Frank Brandt, Darryl Sutton
    Music/Songs & Lyrics: Sammy Cahn, Don Raye, Sammy Fain, Gene
        DePaul, Paul Smith
    Music & Lyrics/Theme: John Debney, Galen R. Brandt
    Music: John Debney
    Company: Walt Disney Television/60 minutes
    Home Video: Walt Disney Home Video #219

Characters and Voices Credited
Peter Pan   Bobby Driscoll
Si/Am ("Lady and the Tramp")   Peggy Lee

Disney's Halloween Treat opened with the mystic sequence from The Sword in the Stone (1963), featuring Merlin and Madame Mim in a wizards' duel, a battle of wits in which they transformed themselves into a variety of animals. The frightful "Night on Bald Mountain" from Fantasia (1940), with its trolls, witches and goblins, followed. Other scenes from Disney movies spotlighted the fiendish Captain Hook from Peter Pan (1952); Cruella De Ville, the wicked villainess of 101 Dalmatians (1960); the evil queen disguised as a peddler woman in Snow White and the Seven Dwarfs (1937); and the terrifying mischievous Siamese Cats from Lady and the Tramp (1955). Incorporated were some scenes from Disney cartoons, including The Skeleton Dance (1929), Pluto's Judgement Day (1933), Lonesome Ghosts (1937), Donald Duck and the Gorilla (1944), Puss Cafe (1949) and Treat or Treat (1952). The final sequence was "The Legend of Sleepy Hollow" from Icabod and Mr. Toad (1949), narrated by Bing Crosby. The special originally aired as part of the prime-time series, Walt Disney (CBS, 1981-1983). Song/Theme: "Disney's Halloween Treat."

DISNEY'S SPORT GOOFY see ALL NEW ADVENTURE OF DISNEY'S SPORT GOOFY, AN; SPORT GOOFY; WALT DISNEY PRESENTS SPORT GOOFY'S OLYMPIC GAMES SPECIAL; WALT DISNEY'S MICKEY, DONALD AND SPORT GOOFY SHOW(S)

DR. SEUSS' HALLOWEEN IS GRINCH NIGHT

Broadcast History
    Premiere: October 29, 1977
    ABC/Saturday 8:00-8:30 PM
    ABC/Repeats: October 26, 1978; October 28, 1979; October 30, 1980
    DIS/Repeats: multiple option, 1986-1987
Executive Producers: David H. DePatie, Friz Freleng
Producer/Creator: Ted Geisel
Director: Gerard Baldwin
Writer/Lyrics: Theodor Seuss Geisel
Music: Joe Raposo, Eric Rogers
Company: Dr. Seuss and A. S. Geisel Productions in association with DePatie-Freleng Enterprises
Home Video: Playhouse Video (CBS-FOX)

Principal Characters and Voices

Grinch	Hans Conreid
Grandpa Josiah	Hal Smith
Grandma Mariah	Irene Tedrow
Ukariah	Gary Shapiro
Max (Grinch's dog)	

Other Voices
    Jack DeLeon, Henry Gibson

Dr. Seuss' Halloween Is Grinch Night sent the townfolk in Whoville running for cover behind bolted doors, plagued by the onset of the eerie "sour-sweet wind," which usually suggested something bad was in the air. Sure enough, it heralded an unwelcome visit from the foul-tempered Grinch, as Grandpa Josiah warned his family members, his wife Mariah, and three grandchildren, the oldest of whom was the brave, bespectacled Ukariah. Atop Mt. Crumpit the Grinch was irritated by the strange night noises. Hitching his unhappy dog Max to the Paraphernalia Wagon, he came rambling down the mountain toward Whoville, provoking alarm. And young, innocent Ukariah, who had left his grandfather's house to go on what he called the "euphemism," promptly got lost and was blown away by the night wind into the path of the Grinch and Max. Carted away through the countryside, where even the ponds had been upset by the wind, Ukariah was taken to Mt. Crumpit where he learned to face up to the scary Grinch and his own fear. The old meanie turned out to be frightened himself of the wind-inspired ghostly noises which whistled through the tunnels and crags atop his retreat, prompting his Whoville visits. So on this Halloween, Ukariah and the Grinch each learned a little lesson about misplaced fear. Television Academy Emmy award (1977-1978), Outstanding Evening Children's Special.

The Dr. Seuss specials moved from CBS to ABC with this program from the imaginative storyteller, Theodor Seuss Geisel, author of more than 40 books, whose witty tongue twisters and catchy rhymes have amused and instructed children for decades. A best-selling author for Random House publishers, Geisel has written nine half-hour animated specials, beginning with Dr. Seuss' How the Grinch Stole Christmas [q.v.].

DR. SEUSS' HORTON HEARS A WHO!

Broadcast History
    Premiere: March 19, 1970
    CBS/Thursday 7:30-8:00 PM
    CBS/Repeats: September 29, 1971, July 31, 1972; April 20, 1973;
        February 4, 1974; March 24, 1975; March 19, 1976; May 13,
        1977; August 4, 1978
Producers: Ted Geisel, Chuck Jones
Director: Chuck Jones
Writer/Lyrics: Theodor Seuss Geisel
Music: Eugene Poddany
Company: Chuck Jones Enterprises in association with The Cat in
    the Hat Productions and MGM-TV
Home Video: MGM-UA Home Video #500176 (Dr. Seuss Video Festival)

Narrator: Hans Conreid

Dr. Seuss' Horton Hears a Who! introduced the storyteller's good-hearted rhyming elephant, who came to the rescue of the microscopic community of Whoville. On the 15th of May, in the Jungle of Nool, in the heat of the day, in the cool of the pool, Horton heard a small noise. It was the sound of a Who and emanated from a dust speck no bigger than a pinhead. The kangaroo and her youngster, and the monkeys known as the Wickersham Brothers, thought him daft. "What rot! ... There aren't any Whos!" Ignoring them, Horton, who behaved generously to all creatures great and small, placed the speck on a clover. "A person's a person ... no matter how small." Snatching Horton's clover, the prankish Wickersham Brothers gave it to Vlad Vlad-i-koff, the bothersome black-bottomed eagle, who flew it far away. "I'll find it or bust," Horton persisted, "I shall find my friends on my small speck of dust." Find them he did, but the Wickershams overcame Horton, tied him up and called him a fool. "Make yourselves heard," he told the Whos, and the Whos made a racket and the elephant smiled, "Do you see what I mean?" They did. And the kangaroo and her young roo in her pouch helped Horton protect them from sun in the summer and rain when it's fall-ish ... "No matter how small-ish!" The special was based on the eponymous book (Random House, 1954) by Dr. Seuss. Songs:

"Repentent Whos," "Old Doc Hoovie," "Be Kind To Your Small Person Friends," "Wickersham Brothers Chante," "Wickersham and Toucanella Hot-Pot Chante," "Make Yourself Heard." George Foster Peabody award (1970) for the Dr. Seuss series, which began in 1966 with Dr. Seuss' How the Grinch Stole Christmas [q.v.].

DR. SEUSS' HOW THE GRINCH STOLE CHRISTMAS

Broadcast History
    Premiere: December 18, 1966
    CBS/Sunday 7:00-7:30 PM
    Sponsor: McDonald's (1985, 1986)
    CBS/Repeats: December 17, 1967; December 22, 1968; December
        21, 1969; December 2, 1970; December 7, 1971; December 4,
        1972; December 10, 1973; December 13, 1974; December 12,
        1975; December 18, 1976; December 10, 1977; December 16,
        1978; December 19, 1979; November 28, 1980; December 16,
        1981; December 18, 1982; December 12, 1983; December 5,
        1984; December 7, 1985; December 17, 1986
Producers: Chuck Jones, Ted Geisel
Director: Chuck Jones
Writer/Lyrics: Theodor Seuss Geisel
Music: Albert Hague, Eugene Poddany
Company: Chuck Jones Enterprises in association with The Cat in
    the Hat Productions and MGM-TV
Record Album: MGM-Leo LES 901
Home Video: MGM-UA Home Video #500176 (Dr. Seuss Video Festival)

Narrator: Boris Karloff

Principal Characters and Voices
Grinch   Thurl Ravenscroft (singing)
Cindy Lou   June Foray

Dr. Seuss' How the Grinch Stole Christmas presented a mean-spirited plot against the Whos in Whoville who liked Christmas a lot. They lived in pumpkin-shaped houses and were animal-like creatures, friendly folks with cute human features. North of Whoville atop Mt. Crumpit, with green skin, red eyes and heart two sizes too small, the Grinch hated Christmas and most of all, the noise of the toys, the wacking and ringing, the feast of roast beast and particularly the singing. Hatching an evil plan he impersonated St. Nick and with his dog Max pulling his sleigh set off with a whip's lick. Arriving in Whoville on Christmas Eve with tippy-toe care, he found their homes dark, no one knew he was there. He took their prepared feast, even their cooked roast beast, gathered up their stockings and all the presents, and only Cindy Lou knew of his presence. She caught him carting off their tree. "I'm taking it home to fix it, dear," said he. Then he rode his laden sleigh 10,000 feet up, with Max's help, of course, to snowy Mt. Crumpet's top. At a quarter to dawn, the Grinch heard a sound that started to grow and with a strange look on his face he began to know. Down below in the square was a throng, the Whos with their voices raised in song. Hand-in-hand the tall, the short and the small, welcomed Christmas without any presents at all. In Whoville they say, the Grinch's heart grew three inches that day; the spirit of Christmas came through and he found new love for the Who. He brought everything back, including the toys, for all of Whoville's girls and boys to enjoy and celebrate just in time, as Boris Karloff happily related in rhyme. Songs: "You're a Mean One, Mr. Grinch!" (Ravenscroft), "Welcome Christmas," "Trim Up the Tree."

The third Yuletide classic following Rudolph, the Red-Nosed Reindeer [q.v.] and A Charlie Brown Christmas [q.v.], the special has been broadcast annually since its debut. Based on the story by Dr. Seuss, CBS paid $315,000 for the film, the highest price for a cartoon special at that time.

DR. SEUSS ON THE LOOSE

Broadcast History
      Premiere: October 15, 1973
      CBS/Monday 8:30-9:00 PM
      CBS/Repeats: October 28, 1974; November 21, 1975; March 9,
         1976; July 12, 1979
Executive Producer: David H. DePatie
Producers: Ted Geisel, Friz Freleng
Director: Hawley Pratt
Writer/Lyrics: Theodor Seuss Geisel
Music: Dean Elliott
Company: DePatie-Freleng Enterprises in association with CBS
Home Video: Playhouse Video #6840 (CBS-FOX)

Host
The Cat in the Hat   Allan Sherman

Narrator
Zax   Hans Conreid

Principal Characters and Voices
Joey/Sam-I-Am   Paul Winchell
Zax/Sylvester McMonkey McBean Bob Holt

Dr. Seuss On The Loose presented a trilogy of stories in rhyme, each introduced in song by the Cat in the Hat. A tale of snobbery began the fun with "The Sneetches With Stars." Sneetches were ostrich-like creatures who lived on beaches; some had stars on their bellies and thought themselves superior to those who had no stars on "thars." "Keep your snoot in the air and remember to snort, we have no truck whatever with the plain-bellied sort." Half were unhappy, when along came a stranger, Sylvester McMonkey McBean, a fix-it-up chappie. He sold stars for \$3 and charged \$10 to take them off, which turned the Sneetch community topsy-turvy and made everyone truly equal. "The Zax" were two travellers, one heading north and the other south, who absolutely refused to step aside when their paths crossed on the prairie of Prax. As the seasons passed, a highway was built over the stubborn Zax and left them there, unbudged, standing still in their tracks. Sam-I-Am was the finicky type, in "Green Eggs and Ham," who would not eat strange-looking food. He would not eat them here or there, would not eat them anywhere; on a train or in the rain, in a box or with a fox, on a boat or with a goat. Until finally it was tasted and savored. Songs: "At the Edge of the Ocean You'll Always Find Sneetches," "On the Prairie of Prax," "Eggs" (Sherman), "Twink, Twink, Twinkle, Twinkle, Lovely Little Star," "A Marshmallow Toast to Belly Stars," "Stars, Stars, Thank Our Lucky Stars," "Abdominable Stars Are Abominable," "Sam, I Am," "He Doesn't Like Green Eggs and Ham," "He Will Eat Them, Anywhere."

DR. SEUSS' PONTOFFEL POCK, WHERE ARE YOU?

Broadcast History
    Premiere: May 2, 1980
    ABC/Friday 8:30-9:00 PM
    ABC/Repeat: July 31, 1981
Executive Producers: David H. DePatie, Friz Freleng
Producers: Ted Geisel, Lee Gunther
Director: Gerard Baldwin
Writer/Lyrics: Theodor Seuss Geisel
Music: Joe Raposo, Eric Rogers
Company: Dr. Seuss and A. S. Geisel Productions in association
    with DePatie-Freleng Enterprises
Home Video: Playhouse Video #6826 (CBS-FOX)

Principal Characters and Voices
Pontoffel Pock   Wayne Morton
Neepha Pheepha   Sue Allen
McGillicuddy   Hal Smith

Other Voices
    Ken Lundie, Don Messick, Joe Raposo

Dr. Seuss' Pontoffel Pock, Where Are You? was the original story of a kind-hearted bungler who felt himself a complete failure. Failing to heed instructions on how to properly operate a canning machine, sending pickles careening everywhere, he was fired from his job in a dill-pickle factory. Wishing to get away from his troubles, Pock was accosted by a sprightly fairy named McGillicuddy, who provided a magical piano that could take him anywhere at the touch of a colored button. On it, Pock was whisked off to Groogen, a Tyrolean kingdom where he managed to make himself so unwelcome with his flying

antics, buzzing the townspeople on his upright, that he was shot
down with their big cannon, the Boomy Gun. Given another chance,
Pock was transported to Casbah-Mopolis, an Arabian kingdom where
he had a romantic escapade with the ravishing eye-dancer, Neepha
Pheepha, who slipped off the piano and was left behind in his attempt to rescue her from a slobbish sheik. Pushing buttons with
reckless abandon and zapping from place to place, Pock was pursued
by the good fairies and in the end learned to like himself. With
restored confidence he returned to his job at the pickle factory.
Songs: "Pull 'Em and Push 'Em," "Alone," "The Piano Will Take You
Away," "Welcome to Groogen," "I'm Feeling Free," "Load Up the
Boomy Gun," "The Great Eye-Ball Dancer," "Pontoffel Pock, Where
Are You?"

DR. SEUSS' THE CAT IN THE HAT

Broadcast History
    Premiere: March 10, 1971
    CBS/Wednesday 7:30-8:00 PM
    CBS/Repeats: April 11, 1972; February 20, 1973; January 4,
        1974; January 31, 1975; March 30, 1976; August 20, 1979
    DIS/Repeats: multiple option, 1985-1986
Executive Producers: David H. DePatie, Friz Freleng
Producers: Chuck Jones, Ted Geisel
Director: Hawley Pratt
Writer/Lyrics: Theodor Seuss Geisel
Music: Dean Elliott, Eric Rogers
Company: DePatie-Freleng Enterprises
Home Video: Playhouse Video #6840 (CBS-FOX)

Principal Characters and Voices
Cat in the Hat   Allan Sherman
Karlos K. Krinklebein   Daws Butler
Boy   Tony Frazier
Girl   Pamelyn Ferdin
Mother   Gloria Camacho
Thing 1   Thurl Ravenscroft
Thing 2   Lewis Morford

Dr. Seuss' The Cat in the Hat brought some wild and whimsical excitement to two children faced with the prospect of rainy day boredom in a musical romp with a dandy score. Left alone when their
mother had to go out, the children were surprised by the visit of
the audacious feline in the red-and-white candy-striped stovepipe
hat. Refusing to leave, for "a cat shouldn't be in when Mother's
out on a rainy afternoon," the madcap mischief-maker wouldn't budge
until he found his missing moss-covered, three-handled family gradunza. Upset at his audacity, a goldfish named Karlos K. Krinklebein was cleared of the theft and as the search went on the singing
and dancing Cat conjured up his helpmates, Thing 1 and Thing 2,

who could find anything under the sun. But alas, it was never found though the search virtually destroyed the house, only to be magically restored by the Cat's sweep-up machine, just before the children's mother returned. Built around the many songs in the score, the film's big musical number was the "Cat's Hat," with the Cat donning headgear from countries around the world as the children, Krinklebein and the Things joined in. The special was based on the eponymous book (Houghton, 1957) by Dr. Seuss. Songs: "Nuthig, Nuthig To Do," (Ferdin, Frazier), "The Old Moss-Covered Three-Handled Family Gradunza," "I'm a Punk," "It Can Be Done," "Sweep Up the Memories" (Sherman), "Calulatus Eliminatus (Where It Is Not)" (Sherman, Ferdin, Frazier), "Cat's Hat" (cast).

DR. SEUSS' THE GRINCH GRINCHES THE CAT IN THE HAT

Broadcast History
    Premiere: May 20, 1982
    ABC/Thursday 8:00-8:30 PM
    ABC/Repeat: August 7, 1983
Executive Producer: David H. DePatie
Producers: Ted Geisel, Friz Freleng
Director: Bill Perez
Writer/Lyrics: Theodor Seuss Geisel
Music: Joe Raposo
Company: Dr. Seuss and A. S. Geisel Productions in association
    with Marvel Productions
Home Video: Playhouse Video #6826 (CBS-FOX)

Voices
    Mason Adams, Joe Eich, Bob Holt, Marilyn Jackson, Melissa Mac-
    kay, Frank Welker, Richard B. Williams

Dr. Seuss' The Grinch Grinches the Cat in the Hat found an usually happy Grinch enjoying a summer outing on a Breezleberry day, motoring contently along in the countryside until he crossed paths with the motoring carefree Cat. Frustrated in his attempts to run down the elusive frolicking feline, the foul-tempered meanie returned to his wicked ways, unhelpful, unfriendly and unkind, swearing vengeance. Back at his lair, the Grinch, aided by his mongrel Max, constructed some elaborate contraptions that turned his victims polka-dot and plaid, garbled musical sounds, sucked the sound from the air and cast dark clouds over the land. By remote control he used the machinery to cause problems for the happy-go-lucky feline. "When your life's full of boulders, just shrug your shoulders," crooned the crafty Cat, who applied a little psychology to change the ways of the psychopathic Grinch. Gathering his friends, he ungrinched the tearful Grinch with a serenade to his wonderful loving mother, making for a lively, lyrical lesson in amiability, courtesy and being considerate of others. Songs: "It's Gonna Be a Breezleberry Day," "Relaxification," "The Master of Everyone's Ears," "The Most Horrible

Things," "Why Is a Grinch?" "Remember Your Mother." Television
Academy Emmy award (1981-1982), Outstanding Animation Program.

DR. SEUSS' THE HOOBER-BLOOB HIGHWAY

Broadcast History
    Premiere: February 19, 1975
    CBS/Wednesday 8:00-8:30 PM
    CBS/Repeats: March 23, 1976; November 15, 1977; September 9,
        1981
    DIS/Repeats: multiple-option, 1986-1987
Executive Producer: David H. DePatie
Producers: Ted Geisel, Friz Freleng
Director: Alan Zaslov
Writer/Lyrics: Theodor Seuss Geisel
Music: Dean Elliott
Company: DePatie-Freleng Enterprises
Home Video: Playhouse Video (CBS-FOX)

Voices
    Bob Holt, Hal Smith

Dr. Seuss' The Hoober-Bloob Highway was the first of the Dr. Seuss
series written especially for television. The highway itself was a
magical ribbon of light that "begins way up above and ends way down
below, and starts far beyond where the Astronauts go." On a floating island at the top, Mr. Hoober-Bloob, assisted by a self-playing
instrument, dispatched the wee ones down the special thoroughfare
to their respective homes on Earth. But not before they were
treated to a vision of their future: "There are really so many places
to send you that's it's really only fair to give some idea of what
goes on down there." So the unborn babies were able to witness
the pros and cons of life on earth and able to choose their home-
towns, described in tongue-twisting verse containing names like
Bodja-Nodja-Stan, North Nizza-Skrinza-Bo and West Watch-a-Ka-Tella.
Things were not always easy, but being there was a joy, with such
delights as sunshine, summer, and just being alive, in this positive
lesson on life's trials and treats. Songs: "The Hoober-Bloob Highway," "Doing Nuthig Among the Daisies," "Ology," "The Things You
Gotta Know," "I've Made a Deal, Bub," "On the Other, Other Hand,"
"It's Fun to be Human," "What Do You Do When the Snorken Goes
Slump?" "A Few Simple Questions."

DR. SEUSS' THE LORAX

Broadcast History
    Premiere: February 14, 1972
    CBS/Monday 8:30-9:00 PM
    CBS/Repeats: March 28, 1973; March 25, 1974; July 19, 1977;
        August 4, 1978

Executive Producer: David H. DePatie
Producers: Friz Freleng, Ted Geisel
Director: Hawley Pratt
Writer/Lyrics: Theodor Seuss Geisel
Music: Dean Elliott
Company: DePatie-Freleng Enterprises
Home Video: Playhouse Video (CBS-FOX)

Narrator: Eddie Albert

Principal Characters and Voices
Lorax/Once-ler   Bob Holt
Boy   Harlen Carraher
Other   Athena Lorde

Dr. Seuss' The Lorax struck a blow for ecology in verse, a poignant
tale about progress gone amok. Geared to the young with an eye
on the world they will inherit, this warning was in the form of a
gnomelike oldster's crusade to save an endangered species, the Truffula Trees. A shortish, brownish, mustachioed little man, the Lorax
lived at the far end of town where the Grickle-grass grew and tried
his best to preserve the forested patch after the Once-ler family
found they could get mighty rich by harvesting the lot. Because
its silken tufts could be knitted into practically anything, the profit-
greedy Once-lers manufactured Thneeds, something all people need.
Down came the Truffulas, up went the factories, and away went the
Bar-ba-loots who thrived on Truffula fruits, the singing Swomee-
Swans who choked on the factory smoke and the Humming-Fish whose
pond was polluted with glump. With the habitat and animals gone,
the Lorax then disappeared too. Later, to an inquiring little boy
who was given the last Truffula seed to plant and nourish, his name
became perfectly clear. "Unless someone like you cares a whole
awful lot, nothing is going to get better. It's not!" The special
was adapted from the Dr. Seuss book. Songs: "Street of the Lifted
Lorax," "Under the Truffula Trees," "To the House of Once-Ler We
Go," "Everybody Do Need a Thneed," "Three Cheers for Good Old
Once-Ler," "Take a Letter," "Aren't You Ashamed, Once-ler," "A
Thought About Something."

DONALD DUCK'S 50TH BIRTHDAY

Broadcast History
    Premiere: November 13, 1984
    CBS/Tuesday 8:00-9:00 PM
    CBS/Repeat: October 29, 1985
Producer/Director: Andrew Solt
Co-Producer/Director: Phillip Savernick
Writers: Peter Elbling, Andrew Solt
Music/Songs & Lyrics: Michael Silversher, Patty Silversher, Will
    Ryan

Music: John Debney, Paul J. Smith
Company: Andrew Solt Productions in association with Walt Disney
Television/60 minutes
Home Video: Walt Disney Home Video

Host: Dick Van Dyke

Guests
Ed Asner, Bruce Jenner, Cloris Leachman, John Ritter, Kenny
Rogers, Donna Summer, Andy Warhol, Henry Winkler, C-3PO and
R2D2

Principal Characters and Voices

Donald Duck	Clarence Nash
C-3PO	Anthony Daniels
R2D2	(electronic)

Donald Duck's 50th Birthday began at the Hollywood/Burbank air-
port with Disney's irascible webfoot bidding farewell as he departed
on Duck One for a personal appearance tour. At the studio, Dick
Van Dyke provided a nostalgic retrospective on Donald's career that
began with The Wise Little Hen (1934) and gained popularity through
150 cartoons, including the Oscar-winner Der Fuehrer's Face (1942),
five feature films and 16 TV programs. Star Wars droids C-3PO
and R2D2 provided an intro-duck-tion to Clarence "Ducky" Nash,
who for 50 years provided the "voice that would drive any sane duck
quackers." Footage of Walt Disney meeting with Donald and later
commenting on the importance of sound in a cartoon were featured.
The various guests presented segments on Donald's film career, his
courtship of Daisy, as a work of art, his television and movie appearances, his wartime experiences, educational films, athletic en-
deavors and as a "duck of all trades." Film clips included the movies
The Three Caballeros (1944) and Saludos Amigos (1942), and the
cartoons The Band Concert (1935), Don Donald (1936), Donald's
Nephews (1938), Donald's Snow Fight (1942), Slide, Donald, Slide
(1949), Trick or Treat (1952), How To Have an Accident at Work
(1959), Donald in Mathmagic Land (1959), Donald and the Wheel
(1961) and others. At the end, Van Dyke presented Donald with a
special birthday cake baked by Daisy. Songs: "Happy, Happy
Birthday To You," "Can You Quack Like Donald Duck?" "Goin'
Quackers."

DOONESBURY SPECIAL, A

Broadcast History
Premiere: November 27, 1977
NBC/Sunday 9:30-10:00 PM
SYN/Repeats: 1980 +
Producers/Directors: John Hubley, Faith Hubley, Garry Trudeau
Writer: Garry Trudeau

A DOONESBURY SPECIAL. © 1977, John and Faith Hubley Films, Ltd.
Courtesy of The Hubley Studio.

Music: Jimmy Thudpacker
Music/Harmonica Solo: John B. Sebastian
Company: John and Faith Hubley Films in association with Universal
    Press Syndicate
Distributor: Fox-Lorber Associates/1980-
Home Video: Pacific Arts

Principal Characters and Voices

Zonker Harris	Richard Cox
Joanie Caucus	Barbara Harris
Mike	David Grant
Mark Slackmeyer/Ralphie	Charles Levin
B.D.	Richard Bruno
Boopsie	Rebecca Nelson
Rev. Scot Sloan	Rev. William Sloane Coffin, Jr.
Referee	Jack Gilford
Kirby	Mark Baker
Frank	Eric Elice
Calvin	Ben Halley, Jr.
Sportscaster	Will Jordan
Ellie	Linda Baer
Howie	Eric Jaffe
Jeannie	Michelle Browne

Rufus	Thomas Baxton
Magus	Lenny Jackson
Virgin Mary	Patrice Leftwich
Jimmy Thudpacker	Jimmy Thudpacker

A Doonesbury Special took an ironic look at contemporary society as Zonker Harris and his friends were faced with the conclusion of an era--the age of the activist sixties. Seeing Jimmy Thudpucker on TV sent Zonker back down memory lane to flower child time, college campus bombings and cynical observations about both political extremes. Flashback sequences contrasted a peace demonstration, a classic confrontation with the National Guard and the football huddle debates between B.D. and Zonker, with the present mood of the Waldenites. There was sharp use of put-on jargon ("role models," "valid points," "affirmative action cases"). Joanie Caucus, who was now committed to the care and the conditioning of a new generation at the Walden Day Care Center, suggested concentrating on the future rather than trying to alter the present. As she talked, the scene dissolved to the children's efforts to learn from adults whose values were shifting. Football, validity of the Walden Commune and religion all took pastings, with the youngster's view of the revolution. It was a humorous yet uncompromising view of our changing patterns and lifestyles, acknowledging that transition and process are part of the natural condition and that what is valuable from the past must be reconciled with the exigencies of the future. The best line: "It was against Nixon, it was fun and it was held mostly outside." Songs: "Stop in the Middle," "I Do Believe."

The special was adapted from Garry Trudeau's comic strip, which he began while a college undergraduate as Bull Tales for the Yale Record (1968). Moved to the Yale Daily News (1969), it attracted national attention and was retitled Doonesbury and distributed by the Universal Press Syndicate (October 26, 1970). Original artwork and the story behind the film's creation were published in A Doonesbury Special: A Director's Notebook (Sheed Andrews and McMeel, 1978) by Trudeau.

DOROTHY IN THE LAND OF OZ see THANKSGIVING IN THE LAND OF OZ

DOWN AND OUT WITH DONALD DUCK

Broadcast History
    Premiere: March 25, 1987
    NBC/Wednesday 8:00-9:00 PM
Producers: Scot Garen, Jolie Albrecht
Director: Scot Garen
Writers: Jolie Albrecht, Katharine Sloan, Scot Garen, Stan Freberg
Music: Christopher L. Stone
Company: Garen-Albrecht Productions in association with Walt Disney Television/60 minutes

Narrator: Stan Freberg

Principal Characters and Voices
Donald Duck/Daisy Duck/
    Huey/Dewey/Louie   Tony Anselmo
Professor Ludwig von Drake   Albert Ash
Mickey Mouse   Les Perkins
Goofy/Peg-Leg Pete   Will Ryan
Announcer   Harry Shearer

Down and Out With Donald Duck investigated the dour duck's fowl
ways in clips culled from the Disney studio library. A 60 Minutes-
style report, the "duckumentary" chronicled the "quackup" of the
Disney star. When Donald threw a colossal tantrum on the set, his
studio dumped him, his fans stopped clamoring for autographs and
even Daisy, his long-suffering girlfriend, threatened to leave him.
Finally acknowledging his problem, Donald desparately sought new
ways to keep his cool. Friendless and alone, he was forced to take
odd jobs, such as working as a forest ranger, in scenes from his
various films, until he could convince the studio that he had his
fierce temper under control. The special was compiled and edited
from 30 hours of cartoons without one frame of new animation added.

EASTER BUNNY IS COMIN' TO TOWN, THE

Broadcast History
    Premiere: April 6, 1977
    ABC/Wednesday 8:00-9:00 PM
    ABC/Repeats: March 20, 1978; April 14, 1979; April 5, 1980
    SYN/Repeats: 1985 +
Producers/Directors: Arthur Rankin, Jr., Jules Bass
Writer: Romeo Muller
Music: Maury Laws, Bernard Hoffer
Lyrics: Jules Bass
Company: Rankin-Bass Productions/60 minutes
Distributor: Lorimar Syndication ("Animated Holiday Specials")/
    1985-
Home Video: Children's Video Library (Vestron)

Narrator
S. D. Kluger   Fred Astaire

Principal Characters and Voices
Sunny, the Easter Bunny   Skip Hinnant
Chugs   Robert McFadden
Hallelujah Jones   Ron Marshall
King Bruce   James Spies
Lily Longtooth   Meg Sargent

THE EASTER BUNNY IS COMIN' TO TOWN. © 1977, Rankin/Bass
Productions, Inc. Courtesy of Rankin/Bass Productions and Lorimar
Syndication.

Other Voices
    Gia Andersen, George Brennan, Stacey Carey, Jill Choder, Karen
    Dahle, Laura Dean, Michael McGovern, Ray Owens, Allen Swift

The Easter Bunny Is Comin' to Town incorporated tales about the
origins of the holiday traditions and symbols, narrated by Fred
Astaire as S. D. Kluger, previously the storyteller of Santa Claus
Is Comin' to Town [q.v.]. This time, the small town mailman returned with letters and questions for the Easter Bunny. The story
began in the village of Kidville, a place which was run and inhabited
only by children. One Easter Morning they found a newcomer, Sunny,
a sad baby bunny. Sunny grew up happily but liked to venture to
a nearby town where only grown-ups lived and children were pro-
hibited except for 7-year-old King Bruce. As a gesture of friendship, Sunny started bringing Bruce painted eggs, the first decorated
Easter eggs. Every Easter thereafter, the rabbit would invent another tradition, like egg rolling, jellybeans and chocolate bunnies.
Bruce's hard-hearted, domineering aunt, Lily Longtooth, was raving
mad about the joy and excitement Easter created in the grown-up
town and encouraged her nephew to cause all sorts of trouble for
Sunny and his friends, Chugs and Hallelujah Jones. But when she
saw an Easter lily, finally she too accepted the love of Easter Day.
The special featured "The Little Engine Who Could" and was filmed
using stop-motion animated puppets (Animagic). Songs: "The Easter

Bunny Is Comin' to Town" (Astaire), "The Little Engine Who Could,"
"Someone's Gotta Take a Taste," "You Think Nobody Loves You
(But They Do!)," "Big Rock Candy Mountain," "Trainyard Blues,"
"Think You Can Do," "What Came First, the Chicken or the Egg?"

EASTER FEVER
(aka THE JACK RABBIT STORY)

Broadcast History
    Premiere: March 30, 1980
    CBC/Sunday 7:00-7:30 PM
    SYN/local station option (KNBC, Los Angeles, April 1, 1980,
        Tuesday 7:30-8:00 PM PST)
    SYN/Repeats: 1981 +
Executive Producers: Robert Foster, Ted Kernaghan, Nigel Martin
Producers: Patrick Loubert, Michael Hirsh
Associate Producer/Writer: Larry Mollin
Directors: Ken Stephenson, Gian Celestri, Greg Duffell
Music: John Sebastian
Company: Nelvana Limited, Toronto, Canada, in association with
    the CBC
Distributor: Viacom Enterprises/1980-
Home Video: Warner Home Video #30009 ("Nelvanamation II")

Principal Characters and Voices
Jack (Easter Bunny)   Garrett Morris
Don Rattles/Steed Martin   Maurice LaMarche
Santa Claus/Baker   Chris Wiggins
Madame Malegg   Jeri Craden
Aardvark   Jim Henshaw
Scarlett O'Hare   Catherine O'Hara
Scrawny Chicken   Melleny Brown
Ratso Rat   Larry Mollin
Announcer   Don Ferguson

Easter Fever raked the Easter Bunny over the coals when Jack's
friends gathered to celebrate and honor him on the eve of his retirement from show business at the Fryer's Club Roast. The hosts were
Don Rattles, a venom-tongued serpent, and Steed Martin, a wild and
crazy gnu. After Jack made his entrance as a song-and-dance man,
three guests of honor told about an important event in his life
through flashback scenes. Santa Claus told how Jack became the
one and only Easter Bunny; Ratso Rat related how Jack fell in love
one Spring and met his wife, Scarlett O'Hare; and Scrawny Chicken
recounted Jack's confrontation and adventure with Madam Malegg, the
mad chef who stole his Easter Eggs. Throughout the "roast," an
aardvark that worked in the kitchen plotted to prevent Jack's retirement and at the end succeeded in getting to the dais. In an im-
passioned plea, the aardvark explained why he should not hang up

his basket for greener pastures. Touched at the argument, Jack resolved to stay on as the Easter Bunny, on one condition: that the "roast" be held every year and he would not have to be present. Songs included: "Easter Has Been Very Good to Me" (Jack).

EASTER IS

Broadcast History
Premiere: March 1974
SYN/local station option (WLS, Chicago, April 14, 1974, Sunday 1:00-1:30 PM CST)
SYN/Repeats: 1975 +
Executive Producer: Dr. Martin J. Neeb, Jr.
Producer: Rev. Ardon D. Albrecht
Director: Dorse A. Lanpher
Writer: Michael Halperin
Music: Jimmy Haskell
Lyrics: Guy Hemric
Company: Screen Images for Lutheran Television
Distributor: International Lutheran Layman's League/1985-
Home Video: United Entertainment

Principal Characters and Voices

Benji	David Kelly
Schoolteacher	Leslie Uggams
Martin	Philip Morris
Waldo (Benji's dog)	

Other Voices
Joan Gardner, Shelley Hines, Darla Hood, Dina Lynn, Bob Norris, Gary Shapiro, Dru Stevens, Les Tremayne

Easter Is had Benji so worried about his lost dog Waldo that he could not concentrate on drawing an Easter poster to enter in the school contest. He was about ready to give up the search when a mysterious phone-caller demanded, "Be at Sam's garage in half an hour with five bucks or you'll never see your dog again." Benji scraped up the money, but when he arrived Waldo was gone, the rope was chewed through and there was blood on the window. Of course there couldn't be anything but a happy ending to an Easter show, and Waldo's dramatic return on Easter morning gave Benji a great idea for his poster about Easter's deeper Christian meaning. Songs: "His Love," "Not a Day Goes By," "Easter Gift" (Uggams).

EMPEROR'S NEW CLOTHES, THE

Broadcast History
Premiere: February 21, 1972

ABC/THE ENCHANTED WORLD OF DANNY KAYE: THE EMPEROR'S
NEW CLOTHES, Monday 8:00-9:00 PM
SYN/Repeats: 1985 +
Producers/Directors: Arthur Rankin, Jr., Jules Bass
Associate Producer: Herbert Bonis
Writer: Romeo Muller
Music: Maury Laws
Lyrics: Jules Bass
Company: Rankin-Bass Productions/60 minutes
Distributor: Viacom Enterprises/1986-

Narrator
Marmaduke   Danny Kaye

Principal Characters and Voices
Emperor Klockenlocher   Cyril Ritchard
Princess Klockenlocher   Imogene Coca
Mufti   Allen Swift
Jaspar   Robert McFadden

The Emperor's New Clothes starred Danny Kaye as the voice of Marmaduke in a musical adaptation of the story by Hans Christian Andersen. Introduced by Kaye, who brought the storyteller to life in a
1952 RKO movie, it was a whimsical account of the vain Emperor
Klockenlocher, who allowed himself to be bamboozled into ordering a
suit of clothing made from "invisible cloth." He paid one million
Grinklens for the invisible suit tailored by Marmaduke, a con-man-
turned-tailor. "I see what I want to see," said the Emperor, who
proved his point when he led a parade in the all-together. Even the
court went along with the eccentricity of their monarch until a brave
little boy finally voiced the truth about his appearance. The special
was filmed using stop-motion animated puppets (Animagic) with some
live-action portions shot on location in Denmark. Songs: "Come
Along With Me," "Creation," "The Tailor's Song," "Clothes Make the
Man," "I See What I Want to See" (all Kaye).

ENCHANTED WORLD OF DANNY KAYE, THE   see EMPEROR's NEW
CLOTHES, THE

EVERYBODY RIDES THE CAROUSEL

Broadcast History
    Premiere: September 10, 1976
    CBS/A MOBIL SHOWCASE PRESENTATION, Friday 8:00-9:30 PM
    Sponsor: Mobil Oil
    SYN/Repeats: 1980 +
Producers: John Hubley, Faith Hubley
Director: John Hubley
Writers: John Hubley, Faith Hubley

Music: William Russo
Soloists: Dizzy Gillespie, Larry Adler, Benny Carter
Company: The Hubley Studio/90 minutes
Distributor: Fox-Lorber Associates/1980-

Hostess: Cicely Tyson

Narrator: Alvin Epstein

Principal Characters and Voices

Mother	Judith Coburn
Baby #1/Maura #2/Adolescent #4	Georgia Hubley
Baby #2	Ray Hubley
Baby (cries)/Emily/Adolescent #5	Emily Hubley
Babies' Relative #1/Cafeteria Woman	Jane Hoffman
Babies' Relative #2	Lou Jacobi
Babies' Relative #3	Lane Smith
Babies' Relative #4	Eleanor Wilson
Maura #1	Maura Washburn
Maura's Mother	Linda Washburn
Maura's Father	Mike Washburn
Bruce/Student #2	Bruce E. Smith
Bruce's Mother	Jane E. Smith
Bruce's Father	Mortimer Shapiro
Student #1	John Infantanza
Boy	Leeds Atkinson
Girl	Jenny Lumet
Oracle	Jo Carrol Stoneham
Adolescent #1	Alvin Mack
Adolescent #2	Michael Hirst
Adolescent #3	Barbara Gittleman
Lovers	Charles Levin
	Meryl Streep
Dinah	Dinah Manoff
Dinah's Father	John Randolph
Dinah's Mother	Sarah Cunningham
Tulane	Tulane Bridgewater
Tulane's Mother	DeeDee Bridgewater
Librarian	William Watts
Couple in Bed	Lawrence (David) Pressman/ Lanna Saunders
Cafeteria Man	Jack Gilford
Halloween Woman	Juanita Moore
Halloween Man	Harry Edison

Everybody Rides the Carousel, in three half-hour segments, delineated psychiatrist Erik H. Erikson's concept of the eight stages of the human life-cycle, depicting the growth of a human being through a series of challenges and conflicts inherent in each stage of development. The pedantic fablelike story displayed a genuine gift for whimsy and used graceful, fluid, human characters in a visual metaphor of a carousel and eight rides: infancy, toddler, childhood, school, adolescence, young adulthood, maturity, and old age. The struggle between opposing inner forces in each stage was symbolized by the animated characters, which were seen to exist and compete for hegemony within the individual. In one scene from childhood, when a little girl's parents laughed at her drawing, she turned into a monstrous bird and thrashed them. And in a schoolroom scene, students expanded and contracted in size according to their skills. The treatment of death was particularly adroit and dealt with the subject frankly, without fear or sentimentality. The film's voice characterizations were mostly improvisations. Large doses of Erikson's theory were administered in the various segments.

FABULOUS SHORTS, THE

Broadcast History
   Premiere: October 17, 1968
   NBC/Thursday 7:30-8:00 PM
   Sponsor: Timex
Executive Producer/Writer: Lee Mendelson
Producers/Directors: Walt DeFaria, Sheldon Fay, Jr.
Associate Producer: David Crommie
Music: John Scott Trotter
Company: Lee Mendelson Productions/60 minutes

Host: Jim Backus

The Fabulous Shorts featured many of the Motion Picture Academy's Oscar-winning cartoons. The show traced Walt Disney's achievements from Steamboat Willie (1928), which introduced Mickey Mouse, to his Oscar-winning Flowers and Trees (1932), The Old Mill (1937), Ferdinand the Bull (1938), Der Fuehrer's Face (1942) with Donald Duck and Lend a Paw (1941) with Mickey Mouse. Included in the compilation were some contemporary efforts like John Snyder of Rembrandt Studios' Munro (1960), Jules Feiffer's sly tale of a 4-year-old army draftee; John and Faith Hubley's Moonbird (1959), narrated by the artists' sons; Dusan Vukotick of Zagreb Film, Yugoslavia's Ersatz, the first foreign Oscar-winner; two illustrated tunes from Storyboard with Herb Alpert and Tijuana Brass, Tijuana Taxi and Spanish Flea (1966); and The Critic (1963), a Mel Brooks--Ernest Pintoff creation. Also clips from the Warner Bros. Cartoons' Tweetie Pie (1947), Knighty Knight Bugs (1958), Speedy Gonzales (1955), For Scent-imental Reasons (1949) and DePatie-Freleng's The Pink Phink (1964). Mel Blanc showed how a Bugs Bunny cartoon was made, and Jim Backus offered a few words about Mr. Magoo, who starred in two winners for UPA, When Magoo Flew (1954) and Mister Magoo's Puddle Jumper (1956).

FAERIES. © 1981, Tomorrow Entertainment, Inc. Courtesy of Lee
Mishkin Animation.

FAERIES

Broadcast History
    Premiere: February 25, 1981
    CBS/Wednesday 8:30-9:00 PM
    CBS/Repeats: July 31, 1982; August 13, 1983
Executive Producer: Thomas Moore
Producers: Norton Virgien, Fred Hellmich, Lee Mishkin
Directors: Lee Mishkin, Fred Hellmich
Writers: Christopher Gore, Alan Aldrich, Lee Mishkin
Company: MHV and Friends in association with Tomorrow Entertainment
Home Video: Family Home Entertainment

Principal Characters and Voices

Faerie King/Shadow	Hans Conreid
Oisin	Craig Schaefer
Princess Niamh	Morgan Brittany
Puck/Fir Darrig	Frank Welker
Kobold	Bob Arbogast
Hags	June Foray /
	Linda Gary

Trows/Hunters	Mel Wells/
	Frank Welker/
	Bob Arbogast

Faeries depicted the sprites in several forms, based on the 1978 book by Brian Froud. Oisin, the only human character in the special, was a hunter who followed a deer that led him into a mushroom cluster. Magically, the mushrooms turned into faeries and danced before him. The Trows explained that they were in danger and that only a mortal could save them. Princess Niamh used her magic to turn the middle-aged Oisin into a 15-year-old boy and to take him away from the human world to meet her father, the Fairy King. The King had made a mistake by giving life to his own shadow and now the evil spectre occupied the throne at Squalorweb and was trying to conquer the faerie world and also marry the Princess. Accompanied by Puck, whom Shakespeare made the most famous faerie in history, and possessed of a magic ring, Oisin set off the for shadow's lair, Squalorweb Castle. Along the way he encountered different clans of faeries, including redcaps, whose head gear had been dyed in blood, and Fir Darrig, a Kobold whose clan carried candles on their hats because they lived in mines in Germany. With their help he found the castle and the shadow. Illuminated by a candle, Oisin's shadow dueled the Faerie King's shadow in the final triumphant showdown. Songs: "How About a Kobold Stew," "To the Shadow."

FAMILY CIRCUS CHRISTMAS, A

Broadcast History
    Premiere: December 18, 1979
    NBC/Tuesday 8:30-9:00 PM
    NBC/Repeats: December 5, 1980; December 20, 1981
Producer: Edward F. Cullen
Associate Producer: Saul Kasden
Director: Al Kouzel
Writer: Joseph C. Cavella
Music: Tom McIntosh
Lyrics: Jay Livingston, Ray Evans
Company: Cullen-Kasden Productions in association with the Register & Tribune Syndicate
Distributor: Fremantle International/1982-
Home Video: Family Home Entertainment

Principal Characters and Voices

Mommy	Anne Costello
Daddy	Bob Kaliban
Billy	Mark McDermott
Dolly	Missy Hope
Jeffy/P.J.	Nathan Berg
Santa Claus	Allen Swift
Barfy (pet dog)	

Vocalist: Sarah Vaughan

A Family Circus Christmas followed the dreams and adventures of
the imaginative household children at Christmastime. The story was
pegged on Jeffy's request to Santa Claus for a very special gift,
one that even stumped the jolly gent. The boy asked for Santa to
bring his "Granddad down from Heaven." Santa encouraged Jeffy
to believe in the spirit of Christmas, and through his dream and a
fantasy sequence, Granddad made the trip to enjoy a very merry
Christmas with the children. Song/Theme: "The Dreamer" (Vaughan).
     The special was the second of three films based on Bil Keane's
enduring domestic cartoon panel modelled on his own family, following A Special Valentine with the Family Circus [q.v.].

FAMILY CIRCUS EASTER, A

Broadcast History
     Premiere: April 8, 1982
     NBC/Thursday 8:30-9:00 PM
     NBC/Repeat: April 1, 1983
Producer: Edward F. Cullen
Associate Producer: Saul Kasden
Director: Dave Brain
Writer: Joseph C. Cavella
Music: Tom McIntosh
Lyrics: Gerry Glombecki
Company: Cullen-Kasden Productions in association with the Register
     & Tribune Syndicate
Home Video: Family Home Entertainment

Principal Characters and Voices
Mommy   Anne Costello
Daddy   Bob Kaliban
Billy   Mark McDermott
Dolly   Missy Hope
Jeffy/P.J.   Nathan Berg
Easter Bunny   Dizzy Gillespie
Barfy (pet dog)

A Family Circus Easter incorporated a musical fantasy with the family
children taking a magical trip to ask the Easter Bunny how to hide
eggs. The story followed the experiences of the children, Billy,
Dolly and Jeffy, as they tried to make a happy Easter holiday for
their baby brother P.J., setting out Easter Eggs in the yard. When
a rabbit turned up, the children boxed it in until, eventually, the
real Easter Bunny arrived on the scene. He helped answer, in song,
their nagging question of why the Easter Bunny hides his eggs. It
was based on Bil Keane's comic-panel characters. Songs: "Hey There,
Easter Bunny," "Now You See It, Now You Don't" (Gillespie).

FAMILY CIRCUS VALENTINE, A   see SPECIAL VALENTINE WITH
THE FAMILY CIRCUS, A

FAMILY DOG, THE

Broadcast History
    Premiere: February 16, 1987
    NBC/AMAZING STORIES, Monday 8:30-9:00 PM
    NBC/Repeat: September 11, 1987
Executive Producer: Steven Spielberg
Producer: David E. Vogel
Producers/Animation: Brad Bird, Alexander King
Associate Producer: Cleve Reinhard
Director/Writer: Brad Bird
Music/Theme: John Williams
Music: Danny Elfman, Steve Bartek
Company: Hyperion-Kushner-Locke Productions in association with
    Amblin Entertainment and Universal Television

Principal Characters and Voices
Father   Stan Freberg
Mother   Mercedes McCambridge
Billy   Scott Menville
Baby Sister   Annie Potts
Family Dog

Other Voices
    Jack Angel, Brooke Ashley, Brad Bird, Marshall Efron, Stanley
    Ralph Ross

The Family Dog was a trilogy of comic stories centering around a sub-
urban middle-class family and their put-upon pet pooch. The tales
were seen from the perspective of the family dog, an unusual breed,
something of a cross between a bull terrier and a large rat. The
first segment took place on a typical Saturday afternoon that quickly
turned nightmarish when all of the dog's attempts at rest and relaxa-
tion failed due to the torments inflicted by the children, the goggle-
eyed little hellion Billy and his chubby baby sister, who looked like
a fireplug with a Pippi Longstocking hairdo. Next came an assortment of adventures depicted in the family's home movies of last
Christmas, as captured in fabulous 8mm by Uncle Bud. Third, the
mutt's inability to keep thieves from burglarizing the household prompted a frustrated Dad to enroll him in Gerta La-Strange's attack-dog
school. To unmask the culprits, the dog hung out at the Rat's Nest
and became a hero when he helped capture the two robbers. Back
home, pampered and dining on sirloin steak from Mom, who had
lamented being "a short-order cook for a dog" and now called him
"our little hero," the dog created a ruckus when he mistakenly took
Dad, who was accidentally locked out of the house, for a prowler.
    The film was promoted as "A Special Animated Adventure" and

was one of the few fully articulated new cartoons featuring original characters. It was created by Brad Bird and aired as an episode of Steven Spielberg's Amazing Stories (NBC, 1985-1987).

FAT ALBERT CHRISTMAS SPECIAL, THE

Broadcast History
   Premiere: December 18, 1977
   CBS/Sunday 7:00-7:30 PM
   CBS/Repeats: November 27, 1979; December 24, 1980
   SYN/Repeats: 1984 +
Executive Producer: William H. Cosby, Jr.
Producers: Louis Scheimer, Norman Prescott
Director: Hal Sutherland
Writers: Bill Danch, Jim Ryan
Music: Yvette Blais, Jeff Michael
Company: Filmation in association with Bill Cosby Productions
Distributor: Group W Productions/1984-

Principal Characters and Voices

Fat Albert/Mushmouth/Bill	Bill Cosby
Russell	Jan Crawford
Weird Harold	Gerald Edwards
Rudy	Eric Suter

Other Voices
   Erika Carroll, Eric Greene, Kim Hamilton, Julius Harris, Ty Henderson

The Fat Albert Christmas Special presented another twist on Charles Dickens' Scrooge tale when the Cosby kids were threatened with eviction from their junkyard lean-to clubhouse by tightwad owner Tyrone. The bad news came while they were rehearsing their Christmas pageant. Meantime, with his father out of work and his mother about to give birth with nowhere to stay, little Marshall became involved with the gang, who rescued him when he ran away. During their search for a place for his mother to have her child, Fat Albert and his pals uncovered the reason for Tyrone's Scrooge-like meanness, which was resolved when brotherly love in north Philly won out again.

   The special was the third in a series of five Fat Albert specials that began with Hey, Hey, Hey, It's Fat Albert [q.v.]. The Christmas, Easter and Halloween specials were incorporated in the 90-episode weekday-strip series, Fat Albert and the Cosby Kids (SYN, 1984-), packaging new films and the off-network series, Fat Albert (CBS, 1972-1984), described in Children's Television, Part I (Scarecrow, 1983), pp. 99-100.

FAT ALBERT EASTER SPECIAL, THE

Broadcast History
  Premiere: April 3, 1982
  CBS/Monday 8:30-9:00 PM
  CBS/Repeat: March 30, 1983
  SYN/Repeats: 1985 +
Executive Producer: William H. Cosby, Jr.
Producers: Louis Scheimer, Norman Prescott
Creative Director: Don Christensen
Writers: Bill Danch, Dan DiStefano
Music: Yvette Blais, Jeff Michael
Company: Filmation in association with Bill Cosby Productions
Distributor: Group W Productions/1984-

Principal Characters and Voices
Fat Albert/Mushmouth/Bill/
  Mudfoot   Bill Cosby
Russell   Jan Crawford
Rudy   Eric Suter
Weird Harold   Gerald Edwards

The Fat Albert Easter Special brought home the spirit of rebirth to Fat Albert and his friends when they tried to spruce up mean old Mudfoot's ramshackle place. After explaining to his pals that Easter eggs were a symbol of the new life and rebirth that are synonymous with the holiday, Fat Albert joined the gang to observe the joy of Easter by rejuvenating their elderly acquaintance's home. A practical joke by the smark aleck Rudy, however, led to the elderly Mudfoot's serious injury and hospitalization. Disguising himself as a doctor, Fat Albert convinced the despondent man that there were good reasons for living and sped him on his way to recovery and a big welcome home from the Cosby kids. Earlier, the whole crew took time out from their task to watch their favorite TV show, "The Adventures of the Brown Hornet," a masked do-gooder with the tenacity of Superman and the finesse of Inspector Clouseau who roamed far out in space, in equally far out bizarre adventures. His sidekicks were Tweeter Belle and Stinger, and the program-within-the-program concerned the space hero's retrieval of stolen Easter eggs.

FAT ALBERT HALLOWEEN SPECIAL, THE

Broadcast History
  Premiere: October 24, 1977
  CBS/Monday 8:30-9:00 PM
  CBS/Repeats: October 25, 1978; October 22, 1979; October 27, 1981
  SYN/Repeats: 1984 +
Executive Producer: William H. Cosby, Jr.
Producers: Louis Scheimer, Norman Prescott

THE FAT ALBERT HALLOWEEN SPECIAL. © 1984, Wm. H. Cosby,
Jr. Courtesy of Group W Productions and Filmation.

Director: Hal Sutherland
Writers: Bill Danch, Jim Ryan
Music: Yvette Blais, Jeff Michael
Company: Filmation in association with Bill Cosby Productions
Distributor: Group W Productions/1984-

Principal Characters and Voices

Fat Albert/Mushmouth/Bill   Bill Cosby
Russell   Jan Crawford
Weird Harold   Gerald Edwards

| Rudy | Eric Suter |
| Others | Erika Carroll |

The Fat Albert Halloween Special carried an educational message on the do's and don'ts of trick-or-treating when trouble-maker Devery masterminded a scheme to scare the neighborhood's old people. Dressed up in their Halloween costumes, Fat Albert and friends Mushmouth, Bucky, Russell, Bill, Dumb Donald, Weird Harold and Rudy decided to take in a horror movie which inspired them to re-create some scary moments in the neighborhood. As usual, Fat Albert's inherent sense of right and wrong came into play, and what happened to them at creepy old lady Bakewell's house taught them another valuable lesson about people.

FIRST CHRISTMAS, THE
(The Story of the First Christmas Snow)

Broadcast History
    Premiere: December 19, 1975
    NBC/Friday 8:00-8:30 PM
    Sponsor: Frito-Lay
    NBC/Repeats: December 18, 1976; December 15, 1979
    SYN/Repeats: 1985 +
Producers/Directors: Arthur Rankin, Jr., Jules Bass
Writer: Julian P. Gardner
Music: Maury Laws
Lyrics: Jules Bass
Company: Rankin-Bass Productions
Distributor: Lorimar Syndication ("Animated Holiday Specials")/
    1985-

Narrator
Sister Theresa   Angela Landsbury

Principal Characters and Voices
Father Thomas   Cyril Ritchard
Lukas   David Kelly
Sister Catherine   Iris Rainer
Sister Jean   Joan Gardner
Louisa   Dina Lynn

Other Voices
    Sean Manning, Don Messick, Hilary Momberger, Dru Stevens,
    Greg Thomas

The First Christmas, subtitled "The Story of the First Christmas Snow," was a poignant tale set in a small Abbey in the south of France in 1845, narrated by Angela Landsbury as Sister Theresa. As the nun was writing at her desk one day, a lightning bolt struck a boy, Lukas, who was out in the field nearby. When Sister Theresa ran to offer help, a card fell from her habit--the first Christmas card. Now blind, Lukas had Sister Theresa to care for him, and while recuperating at the Abbey he befriended young Louisa. As Christmas approached, Lukas longed for his first snowfall. "Even if I don't see it," he said, "I could feel it," and segued into the sentimental favorite, "I'm Dreaming of a White Christmas." One day, while he was walking outside with Louisa, Lukas felt something cold and wet on his face. He thought it was rain, but when Louisa told him it was snow he asked her to tell him what snow looked like. Louisa described the snowfall so vividly that he believed he could see it in his mind's eye. In reality, he had begun to see it for the first time as a miracle had restored his sight on a glorious white Christmas. Songs: Irving Berlin's "White Christmas" (Lukas), "The First White Christmas," "Christmas Snow Is Magic," "Save a Little Christmas."

FIRST EASTER RABBIT, THE

Broadcast History
Premiere: April 9, 1976
NBC/Friday 8:00-8:30 PM
NBC/Repeat: April 9, 1977
CBS/Repeats: March 19, 1978; April 7, 1979; April 9, 1981
SYN/Repeats: 1986 +
Producers/Directors: Arthur Rankin, Jr., Jules Bass
Writer: Julian P. Gardner
Music: Maury Laws
Lyrics: Jules Bass
Company: Rankin-Bass Productions with animation by Toru Hara and Tsuguyuki Kubo
Distributor: Lorimar Syndication ("Animated Holiday Specials")/1986-

Narrator
Great Easter Bunny   Burl Ives

Principal Characters and Voices
Stuffy	Robert Morse
Flops	Stan Freberg
Zero/Spats	Paul Frees
Mother	Joan Gardner
Whiskers	Don Messick
Glinda	Dina Lynn

Vocalists
Burl Ives, Robert Morse, Christine Winter

The First Easter Rabbit told the story of Stuffy, a rabbit with a special mission, narrated by Burl Ives as the Great Easter Bunny. Stuffy was a toy bunny, a Christmas present to the young Glinda, magically brought to life by a kind fairy as the "First Easter Rabbit."

His new role called for him to dispense baskets full of Easter eggs to the children, but first he had to venture to Easter Valley, near the North Pole. It was a remarkable place with a large workshop for decorating eggs and making baskets and Easter bonnets and where Santa Claus was on hand to welcome him. Learning that Glinda was ill, Stuffy made a trip to her village and told her of his plans for Easter. They planned to meet on Easter Sunday, but a nasty bunny destroyed the Golden Easter Lily and a frozen fiend named Zero threatened to put a chill on Stuffy's debut by blowing a blizzard his way. Just in time, Santa rescued the baskets and freezing workers from Easter Valley, the evil rabbit restored the Golden Lily and the Easter parade was on. The special was loosely adapted from the book, The Velveteen Rabbit, and filmed with stop-motion animated puppets (Animagic). Songs: Irvin Berlin's "Easter Parade," "There's That Rabbit."

FIVE WEEKS IN A BALLOON

Broadcast History
    Premiere: November 24, 1977
    CBS/FAMOUS CLASSIC TALES, Thursday 3:30-4:30 PM
    Sponsor: Kenner Products (Toy Group, General Mills)
    CBS/Repeats: September 30, 1978; November 22, 1981
    SYN/Repeats: 1982 +
Executive Producer: Neil Balnaves
Producer: Doug Paterson
Director: Chris Cuddington
Writer: Kimmer Ringwald
Music: Australian Screen Music
Company: Hanna-Barbera Productions, Sydney, Australia (Southern
    Star Productions)/60 minutes
Distributor: Worldvision Enterprises/1982-
Home Video: Worldvision

Narrator: John Stephenson

Principal Characters and Voices
Dr. Samuel Fergusson/Duke of Salisbury	Laurie Main
Oliver	Loren Lester
Queen Victoria	Cathleen Cordell
Irumu/King Umtali	Brooker Bradshaw
Le Griffe/1st & 2nd Poacher	Johnny Hayner
Native	Gene Whittington

Five Weeks in a Balloon followed the adventure of a trio ballooning across the wilds of nineteenth-century Africa, based on the book by Jules Verne. In 1862 London, Dr. Samuel Fergusson, a famed and respected explorer, and his Texas-educated nephew Oliver were invited to Windsor Castle by Queen Victoria to meet Irumu, Emissary of the Bantu King Umtali. Irumu revealed that the King desired to make a birthday present to the Queen of "the eye of the cat," a priceless diamond located on Devil's Peak deep in Bantu land, and needed their help. Deciding to complete their journey over Africa by hot-air balloon, a feat never attempted before, the Doctor, Oliver and Irumu embarked for Cairo. Meanwhile, the Duke of Salisbury, also privy to the meeting, plotted to obtain the diamond for himself and hired as a guide Le Griffe, a treacherous thug. Lifting off on their flight from Cairo, the trio encountered tornadoes and terrifying hazards, all the time pursued by the Duke and Le Griffe. After a battle of wits and a display of raw courage when both parties reached the peak at the same time, the Doctor, Oliver and Irumu prevailed in claiming the diamond for Queen Victoria.

FLASH GORDON--THE GREATEST ADVENTURE OF THEM ALL

FLASH GORDON--THE GREATEST ADVENTURE OF THEM ALL.
© 1978, King Features Syndicate, Inc. Courtesy of Group W Productions and Filmation.

Broadcast History
    Premiere: August 21, 1982
    NBC/Saturday 8:00-10:00 PM
    NBC/Repeats: September 5, 1982; September 26, 1982
    Executive Producers: Norm Prescott, Lou Scheimer
    Producer: Don Christensen
    Director: Gwen Wetzler
    Sequence Directors: Marsh Lamore, Kay Wright
    Writer: Samuel A. Peeples
    Music: Yvette Blais, Jeff Michael
    Company: Filmation Studios/120 minutes

Principal Characters and Voices
Flash Gordon   Robert Ridgely
Dale Arden   Diane Pershing
Dr. Zarkov   David Opatoshu
Ming the Merciless   Bob Holt
Vultan   Vic Perrin
Princess Aura   Melendy Britt
Prince Barin   Robert Douglas
Thun   Ted Cassidy

Flash Gordon--The Greatest Adventure of Them All presented the
indomitable space hero in his first full-length animated space fantasy
made for television. A superb athlete and Olympic triple-gold medal-
ist, the golden-haired Flash was now portrayed as a State Department
employee in Warsaw in 1939, where he learned that Earth was threatened not only by Hitler but one of his allies, Ming the Merciless,
and Ming's advanced scientific powers on the planet Mongo. Gordon
blasted off from Earth with Dr. Zarkov, a Nobel-prize scientist
dedicated to peace, and Dale Arden, an American reporter, and
headed for Mongo in a valiant effort to negotiate and save the universe. Before long the heroic trio were involved not only with the
evil emperor Ming and his minions and the sexy and nasty Princess
Aura, but with Prince Barin from the planet Aboria, Thun and his
lion people, Vultan and his hawkmen, and assorted apemen, dino-
saurs, Amazon warriors, lizard women and other genetic mutations.
    A straightforward, adventure-filled scenario with wonderfully
imaginative creatures, the film was scripted by Samuel A. Peeples,
who wrote the pilot for Star Trek (NBC, 1966-1969), and was based
on the newspaper comic (January 7, 1934) created by Raymond Chand-
ler for the King Features Syndicate. Partly to defray the $2.4 mil-
lion production, the studio pre-sold foreign TV and theatrical rights
but was barred from releasing the film to theaters domestically by
part-owner Dino De Laurentiis to protect his own live-action version
of Flash Gordon (Universal, 1980). NBC billed it as "the first full-
length animated adult space fantasy ever produced for television."
Described by TV Guide critic Judith Crist as, "Great stuff and
delectable nonsense," various scenes from the film, along with new
footage, were used for the Saturday morning series, The New Adventures of Flash Gordon (NBC, 1979-1980/1982-1983), described in
Children's Television, Part I, (Scarecrow, 1983), pp. 197-198.

FLASHBEAGLE   see   IT'S FLASHBEAGLE, CHARLIE BROWN

FLIGHT OF DRAGONS, THE

Broadcast History
    Premiere: August 3, 1986
    ABC/AN ABC MOVIE PRESENTATION, Sunday 7:00-9:00 PM
    SYN/Repeats: 1987 +
Producers/Directors: Arthur Rankin, Jr., Jules Bass
Associate Producers: Masaki Iizuka, Lee Dannacher
Directors/Animation: Katsuhisa Yamada, Fumihiko Takayama
Writers: Romeo Muller, Jeffrey Walker
Music & Lyrics/Title Song: Maury Laws, Jules Bass
Music: Maury Laws
Company: Rankin-Bass Productions/120 minutes
Home Video: Vestron

Principal Characters and Voices

Peter Dickenson	John Ritter
Carolinus	Harry Morgan
Ommadon	James Earl Jones
Smrgol	James Gregory
Gorbash	Cosie Costa
Arak	Victor Buono
Danielle	Nellie Bellflower
Princess Melisande	Alexandra Stoddart
Pawnbroker	Larry Storch

Other Voices
    Jack Lester, Robert McFadden, Don Messick, Ed Peck

Vocalist: Don McLean

The Flight of Dragons followed a young Boston writer, Peter Dickenson, who travelled back to a time between the waning Age of Magic
and the dawning Age of Science. It began when the Green Wizard
of All Nature, Carolinus, realizing man's machinery was destroying
his magical kingdom, summoned his three brothers to the Temple of
All Antiquity. Mounted on his dragon Gorbash, Carolinus flew off
to meet Solarius, the Blue Wizard of space, oceans and mountains;
Lo Tajal, the Yellow Wizard of light and air; and Ommadon, the Red
Wizard of black magic and Lord of the devil's domain. The three
good brothers agreed to create an enchanted retreat from the scientific age, but Ommadon would not concede and vowed to provoke man
to destroy himself, leaving the world free for his devilish magic.
Realizing that Ommadon had to be stopped, but forbidden to war
against their blood, the good three decided to enlist others to steal
his Red Crown, the source of his dark power. Searching the future,
Carolinus found a descendent of Great Peter, the Dragon Master, in
a Boston pawnship. Peter was fascinated by the legendary creatures

and was playing a chess-like game he had invented, "The Flight of Dragons." Taking Peter back in time, Carolinus outfitted him properly for the task and introduced him to his niece, Princess Melisande, with whom Peter fell in love. Meanwhile, under Ommadon's spell, all the other dragons had gone over to help him protect his crown. Aware of Peter's presence, he dispatched his terrifying dragon Bryagh, who swept Peter up in his claws. Young Gorbash flew in pursuit while Carolinus tried an incantation, but his fading magic went wrong and in a flash Gorbash and Peter were merged in the young dragon's body. So it remained throughout the quest, joined by Sir Orrin Neville Smythe astride his horse Lancer, Carolinus's aging dragon Smrgol, and aided also by Arak the Wolf, Danielle of the Woodlands and the Elf Giles. What followed was their battles against hordes of demons and monsters such as the Sandmirks, the Ogre of Gormly Keep, the Worm of Sliggoth and legions of Flying Dragons. Using the Shield of Saturn and the Golden Flute, Peter ultimately grabbed the crown from a defeated Ommadon, hideously transformed into a scaly, many-horned, seven-headed dragon. As a dome of invisibility grew over the magic realm of Carolinus and his brothers for all time, the scene faded to the pawnshop with Peter and the Pawnbroker again playing his game when Melisande entered and they embraced. Song/Theme: "The Flight of Dragons" (McLean).

The two-hour made-for-TV movie was based on the eponymous book by Peter Dickenson, designed by Wayne Anderson, with additional material from the book, The Dragon & The George by Gordon R. Dickson.

FLINTSTONE CHRISTMAS, A

Broadcast History
    Premiere: December 7, 1977
    NBC/Wednesday 8:00-9:00 PM
    NBC/Repeat: December 11, 1978
Executive Producers: William Hanna, Joseph Barbera
Producer: Iwao Takamoto
Associate Producer: Alex Lovy
Director: Charles A. Nichols
Writers: Duane Poole, Dick Robbins
Music: Hoyt Curtin, Paul DeKorte
Company: Hanna-Barbera Productions/60 minutes
Distributor: Worldvision Enterprises

Principal Characters and Voices

Fred Flintstone	Henry Corden
Barney Rubble	Mel Blanc
Betty Rubble/Pebbles Flintstone	Gay Hartwig
Wilma Flintstone	Jean VanderPyl
Bamm Bamm Rubble	Lucille Bliss

Mrs. Santa	Virginia Gregg
Real Santa	Hal Smith
Ed the Foreman/Otis	Don Messick
Mr. Slate	John Stephenson

A Flintstone Christmas had Fred pinch-hitting for Santa after he sprained an ankle falling from the Flintstone's roof on Christmas Eve. Actually, it was Barney Rubble's suggestion, since Fred was to play Santa at the Ladies Auxiliary Christmas party for underprivileged children, but when Fred protested Santa overcame his objections. With a magical wave of his arms, Santa dressed Fred in a complete outfit and put an elf suit on Barney. All went well, except Fred's attempts to get back up the chimneys, until in a fierce winter storm the gifts were lost. Dismayed, Fred and Barney used the sleigh's CB radio to contact Santa, who instructed them to order the reindeer home, where Mrs. Claus had prepared a new sack of toys. Meanwhile, back at the Bedrock party, Wilma, Betty, and Mr. Slate, Fred's boss, were furious that he had not arrived, and the children, including 7-year-old Pebbles and young Bamm Bamm, were growing restless awaiting Santa. Nearly finished with their deliveries, Fred and Barney remembered the party and pushed the sleigh's high speed button, arriving just as Mr. Slate declared to Wilma that Fred was fired. Magically filling their empty sack with toys for the children, and wishing all a Merry Christmas, Fred and Barney hurried back to return Santa's clothes, sleigh and reindeer. When Wilma, Betty and their children arrived, the pair tried to explain why they were late, but their spouses wouldn't believe them. Hearing sleigh bells outside, Pebbles and Bamm Bamm rushed to the window, where they were joined by Fred and Barney to see Santa riding off in his sleigh. Songs: "[Meet] The Flintstones (Theme)," "Christmas Is My Favorite Time of Year," "Dino the Dinosaur."

It was the first special starring the most enduring, created-for-TV cartoon-family and friends on television. The Stone Age characters have been around in one form or another since their prime-time debut September 30, 1960 on The Flintstones (ABC, 1960-1966), a hit series which was followed by a string of Saturday morning shows, all described in Children's Television, Part I (Scarecrow, 1983), pp. 103-109, 216-217. In the 1980s, they have been continued in the Saturday morning series, The Flintstones Comedy Show (NBC, 1980-1982), The Flintstone Funnies (NBC, 1982-1984) and as toddlers in The Flintstone Kids (ABC, 1986-). The characters also appeared in an animated movie, A Man Called Flintstone (COL, 1966) and in several made-for-TV movies including The Jetsons Meet the Flintstones, optioned by the FOX network for 1987-1988.

FLINTSTONES: FRED'S FINAL FLING, THE

Broadcast History
   Premiere: October 18, 1981
   NBC/Sunday 7:00-7:30 PM
   NBC/Repeat: August 1, 1982

THE FLINTSTONES: FRED'S FINAL FLING. © 1981, Hanna-Barbera Productions, Inc. Courtesy of Hanna-Barbera Productions and TECO. Entertainment.

Executive Producers: William Hanna, Joseph Barbera
Producer: Alex Lovy
Directors: Oscar Dufau, Ray Patterson
Writer: Bob Ogle
Music: Hoyt Curtin, Paul DeKorte
Company: Hanna-Barbera Productions
Distributor: Worldvision Enterprises

Principal Characters and Voices

Fred Flintstone/Monkey #2/ Turtle #2	Henry Corden
Wilma Flintstone/Pebbles/ Elephant	Jean VanderPyl
Barney Rubble/Dino/Monkey #3	Mel Blanc
Betty Rubble/Nurse/Turtle #1	Gay Autterson
Frank Frankenstone/Dinosaur/ Monkey #1	John Stephenson
Doctor/Fish #1/Fish #2/Parrot/ Pigasaurus	Don Messick

The Flintstones: Fred's Final Fling relied upon a diagnostic foulup-- during his annual physical a nurse confused Fred's X-ray with that of Frank Frankenstone. Alarmed when he noted the mechanical insides of the monster, the doctor told Fred he had 24 hours to live. Dazed by the news, Fred pondered his end and realized how little he had done for others, vowing to make it up in his last hours. He began by giving Barney his new fishing rod, bowling ball and golf clubs. Leaving the house on a mysterious mission, he returned in a new car, wearing a Santa Claus costume, with toys for Pebbles, a big bone for Dino and presents for Wilma. Piling Wilma and the Rubbles in the new car, he took them to Bedrock's best Mexican restaurant, the La Coo Coo Rocko. After happily dancing until midnight, Fred decided to take everyone roller-skating, where he recaptured his happy times spend with Wilma, including their wedding day, via flashbacks. Wearily falling asleep, Fred was surprised when he awakened the next afternoon and tried to explain to Wilma his plight, but learned the Doctor had called and apologized for the mixup. Celebrating his reprieve at La Coo Coo Rocko, Fred vowed to always do nice things for people and told Wilma he had to be in Heaven anyway, holding an angel like her in his arms.

The program was one of three telecast in October 1981 and repeated in Summer 1982 in a special prime-time series.

FLINTSTONES: JOGGING FEVER, THE

Broadcast History
    Premiere: October 11, 1981
    NBC/Sunday 7:00-7:30 PM
    NBC/Repeat: July 25, 1982
Executive Producers: William Hanna, Joseph Barbera

Producer: Alex Lovy
Director: Ray Patterson
Writer: Bob Ogle
Music: Hoyt Curtin, Paul DeKorte
Company: Hanna-Barbera Productions
Distributor: Worldvision Enterprises

Principal Characters and Voices

Fred Flintstone/Workman #2	Henry Corden
Wilma Flintstone/Pebbles/ Nurse #1	Jean VanderPyl
Barney Rubble/Dino/Turtle	Mel Blanc
Betty Rubble/Nurse #2	Gay Autterson
Frank Frankenstone/Mr. Slate/ Dinosaur/Pterodactyl/Bird/ Snake	John Stephenson
Creeply/Announcer	Frank Welker
Control Tower Operator/Workman #1/Hipposaurus	Wayne Norton

The Flintstones: Jogging Fever found everyone in Bedrock out for a morning run, except Fred who sat down to a big breakfast. Wilma noted he was getting flabby, but Fred insisted he was still in great shape. Exasperated when all the workers talked about was jogging at their annual company physical, Fred fared poorly and Mr. Slate called him a disgrace, warning him to "shape up or ship out." Vowing to prove he was in shape by becoming the first Bedrock entrant in the big Rockston Marathon, Fred became an overnight celebrity interviewed by reporters and an inspiration to children. Wearing a jacket embroidered "The Stoneage Stallion," Fred hit the road Rocky-style and began training under the eye of his coach, Barney. Tormented by doubt about his endurance, yet determined not to disgrace his family, Fred entered the race but could not stay on course for long. He was straining 10 miles behind several finalists when a turtle passed him, but pushed on to enter the darkened stadium, where matches were lit revealing Wilma and his fans waiting for him. Though he finished last, they considered him a winner for his fortitude and carried him exhausted and asleep back to Bedrock.

The program was one of three in a special prime-time special series aired in October 1981.

FLINTSTONES' LITTLE BIG LEAGUE, THE

Broadcast History
Premiere: April 6, 1978
NBC/Thursday 8:00-9:00 PM
NBC/Repeat: October 10, 1980
Executive Producers: William Hanna, Joseph Barbera
Associate Producer: Neil Balnaves

Director: Chris Cuddington
Writer: Jameson Brewer
Music: Hoyt Curtin, Paul DeKorte
Company: Hanna-Barbera Productions, Sydney, Australia (Southern
    Star Productions)/60 minutes
Distributor: Worldvision Enterprises
Home Video: Worldvision

Principal Characters and Voices

Fred Flintstone	Henry Corden
Barney Rubble/Dino	Mel Blanc
Wilma Flintstone	Jean VanderPyl
Betty Rubble	Gay Hartwig
Pebbles Flintstone	Pamela Anderson
Bamm Bamm Rubble	Frank Welker
Officer	Ted Cassidy
Judge	Herb Vigran
Dusty	Lucille Bliss
Lefty	Randy Gray
Other Voices	Don Messick/John Stephenson

The Flintstones' Little Big League placed old friends Fred and
Barney Rubble on opposing sides, as coaches of competing baseball
teams. After Barney abandoned their weekly bowling game to manage
the little league Sandstone Sluggers, led by his son Bamm Bamm who
slugged every ball out of the park, Fred angrily stormed back home.
Unable to fathom her father's grouchiness, Pebbles asked her mother
what was wrong. "He's suffering from a terrible illness called re-
jection--complicated by chronic and recurring attacks of stabbing
envy," replied Wilma. Called into his boss's office next morning,
Fred was approached by Mr. Slate to coach the Bedrock Broncos, a
small-fry team he sponsored, which had to win the little league world
series "as Judge Slade's son is on the team." Assuring Mr. Slate
the pennant, Fred met with his players and after two grueling hours
had assigned each to the bench. After scouting the opposition and
convinced his team were hapless losers, panicky Fred realized that
his own daughter might be the answer when he watched her catch a
foul ball and pitch it back in to the catcher's mitt. On the eve of
the big game, a suspicious Fred and Barney spent the night keeping
an eye on each other, but finally fell asleep. Awakening, they
rushed to the park where the game had already begun with Wilma
and Betty as coaches. The game ended in a tie, and star pitcher
Pebbles and slugger Bamm Bamm climbed into the stands to tell their
fathers, who were sound asleep. The special slipped in a moral on
fair play and how effort, not the final result, was the most important
quality to cherish and pass on to progeny.

FLINTSTONES MEET ROCKULA AND FRANKENSTONE, THE

Broadcast History
    Premiere: October 3, 1980

NBC/Friday 8:00-9:00 PM
NBC/Repeat: August 8, 1982
Executive Producers: William Hanna, Joseph Barbera
Producer: Alex Lovy
Associate Producer: Neil Balnaves
Directors: Ray Patterson, Chris Cuddington
Writer: Willie Gilbert
Music: Hoyt Curtin, Paul DeKorte
Company: Hanna-Barbera Productions, Sydney, Australia (Southern
　Star Productions)/60 minutes
Distributor: Worldvision Enterprises
Home Video: Worldvision

Principal Characters and Voices

Fred Flintstone	Henry Corden
Wilma Flintstone/Frau G.	Jean VanderPyl
Barney Rubble	Mel Blanc
Betty Rubble	Gay Autterson
Count Rockula	John Stephenson
Frankenstone	Ted Cassidy
Monty Marble	Casey Kasem
Igor/Wolf	Don Messick
Silica/Bat	Lennie Weinrib

The Flintstones Meet Rockula and Frankenstone opened with Fred,
Wilma and the Rubbles decked out in crazy outfits, hoping to be
prize-winners on Monty Marble's "Make a Deal or Don't," filmed in
downtown Bedrock. Fred and Wilma won a romantic trip to Rockysl-
vania and a stay at Count Rockula's castle, and Barney and Betty
gave up their prize money to accompany them. The foursome arrived just in time for the monster ball featuring a mob of people
clad in bizarre costumes gyrating to disco music. Wandering down
to the subterranean lab, Fred and Barney found Frankenstone, who
suddenly awakened from his 500-year sleep and raised his creator,
Count Rockula, who scared all the guests away except for the Flintstones and the Rubbles, who had retired earlier. While Fred and
Barney sneaked down to grab a snack, the Count mistook Wilma for
his old bride and carted her down a secret passage. After they
found Wilma, disguised as a mummy to avoid her captor, they all
skinnied down a sheet-rope and escaped after being chased by the
monster. Trying to stop them, Count Rockula flew on ahead but
believed it time to retire after Barney's imitation rooster-crow, "Yabba
Dabba Doo!" Happy to be home and over their scary adventure,
Wilma was in the kitchen when a bat flew through the window and
the transformed Count appeared to offer her a beautiful life full of
riches. As the crafty Wilma enumerated all the duties the married
Count would have to perform, Rockula shrank to bat-size and flew
off in fright.

FLINTSTONES' NEW NEIGHBORS, THE

Broadcast History
  Premiere: September 26, 1980
  NBC/Friday 8:00-8:30 PM
Executive Producers: William Hanna, Joseph Barbera
Producer: Alex Lovy
Director: Carl Urbano
Writer: Willie Gilbert
Music: Hoyt Curtin, Paul DeKorte
Company: Hanna-Barbera Productions
Distributor: Worldvision Enterprises

Principal Characters and Voices

Fred Flintstone/Scorpion	Henry Corden
Wilma Flintstone/Pebbles	Jean VanderPyl
Barney Rubble/Dino	Mel Blanc
Betty Rubble	Gay Autterson
Bamm Bamm/Vulture	Don Messick
Frank Frankenstone/Rockelle	John Stephenson
Oblivia Frankenstone	Pat Parris
Stubby Frankenstone	Jim McGeorge
Hidea Frankenstone	Julie McWhirter
Creeply/Mother Pterodactyl	Frank Welker
Pterodactyl Chicks	Don Messick/Mel Blanc/Frank Welker

The Flintstones' New Neighbors introduced a gruesome family who
moved their creepy looking house on a lot next door to Fred and
Wilma. Furious and believing the neighborhood was going to the
dinos, Fred wanted nothing to do with the clan, but Wilma insisted
they welcome their new neighbors. Frank Frankenstone, a mon-
strously big fellow with large neck bolts, greeted the Flintstones and
invited them into a grotesquely furnished home where they witnessed
his wife, Oblivia, making new curtains with a spider; their son,
Stubby, digging graves in the cellar; and their teenage daughter,
Hidea, playing her record "Cemetery Serenade" at full blast. When
Oblivia asked their maid Rockelle to serve refreshments, a huge
hairy arm stretched out from the kitchen to present Fred with a
tray of sautéed scorpion and one tidbit bit Fred on the nose. Parting company with the Rubbles because he wanted to drive the Frankenstones away, Fred refused to go picnicking with them at the Washington's Birthday outing. When Pebbles wandered away and fell over
a cliff unharmed into a pterodactyl's nest, Barney finally lured the
mother bird away as Frank helped Fred rescue her. After their
hairbreadth escape from the pterodactyl, Fred apologized to everyone and heartily accepted the Frankenstones as friends.
    The special, along with The Flintstones Meet Rockula and Frank-
enstone [q.v.], preceded the November 22, 1980 debut of The
Frankenstones as a component of the Saturday morning series, The
Flintstones Comedy Show (NBC, 1980-1982), described in Children's
Television, Part I (Scarecrow, 1983), pp. 103-109.

FLINTSTONES' 25TH ANNIVERSARY CELEBRATION, THE

Broadcast History
    Premiere: May 20, 1986
    CBS/Tuesday 8:00-9:00 PM
Executive Producers: William Hanna, Joseph Barbera, Joe Taritero
Producers: Robert Guenette, Peter Wood
Producer/Animation: Gerard Baldwin
Associate Producer: Fred Rosen
Director: Robert Guenette
Directors/Animation: Frank Adrina, Oliver "Lefty" Callahan, Robert
    Goe, Richard Leon, Jay Sarbry
Writers: Tom Ruegger, John K. Ludin, Charles M. Howell IV
Music: Hoyt Curtin, Tom Worral, Ron Jones
Company: Hanna-Barbera Productions with Robert Guenette Produc-
    tions/60 minutes

Cast
    Tim Conway
    Harvey Korman
    Vanna White

Principal Characters and Voices
Fred Flintstone   Alan Reed/Henry Corden
Wilma Flintstone   Jean VanderPyl
Barney Rubble   Mel Blanc
Betty Rubble   Bea Benaderet
Yogi Bear/Huckleberry Hound/
    Quick Draw McGraw   Daws Butler
Scooby-Doo/Scrappy-Doo   Don Messick

The Flintstones' 25th Anniversary Celebration saluted the silver
jubilee of the popular Stone Age family with nostalgic clips from
past episodes and new animation featuring the characters. Live-
action segments starring Tim Conway, Harvey Korman and Vanna
White served to introduce the cartoon scenes; Conway as an archeolo-
gist discovered cave paintings of Fred Flintstone and Barney Rubble,
and as a college professor explored the origins of the phrase "Yabba
Dabba Doo!" with a classroom of not-so-attentive Hanna-Barbera
characters, Yogi Bear and others, and documented a list of Fred
Flintstone firsts including fire and his split-level cave. In "60 Sand-
Pebbles," the paradigm of Stone Age investigative reporting, clips
and interviews with Fred and Wilma Flintstone provided an in-depth
look at their marriage over the years, which Wilma described as "a
two-way street, filled with potholes." As reporter Diane Sawstone,
Vanna White moderated the segment, "The World's First Family."
Bowling buddies Conway and Korman knocked over a few pins while
reminiscing about their old pals Fred and Barney, roasting everything
from Fred's wardrobe to Barney's short stature. And lastly, Fred
and Wilma donned evening wear to highlight their 25 years together
via flashbacks and drove off with Betty and Barney beneath a bright

prehistoric moon as they looked forward to another 25 years. Songs: "[We're] The Flintstones" (Theme), "Listen to the Rockin' Bird," "Yabba Dabba Doo!" (Fred), "Do You Remember?" (Fred and Wilma).

FLINTSTONES: WIND-UP WILMA, THE

Broadcast History
    Premiere: October 4, 1981
    NBC/Sunday 7:00-7:30 PM
    NBC/Repeat: March 7, 1982
Executive Producers: William Hanna, Joseph Barbera
Producer: Alex Lovy
Associate Producer: Doug Paterson
Directors: Carl Urbano, Geoffrey Collins
Writer: Len Janson
Music: Hoyt Curtin, Paul DeKorte
Company: Hanna-Barbera Productions
Distributor: Worldvision Enterprises

Principal Characters and Voices

Fred Flintstone/Turtle #2/	
Elephant	Henry Corden
Wilma Flintstone/Pebbles/	
Clothespin Bird	Jean VanderPyl
Barney Rubble/Dino/Crook #2	Mel Blanc
Betty Rubble/Female Cop/	
Cuckoo Bird	Gay Autterson
Frank Frankenstone/Animal/ La	
Shale/ Rocky	Julie McWhirter
Announcer/Bird #1/Turtle #1	Don Messick
Mean/Checker/Crook #1	Joe Baker
Stub/Cop	Jim McGeorge
Sheep/Rooster/Umpire/Reporter	
#1/Thief/1st Man/Voice	Paul Winchell
Creeply/Bird #2/Finrock	Frank Welker

The Flintstones: Wind-Up Wilma made Fred's wife a temporary bread-winner and celebrity when she angrily pitched a melon, beaning two thiefs making off with her grocery money at the supermarket. The whole town watched her on the TV news, including Bedrock Dodger owner Charley Finrock and manager Tommy La Shale, who decided a lady pitcher might boost their poorly attended baseball games. Until he learned they had offered her 1,000 clams, chauvinistic Fred refused to let her join the team. Reluctantly, he stayed home to watch Pebbles while Wilma reported for practice. Amazing the coaches with ten perfect pitches, Wilma went home to rest up for the next day's game. Exhausted after caring for Pebbles and the Frankenstone's monstrous children, Fred schemed with Dino and Pebbles, to no avail, to keep Wilma awake all night and too tired to play. Despite their efforts, she was called in the ninth inning to face the biggest, toughest hitter in baseball and struck him out to help the Dodgers win the game. A delighted Fred's pride was hurt when reporters refered to him only in passing as her husband. Then as Wilma demonstrated her pitching technique she seized her cramped arm and claimed she had developed "pitcher's elbow," telling Fred she could never play again. Of course, the family was glad to have her back. Later, when Wilma stopped another robbery at the supermarket with her famous melon wind-up, Fred realized that she had sacrificed her promising baseball career for his sake. Exuberantly, Fred called her "the greatest," and together they escaped and headed home before the reporters arrived.

FLUPPY DOGS   see   DISNEY'S FLUPPY DOGS

FOR BETTER OR FOR WORSE: THE BESTEST PRESENT

Broadcast History
    Premiere: December 9, 1985
    CTV/Monday 7:30-8:00 PM
    CTV/Repeat: December 19, 1986
    HBO/Repeats: multiple option, December 1-23, 1986
    CRC/Repeat: LE PLUS BEAU DES CADEAUX, December 26, 1986,
        Friday 4:30-5:00 PM
    SYN/Repeats: 1986 +
Executive Producer: William H. Stevens, Jr.
Producer: Hugh Campbell
Associate Producer: Alison Clayton
Director: Sebastian Grunstra
Writer/Creator: Lynn Johnston
Music/Songs & Lyrics: Bob Chimbel, Merry Chimbel
Music: Gary David Morton
Company: Atkinson Film-Arts, Ottawa, Canada, in association with
    Telefilm Canada
Distributor: Crawleys International/1986-
Home Video: Family Home Entertainment

Principal Characters and Voices

Michael Patterson	Aaron Johnston
Elizabeth "Lizzy" Patterson	Katherine Johnston
Elly Patterson	Abby Hagyard
John Patterson	William H. Stevens, Jr.
Walter Lederhaus	Billy Van
Connie	Anna MacCormick
Lawrence	Dominic Bradford
Farley (the sheepdog)	

Vocalist: Scott Binkley

For Better or for Worse: The Bestest Present portrayed the mini-catastrophes of an average family's Christmas adventure. In the midst of a heavy storm, housewife Elly Patterson bundled her two children, Michael and Lizzy, into the family car for a trip to busy Philpott's department store and some holiday shopping. During the frenzied gift-hunting, three-year-old Lizzy lost her favorite stuffed-bunny and was heart-broken. Attempting to locate the toy, brother Michael placed an ad in the lost-and-found column of the local paper. A lonely, embittered widower, Walter Lederhaus, an elderly night-watchman at the store, retrieved the bunny and rediscovered the meaning of a family Christmas in a touching celebration when he accepted John and Elly Pattersons' invitation to share Christmas dinner. The special was based on cartoonist Lynn Johnston's syndicated comic strip for the Universal Press Syndicate. Songs: "For Better or For Worse" (Theme), "Oh, Little Girl of Mine," "First Day of Snow."

FOURTH KING, THE

Broadcast History
Premiere: December 23, 1977
NBC/Friday 8:30-9:00 PM
Executive Producer: Renato M. Pachetti
Producers: Alvin Cooperman, Bruno Caliandro
Writers: Alvin Cooperman, Seymour Reit
Music: Ralph Affoumado, Eddie Sauter, Elliot Lawrence
Lyrics: Alvin Cooperman
Company: RAI Television Productions, Italy, in association with NBC

Principal Characters and Voices
Lion	Ted Ross
Sparrow	Laurie Beechman
Turtle	Arnold Stang
Beaver	Bob McFadden
Rabbit	Ed Klein

The Fourth King explained how the animal kingdom discovered and celebrated the birth of Christ, complete with original songs created for the occasion. Produced for the Christmas season and originally televised in Italy on RAI Television, the voices were redubbed in English for its NBC debut.

FREEDOM IS

Broadcast History
Premiere: Summer 1976
SYN/local station option
Sponsors: Reader's Digest, McDonald's, Wrigley Gum
Executive Producer: Martin J. Neeb, Jr.
Production Executive: Rev. Ardon D. Albrecht
Writer: Don Hall

Music: Jimmy Haskell
Lyrics: Don Hinchey
Company: Screen Images for Lutheran Television
Distributor: International Lutheran Layman's League/1985-

Principal Characters and Voices

Benji	David Kelly
Jeremiah Goodheart	Jonathan Winters
Samuel	Richard Roundtree
Ben Franklin	Joseph Cotton
John Adams	Edward Asner
Thomas Jefferson	Dan Dailey
Jason	Philip Morris
Waldo (Benji's dog)	

Freedom Is transported young Benji and his dog Waldo back to the Revolutionary War via a dream sequence. Benji and Waldo met Jeremiah Goodheart, who had been entrusted with a letter to deliver to the Second Continental Congress in Philadelphia. The letter, meant for John Adams, explained that the British were in Boston Harbor and that a quick decision was needed on whether the colonies would declare themselves independent. Because of his haste, Jeremiah lost the letter, and Benji volunteered to search for it, aided by his new friend, the slave boy Jason. The two discovered the letter on a bridge and after it was delivered to Jeremiah, Benji asked Thomas Jefferson if this meant that Jason and his father Samuel would be set free. Jefferson explained that he had written against slavery in the first draft of the declaration but that some delegates believed they would lose too much money if they freed their slaves. He urged Benji to keep the spirit of freedom alive so that someday Samuel and Jason could also be free. Benji returned with a lesson that freedom was still growing and that it was up to persons like himself to help continue its growth. Songs: "Freedom Is," "The Search," "Freedom Is, March."

The special was the only national TV program for the 1976 Bicentennial Celebration sponsored by a national religous denomination. The $200,000 for the film was funded totally by the children and youth of the Lutheran Church, Missouri Synod.

FROM THE EARTH TO THE MOON

Broadcast History
    Premiere: c1976
    SYN/local station option
Producer: Walter J. Hucker
Director: Richard Slapczynski
Writer: John Palmer
Music: Richard Bowden
Company: Air Programs International, Sydney, Australia/60 minutes
Distributor: D. L. Taffner ("Animated Classics for Children")/1985-

Voices
    Alistair Duncan, Ron Haddrick, Phillip Hinton, Shane Porteous

From the Earth to the Moon was Jules Verne's adventurous account of the Gun Club and their attempt to reach the moon with a projectile fired from an extremely long cannon. Set just after the Civil War, the Frenchman Michel Arden, president of the club General Barbicane and his rival Captain Nicholl manned the "vessel." Transcending the earth's atmosphere, the crew took delight in the discovery of weightlessness. But forced to alter their course by a meteor, they were dismayed to discover that they had to land on the dark side of the moon, where they encountered smoking volcanos, sulphuric air and the ruins of a once magnificent city. Chased by monsterous robots, they boarded their craft and sped back to earth, crashing into the ocean, where they were rescued and given a hero's welcome. The flight was envisaged by Verne more than 100 years before Apollo 11 landed on the moon.

FROSTY THE SNOWMAN

Broadcast History
    Premiere: December 7, 1969
    CBS/Sunday 7:30-8:00 PM
    Sponsors: Kodak, Swift & Company
    CBS/Repeats: December 5, 1970; December 5, 1971; December 4,
        1972; December 10, 1973; December 8, 1974; December 12,
        1975; December 17, 1976; December 10, 1977; November 30,
        1978; December 8, 1979; November 28, 1980; November 27,
        1981; December 21, 1982; December 14, 1983; December 11,
        1984; December 7, 1985; December 12, 1986
Producers/Directors: Arthur Rankin, Jr., Jules Bass
Writer: Romeo Muller
Music & Lyrics/Title Song: Jack Rollins, Steve Nelson
Music: Maury Laws
Lyrics: Jules Bass
Company: Rankin-Bass Productions
Distributor: Viacom Enterprises/1987-
Record Album: MGM SE 4733

Narrator
Jimmy Durante   Jimmy Durante

Principal Characters and Voices
Frosty   Jackie Vernon
Professor Hinkle   Billy De Wolfe
Karen   June Foray
Santa Claus   Paul Frees

Frosty the Snowman presented the happy-go-lucky character "who came to life one day." It was Christmas Eve, and the children had built a snowman with a corncob pipe, button nose and two eyes made of coal. Topping him off with a magic hat that belonged to an unsuccessful magician, suddenly the youngsters found him alive, transformed from a lifeless snow figure into a lovable song-and-dance man. Threatened with a meltdown by rising temperatures, Frosty sought the safety of colder climes via train, pursued by the villainous Professor Hinkle who wanted back his magic hat. Accompanied by Karen, his little benefactress, Frosty weathered a string of mishaps enroute and the schemes of Hinkle to safely arrive at the North Pole for a joyous meeting with Santa Claus, who promised Hinkle a new hat if he mended his wicked ways. Jimmy Durante appeared as an animated character to narrate the film and sing the many new verses to the song, written by Jack Rollins and Steve Nelson. Song/ Theme: "Frosty the Snowman" (Durante).

Broadcast annually since 1969, the special is the fourth animated Yuletide classic, following Rudolph, the Red-Nosed Reindeer [q.v.], A Charlie Brown Christmas [q.v.] and Dr. Seuss' How the Grinch Stole Christmas [q.v.]. Frosty was also featured in two other films, Frosty's Winter Wonderland [q.v.] and Rudolph and Frosty [q.v.].

FROSTY'S WINTER WONDERLAND

Broadcast History
  Premiere: December 2, 1976
  ABC/Thursday 8:00-8:30 PM
  Sponsor: Parker Brothers
  ABC/Repeats: December 3, 1977; December 13, 1978; November
    25, 1979; December 23, 1981; December 1, 1982
  SYN/Repeats: 1986 +
Producers/Directors: Arthur Rankin, Jr., Jules Bass
Writer: Romeo Muller
Music: Maury Laws
Lyrics: Jules Bass
Company: Rankin-Bass Productions with animation by Toru Hara and
  Tsuguyuki Kubo
Distributor: Lorimar Syndication ("Animated Holiday Specials)/1986-
Home Video: Lightning Video (with LEPRECHAUN'S CHRISTMAS GOLD)

Narrator: Andy Griffith

Principal Characters and Voices

Frosty	Jackie Vernon
Crystal the Snowgirl	Shelley Winters
Jack Frost	Paul Frees
Parson	Dennis Day
Children/Others	Shelley Hines
	Eric Stern
	Manfred Olea
	Barbara Jo Ewing

Vocalists: The Wee Winter Singers

FROSTY'S WINTER WONDERLAND. © 1976, Rankin/Bass Productions, Inc. Courtesy of Rankin/Bass Productions and Lorimar Syndication.

Frosty's Winter Wonderland starred the holiday season's favorite snow-man, who decided to vacation in the more hospitable South. It was lonely up there at the North Pole, and Frosty wanted to join his friends. Aiming to please, the young children built him a snowgirl, Crystal. The two happy snow people fell in love and were preparing to marry when angry Jack Frost, left alone at the North Pole, played a dirty trick on the pair and froze Frosty lifeless. But Crystal brought him to life when she gently bussed him on the cheek. Quickly, the children built a snowparson to marry the pair, and Jack Frost, overjoyed to get away from his bleak post, turned up as best man at Crystal's suggestion. Frosty took Crystal as his wife and, in the happy ending, they returned to the North Pole along with Jack. The special was a musical sequel to Frosty the Snowman [q.v.]. Songs: "Frosty the Snowman," "Winter Wonderland" (Griffith & Cast).

GARFIELD GOES HOLLYWOOD

Broadcast History
    Premiere: May 8, 1987
    CBS/Friday 8:00-8:30 PM
    Sponsor: McDonald's, Carnation
Producer/Director: Phil Roman
Writer/Creator: Jim Davis

Music & Lyrics: Ed Bogas, Desiree Goyette
Company: Film Roman in association with United Media

Principal Characters and Voices

Garfield	Lorenzo Music
Jon Arbuckle	Thom Huge
Odie/Bob/Grandma Fogerty/	
Announcer	Gregg Berger
Herbie	Nino Tempo
M.C.	Frank Welker

Vocalists
Desiree Goyette, Thom Huge, Lorenzo Music, Lou Rawls

Garfield Goes Hollywood provided the pasta-loving fat cat a chance
at fame and fortune when he joined with Jon and his dog Odie to
enter a local TV contest.   In a rare display of team spirit, the self-
centered Garfield, who could barely tolerate his perennial optimistic
owner and his gushy well-meaning dog, became a member of their
makeshift 1950s rock 'n' roll trio, Johnny Bop and the Two-Steps.
Up against such competition as five tap-dancing pigeons, Mountain
Man Dan and his dog Blue, Pierre and his talking parrot, and a
clumsy roller-skating bear, they entered WBOR-TV's "Pet Search,"
which offered $1,000 to the most talented animal act.   Amazingly,
they won and headed for Hollywood and the national "Pet Search"
finals, offering a top prize of one million dollars, film studio contracts, lavish new homes and other show business accoutrements
Just one look after arriving in Tinseltown and Garfield knew he must
realize his dream, life in the fast lane in the lap of luxury.   With
self-indulgent cunning, he determined to do whatever was necessary
to win the contest, including dumping Jon from the act.   So Garfield
and Odie went it alone as the dancing Armandos against the Lemon
Sisters, four chickens, and the tumbling Garbanzo Brothers, a group
of dogs.   "I didn't know dogs could tumble," said Jon.   "Yeah, but
are they housebroken?" Garfield groused.   Then came the last act,
Desiree the Classical Cat, a feline singer who won the top prize.
Songs: "They Love Us" (Music), "My Dog Blues" (Bogas), "Hollywood Island" (Rawls), "Wizard of Love" (Huge), "Classical Cat"
(Goyette).
     The special was the sixth in the Garfield series, based on the
comic character created by Jim Davis, which began with Here Comes
Garfield [q.v.].   The misanthropic alley cat was born in 1976, two
years before his first comic strip, Garfield the Cat, appeared in
January 1978 for United Feature Syndicate.   By age four, Garfield
ranked with the superstrips and in 1987 was carried in more than
1,900 newspapers worldwide.   Setting a new record, Davis was the
first author ever to have three, four, five, six and then seven Garfield books on a national bestseller list at the same time.   The premiere puss was modeled and named after Davis's Grandfather Garfield,
"a huge, stubborn, opinionated, cantankerous man."

GARFIELD IN PARADISE

Broadcast History
Premiere: May 27, 1986
CBS/Tuesday 8:00-8:30 PM
Sponsor: McDonald's
CBS/Repeat: January 16, 1987
Executive Producer: Jay Poynor
Producer/Director: Phil Roman
Writer/Creator: Jim Davis
Music & Lyrics: Ed Bogas, Desiree Goyette
Company: Film Roman in association with United Media

Principal Characters and Voices

Garfield	Lorenzo Music
Jon Arbuckle	Thom Huge
High Rama Lama	Wolfman Jack
Hotel Clerk/Salesman	Frank Nelson
Odie Pigeon	Gregg Berger
Owooda	Desiree Goyette
Mai Tai/Stewardess	Julie Payne
Monkey	Nino Tempo
Woman/Cat	Carolyn Davis
B.G. Voices	Hal Smith

Vocalists
Desiree Goyette, Thom Huge, Lorenzo Music, Lou Rawls

Garfield in Paradise erupted into a comic calamity when the finicky feline traveled through a timewarp of sorts. Feeling blah and needing a change, Jon decided that a mellow tropical vacation would be just the ticket. With dreams of a plush Hawaiian paradise, his cool cat Garfield joined him. But Paradise World was anything but paradise when Jon and Garfield arrived at the less-than-plush resort and settled in their flea-infested accomodations. And to make matters worse for Garfield, Odie stowed away in his luggage. "I'm traveling third class with a fourth-class owner to a fifth-class motel to sleep with a sixth-class mutt," said the grouchy, cynical cat. His spirits were restored when they visited the tropical village of a remote tribe, the duck-tailed Ding Dongs, whose members remained locked in the benighted year 1957 when they discovered beach movies and began worshipping their cars. In this 1950s rock-and-roll haven of hot-rodding natives, they encountered the tribe's hip leader, the High Rama Lama; Jon found romance with the village princess, Owooda; and Garfield was smitten with her cat Mai Tai. When a rumbling volcano, Honny Looey-Ha, threatened to destroy the village, the High Rama prepared to offer the princess as a sacrifice. But Owooda was rebuffed by the volcano, which only wanted Jon's 1950s rental car, and in the ensuing sacrifice Odie rode it into a fiery fate. Remorseful over the apparent loss of his pal, Garfield and the others rejoiced when Odie climbed out unharmed. Songs: "Aloe Hawaii," "Beauty and the Beach," "It Was You" (Huge), "Chrome" (Rawls), "Orchids" (Goyette), "So Long, Old Friend" (Music).

GARFIELD IN THE ROUGH

Broadcast History
    Premiere: October 26, 1984
    CBS/Friday 8:00-8:30 PM
    Sponsors: McDonald's, Kellogg's
    CBS/Repeats: March 23, 1985, August 21, 1987
Executive Producer: Jay Poynor
Producer/Director: Phil Roman
Writer/Creator: Jim Davis
Music & Lyrics: Ed Bogas, Desiree Goyette
Company: Film Roman in association with United Media

Principal Characters and Voices
Garfield   Lorenzo Music
Jon Arbuckle   Thom Huge
Odie/Ranger #1/Announcer   Gregg Berger
Ranger #2   George Wendt

GARFIELD IN THE ROUGH. © 1984, United Feature Syndicate, Inc. Courtesy of Paws, Inc., Film Roman and United Media.

Dicky Beaver	Hal Smith
Billy Rabbit	Orson Bean
Girl Cats/Arlene	Desiree Goyette

Vocalists
Desiree Goyette, Thom Huge, Lou Rawls

Garfield in the Rough placed the rotund and acerbic feline in an ill-fated adventure in the great outdoors. Bored with their morning routine of coping with the playful Odie, the same old food and their colorless life, Jon suggested they needed a vacation. Fantasizing on a life of sun and surf with a Hawaiian chieftan's daughter, a pretty señorita in Acapulco and a gondola ride with a contessa in Venice, the orange feline was less than enthusiastic over Jon's intended camping junket to Lake Wobegone. Failing to thwart the trip, a reluctant Garfield faced misadventure in what he discerned as a forest primeval, ridden with "inconvenience, dampness, filth and second-rate food." Afraid of the cat-eating animals "out there," the timid tabby met two beasts, Billie the rabbit and Dickie the beaver, but fun turned to fear when he learned that a black panther had escaped from the zoo. Hastening to warn Jon, Garfield and Odie were terrorized when the big cat with yellow eyes pounced on their campsite. Setting his teeth and claws in the animal's back, Garfield was thrown up against a tree by the panther, who was tranquilized by the Forest Ranger's dart just in time to save another of the cat's nine lives. After assuming his hero's role with his usual bluff bravado, Garfield fainted when he opened the door and saw the piercing yellow eyes of a small cat. The special was the third in the series based on Jim Davis's popular newspaper comic. Songs: "In The Rough," "Camping Is My Life," "Fear," "So Long, Old Friend," "R & R," "Music of Nature." Television Academy Emmy award (1984-1985), Outstanding Animation Program.

GARFIELD ON THE TOWN

Broadcast History
    Premiere: October 28, 1983
    CBS/Friday 8:00-8:30 PM
    Sponsors: McDonald's, Kellogg's
    CBS/Repeats: March 10, 1984; December 28, 1985
Executive Producer: Jay Poynor
Producers: Lee Mendelson, Bill Melendez
Director: Phil Roman
Writers: Jim Davis, Lorenzo Music
Music & Lyrics: Ed Bogas, Desiree Goyette, "Home" co-written with
    Roberta Vandervort
Company: In association with United Media. Lee Mendelson-Bill
    Melendez Productions

GARFIELD ON THE TOWN. © 1983, United Feature Syndicate, Inc.
Courtesy of Paws, Inc., Film Roman and United Media.

Principal Characters and Voices

Garfield	Lorenzo Music
Jon Arbuckle	Thom Huge
Raoul	George Wendt
Ali Cat	Gregg Berger
Mom	Sandi Hug
Doc	Julie Payne
Grandfather	Lindsay Workman
Girl Cat #2 & #3	Allyce Beasley
Girl Cat #1	Desiree Goyette
Odie (the dog)	

Vocalists
   Desiree Goyette, Lou Rawls

Garfield on the Town was the second adventure of the orange feline,
who met the toughest, meanest gang of cats around. Watching Garfield and Odie, the dog, playing demolition derby in the living room,
Jon Arbuckle decided that Garfield was hyperactive and it was time
for a visit to the vet. Enroute, Garfield escaped from the car into
the city streets where he tried unsuccessfully to "howl" with three
female cats. Now facing nighttime and forced to scrounge for food,
Garfield prowled the alleys for a choice garbage can but met up with

a tough alley cat, appropriately named Ali, and his gang, the Claws. They chased him into the kitchen of the deserted Italian restaurant where he had been born. There he was reunited with his long-lost mother and his cousins, his brother Raoul and his grandfather, all mousers who put him through a test of his cathood--catching a mouse. But Garfield disdained mice, "Show me a good mouser and I'll show you a cat with bad breath." Besides, "Their tiny little bones might stick in my throat." After a lookout spotted the Claws, who wanted the orange "lardball," the mousers decided to fight and won the ensuing rumble. Far from brave and not one of their kind, Garfield was asked to leave. "You wouldn't survive here. You have a good life, an easy life. We all envy you," said his mother sadly. Meanwhile, Jon and Odie, searching for Garfield, found the despondent cat in a rainstorm and took him home where he feasted on lasagne. After he was tucked in bed, his mother appeared at the window, and spotting her as she scurried away, Garfield shouted, "Thanks Mom, for everything!" Songs: "Just Another Crazy Day," "Startin' From Scratch," "Home," "We Bad." Television Academy Emmy award (1983-1984), Outstanding Animation Program.

GARFIELD'S HALLOWEEN ADVENTURE

Broadcast History
   Premiere: October 30, 1985
   CBS/Wednesday 8:00-8:30 PM
   Sponsor: McDonald's
   CBS/Repeat: October 24, 1986
Executive Producer: Jay Poyner
Producer/Director: Phil Roman
Writer/Creator: Jim Davis
Music: Ed Bogas, Desiree Goyette
Company: Film Roman in association with United Media

Principal Characters and Voices

Garfield	Lorenzo Music
Jon Arbuckle/Binky the Clown	Thom Huge
Odie/TV Announcer	Gregg Berger
Old Man	Lindsay Workman
Woman	Desiree Goyette

Vocalists
   Lorenzo Music, Lou Rawls

Garfield's Halloween Adventure was a tale of greed and ghosts on the favorite holiday of the all-too-human comic-strip cat. "It's not like those other stupid holidays," he explained, "there's no dumb bunny, no fireworks, no relatives, just candy, candy, candy...." After watching Binky the Clown on TV, the greed-inspired Garfield enlisted Odie the dog for some trick-or-treating, hoping for two bags of goodies instead of one. Searching through Jon's attic for an

GARFIELD'S HALLOWEEN ADVENTURE. © 1985, United Feature
Courtesy of Paws, Inc., Film Roman and United Media.

appropriate costume, Garfield outfitted himself as Orange Beard the
Pirate Cap'n and Odie as "me First Mate." Hitting the sidewalks of
suburbia, "Lootin' always be a good time," growled the feline pirate,
and we've "gotta village to pillage." Commandeering a rowboat to
reach the homes on the other side of the river, the mates were soon
shipwrecked and forced to take refuge in a haunted house on an eerie
island. "You've picked a poor night to come visiting, my friends,"
said their ethereal host, an old man who warned them about the 100-
year-old pirates' treasure "they" were returning for at midnight.
Consumed with fright, the pair hid from their ghostly pursuers,
prompting Garfield to promise that if they ever got back to land,
"I'm going to give up this pirate business" and "stop pretending I'm
something I'm not." Return they did after Odie saved Garfield from
near drowning and Garfield returned the pirates' treasure ring he
had filched. Safe at home after their harrowing escapade, Garfield,
at great personal sacrifice, gave Odie half his candy. Songs: "This
Is the Night," "Scaredy Cat" (Rawls), "What'll I Be?" (Music). Television Academy Emmy award (1985-1986), Outstanding Animation Program.

GET ALONG GANG, THE see ADVENTURES OF THE GET ALONG
    GANG, THE

GLO FRIENDS SAVE CHRISTMAS, THE

Broadcast History
    Premiere: 1985
    SYN/local station option (KTLA, Los Angeles, November 29, 1985,
        Friday 7:00-7:30 PM PST)
    SYN/Repeats: 1986 +
Executive Producers: Joe Bacal, Tom Griffin, John Claster, Margaret
    Ann Loesch
Producers: Mike Joens, Lee Gunther
Writer: George Arthur Bloom
Music: Tommy Goodman
Lyrics: Barry Harman
Company: Sunbow Productions in association with Marvel Productions
Distributor: Claster TV Productions/1985-
Home Video: Children's Video Library (Vestron)

Principal Characters and Voices
Santa Claus   Carroll O'Connor
Blanche, Wicked Witch of North
    Pole   Sally Struthers

Other Voices
    Charlie Adler, Jill Choder, Townsend Coleman, Laura Dean, Pat
    Fraley, Ellen Gerstell, Renae Jacobs, Mona Marshall, Michael Mich,
    Lorenzo Music, Laurie O'Brien, Patti Parris, Susan Silo, Frank
    Welker

The GLO Friends Save Christmas began on Christmas Eve as the little
creatures who gave off a friendly glow were preparing for the Yule
festivities in Gloland. Meantime, Blanche, the Wicked Witch of the
North Pole, hatched a fiendish plot to stop Santa from delivering his
sleigh of goodies. As she told Moose, disgruntled because Santa did
not pick him to pull his sleigh, "From this night forth, I'll be known
as the Witch who stopped Christmas!" Using her Icicle Wand to brew
up snowstorms, hailstorms and rainstorms to no avail, in desperation
she cast a spell on the forest and like gnarled fingers the trees plucked
Santa and his reindeer out of the sky. Blanche imprisoned them in
an icicle cage. Glo Friends Shuttlebug and Dragonflyer witnessed
Santa's plight and raced back to Gloland where a search party was
organized. Splitting into two groups, the Glo Friends, led by Dragonflyer, found the banished turncoat Moose with his antlers entangled
in the trees while Gloworm and his Glo Friends were swallowed up
by some bewitched Ice Flowers. Rescued by Dragonflyer, together
Gloworm and all the Glo Friends reached Santa's cage, led by the
grateful freed Moose. Glowing as hard as they could, they melted
the ice beneath Blanche, tossing her into the drink, and Glohopper
caught her Icicle Wand, which melted in his hand as Santa's cage
turned to water. With Moose helping to pull the sleigh and the Glo
Friends lighting a path through the night sky, Santa Claus continued
on his appointed rounds. Songs: "Say Goodbye to Christmas," "The

What If There's No Christmas Blues?" "A Time To Be Brave," "Glow, Everybody Glow!"
The special reunited the voices of Carroll O'Connor and Sally Struthers, remembered as Archie Bunker and daughter Gloria on All in the Family (CBS, 1971-1983). A series, GLO Friends, was distributed as a component of the 65-episode weekday-strip series, My Little Pony and Friends (SYN, 1986-). The GLO Friends characters were adapted from the Hasbro toy line.

GNOMES

Broadcast History
    Premiere: November 11, 1980
    CBS/Tuesday 8:00-9:00 PM
    CBS/Repeats: August 28, 1982; August 27, 1983
    SYN/Repeats: 1984 +
Executive Producers: Thomas W. Moore, Anne E. Upson
Producer/Director: Jack Zander
Writers: Sam Moore, Maurice Rapf
Music: Neil Warner
Lyrics: Phyllis Levinson
Company: Zanders Animation Parlor in association with Tomorrow
    Entertainment/60 minutes
Distributor: DFS Program Exchange/1984-
Home Video: Magic Window (RCA/COL #60640)

Narrator: Lee Richardson

Voices
    Arthur Anderson, Rex Everhart, Anne Francine, Hetty Galen,
    Gordon Halliday, Bob McFadden, Corrinne Orr, Joe Silver

The Gnomes, the six-inch, ten-ounce peace-loving woodland creatures, battled their archenemies the villainous Trolls in this fantasy film. Known as "friends to all, man and mice alike," the heroes' life-span was 400 years. Arrayed against them were the Trolls, "loathsome creatures who are never happier than when they're thundering about, smashing and causing trouble." The story centered on one woodland Gnome family and the impending marriage of their eldest son, who was 101 years old, finally old enough to tie the knot. But the prospective groom and his bride were kidnapped by the Trolls, setting the stage for a knockdown battle that ensued. On the Gnomes side were such friendly woodfolk as a boar, bear, birds and beaver, who came to their aid. Based loosely on the Netherlands book by Wil Huygen and illustrator Rien Poortvliet, the special was enhanced by spirited original music.

GOLDILOCKS

Broadcast History
    Premiere: March 31, 1970
    NBC/Tuesday 8:30-9:00 PM
    Sponsors: E & B Carpet Mills; Sun Maid
    NBC/Repeat: October 24, 1970
Producers: David H. DePatie, Friz Freleng
Co-Producers: Richard M. Sherman, Robert B. Sherman
Associate Producer: Walter N. Bien
Director/Live Action: Marc Breaux
Director/Animation: Lee Mishkin
Writer: A. J. Carothers
Music/Songs & Lyrics: Richard M. Sherman, Robert B. Sherman
Music: Doug Goodwin
Company: DePatie-Freleng-Mirisch Productions in association with
    NBC
Record Album: Disneyland 3511
Home Video: In Release

Principal Characters and Voices

Goldilocks	Mary Frances Crosby
Papa Bear	Bing Crosby
Mama Bear	Kathryn Crosby
Baby Bear	Nathaniel Crosby
Bobcat	Paul Winchell
Others	Avery Schreiber

Goldilocks combined touching pleas for both brotherhood and a respect for nature in this live-action and animated updating of the
"Goldilocks and the Three Bears" fairytale.   While on a camping trip
with her family, Mary Frances Crosby fell asleep and dreamed she
was Goldilocks, with the other Crosby family members voicing the
family of animated-cartoon bears.   It was a swinging place, where
Papa Bear played golf, but her incursion in the woodlands alarmed
the other animals, afraid more humans would follow.   A ruckus developed when a militant bobcat led a protest march on the golf links
over concern for human encroachment on the environment.   Papa
Bear reconciled their concern with his persuasion for a peaceful
brotherhood of animals and humans to share responsibility for the
ecology.   At the close Mary awoke to find herself with her real family
in the woods.   Songs: "Take a Longer Look" (Bing), "Don't Settle
For Less" (Mary).

GREAT BEAR SCARE, THE

Broadcast History
    Premiere: October 1982
    SYN/local station option
Executive Producer: Thomas A. Mayfield

Producer: Mary L. Roscoe
Director: Hal Mason
Writer: John Barrett
Music: William Loose, Edward Yelin
Company: DimenMark Films
Distributor: WesternWorld Television/1986-
Home Video: Family Home Entertainment

Principal Characters and Voices

Ted E. Bear	Tom Smothers
Patti Bear	Sue Raney
Professor Werner Von Bear	Hans Conreid
Dracula	Louis Nye
C. Emory Bear	Hal Smith
Miss Witch	Lucille Bliss
Luther (Miss Witch's cat)	

The Great Bear Scare found everyone in Bearbank, a unique community carved out of the forest, preparing for the upcoming Halloween festivities. Some miles to the north, a group of characters on foreboding Monster Mountain were hatching a nasty plot. This year Count Dracula, his secretary Miss Witch, Luther, her green-eyed cat, and assorted goblins, ghouls and weirdos decided to terrorize the residents of Bearbank, noted for its Organic Honeyworks, and ruin their holidays. Heeding rumors about this menace, the residents selected the green polka-dot tie wearing Theodore Edward Bear, Ted E. Bear to all who knew him, to find out what the dastardly bunch in their computerized War Room were up to. Ted worked for the Bureau of Bear Affairs, a busy "bearocracy" headed by C. Emory Bear, that looked after things bears could do nothing about. He sought the advice of a quiet philosopher, Bum Bear, Superintendent of Flowers at Honey Acres, and the learned Werner Von Bear, Professor of Probabilities at Grizzly University. Ted's special friend, Patti Bear, Anchorbear for the KBAR-TV "Bear Witness News," was assigned to cover the event. Naturally, all ended happily with Ted E. Bear a local hero after putting Bearbank's fears to rest and underscoring the moral that the only thing to be feared is fear itself.

The Honorary Chairbear for the National Kidney Foundation, Ted E. Bear was also featured in The Bear Who Slept Through Christmas [q.v.].

GREAT CHRISTMAS RACE, THE

Broadcast History
   Premiere: 1986
   SYN/local station option (KABC, Los Angeles, November 11, 1986,
      Sunday 9:30-10:00 AM PST)
   SYN/Repeats: 1987 +
Executive Producer: Philip Kent
Producer: Robert Halmi

Co-Producer/Creator: Roger Himmel
Associate Producers: Dan Martin, Denise Sickinger
Writer: Venable Herndon
Music: Irwin Fisch, Alan Sneeling
Lyrics: Guy Mazzeo, Roger Himmel
Company: Blair Entertainment in association with Pannonia Film,
  Budapest, Hungary
Distributor: Blair Entertainment/1986-

Principal Characters and Voices

Lollipop Dragon	Gary Wilmot
Princess Gwendolyn	Jill Lidstone
Prince Hubert	Pat Starr
Blue Eyes	Karen Fernald
Glider/Queen	Eva Hadden
Baron Bad Blood	Stephen Thorne
Cosmo the Cunning/King	Dennis Greashan
Cuddles	(non-speaking)

The Great Christmas Race squared-off the Lollipop Dragon against
Baron Bad Blood in an event where victory could mean that the
world would be filled with liver-flavored lollipops at Christmastime.
A large creature with a great green tummy, the Lollipop Dragon
dwelled in Tumtum, a medieval-fantasy land where the major industry
was a lollipop factory. His best friends were the children of the
King and Queen, Princess Gwendolyn and Prince Hubert, and three
baby dragons, Blue Eyes, Glider and Cuddles. They were pitted
against the evil knight, Baron Bad Blood, and his henchman, Cosmo
the Cumming. Released from a spell and no longer a part of the
forest, the Baron entered an annual race in Tumtum which rewarded
the winner with an etching of his face on a commemorative Christmas
lollipop in the flavor of his choosing. And the Baron's favorite flavor
was liver. Setting out to win at any cost and using the foulest means
he could muster, the Baron was finally thwarted by the Lollipop Dragon and his friends, who saved the Lollipop Factory from ruin and
children everywhere from decades of foul-tasting confections.
    The special was based on "The Lollipop Dragon," an animated-
filmstrip character used as a classroom teaching aid, under license
from the Lollipop Dragon Trust and introduced in The Magic Lollipop
Adventure [q.v.].

GREAT EXPECTATIONS

Broadcast History
    Premiere: Fall 1984
    SYN/local station option
Executive Producers: Tom Stacey, George Stephenson
Producer: Eddy Graham
Director: Jean Tych
Writer: Alex Buzo

Music: Richard Bowden, Billy Burton
Company: Burbank Films, Sydney, Australia/90 minutes
Distributor: Twentieth-Century Fox Television ("Charles Dickens
    Classics")/1984-

Voices
    Barbara Frawley, Marcus Hale, Philip Hinton, Simon Hinton, Liz
    Horne, Bill Kerr, Moya O'Sullivan, Robin Stewart

Great Expectations, adapted from the 1861 novel by Charles Dickens,
followed Philip (Pip) Pirrip through a series of fateful circumstances
as he changed from a boy of false standards to a man of character.
Orphaned as a boy, Pip's great expectations were realized when he
was given a fortune by an unknown benefactor. Forsaking his humb-
ler friends, Pip moved to London to become a gentleman but fell into
misfortune over bad debts. After being saved by his brother-in-
law, Joe Gargery, he returned home to honest work, was reunited
with his early love Estella and changed his ways.

GREAT HEEP, THE

Broadcast History
    Premiere: June 7, 1986
    ABC/Saturday 8:00-9:00 PM
Executive Producer: Miki Herman
Producers: Michael Hirsh, Patrick Loubert, Clive A. Smith
Supervising Producer: Lenora Hume
Directors: Clive A. Smith, Gord Stanfield
Writer: Ben Burtt
Music: Patricia Cullen, Patrick Gleeson
Company: Nelvana Limited, Toronto, Canada, in association with
    Hanho Heung-Up and Mi-Hahn Productions, Seoul, Korea, for
    Lucasfilm/60 minutes

Principal Characters and Voices

C-3PO	Anthony Daniels
R2D2	(electronic)
Great Heep	Long John Baldry
Mungo Baobab	Winston Rekert
Admiral Screed	Graeme Campbell
Fridge	Noam Zylberman
Captain Cag/Announcer	Dan Hennessey
Darva/KT-10	Melleny Brown

The Great Heep hinged on a valuable fuel source discovered on the
distant planet Biitu, somewhat resembling a futuristic Arabian fantasy-
land. Enroute to new jobs with the merchant explorer Mungo Baobab
at a farm colony on Biitu, droids C-3PO and R2D2 were hijacked from
Captain Cag's spaceship by the robot-minions of a gigantic combustion-
driven droid, The Great Heep, who was dispatched by the Empire to

take control of the planet and their mining operations, which were turning Biitu into a wasteland. Admiral Screed commanded the Empire forces overseeing the ore shipments. In the clutches of the lethal Heep, Mungo was placed behind bars, C-3PO enslaved to work the mines and R2D2 placed in a R2-unit Harem to await his fate, where he met a girlfriend droid, KT-10. As they soon learned, the behemoth Heep snacked on R2 units to recharge its evil mechanism. Harrowing experiences and brushes with death ensued as the two robots and Mungo escaped their captors with the aid of the native boy Fidge, who stole bulldozer and knocked in the Harem wall, freeing the captive R2 units. Gaining control of Screed's cargoship, R2D2 battled the Heep in the final showdown, destroying a mast supporting an energy canopy over the planet that held back the elements to allow the mining and causing a downpour of rain to extinguish the Heep's power source. Captain Cag returned to rescue Mungo and the droids, and the planet reverted to its peaceful natives.

The celebrated Lucasfilm droids were spin-offs from the all-time movie hit Star Wars (TCF, 1977) and appeared in their own Saturday morning animated series, The Ewoks and Star Wars Droids Adventure Hour and The All New Ewoks (ABC, 1985-1987).

GREAT PUMPKIN see IT'S THE GREAT PUMPKIN, CHARLIE BROWN

GREAT SANTA CLAUS CAPER, THE see RAGGEDY ANN AND ANDY IN "THE GREAT SANTA CLAUS CAPER"

GREATEST STORIES OF ALL see KINGDOM CHUMS

GRINCH GRINCHES THE CAT IN THE HAT, THE see DR. SEUSS' THE GRINCH GRINCHES THE CAT IN THE HAT

GROVER MONSTER CARTOON SPECIAL, THE see JEAN MARSH CARTOON SPECIAL, THE

GULLIVER'S TRAVELS

Broadcast History
    Premiere: November 18, 1979
    CBS/FAMOUS CLASSIC TALES, Sunday 2:00-3:00 PM
    Sponsor: Kenner Products (Toy Group, General Mills)
    CBS/Repeat: November 9, 1980
    SYN/Repeats: 1981 +
Executive Producer: Doug Paterson
Director: Chris Cuddington
Writer: Kimmer Ringwald

Music: Australian Screen Music
Company: Hanna-Barbera Productions, Sydney, Australia (Southern Star Productions)/60 minutes
Distributor: Worldvision Enterprises/1981-
Home Video: Worldvision

Principal Characters and Voices

Gulliver/Lillaputian/Mob Member #1	Ross Martin
Filmnap/Jester/Pirate	Hal Smith
Bolgolam/Lillaputian King/ Brobdingnag King	John Stephenson
Reldresal/Old Fisherman/ Blefuscu King	Don Messick
Farmer/Brobdingnag Minister/ Mob Member #2	Regis Cordic
Lillaputian Queen/Brobdingnag Queen	Julie Bennett
Farmer's Wife/Glumdalclitch	Janet Waldo

Gulliver's Travels was a rather liberal adaptation of the first two parts of Jonathan Swift's 1726 eponymous novel. Seeking to improve the needs of his family, Lemuel Gulliver embarked from England on what proved to be a dangerous voyage. Shipwrecked and marooned on a strange island, he was captured by little people the size of his thumb in the land of Lilliput. Believing he was a giant sent by their Blefuscuan enemies, he was spared by the king but mistrusted by Bolgolam and the sinister Filmnap, who lured him into the clutches of the Blefuscuan Navy. Returning with their entire fleet in a fishing net, Gulliver endeared himself to the Lilliputians until he violated their rules, tripped up by Bolgolam. After swimming to Blefuscu, Gulliver was sucked up by a whirlpool and deposited in Brobdingnag, a land where clouds were green, and sand was blue and everything was gigantic; even a blade of grass towered over his head. Discovered by a farmer and made into a plaything by his daughter Glumdalclitch, Gulliver finally wound up in the childless King and Queen's castle when Glumdalclitch was made a ward of the court. In the garden Gulliver was swooped up by an eagle that carried him out to sea, where he swam to a ship and was rescued by his own people. After they attempted to steal the fortune he had accumulated, Gulliver escaped again to land on the shores of England. Reflecting on his adventures, Gulliver realized that nothing was so great or so small, other than by comparison, and a worldwide search for riches was unnecessary because they surrounded him in the embodiment of his family. He had always been a wealthy man.

    A prior Hanna-Barbera Saturday morning animated-fantasy concerned Gulliver's son, Gary, in The Adventures of Gulliver (ABC, 1968-1970), described in Children's Television, Part I (Scarecrow, 1983), pp. 8-9. Fleischer Studios also produced the animated movie, Gulliver's Travels (PAR, 1939), based on the story.

HALLOWEEN IS GRINCH NIGHT   see DR. SEUSS' HALLOWEEN IS
   GRINCH NIGHT

HALLOWEEN WHO-DUN-IT?

Broadcast History
   Premiere: 1977
   SYN/local station option
Producers: Art Clokey, Ruth Clokey
Directors: Art Clokey, Raymond Peck
Writer: Nancy Moore
Music: John Seely, Patricia Beck
Company: Clokey Productions for the Lutheran Church in America
Distributor: Department of Telecommunications, Lutheran Church in
   America/1985-

Principal Characters and Voices
Davey Hanson/Sally Hanson/
   Mary Hanson   Norma McMillan/Nancy Wible
Goliath/John Hanson   Hal Smith

Halloween Who-Dun-It? provided another lesson in Christian living
demonstrated through the everyday experiences of Davey Hanson and
his dog Goliath. Dressed as a man from Mars, Davey attended the
town Halloween party and won a toy that fired missiles. Later,
Davey, Sally in her witch's costume and Goliath, outfitted as a tiger,
went off trick-or-treating and became engaged in the usual Halloween
mischief, carried away by the assumption that no one could tell who
was behind their disguises. Some damage was done and feelings
were hurt, not resolved until they all faced the realization that masks
could not hide their deeds from God. Realizing they were responsible
for their own actions, they repented and made amends. The half-
hour film was the last of six stop-motion animated puppet specials
starring Davey and Goliath.

HAPPILY EVER AFTER

Broadcast History
   Premiere: October 21, 1985
   PBS/WONDERWORKS, (KCET, Los Angeles) Monday 8:00-9:00 PM
      PST
   PBS/Repeats: multiple, 1986 +
Executive Producers: Henry Winkler, Roger Birnbaum
Producers/Original Story: Linda Balahoutis, Marilyn Katzenberg
Producer/Director (London): Steven Melendez
Associate Producer (London): Graeme Spurway
Director: Bill Melendez
Writer: Bill Scott
Music: Randy Edelman

HAPPILY EVER AFTER. © 1985, JZM-Bill Melendez Productions.
Courtesy of the Public Broadcasting Service.

Lyrics: Randy Edelman, Bill Scott
Company: JZM-Bill Melendez Productions in association with WONDER-
   WORKS and Bill Melendez Productions, London, England/60 min-
   utes

Narrator: Carol Burnett

Principal Characters and Voices
Molly Conway   Cassandra Coblentz

Alice Conway	Carrie Fisher
Carl Conway	Henry Winkler
Tommy Johnson	Danny Colby
George Johnson	Danny DeVito
Rose Johnson	Rhea Perlman
Joey Fabrizio	Jeremy Schoenberg
Dom Fabrizio	Dana Ferguson
Mary O'Connell	Gini Holtzman
Darlene Kashitani	Karrie Ullman
Woody Coleman	Carl Stevens
Molly's Daughter	Keri Houlihan
What's His Name	Brett Johnson

Happily Ever After was a portrait of troubled youngsters and bicker-
ing parents in the shadow of divorce. It was a bitter-sweet look
look at how one family handled a problem familiar to many children;
about a girl, Molly Conway, who struggled to come to terms with
her parents, Carl and Alice, when their marriage turned sour. A
lovable, carefree child with a vivid imagination, Molly was confused,
hurt and blaming herself as her parents' problems became irreconcil-
able. When they decided to divorce, Molly and her set of offbeat,
quirky friends, who called themselves the Skywalkers, devised a plan
to bring them together again. The Skywalkers helped Molly earn
enough money to buy her mother a gift, pretending it was from her
father. When the "foolproof" idea backfired, she decided to run
away, hoping to make her parents realize they were breaking up the
family. She and Tommy Johnson, whose parents George and Rose
were also arguing, ran away together, but even that plan did not
work when they were quickly found. That left Molly in a blue funk
that colored her big speech as the Fairy Godmother in the rehearsal
for the class play, Cinderella. "Live happily ever after!" Molly
snorted, "That's just dumb! It doesn't happen." The program interwove circus-type dream sequences that reflected Molly's topsy-turvy
vision of her plight. Molly had to accept the inevitable when her
father moved out and she and her mother stayed together. Through
the support of her friends and teacher Miss McCullough, Molly finally
realized it was still possible to live "happily ever after." Songs:
"Give Life All You've Got!" (Jackie DeShannon), "Skywalker's Rule."
    The program was a special animated presentation on Wonder-
works, an anthology series from the PBS Children's and Family Con-
sortium. Jay Rayvid of WQED/Pittsburgh was the executive director,
and Lee Polk was the executive producer of the series. Major funding was provided by the Corporation for Public Broadcasting and
public television stations, with additional funding from the National
Endowment for the Arts.

HAPPY ANNIVERSARY, CHARLIE BROWN

Broadcast History
    Premiere: January 9, 1976
    CBS/Friday 8:00-9:00 PM

HAPPY ANNIVERSARY, CHARLIE BROWN. © 1976, United Feature
Syndicate, Inc. Courtesy of Charles M. Schulz Creative Associates
and United Media.

Producers: Lee Mendelson, Warren Lockhart
Director/Writer: Lee Mendelson
Directors/Animation: Bill Melendez, Phil Roman
Music: Vince Guaraldi
Company: Lee Mendelson Productions in association with Charles M.
    Schulz Creative Associates and United Feature Syndicate/60 minutes

Host: Carl Reiner

Special Guest Star: Charles Schulz

Principal Characters and Voices

Charlie Brown	Duncan Watson
Schroeder	Greg Felton
Sally Brown	Gail M. Davis
Lucy Van Pelt	Lynn Mortensen
Linus Van Pelt	Liam Martin
Peppermint Patty	Stuart Brotman

Happy Anniversary, Charlie Brown celebrated the 25th year of the
Peanuts comic strip and included highlights of 14 Charlie Brown TV
specials. The program was built around an interview with Charles

Schulz, who told how his comic strip began as Li'l Folks in the late forties in the St. Paul Pioneer Press, rechristened Peanuts by the editors for its United Feature Syndicate debut, October 2, 1950. The most successful comic strip of all times, the feature is seen in more than 1,900 newspapers worldwide--an estimated 100 million readers in some 70 countries. Schulz discussed what he thought of its popularity and where he got his ideas for the strip. He also profiled its familiar faces like Charlie Brown ("based a good deal on myself"), the ever-cranky Lucy, piano prodigy Schroeder and Linus ("the group's most well-rounded person"). Then he delved into the more recent arrivals, like Peppermint Patty, whom Schulz said represented a new trend among kids to be independent and speak out, and Snoopy's fine feathered friend Woodstock. The clips from the prior TV specials included one of Snoopy's most memorable moments as a First World War flying ace locked in combat with the Red Baron. Television Academy Emmy award (1975-1976), Best Documentary.

HAPPY BIRTHDAY, CHARLIE BROWN

Broadcast History
   Premiere: January 5, 1979
   CBS/Friday 8:00-9:00 PM
   Sponsor: Interstate Brands
Producer/Director/Writer: Lee Mendelson
Associate Producers: Martha Grace, Paul Preuss, Ron Nelson
Director/Animation: Bill Melendez
Company: Lee Mendelson Productions in association with Charles M.
   Schulz Creative Associates and Bill Melendez Productions/60 minutes

Hostess: Phyllis George

Special Guest Star: Charles Schulz

Principal Characters and Voices

Charlie Brown	Arrin Skelley/Peter Robbins
Linus Van Pelt	Daniel Anderson
Sally Brown	Annalisa Bortolin
Marcie	Casey Carlson
Lucy Van Pelt	Sally Dryer-Barker/Michelle Muller
Dolores	Leticia Ortiz
Peppermint Patty	Laura Planting
Franklin	Ronald Hendrix

Vocalists
   Don Potter, Becky Reardon, Larry Finlayson

Happy Birthday, Charlie Brown saluted the beginning of the Peanuts comic-strip's 30th year and 15th year on network television. At his home in Santa Rosa, California, creator Charles M. Schulz talked with Phyllis George about his 30-year-old feature, focusing on what made his comic's characters tick along with his favorite scenes from past TV productions. Included were Snoopy dancing to Schroeder's piano music (1971) and the beagle's wrist-wrestling duel with Lucy (1969) and brief stint as an Alaskan sled dog (1978). Also included were clips from the Peanuts movies, Race for Your Life, Charlie Brown (1977) and Bon Voyage, Charlie Brown (1980), and Snoopy in animation doing "Suppertime" from the stage play, You're a Good Man, Charlie Brown (1967). Other highlights were a film clip of the Apollo 10 space shot with the modules named for Charlie Brown and Snoopy, a montage of magazine covers featuring the Schulz characters and scenes from several of his four network ice shows. Brought together for the reunion were some of the original voice cast members, including Peter Robbins (Charlie Brown, 1965-1969) and Sally Dryer (Lucy Van Pelt, 1966-1968) and the new voices for You're the Greatest, Charlie Brown [q.v.]. Songs: "The Big Bow Wow," "Suppertime" (Potter), "Happiness Is..." (Reardon, Finlayson), "You're a Good Man, Charlie Brown" (cast).

Happy Birthday, Charlie Brown (Random House, 1979), a book supplement to the program by Lee Mendelson in association with Charles Schulz, covered in more detail the dual anniversaries with original artwork from the various specials, movies and comic strips.

HAPPY BIRTHDAY, DONALD DUCK

Broadcast History
    Premiere: November 21, 1956
    ABC/DISNEYLAND, "At Home With Donald Duck," Wednesday 7:30-
      8:30 PM
    ABC/Repeat: May 8, 1957
    NBC/Repeats: THE WONDERFUL WORLD OF DISNEY, November
      7, 1976; HAPPY BIRTHDAY, DONALD DUCK, April 4, 1979,
      Wednesday 8:00-9:00 PM
Producer: Walt Disney
Directors: Jack Hannah, C. August Nichols
Writers: David Detiege, Albert Pertino, Nick George, Bill Berg, Milt
    Schaffer, Dick Kurney
Music: Joseph S. Dubin, Oliver Wallace
Company: Walt Disney Television/60 minutes

Principal Character and Voice
Donald Duck   Clarence Nash

Happy Birthday, Donald Duck was built around the Disney cartoon Donald's Happy Birthday (1949). When Donald's mischievous nephews, Huey, Dewey and Louie, planned a special birthday surprise for their uncle, the irascible duck caught them with a box of cigars. Not realizing the gift was for him, Donald forced them to smoke the stogies until they turned green in the face. Conscience stricken after he discovered a birthday card in the box for him, Donald threw a party to make amends, deciding to entertain his nephews with cartoons of his favorite star, himself. Having seen those films many times before, his nephews substituted cartoons starring Mickey Mouse, Goofy and Pluto. Featured were the Disney shorts Foul Hunting (1947), Pluto's Blue Note (1947), Mickey and the Seal (1948) and Sea Salts (1949).

First broadcast on NBC in 1976, the film was reedited, retitled and aired as a special in 1979. The film premiered on Disneyland (ABC, 1954-1958), one of the prime-time series of Walt Disney, described in Children's Television, Part II, (Scarecrow, 1985), pp. 542-547.

HAPPY EASTER

Broadcast History
    Premiere: 1967
    SYN/local station option
Producers: Art Clokey, Ruth Clokey
Directors: Art Clokey, Raymond Peck
Writer: Nancy Moore
Music: John Seely, Patricia Beck
Company: Clokey Productions for the Lutheran Church in America
Distributor: Department of Telecommunications, Lutheran Church in
    America/1985-

Principal Characters and Voices
Davey Hanson/Sally Hanson/
    Mary Hanson   Norma McMillan/Nancy Wible
Goliath/John Hanson   Hal Smith

Happy Easter dealt with the death of a relative, providing another lesson in Christian living from everyday experience for Davey Hanson. The Wednesday before Easter Sunday, Davey visited his adored paternal grandmother; they played baseball together, baked a cake and planned to attend the Easter pageant on Sunday. Unexpectedly, on Thursday his grandmother died. Davey's grief overwhelmed him until he watched a rehearsal of the Passion Play. Then he understood why his grandmother always said Easter was a happy time, as Jesus, after earthly death, still lives, and God who raised Him made the same promise to everyone. It was the third of six half-hour, stop-motion animated puppet specials produced by the Lutheran Church in America and telecast with the others on more than 200 stations in the U.S. and on six continents in five languages.

HAPPY NEW YEAR, CHARLIE BROWN!

Broadcast History
    Premiere: January 1, 1986
    CBS/Wednesday 8:30-9:00 PM
    Sponsors: Nabisco Brands, Peter Paul Cadbury
    CBS/Repeat: January 1, 1987

Executive Producer: Lee Mendelson
Producer/Director: Bill Melendez
Writer/Creator: Charles M. Schulz
Music: Desiree Goyette, Ed Bogas
Company: Lee Mendelson-Bill Melendez Productions in association
  with Charles M. Schulz Creative Associates and United Feature
  Syndicate.
Home Video: Kartes Video Communications

Principal Characters and Voices

Charlie Brown	Chad Allen
Lucy Van Pelt	Melissa Guzzi
Linus Van Pelt	Jeremy Miller
Peppermint Patty	Kristi Baker
Sally Brown	Elizabeth Lyn Fraser
Schroeder	Aron Mandelbaum
Marcie	Jason Mendelson
Snoopy	
Woodstock	

Happy New Year, Charlie Brown rang in 1986 with a big bash, a rousing, romantic auld lang syne complicated by Charlie's dreaded homework assignment. Just before Christmas vacation began, his worst
fears were realized when the teacher announced a task condemning him
to days of drudgery. The assignment: read and write a book report
on Leo Tolstoy's epic novel, War and Peace, more than 1,100 pages
long. "Good grief!" No such gloom and doom hovered around Lucy,
Marcie and Peppermint Patty, who were determined to throw a memorable New Year's Eve party, one that would make their romantic dreams
come true. Lucy, of course, set her sights on piano-playing Schroeder
as the perfect date, while Marcie aimed to escort philosophizing Linus
and Patty planned to corral good ol' Charlie himself. Of course the
boyfolk were less than interested; Schroeder preferred to see life
as a sonata, Linus remained coldly philosophical and Charlie was too
consumed with anxiety about his book report and courted disaster by
inviting the Little Red-Haired Girl. Nevertheless, Lucy enrolled the
gang in dancing lessons to prepare for the party. While Charlie,
with War and Peace in his lap, watched from the sidelines, his pals,
including Snoopy and Woodstock, learned a bushel of new steps.
Fearing he might miss the festivities because he still hadn't finished
the book, on the night of the party Charlie resolved not to be so
"wishy-washy" and decided to read it there. At the party he found
time to join in a no-holds-barred game of "Musical Chairs" and to tell
Patty his resolution, "Never volunteer to be a program chairman."
Song: "Slow, Slow, Quick, Quick."

HAPPY PRINCE, THE

Broadcast History:
  Premiere: 1975
  SYN/local station option

Executive Producers: Murray Shostak, Michael Mills
Producer: Gerald Potterton
Director: Sebastian Grunsta
Music: Ron Goodwin
Company: A Reader's Digest Presentation in association with Gerald
    Potterton Productions, Montreal, Canada
Distributor: LBS Communications ("LBS Children's Theatre")/1983-
    1985
Record Album: Capitol/Reader's Digest SQ 6426
Home Video: Random House Home Video

Principal Characters and Voices
Statue   Christopher Plummer
Swallow   Glynis Johns

The Happy Prince was a bittersweet tale of a royal statue and the
small swallow who befriended it. Together, as they overlooked the
village square, they came to understand the hopes and needs of the
townspeople who moved about them. The film was based on the story
by Oscar Wilde which reasserted the author's belief that his stories
were "meant partly for children and partly for those who have kept
the childlike faculties of wonder and joy."

HARLEM GLOBETROTTERS MEET SNOW WHITE, THE

Broadcast History
    Premiere: September 27, October 4, 11 & 18, 1980
    NBC/FRED AND BARNEY MEET THE SHMOO, (4 part serial),
        Saturdays 9:00-10:30 AM
    SYN/Repeats: local station option (part of a 2-hour special, KCOP,
        Los Angeles, October 26, 1985, Saturday 2:00-4:00 PM PST)
    Sponsor: Tonka Toys
Executive Producers: William Hanna, Joseph Barbera
Producers: Alex Lovy, Art Scott
Directors: Oscar Dufau, Carl Urbano
Writer: Willie Gilbert
Music: Hoyt Curtin, Paul DeKorte
Company: Hanna-Barbera Productions/60 minutes
Distributor: Worldvision Enterprises/1985-

Principal Characters and Voices
"Curly" Neal   Stu Gilliam
Geese   John Williams
Marques   Robert DoQui
Li'l John   Buster Jones
Dunbar   Adam Wade
Nate   Scatman Crothers
"Baby Face" Paige   Mork Davitt
Snow White   Russi Taylor
Prince   Michael Bell

Marva	Diane McCannon
Queen of Grimmania	Gay Autterson
Count Revolta	John Stephenson

The Harlem Globetrotters Meet Snow White altered the course of fairy-tale history through a series of magical events surrounding the basketball team's exhibition game in the land of the Grimm Brothers at Grimmania castle. Made up to look homely, young Marva, the wicked Grimmanian Queen's beautician, explained that the jealous Queen could not tolerate anyone fairer than herself and had disposed of Snow White with a poisoned apple. On a rampage because her computerized mirror was on the blink, the Queen ordered her toady, Count Revolta, to have it repaired while the Globetrotters entertained with a show of dexterity. Mistakenly, "Baby Face" Paige dumped a bucket of water on the vain Queen who, infuriated, ordered the Globetrotters imprisoned. In their scrambling escape the team became lost in the forest, where they found Snow White alive and awake, hiding out at the home of the Seven Dwarfs. Despite their efforts, the Queen located Snow White in her mirror, finally slipped her a deadly apple and zapped a disguised Carpathian Prince into a frog for fear his kiss would awaken her. Deciding to find a prince to rouse the girl, Marques instead suggested they find a frog who might be a spellbound prince. Meanwhile, Count Revolta incarcerated the sleeping Snow White in the castle dungeon where the Globetrotters, who were out frog-hunting, were soon imprisoned as well. Promising to return Snow White if they could beat her Gargoyle team, the Queen's challenge was accepted by the Trotters, but when they finally won the treacherous game she reneged. Luckily, the frog prince awakened Snow White with a kiss and restored to his human form, he and his princess made plans to leave for his Carpathian home. The furious Queen objected until Geese convinced her that with Snow White out of her kingdom, she'd again reign as the fairest in the land.

Originally serialized on NBC, the hour-long film was syndicated as part of a two-hour special with Pound Puppies [q.v.] and Star Fairies [q.v.]. Previously, the team appeared in two Saturday morning series, Harlem Globetrotters (CBS, 1970-1973/NBC, 1978, 1979-1980), described in Children's Television, Part I (Scarecrow, 1983), pp. 131-134.

HE-MAN AND SHE-RA--A CHRISTMAS SPECIAL

Broadcast History
    Premiere: 1985
    SYN/local station option (KCOP, Los Angeles, November 29, 1985,
        Friday 4:00-5:00 PM PST)
    Sponsor: Mattel
    SYN/Repeats: 1986 +
Executive Producer: Louis Scheimer
Producers: Arthur H. Nadel, Joseph A. Mazzuca
Directors: Bill Reed, Ernie Schmidt

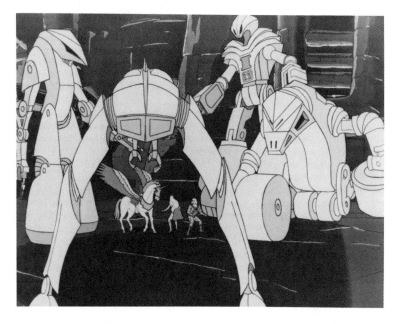

HE-MAN AND SHE-RA--A CHRISTMAS SPECIAL. © 1985, Mattel, Inc. Couretsy of Group W Productions and Filmation.

Writers: Don Heckman, Bob Forward
Music: Shuki Levy, Haim Saban
Company: Filmation/60 minutes
Distributor: Group W Productions/1985-

Principal Characters and Voices

Adam/He-Man	John Erwin
Adora/She-Ra	Melendy Britt
Skeletor	Alan Oppenheimer
Madam Razz/Shadow Weaver	Linda Gary
Hordak/Bow	George DiCenzo
Orko	Eric Gunden (pseud.)

Other Voices
 Lana Beeson, Erika Scheimer, R. D. Robb

He-Man and She-Ra--A Christmas Special exposed that diabolical doer of dastardly deeds and persisent nemesis of He-Man, Skeletor, to the joys of the holiday season. Orko, the little friend of Prince Adam/He-Man triggered the action when the Sky Spy spaceship on which he was playing accidentally took off and landed on Earth.

There Orko learned about Christmas customs from two youngsters, Miguel and Alicia, and attempted to learn "Jingle Bells." Out to stop the spread of the holiday spirit, the ever-villainous Skeletor and Hordak, working under orders of the evil Prime Horde, kidnapped the children and returned to Eternia, unaware that Orko was an accidental stowaway on their spaceship. Wanting to know what Christmas was all about and why the Prime Horde considered it a threat, Skeletor questioned the children. "It's a wonderful time of the year," Miguel said, "Everyone has a lot of fun." "You mean they get in fights?" asked Skeletor. "No! No! They have fun," Miguel explained. "I like fights," said Skeletor. "And you give each other presents," Miguel added. "And when you open them they explode, right?" "No! They're nice gifts," Miguel told him. But Skeletor had the last word: "Doesn't sound like much fun to me." Eventually, the Christmas message managed to penetrate the thick skull of Skeletor, and in an uncommon change of heart he helped rescue the youngsters. Meanwhile, Princess Adora/She-Ra's pursuit of a powerful crystal, the threat of the Monstroids, the assistance of the Manchines, the rescue of Orko and other incidental adventures were woven throughout the story, which culminated in a celebration at the Royal Palace of King Randor and Queen Marlena, where Prince Adam/He-Man, Princess Adora/She-Ra and all their friends met for a gala Christmas Eve party. Songs: "Christmas on Eternia" (Theme), "Jingle Bells."

The special featured many of the characters from the popular weekday strip-series, He-Man and the Masters of the Universe (SYN, 1983-) and She-Ra, Princess of Power (SYN, 1985-), based on the Mattel action-toy line. He-Man also was starred in the animated movie, Secret of the Sword (Filmation, 1984).

HERE COMES GARFIELD

Broadcast History
    Premiere: October 25, 1982
    CBS/Monday 8:30-9:00 PM
    Sponsor: Kellogg's
    CBS/Repeats: November 26, 1983; May 17, 1985
Executive Producer: Jay Poynor
Producers: Lee Mendelson, Bill Melendez
Director: Phil Roman
Writer/Creator: Jim Davis
Music & Lyrics: Desiree Goyette, Ed Bogas
Company: Lee Mendelson-Bill Melendez Productions in association
    with United Media
Record Album: Epic FE 38136

Principal Characters and Voices
Garfield   Lorenzo Music
Jon Arbuckle   Sandy Kenyon
Hubert   Henry Corden

Reba/Skinny	Hal Smith
Fast Eddie/Fluffy	Hank Garrett
Salesman	Gregg Berger
Little Girl	Angela Lee
Odie (the dog)	
Honey Bun (neighbor's dog)	

Vocalists
   Desiree Goyette, Lou Rawls

Here Comes Garfield marked the first animated appearance of Jim
Davis's flabby tabby. Up to all his old mischief, Garfield feuded
with the playful, slow-witted mutt Odie, awoke his master Jon Arbuckle by trampolining on his stomach and consumed copious amounts
of food. Thrown out of the house to do their roughhousing outside,
Garfield and Odie ran afoul of the dainty Honey Bun, the pampered
dog of their mean neighbors Reba and Hubert, who called the city
pound. Garfield escaped the dog catcher, but Odie was carted away
and locked behind bars. Meantime, Garfield, turned fatter and sas-
sier by midnight snacking on his favorite food, lasagna, was inspired
to rescue his playmate. In turn captured and incarcerated, he
learned from Fluffy the cat and Fast Eddie the dog that Odie had
only until dawn to live. A little girl's visit to the pound provided
an opportunity for Garfield, Odie and all their friends to escape.
Worried over their disappearance, Jon welcomed his happy pets home
the next morning with a steak for Odie and bacon and eggs for Garfield, who unceremoniously splattered the plate on his head. "Home
is where they understand you," said the acerbic fat cat. Songs:
"Here Comes Garfield," "Along About Midnight," "So Long, Old
Friend," "Together Again."

HERE COMES PETER COTTONTAIL

Broadcast History
   Premiere: April 4, 1971
   ABC/Sunday 7:00-8:00 PM
   ABC/Repeat: March 30, 1972
   CBS/Repeats: April 13, 1976; April 8, 1977; March 24, 1978;
       April 10, 1979; March 28, 1980; April 10, 1981
Producers/Directors: Arthur Rankin, Jr., Jules Bass
Director/Animagic: Kizo Nagashima
Writer: Romeo Muller
Music: Maury Laws
Lyrics: Jules Bass
Company: Rankin-Bass Productions in association with Videocraft
   International/60 minutes
Distributor: Viacom Enterprises/1987-

Narrator
Seymour S. Sassafrass   Danny Kaye

HERE COMES PETER COTTONTAIL. © 1971, Rankin/Bass Productions, Inc. Courtesy of Rankin/Bass Productions.

Principal Characters and Voices

Peter Cottontail	Casey Kasem
Irontail	Vincent Price
Antoine/Wellington B. Bunny	Danny Kaye
Donna	Iris Rainer
Bonnie	Joan Gardner

Other Voices
Paul Frees, Greg Thomas, Jeffrey A. Thomas

Here Comes Peter Cottontail answered the sticky question, "What happened when the Easter Bunny overslept and did not give away his eggs one Easter Day?" Set at Eastertime in April Valley, Danny Kaye as storyteller Seymour S. Sassafrass related the events in Peter Cottontail's campaign to become the Chief Easter Bunny. Also coveting the job was the sinister rabbit Irontail, who demanded a contest for the job to see who could give away the most eggs on Easter morning. When Peter overslept, it appeared he had lost the contest. Enter the erudite Sassafrass, who provided his magic Yestermorrowbile to return Peter back to Easter. When the machine went amuck, however, Peter was sent back through all the holidays of the year trying to find people to take his eggs. Finally, on St. Patrick's Day everyone became enchanted with Peter's green eggs and so Peter won the job after all. Inspired in part by the eponymous hit song, popularized by Gene Autry, the musical special used a storyline based on the book, The Easter Bunny Overslept by Priscilla and Otto Friedrich and was filmed using stop-motion animated puppets (Animagic). Songs: "Here Comes Peter Cottontail," "Improvise," "The Puzzle of Life," "Be Mine Today" (Kaye).

HERSELF THE ELF see SPECIAL MAGIC OF HERSELF THE ELF, THE

HE'S YOUR DOG, CHARLIE BROWN

Broadcast History
    Premiere: February 14, 1968
    CBS/Wednesday 8:30-9:00 PM
    Sponsor: Coca-Cola, Dolly Madison
    CBS/Repeats: February 20, 1969; February 15, 1970; February
        13, 1971; February 14, 1972, June 5, 1973
Executive Producer: Lee Mendelson
Producers: Lee Mendelson, Bill Melendez
Director: Bill Melendez
Writer/Creator: Charles M. Schulz
Music: Vince Guaraldi
Company: Lee Mendelson-Bill Melendez Productions in association
    with Charles M. Schulz Creative Associates and United Feature
    Syndicate
Record Albums: Disneyland 2603; 3703 (with book); 403 (single);
    Western Publishing
Home Video: Hi-Tops Video (nee Media Home Entertainment)

Principal Characters and Voices
Charlie Brown   Peter Robbins
Peppermint Patty   Gail DeFaria
Lucy Van Pelt   Sally Dryer
Linus Van Pelt   Christopher Shea
Snoopy   Bill Melendez

He's Your Dog, Charlie Brown--and you have to do something about it, demanded the gang in this Peanuts special. Snoopy had been acting wild, and everyone was complaining. There was only one thing Charlie could do: send Snoopy back to the Daisy Hill Puppy Farm for lessons in "obedience and the social graces." "It's for your own good," he told Snoopy, and he made arrangements for the beagle to stay nearby at Peppermint Patty's house. Setting off with a suitcase and his dog dish on his head, Snoopy had a different idea.

Patty welcomed Snoopy, who made himself at home, fantasizing he
was a First World War flying ace on leave in Paris as he swam and
sunned himself while Patty waited on him for three days. Fed up,
Patty called Charlie, who arrived with a leash to bring Snoopy home.
But Snoopy broke away and returned to Patty's, where she demanded
he do his share of work around the place, washing dishes and win-
dows and mowing the lawn. Caught between work and the leash,
Snoopy accidently broke a dish and was banished to the garage for
the night. Lonesome and homesick, the beagle returned to Charlie's
warm welcome, realizing he had learned a good lesson. Back prone
atop his doghouse the next day, he stretched, yawned and snoozed
contentedly under the bright blue sky.

HEY, HEY, HEY, IT'S FAT ALBERT

Broadcast History
    Premiere: November 12, 1969
    NBC/Wednesday 7:30-8:00 PM
    NBC/Repeats: April 17, 1970; September 12, 1971
Executive Producer: William H. Cosby, Jr.
Producers: Louis Scheimer, Norman Prescott
Director: Hal Sutherland
Writers: Bill Cosby, Jim Ryan, Bill Danch
Music: Herbie Hancock
Company: Filmation in association with Bill Cosby Productions

Principal Characters and Voices
Fat Albert/Mushmouth/Mudfoot/
    Dumb Donald   Bill Cosby
Russell   Stephen Cheatham
Weird Harold   Gerald Edwards
Bucky   Jan Crawford
Rudy   Eric Suter
Weasel
Nolan

Hey, Hey, Hey, It's Fat Albert introduced a group of Bill Cosby's
North Philadelphia childhood chums, derived from his wry memories
and comic tales of his Depression-era neighborhood. Marking the
debut of the sloppy, rotund member of the street gang, Fat Albert,
whose favorite expression was, "Hey, Hey, Hey," was the key player
as Captain Cosby's Eagles prepared to meet the fearsome Green
Street Terrors to contest the Football Tackle Championship of the
entire world. With Fat Albert on their team, the Eagles were confident they could forego practice for a film matinee starring Lon Chaney,
Jr. as the Wolfman. But without Fat Albert the Eagles stood no
chance. And at game time, Fat Albert decided to sit this one out,
maybe even leave the neighborhood, deeply hurt by his teammate's
wisecracks about his overweight size. After apologies were made all
around, Fat Albert was coaxed to return in time to hear their cheers

of victory when he made the winning touchdown run in their game of rough street-football.

The special was the first program to feature cartoon blacks in network prime time. It utilized some unique artwork, with the cartoon characters moving against a continuing film background of buildings, traffic and pro-footballers. Russell, whose lines were muffled by a heavy scarf over his mouth, was recorded by Stephen Cheatham with a jacket draped over his head. Other than Cosby's various voices, only children, all amateurs, were used to voice the parts. Four sequels followed, Weird Harold [q.v.] and the Christmas, Easter and Halloween specials starring Fat Albert [q.v.]. Also, it was the forerunner which sparked the widely acclaimed Saturday morning series, Fat Albert (CBS, 1972-1984), described in Children's Television, Part I (Scarecrow, 1983), pp. 99-100.

HIAWATHA

Broadcast History
    Premiere: September 24, 1972
    SYN/FESTIVAL OF FAMILY CLASSICS, WABC, New York, Sunday
        7:00-7:30 PM
    SYN/Repeats: 1973 +
Producers/Directors: Arthur Rankin, Jr., Jules Bass
Associate Producer: Mary Alice Dwyer
Writer: William J. Keenan
Music: Maury Laws, Jules Bass
Company: Rankin-Bass Productions
Distributor: Viacom Enterprises ("Family Classics")/1986-
Home Video: Prism

Hiawatha told the legend of the brave Indian youth immortalized in Henry Wadsworth Longfellow's epic poem. Growing up under the care of his grandmother, Nokomis, he was a friend to all animals but had to prove his strength and courage among the men in the tribe. When he killed a cougar with his bare hands, Hiawatha earned a place among the braves. A more severe test of his courage followed when his tribe was threatened with starvation under the spell of Pearl Feather, an evil medicine man who was angered over Hiawatha's humiliation of his cowardly son Pau Puk. Guided by his friend and mentor, a crotchety old raven, Hiawatha forced an end to Pearl Feather's spell, and the grateful braves named him their new chief.

HOBBIT, THE

Broadcast History
    Premiere: November 27, 1977
    NBC/Sunday 8:00-9:30 PM
    Sponsor: Xerox
    CBS/Repeat: May 19, 1979
    SYN/Repeats: 1985 +

THE HOBBIT. © 1977, Rankin/Bass Productions, Inc. Courtesy of
Rankin/Bass Productions and Lorimar Syndication.

Producers/Directors: Arthur Rankin, Jr., Jules Bass
Writer: Romeo Muller
Music: Maury Laws, Lois Winter (Chorale)
Lyrics: Jules Bass
Company: Rankin-Bass Productions with animation by Toru Hara and
    Tsuguyuki Kubo/90 minutes
Distributor: Lorimar Syndication ("Animated Holiday Specials")/
    1985-
Record Album: Buena Vista 103 (with book); Disneyland 3819 (with
    book), 103 (single)
Home Video: ABC Video

Principal Characters and Voices

Bilbo Baggins	Orson Bean
Gandalf	John Huston
Thorin Oakenshield	Hans Conreid
Dragon Smaug	Richard Boone
Gollum	Theodore
Elvenking	Otto Preminger
Elrond	Cyril Ritchard

Other Voices
    Jack DeLeon, Paul Frees, Don Messick, John Stephenson

Balladeer: Glenn Yarbrough

The Hobbit followed J.R.R. Tolkien's group of adventurers led by

Bilbo Baggins in a search for treasure in the lands of Middle Earth.
Before he could say, "I'm only a simple Hobbit," Bilbo found himself
playing thief for Thorin, a dwarf who was pretender to the throne
of the King of Under the Mountain. Reluctantly drafted by Gandalf,
the Wandering Wizard, Bildo was assigned the task since there were
an unlucky number of 13 dwarfs and it would take a luckier number
than that to recover their gold from eerie Lonely Mountain and the
dreaded dragon Smaug. Embarking from his Hobbit's hole, Bilbo encountered an incredible array of creatures on his mission: trolls,
goblins, elves and even a colony of humans; giant spiders, eagles
and butterflies, a secret door and a thrush, ancient secrets, horrible
Gollum and his magic ring, a magic sword, the Elvenking and Elrond.
He was pitted against an army of ugly goblins, a slimy denizen who
wanted to eat him and, of course, the terrifying, firebreathing Smaug.
All foes were dispatched with equal aplomb, the trolls with the help
of Gandalf. Through a bit of ingenuity and with the use of the
magical ring, Bilbo regained the Dwarf King's gold and escaped alive.
While happy indeed to be safely home in his quiet Hobbit hole, Bilbo
could never forget his adventure or the treasures it yielded--a magic
ring and a lot of courage. Songs: "The Greatest Adventure,"
"Roads" (Yarbrough), "The Dwarfs of Yore" (Huston), "That's What
Bilbo Baggins Hates," "The Misty Mountains," "Rollin' Down the Hole,"
"In the Valley," "The Mountain King's Return" (Dwarfs), "Down,
Down to Goblin Town," "Funny Little Things" (Goblin chorus), "In
the Valley, Ha! Ha!" (Elves chorus), "Gollum's Riddle" (Sirens).
John Foster Peabody award (1977).

Based on the original Tolkien book (1937), the made-for-TV
feature included a message against war and self service and prompted
a sequel, The Return of the King [q.v.]. A deluxe edition of The
Hobbit with illustrations from the film was published by Harry Abrams.
(1977).

HOOBER-BLOOB HIGHWAY see DR. SEUSS' HOOBER-BLOOB HIGH-
WAY

HOORAY FOR THE THREE WISEMEN

Broadcast History
 Premiere: 1987
 SYN/local station option
Producer: Aldo Raparelli
Director: Manfredo Manfredi
Writers: Guido and Maurizio DeAngellis, Cesare DeNatale
Music and Lyrics: Guido and Maurizio DeAngellis
Music: F. Rodriguez
Company: Cineteam Realizzazioni in association with Radiotelevisione
 Italiana (RAI)/60 minutes
Distributor: Coral International Television/1987-
Record Album: RCA

Principal Characters and Voices

Gaspar	Albert Eddy
Balthasar	Leroy Villanueva
Melchor	Tony McShear
Kid	Dennis Khalili-Borna
Joseph	Michael Connor
Mary	Erica Rose
Herod	Ken Dana
	Michael McComohie (singing)
Shepherd	Simon Prescott

Other Voices
   Janus Blythe, Susan Sacker, Samuel J. Salerno

Hooray for the Three Wisemen was Italy's answer to the contemporary
Japanese cartoon-fantasy heroes, a musical story told in six episodes.
An adverturous legend set in the year 2000, it concerned the Three
Wisemen who arrived on Earth from different planets in a comet-
spaceship on a mission to bring gifts to the newborn "Child." Along
the way they encountered King Herod and his soldiers who hindered
their search, became involved in an adventure in the fantastic land
of Bolliboo and met a kind old shepherd who helped them. The film
was reedited and redubbed by Coral Pictures for English audiences.

HORSE THAT PLAYED CENTERFIELD, THE

Broadcast History
   Premiere: February 24 & March 3, 1979
   ABC/ABC WEEKEND SPECIALS, Saturday 12:00-12:30 PM
   ABC/Repeats: September 29 & October 6, 1979; July 5 & 12,
      1980; June 13 & 20, 1981; June 5 & 12, 1982; May 28 & June
      4, 1983; June 15 & 22, 1985
Executive Producers: Joseph Ruby, Ken Spears
Producer: Jerry Eisenberger
Directors: Rudy Larriva, Manny Perez
Writer: Sheldon Stark
Music: Dean Elliott
Company: Ruby-Spears Enterprises for ABC/60 minutes, 2 parts
Home Video: Playhouse Video (CBS-FOX)

Voices
   John Erwin, Joan Gerber, Allan Melvin, Don Messick, Howard
   Morris, Alan Oppenheimer, Brad Sanders

The Horse That Played Centerfield was a juvenile fantasy about a
losing baseball team that was spurred into winning by a farm horse
that could play better than they could. In Part I, finishing last
every season, the New York Goats were a professional baseball team
with an embarrassing strike-out and error record, the worst in major
league history. "They're not just bad, they're awful," fumed Kevin
Darling, who owned a Florida orange grove near the Goats' spring

training camp in Chatahaches, Florida. During practice, the Goats' centerfielder missed an easy catch, and manager Casey Balloo tried to humiliate his team into performing better by putting Karen Darling's horse Oscar into center field. Surprising them all by making spectacular catches, a skill he had developed with oranges at the Darlings' grove, Oscar was soon the team's regular centerfielder. With Oscar in the lineup, the Goats began to win games, and ultimately the National League Pennant.

In Part II, during the World Series, some gamblers kidnapped the horse, hoping to deprive the Goats of their good luck token and their psychological edge. Disappointed by Oscar's absence, the Goats began to play poorly and after losing the first game Kevin knew he had to do something to recover the team's star centerfielder. With the aid of Phil Furlong, a newspaper reporter, Kevin traced the horse-nappers to a farmhouse not far from a racetrack. Enlisting the aid of the track horses, Kevin and Phil rescued Oscar, apprehended the gamblers, and returned to the stadium. To the wild cheering of the fans, Oscar took to the field, buoying the spirits of the Goats, who won the big game aided by their horse that played centerfield. The two-part special was based on the eponymous 1969 novel by Hal Higdon.

HORTON HEARS A WHO   see   DR. SEUSS' HORTON HEARS A WHO

HOW BUGS BUNNY WON THE WEST

Broadcast History
    Premiere: November 15, 1978
    CBS/Wednesday 8:30-9:00 PM
    CBS/Repeats: September 10, 1979; September 18, 1980; March
        8, 1983; January 13, 1984; May 30, 1984; January 18, 1985;
        September 20, 1985; August 21, 1987
Executive Producer/Director: Hal Geer
Writers: Marc Sheffler, Hal Geer, Tedd Pierce, Warren Foster,
    Michael Maltese
Music: Harper MacKay, Carl Stalling, Milt Franklin, Bill Lava
Company: Warner Bros. Television

Host: Denver Pyle

Principal Characters and Voices
Bugs Bunny/Yosemite Sam/Daffy
    Duck/ Porky Pig/Blacque Jacque
    Shellacque/Nasty Canasta   Mel Blanc

How Bugs Bunny Won the West, through excerpts from previously exhibited cartoons, followed Bugs ranging far and wide through the sprawling, brawling West, using his wiles, wisecracks and wild-and-wooly schemes. Arriving in San Francisco at the dawn of the 1849

Gold Rush, Bugs was a lucky rube whose rabbit's foot was a natural at the gaming table. His winnings provided a stake that sent him hopping off to the California gold fields, where his good fortune continued despite a series of plots to outsmart him, hatched by perfidious prospectors Yosemite Sam and Daffy Duck. In traditional frontier spoofs, Bugs and the cartoon troupe of tenderfoot thespians became involved in a classic barroom confrontation, a hare-brained shootout, a train robbery and assorted chases and misadventures before the West could be reasonably considered won, Bugs Bunny style. Denver Pyle, who starred as Uncle Jesse Duke on The Dukes of Hazzard (CBS, 1969-1984), hosted the program.

I LOVE THE CHIPMUNKS, VALENTINE SPECIAL

Broadcast History
    Premiere: February 12, 1984
    NBC/Sunday 7:00-7:30 PM
    NBC/Repeat: February 13, 1985
Executive Producers: Joseph Ruby, Ken Spears
Producers: Ross Bagdasarian, Janice Karman
Associate Producer: Larry Huber
Director: Charles A. Nichols
Writers: Janice Karman, Ross Bagdasarian, Cliff Ruby, Elana Lesser
Music: Dean Elliott
Company: Ruby-Spears Enterprises in association with Ross Bagdasarian Productions

Principal Characters and Voices

Alvin/Simon/David Seville	Ross Bagdasarian
Theodore/Brittany/Jeanette/ Elenore	Janice Karman
Others	Julie McWhirter Dees
	Frank Welker

I Love the Chipmunks, Valentine Special taught a lesson in honesty and love when Simon and Theodore tried to get their brother Alvin into the Valentine's Day spirit. To the Chipmunks, it meant the arrival of the long-awaited social event of the year, the Valentine's Day dance and a chance to win the prestigious Valentine's Day dance contest. Simon exchanged Valentines with the beautiful Chipette, Jeanette; and Theodore and Elenore swapped Valentine cakes and cookies. But when the popular Brittany attempted an old trick to get Alvin to invite her to the dance, he picked up her dropped handkerchief to blow his nose! Simon and Theodore tried to remedy his oblivious indifference by playing sleep-tapes suggesting his Don Juan irresistibility. Thus hypnotized, Alvin christened himself Captain Chipmunk and rode about, masked and on horseback, winning many young ladies' hearts, including Brittany's. Unaware of his nighttime alter-ego until awakened when he fell in a pool, and before he could confess his masquerade to Brittany, he overheard her voice her

I LOVE THE CHIPMUNKS, VALENTINE SPECIAL. © 1984, Ruby-Spears Enterprises, Inc. and Bagdasarian Productions. Courtesy of Bagdasarian Productions, Ruby-Spears Enterprises and TECO.

preference for Captain Chipmunk over Alvin. Deciding to discontinue competing with himself and turn the tables on Brittany, as Captain Chipmunk he stormed into the big dance dressed in tatters and was anything but charming. Leaving Brittany and her friends in shock, he departed and returned as a tuxedoed Alvin, heartily welcomed by all, and asked Brittany to dance. As they cut some fancy figures to the beat of the Chipette's song, the applause became resounding for the new winners of the Valentine's Day dance contest. Song/ Theme: "The Chipette Song."

INCREDIBLE BOOK ESCAPE, THE

Components
    THE FURIOUS FLYCYCLE, THE GHOST IN THE SHED, MYRA, THE PRACTICAL PRINCESS

Broadcast History
    Premiere: June 3, 1980
    CBS/CBS LIBRARY SPECIAL, Tuesday 3:00-4:00 PM
    Sponsor: General Foods
    CBS/Repeat: November 28, 1980
    SYN/Repeats: 1986 +
Producer: Nick Bosustow
Director/Animation: Sam Weiss
Director/Live Action: Seth Pinsker
Writer: George Arthur Bloom
Music: Larry Wolff
Company: Bosustow Entertainment/60 minutes
Distributor: Coe Film Associates/1986-

Cast
P.J.   Quinn Cummings

Principal Characters and Voices

Mrs. Page	Ruth Buzzi
Myra	Penelope Sundrow
Ghost-in-the-Shed	George Gobel
Princess	Tammy Grimes
Lord Garp/Prince	Arte Johnson
Professor Mickimecki	Hans Conreid
Melvin Spitznagle	Sparky Marcus
Mrs. Spitznagle	June Foray
Mr. Spitznagle	Jack Angel

The Incredible Book Escape starred Quinn Cummings as a young P.J., who inadvertently became locked in the children's reading room at the library after hours. There she encountered some characters from the picturebooks that surrounded her, in a fanciful blend of live-action and animation. The characters she met were Myra, a little girl who could become whomever or whatever she imagined herself to be, from Myra by Barbara Bottner; a determined ghost on a New England farm, from The Ghost in the Shed by Marilynne K. Roach in the collection, Encounters with the Invisible World; a liberated princess with a practical answer to any problem, from The Practical Princess by Jay Williams; and an aspiring young inventor, Melvin Spitznagle, from The Furious Flycycle by Jan Wahl. Each were depicted in a different animation style matching the unique illustrations of the books. They befriended P.J. and eventually came up with a solution that triggered her release from the library. The stories were chosen from the annual United States Library of Congress list of recommended children's books.

INCREDIBLE DETECTIVES, THE

Broadcast History
    Premiere: November 17, 1979
    ABC/ABC WEEKEND SPECIALS, Saturday 12:00-12:30 PM
    ABC/Repeats: March 20, 1980; September 27, 1980
Executive Producers: Joseph Ruby, Ken Spears
Producer: Jerry Eisenberger
Director: Rudy Larriva
Writer: Mark Evanier
Music: Dean Elliott
Company: Ruby-Spears Enterprises
Home Video: Worldvision

Principal Characters and Voices
Madame Chen   Marlene Aragon
Reggie   Laurie Main
Hennesey   Frank Welker
Davey Morrison   Albert Eisenmann

Other Voices
    Stan Freberg, Michael Rye, John Stephenson

The Incredible Detectives premiered three unlikely sleuths, Madame Chen, a slightly vain Siamese cat, Hennesey, a gabby black crow, and Reggie, a sophisticated but stuffy bulldog. They were the pets of the Morrison family. After Mr. Morrison, a government missile scientist, left for work and Davey and his mother left for the museum, Madame Chen sensed trouble ahead for their young master. Sure enough, two scoundrels kidnapped Davey at the museum, and his parents received a ransom note demanding his father's secret missile plans in exchange for the boy. Aware that a bumbling police detective was assigned the case and banking on the cat's intuitive powers, the crow's cunning and the bulldog's deductive reasoning, the three set out to investigate. After surviving a false alarm at the police station, Madame Chen and Reggie were captured by the guards during a wild chase at the museum, but not before Reggie's super sniffer revealed that one of the kidnappers was a guard. Following up this lead, Hennesey overheard that Davey was being held in a secret room at the museum and then managed to rescue the others from the animal shelter. Together they returned to the museum, found the secret room, freed Davey and foiled the hoods. At home, the police detective rewarded the incredible trio with honorary detective badges for a job well done. The program was based on the book by Don and Joan Caufield.

INCREDIBLE, INDELIBLE, MAGICAL, PHYSICAL MYSTERY TRIP, THE

Broadcast History
Premiere: February 7, 1973
ABC/ABC AFTERSCHOOL SPECIALS, Wednesday 4:30-5:30 PM
Sponsors: Oscar Mayer, M & M/Mars, Gillette
ABC/Repeats: October 24, 1973; ABC WEEKEND SPECIALS, March 4, 1978
Executive Producer: Stanley E. Paperny
Producers: David H. DePatie, Friz Freleng
Director/Animation: Herbert Klynn
Director/Live Action: Jim Cates
Writer: Larry Spiegel
Music & Lyrics: Edward Newmark
Company: DePatie-Freleng Enterprises in association with ABC/60 minutes

Cast
Uncle Carl	Hal Smith
Joey	Michael Link
Missy	Kim Richards

Principal Characters and Voices
Timer	Len Maxwell
Joey	Peter Broderick
Missy	Kathy Buch

The Incredible, Indelible, Magical, Physical Mystery Trip introduced children to the wonders of the human body. The acclaimed educational fantasy combined live action with animation to tell the story of two children, miniaturized to germ size by a magical figure, Timer, who gave them a tour through their gluttonous Uncle Carl's body. On their lively musical journey, Joey and Missy met a world of strange inhabitants: General Antigen, who fought tooth decay; a smoke-damaged cell in Lungland; and Admiral Plasma. From them they learned a lesson about body mistreatment from the suffering organs, smoke-clogged lung sacs, a too-full stomach and an overstrained heart. Songs: "Follow Me," "Sailing Down the River," "Have a Heart," "Missy's Song," "The Food Song," "Look on the Bright Side," "The Brain Song."

The successful venture into some basic biology spurred a sequel,

The Magical Mystery Trip Through Little Red's Head [q.v.] and was somewhat similar to All About Me [q.v.].

INTERGALACTIC THANKSGIVING
(aka PLEASE DON'T EAT THE PLANET)

Broadcast History
   Premiere: October 3, 1979
   CBC/Wednesday 8:00-8:30 PM
   SYN/local station option, October 1979 +
   CBC/Repeats: 1980 +
Producers: Michael Hirsh, Patrick Loubert
Director: Clive A. Smith
Writers: Greg Duffell, Don Arioli, Martin Lavut
Music/Songs & Lyrics: John Sebastian with the John Hall Band
Music: Patricia Cullen
Company: Nelvana Limited, Toronto, Canada, in association with the
   CBC
Distributor: Viacom Enterprises/1979-
Home Video: Warner Home Video #4006 ("Nelvanamation")

Principal Characters and Voices
King Goochie   Sid Caesar
Ma Spademinder   Catherine O'Hara
Pa Spademinder   Chris Wiggins
Victoria Spademinder   Jean Walker
Magic Mirror   Martin Lavut
Notfunnyenuf   Derek McGrath
The Bug   Al Waxman
Bug Kid   Toby Waxman
Cromwell (Victoria's Dog)

Intergalactic Thanksgiving (aka Please Don't Eat the Planet) was an ecology-wise tale in outer space, sometime in the distant future, where a group of rocket wagon-trains were on a journey to the unknown, looking for a new place to settle.   One wagon, containing the hard-working, simple-minded Spademinder family, crash-landed on the planet Laffalot, where all the zanies did was joke, kid-around and sing.   The Spademinders explored their new planet and set up a homestead and started gardening.   Observing the Spademinders, the Laffalotions, who survived effortlessly by consuming the planet's soil, were thrown into fits of laughter at the very idea of such toil. However, the Laffalots were eating themselves out of their home. The crust of the planet had to be shored-up continually by the bugs who lived below.   This problem was accidently discovered by young Victoria Spademinder, her dog Cromwell and the Prince, Notfunnenuf, and through their adventures the Laffalotions learned the importance of planting crops to save the soil while the Spademinders were reminded of the value of humor and song in their lives.   The story culminated in the first harvest celebration in outer space, in the true spirit of the Thanksgiving Holiday. Songs: "We Are the Cosmic Farmers," "We Don't Know What's In Store," "Build It up."

IS THIS GOODBYE, CHARLIE BROWN?

Broadcast History
    Premiere: February 21, 1983
    CBS/Monday 8:00-8:30 PM
    CBS/Repeat: February 13, 1984
Producers: Lee Mendelson, Bill Melendez
Director: Phil Roman
Writer/Creator: Charles M. Schulz
Music: Judy Munsen, Steven Riffkin
Company: Lee Mendelson-Bill Melendez Productions in association
    with Charles M. Schulz Creative Associates and United Media
Record Albums: Disneyland 410 (single); Western Publishing
Home Video: Hi-Tops Video

Principal Characters and Voices

Charlie Brown	Brad Kesten
Linus Van Pelt	Jeremy Schoenberg
Lucy Van Pelt	Angela Lee
Peppermint Patty	Victoria Vargas
Marcie	Michael Dockery
Sally Brown	Stacy Heather Tolkin
Schroeder	Kevin Brando
Snoopy	Bill Melendez

Is This Goodbye, Charlie Brown? was a funny yet poignant treatment of the trauma friends suffer when they must separate. Lucy and Linus were moving away from their pintsized friends because their father had been transferred to a new job in another city. News of the development was so appalling to Charlie Brown that he was left speechless. Almost. After all, he was losing Linus, his best friend and his second-baseman. Without Lucy, crabby fussbudget that she was, who would bait Snoopy or give psychiatric advice? Before the final goodbyes could be said, these and some other matters had to be cleared up. Reluctantly, Lucy sold her psychiatry practice to a goateed Snoopy wearing a Viennese homburg, and the enterprising beagle quickly raised the fee from five to 50 cents. And then there was the question of the goodbye party. But that was quickly resolved by another of the bullish beagle's businesses, Joe Cool's Catering, which served up the finest in dog biscuits and kibble. The anticipated finale found Lucy and Linus returning to their home and not leaving their friends after all.

IT WAS A SHORT SUMMER, CHARLIE BROWN

Broadcast History
    Premiere: September 27, 1969

CBS/Saturday 8:30-9:00 PM
Sponsors: Coca-Cola; Dolly Madison, McDonald's, Kellogg's
CBS/Repeats: September 16, 1970; September 29, 1971; September 7, 1972; June 27, 1983
Producers: Lee Mendelson, Bill Melendez
Director: Bill Melendez
Writer/Creator: Charles M. Schulz
Music: Vince Guaraldi, John Scott Trotter
Company: Lee Mendelson-Bill Melendez Productions in association with Charles M. Schulz Creative Associates and United Feature Syndicate
Home Video: Snoopy's Home Video Library/Hi-Tops Video (nee Media Home Entertainment)

Principal Characters and Voices

Charlie Brown	Peter Robbins
Lucy Van Pelt	Pamelyn Ferdin
Linus Van Pelt	Glenn Lelger
Sally Brown	Hilary Momberger
Snoopy	Bill Melendez

It Was a Short Summer, Charlie Brown satirized that universal academic pet peeve--the school composition. On the first day back at school, after the class was assigned to write a 500-word theme on what they did during the summer, Linus raised his hand and asked, "How do you teachers keep coming up with these great new ideas?" Agonizing over things past, Charlie Brown still had 492 words to go as they flashed-back to scenes at their summer camp. Snoopy had more baggage than the others and was paired with Charlie in his tent. Charlie's bed-making demonstration was a failure, but Snoopy showed how to make a bed so tight you could bounce a quarter on it. Then Charlie, his tent-mates and superdog Snoopy competed against the nearby girls' camp in a swim meet, baseball game and a canoe race, all ending in defeat and disaster. Trying to find something at which they could beat the girls, Charlie noticed Snoopy and Linus arm-wrestling and proposed a wrist-wrestling competition with the Masked Marvel, Snoopy, as their champion. Lucy and Snoopy were locked hand and paw, but neither could put the other down. Suddenly, Snoopy kissed Lucy on the nose. "Foul, foul!" she fumed, "The stupid Masked Marvel fouled! I'm the winner, I won!" Linus got an "A" on his vacation paper, and Charlie got a "C." "It was kind of a short summer, wasn't it, Charlie Brown?" asked Linus. "Yes," answered Charlie, "and it looks like it is going to be a long winter."

IT'S A BRAND NEW WORLD

Broadcast History
Premiere: March 8, 1977
NBC/NBC SPECIAL TREAT, Tuesday 4:00-5:00 PM
NBC/Repeats: April 9, 1977; December 5, 1977

Executive Producer: Eddie Elias
Producer: Al Elias
Associate Producers: Peter Runfalo, Anne Scarza
Directors: Ronald Fritz, Dan Hunn
Writers: Romeo Muller, Max Wilk
Music & Lyrics: Al Elias, Andy Badale, Murray Semos, Romeo Muller, Max Wilk
Company: Elias Productions in association with D & R Productions / 60 minutes

Principal Characters and Voices

Teacher/Noah	Joe Silver
Elijah/Samson	Malcolm Dodd
Aaron	Dennis Cooley
Jezebel	Boni Enten
Barnabas	George Hirsch
Samson's Brother	Charmaine Harma

Vocalists
Sylvester Fields, Hilda Harris, Maeretha Stewart

It's A Brand New World was the sixth in a series of afternoon specials for youngsters on the periodic NBC Special Treat (NBC, 1975-1982). A holiday musical about a remedial Bible class for aspiring angels, it told the stories of Noah and Samson in contemporary popular style, illustration, music and song, as seen through the eyes of four fun-loving children. Songs: "It's a Brand New World," "Four Would-Be Angels."

IT'S A MYSTERY, CHARLIE BROWN

Broadcast History
     Premiere: February 1, 1974
     CBS/Friday 7:30-8:00 PM
     Sponsors: Kellogg's, Dolly Madison
     CBS/Repeat: February 17, 1975
Executive Producer: Lee Mendelson
Producer: Bill Melendez
Director: Phil Roman
Writer/Creator: Charles M. Schulz
Music: Vince Guaraldi
Company: Lee Mendelson-Bill Melendez Productions in association with Charles M. Schulz Creative Associates and United Feature Syndicate
Record Albums: Disneyland 409 (single); Western Publishing
Home Video: Kartes Video Communications

Principal Characters and Voices

Charlie Brown	Todd Barbee
Lucy Van Pelt	Melanie Kohn

Linus Van Pelt	Stephen Shea
Sally Brown	Lynn Mortensen
Peppermint Patty	Donna Forman
Marcie	James Ahrens
Pig-Pen	Thomas A. Muller
Snoopy	Bill Melendez

It's a Mystery, Charlie Brown provided a perplexing problem for the Peanuts clan: who stole Woodstock's nest? Snoopy donned his Sherlock Holmes' duds, equipped himself with a calabash pipe and magnifying glass, and with his feathered client at his heels went on the prowl as the world's greatest detective. Sparing no one the Scotland Yard treatment in his search for the neighborhood thief, he gave Charlie Brown the third degree and dusted for fingerprints at Lucy and Linus's home. "He's gone crazy!" shouted Lucy. "Ashes to ashes and dust to dust. Snoopy will find it, and find it he must!" spouted Linus. Marcie rebuffed him, Pig-Pen repulsed him and Peppermint Patty donned a mask and played a game of cops and robbers with him. Finally, Snoopy located his objective in the school science lab, in a glass encased exhibit labelled "Prehistoric Bird's Nest," and returned it to Woodstock's tree. "I've been robbed!" shouted the culprit, Sally, who demanded Snoopy give it back and pressed countercharges. Assuming a peacekeeper role, Charlie suggested Lucy settle the dispute at her psychiatric booth, whose sign she changed to "Legal Aid 7 Cents." As the judge, Lucy ruled in favor of Woodstock. So Sally presented a new science exhibit: a demonstration of Pavlov's experiment using Snoopy to prove a dog would drool if you rang a bell and promised him food. She got an "A" on her exhibit, Woodstock got back his nest and Snoopy stole the show.

IT'S AN ADVENTURE, CHARLIE BROWN

Broadcast History
    Premiere: May 16, 1983
    CBS/Monday 8:00-9:00 PM
    CBS/Repeats: November 5, 1983; September 19, 1987
Producers: Lee Mendelson, Bill Melendez
Directors: Bill Melendez, Phil Roman, Sam Jaimes
Writer/Creator: Charles M. Schulz
Music: Ed Bogas, Desiree Goyette
Company: Lee Mendelson-Bill Melendez Productions in association
    with Charles M. Schulz Creative Associates and United Feature
    Syndicate/60 minutes
Home Video: Snoopy's Home Video Library/Hi-Tops Video (nee Media
    Home Entertainment)

Host: Charles Schulz

Principal Characters and Voices

Charlie Brown	Michael Catalano
Lucy Van Pelt	Angela Lee
Linus Van Pelt	Earl "Rocky" Reilly
Peppermint Patty	Brent Hauer
Marcie	Michael Dockery
Schroeder	Brad Schachter
Ruby	Jenny Lewis
Austin	Johnny Graves
Leland	Joel Graves
Milo	Jason Muller
Camp Kid #1	Brian Jackson
Camp Kid #2	Kevin Brando
Caddymaster	Gerard Goyette, Jr.
Snoopy	Bill Melendez

Announcer: John Hiestand

It's An Adventure, Charlie Brown, an unusual anthology of six Peanuts stories, highlighted some of the favorite newspaper comic strips of creator Charles Schulz, who introduced the animated adaptations. The assortment of adventures evolved as his characters faced individual vicissitudes that involved other members of the Peanuts clan. Along with her pal Marcie, Peppermint Patty, who considered herself well qualified to be a golf caddy even though she believed pars and birdies were bowling terms, got a job at the Ace Country Club, where two wildly competitive women golfers proved to be hazards to each other, the caddies and "the crabbiest golfer at the club," a dogged sport with long floppy ears. In another cartoon, Marcie blew a butterfly off the dozing Patty's nose, convincing Patty that it really turned into an angel and flew away. Patty considered it a "miracle" and felt "chosen" to bring an important message to the world. Unrequited love was the theme for a segment between a smitten Lucy and a musically preoccupied Schroeder, who got so keyed up that he hit Lucy with his piano. She slipped some sheet music in front of him, tricking him into playing a love song which she sang to him. Totally carried away, she danced wildly with Snoopy, the boogying beagle, atop the piano, much to Schroeder's horror. In another vignette, Linus's beloved security blanket started retaliating when Lucy threatened it with the trash burner. Claiming it "hissed" at her, attacked her in her living room and chased her outside, she finally buried it. While Linus suffered withdrawal symptoms during which a compassionate Charlie Brown sat up with him all night, Snoopy unearthed the blanket, only to have Lucy make a kite of it. As it sailed out over the ocean, a rescue team unique to Peanutland attempted to retrieve it. Fearful that he was "cracking up" because everything he saw was round as a baseball, including his head and the sun, Charlie followed the advice of his pediatrician, Dr. Sweet, and took off for two weeks at a dreaded summer camp, where he surprised everyone and, oddly enough, became something of a hero. And when that gluttonous kite-eating tree swallowed

Charlie's first spring kite, he retaliated with fury. Fearing he might be put in jail by the Environment Protection Agency, Charlie ran away and again became a hero, this time to a group of smaller children who wanted him to manage their baseball team, The Goose Eggs. The hour-long program utilized some of the short films of varying lengths, comic strip style, from the Saturday morning series, The Charlie Brown and Snoopy Show (CBS, 1983-1986).

IT'S ARBOR DAY, CHARLIE BROWN

Broadcast History
  Premiere: March 16, 1976
  CBS/Tuesday 8:00-8:30 PM
  Sponsor: Dolly Madison, McDonald's
  CBS/Repeats: March 14, 1977; April 10, 1978; March 24, 1980
Executive Producer: Lee Mendelson
Producer: Bill Melendez
Director: Phil Roman
Writer/Creator: Charles M. Schulz
Music: Vince Guaraldi
Company: Lee Mendelson-Bill Melendez Productions in association
  with Charles M. Schulz Creative Associates and United Feature
  Syndicate
Home Video: Kartes Video Communications

Principal Characters and Voices
Charlie Brown   Dylan Beach
Lucy Van Pelt   Sarah Beach
Sally Brown   Gail M. Davis
Peppermint Patty   Stuart Brotman
Schroeder   Greg Felton
Linus Van Pelt   Liam Martin
Rerun   Vinnie Dow
Frieda   Michelle Muller

It's Arbor Day, Charlie Brown began with Sally Brown telling her class that Arbor Day is "the day when all the ships sail into the arbor." But Sally soon learned, with the help of her heartthrob Linus, that it was a day of beautification and conservation, celebrated by the planting of trees. Love was also in the air with Sally pursuing the romantically uninclined Linus and Peppermint Patty yearning for a reluctant Charlie Brown. Meantime, the gang decided they must do their part for Arbor Day. So they pitched in, at first with trees and then on to everything growable from trailing vines to vegetables. The only one left out of the green-thumb fury was Charlie, who thought they were tidying up the ballpark for the coming game, blissfully unaware that a veritable jungle was being sown in the middle of his beloved baseball field, including a large tree planted on the pitcher's mound. "It's about time we had a little class on the pitcher's mound," said Lucy behind Charlie's back. Somewhat

remorseful at their deed, however, they named it "Charlie Brown
Field." Near the end, Sally read a tribute to the Arbor Day founder,
J. Sterling Morton, quoting from his Arbor Day address of 1894:
"So every man, woman, and child who plants trees shall be able to
say on coming as I come, toward the evening of life, in all sincerity
and truth, 'If you seek my monument, look around you!'"

Rerun joined the cast for the first time in this Peanuts special,
making his entrance on the backseat of his mother's bicycle. Schulz
developed the character while observing the number of small children
strapped and harnessed to various conveyances. "You look at these
little kids hanging on to their elders ... and you wonder what goes
through their minds," he noted. Rerun was "a kind of interpreter
to those silent thoughts and impressions."

IT'S FLASHBEAGLE, CHARLIE BROWN

Broadcast History
    Premiere: April 16, 1984
    CBS/Monday 8:00-8:30 PM
    Sponsors: Nabisco Brands, Peter Paul Cadbury
    CBS/Repeats: January 1, 1985; May 27, 1986
Producers: Lee Mendelson, Bill Melendez
Directors: Bill Melendez, Sam Jaimes
Writer/Creator: Charles M. Schulz
Music & Lyrics: Desiree Goyette, Ed Bogas
Company: Lee Mendelson-Bill Melendez Productions in association with
    Charles M. Schulz Creative Associates and United Media
Home Video: Snoopy's Home Video Library #M335/Hi-Tops Video
    (nee Media Home Entertainment)

Principal Characters and Voices

Charlie Brown	Brett Johnson
Sally Brown	Stacey Ferguson
Schroeder	Gary Goren
Peppermint Patty	Gini Holtzman
Marcie	Keri Houlihan
Linus Van Pelt	Jeremy Schoenberg
School Teacher	Desiree Goyette
Snoopy	Bill Melendez

Vocalists:
    Desiree Goyette, Joey Scarbury, Kevin Brando, Joseph Chemay,
Stacey Ferguson, Gini Holtzman, Brad Kesten, Jessie Lee Smith,
David Wagner

It's Flashbeagle, Charlie Brown cleverly integrated some production
numbers in this musical romp with Snoopy and the Peanuts clan.
Dance fever seized the pooch and he doggedly pursued it to a whole
new lifestyle. Setting up his sound system outside his doghouse,
Snoopy practiced his new steps after dark. He spent hours in the

painstaking ritual as a disco hound, primping in front of a mirror, meticulously blow-drying his hair, brushing his ears, applying cologne and selecting his clothes. Finally donning a flashdance-like sweatshirt, headband and leg warmers, he strutted off to the club. Once on the dance floor, he put on a mind-boggling display of high-stepping acrobatic disco dancing that left his fellow patrons clamoring for more. The strenuous routine forced him to sleep late every morning, which strained his relationship with Charlie Brown, who wistfully lamented, "Some kids have dogs who follow them to school." But Snoopy was not the only one in the grip of the big beat. Peppermint Patty was still having trouble in class, snoozing, flubbing a quiz, and even getting her looseleaf binder stuck on her head. But she shined in physical education. "I wish all the classes were gym," she confessed to Lucy. Once in her leotards she showed why, leading the class in a spirited musical aerobics routine that conclusively proved her contention, "I'm in shape." Also demonstrating she could sing and dance, Lucy took over a well-mannered game of Simon Says, turning it into her own raucous musical number. Even Charlie displayed some unsuspected musical talent, cutting loose and leading the class in a loud and fast-paced barn dance. Still perplexed, however, Charlie could not understand why his beagle was so lifeless in the daytime. "You don't do any of the things that a dog is supposed to do--bark at strangers, bring me in the paper in the morning, bring me my slippers at night," he scolded Snoopy. "There's nothing worse than owning a dog who isn't a dog." Then Charlie found out that Snoopy was still a dog after all, and much more, when he burned up the dance floor. Songs: "It's Flashbeagle, Charlie Brown" (Scarbury/Goyette), "I'm in Shape" (Patty), "Lucy Sez" (Lucy), "Pig Pen Hoe-Down," "It's Snoopy."

Marine Jahan, who performed much of the dancing in the movie Flashdance (PAR, 1983) and Jill Schulz, daughter of Charles Schulz, were models for Snoopy's dancing and Peppermint Patty's aerobics, respectively, through the rotoscope animation technique.

IT'S MAGIC, CHARLIE BROWN

Broadcast History
  Premiere: April 28, 1981
  CBS/Tuesday 8:00-8:30 PM
  CBS/Repeats: March 22, 1982; March 23, 1985
Executive Producer: Lee Mendelson
Producer: Bill Melendez
Director: Phil Roman
Writer/Creator: Charles M. Schulz
Music: Ed Bogas, Judy Munsen
Company: Lee Mendelson-Bill Melendez Productions in association
  with Charles M. Schulz Creative Associates and United Feature
  Syndicate
Home Video: Hi-Tops Video (nee Media Home Entertainment)

Principal Characters and Voices

Charlie Brown	Michael Mandy
Sally Brown	Cindi Reilly
Linus Van Pelt	Earl "Rocky" Reilly
Marcie	Shannon Cohn
Schroeder/Franklin	Christopher Donohoe
Lucy Van Pelt	Sydney Penny
Snoopy	Bill Melendez
Voice	Casey Carlson

It's Magic, Charlie Brown presented the amazing feats and slight of paw of "The Great Houndini," Snoopy, who checked out a library book entitled "How to Perform Magic" and took its message to heart. Performing his first show in front of the neighborhood gang, the prodigious pooch had a few kinks in his act he needed to work out-- such as the solid rings that interlocked but would not come apart, and getting his three-sectional magic closet to release an entrapped Peppermint Patty. Linus fainted dead away when Snoopy was unable to restore the multiple pieces of his scissored blanket. And Lucy was pretty sore at returning to the ground with a resounding thud while being levitated. Topping it all, Snoopy made good ol' Charlie Brown disappear, only to discover that making him visible again was not so easy. "Good grief, they can't see me!" said Charlie later at the baseball field, where after 900 straight losses his team actually won a game on Snoopy's home run. "We finally won a game, and I wasn't even in it," Charlie Brown said, more than just a bit depressed. "I'm doomed," he lamented, "to walk the world as a lost soul." But then he discovered he could sneak up on Lucy, practicing to hold the football for a placekick, and actually boot it off the tee for the first time. After three successful kicks, however, Snoopy waved his wand, Charlie became visible, Lucy yanked the ball and Charlie landed with a back-breaking thump. "Welcome home, Charlie Brown," said the treacherous Lucy. "I did it," said an elated Charlie, "I finally kicked that football!" And during a happy reunion he hugged Snoopy, who levitated a protesting Lucy into limbo.

IT'S THE EASTER BEAGLE, CHARLIE BROWN

Broadcast History
    Premiere: April 9, 1974
    CBS/Tuesday 8:00-8:30 PM
    Sponsors: Kellogg's, Dolly Madison; Cadbury, Nabisco Brands
    CBS/Repeats: March 26, 1975; April 12, 1976; April 4, 1977;
        March 19, 1978; April 9, 1979; March 26, 1986
Executive Producer: Lee Mendelson
Producer: Bill Melendez
Director: Phil Roman
Writer/Creator: Charles M. Schulz
Music: Vince Guaraldi, John Scott Trotter

Company: Lee Mendelson-Bill Melendez Productions in association
with Charles M. Schulz Creative Associates and United Feature
Syndicate

Home Video: Hi-Tops Video (nee Media Home Entertainment)

Principal Characters and Voices

Charlie Brown	Todd Barbee
Lucy Van Pelt	Melanie Kohn
Linus Van Pelt	Stephen Shea
Peppermint Patty	Linda Ercoli
Sally Brown	Lynn Mortensen
Marcie	James Ahrens

It's the Easter Beagle, Charlie Brown observed another holiday in
Peanutland.   All Lucy could think about was another great excuse
for boys to give presents to pretty girls, "a great time of the year
for getting," which enraged Schroeder: "It's a time for renewal--
the start of spring ... All you can think about is gimme, gimme,
gimme!"   "That's called survival, baby!" Lucy retorted.   Meanwhile,
Peppermint Patty's preparations were having trouble getting off the
ground when Marcie used up three dozen eggs, frying, cooking and
boiling them without the shells.   But not to worry, advised Linus,
who insisted that an Easter Beagle would magically appear to hand
out colorful Easter eggs on Easter morning.   With fresh memories on
her mind of their futile vigil spent awaiting the Great Pumpkin, Sally
was skeptical.   "The Easter Beagle will never let you down," said
Linus.   "I know he won't.   But what about you?" Sally retorted.
Practical Lucy couldn't be bothered by her brother's stupid ideas.
"You paint the eggs, you hide the eggs, you find the eggs," she
stated.   Snoopy was busy too, nosing into Woodstock's new birdhouse,
which he accidently trashed and had to replace.   Spying on Lucy as
she hid her eggs, Snoopy quickly gathered them up and distributed
his basket of goodies as the frolicking Easter Beagle, but found it
empty when he came to good ol' Charlie Brown, who could only let
out a big sigh.   At the close, Snoopy kissed an infuriated Lucy on
the cheek and anger turned to joy as she exclaimed: "The Easter
Beagle!"
   The original airing of the show marked the 50th broadcast (including repeats) of a Peanuts special.   In 1977, more than 1,200
viewers, most of them angry parents, flooded the switchboards at
CBS Television City, Los Angeles, complaining vigorously because a
tennis match pushed back the start of the repeated special on the
West Coast.

IT'S THE GREAT PUMPKIN, CHARLIE BROWN

Broadcast History
   Premiere: October 27, 1966
   CBS/Thursday 8:30-9:00 PM
   Sponsors: Coca-Cola; Dolly Madison, McDonald's, Peter Paul Cad-
   bury, Nabisco

CBS/Repeats: October 26, 1967; October 24, 1968; October 26, 1969; October 24, 1970; October 23, 1971; October 28, 1974; October 23, 1976; October 30, 1978; October 22, 1979; October 24, 1980; October 30, 1981; October 25, 1982; October 28, 1983; October 26, 1984; October 30, 1985; October 24, 1986
Executive Producer: Lee Mendelson
Director: Bill Melendez
Writer/Creator: Charles M. Schulz
Music: Vince Guaraldi, John Scott Trotter
Company: Lee Mendelson-Bill Melendez Productions in association with Charles M. Schulz Creative Associates and United Feature Syndicate
Record Albums: Disneyland 2604, 3704 (with book), 404 (single); Western Publishing
Home Video: Snoopy's Home Video Library #M339/Hi-Tops Video (nee Media Home Entertainment)

Principal Characters and Voices

Charlie Brown	Peter Robbins
Lucy Van Pelt	Sally Dryer
Linus Van Pelt	Christopher Shea
Sally Brown	Kathy Steinberg
Peppermint Patty	Lisa DeFaria
Frieda	Ann Altieri

It's the Great Pumpkin, Charlie Brown reflected on the meaning of Halloween to the Peanuts clan. The holiday season meant happiness for Charlie Brown, who was finally invited to a party; heroics for Snoopy, the canine combatant, who engaged the Red Baron in fierce, wild-blue-yonder aerobatics; and the moment of truth for the blanket-toting Linus, who sat in the pumpkin patch awaiting the arrival of the Great Pumpkin, "with a bag of toys for all the good children." Linus talked Sally into joining him in the patch to await the elusive jack-o'-lantern, but only Snoopy arrived in his flying helmet, goggles and scarf, silhouetted against the moon. Furious, Sally abandoned the whole idea and went home. Meanwhile, the rest of the gang went trick-or-treating, and poor ol' Charlie received only rocks in his bag.
     Charlie Brown's lack of success at trick-or-treating inspired viewers throughout the country to send hundreds of bags of candy for him to creator Charles Schulz every time the special aired. The program included Snoopy's first fantasy scene, furiously battling his skillful enemy the Red Baron (who flew a Fokker Triplane in the strips) while astride his Sopwith Camel (his doghouse), five minutes of pantomime which convinced Schulz and the producers that the beagle could become a TV star, albeit silent. Subsequently, Snoopy was made one of the leading characters in You're a Good Sport, Charlie Brown [q.v.] and A Charlie Brown Thanksgiving [q.v.]. Schulz's son Monte, whose avid hobby was First World War model airplanes, was the inspiration for the Red Baron comic strips and animated premise.

IT'S YOUR FIRST KISS, CHARLIE BROWN

Broadcast History
   Premiere: October 24, 1977
   CBS/Monday 8:00-8:30 PM
   Sponsors: Interstate Brands; Peter Paul, McDonald's
   CBS/Repeats: January 8, 1979; January 14, 1980; January 30,
     1981
Executive Producer: Lee Mendelson
Producer: Bill Melendez
Director: Phil Roman
Writer/Creator: Charles M. Schulz
Music: Ed Bogas
Company: Lee Mendelson-Bill Melendez Productions in association
   with Charles M. Schulz Creative Associates and United Feature
   Syndicate
Home Video: Hi-Tops Video (nee Media Home Entertainment)

Principal Characters and Voices
Charlie Brown	Arrin Skelley
Peppermint Patty	Laura Planting
Linus Van Pelt	Daniel Anderson
Lucy Van Pelt	Michelle Muller
Franklin	Ronald Hendrix
Snoopy	
Woodstock	

It's Your First Kiss, Charlie Brown revolved around the Birchwood
School's annual homecoming football game and dance. It was traditional that the celebration could not begin until the homecoming
queen received a kiss, the traditional duty that befell Charlie in
his role as escort of Heather, none other than the stupified tyke's
Little Red-Haired "dream girl." First, Charlie also had to prove his
mettle as place-kicker on Peppermint Patty's team in the big football
game, refereed by Snoopy, who got speared by the down marker when
it was moved by Woodstock. Of course, Lucy was up to all her old
tricks, pulling the ball away just as Charlie was about to kick off
and while trying for the extra point after a scoring run by Patty--
"Chuck, you really goofed-up on that play!" Later, with the score
21 to 20 and a chance to win the game with a field goal, Lucy did it
again and Birchwood lost. "Linus, I made a fool of myself," said
the embarassed Charlie, "How can I face the Little Red-Haired Girl?"
"Look at it this way, Charlie Brown," said Linus, "It's better to get
bad press than no press at all." At the dance, Charlie surprised
everyone when he gave Heather a big kiss and lapsed into an ecstatic
swoon. The next day, Linus reminded Charlie "You were the life of
the party. You lost the game, but sure took honors at the dance."
"Did I do all that?" asked Charlie, trying to recall. "What good is
it to do anything if you can't remember what you did?" "Well," said
Linus, "at least it was your first kiss, Charlie Brown."
     Charles Schulz broke one of his cardinal rules for this special

by portraying Charlie Brown's heartthrob, the Little Red-Haired Girl, for the first time. One of the highest rated _Peanuts_ specials, Patty's crack about "goofing up" the kick brought so many protesting viewer letters saying it was Lucy's fault, not Charlie Brown's, that the words were dubbed out for the repeat broadcasts.

IT'S YOUR 20TH TELEVISION ANNIVERSARY, CHARLIE BROWN

Broadcast History
    Premiere: May 14, 1985
    CBS/Tuesday 8:00-9:00 PM
    CBS/Repeat: February 10, 1987
Executive Producer: Lee Mendelson
Associate Producer: Glenn Mendelson
Director/Live Action: Lee Mendelson
Directors/Animation: Bill Melendez, Phil Roman, Sam Jaimes
Writer/Creator: Charles M. Schulz
Music: Vince Guaraldi, Desiree Goyette, Ed Bogas, Judy Munsen
Company: Lee Mendelson-Bill Melendez Productions in association
    with Charles M. Schulz Creative Associates and United Media Pro-
    ductions/60 minutes

Host: Charles Schulz

It's Your 20th Television Anniversary, Charlie Brown celebrated two successful decades on the network with nostalgic moments from 26 previous _Peanuts_ specials, a rare behind-the-scenes look at what went into their making and some new musical numbers. Creator Charles Schulz was host-raconteur of the milestone animated and live-action hour. Beginning with scenes from the award-winning A Charlie Brown Christmas, which launched the special series in 1965, dozens of acclaimed magical moments of hilarity, love, tears and music that made _Peanuts_ history were screened. In the segment devoted to Snoopy, the beagle battled the Red Baron and arm-wrestled with Lucy in earlier days, was depicted in his "Joe Cool" phase, briefly joined the circus, displayed his various athletic skills and burned up the dance floor as "Flashbeagle." Perennial loser Charlie Brown was viewed from his earliest baseball failures to almost winning a decathalon. Linus awaited the Great Pumpkin again, fought for his beloved blanket and philosophized to his peers. Lucy was shown mellowing slightly but still Charlie's main antagonist. Peppermint Patty, Sally Brown, Marcie, Schroeder and the rest of the clan also demonstrated their distinctive personalities. And segments dubbed in French, German and Japanese were introduced in a tribute to the series' international fans. Showing how music reflected the changing times via a split screen, Snoopy and Marine Jahan were seen with the dogged beagle following the real-life Flashdance star's steps and performing aerobics patterned after Schulz's daughter, Jill, both used as models for the musical numbers. Spilling over the dance floor in a new production number, the _Peanuts_ performed to the beat of "Lets Have a Party," and in top hat, white tie and tails, Snoopy was a dancing, singing whirlwind in the also new "My Big Debut." From his Santa Rosa, California, studio, Schulz, who has drawn the Peanuts comic strip about 13,000 times since its creation in 1950, explained how the characters and stories developed from his own experiences, how he created new ones and how television had influenced them. With the help of producers Lee Mendelson and Bill Melendez, he traced the production of a special, from the story conferences through the techniques of animation to a recording session of the voices. Among the voice-actors introduced were several, now adults, including Peter Robbins who voiced the first Charlie Brown 20 years ago. Schulz paid tribute to the individuals involved in the productions, such as Melendez, responsible for the animation of all the specials, and the late Vince Guaraldi, who composed the distinctive musical scores for the early programs. Songs: "Lets Have A Party," "My Big Debut," "It's Flashbeagle, Charlie Brown," "I'm in Shape."

IVANHOE

Broadcast History
    Premiere: November 27, 1975
    CBS/FAMOUS CLASSIC TALES, Thursday 12:30-1:30 PM
    Sponsor: Kenner Products (Toy Group, General Mills)
    SYN/Repeats: December 13, 1975 +
Producer: Walter J. Hucker
Director: Leif Gram
Writer: John Palmer
Music: Richard Bowden
Company: Air Programs International, Sydney, Australia/60 minutes
Distributor: D. L. Taffner ("Animated Classics for Children")/1983-
Home Video: Classics for Kids (MGM/UA)

Voices
    Alistair Duncan, Barbara Frawley, Chris Haywood, Mark Kelly, John Llewellyn, Helen Morse, Bevan Wilson

Ivanhoe, loosely based on the 1820 romantic adventure by Sir Walter Scott set in feudal twelfth-century England, centered on the young knight who returned from the Crusades in Palestine to find Prince John and his Norman nobles oppressing the people. After Ivanhoe defended the honor of the Saxons at a tournament, defeating the Prince's champion, a web of intrigue developed in which Lady Rebecca, daughter of a rich merchant, was held by Prince John for ransom, and Ivanhoe, wounded at the joust, was held prisoner at a nearby castle. Freed by Robin Hood and his Merry Men, Ivanhoe in turn rescued Rebecca, and King Richard returned to right the wrongs.

JACK AND THE BEANSTALK. © 1967, Hanna-Barbera Productions, Inc. Courtesy of Hanna-Barbera Productions and TECO.

JACK AND THE BEANSTALK

Broadcast History
   Premiere: February 26, 1967
   NBC/Sunday 7:30-8:30 PM
   Sponsor: Your Gas Company
   NBC/Repeat: January 16, 1968
   CBS/Repeat: January 15, 1971
   SYN/Repeats: 1975 +
   DIS/Repeats: multiple option, 1986-1987
Executive Producers: William Hanna, Joseph Barbera
Producer/Director: Gene Kelly
Associate Producer: Bill Perez
Writers: Michael Morris, Larry Markes
Music/Songs & Lyrics: Sammy Cahn, James Van Heusen
Music: Lenny Hayton
Company: Hanna-Barbera Productions/60 minutes
Distributor: Worldvision Enterprises/1979-
Home Video: Worldvision

Cast
Jeremy Keen   Gene Kelly
Jack   Bobby Riha
Mother   Marian McKnight

Principal Characters and Voices

Arnold the Mouse	Chris Allen
Monster Cat	Dick Beals
Princess Serena	Janet Waldo
	Marni Nixon (singing)
Giant	Ted Cassidy
Woggle Bird	Cliff Norton
Others	Jack DeLeon

Announcer: Art Gilmore

Jack and the Beanstalk combined live action and animation in a sterling musical production of the "Once upon a time" favorite. Meeting Jeremy Keen, a Yankee peddler, on his way to market to sell Maude, the family cow, Jack was conned into exchanging the animal for a handful of magical beans. Reprimanded by his mother, who threw the beans out the window, Jack awoke next morning to find not only a sky-high stalk which had sprouted but Jeremy and Maude as well. Together, Jeremy and Jack ventured up the vine, hoping to find fame and fortune at the top. Instead of a pot of gold, however, they found a gruff cartoon giant who made them prisoners in his castle. While escaping, they encountered the captive Princess Serena, forever attached to a golden harp by the giant's black spell. Before they could make their way to safety by finding the giant's flying goose, the giant upset their plan and locked Serena in the treasure room. With the help of Arnold the Mouse and a "Minute Mice" regiment, they located the key, Jeremy's kiss freed Serena from the spell and the three fled on the wings of Lucy, the Golden Goose. Bidding a bittersweet farewell to Jeremy, Serena returned to her kingdom, and the two adventurers, pursued by the giant, made a hasty retreat down the beanstalk, managing to chop it down just in time. Jack's mother, who bore an amazing resemblance to Princess Serena, thanked Jeremy for safely returning her son, invited him in for a cup of tea, and they all lived happily ever after. Songs: "Half Past April and a Quarter to May," "It's Been Nice" (Riha & Kelly), "A Tiny Bit of Faith," "What Does a Woggle Bird Do?" (Kelly), "One Starry Moment" (Nixon), "Stiffen Up," "I Sure Hate Love" (Riha). Television Academy Emmy award (1966-1967), Outstanding Children's Program.

The special reunited the talents of Gene Kelly with Bill Hanna and Joe Barbera, who animated the sequences for Anchors Aweigh (MGM, 1945), in which Kelly danced with Jerry Mouse.

JACK FROST

Broadcast History
    Premiere: December 13, 1979
    NBC/Thursday 8:00-9:00 PM
    NBC/Repeat: December 5, 1980
    SYN/Repeats: 1987 +

Producers/Directors: Arthur Rankin, Jr., Jules Bass
Writer: Romeo Muller
Music: Maury Laws, Jules Bass
Company: Rankin-Bass Productions/60 minutes
Distributor: Lorimar Syndication ("Animated Holiday Specials")/
    1987-
Home Video: Lightning Video

Narrator
Pardon-Me-Pete   Buddy Hackett

Principal Characters and Voices
Jack Frost   Robert Morse
Elisa   Debra Clinger
Kubla Kraus/Father Winter   Paul Frees
TV Announcer   Dave Garroway
Elisa's Father/Danny   Larry Storch
Elisa's Mother   Dee Stratton
Snip   Don Messick
Holly   Diana Lynn

Jack Frost introduced the icy spirit of Winter, who moved from the
South Pole to enjoy wintertime with the children of January Junction.
In the story, told by Pardon-Me-Pete, the world's most famous groundhog, the children there had built a snowwoman, Elisa, who warmed
the invisible Jack's heart. In order to be seen, he struck a deal
with Father Winter that after he defeated Kubla Kraus, a villianous
giant, he would become visible to the beautiful, and now human,
Elisa. So Father Winter granted Jack a season of human life in which
he had to acquire a horse, a home, a wife and a pot of gold. After
battling with the terrible Kraus and his robot knights, the victorious
Jack had a home, a real castle. And there was gold and a robot
horse there too. But before he could propose to Elisa, he found her
preparing to marry a true knight in shining armor. Realizing that
his romantic winter had been but a fantasy, Jack showered the newly-
weds with springtime. The special was filmed using stop-motion animated puppets (Animagic). Songs: "Me and My Shadow," "The Christmas Song," "Jack Frost," "Lonely Being...," "There's the Rub," "She
Is Beautiful," "Just What I Always Wanted," "The Groundhog's Song."

JACK O' LANTERN

Broadcast History
    Premiere: October 29, 1972
    SYN/FESTIVAL OF FAMILY CLASSICS, WABC, New York, Sun-
        day 7:00-7:30 PM
    SYN/Repeats: 1973 +
Producers/Directors: Arthur Rankin, Jr., Jules Bass
Associate Producer: Mary Alice Dwyer
Writer: William J. Keenan

Music: Maury Laws, Jules Bass
Company: Rankin-Bass Productions
Distributor: Viacom Enterprises ("Family Classics")/1986-
Home Video: Prism (with YANKEE DOODLE)

Jack O' Lantern captured the spooky aura of Halloween with a collection of transparent comical ghosts, ghouls and goblins floating in and out of the story about Jack's running battle with Zelda, a broomstick-riding witch, and her henpecked warlock husband, Sir Archibald. It was related to young Michael and his sister Colleen by their grandfather as the scenes unfolded from his memory. An elfish leprechaun with a pumpkin head, Jack was forced to relinquish his magic pot of gold when the youngsters' counterparts of two generations before were captured by Sir Archibald. The day was saved when their grandfather's goat, Billy, butted Sir Archibald into a barn stall, enabling Jack to recover his gold and cancel out Zelda's evil spells.

JACK RABBIT STORY, THE   see   EASTER FEVER

JEAN MARSH CARTOON SPECIAL, THE

Broadcast History
    Premiere: March 10, 1975
    PBS/Monday 7:00-8:00 PM
    PBS/Repeats: multiple, 1975 +
Executive Producer: Zev Putterman
Producer: Dave Connell
Director: Jim Scalem
Writers: Jim Thurman, Norman Stiles
Company: KQED, San Francisco, for PBS/60 minutes

Hosts: Jean Marsh, Grover Monster

The Jean Marsh Cartoon Special featured a collection of animated films for children, including a Road Runner cartoon by Chuck Jones; a monster film by children's book illustrator Maurice Sendak; and products of San Francisco's studio Imagination, Inc., Oscar-winning producer-director John Hubley (The Moonbird, 1959) and other animators. The elements were introduced by Grover Monster, one of the original Muppets seen on Sesame Street (PBS, 1969-) and Jean Marsh, remembered as Rosie the maid in Upstairs, Downstairs (PBS, 1974-1977). In the following month, Marsh was the hostess for the 13-week series, The International Animation Festival (PBS, 1975), which was also produced at KQED, San Francisco, described in Children's Television, Part I (Scarecrow, 1983) pp. 148-149. The program was sometimes logged as The Grover Monster Cartoon Special.

JIM HENSON'S MUPPET BABIES

Broadcast History
Premiere: December 18, 1984
CBS/Tuesday 9:00-9:30 PM
Sponsors: Campbell's Soups, Sears
Executive Producers: Margaret Loesch, Lee Gunther
Producers: Bob Richardson, Jim Henson
Directors: John Gibbs, Gerry Chiniquy, Jeff Hale, Tom Ray, James Walker, Dave Brian, Brad Case, Jeff Hill, Joan Swanson, Norm McCabe
Writer: Jeffrey Scott
Music: Rob Walsh, Alan O'Day, Janis Liebhart, Scott Brownie
Company: Henson Associates (ha!) in association with Marvel Productions

Principal Characters and Voices
Kermit/Beaker	Frank Welker
Piggie	Laurie O'Brien
Fozzie/Scooter	Greg Berg
Rowlf	Katie Lee
Skeeter/Animal	Howie Mandel
Gonzo	Russi Taylor
Nanny	Barbara Billingsley

Jim Henson's Muppet Babies featured the first appearance of the toddler creations in prime time on a CBS Special Presentation. Entitled "Gonzo's Video Show," the Muppet Babies played show-business in their nursery with a videotape camera supplied by Nanny. Piggie primped as the star and assumed the dual role as director, with Kermit as her leading man in an Arabian fantasy. "Carry me off into the sunset," said the piglet to her "great green hunk," staggering under his formidable task. Between scenes Fozzie told his stale jokes ("wukka, wukka, wukka") while the gang staged a rock music video starring the divine swine and taped their own movie adaptation of Star Wars with the stock characters in various roles such as Kermit Skywalker, Princess Piggie, Gonz Solo, Animal Vader, Obe Konabe Rowlf. Song/Theme: "I'm Going to Be a Star" (Piggie).

The program was an episode from the popular Saturday morning Emmy award-winning series, Jim Henson's Muppet Babies (CBS, 1984-1985/1986-), which returned in its second year as the hour-long program, Jim Henson's Muppets, Babies and Monsters (CBS, 1985-1986), and added 12 new stories in the original format for 1986-1987.

JOHNNY APPLESEED

Broadcast History
Premiere: November 5, 1972

SYN/FESTIVAL OF FAMILY CLASSICS, WABC, New York, Sunday
    7:00-7:30 PM
SYN/Repeats: 1973 +
Producers/Directors: Arthur Rankin, Jr., Jules Bass
Associate Producer: Mary Alice Dwyer
Writer: William J. Keenan
Music: Maury Laws, Jules Bass
Company: Rankin-Bass Productions
Distributor: Viacom Enterprises ("Family Classics")/1986-
Home Video: Prism (with BALLAD OF PAUL BUNYAN)

Johnny Appleseed enhanced the story of the folk hero who roamed
the land planting apple seeds that eventually grew to provide fruit
throughout the country. A kind, loving eccentric, this barefoot
Johnny wore an upside-down cooking pot on his head with two birds
perched on the handle and a raccoon squatting on top, his tail hanging down Johnny's back. Eating an apple a day and drinking a quart
of apple juice a day was Johnny's prescription on how to stay healthy
over the winter. He set up an assembly line to bottle "Dr. Appleseed's Winter Comfort Apple Medicine." But some of the townfolk
still liked Doc Staywell's worthless quack medicine and despite Johnny's
warnings, became sick. After Doc finally realized that Johnny's
medicine was better and started filling his own bottles with apple
juice, his scheme was discovered and foiled. Repentant, Doc agreed
to take over as apple seed planter for Johnny's western territory.

JOURNEY BACK TO OZ

Broadcast History
    Premiere: December 5, 1976
    ABC/Sunday 7:00-9:00 PM
    Sponsor: Procter & Gamble
    SYN/Repeat: SFM HOLIDAY NETWORK, December 1978
Producers: Norman Prescott, Louis Scheimer
Directors: Hal Sutherland, Rudy Larriva, Don Towsley, Don Chris-
    tensen
Writers: Fred Ladd, Norman Prescott
Music/Songs & Lyrics: Sammy Cahn, James Van Heusen
Music: Walter Scharf
Company: Filmation/120 minutes
Distributor: SFM Entertainment/1978-
Record Album: Filmation FM 17
Home Video: MGM/UA

Host
Wizard   Bill Cosby

Principal Characters and Voices
Dorothy   Liza Minnelli
Scarecrow   Mickey Rooney

JOURNEY BACK TO OZ. © 1974, Filmation Associates. Courtesy of
Group W Productions.

Tin-Man	Danny Thomas
Cowardly Lion	Milton Berle
Aunt Em	Margaret Hamilton
Mombi (Bad Witch)	Ethel Merman
Glinda (Good Witch)	Rise Stevens
Pumpkinhead	Paul Lynde
Woodenhead	Herschel Bernardi
The Signpost	Jack E. Leonard
Toto (Dorothy's dog)	

Other Voices
    Mel Blanc, Dallas McKennon, Larry Storch

Journey Back to Oz provided Dorothy with some new companions on
her mission to save Oz from the flying villainess. In this sequel
without a Wizard, to the 1939 MGM movie, Bill Cosby was the single
live character, seen in the role of the Host Wizard who spent all his
time in a gaudily decorated hot-air balloon, watching the goings-on
down below. Through his own brand of magic, occasionally he lent
a benevolent hand in the destiny of the little girl, who was swept up
in a Kansas cyclone and once again transported to the magical kingdom.

On her journey to the Emerald City, where the Scarecrow was now King of Oz, Dorothy, with her faithful dog Toto, was joined by Pumpkinhead, scared of his own shadow, and Woodenhead the Horse, admittedly ambitious, who wanted to get to the top without working for it. The Cowardly Lion and the Tin-Man, who she met enroute, bowed out when they learned she was up against Mombi, the Bad Witch. The highlight was the raspy cackling of Ethel Merman as the bellowing voice of Mombi, who did her darndest to thwart Dorothy in her efforts to save Oz from the broom-riding old hag whose newest potion created a herd of magical green elephants. Through a magic box given her by Glinda, the Good Witch, Dorothy not only saved the Scarecrow and his kingdom but regained freedom for its citizens. Based on the books by L. Frank Baum, the 90-minute animated film portion was also released theatrically. Songs: "A Faraway Land" (Dorothy), "I Can't Make Up My Mind," "Keep a Happy Thought," "The Horse on the Carousel," "B-R-A-N-E Spells Brain!" "An Elephant Never Forgets," "You Have Only You," "If You're Gonna Be a Witch--Be a Witch!" "Return to the Land of Oz March," "That Feeling for Home" (Dorothy).

JOURNEY TO THE CENTER OF THE EARTH

Broadcast History
    Premiere: November 13, 1977
    CBS/FAMOUS CLASSIC TALES, Sunday 2:00-3:00 PM
    Sponsor: Kenner Products (Toy Group, General Mills)
    CBS/Repeat: November 23, 1978
    SYN/Repeats: 1979 +
Producer: Walter J. Hucker
Director: Richard Slapczynski
Writer: John Palmer
Music: Richard Bowden
Company: Air Programs International, Sydney, Australia/60 minutes
Distributor: D. L. Taffner ("Animated Classics for Children")/1983-
Home Video: Classics for Kids (MGM/UA)

Voices
    Lynette Curran, Alistair Duncan, Barbara Frawley, Ron Haddrick, Bevan Wilson

Journey to the Center of the Earth was another adaptation of the 1865 classic science-fiction novel by Jules Verne about the mission mounted to unravel the Earth's mysteries by Professor Lindenbrook, who uncovered a lost route deep into the core. In this version Lindenbrook, his friend Alex and guide Hans set out from Reykjavik, Iceland, to descend through the crater of a volcano to an ancient prehistoric world, emerging on the slopes of Mount Stromboli, Italy, to dumbfound Lindenbrook's rival, Professor Kippner, with an authentic dinosaur egg which when cracked revealed a baby dinosaur. It was not associated with the Saturday morning series Journey to the Center of the Earth (ABC, 1967-1969).

KIDNAPPED

<u>Broadcast History</u>
Premiere: October 22, 1973
CBS/FAMOUS CLASSIC TALES, Monday 3:00-4:00 PM
Sponsor: Kenner Products (Toy Group, General Mills)
SYN/Repeats: 1973 +
Executive Producer: Walter J. Hucker
Director: Leif Gram
Writer: John Palmer
Music: John Sangster
Company: Air Programs International, Sydney, Australia/60 minutes
Distributor: D. L. Taffner ("Animated Classics for Children")/1983-
Home Video: Classics for Kids (MGM/UA)

<u>Kidnapped</u> was an animated version of Robert Louis Stevenson's novel set in late 1700s. In Scotland, David Balfour set out to claim his inheritance but learned that his uncle Ebenezer, Master of the House of Shaws, had illegally seized his possessions. Arriving in Queensferry to see the family lawyer, David was lured aboard <u>The Covenant</u> and kidnapped by Captain Hoseason, in the pay of his uncle. Aboard, he met Alan Breck, a rescued Jacobite enroute with gold for Bonnie Prince Charlie, and after repulsing Captain Shuan at sea David was washed overboard. Surviving an attack by a blind beggar and the English king's agent, Colin Campbell, on land, David was reunited with Alan and aided by two highland clan chiefs, James Stewart and Cluny MacPherson. Finally, Alan and the lawyer tricked Ebenezer into confessing his guilt, and Alan was able to resume his journey to France when David was declared the new Master of the House of Shaws.

KING KONG SHOW, THE

<u>Broadcast History</u>
Premiere: September 6, 1966
ABC/Tuesday 7:30-8:30 PM
Executive Producers: Arthur Rankin, Jr., Jules Bass
Producer: Arthur Rankin, Jr.
Director: Jules Bass
Music: Maury Laws
Company: Rankin-Bass Productions in association with Videocraft
International/60 minutes

<u>The King Kong Show</u> was set on the Island of Mondo, a prehistoric island in the Java Sea where Professor Bond, his young son Bobby, and daughter Susan befriended the giant ape with colossal strength. The movie monster launched his cartoon career doing battle with a throwback to the Mesozoic era, an enormous, slimy denizen called Kraken that emerged from the sea.
The special premiered two half-hour episodes from the Saturday

morning series, The King Kong Show (ABC, 1966-1969), described in Children's Television, Part I (Scarecrow, 1983), pp. 164-165. It was the first animated cartoon special and series accomplished in Japan expressly for an American network presentation. Also, it was the first preview of a Saturday morning show aired in prime time on ABC, following the NBC pioneer, The World of Secret Squirrel and Atom Ant [q.v.]. Subsequently, the networks usually presented short scenes from all their new Saturday morning children's shows, later incorporating the whole schedule in special prime-time previews.

KING OF THE BEASTS

Broadcast History
    Premiere: April 9, 1977
    NBC/Saturday 8:00-8:30 PM
    NBC/Repeat: April 19, 1978
    SYN/Repeats: 1985 +
Executive Producer: Charles G. Mortimer, Jr.
Producer/Director: Shamus Culhane
Writers: John Culhane, Charles G. Mortimer, Jr., Shamus Culhane
Music: Michael Colicchio
Lyrics: Wiley Gregor
Company: Shamus Culhane Productions in association with Westfall
    Productions
Distributor: Lorimar Syndication ("Animated Holiday Specials")/
    1986-
Home Video: Children's Video Library (Vestron) (with NOAH'S
    ANIMALS, LAST OF THE RED-HOT DRAGONS)

Principal Characters and Voices

Noah	Henry Ramer
Crocodile	Paul Soles
Lion	Carl Banas
Male Elephant	Murray Westgate
Female Elephant	Bonnie Brooks
Male Giraffe/Camel	Jay Nelson
Polar Bear	Don Mason
Ostrich/Female Penguin	Ruth Springford
Walrus	Jack Mather
Female Baby Croc	Judy Sinclair
Male Baby Croc/Mouse	Cardie Mortimer

The King of the Beasts, which explained how the lion was crowned as leader of the animal world, resurrected the menagerie aboard the Ark in Noah's Animals [q.v.]. The Elephant and Crocodile both thought themselves qualified, while the Polar Bear appeared as the smartest of the lot since he knew he was a worker, not a leader. Once the Ark had come to rest on Mount Ararat, the animals had to track down the Crocodile, who moseyed off to set up a solitary kingdom atop a mountain, joyously singing about being a loner. When the Crocodile finally returned, he nominated himself for the king, claiming he was a hardy bachelor who could devote all his time to the duties of the royal office. But Noah took the croc aside to show him he was mistaken. As a pair of eggs hatched, two emergent baby crocodiles hailed the tough he-croc as "Mama." Furious, the croc launched an all-out campaign for the crown, climaxed by a torchlight parade which accidentally set the Ark on fire. Rushing to the rescue, the heroic Lion disappeared into the flaming interior to save Noah, and the animals rejoiced for they knew he was truly the King of the Beasts. Songs: "Arkadia!" "Me, Myself and I," "Nothing's Ever Going to Worry Me," "The Old Soft Paw," "The Lord Helps Those Who Help Themselves," "Fight, Fight, Fight ... Win, Win, Win," "There Will Be a New Day," "Some Must Take the Platform," "The Polar Tariat," "Goodbye 'Til We Meet Again."

KINGDOM CHUMS: "LITTLE DAVID'S ADVENTURE," THE

Broadcast History
   Premiere: November 28, 1986
   ABC/Friday 8:00-9:00 PM

THE KINGDOM CHUMS: "LITTLE DAVID'S ADVENTURE." © 1986, Capital Cities/ABC, Inc. Courtesy of Capital Cities/ABC.

Executive Producers/Animation: Jean Chalopin, Andy Heyward
Executive Producer/Live Action: Diana Kerew
Producers/Animation: Jean Chalopin, Andy Heyward, Tetsuo Katayama
Associate Producer: Carol Corwin
Directors/Animation: Bernard Deyries, Minoru Okazaki
Director/Live Action: Colin Chilvers
Writers: Jeff Scott, Jeanne Betancourt
Music & Lyrics: Joe Raposo
Company: An ABC Production in association with DIC Enterprises
and Diana Kerew Productions/60 minutes

Cast

Mary Ann	Jenna Van Oy
Peter	Christopher Fitzgerald
Sauli	Andrew Cassese

Principal Characters and Voices

Little David	Scott Menville
	Sandi Patti (singing)
Magical Nose	John Franklin
Christopher/Cat Soldier	Billy Bowles
Goliath/Fox Soldier #3	Jim Cummings
Eliab/Fox Soldier #2	Townsend Coleman
King Saul	Paul Winchell
Rat Soldier/Frog Servant/	
Frog Soldier	Phil Proctor

Vocalists
John Franklin, Sandi Patti, Mitchell Whitfield

The Kingdom Chums: "Little David's Adventure" was an inspirational holiday special based on the Biblical story of David and Goliath. In the live-action opening, Peter's Jewish schoolmate Sauli was harrassed by three bullies, causing him to fall on Birdie, the pet of Peter's sister, Mary Ann. At their home, Sauli felt badly about the bird, but Mary Ann believed her stuffed lion Christopher when he told her to have faith. Then colorful ribbons of light streamed into the room from magical "Love" stars, pulling the three children and Mary Ann's stuffed animals through their computer into an animated world where the toys came alive. Christopher, Magical Nose and Little David, known as the Raccoon of Courage, welcomed the children and explained that they were the Kingdom Chums who rode the Love Light and knew all the world's greatest stories. Accompanying the children on the Love Light beam, Little David transported them to the story of David. There they accompanied him while he delivered supplies to his brothers, fighting with the Israelites, who had been challenged by the Phillistines to a one-on-one confrontation. Taunted by his older brother Eliab, Little David accepted their challenge, met Goliath with a slingshot and stoned and defeated him, demonstrating that with faith instead of fear one had the courage to face life's challenges. Taken by a rainbow back to Magical Nose, who returned them home, in the live-action closing Mary Ann kept the faith and found Birdie alive. And Sauli, who learned a lesson about courage, stood up to the bullies when they accosted him, and they backed off. Songs: "Greatest Stories of All" (Franklin, Patti, Whitfield), "Child of God," "Your Love Makes Me Strong" (Patti).

The film was adapted from the book Little David's Adventure (Word, 1986) by Squire D. Rushnell, ABC Vice-President, Long Range Planning and Children's Programs. An Indian housewife and two-time Grammy award-winner, Gospel singer Sandi Patti (the singing voice of Little David) gained national attention with her powerful rendition of the "Star Spangled Banner" during the gala Liberty Weekend Celebration (ABC, 1986).

KISSYFUR: "BEAR ROOTS"

Broadcast History
    Premiere: December 22, 1985
    NBC/Sunday 7:30-8:00 PM
Executive Producers: Jean Chalopin, Andy Heyward
Producers/Writers: Len Janson, Chuck Menville
Producers/Animation: Tetsuo Katayama, Koichi Ishiguro, Yasumi
    Ishida, Masanori Kobayashi
Associate Producer: Carol Corwin
Directors: Bernard Deyries, Masaaki Osumi
Music: Shuki Levy, Haim Saban
Company: NBC Productions in association with DIC Enterprises

Principal Characters and Voices

Kissyfur	R. J. Williams
Gus	Edmund Gilbert
Jolene	Terence McGovern
Floyd/Stuckey	Stu Rosen
Duane	Neil Ross
Beehonie/Miss Emmy/Toot	Russi Taylor
Lennie	Lennie Weinrib
Uncle Shelby	Frank Welker

Kissyfur: "Bear Roots" introduced a precocious young bear and his father, a big jolly-bear Gus, a pair of big top performers who gave up their nomadic life to take roots among the inhabitants of a happy swampland. Escaping from the circus train, they hooked up with a gang of anthropomorphically cute critters in Paddlecab County who convinced the pair to settle down with them. A father and son team of obnoxious pigs were the kingpins of the otherwise benevolent community of animals. Once the pig-boy insultingly called the cub "Twinkle Toes," and when he became angry over the ridicule it was difficult to understand why one so easily offended would ever admit to the name "Kissyfur." Nonetheless, thanks to his tanbark experiences, the ingratiating little bruin was a talented performer who immediately became a favorite among his peers, and Gus, a wise and imposing figure, soon loomed as a respected community leader. To-gether they saved their new neighbors from an attack by the hungry alligators, Jolene and Floyd.

The first of four Kissyfur specials aired by the network, the concept and characters were created by Phil Mendez. The films were included as episodes of the Saturday morning series, Kissyfur (NBC, 1986-1987), which was promoted as the first animated cartoon series created by a black for NBC. One of the first animated cartoon prop-erties owned by the network, obviously aired in prime time to promote and help amortize the films, the special evoked the critters and Oke-fenokee Swamp setting of Pogo [q.v.].

KISSYFUR: "THE BIRDS AND THE BEARS"

Broadcast History
    Premiere: March 30, 1986
    NBC/Sunday 7:30-8:00 PM
Executive Producers: Jean Chalopin, Andy Heyward
Producers: Len Janson, Chuck Menville
Producers/Animation: Tetsuo Katayama, Koichi Ishiguro, Yasumi
    Ishida, Masamori Kobayashi
Associate Producer: Carol Corwin
Directors: Bernard Deyries, Masaaki Osumi
Writers: Len Janson, Chuck Menville, Gene Ayers
Music: Shuki Levy, Haim Saban
Company: NBC Productions in association with DIC Enterprises

Principal Characters and Voices

Kissyfur	R. J. Williams
Gus	Edmund Gilbert
Jolene	Terence McGovern
Floyd/Stuckey	Stu Rosen
Duane	Neil Ross
Beehonie/Miss Emmy/Toot	Russi Taylor
Lennie	Lennie Weinrib
Uncle Shelby	Frank Welker

Kissyfur: "The Birds and the Bears" featured the same characters seen in the first special and was built around the visit of Miss Emmy Lou's city-wise niece Donna, who visited Paddlecab County and lured Kissyfur and the swamp kids down a path of mischief. In their en-thusiasm to impress Miss Emmy's sophisticated relative, Kissyfur and the swamp kids ran into trouble after building a raft. While floating down the river together, their reckless joyride became a struggle to survive when they were caught up in some raging rapids and pur-sued as a tasty meal by the hungry swamp 'gators, Jolene and Floyd. Coming to their rescue, Gus saved the soaked youngsters and dis-patched the 'gators to another part of the swamp.

KISSYFUR: "THE LADY IS A CHUMP"

Broadcast History
    Premiere: June 1, 1986
    NBC/Sunday 7:30-8:00 PM
Executive Producers: Jean Chalopin, Andy Heyward
Associate Producer: Carol Corwin
Producers/Animation: Tetsuo Katayama, Koichi Ishiguro, Yasumi
    Ishida, Masanori Kobayashi
Directors: Bernard Deyries, Masaaki Osumi
Writers: Charles Kaufman, Mark Nasatir
Music: Shuki Levy, Haim Saban
Company: NBC Productions in association with DIC Enterprises

Principal Characters and Voices

Kissyfur	R. J. Williams
Gus	Edmund Gilbert
Jolene	Terence McGovern
Floyd/Stuckey	Stu Rosen
Duane	Neil Ross
Beehonie/Miss Emmy/Toot	Russi Taylor
Lennie	Lennie Weinrib
Uncle Shelby	Frank Welker

Kissyfur: "The Lady Is a Chump" unfrocked the bear cub's new
nanny as an imposter bent on a tasty meal. Unwittingly, Gus hired
Floyd the 'gator, disguised in a female bear's outfit, to help with
the domestic chores. Floyd could not cook or clean but Gus and
Kissyfur pretended the nanny was wonderful anyway, until the 'gator
lured the swamp kids deep into the swamp where Jolene had a boiling
pot ready for them. Too late, the youngsters realized they had been
tricked but managed to scramble around, eluding the frustrated pair
until the arrival of Gus and Miss Emmy, who had discovered swamp
grass in the nanny's muffins and realized it was a costumed 'gator.
Again, Gus dispatched the hungry pair to a remote corner of the
swamp.

KISSYFUR: "WE ARE THE SWAMP"

Broadcast History
    Premiere: July 6, 1986
    NBC/Sunday 7:30-8:00 PM
Executive Producers: Jean Chalopin, Andy Heyward
Producers/Animation: Tetsuo Katayama, Koichi Ishiguro, Yasumi
    Ishida, Masanori Kobayashi
Associate Producer: Carol Corwin
Directors: Bernard Deyries, Masaaki Osumi
Writer: Gene Ayres
Music: Shuki Levy, Haim Saban
Company: NBC Productions in association with DIC Enterprises

Principal Characters and Voices

Kissyfur	R. J. Williams
Gus	Edmund Gilbert
Jolene	Terence McGovern
Floyd/Stuckey	Stu Rosen
Duane	Neil Ross
Beehonie/Miss Emmy/Toot	Russi Taylor
Lennie	Lennie Weinrib
Uncle Shelby	Frank Welker
Flo	Marilyn Lightstone

Kissyfur: "We Are the Swamp" placed the cub and the swamp kids in a magical place high in a tree, complete with food and a swimming hole. Lured to the lair by an old buzzard named Flo, during a drought which made everyone miserable, Kissyfur and the kids tried to leave but Flo and her snake Reggie prevented their departure. While their parents searched for them, they were forced to cook and clean and soon learned they were the main dish for dinner, which scared them into evasive action. Lurking nearby, the 'gators Jolene and Floyd also wanted a bite of them. Finally discovered by Gus and Miss Emmy, they were rescued. Flo and Reggie were dispatched far, far away as the rains came and everything returned to normal. The Moral: Don't trust strangers.

LAND OF OZ, THE   see   THANKSGIVING IN THE LAND OF OZ

LAST OF THE CURLEWS

Broadcast History
    Premiere: October 4, 1972
    ABC/ABC AFTERSCHOOL SPECIALS, Wednesday 4:30-5:30 PM
    ABC/Repeat: March 7, 1973
Producers/Directors: William Hanna, Joseph Barbera
Associate Producer: Lew Marshall
Director: Charles A. Nichols
Writer: Jameson Brewer
Music: Hoyt Curtin, Paul DeKorte
Company: Hanna-Barbera Productions/60 minutes
Distributor: Worldvision Enterprises

Narrator: Lee Vines

Principal Characters and Voices

Stan	Ross Martin
Mark	Vinnie Van Patten
Bird calls	Ginny Tyler

Last of the Curlews depicted the poignant plight of the tall, stately shore bird as the last of the species, a male and female,

LAST OF THE CURLEWS. © 1972, Hanna-Barbera Productions, Inc.
Courtesy of Hanna-Barbera Productions and TECO.

searched unsuccessfully in the northland for a mate. Not for a decade had the Eskimo curlew been sighted; the last two were photographed on the Texas coast. With the seasonal change, the scene switched to the birds' long migration to South America through violent storms, shifting cloudscapes and errant winds; of the meeting of the pair on the Patagonian seacoast; of their mating dance, vivid and exotic; and of their struggles to complete their migration back to the Arctic. Then, focusing on an autumnal woodland in the far north, there was a glimpse of a crystal-clear lake surrounded by a forest alive with wild creatures. A rifle crack underscored it was also alive with enemies. Two hunters, father and son, checked the webbing on a travois. "Strong enough to hold our buck when we get him," said Stan with anticipation. Shying away, his son Mark asked, "Do we have to drag him around after we shoot him?" Uneasily watching his father clean and oil the guns, Mark could not match his dad's enthusiasm for the hunt. At the sight of his first big buck, Mark hesitated, his finger frozen on the trigger. His hesitation seemed warranted soon after, when he picked up the dead body of the last female Eskimo curlew, senselessly shot by a farmer in a plowed field. The cartoon lesson about respect for wildlife was based on the book by Jameson Brewer and targeted for an audience 8 years old and up. Television Academy Emmy award (1972-1973), Outstanding Achievement in Children's Programming--Informational/Factual.

LAST OF THE MOHICANS, THE

Broadcast History
Premiere: November 27, 1975
CBS/FAMOUS CLASSIC TALES, Thursday 4:30-5:30 PM
Sponsor: Kenner Products (Toy Group, General Mills)
CBS/Repeat: November 25, 1981
SYN/Repeats: December 15, 1975 +
Executive Producers: William Hanna, Joseph Barbera
Producer: Neil Balnaves
Director: Chris Cuddington
Writer: Draper Lewis
Music: Hoyt Curtin, Paul DeKorte
Company: Hanna-Barbera Productions, Sydney, Australia (Southern Star Productions)/60 minutes
Distributor: Worldvision Enterprises/1979-
Home Video: Worldvision

Principal Characters and Voices

Hawkeye	Mike Road
Uncas	Casey Kasem
Chingachook	John Doucette
Cora Munro	Joan Van Ark
Alice Munro	Kristina Holland
Duncan Heyward	Paul Hecht

Magua/Soldier	Frank Welker
Colonel Allan Munro/Delaware	
Chief	John Stephenson

The Last of the Mohicans, based on James Fenimore Cooper's second novel (1826) of his five Leatherstocking Tales of frontier life, took place in the wilderness of northern New York State in 1757, during the French and Indian war. The scout Hawkeye (Natty Bumppo) and his Mohican friends Chingachook and his son Uncas were engaged in a struggle to rid the forest of the traitorous Indian Magua and his Huron band of renegades, allied with the French. During the campaign for Fort William Henry on Lake George, under attack by the French and Indians, Commander Allan Munro's daughters, Cora and Alice, enroute under the escort of the latter's fiancé, Major Duncan Heyward, were captured by Magua but rescued and conveyed to the ravaged Fort by Hawkeye. In the battle, Chingachook was killed while saving his son's life. Planning to leave for Fort Ticonderoga, where they believed the Colonel had gone with his troops, they set up camp but the girls were kidnapped again. Hawkeye and Duncan managed to free Cora from Magua, but Alice, sent to a Delaware camp nearby, was recaptured with her rescuer Uncas. After learning that Uncas was the son of their late friend Chingachook, however, the Delawares freed them and agreed to help defeat the renegades, causing Magua's men to retreat. Arriving exhausted at Fort Ticonderoga, Hawkeye reunited the girls with their father. Cora settled down there with Major Heyward while Alice rode off into the forest with Uncas, the last of the Mohicans, to try to re-establish his tribe.

LAST OF THE RED-HOT DRAGONS, THE

Broadcast History
Premiere: April 1, 1980
NBC/Tuesday 8:30-9:00 PM
SYN/Repeats: 1986 +
Executive Producer: Charles G. Mortimer, Jr.
Producer/Director: Shamus Culhane
Supervisor/Animation: Angelo Beretta
Writers: Charles G. Mortimer, Jr., Shamus Culhane, John Culhane
Music: Michael Colicchio
Lyrics: Wiley Gregor
Company: Shamus Culhane Productions with Erredia 70, Milano, Italy, in association with Westfall Productions
Distributor: Lorimar Syndication ("Animated Holiday Specials")/ 1986-
Home Video: Children's Video Library (Vestron) (with NOAH'S ANIMALS, KING OF THE BEASTS)

Principal Characters and Voices
Dragon	John Culhane

King Lion	Carl Banas
Crocodile	Paul Soles
Elephant	Murray Westgate
Penguin	Ruth Springford
Polar Bear	Don Mason
Baby Girl Crocodile	Judy Sinclair
Baby Boy Crocodile	Cardie Mortimer

The Last of the Red-Hot Dragons featured a ancient flying dragon who regained his talent for breathing fire just in time to save some of Noah's Animals [q.v.] who were marooned at the North Pole. Dispersing after surviving the flood, King Lion, Elephant, Crocodile and the baby crocs set off for the Nile, while Polar Bear, Penguin, Seal and others headed for the North Pole. However an accident trapped the Artic-bound animals in an ice cave. In an attempt to summon help, Polar Bear sent a frantic S.O.S. around the world which was eventually heard by King Lion's group. Emerging from the Nile mud and finally convinced he could fly again, the Dragon, who survived the flood by holding his breath beneath the sea for 40 days and 40 nights, a feat which had also doused his fiery flame, transported King Lion's entourage to the Pole for a rescue attempt. Trying to pierce the block of ice covering the cave's mouth with his tail, the Crocodile only succeeded in making the tip red-hot. It was then that the baby crocs hit upon the idea of using the tip to light the Dragon's fire, and his blowtorch breath melted the ice slab quickly. Surrounded by the admiring throng of animals, the venerable Dragon showed off by blasting a phenomenal fireworks display into the sky. Songs: "I'm the Last of the Red-Hot Dragons," "We Like Ice," "What a Way To Go."

LEGEND OF HIAWATHA, THE

Broadcast History
Premiere: November 24, 1983
CBS/KENNER FAMILY CLASSICS, Thursday 11:00-12:00 AM
Sponsor: Kenner-Parker Products (Toy Group, General Mills)
NBC/Repeat: NBC SPECIAL TREAT, December 4, 1984
SYN/Repeats: 1985 +
Producers: William H. Stevens, Jr., Hugh Campbell
Director: Sebastian Grunstra
Writer: Alvin Schwartz
Company: Atkinson Film-Arts, Ottawa, Canada, in association with Triple Seven Concepts/60 minutes
Distributor: Toy Group, General Mills/1985-
Home Video: Family Home Entertainment

Voices
Tim Atkinson, Barry Edward Blake, Gary Chalk, Arline Van Dine, Les Lye, Anna MacCormick, Michael Voss

The Legend of Hiawatha, based on Henry Wadsworth Longfellow's 1855 poem, followed the legendary Indian hero, half man, half god, sent to his people to teach them the ways of progress and survival. After searching across deserts and mountains for the North Wind, his mythical father, Hiawatha found love with the beautiful maiden Minnehaha and battled the evil Pearl Feather, a magical creature that had cast a plague over her and the people in his village. Before leaving to meet Minnehaha in another land, Hiawatha exorted his people to meet all things with courage: "Even in a moment of defeat, those who do not lose heart, who keep alive their hope for tomorrow, will best meet the challenges to come. That is the most important teaching I can leave you."

LEGEND OF ROBIN HOOD, THE

Broadcast History
Premiere: November 14, 1971
CBS/FAMOUS CLASSIC TALES, Sunday 5:00-6:00 PM
Sponsor: Kenner Products (Toy Group, General Mills)

THE LEGEND OF ROBIN HOOD. © 1983, D. L. Taffner/Limited. Courtesy of D. L. Taffner/Limited.

CBS/Repeats: November 11, 1972; September 30, 1973
SYN/Repeats: 1974 +
Producer: Walter J. Hucker
Director: Zoran Janjic
Writer: Alexander Buzo
Music: John Sangster
Company: Air Programs International, Sydney, Australia/60 minutes
Distributor: D. L. Taffner ("Animated Classics for Children")/1985-
Home Video: Classics for Kids (MGM/UA)

Voices
    Tim Elliott, Peter Guest, Ron Haddrick, John Kingley, John
    Llewellyn, Helen Morse, Brenda Senders

The Legend of Robin Hood relived the tales about Robin of Locksley,
the thirteenth-century bowman who acquired the name Hood from his
headpiece. With his outlawed Merry Men in Sherwood Forest, Robin
remained loyal to the crusading King Richard and campaigned to rid
England of the evil Prince John and to restore justice to the poor.
To enhance the score, composer John Sangster blended modern music
with medieval sounds performed by the Renaissance Players, an
Australian group.

LEPRECHAUN'S CHRISTMAS GOLD, THE

Broadcast History
    Premiere: December 23, 1981
    ABC/Wednesday 8:30-9:00 PM
    ABC/Repeat: December 20, 1983
    SYN/Repeats: 1985+
Producers/Directors: Arthur Rankin, Jr., Jules Bass
Writer/Lyrics: Romeo Muller
Music: Maury Laws
Company: Rankin-Bass Productions
Distributor: Lorimar Syndication ("Animated Holiday Specials")/1985
Home Video: Lightning Video (with FROSTY'S WINTER WONDERLAND)

Narrator
Barney Killakilarney   Art Carney

Principal Characters and Voices
Faye Killakilarney   Peggy Cass
Dinty Doyle   Ken Jennings
Old Mag   Christine Mitchell
Child/Others   Glynis Bieg/Michael Moronosk

The Leprechaun's Christmas Gold told the legend of how the wee folk
brought the gold to Ireland. It was about a young cabin boy, Dinty
Doyle, who discovered Christmas on an uncharted island inhabited
by the Killakilarney clan of leprechauns. Unwittingly, Dinty also

unearthed a wicked banshee, Old Mag, with whom the leprechauns had a running battle. The caterwauling banshee always was able to trick an innocent leprechaun into handing over the isle's pot of gold at the end of the rainbow. Furiously searching to find the clan's treasure before Christmas morning, this year she duped Dinty into revealing the location. However, as Old Mag reached the golden treasure, the light had set in; it was Christmas morning and the banshee was too late. Her spirit was washed out to sea as Dinty's ship returned to take them all back home to Ireland. Art Carney lent his Irish brogue as the narrator, Barney, the eldest Killakilarney. The special was filmed using stop-motion animated puppets (Animagic). Songs: "Christmas in Killarney," "Golden Gold of Ireland."

LIBERTY AND THE LITTLES

Broadcast History
Premiere: October 18, 25 & November 1, 1986
ABC/ABC WEEKEND SPECIALS, Saturday 12:00-12:30 PM
Executive Producers: Jean Chalopin, Andy Heyward
Producer: Joellyn Marlow
Writer: Marc Scott Zicree
Music: Shuki Levy, Haim Saban
Company: ABC Entertainment Productions in association with DIC Enterprises/90 minutes, 3 parts

Principal Characters and Voices

Tom Little	David Wagner
Lucy Little	Bettina Rush
Grandpa Little	Alvy Moore
Dinky Little	Robert David Hall
Helen Little	Patti Parris
William Little	Gregg Berger
Michelle/Pierre	Katie Lee
Père Egalitaire	Jim Morgan
General/Massey	Earl Boen

Liberty and the Littles, in Part I, found the tiny clan--Dinky, Grandpa, parents William and Helen, young Tom and Lucy--enroute to the Statue of Liberty's 100th anniversary in Dinky's plane when a terrible thunderstorm forced them down on Liberty Island. Chased by a guard dog, the family ran toward the statue and accidently opened a secret entrance just in time. Inside they discovered a "little" nineteenth-century town with the townspeople dressed in tattered clothes and speaking with French accents, but otherwise resembling the Littles with pointy ears and tails. On orders of the General, the Littles were captured by soldiers, who claimed they were demons. With the aid of two children, Michelle and Pierre, the Littles escaped, but William and Helen were recaptured. Searching for an old man, Père Egalitaire, said to hold the key to saving the parents, they

LIBERTY AND THE LITTLES. © 1986, Capital Cities/ABC, Inc.
Courtesy of Capital Cities/ABC.

climbed up in the arm of the statue but Dinky fell, landing safely. Forced by pursuing soldiers onto the scaffolding, which gave way, they were rescued by Dinky in his repaired plane. Meantime, outside, Massey the Magician ominously told Mr. Fuller, coordinator of the unveiling ceremonies, that the statue held a secret that once revealed would make him the greatest magician in the world. And while the party flew back to the statue to rescue William and Helen, Massey waved his magic wand and the statue disappeared.

In Part II, when the Littles flew closer they realized that the disappearance was an illusion; at Massey's command, workman inside released mirrored plastic which covered Lady Liberty. Angry over his trick, Fuller fired Massey, who vowed to make the statue disappear for good. Overhearing the threat, Grandpa and the children followed Massey to Manhattan and learned that he planned to melt Miss Liberty with a secret formula. Grandpa and Dinky decided to warn the Bigs, and Tom and Lucy set off to the Empire State Building tower, a drawing of which they spotted inside the statue's hand. At the statue, William and Helen were put on trial before the General, who threatened to torture them until they confessed to being demons. Grandpa and Dinky, in attempting to warn the Bigs by typing out a message on a newspaper's computer, barely evaded a security guard when Dinky fell onto a conveyor belt leading to the printing press. In the Empire State Building tower, Tom and Lucy found Père Egalitaire, who mistook them for the General's men and threatened to destroy them.

In Part III, Père Egalitaire realized the Littles were not sent by the General but refused to help save William and Helen. By shutting down the power, Grandpa managed to save Dinky from the presses, and they flew off to join Tom and Lucy at the Empire State Building. There Grandpa finally enlisted the aid of Père Egalitaire, who revealed how the French Littles came to the United States and that the General took dictatorial command as a teenager. Meanwhile, Massey prepared a remote control plane to fly over the statue and release his melting formula. And at the statue, the General tied William and Helen to a post inside the torch, so when it was lit the heat would force their confession. Grandpa and Dinky set out to intercept Massey's plane, while Père Egalitaire and the children went to rescue the parents. As the unveiling ceremonies began, Grandpa and Dinky managed to get inside of Massey's plane and divert it as Père Egalitaire convinced the French Littles to rise up against the General and fight for liberty and was able to save William and Helen before the torch was lit. After boasting of his plans on TV, Massey was apprehended and the ceremonies went smoothly. Thanking the Littles for their freedom, the French Littles decided to hold elections, try the General and become a democracy.

Based on the books by John Peterson, the specials featured the central "Little" characters from the successful Saturday morning series, The Littles (ABC, 1983-   ), about a clan of mouse-sized human-like creatures living in the walls of homes, facing human and animal-sized dangers at every turn. The characters were also starred in the animated movie, Here Comes the Littles (DIC, 1985).

THE LIFE AND ADVENTURES OF SANTA CLAUS. © 1985, Rankin/
Bass Productions, Inc. Courtesy of Rankin/Bass Productions.

LIFE AND ADVENTURES OF SANTA CLAUS, THE

Broadcast History
Premiere: December 17, 1985
CBS/Tuesday 8:00-9:00 PM
CBS/Repeat: December 2, 1986
Producers/Directors: Arthur Rankin, Jr., Jules Bass
Supervising Producer: Lee Dannacher
Director/Animagic: Masaki Iizuka
Writer/Lyrics: Julian P. Gardner
Music: Bernard Hoffer
Company: Rankin-Bass Productions in association with Pacific Anima-
tion Tokyo, Japan/60 minutes

Principal Characters and Voices

Great Ak	Alfred Drake
Santa	Earl Hammond
Santa (as youth)	J. D. Roth
Tingler	Robert McFadden
Necile	Lesley Miller
King Awgwa	Earle Hyman
Wind Demon	Larry Kenney
Weekum	Joey Grasso

Children	Amy Anzelowitz/Josh Blake/Ari Gold/Jamie Lisa Murphy
Others	Lynne Lipton Peter Newman

Vocalists
Al Dana, Margaret Dorn, Arlene Martell, Marty Nelson, David Ragaini, Robert Ragaini, Annette Sanders

The Life and Adventures of Santa Claus told how Claus, born a mortal, became immortal by providing pleasure to children on Christmas day. The fanciful musical began "an age ago" in the Forest of Bursee, populated by various chimerical Immortals, born to their state, who had no children or kin. Led by the Great Ak, they were called to a roundtable meeting to discuss granting immortality to Claus, whom they had adopted 60 years before, facing the spectre of death after Christmas. Related in a flashback, he was found abandoned as a babe, raised by the Immortals and named Claus, or Little One. When he was grown, Claus was given a tour of the world by the Great Ak and reluctantly returned to mortal existence to alleviate man's endless examples of inhumanity to man. Moving to the snow-covered Laughing Valley of Ho Ha Ho, he settled down as a kindly old bachelor and began his tradition of Christmas giving by making little gifts for a nearby orphanage. Soon his expanded efforts incurred the wrath of the dreaded Awgwas, child-hating nasty creatures allied with cobras and black widow spiders, who spent their time trying to make children misbehave and do terrible things. They conspired to halt Claus's toy-making operations. Laboring to bring love and joy to an unjust world, Claus did not lack for help. When his sleigh became weighed down with gifts, the reindeer lent a helping hoof. And when the Awgwas turned truly evil, the Great Ak returned to offer his magical powers, because "it is the law that good shall overcome evil," and dispatched them forthright. Finally, Claus's selflessness and efforts to cheer up children with toy presents earned him a reputation as a saint, adding Santa to his name, and was rewarded immortality to keep doing his thing. Filmed using stop-motion animated puppets (Animagic), the holiday special was based on the 1902 story by Oz creator L. Frank Baum and carried a CBS "Read More About It" book project message. Songs: "Ora E Sempré," "Babe in the Woods," "Big Surprise," "Ho-Ha-Ho!" "A Child."

LIFE IS A CIRCUS, CHARLIE BROWN

Broadcast History
    Premiere: October 24, 1980
    CBS/Friday 8:00-8:30 PM
    CBS/Repeats: January 11, 1982; January 17, 1983
Executive Producer: Lee Mendelson
Producer: Bill Melendez
Director: Phil Roman

LIFE IS A CIRCUS, CHARLIE BROWN. © 1979, United Feature
Syndicate, Inc. Courtesy of Charles M. Schulz Creative Associates
and United Media.

Writer/Creator: Charles M. Schulz
Music: Ed Bogas, Judy Munsen
Company: Lee Mendelson-Bill Melendez Productions in association
with Charles M. Schulz Creative Associates and United Feature
Syndicate
Home Video: Hi-Tops Video (nee Media Home Entertainment)

Principal Characters and Voices

Charlie Brown	Michael Mandy
Peppermint Patty	Brent Hauer
Paula	Casey Carlson
Schroeder	Christopher Donohoe
Linus Van Pelt	Earl "Rocky" Reilly
Lucy Van Pelt	Kristen Fullerton
Marcie	Shannon Cohn
Snoopy	Bill Melendez

Life Is a Circus, Charlie Brown followed the adventures of Snoopy,
who left home and became a big top star. Smitten by a fancily
preened French poodle named Fifi, a performer in a traveling circus
which came to town, the beagle trailed her into a tent to win her
affection and wound up part of the act: Miss Polly and her Poodles.
"Boy! Pretty great, Chuck! Your dog is a circus clown!" said Peppermint Patty. "Circus Clown!?" replied Charlie, "He should be
home guarding the house!" But when the circus left town, Snoopy
followed Fifi on board the train to the next show. Soon Snoopy was
billed as "Hugo the Great," stealing center ring--and loving it--with
his antics on a unicycle, the high wire and ultimately, the trapeze.
He was his poodle partner's heart-throb. Meanwhile, Charlie Brown,
who understandably was down in the dumps, said, "I don't want to
stand in his way, Linus. But after all, he got his food and lodging
from me. I expected some loyalty." But Charlie received cold comfort from Linus: "It's difficult not to be attracted by romance and
excitement, Charlie Brown. There's more to life than a plastic supper
dish." Lucy, convinced the beagle would not return, closed up his
doghouse with the sign, "Premises Condemned." Spurned by Fifi,
who preferred circus life after they ran away when Polly was pushed
by Snoopy into a vat in which she "color coordinated" the beagle
pink, the heartbroken pooch returned to good ol' Charlie Brown's,
took a shower, donned his sleeping cap and retired prone atop his
dog house, newly adorned by a neon sign, "Hugo the Great." Television Academy Emmy award (1980-1981), Outstanding Animated Program.

LION, THE WITCH, AND THE WARDROBE, THE

Broadcast History
Premiere: April 1 & 2, 1979
CBS/Sunday, Monday 8:00-9:00 PM
Sponsor: Kraft Foods
CBS/Repeat: April 22 & 23, 1980

THE LION, THE WITCH AND THE WARDROBE. © 1979, Children's
Television Workshop. Courtesy of Bill Melendez Productions.

Executive Producer: David Connell
Producer: Steven C. Melendez
Supervising Director: Bill Melendez
Directors: George Dunning, Bob Balzer, Nick Spargo, Edric Radage
Writers: David D. Connell, Bill Melendez
Music: Michael J. Lewis
Company: A Children's Television Workshop Production in associa-
   tion with Bill Melendez Productions and in cooperation with the
   Episcopal Radio-TV Foundation; by Bill Melendez Productions,
   T.V. Cartoons and Pegbar Productions, London, England/120
   minutes, 2 parts
Home Video: Vestron Entertainment #4194

Principal Characters and Voices

Lucy	Rachel Warren
Susan	Susan Sokol
Peter	Reg Williams
Edmund	Simon Adams
Mr. Tumnus	Victor Spinetti
Professor	Dick Vosburgh
Mr. Beaver	Don Parker
Mrs. Beaver	Liz Proud
Aslan	Stephen Thorne
White Witch	Beth Porter

The Lion, the Witch and the Wardrobe began with the discovery of the magical and mythical land of Narnia by four children--Lucy, Susan, Peter and Edmund--who were evacuated from London during the Blitz to an old English country home. Stepping over a magic line in the back of a wardrobe closet, they found their way into the mysteries of Narnia, where it was "always winter and never Christmas" and which at the time was under the spell of the villainous White Witch. In their adventures they met some of the residents, including a beaver family and Aslan (the Turkish word for "lion"), who emerged as the heroic character in the fantasy tale, a noble beast who with the help of the children challenged the Witch's tyrannic rule. The film was almost a word-for-word adaptation of the first book in C. S. Lewis's The Chronicles of Narnia. Television Academy Emmy award (1978-1979), Outstanding Animation Program.

The special focused on the first of seven children's classics written by Lewis, originally published as The Chronicles of Narnia from 1950 to 1956 in Great Britain and in the 1960s by the MacMillan Company in the U.S. Produced as two hour-long specials, which portrayed basic pro-social qualities such as honesty, loyalty and friendship, each of the three parts of the story were animated by a different studio. Kraft Foods committed more than $3 million to the project to introduce the classic literature adventure to an American audience, and the advertising and promotion campaign for the show was described as "the largest in Kraft's history." Joan Ganz Cooney, president of the Children's Television Workshop, developed the project and negotiated the rights with the Episcopal Radio-TV Foundation, which had been assigned the broadcast rights by the trustees of the Lewis estate. It was the first commercial entertainment program undertaken by CTW, which produced the Emmy award-winning educational series, Sesame Street (NET/PBS, 1969-), The Electric Company (PBS, 1971-1981), 3-2-1 Contact! (PBS, 1980-) and others, described in Children's Television, Part II (Scarecrow, 1985), pp. 157-159, 442-445, 508-509.

LITTLE BROWN BURRO, THE

Broadcast History
     Premiere: December 1978
     SYN/local station option (WABC, New York, December 13, 1978,
          Wednesday 7:30-8:00 PM)
     CTV/December 15, 1978, Friday 7:00-7:30 PM
     SYN/Repeats: 1979 +
Executive Producer: Donald W. Reid
Producer: Beryl Friesen
Associate Producer: William H. Stevens, Jr.
Directors: Vic Atkinson, Pino Van Lamsweerde
Writers: Paul Friesen, Christine Atkinson
Music: Lucio Agostini
Lyrics: Beryl Friesen
Company: Titlecraft with Atkinson Film-Arts, Ottawa, Canada, in
     association with D. W. Reid Films

Distributor: Crawleys International ("Cartoon Classics")/1986-
Home Video: Embassy Home Entertainment

Narrator: Lorne Greene

Principal Characters and Voices
Little Brown Burro   Bonnie Brooks
Omar   Paul Soles

Other Voices
    Carl Banas, Nick Nichols, Henry Ramer

Vocalists: Westboro United Church Children's Choir

The Little Brown Burro was a Christmas story woven around the
Nativity, set against a rich Middle East backdrop, following the adventures of a rejected and forlorn burro. Despised and belittled
by man and animal alike, he began to believe his detractors--that
he could serve no useful purpose. Through a series of humorous
and sometimes poignant incidents, the vulnerable burro's self-confidence
was buoyed by a desert rat, Omar, a despised creature whose ingenuity and fortitude made him a natural survivor. Separated from
his friend, the little burro wound up in an auction, where the other
animals brought high prices, sold for only one piece of silver to a
man, Joseph, who could afford no more. Reencountering Omar, the
burro rejected his friend's musical invitation to travel to Cathay and
discover the delights of the world. With his new self-assurance, the
burro followed his humble intuition and exercised his own judgment--
to prove his worth, do the best he could and make his own contribution. He decided to carry "the woman" on his back, journeying with
Joseph on a special night to Bethlehem. There he was witness to
the Nativity, joined by the Wise Men, angels and Omar as well. The
special was based on an original radio play by Paul Friesen. Songs:
"No One Cares If I Go or Stay," "I Have a Feeling I Can't Explain"
(Burro), "It's All a Matter of Attitude," "The Wonders of Cathay"
(Omar).

LITTLE DRUMMER BOY, THE

Broadcast History
    Premiere: December 19, 1968
    NBC/Thursday 7:30-8:00 PM
    Sponsor: U.S. Natural Gas Association
    NBC/Repeats: December 18, 1969; December 16, 1970; December
        14, 1971; December 10, 1972; December 9, 1973; December 15,
        1974; December 14, 1975
    SYN/Repeats: 1982 +
Producers/Directors: Arthur Rankin, Jr., Jules Bass
Director/Animation: Takeo Nakamura
Writer: Romeo Muller

Music & Lyrics/Title Song: Katherine Davis, Henry Onorati, Harry
    Simeone
Music: Maury Laws
Lyrics: Jules Bass
Company: Rankin-Bass Productions
Distributor: Viacom Enterprises/1986-

Narrator: Greer Garson

Principal Characters and Voices
Aaron   Teddy Eccles
Haramed   José Ferrer
Ali/Others   Paul Frees

Vocalists: The Vienna Boys' Choir

The Little Drummer Boy told the touching story of Aaron, orphaned
by bandits, who had only one desire in life, to care for his lamb,
camel and donkey. Kidnapped by Haramed, the boy was made a
member of a band of itinerant muscians and his camel was sold to
one of the Three Wise Men enroute to Bethlehem to honor the Christ
Child. Gaining his freedom with the aid of the other two animals,
Aaron journeyed to Bethlehem to reclaim his camel and arrived at
the manger as the three kings were offering their gifts to the baby
Jesus. Aaron could offer only one gift, a song. But the song was
the one gift which engaged the infant's attention. Miraculously,
Aaron's lamb, injured by a Roman soldier, was healed. One of the
classic Christmas films, based on the title song and narrated by the
soothing voice of Greer Garson, the special was filmed using stop-
motion animated puppets (Animagic). Songs: "The Little Drummer Boy"
(Vienna Boys' Choir), "One Star in the Night," "Why Can't the
Animals Smile?" "The Goose Hangs High."

LITTLE DRUMMER BOY, BOOK II

Broadcast History
    Premiere: December 13, 1976
    NBC/Sunday 7:00-7:30 PM
    Sponsor: U. S. Natural Gas Association
    NBC/Repeats: December 23, 1977; December 21, 1978; December
       23, 1980
    SYN/Repeats: 1985 +
Producers/Directors: Arthur Rankin, Jr., Jules Bass
Writer: Julian P. Gardner
Music & Lyrics/Title Song: Katherine Davis, Henry Onorati, Harry
    Simeone
Music: Maury Laws
Lyrics: Jules Bass
Company: Rankin-Bass Productions
Distributor: Lorimar Syndication ("Animated Holiday Specials")/1985-

THE LITTLE DRUMMER BOY, BOOK II. © 1976, Rankin/Bass Productions, Inc. Courtesy of Rankin/Bass Productions and Lorimar Syndication.

Narrator: Greer Garson

Principal Characters and Voices

Brutus	Zero Mostel
Aaron	David Jay
Melchoir	Allen Swift
Simeon	Ray Owens
Plato	Robert McFadden

Little Drummer Boy, Book II was a replacement for the original story which NBC aired for eight consecutive years. In this sequel, Aaron and one of the wise men, Melchoir, ventured to see the bellmaker, Simeon, who twenty years ago had constructed a set of pure silver carillon bells which should now be heard--for "the Babe unto us is born." But Simeon's bells were repossessed by tax collectors, and Aaron set off to find them. At the tax collector's camp the boy performed on his drums for the men, who taunted him and threw his drums and sticks on the fire--the bells were to be melted next. But while the soldiers were engaged in tormenting the boy, the camp animals slyly carted the silver bells to Melchoir and Simeon, who waited nearby. Everyone was happy, except Aaron, whose drums were destroyed, so Simeon made him a new set. Setting out for Bethlehem with people flocking along behind, Aaron played his drums as he marched off to see the Babe in the manger. A sequence featuring the Vienna Boys' Choir singing the title song appeared at the end. The special was filmed using stop-motion animated puppets (Animagic). Songs: "Do You Hear What I Hear," "The Little Drummer Boy" (The Vienna Boys' Choir).

LITTLE MERMAID, THE

Broadcast History
    Premiere: February 4, 1974
    CBS/Monday 8:00-8:30 PM
    CBS/Repeat: January 31, 1975
    SYN/Repeats: 1977 +
Producers: Christine LaRocque, Murray Shostak
Director: Peter Sander
Writers: Peter Sander, Christine LaRocque
Music: Ron Goodwin
Company: A Reader's Digest Presentation in association with Gerald Potterton Productions, Montreal, Canada
Distributor: LBS Communications ("LBS Children's Theatre")/ 1983-1985
Record Album: Capitol/Reader's Digest SQ 6417
Home Video: Random House Home Video

Narrator: Richard Chamberlain

The Little Mermaid presented Hans Christian Andersen's classic tale of a mermaid who was content to live and play beneath the sea until, during a fearful storm at sea, she saved the life of a young prince. Though he was unaware of her deed and of his debt to her, the mermaid came to love him and in so doing longed to take a human form and become his bride.

LITTLE RASCALS CHRISTMAS SPECIAL, THE

Broadcast History
    Premiere: December 3, 1979
    NBC/Monday 8:30-9:00 PM
    NBC/Repeats: December 15, 1980; December 20, 1981
SYN/Repeats: 1984 +
Executive Producers: Robert L. Rosen, Robert A. King
Producers: Romeo Muller, Fred Wolf
Directors: Charles Swenson, Fred Wolf
Writer: Romeo Muller
Music: Greig McRitchie
Company: A King World Presentation in association with Muller-Rosen Productions and Murakami-Wolf-Swenson Films

THE LITTLE MERMAID. © 1974, Potterton Productions, Ltd. Courtesy of LBS Communications.

THE LITTLE RASCALS CHRISTMAS SPECIAL. © 1979, King World, Inc. Courtesy of KingWorld and RLR Associates

Distributor: King World Enterprises/1984–
Home Video: Family Home Entertainment #F345

Principal Characters and Voices

Alfalfa	Jimmy Gatherum
Spanky	Phillip Tanzini
Darla	Randi Kiger
Stymie	Al Jocko Fann
Porky	Robby Kiger
Mom	Darla Hood Granson
Sidewalk Santa	Jack Somack
Butcher	Matthew (Stymie) Beard
Man	Cliff Norton
Sales Clerk	Frank Nelson
Delivery Man	Melville A. Levin
Uncle Hominy	Hal Smith
Sales Lady	Naomi Lewis
Tough Kid	Ike Eisenmann
Pete the Pup	

The Little Rascals Christmas Special captured some nostalgic visions of the Depression-Era neighborhood youngsters as they prepared for the holiday. In their rickety clubhouse, president Alfalfa called the gang together to select a new name, the Royal Reindeer Lodge, since their old one, Woodchucks, had nothing to do with Christmas. They also adopted a new salute, "Ho, Ho, Ho!" Longing for an expensive Blue Comet train for Christmas, Porky and Spanky believed their Mom ordered the train over the phone from Santa. Overhearing their conversation about it with a sidewalk Santa, she decided to make their wish come true by returning a much-needed winter coat she had saved for all year to purchase the train. When she became sick from the cold, Porky and Spanky set out to get her a warm coat. To no avail, the Rascals pitched in to help earn money using several of Alfalfa's zany schemes. Finally, Porky and Spanky decided to exchange the train for the coat, but enroute to the store two tough kids ran off with it, witnessed by the sidewalk Santa. Gathered at the clubhouse for their Christmas Eve festivities, the Rascals were surprised when the sidewalk Santa turned up with a new coat for Mom that he had purchased with his wages. He brought gifts for the children, and under his stern eye the culprits presented Porky and Spanky with their deluxe Blue Comet. Song/Theme: "The First Noel."

This was the first animated-cartoon version of the Little Rascals, whose live-action shorts produced by Hal Roach presented a view of irrepressible childhood that was close to Tom Sawyer and Huck Finn in its innocence and rich period detail. The film spurred a Saturday morning series, The Little Rascals (ABC, 1982-1984). Two of the original cast members taped voiceovers for the special: Matthew Beard, who played Stymie, and Darla Hood (Granson), who was the original Darla in the Our Gang Comedies, televised under several titles including The Little Rascals (SYN, 1955-), described in Children's Television, Part II (Scarecrow, 1985), pp. 296-299.

LORAX, THE   see   DR. SEUSS' THE LORAX

MAD, MAD, MONSTERS, THE

Broadcast History
    Premiere: September 23, 1972
    ABC/ABC SATURDAY SUPERSTAR MOVIE, Saturday 9:30-10:30
       AM
    ABC/Repeats: 1973-1974
    SYN/Repeats: 1975 +
Producers/Directors: Arthur Rankin, Jr., Jules Bass
Writers: William J. Keenan, Lou Silverstone
Music: Maury Laws
Lyrics: Jules Bass
Company: Rankin-Bass Productions/60 minutes

Distributor: Viacom Enterprises/1986-
Home Video: Prism #1213 (Prism Entertainment)

The Mad, Mad Monsters resurrected some well known movie aberra-
tions for this comedy romp. Baron von Frankenstein engineered a
new monstress intended as the perfect bride for his original creation.
Hiring the ballroom of the Transylvania-Astoria on Friday the 13th
for the wedding, the Baron invited his friends, among them the Creature, the Invisible Man and his invisible wife, the Mummy, Count
Dracula, the Wolfman and his own assistant Igor. What ensued was
outrageous chaos, especially after all the panic-stricken "normal"
guests fled the hotel en masse.
        The special was originally telecast on The ABC Saturday Super-
star Movie (ABC, 1972-1974), described in Children's Television,
Part I (Scarecrow, 1983), pp. 5-7.

MAD, MAD, MAD COMEDIANS, THE

Broadcast History
    Premiere: April 7, 1970
    ABC/Tuesday 8:00-8:30 PM
Director/Animator: Bruce Stark
Company: Bruce Stark with ABC

Principal Characters and Voices

Jack Benny	Jack Benny
George Burns	George Burns
Marx Brothers	Groucho/Chico/Harpo Marx
Smothers Brothers	Tom and Dick Smothers
Christopher Columbus	Flip Wilson
George Jessel	George Jessel
Phyllis Diller	Phyllis Diller
Jack E. Leonard	Jack E. Leonard
Henny Youngman	Henny Youngman
W. C. Fields	Paul Frees

The Mad, Mad, Mad Comedians matched animated caricatures of some
well known comedians to excerpts taken from recordings of their
radio programs and TV sketches. Jack Benny and George Burns
traded gags in Benny's Maxwell car; the Marx Brothers were seen in
a sketch about Napoleon and Josephine; and Flip Wilson was captured
in his campy impersonation of Christopher Columbus. The Smothers
Brothers provided their own brand of humor and two songs: "The
Slitheree Dee" and "The Troubadour." The concept and artwork
were supplied by Bruce Stark.

MAGIC LOLLIPOP ADVENTURE, THE

Broadcast History
    Premiere: 1986

SYN/local station option (KABC, Los Angeles, October 26, 1986, Sunday 3:00-3:30 PM PST)
SYN/Repeats: 1987 +
Executive Producer: Philip Kent
Producer: Robert Halmi
Co-Producer/Creator: Roger Kimmel
Associate Producers: Dan Martin, Denise Sickinger
Writer: Venable Herndon
Music: Alan Sneeling, Irwin Fisch
Lyrics: Roger Himmel, Guy Mazzeo
Company: Blair Entertainment in association with Pannonia Film, Budapest, Hungary
Distributor: Blair Entertainment/1986-

Principal Characters and Voices

Lollipop Dragon/Hairy Troll	Gary Wilmot
Cosmo the Cunning/King/ Herald	Dennis Greashan
Baron Bad Blood	Stephen Thorne
Blue Eyes	Karen Fernald
Magic Mirror/Prince Hubert	Pat Starr
Princess Gwendolyn	Jill Lidstone
Glider/Queen/Lady of the Forest	Eva Hadden

The Magic Lollipop Adventure marked the animated-special debut of the green Lollipop Dragon, a large flying-creature with three buck teeth and purple, droopy eyelids. No fire-breather, he was a gentle sort who lived on hugs and lollipops in Tumtum, a medieval fantasy land where the major industry was a lollipop factory. With three baby dragons, Cuddles, Blue Eyes and Glider, he passed most his days with his best friends, Princess Gwendolyn and Prince Hubert, the children of the King and Queen. Baron Bad Blood and his toady Cosmo the Cunning were their enemies. Seeking to ruin the delicious taste of Tumtum lollipops, Bad Blood stole the Magic Wand that gave them their pleasing flavor and kidnapped the baby dragons as hostages. Managing to get inside Blood Castle, the Dragon and the children confronted and battled the evil Baron and Cosmo, released the baby dragons and secured the Magic Wand which was returned to the King and Queen of Tumtum. During their escape, the Baron was turned into a gnarled and harmless old tree, until the spell was broken in the sequel, The Great Christmas Race [q.v.]. Songs: "Let the Magic Surround You," "Sing a Happy Song," "We'll Be Friends Forever."

Created in 1969 by writer Roger Himmel and artists Luther Peters and Connie Ross, the Lollipop Dragon was developed for classroom animated-filmstrips to teach children math, science, reading, morals and ethics. Through the Society for Visual Education, he has been seen in instructional programs by 20 million children in schools and churches throughout the U.S., Canada and Great Britain. The specials, as well as a line of toys and novelties, were licensed by the Lollipop Dragon Trust.

MAGICAL MYSTERY TRIP THROUGH LITTLE RED'S HEAD, THE

Broadcast History
    Premiere: May 15, 1974
    ABC/ABC AFTERSCHOOL SPECIALS, Wednesday 3:30-4:30 PM
    ABC/Repeats: December 11, 1974; ABC WEEKEND SPECIALS,
        April 29, 1978
Producers: David H. DePatie, Friz Freleng
Director: Herbert Klynn
Writer: Larry Spiegel
Music: Dean Elliott
Lyrics: Johnny Bradford
Company: DePatie-Freleng Enterprises/60 minutes

Principal Characters and Voices
Timer   Lennie Weinrib
Carol   Diane Murphy
Larry   Ike Eisenmann
Little Red   Sarah Kennedy
Mother/Adeline/Diane   Joan Gerber

The Magical Mystery Trip Through Little Red's Head took an animated
look, with some live-action portions, at some basic senses and emotions. Based on the tale of "Little Red Riding Hood," updated as a
fantastic trip into the human mind, two youngsters reduced to microscopic size took a fantastic trip through their older sister's head,
where they learned an important lesson about their feelings and how
to deal with them. Timer, the keeper of body time, guided Carol
and Larry in their exploration during Little Red's perilous trip to
her Grandmother's house. Along the way they visited choice, percep-
tion, dreams and the center of the brain. They discovered how Little
Red reacted to events on the trip and how she coped with such emotions as puppy love and particularly fear--how helpful it was to discuss their fears with someone else. The musical odyssey was a sequel to the acclaimed trip through the human body, The Incredible,
Indelible, Magical, Physical Mystery Trip [q.v.]. Songs: "Timer's
Song," "All Aboard," "Go Take a Walk in the Sunshine," "Come With
Me" (Timer), "Nightmare Song" (Carol, Larry), "Squirter's Song,"
"You've Got to Learn to Relax," "Butterflys and Bushes."

MARCO POLO (aka THE TRAVELS OF MARCO POLO)

Broadcast History
    Premiere: 1972
    SYN/local station option
Executive Producer: Walter J. Hucker
Director: Leif Gram
Writer: John Palmer
Music: Richard Bowden
Company: Air Programs International, Sydney, Australia/60 minutes

Distributor: D. L. Taffner ("Animated Classics for Children")/1983-
Home Video: Classics for Kids (MGM/UA)

Voices
    Alistair Duncan, Tim Elliott, Ron Haddrick, Mark Kelly, John
    Llewellyn, Helen Morse

Marco Polo was set in 1260 AD in China, where Kubla Khan was warr-
ing against Siang-yan Fu, a city that dared to resist him. The siege
continued until Marco Polo and his servant Ton-Ton returned from a
mission to suggest a new way to breach the walls. Because of his
help, Marco became a great favorite of the Khan but the enemy of
Achmac, the Khan's general. After surviving Achmac's poison, Marco
was dispatched to save the Province of Yunnan from the invading
King of Burma and to escort the Khan's daughter, Kokachin, to
Persia, before returning home. The story was based on the original
journals of Marco Polo, and the film featured costumes and settings
attributed to the period.

MASTER OF THE WORLD

Broadcast History
    Premiere: October 23, 1976
    CBS/FAMOUS CLASSIC TALES, Saturday 1:00-2:00 PM
    Sponsor: Kenner Products (Toy Group, General Mills)
    SYN/Repeats: 1977 +
Producer: Walter J. Hucker
Director: Leif Gram
Writer: John Palmer
Music: Richard Bowden
Company: Air Programs International, Sydney, Australia/60 minutes
Distributor: D. L. Taffner ("Animated Classics for Children")/1983-
Home Video: Classics for Kids (MGM/UA)

Voices
    Tim Elliott, John Ewart, Ron Haddrick, Judy Morris, Matthew
    O'Sullivan

Master of the World was an adaptation of Jules Verne's nineteenth-
century tale about an incredible flying machine, The Terror, commanded by a mad inventor, Captain Robur, the so-called "Master of
the World." Assigned to investigate a tremendous explosion at Eagle's
Nest, a hilltop not far from Morgantown, North Carolina, Inspector
Strock of the Federal Police tracked the machine to Lake Erie, where
he was captured and held prisoner aboard the craft. Breaking free,
Strock confronted Robur but was unable to stop his plan to destroy
Washington, D.C. Then nature intervened when a bolt of lightning
struck the machine, sending it plunging into Chesapeake Bay where,
miraculously, Strock was rescued by the Navy.

MAYDAY FOR MOTHER see DENNIS THE MENACE: MAYDAY FOR MOTHER

MERRY MIRTHWORM CHRISTMAS, A

<u>Broadcast History</u>
   Premiere: November-December 1984
   SHO/various days, times
   NIK/Repeats: multiple option, 1985
   SEL/Repeats: multiple option, 1985
   SYN/Repeats: 1986 +
Producers/Directors/Writers: Jerry Reynolds, Russ Harris
Associate Producer: Michael N. Ruggiero
Music: Pete Schmutte
Lyrics: Jerry Reynolds
Company: Perennial Pictures
Distributor: Perennial Pictures/1986-
Home Video: Family Home Entertainment

<u>Principal Characters and Voices</u>
Bert Worm/Teddy Toddlers/
   Wilbur Diggs/Baggs   Jerry Reynolds
Crystal Crawler   Rachel Rutledge

A MERRY MIRTHWORM CHRISTMAS. © 1985, Mirthworm, Ltd./ Perennial Pictures Film Corporation. Courtesy of Perennial Pictures Film Corporation.

Wormaline Wiggler   Miki Mathioudakis
Eulalia Inch/Agnes/Dribble   Peggy Nicholson
Mayor Filmore Q. Pettiworm/
   Eudora Vanderworm   Russ Harris

A Merry Mirthworm Christmas introduced the citizens of Wormingham and Bert Worm, a clumsy newcomer, whose help botched preparations for the annual holiday pageant at town Hall. Outraged, Wormaline Wiggler, the haughty Chairworm for the Social Committee, and her dim-witted servant, Teddy Toddlers, ostracized Bert since he could not contribute anything worthwhile and banned him forthwith. Befriended by Crystal Crawler, who tried to persuade him to attend anyway, Bert decided instead to find a place where he could "fit in" better. At the celebration, Crystal berated Wormaline and others in front of the Mayor for their treatment of Bert and moved the crowd to make amends: "After all, everyone deserves a second chance." Wilbur Diggs organized a search party to locate Bert, who had fallen asleep in the Town Hall. Embarrassed, Bert prepared to leave again because he had nothing to contribute, but after Crystal pulled him aside, Bert lead everyone in a joyful song finale. His ability to sing made the perfect contribution to the Christmas celebration. Diggs summed it up: "All it takes is a little patience and understanding. Everybody fits in somewhere." Song/Theme: "No One Could Say I Didn't Try."

MICKEY'S CHRISTMAS CAROL

Components
   THE ART OF SKIING (1941), DONALD'S SNOW FIGHT (1942),
   PLUTO'S CHRISTMAS TREE (1952)

Broadcast History
   Premiere: December 10, 1984
   NBC/Monday 8:00-9:00 PM
   NBC/Repeats: December 22, 1985; December 15, 1986
Executive Producer: Ron Miller
Producer/Director: Burny Mattinson
Producer (TV): Marc Stirdivant
Writers: Burny Mattinson, Tony L. Marino, Ed Gombert, Don Griffith, Alan Young, Alan Dinehart
Music/Song & Lyrics: Irwin Kostal, Frederick Searles
Music: Irwin Kostal
Music (TV): John O'Kennedy, Paul J. Smith
Company: Walt Disney Television/60 minutes
Record Albums: Disneyland 3811 (with book); Disneyland 3825 (Radio Shack release with book); Disneyland 3109 (picture disk)
Home Video: Walt Disney Home Video ("Mickey's Christmas Carol")

Principal Characters and Voices
Mickey Mouse (Bob Cratchit)   Wayne Allwine

Uncle Scrooge McDuck (Ebenezer Scrooge)	Alan Young
Donald Duck (Fred)	Clarence Nash
Goofy (Ghost of Jacob Marley)	Hal Smith
Jiminy Cricket (Ghost of Christmas Past)	Eddie Carroll
Willie the Giant (Ghost of Christmas Present)/Black Pete (Ghost of Christmas Future)	Will Ryan
Morty (Tiny Tim)	Susan Sheridan
Daisy Duck (Isabel)	Pat Parris
Minnie Mouse (Mrs. Cratchit)	(non-speaking)

Mickey's Christmas Carol presented a Disney version of Dickens' classic, casting the studio's stock characters in the various roles. Mickey starred as the underpaid clerk Bob Cratchit, McDuck as the miserly Scrooge, Goofy rattled his chains as the Ghost of Jacob Marley, Jiminy Cricket flew away with Scrooge via his open umbrella as the Ghost of Christmas Past, Willie the Giant (Mickey and the Beanstalk) plucked Scrooge up in his hand as the Ghost of Christmas Present, Mickey's nemesis Pete led Scrooge to his graveyard as the Ghost of Christmas Future, Minnie Mouse was seen as Mrs. Cratchit, Daisy Duck as Scrooge's former sweetheart Isabel, Donald as Scrooge's nephew Fred and Mickey's nephew Morty as Tiny Tim. In the supporting cast were such animated stalwarts as Chip 'n' Dale, Clarabelle Cow, Horace Horsecollar and Ratty and Moley (Wind in the Willows). After Scrooge's repentance, all ended happily with his merry visit with Bob's family and the lame Tiny Tim on Christmas Day. "A toast to all the Cratchits!" he said. Three vintage Disney cartoons rounded out the hour. Song/Theme: "Oh, What a Merry Christmas Day."

By itself, Mickey's Christmas Carol was aired in multiple runs on the Disney Channel (CTV), premiering on December 1, 1984 and repeated in December 1985 and December 1986. Initially released theatrically in 1983 at Christmas, it was the first film produced in thirty years starring Mickey, then 55, and whose last short cartoon was The Simple Things (1953). On his 50th birthday in 1978, Mickey received the 1,700th star on Hollywood's Walk of Fame, the first given to an animated cartoon character.

MIRTHWORM MASQUERADE, A

Broadcast History
    Premiere: April 11, 1987
    SYN/WCBS, New York, Saturday 7:30-8:00 PM
Producers/Directors/Writers: Jerry Reynolds, Russ Harris
Associate Producer: Michael N. Ruggiero
Music/Lyrics: Jerry Reynolds
Company: Perennial Pictures
Distributor: Perennial Pictures/1986-
Home Video: Family Home Entertainment

Principal Characters and Voices

Bert Worm/Teddy Toddlers/ Wilbur Diggs/Baggs/Homer/ Prince Pringle/Armbruster	Jerry Reynolds
Crystal Crawler/Gertie	Rachel Rutledge
Wormaline Wiggler	Miki Mathioudakis
Agnes/Dribble/Eulalia Inch	Peggy Nicholson
Eudora Vanderworm/Mayor Filmore Q. Pettiworm	Russ Harris
Brooks	Michael N. Ruggiero
Chester/Arnold	Adam Dykstra

A Mirthworm Masquerade depicted the further adventures of those wiggly inhabitants of Wormingham at the annual masked ball. Breaking his date with Crystal Crawler because of threats of losing his job and never working in the town again, Bert Worm reluctantly donned a costume as Prince Pringle of Pennequay, who had reneged as the escort for Bert's new employer, Wormaline Wiggle, determined to become Queen of the Masquerade Ball. Filled with disgust at the phony pretense, Bert ripped off his disguise after overhearing the Mayor counting the votes for Queen, which Crystal won by a landslide, and set off to fetch her. At the arrival of the real Prince, the furious Wormaline, believing him to be the masked Bert, created a ugly scene revealing her nasty plan to all. Bert returned with Crystal in time to see her officially crowned. His old friend Wilbur Diggs, impressed with Bert's honesty and spunk offered him a job in his workshop, and a jubilant Bert and a radiant Crystal enjoyed the best Mirthworm Masquerade ever. Song/Theme: "Who Is Who?"

MISS SWITCH TO THE RESCUE

Broadcast History
    Premiere: January 16 & 23, 1982
    ABC/ABC WEEKEND SPECIALS, Saturday 12:30-1:00 PM
    ABC/Repeats: April 24 & May 1, 1982; June 18 & 25, 1983; February 9 & 16, 1985; July 5 & 12, 1986; April 4 & 11, 1987
Executive Producers: Joseph Ruby, Ken Spears
Director: Charles A. Nichols
Writer: Sheldon Stark
Music: Dean Elliott, Paul DeKorte
Company: Ruby-Spears Enterprises/60 minutes, 2 parts

Principal Characters and Voices

Miss Switch/Guinevere	Janet Waldo
Rupert P. Brown III/Peatmouse	Eric Taslitz
Amelia Matilda Daley	Nancy McKeon
Mordo	Hans Conreid
Smirch	Hal Smith
Banana/Conrad	Phillip Tanzini

MISS SWITCH TO THE RESCUE. © 1982, Ruby-Spears Enterprises,
Inc. Courtesy of Ruby-Spears Enterprises and TECO.

Bathsheba/Saturna (Crone)	June Foray
Witch's Book/Old Salt/Mayor	Walker Edmiston
Teacher/Barmaid	Anne Lockhart
Hector	Alan Dinehart

Miss Switch to the Rescue involved an indomitable good witch who
hid her identity as a substitute teacher and who aided young Rupert
when his friend Amelia was kidnapped. In Part I, after a mysterious
old crone gave Rupert a bottle containing a little man, he unwittingly
released the evil warlock Mordo, vengeful toward those who imprisoned
him, who took Amelia back to a New England town in the 1600s. Miss
Switch, Rupert and her cat Bathsheba zapped back and located Mordo
on a pirate ship as he was about to turn the mayor and Amelia into
trolls. Rescuing the pair and returning home, they found that Rupert had only the mayor's coat--Mordo succeeded in turning him into
a troll--and the old crone was actually the bad witch Saturna, whom
the children had helped Miss Switch to banish in The Trouble With
Miss Switch [q.v.]. Seeking her revenge as well, Saturna caused
Amelia to disappear into thin air.

In Part II, Miss Switch temporarily turned back time, and Amelia became visible again. Rushing back to the school lab, they created a potion to keep her there for good. Aware of their actions, Saturna and Mordo, with his pirate henchmen and his troll-mayor, flew his pirate ship to the school and kidnapped all the children. Miss Switch, Rupert, Amelia and Bathsheba chased Mordo on her broomstick to the Island of Fire and Ice, where Saturna had laid a trap for them. Following their mishaps while disguised as penguins, Amelia began to fade for good when she persuaded the troll-mayor, her 300-years-removed grandfather, to drink Miss Switch's potion, restoring both to normalcy. Miss Switch spirited the captured children out of Saturna's cave as it began to break apart, causing the entrapment of the evil pair in a block of ice. The mayor returned to the 1600s and Miss Switch returned the children, who remembered nothing of their adventures, to their classroom. She reminded Rupert and Amelia that revenge was hateful and love was always stronger than hate and flew off on her broomstick with Bathsheba. The two-part sequel was based on characters created by Barbara Brooks Wallace in The Trouble With Miss Switch (Abingdon, 1971).

MR. MAGOO'S CHRISTMAS CAROL

Broadcast History
   Premiere: December 18, 1962
   NBC/Tuesday 7:30-8:30 PM
   Sponsor: Timex
   NBC/Repeats: December 13, 1963; December 18, 1964; December
      17, 1965; December 17, 1966; December 16, 1967
   SYN/Repeats: 1970 +
Executive Producer: Henry G. Saperstein
Producer: Lee Orgel
Director: Abe Levitow
Writer: Barbara Chain
Music/Songs & Lyrics: Jule Styne, Bob Merrill
Music: Walter Scharf
Company: UPA Pictures/60 minutes
Distributor: UPA Productions of America/1986-
Home Video: Paramount Home Video #2320

Principal Characters and Voices

Character	Voice
Ebenezer Scrooge (Mr. Magoo)	Jim Backus
Bob Cratchit	Jack Cassidy
Tiny Tim/Christmas Past	Joan Gardner
Belle Fezzlwig	Jane Kean
Marley's Ghost	Royal Dano
Brady/James	Morey Amsterdam
Christmas Present	Les Tremayne
Old Fezzlwig/Undertaker/ Men	Paul Frees
Mrs. Cratchit/Children	Laura Olsher

MR. MAGOO'S CHRISTMAS CAROL. © 1962, UPA Pictures, Inc.
Courtesy of UPA Productions of America.

Young Scrooge   Marie Matthews
Stage Manager/Billings/Milkman   John Hart

Mr. Magoo's Christmas Carol reprised the Yuletide Dicken's classic
with the myopic Magoo playing it somewhat straight in his portrayal
of Ebenezer Scrooge. The setting was a Broadway theater where
Magoo was starring in a stage presentation of the story, and during
his curtain call he accidentally, and literally, brought down the house
(Cratchit's). A lively musical score enhanced the tale of the miser,
whose own view of life was clouded and faulty until one strange
Christmas Eve. Confronted by the ghosts of his partner Marley,
Christmas Past, Christmas Present and Christmas Future, Scrooge
realized the evil of his ways and repented, making it a Merry Christ-
mas for his faithful employee Bob Cratchit and his sickly son Tiny
Tim, who was a dead ringer for tow-headed Gerald McBoing Boing.
Songs: "It's Great to be Back on Broadway," "Ringle, Rangle,"
"All Alone in the World," "We're Despicable," "The Lord's Bright
Blessings," "Winter."

Commissioned by Timex, the program was the first made-for-
TV animated cartoon special. It followed Mr. Magoo's only movie,
1001 Arabian Nights (COL, 1959), and a 155-episode five-minute TV
series, Mr. Magoo (SYN/1960-1975). It also inspired the studio and
network to star the character in portrayals of literary and historical
figures in a new prime-time series, The Famous Adventures of Mr.
Magoo (NBC, 1964-1965), described in Children's Television, Part I
(Scarecrow, 1983), pp. 193-196.

MR. MAGOO'S STORYBOOK SNOW WHITE

Broadcast History
    Premiere: 1964-1965
    NBC/THE FAMOUS ADVENTURES OF MR. MAGOO, Saturday 8:30-
        9:00 PM
    SYN/Repeat: MR. MAGOO'S STORYBOOK, WCBS, New York,
        November 26, 1970, Thursday 9:00-11:00 AM
    SYN/Repeats: MR. MAGOO'S STORYBOOK SNOW WHITE, 1975 +
Executive Producer: Henry G. Saperstein
Directors: Abe Levitow, Bob McKimson, Gerard Baldwin
Writer: George Gordon
Music: Carl Brandt
Company: A Henry G. Saperstein Production by UPA Pictures/60
    minutes
Distributor: UPA Productions of America/1986-
Home Video: Paramount Home Video

Narrator: Howard Morris

Principal Characters and Voices
Axlerod/Bartholomew/Cornelius/
    Dexter/Eustes/Ferdinand/
    George (Mr. Magoo)   Jim Backus

MR. MAGOO'S STORYBOOK SNOW WHITE. © 1964, UPA Pictures,
Inc. Courtesy of UPA Productions of America

Snow White	Julie Bennett
Queen/Bertha the Peddler/	
Zelda the Gypsy/Old Crone	Joan Gardner
Prince Valor	Howard Morris
Demon/Hunter	Marvin Miller
Blazer (baby dragon)	

Mr. Magoo's Storybook Snow White starred the indominable dimsighted
oldster in the role of the Seven Dwarfs, each with a distinct personality. Axlerod was their leader and an accountant, Bartholomew an
inventive wizard, Cornelius a magician, Dexter a legal expert, George
a dreamer, and Eustes and Ferdinand had no special talent, but
mining gold was a tough job and somebody had to do it. Escaping
from her stepmother, the wicked Queen, who was jealous of her
beauty, Snow White fled into the forest, was released by the Hunter
sent to kill her and stumbled upon the home of the Seven Dwarfs,
who sheltered and tried to protect her. Using his wizardry, Bartholomew accidentally conjured up a fire-breathing baby dragon, Blazer,
who became Snow White's pet. Consulting the Demon in her mirror,
the Queen learned that Snow White was still the fairest in the land
and tried to kill her while disguised as Bertha the Peddler and Zelda
the Gypsy, using magic bodice laces and a hair comb, all foiled by
the Dwarfs. She finally succeeded as an Old Crone with a poisoned
apple, and a comatose Snow White was laid to rest in a glass coffin.
Searching for his true love, Prince Valor finally found her, apparently

dead, and begged the Dwarfs for the coffin. When it was moved the piece of apple was dislodged from her throat, Snow White awoke and lived happily ever after, married to her Prince on the other side of the forest.

Originally two episodes of the prime-time series (NBC, 1964-1965), the film was syndicated in several packages, most recently with Mr. Magoo's Christmas Carol [q.v.], Mr. Magoo's Treasure Island [q.v.] and Uncle Sam Magoo [q.v.]. Also, four two-hour TV movies were spliced together from the NBC episodes, syndicated as Mr. Magoo in the King's Service, Mr. Magoo in Sherwood Forest, Mr. Magoo in Favorite Heroes and Mr. Magoo, Man of Mystery.

MR. MAGOO'S TREASURE ISLAND

Broadcast History
    Premiere: 1964-1965
    NBC/THE FAMOUS ADVENTURES OF MR. MAGOO, Saturday 8:30-
        9:00 PM
    SYN/Repeat: MR. MAGOO'S TREASURE ISLAND, WCBS, New York,
        October 12, 1967, Thursday 9:00-10:00 AM
    SYN/Repeats: 1968 +
Executive Producer: Henry G. Saperstein
Directors: Abe Levitow, Bob McKimson, Steve Clark
Writer: George Gordon
Music: Carl Brandt
Company: A Henry G. Saperstein Production by UPA Pictures/60
    minutes
Distributor: UPA Productions of America/1986-
Home Video: Paramount (MISTER MAGOO'S TREASURE ISLAND)

Principal Characters and Voices
Long John Silver (Mr. Magoo)   Jim Backus
Jim Hawkins   Dennis King
Jarvis   Marvin Miller

Other Voices
    Paul Frees, Joan Gardner, Dal McKennon

Mr. Magoo's Treasure Island was told by young Jim Hawkins, whose mother kept the Admiral Benbow Inn. An old sea dog arrived at the Inn and hired Jim to keep watch for other sailors, but despite all his precautions he was served with the black spot which meant death. Jim and his mother barely escaped a deadly fate themselves, when Blind Pew, Black Dog and other pirates came upon the Inn in search of the old salt's papers. Snatching the packet, Jim, along with Dr. Livesey and Squire Trelawney, determined to find the buried treasure shown on a map among the papers. They fitted out a ship and hired hands, among them the rapscallion Long John Silver, portrayed by the irrascible Mr. Magoo, and his confederates who were also in search of the treasure. Hidden in a barrel, Jim overheard plans for the crew to mutiny and warned his companions. During the ensuing battle, Jim managed to escape and discovered Ben Gunn, a marooned sailor, who already had found the cache. After a battle on the island between the pirates and Jim's party, they managed to get safely aboard the ship with the treasure, which was partly looted by Long John Silver on the trip home.

MISUNDERSTOOD MONSTERS

Components
BEAUTY AND THE BEAST, CREOLE, THE RELUCTANT DRAGON

Broadcast History
Premiere: April 7, 1981
CBS/CBS LIBRARY SPECIALS, Tuesday, 3:00-4:00 PM
CBS/Repeats: January 1, 1982
SYN/Repeats: 1986 +
Producer: Nick Bosustow
Director/Animation: Sam Weiss
Director/Live Action: Seth Pinsker
Writer: George Arthur Bloom
Music: Larry Wolff
Company: Bosustow Entertainment/60 minutes
Distributor: Coe Film Associates/1986-

Host: Meeno Peluce

Narrators
John Carradine, James Earl Jones, Mickey Rooney

Principal Characters and Voices

Mouth	Avery Schreiber
Creole	Mickey Rooney
Bird	Georgia Engel
Alligator	Arte Johnson
Reluctant Dragon	Alan Sues
St. George	Louis Nye
Boy	Sparky Marcus
Beauty	Claire Bloom
Beast	Michael York

Misunderstood Monsters taught tough lessons of life to a misguided youth, portrayed in filmed scenes by Meeno Peluce of The Bad News Bears (CBS, 1979) and Voyagers (NBC, 1982-1983). The stories were fragilely linked by the boy who learned a few spouted verities from a disembodied floating mouth. The tales included: Creole, from the book by Stephen Cosgrove, featured a misshapened-but-kind bird who made friends with an addlepated alligator in a simple tale well told by Mickey Rooney; The Reluctant Dragon, Kenneth Grahame's 1898 English fairytale, whimsically reworked the legend of St. George

and the Dragon with John Carradine's off-camera sonority; and Mari-
anne Mayer's version of Beauty and the Beast, narrated by James
Earl Jones, wove enchantment and poignancy into a story of love
and fidelity but provided no explanation for the prince's initial dis-
figurement.

The anthology was one of three animated presentations on the
CBS Library Specials (CBS, 1979-1982), which featured recommended
children's books from the annual lists of the United States Library
of Congress.

MOBY DICK

Broadcast History
    Premiere: c1975
    SYN/local station option
Executive Producer: Walter J. Hucker
Director: Leif Gram
Writer: John Palmer
Music: Richard Bowden
Company: Air Programs International, Sydney, Australia/60 minutes
Distributor: D. L. Taffner ("Animated Classics for Children")/1983-
Home Video: Classics for Kids (MGM/UA)

Voices
    Alistair Duncan, Tim Elliott, Ron Haddrick, Mark Kelly, John
    Llewellyn

Moby Dick was a literal adaptation of Herman Melville's 1851 novel
about the obsessed Captain Ahab and his ship Pequod, searching
for the great white whale that took his leg. The tragic tale of the
sea recounted the exploits of the crew, Starbuck, Queequeg the har-
poonist and Ishmael, the only survivor.

MOUSE ON THE MAYFLOWER

Broadcast History
    Premiere: November 23, 1968
    NBC/Saturday 7:30-8:00 PM
    NBC/Repeat: November 25, 1971
    SYN/Repeats: 1975 +
Producers/Directors: Arthur Rankin, Jr., Jules Bass
Writers: Romeo Muller, Arthur Rankin, Jr.
Music: Maury Laws
Lyrics: Jules Bass
Company: Rankin-Bass Productions/60 minutes
Distributor: Viacom Enterprises/1986-

MOUSE ON THE MAYFLOWER. © 1968, Rankin/Bass Productions, Inc. Courtesy of Rankin/Bass Productions and Viacom Enterprises.

Narrator
Willum Mouse   Tennessee Ernie Ford

Principal Characters and Voices
Miles Standish   Eddie Albert
John Alden   John Gary
Priscilla Mullens   Joanie Sommers
William Bradford/Quizzler/
    Others   Paul Frees
Indian Mouse/Scurv/Others   June Foray

Mouse on the Mayflower gave an eyewitness report, from a rodent named Willum, of the Pilgrims' 1620 voyage and their landing on Plymouth Rock. According to the astute and erudite mouse, the trip was musical and comical as well as historical and explained how he became the tiniest hero in the New World, beginning with the decision to sail to America where the Pilgrims could worship without oppression. On board the Mayflower were Miles Standish, John Alden, Priscilla Mullens, William Bradford, assorted other Pilgrims and the sinister seamen, Quizzler and Scurv, who sought to sabotage the effort for their own gain. Stormy seas threatened to capsize the frail craft, but with the help of Willum the Pilgrims were able to repair the Mayflower, foil Quizzler and Scurv, and continue safely. In the wilderness they built a colony, Plymouth, and formed a set of laws, the Mayflower Compact. The neighboring Indians were friendly despite the despicable Quizzler's and other scoundrels' attempts to incite a war, a crisis quickly resolved by spunky Willum and his good friend, an Indian mouse. Again with Willum's help, the brave colony survived a cruel winter and sickness. The little hero also was present at the first Thanksgiving feast and observed the famous scene in which John Alden, carrying a message from Miles Standish, was told by Priscilla, "Speak for yourself, John." Songs: "Mayflower," "Elbow Room," "One Day," "Time, Stand Still," "This Land," "When She Looks at Me," "Good Times," "November."

MOWGLI'S BROTHERS

Broadcast History
    Premiere: February 11, 1976
    CBS/Friday 8:30-9:00 PM
    CBS/Repeats: May 6, 1977; April 4, 1978; June 16, 1979; August
       19, 1981
    SYN/Repeats: 1983-1985 ("LBS Children's Theatre"); 1986 +

MOWGLI'S BROTHERS. © 1976, Chuck Jones Enterprises. Courtesy of LBS Communications.

Executive Producer: Chuck Jones
Producer: Oscar Dufau
Directors: Chuck Jones, Hal Ambro
Writer: Chuck Jones
Music: Dean Elliott
Company: Chuck Jones Enterprises
Distributor: Berle Adams/1986-
Home Video: Family Home Entertainment

Narrator: Roddy McDowall

Principal Characters and Voices
Mowgli/Shere Khan/Akela/
   Tabaqui/Bagheera/Baloo   Roddy McDowall
Mother Wolf   June Foray

Mowgli's Brothers, the last of a trilogy adapted from Rudyard Kipling's The Jungle Book (1894) by Chuck Jones, was a story of a human baby adopted by a pair of compassionate wolves. Aided by Baloo, a sleepy brown bear that taught the wolf cubs the Law of the Jungle, and a black panther, Bagheera, the wolves prevailed on the great gray leader, Akela, and the Seeonee Pack to accept the child as one of their own. Named Mowgli ("little frog") by his animal friends, the boy grew to age 11 unaware he was different from the others until called upon to use his human wits to save himself and his lupine mentor, fading with age, from the scheming and vengeful tiger Shere Khan and his cowardly cohort, the jackal Tabaqui. Capping the essence of the tale--the value of loyalty and self-awareness--Mowgli turned to man's "red flower" (fire) to conquer their enemies and realized he was different than his four-footed friends.

MUPPET BABIES see JIM HENSON'S MUPPET BABIES

MY LITTLE PONY

Broadcast History
   Premiere: April 1984
   SYN/local station option (KCBS, Los Angeles, April 16, 1984,
      Monday 7:30-8:00 PM PST)
   Sponsor: Hasbro Toys
   SYN/Repeats: October 6, 1984 +
Executive Producers: Joe Bacal, David H. DePatie, Tom Griffin
Producers: Bob Richardson, Karl Geurs, Lee Gunther
Directors: Gerry Chiniquy, Milt Gray, Tom Ray, Nelson Shin
Writer: George Arthur Bloom
Music/Theme: Ford Kinder, Spencer Michlin
Music/Songs & Lyrics: Tommy Goodman, Barry Harman
Music: Johnny Douglas
Company: Sunbow Productions in association with Marvel Productions

MY LITTLE PONY. © 1984, Sunbow Productions, Inc. Courtesy of
Sunbow Productions and Claster TV Productions.

Distributor: Claster TV Productions/1984-
Home Video: Children's Video Library #1400 (Vestron)

Principal Characters and Voices
Firefly   Sandy Duncan
Moochick   Tony Randall

Other Voices
    Charlie Adler, Tammy Amerson, Fran Brill, Victor Caroli, Laura
    Dean, Carol Goodheart, Lani Groves, Yolanda Erica, Lee Lewis,
    Lynne Lipton, Ullanda McCullough, Gerrianne Raphael, Ron Taylor

My Little Pony centered around the adventures of 13-year-old Megan
and her pony friends that lived in the magical Dream Valley. Their
idyllic life was shattered when the evil half-horse Tirac had the
Stratadons kidnap some ponies to draw his dark chariot and whisked
them off to his gloomy Midnight Castle. Aided by Firefly, a winged-
pony carrying Megan, the cute equines set off to rescue their friends,
first seeking out Moochick, an accentric and venerable magician who
explained that they must use the "Rainbow of Light" in order to defeat the sorcerer's darkness, "the night that never ends." With
Moochick's help, they found a small piece of rainbow contained within a silver locket. Once inside the Castle, and with help from Scor-
pan, Tirac's turncoat second-in-command, the ponies confronted his
evil "Rainbow of Darkness" with the powers from their small bit of
the "Rainbow of Light." Miraculously, it was transformed into a
beautiful rainbow, and Tirac's nasty bunch of rascals were turned
into serene forest animals and butterflys. Defeated, Tirac was swept
into the sky with his foreboding abode, and back at Dream Castle,
Megan and all the ponies rejoiced. Songs: "My Little Pony" (Theme),
"They'll Be Dancing On Air When They Meet You!" (Duncan), "Count
Upon the Sea Ponies" (chorus), "A Piece of Rainbow" (Randall), "It's
a Brand New Day."
    The tuneful tale featured characters adapted from the Hasbro
doll and toy line, which also was the basis for the 65-episode weekday strip-series, My Little Pony and Friends (SYN, 1986-), and
the animated feature, My Little Pony: The Movie (DeLaurentiis,
1986).

MY LITTLE PONY--ESCAPE FROM CATRINA

Broadcast History
    Premiere: April 1985
    SYN/local station option (KTLA, Los Angeles, April 13, 1985,
        Saturday 7:30-8:00 PM PST)
    Sponsor: Hasbro Toys
    SYN/Repeats: November 23, 1985 +
Executive Producers: Joe Bacal, Tom Griffin, Margaret Loesch, Lee
    Gunther
Producer: Karl Geurs

Director: Jay Bacal
Writer: George Arthur Bloom
Music: Tommy Goodman
Lyrics: Barry Harman
Company: Sunbow Productions in association with Marvel Productions and Toei Animation, Tokyo, Japan
Distributor: Claster TV Productions/1985-
Home Video: Children's Video Library (Vestron)

Principal Characters and Voices

Rep — Paul Williams
Catrina — Tammy Grimes

Other Voices

Charlie Adler, Tammy Amerson, Ivy Austin, Laura Dean, Denny Dillon, Patience Jarvis, Lynne Lambert, Ullanda McCullough, Alice Playten

My Little Pony--Escape From Catrina continued the myth of 13-year-old Megan as the young heroine arrived on the back of skydancer at Dream Castle, where a costume ball was planned in her honor. While she met and played with all the new Baby Ponies in the nursery, evil lurked nearby. The cat-like Catrina and her chameleon sidekick Rep were chasing Bushwoolies, round furry critters who had escaped from Catrina's underground lair where they were enslaved and forced to brew the Witchweed Potion which gave her great powers. Unable to recapture the elusive Bushwoolies, Catrina plotted to replace them and captured Baby Surprise and the magical Rainbow Locket, swearing she would throw both in the Vortex unless the Baby Ponies did her menial work. Disenchanted with his treacherous mistress and longing for the "good ol' days" of fun and happiness, Rep helped save the day by coming to the aid of the Baby Ponies, Baby Surprise and Megan, who retrieved the locket in a series of escapades. In the confusion, Catrina wound up in the Vortex, and Rep promised to save her only if she destroyed the Witchweed Machine, whereupon she became her old fun-filled self again and they all joined in the Grand Parade of Costumes at the Dream Castle Ball. Songs: "Let's Not Take a Nap!" (Megan), "Good Ol' Days" (Williams), "Dressed Like a Dream" (Sea Ponies).

MY SMURFY VALENTINE

Broadcast History

Premiere: February 13, 1983
NBC/Sunday 7:00-7:30 PM
Executive Producers: William Hanna, Joseph Barbera
Producer/Director: Gerard Baldwin
Writers: Peyo, Yvan Delporte, Gerard Baldwin, Len Janson, Chuck Menville
Music: Hoyt Curtin, Paul DeKorte

Company: Hanna-Barbera Productions in association with SEPP International

Principal Characters and Voices

Papa Smurf/Azrael/Vulture	Don Messick
Harmony/Greedy/Ogre	Hamilton Camp
Handy/Lazy/Grouchy	Michael Bell
Vanity	Alan Oppenheimer
Brainy/Serpent/Ogre	Danny Goldman
Clumsy/Bear/Serpent #1	Bill Callaway
Smurfette	Lucille Bliss
Gargamel	Paul Winchell
Jokey/Smurfberry Bird	June Foray
Poet/Hefty/Cat	Frank Welker
Cupid	Joe Besser
Chlorhydris	Amanda McBroom

My Smurfy Valentine imparted a lesson about love and friendship as the Smurfs saved the world from the darkest day and hard-hearted Wizard Gargamel met his malevolent mate. The Smurfs snow-covered mushroom village was abuzz with preparations for Cupid's yearly visit, and a frustrated Smurfette wrote to Cupid asking for a dashing Prince Smurfing. Intercepting her note, Gargamel lured her into his clutches as bait, hoping to entrap the rescuing Smurfs. Meanwhile, Chlorhydris, a chiseling sorceress, promised Gargamel gold for his cat Azrael, needed to cast her evil spell at the Magic Wishing Well that would cause a total eclipse of the sun. During the darkness, she planned to unleash all the evil in the world. After greedy Gargamel handed over Azrael and, goldless, was imprisoned, Smurfette escaped and headed for the well but was intercepted by Cupid who told her she could only find love in her own heart. Throwing Azrael in the well, Chlorhydris was about to make her wicked wish when out popped Gargamel with the cat on his head. While the Smurfs pummelled her with snowballs to prevent her from uttering the dreaded spell, Chlorhydris fell into a smitten Gargamel's arms as they succumbed to Cupid's love arrows. Jumping to the well to wish for her Prince Smurfing, Smurfette noticed Azrael about to pounce on Papa Smurf, had a change of heart and instead wished them all back home. Safe at their village, the little blue folk rejoiced around a huge Valentine's cake, except Grouchy, who had avoided Cupid's arrows, leaving the love cherub a challenge for next year.

MYSTERIOUS ISLAND, THE

Broadcast History
Premiere: November 15, 1975
CBS/FAMOUS CLASSIC TALES, Saturday 1:00-2:00 PM PST
Sponsor: Kenner Products (Toy Group, General Mills)
CBS/Repeat: November 25, 1976
SYN/Repeats: 1977 +

Executive Producer: Walter J. Hucker
Director: Leif Gram
Writer: John Palmer
Music: Richard Bowden
Company: Air Programs International, Sydney, Australia/60 minutes
Distributor: D. L. Taffner ("Animated Classics for Children")/1983-
Home Video: Classics for Kids (MGM/UA)

Voices
Alistair Duncan, Tim Elliott, Ron Haddrick, Mark Kelly, John
Llewellyn

The Mysterious Island was based on Jules Verne's nineteenth-century
tale about five Confederate prisoners who escaped in a hot-air balloon from the siege at Richmond, Virginia, during the Civil War.
The journalist Gideon, young Herbert, black Neb, Northern Army
Captain Harding and sailor Captain Jack, with their dog Top, were
blown by a storm to a remote Pacific island where they discovered
Ayrton, a demented castaway who regained his senses. The story
recounted their survival, including an attack by pirates, their efforts to build a boat, their rescue by Captain Nemo and his submarine
Nautilus and the destruction of the volcanic Mysterious Island, so
named for the many strange and unexplained events that occurred
there.

NESTOR, THE LONG-EARED CHRISTMAS DONKEY

Broadcast History
Premiere: December 3, 1977
ABC/Saturday 8:30-9:00 PM
ABC/Repeats: December 13, 1978; December 7, 1979
SYN/Repeats: 1985 +
Producers/Directors: Arthur Rankin, Jr., Jules Bass
Writer: Romeo Muller
Music/Title Song: Gene Autry, Don Pfrimmer, Dave Burgess
Music: Maury Laws
Lyrics: Jules Bass
Company: Rankin-Bass Productions
Distributor: Lorimar Syndication ("Animated Holiday Specials")/1985-

Narrator/Balladeer: Roger Miller

Principal Characters and Voices
Nestor	Erik Stern
Nestor's Mother	Linda Gary
Tillie	Brenda Vaccaro
Olaf	Paul Frees
Girl Donkey #1	Iris Rainer
Girl Donkey #2	Shelley Hines
Roman Soldier	Don Messick

Nestor, the Long-Eared Christmas Donkey, in this special, was the name given the domestic ass that carried Mary to Bethlehem. Burdened with oversized ears, ridiculed and friendless, Nestor was an orphan whose mother had perished in a blinding snowstorm. Traveling south, the donkey encountered a young cherub who took him on a journey to Bethlehem. On the way he met Mary, heavy with child, and Joseph, who were looking for a donkey. Happily, Nestor rendered his services and, with Joseph leading him, carried Mary across the desert under a guiding star. During a driving sandstorm, Nestor protected Mary with his pendulous ears. When they reached shelter in Bethlehem, Mary safely delivered a healthy baby boy and a fulfilled and contented Nestor watched as kings and shepherds approached the manger under the light of the star. The film was based on the title song and used stop-motion animated puppets (Animagic). Songs: "Nestor, the Long-Eared Donkey," "Don't Laugh and Make Somebody Cry," "Follow the Angels."

NEW MISADVENTURES OF ICHABOD CRANE, THE

Broadcast History
    Premiere: October 21, 1979
    CBC/Sunday 7:30-8:00 PM
    SYN/local station option, October 1979
    SYN/Repeats: 1980 +
Executive Producer: Lou Reda
Producer: Beryl Friesen
Associate Producer: William H. Stevens, Jr.
Director: Vic Atkinson
Writer: Michael Paul
Music: Lucio Agostini
Lyrics: Beryl Friesen
Company: Titlecraft-Lou Reda Productions in association with Atkinson Film-Arts, Ottawa, Canada, and CBC
Distributor: Crawleys International/1986-
Home Video: Embassy Home Entertainment

Principal Characters and Voices

Ichabod Crane	The Amazing Kreskin
Washington	Pat Buttram
Wolf	George Lindsey
Velma Van Dam	Hazel Shermet
Rip Van Winkle	Larry Mann
Mayor	Monty Morgan

Vocalist: Bobby Van

The New Misadventures of Ichabod Crane transformed Washington Irving's cowardly schoolteacher into a reluctant hero. One dark Halloween night when all manner of awesome beings stalked the land, the quiet village of Sleepy Hollow was suddenly shattered by unearthly

THE NEW MISADVENTURES OF ICHABOD CRANE. © 1979, C.F.I.
Investments. Courtesy of Lou Reda Productions and Crawley Films
Limited.

screams from the Headless Horseman. But this time the spirit was
manifested by witch extraordinaire, Velma Van Dam, whose spellbind-
ing ways she hoped would win her a witch-of-the-year award. In
her craggy shack at Wrung Neck Roost, with her comic orange cat
underfoot, Velma conjured up devious dreadful things with which to
plague the peaceful townsfolk. Luckily for them, Ichabod Crane,
the redoubtable expert on all things spooky and magical, bumbled
and blustered to the rescue. Hot in pursuit of the pumpkin-headed
ghost, Ichabod was aided by a trio of equally reluctant companions:
Washington, his swayback horse, terrified of everything, especially
long covered bridges; Wolf, his weak-kneed trusty bloodhound; and
Rip Van Winkle, blunderbus at the ready, who slept his way through
their series of misadventures. 'Most all he said was, "Zzzzzzz!"
Turning Rip into a possum, Velma cooked up more potent spells in
her hilltop hideaway until finally Ichabod pilfered her magic spell
book and blundered through the incantations to evade a band of
marching scarecrows sent to retrieve it. Outwitting Velma, Ichabod
saved the day at Sleepy Hollow. Song/Theme: "Icabod Crane" (Van).

NEW YEAR PROMISE

Broadcast History
Premiere: January 1967
SYN/local station option
Producers: Art Clokey, Ruth Clokey
Directors: Art Clokey, Raymond Peck
Writer: Nancy Moore
Music: John Seely, Patricia Beck
Company: Clokey Productions for the Lutheran Church in America
Distributor: Department of Telecommunications, Lutheran Church
  in America/1985-

Principal Characters and Voices
Davey Hanson/Sally Hanson/
  Mary Hanson   Norma McMillan/Nancy Wible
Goliath/John Hanson   Hal Smith

New Year Promise concerned a resolution made by Davey Hanson to
not yell at his little sister in the coming year. When he decided
that the only way he could keep his promise was not to talk to her
at all, Sally was hurt and ran away from home, leaving a note: "You
don't love me. I have gone away forever." With Goliath, his dog,
Davey began a search for his sister. Too late he realized that he
should have promised, "I'll be nice to Sally," and after setbacks,
fears and adventures, the pair found Sally in time to reach the
church and ring and big bell that tolled the coming of the New Year
and its promises. Another half-hour message of love and life demonstrated through Christian living, the special featured the puppets
from the religious series, Davey and Goliath (SYN, 1962-).

NICHOLAS NICKLEBY

Broadcast History
Premiere: Fall 1984
SYN/local station option
Executive Producers: Tom Stacey, George Stephenson
Producer: Eddy Graham
Director: Jean Tych
Writer: Alex Buzo
Music: Richard Bowden, Billy Burton
Company: Burbank Films, Sydney, Australia/90 minutes
Distributor: Twentieth-Century Fox Television ("Charles Dickens
  Classics")/1986-

Nicholas Nickleby, based on the 1839 novel by Charles Dickens, followed the life and adventures of the high-spirited, independent young
man. Left penniless at the death of his father under guardianship
of his money-mad uncle, Ralph Nickleby, Nicholas became a tutor,
actor and accountant involved in a series of misadventures. Nicholas

freed his sister from the clutches of Sir Mulberry Hawk, suffered
the death of his half-wit friend, Smike, the suicide of Ralph, murder
of his partner Gride, banishment of headmaster Wackford Squeers
and married Madeline Bray.

NIGHT BEFORE CHRISTMAS, THE (A Visit from St. Nicholas)

Broadcast History
    Premiere: 1968
    SYN/local station option (KNXT, Los Angeles, December 21, 1968,
        Saturday 4:30-5:00 PM PST)
    SYN/Repeats: 1969 + ; 1974 (ABC O&O: RAINBOW SUNDAE)
Executive Producer: Bill Turnbull
Producer: Adrian Woolery
Director: Jim Pabian
Writer: Dick Woellhaf
Music: Ken Darby, Bill Turnbull; Norman Luboff (Chorale)
Lyrics: Clement Clark Moore, Louise Turnbull
Company: ELBA Productions in association with Playhouse Pictures
Distributor: Golden Phoenix Communications/1974-

Host: Art Linkletter (1968)

Voices
    Douglas Crowther, Barbara Eiler, Virginia Gregg, Hal Smith, Olan
    Soule, Laura Turnbull, Shari Turnbull

Vocalists
    Bill Cole, Eleanor Geffert, Diana Lee, Thurl Ravenscroft, Julie
    Rinker and the Norman Luboff Choir

The Night Before Christmas developed as a story Clement Clark Moore
wrote for his ailing daughter. Leaving his home just before Christmas for a speaking engagement, Professor Moore promised to bring
his children, Emily, Clement and Charity, a gift upon his return.
In particular, Charity wanted a book on Santa Claus, but Moore could
not find one. After Charity took ill with pneumonia and he rushed
home to her side, he penned "A Visit From St. Nicholas," which was
animated with scenes from the original verse and musically related
by the Norman Luboff Choir. Miraculously, Charity was cured and
a Merry Christmas was had by all. The film carried a dedication to
the children of the world. Art Linkletter hosted the initial broadcast. Songs: "'Twas the Night Before Christmas," "The Morning
of Christmas," "Savory Serenade," "Wintertime," "Lullaby Time."

NIGHT THE ANIMALS TALKED, THE

Broadcast History
    Premiere: December 9, 1970

ABC/Wednesday 7:30-8:00 PM
ABC/Repeats: December 17, 1971; December 15, 1972; December 15, 1973; December 24, 1977
SYN/Repeats: 1979 +
Producers/Directors: Pablo Zavala, Sheldon Riss
Music/Songs & Lyrics: Sammy Cahn, Jule Styne
Company: Zavala-Riss Productions
Distributor: Worldvision Enterprises/1986-

Principal Characters and Voices

Donkey	Frank Porella
Ox	Joe Silver
Cow	Pat Bright
Goat	Bob Kaliban

The Night the Animals Talked recreated that wonder-filled night two thousand years ago when legend has it that animals first talked. It was an animated musical parable of the Nativity, witnessed through the eyes of the animals who were snug in their mangers on a cold, crisp winter night in Bethlehem. Seeking shelter, a man and a woman who was expecting a child appeared at the barn door with their donkey. Suddenly, the animals had the miraculous ability to express their feelings in words. Confused by their wondrous gift, at first the animals abused it--the cow wouldn't move an inch to make room for the strange donkey--behaving with envy, spite and selfishness, just like humans. All was resolved, however, by the dog who pleaded with the animals to accept their visitors with tenderness and faith. Songs: "Parable," "It's Great to Communicate," "Let's Not Behave Like People," "A Place Like This," "The Greatest Miracle of All."

NO MAN'S VALLEY

Broadcast History
    Premiere: November 23, 1981
    CBS/Monday 8:30-9:00 PM
    Sponsor: General Mills
    CBS/Repeat: September 12, 1982
    SYN/Repeats: 1984 +
    USA/Repeats: multiple option, 1986-1987
Executive Producers: Lee Mendelson, Phil Howort
Producer: Bill Melendez
Directors: Bill Melendez, Phil Roman
Writers: Christopher Brough, Frank Buxton
Music: Desiree Goyette, Ed Bogas
Company: Lee Mendelson-Phil Howort Productions in association with Frank Fehmers Productions and Bill Melendez Productions
Distributor: Lee Mendelson Productions/1984-
Home Video: Family Home Entertainment

Principal Characters and Voices

Elliot	Frank Buxton
Chief	Henry Corden
Abe	Art Metrano
George	Hal Smith
Nipponia	Chanin Hale
Fred Firmwing	Arnold Stang
Père David	Barney Phillips
Daniel	Joe E. Ross
Pat	Desiree Goyette
Nobody Panda	Richard Deacon
Herman	John Stephenson

No Man's Valley mixed the bitter and the sweet in a story about a covey of California condors that faced eviction from their cliffside home by a construction crew. To seek help, the chief condor dispatched a fledgling named Elliot on a mercy mission: fly to a "lost horizon," a place called No Man's Valley for endangered and extinct animals, and organize a rescue effort. Elliot arrived safely and found the comic inhabitants--Pat the passenger pigeon, Abe the abbysinian jackal, Daniel the Indian elephant, Fred Firmwing the rare butterfly, Louis the French garlic toad, Irma and Herman the Arabian oryx, Father David the Père David's deer, Nipponia the Japanese crested ibis, Lonesome George the Galapagos turtle, and Nobody Panda from China--greatly concerned about giving up their secret Shangri-La for an encounter with man. A plea for conservation and a tribute to people who care about nature, the wilderness and endangered species, the special was adapted from a series of books on No Man's Valley developed by Frank Fehmers Publishing, The Netherlands, based on an original idea by Harrie Geelen and Imme Dros and original art concepts by Michael Jupp and Elsa Godfrey. Song/Theme: "Welcome To No Man's Valley" (Goyette).

NOAH'S ANIMALS

Broadcast History
    Premiere: April 5, 1976
    ABC/Monday 8:00-8:30 PM
    NBC/Repeat: December 25, 1977
    SYN/Repeats: 1986 +
Executive Producer: Charles G. Mortimer, Jr.
Producer/Director: Shamus Culhane
Writers: Charles G. Mortimer, Jr., Shamus Culhane, John Culhane
Music: Michael Colicchio
Lyrics: Wiley Gregor
Company: Shamus Culhane Productions in association with Westfall
    Productions
Distributor: Lorimar Syndication ("Animated Holiday Specials")/1986-
Home Video: Children's Video Library (Vestron) (with KING OF THE
    BEASTS, LAST OF THE RED-HOT DRAGONS)

NOAH'S ANIMALS. © 1976, Shamus Culhane Productions, Inc.
Courtesy of Shamus Culhane Productions and Lorimar Syndication.

Principal Characters and Voices

Noah	Henry Ramer
Crocodile	John Soles
Female Elephant	Bonnie Brooks
Male Giraffe/Camel	Jay Nelson
Ostrich	Ruth Springfield
Polar Bear	Don Mason
Lion	Carl Banas
Walrus	Jack Mather
Male Elephant	Murray Westgate
Female Baby Croc	Judy Sinclair
Male Baby Croc	Cardie Mortimer
Others	Wendy Thatcher

Noah's Animals fantasized about the Ark goings-on, told from the
animals' point of view within the general Biblical storyline. Chaos
reigned in the animal world when Lion took charge and directed the
animals' attention to Noah and his family, building the Ark. Noah's
dog explained its purpose. Quickly the animals accepted Noah's invitation to join him on the ship, yet even when the rain stopped
after 40 days and nights, no one sighted land. Noah became grim
and the animals began to lose hope, but Lion told them to believe
in Noah and have faith. However, led by the grouchy Crocodile,
not altogether without reason the chief villain since he was one of

the few recruits who did not bring a mate aboard for the voyage, the animals threatened to revolt after their bout of boredom and restlessness. Crocodile recruited some self-servers and set off to find land. Noah then sent out the Dove, who returned with an olive branch. Land was nearby, the Ark came to rest peacefully on a mountaintop and life had returned to Earth. Songs: "The Lord Shall Provide," "Floating Free," "The Lord Is My Shepherd," "The Different Song (It Was Meant to Be)," "An-ark-y," "Share and Share Alike," "Never, Never Give Up."

The program had a budget of $225,000 at a time when Saturday morning cartoon series were produced for $75,000 per episode. The special spawned two sequels, The King of Beasts [q.v.] and Last of the Red-Hot Dragons [q.v.].

NOTORIOUS JUMPING FROG OF CALAVERAS COUNTY, THE

Broadcast History
    Premiere: 1983-1984
    SYN/local station option
Producer: Severo Perez
Director: Dan Bessie
Music: Ernie Sheldon
Company: Severo Perez
Distributor: LBS Communications ("LBS Children's Theatre")/1983-
    1985

The Notorious Jumping Frog of Calaveras County was an adaptation of Mark Twain's famous 1865 short story set in the mining community of Angel's Camp, California. Bragging about his educated frog, Dan'l Webster, the Rev. Leonidas W. "Jim" Smiley bet a stranger $40 Dan'l could outjump any frog in the county. But while Jim was out finding a competitor, the stranger fed Dan'l buckshot and, when the frog failed to move and his own frog jumped spritely, won the wager. The half-hour film captured the story's lovingly cynical look at human nature, filled with Twain's own unique brand of wry humor.

NUTCRACKER, THE

Broadcast History
    Premiere: November 25, 1978
    CBS/Saturday 1:30-2:00 PM
    Sponsor: Kenner Products (Toy Group, General Mills)
    CBS/Repeat: November 27, 1980
    SYN/Repeats: 1983 +
Director: B. Stepantsev
Writers: B. Larin, B. Stepantsev
Music: Peter Ilich Tchaikovsky
Company: Soyuzmultfilm Studios, Moscow, U.S.S.R.
Distributor: LBS Communications ("LBS Children's Theatre")/1983-
    1985

The Nutcracker opened with a comely housemaid tidying up after a
prosperous European family enjoyed its traditional holiday party.
The children had left a nutcracker, a soldier, among the other toys
under the tree. Fascinated by the wooden doll, the maid fantasized
that he gallantly defended the King and Queen of Snow against the
three-headed King of Mice and his army of rodents. Returning to
reality, she discovered the angry King of Mice had once again materialized. Bent on revenge, he zapped the girl to doll size in hopes
of destroying her. With his army of toys, the brave Nutcracker
hastened to her defense, and in the ensuing battle the King of Mice
was vanquished. Magically, the Nutcracker became a prince, the
maiden a princess, and they danced away on snowflakes to the castle
of the King and Queen of Snow, where they lived happily ever after.
The film, based on the classic tale by E. T. A. Hoffmann and set
to ballet music (1892) by Tchaikovsky, was an import from the Soviet
Union.

OFF ON A COMET

Broadcast History
    Premiere: c1976
    SYN/local station option
Producer: Walter J. Hucker
Director: Richard Slapczynski
Writer: John Palmer
Music: Richard Bowden, John Sangster
Company: Air Programs International, Sydney, Australia/60 minutes
Distributor: D. L. Taffner ("Animated Classics for Children")/1983-

Voices
    Barbara Frawley, Ron Haddrick, Philip Hinton, Shane Porteous,
    Bevan Wilson

Off On a Comet told the story of French Captain Hector Servadac,
who incredibly found himself adrift in space on a comet which grazed
the earth's surface. Also marooned on the comet, as it travelled across
the skies, were a Russian Count, his crew and yacht, a young Italian
girl and her pet goat, a band of Spaniards and an extremely selfish
merchant trader. The entire colony attempted to live peacefully together, using their skills and adapting to their environment. One day
they learned of an isolated astronomer who calculated that the comet
would soon collide with the earth once again. Using the sails from the
yacht, the colony constructed a hot-air balloon to carry them back to
earth safely, thanks to the professor's calculations. The film was
adapted from Jules Verne's 1877 novel, Hector Servadac; Travels and
Adventures through the Solar System.

OLD CURIOSITY SHOP, THE

<u>Broadcast History</u>
    Premiere: 1984
    SYN/local station option
    SEL/Repeats: multiple option, November 4, 1984 +
    SYN/Repeats: 1985 +
Executive Producers: Tom Stacey, George Stephenson
Producer: Eddy Graham
Director: Warwick Gilbert
Writer: Alex Buzo
Music: John Stuart
Company: Burbank Films, Sydney, Australia/90 minutes
Distributor: Twentieth-Century Fox Television ("Charles Dickens Classics")/1984-
Home Video: Vestron Entertainment

<u>Voices</u>
    John Benton, Jason Blackwell, Wallas Eaton, Penne Hackforth-Jones, Brian Harrison, Doreen Harrop, Ross Higgins, Sophie Horton, Jennifer Mellett

<u>The Old Curiosity Shop</u> adapted Charles Dickens' 1841 sentimental novel that dealt with pathetic Little Nell, her grandfather who lived at the shop, indebted to the vicious dwarf Quilp, and Christopher (Kit) Nubbles, a faithful friend. To save her grandfather, Little Nell went off with Quilp on the road to beg and after much misery and hardship died, shortly before her grandfather's death. Kit's story was happier, and after his marriage he kept the story of Little Nell alive by relating it to his children.

OLIVER AND THE ARTFUL DODGER

<u>Broadcast History</u>
    Premiere: October 21 & 28, 1972
    ABC/ABC SATURDAY SUPERSTAR MOVIE, Saturday 9:30-10:30 AM
    ABC/Repeats: 1973-1974
    SYN/Repeats: 1976 +
    HBO/Repeats: multiple option, April 29, 1986 +
Executive Producers: William Hanna, Joseph Barbera
Directors: Alex Lovy, Lew Marshall, Jan Green, George Singer
Writers: Blanche Hanalis, Ruth Brooks Flippen
Music/Songs & Lyrics: Denby Williams, Joseph Roland, Hoyt Curtin
Music: Hoyt Curtin, Paul DeKorte
Company: Hanna-Barbera Productions/120 minutes
Distributor: Worldvision Enterprises/1979-
Home Video: Worldvision

<u>Narrator</u>: Michael Evans

Principal Characters and Voices

Oliver	Gary Marsh
The Dodger/Fishmonger	Mike Bell
Flip/Boy	John Walmsley
Deacon/Happy Harry/Twig	Darryl Pollack
Louisa/Lilibit	Pamelyn Ferdin
Snipe/Furniture Man	Dick Dawson
Mrs. Puddy/Rose/Tess/Old Hag	Joan Gerber
Mr. Bumble/Coachman	Ronald Long
Mrs. Grunch/Mistress Dreadly/Farmer's Wife/The Old Crone	Anna Lee
Mr. Grunch/Goodfriend/Butcher/Mr. Brownlow/Mr. Highbottle	John Stephenson
The Doctor/Farmer/Constable/Master Dreadly	Bernard Fox
Pastry Cook/House Agent/Midget/Workman/Hero (Dog)	Don Messick

Oliver and the Artful Dodger embellished Charles Dickens' 1838 story
and characters from Oliver Twist set in nineteenth-century England.
Saving the little girl Lilibit from the clutches of Bumble, who enslaved
starving orphans in the workhouse, the quick-witted Dodger took
her home where she met some other street children: Harry, who
burst into tears on any occasion; Deacon, who had a bleak outlook
on life; and Flip, who liked to steal things. Meantime, the Dodger's
old friend, Oliver Twist, was named heir to the benevolent and
wealthy Mr. Brownlow, who died before revealing his will's hiding
place, a secret drawer. After putting Oliver and his foster mother
Mrs. Puddy out in the street and selling the furniture, the dead
man's wicked nephew Snipe learned of the will and set out to destroy
it. Oliver explained his plight to the Dodger, and together with the
other orphans they raced through grimy alleys and journeyed into
the countryside to find the lost inheritance, one step ahead of Snipe,
meeting a host of Dickensonian characters. At Master Dreadly-on-
Thames' house, they finally succeeded, thanks to their dog, Hero.
Escaping capture by Snipe and Bumble on their return, Oliver found
a barrister to see to his affairs and bought his old home for an
orphanage. Realizing he could never live in such a posh place, the
Dodger and Twig, another orphan, resumed selling old iron and
rescuing ragamuffins.

The film was originally telecast on The ABC Saturday Superstar Movie (ABC, 1972-1974), described in Children's Television,
Part I (Scarecrow, 1983), pp. 5-7.

OLIVER TWIST

Broadcast History
    Premiere: April 14, 1981
    NBC/NBC SPECIAL TREAT, Tuesday 4:00-5:00 PM
    HBO/Repeats: multiple option, 1987

Executive Producer: Jacqueline Smith
Producers: Louis Scheimer, Norman Prescott
Director: Hal Sutherland
Music: George Blais
Company: Filmation in association with Warner Bros. Television/60
minutes

Principal Characters and Voices
Oliver Twist   Josh Albee
Fagin   Les Tremayne
Squeaker the Cricket

Other Voices
Phil Clark, Cathleen Cordell, Michael Evans, Lola Fischer, Robert
Holt, Davy Jones, Larry D. Mann, Dallas McKennon, Billy Simp-
son, Larry Storch, Jane Webb, Helene Winston

Oliver Twist was an animated-musical version of Charles Dickens'
classic novel about an orphan boy in mid-nineteenth century London
who found that he was really an heir to a large fortune. The story
featured some of Dickens' most delightful villains: Fagin, Mr. Bumble, The Artful Dodger and Bill Sikes. In this adaptation, Oliver
was paired with a new companion, Squeaker the Cricket, and together
they met adversity with cheerful courage in their search for his inheritance. Originally a 75-minute movie released on May 1, 1974
by Warner Bros., the film was reedited for the NBC telecast.

OLIVER TWIST

Broadcast History
Premiere: 1984
SYN/local station option
HBO/Repeats: multiple option, 1984-1985
SYN/Repeats: 1985 +
NIK/Repeats: multiple option, 1986-1987
Executive Producer: Tom Stacey
Producer: George Stephenson
Directors: Richard Slapczynski, Jean Tych
Writer: John Palmer
Music: Richard Bowden
Company: Burbank Films, Sydney, Australia (1983)/90 minutes
Distributor: Twentieth-Century Fox Television ("Charles Dickens
Classics")/1984-
Home Video: Vestron #3056

Voices
Faye Anderson, Bill Conn, Wallas Eaton, Barbara Frawley, Ross
Higgins, Sean Hinton, Robin Ramsey, Derani Scarr, Robin Stewart

Oliver Twist was a 90-minute adaptation of the Charles Dickens' tale

OLIVER TWIST. © 1984, 20th-Century Fox Film Corporation. Courtesy of Twentieth-Century Fox Television.

set in London at the first part of the nineteenth century, a story of poverty, the horrors of the workhouse and the underworld and about the orphan who struggled to survive and find his inheritance.

OLYMPINKS see PINK PANTHER IN "OLYMPINKS"

ON VACATION WITH MICKEY MOUSE AND FRIENDS

Broadcast History
    Premiere: March 7, 1956
    ABC/DISNEYLAND, "On Vacation," Wednesday 7:30-8:30 PM
    NBC/Repeat: ON VACATION WITH MICKEY MOUSE AND FRIENDS,
        April 11, 1979, Wednesday 8:00-9:00 PM
    ABC/Repeat: THE DISNEY SUNDAY MOVIE ("Disney Summer
        Classics"), June 29, 1986, Sunday 7:00-8:00 PM
Producer: Walt Disney
Directors: Jack Hannah, C. August Nichols
Writers: Dave Detiege, Al Bertino, Ralph Wright, Riley Thompson,
    Milt Schaffer, Eric Gurney
Music: Oliver Wallace, Paul J. Smith
Company: Walt Disney Television/60 minutes
Home Video: Walt Disney Home Video

Host
Jiminy Cricket   Cliff Edwards

Principal Characters and Voices
Mickey Mouse   Wayne Allwine
Donald Duck   Clarence Nash

On Vacation with Mickey Mouse and Friends chronicled the wacky
leisure-time activities of the familiar Disney characters when Jiminy
Cricket was tabbed to produce a television show and went searching
to round up his star attractions. The cartoons featured Mickey
Mouse playing golf with his caddy Pluto, who matched wits with a
goofy gopher, a bee and a persistent wad of bubble gum in Canine
Caddy (1941) and Bubble Bee (1949); Goofy on a fishing trip with
his able assistant Wilbur, Jiminy's grasshopper nephew, in and out
of trouble in Goofy and Wilbur (1939); Donald Duck, who ducked
away to the Bar-None Dude Ranch and his encounter with Rover
Boy #6 and a bucking-bull in Dude Duck (1951); and Mickey Mouse,
Donald Duck and Goofy in their madcap ride in Mickey's Trailer
(1938). When the gang was finally assembled, Jiminy and the stars
joined Minnie Mouse in Hawaii in Hawaiian Holiday (1937). But tired
of it all, Jiminy decided it was time for his own vacation and air-
mailed himself to Catalina Island. Songs: "She'll Be Coming Around
the Mountain When She Comes" (Goofy), "Springtime in the Rockies"
(Donald), "On the Beach at Wakiki."
    Under the above title, the film was aired as a NBC special in
1979. It premiered as "On Vacation," an episode of the prime-time
series, Disneyland (ABC, 1954-1959), described in Childrens Television, Part II (Scarecrow, 1985), pp. 542-547.

PAC-MAN HALLOWEEN SPECIAL, THE

Broadcast History
    Premiere: October 30, 1982
    ABC/Saturday 8:30-9:00 PM
Executive Producers: William Hanna, Joseph Barbera
Producer: Kay Wright
Story Editor: Jeffrey Scott
Music: Hoyt Curtin, Paul DeKorte
Company: Hanna-Barbera Productions

Principal Characters and Voices
Pac-Man   Marty Ingels
Ms. Pac   Barbara Minkus
Baby Pac   Russi Taylor
Chomp Chomp   Frank Welker
Sour Puss   Peter Cullen
Mezmaron   Alan Lurie
Sue Monster   Susan Silo
Inky Monster   Barry Gordon

Blinky Monster/Pinky Monster	Chuck McCann
Clyde Monster	Neilson Ross

The Pac-Man Halloween Special was lifted from the Saturday morning series, Pac-Man (ABC, 1982-1984), and broadcast as a prime-time special. An episode titled "Trick or Chomp," it featured the familiar Pac-cast of characters: the happy-go-lucky round fellow Pac-Man; his wife, Ms. Pac; the family pets Chomp Chomp the dog and Sour Puss the cat; and their energetic Pac-Baby, whose first Halloween was almost a disaster when the trick-or-treating family ran into Mezmaron and his chomping Ghost Monsters. Fortunately, the family ate their treats--power pellets--and the Ghosts were swiftly eradicated. Both the film and the series were inspired by the popular Atari video game.

PAUL BUNYAN see BALLAD OF PAUL BUNYAN, THE

PETER AND THE MAGIC EGG

Broadcast History
    Premiere: March 1983
    SYN/local station option (KNXT, Los Angeles, March 26, 1983,
        Saturday 7:00-7:30 PM PST)
    Sponsors: Quaker Oats, Atari, Green Spot soft drinks
    SYN/Repeats: 1984 +
    HBO/Repeats: multiple option, March 11, 1986 +
Executive Producer: Robert L. Rosen
Producers: Romeo Muller, Fred Wolf
Director: Fred Wolf
Writer: Romeo Muller
Music: Mark Volman, Howard Kaylan
Lyrics: Romeo Muller
Company: RLR Associates in association with Murakami-Wolf-Swenson
    Films
Distributor: Sunbow Productions/1987-

Principal Characters and Voices

Uncle Amos Egg	Ray Bolger
Tobias Tinwhiskers/Cotton	Bob Ridgely
Peter Paas	Al Eisenmann
Terrence	Charles Woolf
Feathers	Joan Gerber
Lollychops	Russi Taylor
Papa Doppler/Kookybird	Bob Holt

Peter and the Magic Egg was an Easter tale spun by Amos Egg, a large, Humpty Dumpty-like farmer, set in Pennsylvania Dutch country on the Doppler egg farm, whose mortgage was about to be foreclosed by Tobias Tinwhiskers, a huge robot-like villain. Wishing for a

PETER AND THE MAGIC EGG. © 1983, RLR Associates, Inc. Courtesy of RLR Associates.

"Wonderment" to help them, the Dopplers found Peter Paas, a tiny baby nearly buried among the eggs in the hen house, who grew a year every month and after one year was 12-years-old. A Bunyanesque-folk hero, he could plow a field in several minutes while building a fence at the same time and had great rapport with the animals, to which he gave nicknames: the rabbit became "Cotton," the duck "Feathers," the lamb "Lollychops" and the turtle "Terrence." Peter took the animals to meet his mother, Mother Nature, who provided a contract to supply all the eggs for the Easter Bunny. Working overtime, the chickens laid the eggs, the Dopplers and other animals dyed them, the Easter Bunny delivered them on Easter morning and the farm was saved. Enraged, Tinwhiskers challenged Peter to a plowing contest and caused him to fall into an old abandoned well and a deep trance. Seeking help from Mother Nature, the animals were given a large egg which could awaken Peter and took turns at the hatching job. The egg was snatched by Tinwhiskers, who was chased by the Easter Bunny, and when he tripped and toppled into the well it cracked and Kookybird emerged. Half bird, half baggy-pants comedian, he danced about telling awful old jokes, and the laughter from the farm folk awakened Peter. Peter joined the others in celebration and their laughter converted Tinwhiskers to his old self, Tobias Toot. Totally reformed, he took Peter's place, working for the Dopplers, when Mother Nature called Peter to other places, his "Wonderment" to bring.

The special was produced in cooperation with the PAAS company, maker of Easter Egg dyes, decorations and novelties.

PICKWICK PAPERS, THE

Broadcast History
    Premiere: 1985
    SYN/local station option
Executive Producers: Tom Stacey, George Stephenson
Producer: Eddy Graham
Director: Warwick Gilbert
Writer: Alex Buzo
Music: John Stuart
Company: Burbank Films, Sydney, Australia/90 minutes
Distributor: Twentieth-Century Fox Television ("Charles Dickens Classics")/1985-
Home Video: Vestron Entertainment

The Pickwick Papers, adapted from Charles Dickens' 1837 novel, one of the author's most quoted books, presented humorous episodes about the goings-on and foibles of the Pickwick Club. Founded by the genial Samuel Pickwick, the members included romantic Tracy Tupman, poetic Augustus Snodgrass, and sporting Nathaniel Winkle. The story was a collection of their escapades and incidents with a host of exaggerated Dickensonian characters, mostly caricatures.

PINK PANTHER IN "A PINK CHRISTMAS"

Broadcast History
    Premiere: December 7, 1978
    ABC/Thursday 8:30-9:00 PM
    ABC/Repeat: December 16, 1979
    SYN/Repeats: 1983 +
Producers: David H. DePatie, Friz Freleng
Director: Bill Perez
Writers: John W. Dunn, Friz Freleng
Music/Theme: Henry Mancini
Music: Doug Goodwin
Lyrics: John Bradford
Company: DePatie-Freleng Enterprises in association with Mirisch-Geoffrey Productions
Distributor: MGM-UA Television Syndication/1983-

Principal Character
Pink Panther   (non-speaking)

The Pink Panther, featured in "PINK AT FIRST SIGHT," "A PINK CHRISTMAS" and "OLYMPINKS." © 1978, Mirisch-Geoffrey DePatie-Freleng Enterprises. Courtesy of MGM/UA Entertainment (now Turner Entertainment)

Pink Panther in "A Pink Christmas" focused on the lanky and mute feline, frozen and friendless on a Central Park bench in the New York City of the 1890s. Broke and trying to obtain food and shelter from the cold during the Christmas season, the Panther concocted all kinds of harebrained schemes which backfired. In despair, the Panther did his best to get tossed in a warm jail cell for a good meal on Christmas Eve, but was frustrated in his attempts to even get arrested by the compassion of the police during the holidays. Fortuitously, the true spirit of Christmas came to his rescue. The special was based on the O. Henry story, The Cop and the Anthem.

The title character, created by veteran animator Friz Freleng for Blake Edwards' movie, The Pink Panther (MGM, 1964), inspired a series of animated short-films released through United Artists, recycled in various Saturday morning series, The Pink Panther (NBC, 1969-1978/ABC, 1978-1979), described in Children's Television, Part I (Scarecrow, 1983), pp. 220-223. It also prompted a toddler spin-off series, Pink Panther and Sons (NBC, 1984-1985/ABC, 1986-1987).

PINK PANTHER IN "OLYMPINKS"

Broadcast History
    Premiere: February 22, 1980
    ABC/Friday 8:00-8:30 PM
    SYN/Repeats: 1983 +
Producers: David H. DePatie, Friz Freleng
Director: Friz Freleng
Writers: Friz Freleng, John W. Dunn, David Detiege
Music/Theme: Henry Mancini
Music: Doug Goodwin
Company: DePatie-Freleng Enterprises in association with Mirisch-
    Geoffrey Productions
Distributor: MGM-UA Television Syndication/1983-

Principal Character
Pink Panther   (non-speaking)

Pink Panther in "Olympinks" gathered the world's greatest collection of athletes to compete in the famous Winter Olympics. An early arrival was the Pink Panther, the miming mute master of mayhem who blissfully cavorted in and around the various contests, leaving chaos in his wake. The crux of the story had the Pink Panther competing against a small, indeterminate creature whose chief virtue was that he wanted to win and whose chief liability was that he wanted to win at any cost. When the trumpets finally summoned the winner, however, it was none other than the suave pink cat who sauntered up to claim the gold medal. The special was initially aired during the 1980 Lake Placid Winter Olympic Games.

PINK PANTHER IN "PINK AT FIRST SIGHT"

Broadcast History
   Premiere: May 10, 1981
   ABC/Sunday 7:30-8:00 PM
   ABC/Repeat: May 29, 1982
   SYN/Repeats: 1983 +
Executive Producer: David H. DePatie
Producer: Lee Gunther
Director: Bob Richardson
Supervising Directors: Nelson Shin, Art Vitrello
Writers/Lyrics: Owen Crump, D. W. Owen
Music/Theme: Henry Mancini
Music: Stephen DePatie
Company: Marvel Productions in association with Mirisch-Geoffrey
   Productions and DePatie-Freleng Enterprises
Distributor: MGM-UA Television Syndication/1983-
Home Video: MGM-UA Home Video #400489

Principal Character
Pink Panther   (non-speaking)

Voices
   Weaver Copeland, Brian Cummings, Marilyn Schreffler, Hal Smith,
   Frank Welker

Pink Panther in "Pink at First Sight" followed the misadventures of
the lovestruck Pink Panther, who fantasized a romance with every
female he met. To earn money, and by pantomiming to a recording
of Enrico Caruso singing "I Pagliacci," he landed a job on Valentine's
Day with Swifty's Messenger Service, which hired out entertainers
to deliver gifts. During his frenzied deliveries via his motorbike,
miming to cassettes on a portable taperecorder, he managed to break-
up a jealous husband's marriage, a valuable violin and a celebration
for the leader of a gangland mob with a gift-wrapped bomb. On the
lam from the thugs, he wound up in the local park, where his fantasy of a pretty she-panther turned into reality as one saundered
by and dropped her hanky, embroidered "Be My Valentine."

PINOCCHIO'S CHRISTMAS

Broadcast History
   Premiere: December 3, 1980
   ABC/Wednesday 8:00-9:00 PM
   ABC/Repeat: December 24, 1982
   SYN/Repeats: 1985 +
Producers/Directors: Arthur Rankin, Jr., Jules Bass
Associate Producer: Masaki Iizuka
Directors/Animagic: Akikazu Kono, Ichiro Komuro
Writer: Romeo Muller

Music: Maury Laws
Lyrics: Julian P. Gardner
Company: Rankin-Bass Productions in association with Pacific Animation, Tokyo, Japan/60 minutes
Distributor: Lorimar Syndication ("Animated Holiday Specials")/1985-

Principal Characters and Voices

Pinocchio	Todd Porter
Geppetto	George S. Irving
Maestro Fire-Eater	Alan King
The Cat	Pat Bright
Julietta/Lady Azura	Diane Leslie
Children	Tiffany Blake
	Carl Tramon
	Alice Gayle

Other Voices
    Gerry Matthews, Robert McFadden, Ray Owens, Allen Swift

Pinocchio's Christmas featured Carlo Collodi's most famous puppet creation in a musical tale that found the lad conned out of money intended for Papa Geppetto's gift. It began with the mischievous marionette and Geppetto preparing for the holidays in their village in the Italian Alps. To earn money for the present, Pinocchio joined a puppet show produced by Maestro Fire-Eater, who promised to turn him into a show business star. There he met a lovely girl, Julietta, fell in love and eloped. Along the way met up with the sly old fox and cat, the Cricket and Lady Azura. Angry over the loss of his star performer, Maestro Fire-Eater set out to make retribution while Papa Geppetto became alarmed at Pinocchio's disappearance. The magical Lady Azura had whisked the marionettes to safety in her chalet. There Pinocchio fabricated a story about his recent escapade and his nose grew proportionately with every lie. Badly frightened, Pinocchio then watched as his nose returned to normal when he told the truth. Still without a present for Geppetto, Pinocchio presented himself to his grieving father, who was overcome with happiness. And when Lady Azura arrived with Julietta, all toasted happily to the joy of Christmas. The special was filmed using stop-motion animated puppets (Animagic). Songs: "What Gifts to Buy," "Knock On Wood," "Let 'em Laugh," "The Whole Truth," "The Perfect Gift," "The Very Best Friend I Ever Had," "Let's Go Dancin'," "Wicked Glee."

PLAY IT AGAIN, CHARLIE BROWN

Broadcast History
    Premiere: March 28, 1971
    CBS/Sunday 7:00-7:30 PM
    Sponsors: Interstate Brands, Coca-Cola
    CBS/Repeats: April 11, 1972; February 11, 1973
Producers: Lee Mendelson, Bill Melendez

Director: Bill Melendez
Writer/Creator: Charles M. Schulz
Music: Vince Guaraldi, John Scott Trotter
Music/Piano Soloist: Lillian Steuber
Company: Lee Mendelson-Bill Melendez Productions in association
    with Charles M. Schulz Creative Associates and United Feature
    Syndicate
Home Video: Hi-Tops Video (nee Media Home Entertainment)

Principal Characters and Voices

Charlie Brown	Chris Inglis
Lucy Van Pelt	Pamelyn Ferdin
Schroeder	Danny Hjeim
Peppermint Patty	Christopher DeFaria
Sally Brown	Hilary Momberger
Frieda	Linda Mendelson
Linus Van Pelt	Stephen Shea

Play It Again, Charlie Brown placed piano prodigy Schroeder at
center-stage, practicing on his toy baby grand, annoyed at the repeated amorous antics of Lucy, who for years had tried to get his
attention. "You don't like me, do you Schroeder?" asked Lucy sweetly.
"No," Schroeder replied, "I never have liked you, and I doubt very
much if I ever will like you!" Persisting, Lucy tried to elicit a kiss
from her reluctant musician but got slurped by Snoopy instead.
When she finally did manage to buss Schroeder, he screamed, "I've
been poisoned!... Get me some hot water!!" Seated in the patient's
chair of her psychiatric booth, a frustrated Lucy confessed, "If the
girls in Women's Lib ever found out how I throw myself at that man,
they'd take away my life membership." After seeking help from many
quarters, finally Peppermint Patty offered a practical solution: why
not win Schroeder's favor by inviting him to give his first recital at
the P.T.A. Benefit Show? But after Lucy set Schroeder for his professional debut, the scheme faltered when he learned that Patty had
nixed Beethoven on the program and instead he would be playing
rock music with a backup combo: Pig Pen on drums, Charlie Brown
on banjo and Snoopy on the bass. Pressed by Lucy, who suggested
something quieter than rock music, Schroeder gave in and started to
rehearse with the group, then abruptly stopped and, with his
head in his hands, said sadly, "I've sold out ... like everybody
else, I've sold out!" Backstage on the day of the concert, Schroeder
could not go through with it, offered his apologies and stormed out.
Afterwards, still pursuing her heartthrob, Lucy asked, "How come
you never send me flowers?" "Because I don't like you," repeated
Schroeder. "The flowers wouldn't care!" she said angrily.
    Pianist/harpsicordist Lillian Steuber played the Beethoven so-
natas for the special. A music luminary in his own right, Schroeder
and his toy piano have been immortalized in a stained glass window
of the Westminster Presbyterian Church, Buffalo, New York.

PLEASE DON'T EAT THE PLANET   see   INTERGALACTIC THANKS-
GIVING, AN

POGO'S SPECIAL BIRTHDAY SPECIAL

Broadcast History
   Premiere: May 18, 1969
   NBC/Sunday 8:00-8:30 PM
   NBC/Repeats: February 22, 1970; February 20, 1971
   SYN/Repeats: 1975 +
Producer/Director: Chuck Jones
Co-Director: Ben Washam
Writer/Lyrics: Walt Kelly
Music: Norman Monate, Walt Kelly, Eugene Poddany
Company: Chuck Jones Enterprises in association with MGM-TV
Distributor: MGM-UA Television Syndication/1982-
Home Video: MGM/UA

Principal Characters and Voices

Pogo Possum/Mam'selle Hepzibah	June Foray
Porky Pine/Bunny Rabbit/ Basil the Butterfly	Chuck Jones
P.T. Bridgeport the Bear/Albert the Alligator/Dr. Howland Owl	Walt Kelly
Churchy-la-Femme/Beauregard Bugleboy	Les Tremayne

Pogo's Special Birthday Special proved calendars and logic meant
nothing in Okefenokee, a swampland community where every critter
tried to impose his own idiosyncrasies. In the story, they were
actively involved in a support-your-favorite-holiday campaign. Pogo's
contrary friend, Albert the Alligator, and the bloodhound Beauregard
Bugleboy, the epitome of war veterans everywhere, were pushing
Christmas as the swamplands top choice while they argued over the
lyrics of "Deck the Halls." Meantime, the crackbrained experimenter
Dr. Howland Owl and the upstanding and nosy turtle Churchy-la-
Femme were hawking Fourth of July firecrackers; the secretive and
spiffy Porky Pine was in a Valentine mood; and Bunny Rabbit was
lobbying for a holiday every day. Porky Pine was also an orphan,
so Pogo the sagacious, modest and tolerant little opossum and the
coy skunk Mam'selle Hepzibah planned a Family Birthday party to
surprise him, which became the Okefenokee clan's favorite special
holiday.
   The special was the first Pogo animated film to feature the
characters of cartoonist Walt Kelly (1913-1973), who introduced Albert
and Pogo briefly in comic books before they were transferred to a
newspaper strip for the New York Star (1948-1949), subsequently
distributed by the Hall Syndicate until discontinued in 1975. The
film carried a credit to "Todd Kausen, age 7, who had the idea for

the Family Birthday." The characters were revived by Kelly's widow, Selby, and his son Stephen, for the animated-puppet movie Pogo For President (WB, 1980).

POINT, THE

Broadcast History
    Premiere: February 2, 1971
    ABC/Tuesday 7:30-9:00 PM
    ABC/Repeat: December 7, 1974
Producer/Director: Fred Wolf
Writer: Norman Lenzer
Music: Harry Nilsson
Company: Nilsson House Music in association with Murakami-Wolf
    Films/90 minutes
Record Album: RCA LSPX 1003; RCA AYL1 3811 (reissue)
Home Video: Vestron #4415

Narrator
Father   (1971) Dustin Hoffman
                                (1974) Alan Barzman
                                (1986) Ringo Starr

THE POINT. © 1971, Nilsson House Music, Inc. and Murakami-Wolf Films, Inc. Courtesy of Murakami-Wolf Films.

Principal Characters and Voices

Son/Oblio	Michael Lookinland
The King/Leafman/Oblio's Father	Paul Frees
The Count	Lennie Weinrib
Rockman	Bill Martin
Oblio's Mother	Joan Gerber
Count's Son	Buddy Foster
Arrow (Oblio's dog)	

The Point was a morality play about the ills of prejudice, a musical
fable that poked fun at conformity. The principal character was
young Oblio, the first boy born with a round head in the Land of
Point, which was populated by pointy-headed people. Declared an
outlaw, Oblio was exiled with his dog Arrow to the Point-less Forest.
Told by a father to his son, the story centered around the many
strange creatures Oblio encountered there, among them the giant
bees, a three-headed man, an old Rockman with a wonderful disposition, and a tree known as Leafman in the leaf-selling business.
Oblio's adventures taught him that things do not have to be pointed
to have a point in life and that prejudice is a pretty silly thing.
The fantasy was based on a story by songwriter Harry Nilsson ("Everybody's Talkin'"), who also composed and performed the songs in the
score. Songs: "Me and My Arrow," "Everything's Got 'em," "Pole
High," "Think About Your Troubles," "Life Line, " "P.O.V. (Point
of View) Waltz," "Are You Sleeping?"
    The first U.S. made-for-TV animated movie (74 minutes), the
score included the original hit song "Me and My Arrow," the only
one from an animated TV special. Ringo Starr narrated the home
video cassette version (1986).

PONTOFFEL POCK, WHERE ARE YOU? see DR. SEUSS' PONTOFFEL
    POCK, WHERE ARE YOU?

POOCHIE

Broadcast History
    Premiere: 1984
    SYN/local station option (KTLA, Los Angeles, June 2, 1984, Satur-
        day 7:00-7:30 PM PST)
    Sponsors: Mattel, Post Pebbles Cereal
    SYN/Repeats: October 19, 1984 +
Executive Producers: Jean Chalopin, Andy Heyward
Producers: W. R. Kowalchuk, Jr., Shigeru Akagawa
Director: Kazuo Terada
Writer: Malcolm Marmorstein
Music: Shuki Levy, Haim Saban
Company: DIC Enterprises in association with Mattel

Distributor: LBS Communications/1984-
Home Video: Children's Video Library #1509

Principal Characters and Voices
Poochie   Ellen Gerstell
Hermes   Neil Ross
Zipcode   Fred Travelena
Koom   Jennifer Darling
Danny Evans   Katie Leigh

Poochie presented a clever career-canine, a cute pink dog with a
heart of gold who wrote a popular advice column "Dear Poochie" for
World Now magazine. Hermes was her micro-chip sidekick, and the
robot Zipcode kept track of her mail. Her adventures began when
young Danny Evans and his father became separated while on an
archaeological dig at the Pyramids in Egypt. Alone and being chased
by thugs, Danny wrote a letter addressed to Poochie's column describing his plight and asking for help. Responding to his urgent
message, Poochie and Hermes flew their jet to Cairo and then set
off to the pyramid where the archaeologist and his son were last seen
together. There they discovered Danny hiding in a mummy case
and a secret door that led underground to a beautiful but dangerous
civilization (worshipping Isis, entombed atop the forbidden Pyramid)
and governed by the young Priestess, Koom. To protect the sanctity
of the tomb, Koom's counsel called for the death of the intruders,
and Hermes and Danny were thrown into a cell occupied by his father.
After rescuing the trio, Poochie, atop the tomb, impersonated a riled
Isis with special effects created by Hermes. Believing Isis had spoken,
Koom released them all after they were subjected to whiffs of the
sleeping flower, which erased their memories of the hidden city.
The title character was based on the Mattel doll line. Song/Theme:
"Poochie."

POPEYE CATCHES DISCO FEVER   see   POPEYE SHOW, THE

POPEYE IN SWEETHEARTS AT SEA   see   POPEYE VALENTINE
    SPECIAL, THE

POPEYE SHOW, THE
(aka POPEYE CATCHES DISCO FEVER)

Broadcast History
    Premiere: September 13, 1978
    CBS/Wednesday 8:00-8:30 PM
Executive Producers: William Hanna, Joseph Barbera
Producer: Art Scott
Directors: Ray Patterson, Carl Urbano
Writers: Glenn Leopold, Dalton Sandifer, Jack Hanrahan, Tom
    Dagenais, Larz Bourne

Music: Hoyt Curtin, Paul DeKorte
Company: Hanna-Barbera Productions in association with King Features Entertainment

Principal Characters and Voices

Popeye	Jack Mercer
Olive Oyl	Marilyn Schreffler
Bluto	Allan Melvin
Wimpy	Daws Butler

The Popeye Show combined four excerpts from the Saturday morning series, The All-New Popeye Hour (CBS, 1978-1981), in a primetime special. The segments included a spoof of a classic western, Popeye as a pilot who transformed his old biplane into a jet by putting spinach in the carburetor, Popeye as a knight who rescued princess Olivette from Sir Bluto the Rotten, and, for contemporary measure, a disco spoof titled "Spinach Fever."

The characters were incorporated in some new episodes for a half-hour Saturday morning series, The Popeye Show (CBS, 1981-1983), along with a spin-off, Private Olive Oyl (CBS, 1981-1983). The spinach-eating old salt was again revived for Popeye and Son (CBS, 1987-   ). The original theatrical cartoons, televised since September 10, 1956 with some new color cartoons produced in 1961-1962, comprise the longest, continuous syndicated cartoons still seen on television. A compilation from the original cartoons was released as the movie, The Popeye Follies: His Times and Life (Max Fleischer, 1973). The earlier Popeye series are described in Children's Television, Part I (Scarecrow, 1983), pp. 225-229.

POPEYE VALENTINE SPECIAL, THE
(aka POPEYE IN SWEETHEARTS AT SEA)

Broadcast History
   Premiere: February 14, 1979
   CBS/Wednesday 8:30-9:00 PM
   CBS/Repeats: February 13, 1980; January 30, 1981; February 2, 1982
Executive Producers: William Hanna, Joseph Barbera
Associate Producers: Neil Balnaves, Alex Lovy
Director: Oscar Dufau
Writers: Tom Dagenais, John V. Hanrahan
Music: Hoyt Curtin, Paul DeKorte
Company: Hanna-Barbera Productions in association with King Features Entertainment

Principal Characters and Voices

Popeye	Jack Mercer
Olive Oyl/Sea Hag/ Bathing Beauty #1	Marilyn Schreffler
Bluto	Allan Melvin

THE POPEYE VALENTINE SPECIAL. © 1979, King Features Syndicate, Inc. © 1979, Hanna-Barbera Productions, Inc. Courtesy of Hanna-Barbera Productions, TECO and King Features Entertainment.

Wimpy	Daws Butler
King Neptune/Man-in-the-moon	Barney Phillips
Jeep/Princess/Bathing	
Beauty #2	Ginny McSwain

The Popeye Valentine Special packed the familiar cast of characters off to sea on a Valentine's Day Sweetheart Cruise, where Olive Oyl, believing herself spurned by the sailor, donned a disguise to find her Mr. Right. Vowing not to let his "sweet patootie go sailin' out of my life," Popeye finagled the captain, Wimpy, to take him on board. Flaunting his new continental air, Bluto and Olive set to charming each other, though Jeep tried to warn her, while the Sea Hag decided her Mr. Right was Popeye and schemed to get him. Among the escapades that followed, Popeye was thrown overboard into the clutches of the matrimony-minded Sea Hag and rescued by a swordfish; disguised as Princess Aqualia, the Hag offered gold to Bluto to take Popeye away from Olive; Bluto kept disposing of the sailor in various ways; and the Hag zapped Olive into a 100-year sleep and Popeye protected the sleepwalking Olive from dangers. Frustrated over Popeye's unswerving love for Olive, the Hag conjured up a storm that threatened the ship, bouncing Popeye into the galley where he found a can of spinach and used his super strength to rivet the disintegrating ship back together. Disguising a kayoed Bluto as himself, Popeye surrendered his look-alike to the Hag, who terminated the storm and her spell on Olive. As the disguised Bluto and the Hag were joined in matrimony by Wimpy, Popeye and Olive were coupled in the cruise's big disco dance. Drawn to the romantic moonlight outside, they embraced, Popeye professed his love and Olive confessed he was always her Mr. Right. Song/Theme: "Mr. Right" (Olive).

POUND PUPPIES

Broadcast History
    Premiere: 1985
    SYN/local station option, (part of a 2-hour special, KCOP, Los
        Angeles, October 26, 1985, Saturday 2:00-4:00 PM PST)
    Sponsor: Tonka Toys
Executive Producers: William Hanna, Joseph Barbera
Producer: Kay Wright
Writer: Tom Ruegger
Music: Hoyt Curtin, Paul DeKorte
Company: Hanna-Barbera Productions
Distributor: Worldvision Enterprises/1985-
Home Video: Family Home Entertainment

Principal Characters and Voices

Cooler	Dan Gilvezan
Violet/TV Newscaster	Gail Matthius
Scrounger	Ron Palillo
Bright Eyes/Mom	Adrienne Alexander
Howler/Fat Cat	Frank Welker
Barkerville/Dad	Alan Oppenheimer
Mayor Fisk	Sorrell Brooke
Chief Williams	Garrett Morris
Bigelow	Jonathan Winters
Tubbs/Pound Puppy #4	Avery Schreiber
Nabbitt/Pound Puppy #3	Henry Gibson
The Nose	Jo Anne Worley
Flack/Nathan/Pound Puppy #1	Charles Adler
Itchy/Snitchy/Louie	Don Messick
Fist/Pound Puppy #2	Ed Begley, Jr.
Mother Superior/Old Lady	June Foray
Doc West/Chelsea	Victoria Carroll
Sarah	Laura Duff

Pound Puppies focused on the exploits of Cooler and his canine co-
horts, whose mission was to find homes for the stray puppies rounded
up by Dabney Nabbitt, a diligent but sloppy dogcatcher. Operating
out of his Pound Puppy Mission Control Center, located in the depths
of the City Pound, which housed makeshift doggy computers and
gadgets to match a puppy with the perfect family, Cooler had no
more difficulty in concealing the Center's activities from Pound Super-
visor Bigelow than he had in engineering 762 previous escapes. Once
the match was made, the happy pooch traveled via the Underground
Pupway, a network of tunnels beneath the city, to his new home.
Messages were passed back and forth all over town by the Canine
Grapevine, a barking relay system. Cooler's crew included Bright
Eyes, whose powers of observation rivaled state-of-the-art surveil-
lance electronics; Barkerville, a cool Brit with a flair for organiza-
tion; Howler, a zany who would attempt anything; and Scrounger,
who rummaged through trash cans and distracted Doberman guard
dogs Itchy and Snitchy at strategic moments. Other nemeses were
Fat Cat, Bigelow's malicious pet, and Mayor Fisk, who threatened
to replace the incompetent Bigelow with someone who might expose
their operations. Their schemes paid off when four liberated Pound
Puppies found homes with delighted children and Violet, who was
dognapped for ransom, escaping only to be impounded, was returned
home by Cooler and his capable crew, who saved Bigelow's job by
crediting him with the capture of the dognappers.

Inspired by the doggie dolls, the film was aired in a two-hour
special with Star Fairies [q.v.] and The Harlem Globetrotters Meet
Snow White [q.v.]. Originally featuring four breeds--bulldog, hound,
spaniel and terrier--the Pound Puppies were created by designer
Mike Bowling in 1984. In 1985, Tonka Toys sold three million pups,
the fourth most popular toy of that Christmas season. The special
was followed by a Saturday morning series, Pound Puppies (ABC,
1986-   ).

PRINCE AND THE PAUPER, THE

Broadcast History
    Premiere: November 26, 1972
    CBS/FAMOUS CLASSIC TALES, Sunday 5:00-6:00 PM
    Sponsor: Kenner Products (Toy Group, General Mills)
    CBS/Repeat: November 11, 1973
    SYN/Repeats: 1974 +
Executive Producer: Walter J. Hucker
Director: Chris Cuddington
Writer: John Palmer
Music: Richard Bowden
Company: Air Programs International, Sydney, Australia/60 minutes
Distributor: D. L. Taffner ("Animated Classics for Children")/1983-
Home Video: Classics for Kids (MGM/UA)

Voices
   Rosemary Butcher, Alistair Duncan, Tim Elliott, Barbara Frawley,
   Ron Haddrick, John Llewellyn, Richard Meikle, Brenda Senders

The Prince and the Pauper was a straightforward adaptation of Mark
Twain's 1882 novel about a sixteenth-century English beggar, 10-
year-old Tom Canty, who changed places with his double, Edward,
Prince of Wales (later Edward VI), whose harrowing experiences
taught him the necessity of being a just ruler. After three weeks,
Edward managed to return in time to be crowned King when he was
able to prove his heritage by bringing forth the great seal of England from its hiding place. Administering justice and compassion as
needed to those involved in his ordeal, Edward made Tom the "King's
Ward" and promised him the Throne's protection for all his life, "for
let no man forget you have once been King of England."

PUFF AND THE INCREDIBLE MR. NOBODY

Broadcast History
   Premiere: May 17, 1982
   CBS/Monday 8:00-8:30 PM
   CBS/Repeat: August 30, 1985
   HBO/Repeats: multiple option, September 17, 1985 +
   SYN/Repeats: 1986 +
Executive Producers: Robert L. Rosen, Kevin Hunter
Producers: Peter Yarrow, Romeo Muller, Fred Wolf
Director: Fred Wolf
Writer: Romeo Muller
Music: Peter Yarrow, David Campbell
Company: A Yarrow-Muller Presentation produced at Murakami-
   Wolf-Swenson Films for the My Company
Distributor: Sunbow Productions/1987-
Home Video: Children's Video Library (Vestron)

Principal Characters and Voices
Puff   Burgess Meredith
Terry   David Mendenhall
Mr. Nobody   Robert Ridgely
Girl   Diana Dumpis
Boy   Billy Jacoby
Mom   Joan Gerber
Dad   Bob Holt
Professor K   Hal Smith

Puff and the Incredible Mr. Nobody solved the problems of an artistically precocious boy, Terry, a very gifted but insecure child. Because he was different, Terry was not accepted by the other children, who made fun of him. Alone and miserable, he created an
imaginary friend, Mr. Nobody, an incredible talking duck who wore
a saucepan with a feather for a hat. No one could see Mr. Nobody

PUFF AND THE INCREDIBLE MR. NOBODY. © 1982, The My Company. Courtesy of RLR Associates and Murakami-Wolf-Swenson Films.

but Terry, who felt more secure when his pal was at his side. The child gave Mr. Nobody all the credit for his own talents, of which he was ashamed, and when an art teacher reprimanded Terry for a particularly fanciful picture, he decided, "From here on, I'll tell them Nobody did it. Then I won't get blamed." Soon Terry began to believe what he had started out to pretend, that his abilities to make up songs, games, paint pictures and tell jokes originated with Mr. Nobody. But a later conflict with his father over his fantasizing caused his friend to disappear. Arriving on the scene, Puff the Magic Dragon took Terry in tow on a challenging journey in the Fantaverse to search for the elusive Mr. Nobody. At first Terry found that he did not have any ideas for a joke or a poem, necessary attributes for getting along in the Fantaverse. With Puff's help, Terry soon found that he had more creative resources than he thought and came to terms with his own abilities. When he met Mr. Nobody again, Terry realized that his duck was actually a part of his own personality. Through the efforts of Puff and Mr. Nobody, Terry returned to the real world, proud of his talents, intelligence and able to cope. Song/Theme: "Puff the Magic Dragon."

PUFF THE MAGIC DRAGON

Broadcast History
Premiere: October 30, 1978
CBS/Monday 8:30-9:00 PM
Sponsors: Kenner Products, Hershey Foods
CBS/Repeats: September 10, 1979; April 28, 1981
SYN/Repeats: 1986 +
Executive Producers: Robert L. Rosen, Kevin Hunter
Producers: Peter Yarrow, Romeo Muller
Directors: Charles Swenson, Fred Wolf
Writer: Romeo Muller
Music: Peter Yarrow, David Campbell
Company: A Yarrow-Muller Presentation produced at Murakami-Wolf-Swenson Films for the My Company
Distributor: Sunbow Productions/1987-
Home Video: Children's Video Library (Vestron)

Principal Characters and Voices

Puff	Burgess Meredith
Jackie Draper	Phillip Tanzini
Pirate/Pieman/Sneeze	Bob Ridgely
Mother/Star	Maitzi Morgan
Father	Peter Yarrow
Bald Doctor	Regis Cordic
Tall Doctor	Frank Nelson
Short Doctor	Charles Woolf

Puff the Magic Dragon depicted the adventures of Jackie Draper, an ailing young boy, and Puff, a magical dragon. A silent, timid and withdrawn child for whom doctors held little hope, Jackie was surprised when Puff magically appeared: "I've come to help you help yourself." Puff offered him some important advice: "The first step of not being afraid is to see things as they really are." Transforming the boy from Jackie Draper to Jackie Paper, Puff took the lonely little tyke on a journey to his mysterious island, Honah Lee. With Puff's help and encouragement, Jackie learned how to face new situations and solve difficult problems without retreating into his silent shell. Along the way, they met a giant Pirate who longed to be a Baker at heart; rescued a tiny falling star from a skyfull of angry clouds; and finally arrived at Honah Lee, which was inexplicably barren, desecrated by the Living Sneezes. But Puff had worked his magic well in the transformation of Jackie, who was strong enough to take charge of the situation. He cured the Living Sneezes by brewing them a great vat of chicken soup and saved Honah Lee from further destruction. After Puff transported the boy back to reality as Jackie Draper and the lad discovered that he could talk, he admonished Jackie "to face growing up ... to go beyond childish fancies, such as a dragon, and not need them anymore--unless absolutely necessary." Songs: "Puff the Magic Dragon," "Weave Me the Sunshine," "Built Me a Boat."

The special was the first in the series based on "Puff the Magic Dragon," the classic hit song by Peter Yarrow and Leonard Lipton, made famous by the singing group Peter, Paul and Mary in the 1960s.

PUFF THE MAGIC DRAGON IN "THE LAND OF THE LIVING LIES"

Broadcast History
    Premiere: November 17, 1979
    CBS/Saturday 8:00-8:30 PM
    Sponsor: Kenner Products, Kellogg's
    CBS/Repeat: October 22, 1980
    SYN/Repeats: 1986 +
Executive Producers: Robert L. Rosen, Kevin Hunter
Producers: Peter Yarrow, Romeo Muller, Charles Swenson, Fred
    Wolf
Directors: Charles Swenson, Fred Wolf
Writer: Romeo Muller
Music: Peter Yarrow, David Campbell
Company: A Yarrow-Muller Presentation produced at Murakami-Wolf-
    Swenson Films for the My Company
Distributor: Sunbow Productions/1987–
Home Video: Children's Video Library CA2537 (Vestron)

Principal Characters and Voices

Puff	Burgess Meredith
Sandy	Mischa Lenore Bond
Talking Tree	Alan Barzman
Kid Umpire/Boy Who Cried Wolf/Boy With Huge Ears	Ike Eisenmann
Mother/Talking Pumpkin/ Little Girl	Joan Gerber
Judge/Bailiff/Zealot	Gene Moss
Baron Munchausen/Snake/ Attorney/Basketball Player	Robert Ridgely
Father	Peter Yarrow

Puff the Magic Dragon in "The Land of the Living Lies" was a tale about the magic dragon who helped a guilt-ridden little girl learn the truth about herself. Gifted with a wonderful imagination, Sandy was fond of telling stories about make-believe places and persons until an emotional upheaval in her life left her unable to cope with her fantasies and the tales became outright lies. After Puff ballooned into her life and they became friends, together they traveled to the fantastic and fearsome Land of the Living Lies, where fibs and tall tales were a way of life, and they encountered such famous liars as the Boy Who Cried Wolf, Baron Munchausen and Pinocchio. Along the way Sandy was arrested for a crime she did not commit, normal procedure there, and told the biggest whopper of them all, a lie of self-deception. Puff patiently explained about different sorts of lies, ranging from the harmless social lies to cruel lies that could hurt others and the lies we tell ourselves to hide from the truth. Surrounded by un-truth, Sandy soon learned to hate lying and realized she was not responsible for her parent's divorce, the underlying reason for her lapse into prevarication. Able now to face the real world, Sandy was transported by the jolly green dragon to her home, where she decided to put her fertile imagination to good use as a writer. Song/Theme: "Puff the Magic Dragon."

PUMPKIN FULL OF NONSENSE, A see ADVENTURES OF THE SCRABBLE PEOPLE IN "A PUMPKIN FULL OF NONSENSE," THE

PUMPKIN WHO COULDN'T SMILE, THE see RAGGEDY ANN AND ANDY IN "THE PUMPKIN WHO COULDN'T SMILE"

PUPPY SAVES THE CIRCUS, THE

Broadcast History
    Premiere: September 12, 1981
    ABC/ABC WEEKEND SPECIALS, Saturday 12:00-12:30 PM
    ABC/Repeats: March 6, 1982; October 23, 1982; March 3, 1984
Executive Producers: Joseph Ruby, Ken Spears
Director: Rudy Larriva
Writer: Sheldon Stark
Music: Dean Elliott, Paul DeKorte
Company: Ruby-Spears Enterprises

Principal Characters and Voices

Petey	Sparky Marcus
Dolly	Nancy McKeon
Tommy	Tony O'Dell
George Goodbee/Sligh	Alan Young
Gloria Goodbee	Janet Waldo
Emily	Linda Gary
Dad/Abdullah	John Stephenson
Kiki/Vet	Alan Dinehart
Tiger/Lead Pony/Clown	Frank Welker

The Puppy Saves the Circus told how Petey suffered a bout of amnesia and saved the nearly bankrupt Goodbee Giant Travelling Circus before he was reunited with his family. After a collision with a car driven by George Goodbee and his daughter Gloria, Petey was picked up by the friendly-but-broke circus owner, who took him to his vet. Amazed at his resemblance to one of his deceased stars, "Rags, the Wonder Dog," the circus owner trained Petey, whose memory was blank, as a replacement act. Petey became "Rags II, the Funny Wonder Puppy" and received top billing. Thereby, he incurred the wrath of Abdullah and Sligh, two clown caitiffs planning to swindle the owner. On the night Petey's family visited the circus, the villains plotted to grease Petey's tightwire, causing his downfall. The skullduggery was overheard by the sea lion, who told Kiki, the feisty spider monkey and Petey's best friend, who alerted the other animals. Just in time, Kiki shoved the stilt clown forward and the puppy dropped unharmed into his pants. As the animals charged after the clowns, Petey was accidentally bumped by their truck, awakened to regain his memory and jumped happily into the arms of Tommy, the boy who loved him.

The show opened the fifth season of the ABC Weekend Specials and was the fourth in the series based on The Puppy Who Wanted a Boy [q.v.].

PUPPY WHO WANTED A BOY, THE

Broadcast History
    Premiere: May 6, 1978
    ABC/ABC WEEKEND SPECIALS, Saturday 12:00-12:30 PM
    ABC/Repeats: September 23, 1978; January 21, 1979 (Sunday
        7:00-7:30 PM), October 27, 1979
Executive Producers: Joseph Ruby, Ken Spears
Producer: Jerry Eisenberg
Director: Rudy Larriva
Writer: Barbara Corday Avedon
Music: Dean Elliott, Paul DeKorte
Company: Rudy-Spears Enterprises

Principal Characters and Voices
Sonny/Petey   Todd Turquand
Tommy   John Joseph Thomas

Other Voices
    Mike Bell, Joan Gerber, Bob Holt, Larry Mann, Hazel Shermet,
    Frank Welker

The Puppy Who Wanted a Boy followed the harrowing adventures of a pup born into a large litter in a small town where there were not enough adoptive boys and girls to go around. So the heartsick runt trotted off to the city to find a boy of his own. Wandering through the city, undeterred by the falling snow and howling wind, the pup was about to give up hope when he met an older and wiser dog that advised him: "If there is something you want, you have to go after it. If you don't you'll be disappointed in yourself for the rest of your life." His search was sidetracked, however, when he was entrapped with some other dogs by Popov, a reprobate who sold them for experimental research. Helped by the other captive canines, the pup managed to outwit Popov's evil cat Katuska, escaped from his cage and continued on. Tired and hungry, he heard the sobs of 12-year-old Tommy, sitting in front of the "Public Home for Boys." Sensing Tommy's loneliness, he nuzzled up to the child and licked

THE PUPPY WHO WANTED A BOY. © 1978, Ruby-Spears Enterprises.
Courtesy of Capital Cities/ABC, Ruby-Spears Enterprises and TECO.

his hand. Tommy took the dog inside and, as the other boys gathered around, begged Miss Miller, the head-mistress, to let him keep
the dog. At last the puppy had found his own boy, an orphan much
in need of his love and friendship, a warm home and a new name--
Petey.

Adapted from the sentimental story by Catherine Woolley, the
special's warm reception inspired a string of three sequels and the
Saturday morning series, The Puppy's New Adventures (ABC, 1982-
1983), The Puppy's Further Adventures (ABC, 1983-1984) and The
Puppy's Great Adventures (ABC, 1984-1985/CBS, 1986).

PUPPY'S AMAZING RESCUE, THE

Broadcast History
    Premiere: January 26, 1980
    ABC/ABC WEEKEND SPECIALS, Saturday 12:00-12:30 PM
    ABC/Repeats: May 3, 1980; September 6, 1980; March 26, 1983
Executive Producers: Joseph Ruby, Ken Spears
Producer: Jerry Eisenberger
Director: Rudy Larriva
Writer: Sheldon Stark
Music: Dean Elliott, Paul DeKorte
Company: Ruby-Spears Enterprises

Principal Characters and Voices
Petey   Bryan Scott
Tommy   John Joseph Thomas
Dolly   Nancy McKeon

Other Voices
   Hettie Lynn Hurtes, John Stephenson, Janet Waldo, Frank Welker

The Puppy's Amazing Rescue opened high up in the snow-covered
mountains, where Petey, his canine friend Dolly and his master Tommy
and his parents were enjoying a winter holiday in their cabin. There
to celebrate Tommy's birthday, the boy and his dad took the pups
for a first run on his new sled. Caught in a massive snowslide,
Petey and Dolly cascaded down the slopes and were separated from
the pair. Searching for Tommy and his father, the lost pups encountered a hungry grizzly that chased them into an icy stream where a
friendly beaver rescued them from a watery grave. Still looking for
their cabin, they stumbled accidentally into a similar one inhabited
by Karl and Erica, a pair of cruel poachers out to catch the grizzly,
who decided to use the puppies for bait. Just as the huge bear approached the trap, a sympathetic raccoon freed the pair. Hurrying
off on their search, they had another harrowing escape from the
poachers' menacing hawk before locating Tommy and his dad stranded
on a narrow ledge. With the grizzly and trappers hot on his trail,
Petey managed to outwit them all, rescued the helpless humans and
entrapped the poachers for the sheriff.

PUPPY'S GREAT ADVENTURE, THE

Broadcast History
   Premiere: February 3, 1979
   ABC/ABC WEEKEND SPECIALS, Saturday 12:00-12:30 PM
   ABC/Repeats: May 12, 1979; September 22, 1979
Executive Producers: Joseph Ruby, Ken Spears
Producer: Jerry Eisenberg
Director: Rudy Larriva
Writer: Sheldon Stark
Music: Dean Elliott, Paul DeKorte
Company: Ruby-Spears Enterprises

Principal Characters and Voices
Petey   Bryan Scott
Tommy   John Joseph Thomas
Dolly   Nancy McKeon

Other Voices
   Scatman Crothers, Joan Gerber, Allan Melvin, John Stephenson,
   Frank Welker

The Puppy's Great Adventure detailed the further escapades of the
pup Petey and the orphan Tommy in this first sequel to The Puppy
Who Wanted a Boy [q.v.]. Tommy was adopted by a wealthy jeweler
and his wife, and Petey's happiness turned to bitter sorrow when
Tommy's stepfather refused to take him too and the pup was left behind at the orphanage. Fleeing the home, Petey set out to find his

young master. Hopping a freight train, he met two rascally hobo-canines, and during the hazardous ride the three dogs narrowly escaped from an angry brakeman. Eventually, Petey ended up in Loveton, where Tommy lived. With the help of a firehouse dog, Petey met a plucky female pup, Dolly, who lived next door to Tommy. Inadvertently, the puppies overheard a plan to rob the stepfather's safe. In an attempt to warn the family, Petey was blamed for steal-ing a valuable diamond. Only by his and Dolly's resourcefulness were they able to escape impending peril and expose the real culprits. Hailed a hero, Petey was joyfully reunited with Tommy when his adopted parents realized that there was indeed a place for the pup in their household. The special was based on the character created by Jane Thayer.

PUSS-IN-BOOTS

Broadcast History
    Premiere: December 9, 1972
    SYN/FESTIVAL OF FAMILY CLASSICS, WABC, New York, Sunday
        7:00-7:30 PM
    SYN/Repeats: 1973 +
Producers/Directors: Arthur Rankin, Jr., Jules Bass
Associate Producer: Mary Alice Dwyer
Writer: Sandy Glass
Music: Maury Laws, Jules Bass
Company: Rankin-Bass Productions
Distributor: Viacom Enterprises ("Family Classics")/1986-
Home Video: Prism (with A CHRISTMAS TREE)

Puss-in-Boots featured a brash cat, Orlando, who donned a feathered cap and pair of boots, too small for his master Jacques, which pos-sessed magical powers. Wearing them, Orlando had the ability to talk. The epitomy of the eternal con artist, the foxy feline immedi-ately began to sweet-talk the gullible king, intending to elevate his master, despite the latter's lack of wealth or rank, into a position where he could woo the king's daughter. In love with the girl from first sight, Jacques married the Princess and lived happily ever after, thanks to the success of Orlando's wily stratagems.

RACCOONS AND THE LOST STAR, THE

Broadcast History
    Premiere: December 1983
    SYN/local station option (KNBC, Los Angeles, December 1 & 2,
        1983, Thursday & Friday 7:30-8:00 PM PST)
    Sponsors: Wrigley, Proctor & Gamble, Tonka Toys
    CBC/December 14, 1983, Wednesday 8:00-9:00 PM
    CBC/Repeats: 1984 +
    SYN/Repeats: 1984 +

THE RACCOONS AND THE LOST STAR. © 1983, Gillis-Wiseman Productions, Inc. Courtesy of Evergreen Marketing, Inc.

Executive Producer: Sheldon Wiseman
Producer: Kevin Gillis
Directors: Kevin Gillis, Paul Schibli
Writer: Juliet Packer
Music: Kevin Gillis, Jon Stroll
Company: Gillis-Wiseman Productions, Ottawa, Canada, in association with Atkinson Film-Arts, Ottawa, Canada/60 minutes
Distributor: Crawley's International/1986-
Record Albums: Polgram/Starland Records
Home Video: Embassy Home Entertainment

Narrator: Rich Little

Principal Characters and Voices
Bert Raccoon/Pig General	Len Carlson
Ralph Raccoon	Bobby Dermer
Melissa Raccoon	Dottie West
Julie	Tammy Bourne
Tommy	Hadley Kay
Dan	John Schneider
Schaeffer (Julie and Tommy's dog)	Carl Banas
Cyril Sneer/Snag	Michael Magee
Cedric Sneer/Pig General	Fred Little
The Pig General	Nick Nichols
Sophia Tutu/Broo	Sharon Lewis

The Raccoons and the Lost Star restored peace to the planets, this time in a space-age adventure filled with high tech gadgetry. The large cast included: Bert Raccoon, a courageous but somewhat inept friend of all the animals and his best friends, Ralph and Melissa Raccoon, the leader of the Raccoons and his wife; Schaeffer, an awkward but compassionate sheepdog that befriended the Raccoons; Broo, a puppy resembling Schaeffer wearing "the gold star" on a blue ribbon around his neck; Cyril Sneer, a nefarious pink aardvark and crazed military commander trying to dominate Earth and its creatures; Cedric Sneer, his bungling wimpish son in love with Sophia Tutu, another aardvark-like creature who teamed up with Schaeffer and the Raccoons; Snag, Cyril's blue dog-like aardvark; the Pig Generals, who echoed all of Sneer's orders; the Bears, Cyril's thug-like army and look-alikes who acted in unison; Julie, an 8-year-old who was sensitive and bright; Tommy, her 9-year-old inquisitive and trusting brother; and Dan, their forest ranger father. On a far-away planet, Cyril plotted to conquer Earth from his hollowed-out mountain labyrinth of machines and rocketry. The hitch was the lost gold star, hanging from the neck of Broo, which had to be recovered to power his technological wizardry. Mysteriously hurled through space to Cyril's planet, Schaeffer became involved in his diabolical plan but cannily connived with the Raccoons, Sophia and Broo to thwart the cigar-chomping, power-mad aardvark ruler. Courage, friendship and unwavering determination were the underlying educational themes of this third special of the Raccoons series, which also enjoyed multiple runs on the BBC. Songs: "Calling You," "Shining" (Schneider); "Lions and Tigers," "Fallin 'Fallin'" (West); "One More Night," "Friends" (Schneider, West)

RACCOONS CHRISTMAS SPECIAL see CHRISTMAS RACCOONS, THE

RACCOONS ON ICE

Broadcast History
    Premiere: December 20, 1981
    CBC/Sunday 7:00-7:30 PM
    CBC/Repeats: 1982 +
    SYN/local station option, 1982; (KNBC, Los Angeles, April 13,
       1982, Tuesday 7:30-8:00 PM PST)
    Sponsors: General Foods, Warner Lambert, LJN Toys, Tomy Toys,
       Sunkist
    SYN/Repeats: 1982 +
    DIS/Repeats: multiple option, January 1983 +
Executive Producer: Sheldon S. Wiseman
Producer: Kevin Gillis
Directors: Kevin Gillis, Paul Schibli
Writer: Juliet Packer
Music: Kevin Gillis, Jon Stroll

Company: Gillis-Wiseman Productions, Ottawa, Canada, in associa-
   tion with Atkinson Film-Arts, Ottawa, Canada
Distributor: Crawley's International/1986-
Record Albums: Polygram/Starland Records
Home Video: Embassy Home Entertainment

Narrator: Rich Little

Principal Characters and Voices

Bert Raccoon	Len Carlson
Ralph Raccoon	Bobby Dermer
Melissa Raccoon	Rita Coolidge
Schaeffer	Carl Banas
Cyril Sneer/Snag	Michael Magee
Cedric Sneer	Fred Little
Sophia Tutu	Sharon Lewis
Julie	Tammy Bourne
Tommy	Hadley Kay
Ferlin	Danny Gallivan

Vocalist: Leo Sayer

The Raccoons on Ice had an environmental theme and focused on the
sport of ice hockey. In a winter snowland "somewhere a long ways
off, and just over the horizon" in the Evergreen Forest, the gentle
raccoons played hockey on the frozen lake. A sequel to the acclaimed
The Christmas Raccoons [q.v.], Bert, Melissa, Ralph and the rest
of the critters were often abetted by a goofy sheepdog Schaeffer,
the pet of 8-year-old Julie and 9-year-old Tommy, the children of
Dan the forest ranger. The Raccoons were constantly harassed by
Cyril Sneer, a snarling, villainous pink aardvark and his offspring,
the wimpish, myopic accountant Cedric; Cedric's girlfriend Sophia
Tutu, appropriately so attired; and Cyril's sniveling, dog-like blue
aardvark Snag. All was placid until it was discovered that the greedy
Sneer planned to bury the lake under a giant sports stadium, the
Fabulous Forum, a superdome with tacky taco stands and more hype
than Madison Square Garden, thus introducing the environmental-
protection issue. To save and preserve Evergreen Lake, everything
hinged on a brutal hockey game with the courageous Raccoons,
Schaeffer and a surprise defector Cedric pitted against Sneer's Brutish Bears, all of whom bore an uncanny resemblance to Leonid Brezh-
nev. Songs: "Takin' My Time," "You Can Do It" (Sayer);
"Some Days" (Coolidge); "To Have You" (Coolidge & Sayer).
   The special was syndicated to about 150 U.S. TV stations and
aired in April 1982 as the National Hockey League swung into the
Stanley Cup playoffs. The challengers' jerseys were a facsimile of
those of the New York Islanders, 1981-83 Stanley Cup champions.
The program was also telecast on the BBC and was the first animated
special produced in North America selected for viewing on the Disney
Channel (CTV).

RAGGEDY ANN AND ANDY IN "THE GREAT SANTA CLAUS CAPER"

Broadcast History
  Premiere: November 30, 1978
  CBS/Thursday 8:30-9:00 PM
  Sponsor: Kellogg's
  CBS/Repeats: December 10, 1979; December 9, 1980
  SYN/Repeats: 1984 +
Producer/Director/Writer: Chuck Jones
Music: Earl Robinson
Company: Chuck Jones Enterprises in association with Bobbs-Merrill
Distributor: Harmony Gold/1984-
Home Video: MPI (with "THE PUMPKIN WHO COULDN'T SMILE")

Principal Characters and Voices

Raggedy Ann/Comet	June Foray
Raggedy Andy	Daws Butler
Alexander Graham Wolf/Santa	Les Tremayne
Raggedy Arthur (Ann & Andy's dog)	

Raggedy Ann and Andy in "The Great Santa Claus Caper" took the cloth-and-yarn siblings to the North Pole at the insistence of one of Santa's reindeers. The plot revolved around Alexander Graham Wolf (alias "the Big Bad Wolf"), who invented Gloopstik, "the wonder plastic of the 20th-century," which could solidify anything in an unbreakable plastic cube and keep it new forever. Planning to use his Gloopstik Machine to sabotage Christmas for children all over the world, the Wolf headed for Santa's workshop. Learning of the dastardly scheme, Comet, one of Santa's reindeers, sped for help to Raggedy Ann, Raggedy Andy and Raggedy Arthur, their skateboarding sheepdog pal. Arriving at Santa's they found the Wolf had already Gloopstuk all the toys so children could not play with them, and Arthur was thrown into the Gloopstik machine as well. The Wolf tried to throw Andy in too, but the effort backfired when he became Gloopstuk himself. Telling Arthur they still loved him, Ann and Andy broke the Gloopstik cube with the power of love and freed their dog. Vowing to be a "Big Good Wolf" if he ever got unstuck, Alexander begged Ann and Andy for his freedom. In an aside to the audience, Raggedy Ann asked if they wanted their presents sealed forever; the resounding answer "no" shattered all the Gloopstuk gifts just in time for Santa's yearly sleigh ride and freed the Wolf too.

  Based on the rag doll characters in the Raggedy Ann (1918) and Raggedy Andy (1920) stories by Johnny Gruelle, the special introduced Raggedy Arthur, a flop-eared sheepdog of obscure pedigree who was "invented" by Chuck Jones. The original pair made their film debut in Max Fleischer's two-reel featurette, Raggedy Ann and Raggedy Andy (1940), appeared in his cartoons Suddenly It's Spring (1944) and The Enchanted Square (1947) and returned to the big screen in the Lester Osterman animated movie, Raggedy Ann and

Andy: A Musical Adventure (TCF, 1977), voiced by Didi Conn and Mark Baker, which introduced "The Camel with the Wrinkled Knees." Jerome Kern wrote the song "Raggedy Ann" for the stage musical Stepping Stones (1923) and another short-lived Broadway musical opened in October 1986. The Gruelle characters have appeared in countless books published by Bobbs-Merrill owned by Macmillan, and more than 800 Raggedy Ann products have been marketed from 110 licensees in the United States alone.

RAGGEDY ANN AND ANDY IN "THE PUMPKIN WHO COULDN'T SMILE"

Broadcast History
    Premiere: October 31, 1979
    CBS/Wednesday 8:30-9:00 PM
    Sponsor: Kellogg's
    SYN/Repeats: 1984 +
Producer/Director/Writer: Chuck Jones
Associate Producer: Mary Roscoe
Music: Earl Robinson
Company: Chuck Jones Enterprises in association with Bobbs-Merrill
Distributor: Harmony Gold/1986-
Home Video: MPI (with "THE GREAT SANTA CLAUS CAPER")

Principal Characters and Voices

Raggedy Ann/Aunt Agatha	June Foray (Mrs. Hobart Donavan)
Raggedy Andy	Daws Butler
The Pumpkin	Les Tremayne
Ralph	Steven Rosenberg
Raggedy Arthur (Ann & Andy's dog)	

Raggedy Ann and Andy in "The Pumpkin Who Couldn't Smile" resolved the plight of a dejected little boy and a woebegone pumpkin who longed for a home on Halloween eve. Forbidden to take part in the neighborhood trick-or-treat fun, Ralph was a lonely boy whose spinsterish and strict Aunt Agatha even refused to consider having a pumpkin in the house because of danger "from fires and fruit flies." With reluctant but loyal support from Raggedy Andy, Raggedy Ann was determined to find one for Ralph. "If there's a little boy here who needs a pumpkin, there just has to be a pumpkin out there someplace that needs a little boy." Indeed there was, a glum, left-behind failure of a Jack O' Lantern whose carved-on face was a mockery of the decorator's art. The trick was how to get the pumpkin and boy together. The solution was Raggedy Arthur and his skateboard and the start of a frolicksome pumpkin chase involving goblins, ghosts, black cats, rag dolls, trick-or-treaters and the local police. And the treat was due to the resourcefulness of Ann, Andy and the flop-eared Arthur, when the pumpkin realized its dream, Ralph found his smile again and a more sympathetic Aunt Agatha relived memories of long-lost youth.

RAINBOW BRITE: PERIL IN THE PITS

Broadcast History

Premiere: June 1984
SYN/local station option (KTTV, Los Angeles, June 27, 1984,
Wednesday 4:30-5:00 PM PST)
Sponsor: Mattel
SYN/Repeats: December 3, 1984 +
Executive Producers: Jean Chalopin, Andy Heyward
Producer: Tetsuo Katayama
Directors: Osamu Dezaki, Akio Sugino
Writer: Woody Kling
Music: Shuki Levy, Haim Saban
Company: A Hallmark Properties Presentation in association with
DIC Enterprises
Distributor: SFM Entertainment/1984-
Home Video: Children's Video Library #1507 (Vestron)

Principal Characters and Voices

Rainbow Brite	Bettina Rush
Starlite/Spectran	Andre Stojka
Brian	Scott Menville
Murky Dismal	Peter Cullen
Lurky/Buddy Blue/Puppy Brite	Patrick Fraley
Twink/Shy Violet/Indigo/	
La La Orange	Robbie Lee
Krys	David Mendenhall
Count Blogg	Jonathan Harris
Stormy	Marissa Mendenhall
Princess/Moonglow/Tickled Pink	Ronda Aldrich
Patty O'Green/Red Butler/Can-	
ary Yellow/Castle Creature	Mona Marshall

Rainbow Brite: Peril in the Pits centered on the adventures of a
little girl who brought color back to the world. She lived in Rainbowland with Starlite, the magical talking and flying horse, Twink
and the other sprites, and her special friends the Color Kids:
Buddy Blue, Shy Violet, Indigo, La La Orange, Tickled Pink, Patty
O'Green, Red Butler and Canary Yellow. Little Brian was rejected
by his school baseball team, and Rainbow Brite tried to lift the boy's
spirits by sending him his own special rainbow. Accidentally, Brian
stepped in front of the rainbow's path and colorful stripes appeared
across his face, requiring him to visit Rainbowland, for it was only
there that Rainbow Brite had the power to remove them. Once there,
Brian was caught up in a battle between Rainbow Brite and Murky
Dismal and Lurky, the two gloomy characters who lived in "the Pits"
and who were determined to make the blue skies gray. Brian, along
with Rainbow Brite's other friends, came to her aid and triumphed
over Murky and Lurky's evil ways and in the end, of course, the
world remained a beautiful and wonderful place.

RAINBOW BRITE: THE BEGINNING OF RAINBOW LAND

Broadcast History
    Premiere: April 1985
    SYN/local station option (KTTV, Los Angeles, April 15 & 16,
        1985, Tuesday & Wednesday 3:00-3:30 PM PST)
    Sponsor: Mattel
    SYN/Repeats: 1985 +
Executive Producers: Andy Heyward, Jean Chalopin
Producer: Tetsuo Katayama
Associate Producer: Rita Rokisky
Director: Bernard Deyries
Writer: Howard Cohen
Music: Shuki Levy, Haim Seban
Company: A Hallmark Properties Presentation in association with
    DIC Enterprises/60 minutes, 2 parts
Distributor: SFM Entertainment/1985-
Home Video: Children's Video Library #1523 (Vestron)

Principal Characters and Voices

Rainbow Brite	Bettina Rush
Starlite/Spectran	Andre Stojka
Brian	Scott Menville
Murky Dismal	Peter Cullen
Lurky/Buddy Blue/Puppy Brite	Patrick Fraley
Twink/Shy Violet/Indigo/	
La La Orange	Robbie Lee
Krys	David Mendenhall
Count Blogg	Jonathan Harris
Stormy	Marissa Mendenhall
Princess/Moonglow/Tickled Pink	Ronda Aldrich
Patty O'Green/Red Butler/Can-	
ary Yellow/Castle Creature	Mona Marshall

Rainbow Brite: The Beginning of Rainbowland related the legend
about the history of Rainbowland, its inhabitants and the brave little
girl who brought color and happiness to the world. In Part I, the
World was dark and scary--a colorless wasteland ruled by an Evil
Force that took the form of wind, storm and giant rocks. Weary
creatures called sprites trudged across the desolate landscape. A
sudden burst of light that resembled a comet whooshed through the
sky and hovered over the ground. The hugh fireball suddenly disappeared and left standing there was a little girl. A voice from beyond gave her a few last words of advice: "Find the light and color
of this land and set it free--find the rainbow." Later known as Rainbow Brite, she set off on her quest and met Twink, a frightened
sprite who was running away and who told her the rainbow was in
the evil ruler's eerie castle. As they approached the dreaded lair,
they came upon a field of frozen statues--sprites that had been
turned to ice because they had ventured too close. Among them was
a frozen horse. Amazed at his beauty, Rainbow stroked his neck,

kissed him and the horse, named Starlite, leaped into life. After learning from Starlite that they would need a magic belt to gain entry into the castle, Twink and Rainbow were carried away by the horse on a search. Meanwhile, the Evil Force created a ferocious storm to stop the threesome and sent out two henchmen, Murky Dismal and Lurky, to capture them. A storm enraged river erupted down upon Rainbow, Twink and Starlite, separating Rainbow, who called out to the Good Force beyond to no avail. Suddenly, she noticed a soft glowing light and a baby tossed around in the river. With the aid of Starlite and Twink, she brought the baby to safety and took refuge in a riverbank cave, where they found an ancient, rusted belt. Rainbow strapped it around her waist and the cave was filled with brilliant colors. While not yet possessing all the necessary magic, the belt was the key to the castle.

In Part II, Rainbow discovered that the magic belt not only projected colors, but also images of the Color Kids, the keepers of the enchanted Star Sprinkles that could make the world full of color. Banished by the Evil Force to the seven corners of the land, only the person who wore the magic belt could set them free. In seven daring adventures, Rainbow and her friends rescued the Color Kids, but she still did not possess the power to activate the hints of color that surrounded them. Before she reached the castle, Murky Dismal and Lurky kidnapped the baby and Rainbow gave chase, gaining entry through the use of the belt. After confronting the Evil Force, it appeared she would have to choose between giving up the belt and rescuing the baby. But, miraculously, the baby was transformed into an ascending, glowing white light. Originating from it was the voice of Rainbow's Good Force and the Star Sprinkles, which pelted Rainbow's belt, causing a glorious rainbow to burst forth. It became Rainbow's gleaming sword and defeated the Evil Force. Finally, Rainbow possessed the power to spread color over the land, drove Murky Dismal and Lurky to the pits of Rainbowland and was able to undertake her further adventures.

The two-part special was often combined with the others to comprise a five-part Rainbow Brite mini-series which was syndicated beginning in the 1984-1985 season. The programs were a presentation of Hallmark Properties, which licensed a doll line and other novelties based on the characters and name. The property was also adapted for a 13-week series, one of three elements in Kideo TV (SYN, 1986-), a 90-minute show aired usually on Sunday mornings, distributed by LBS Communications, and the movie, Rainbow Brite and the Star Healer (WB, 1985).

RAINBOW BRITE: THE MIGHTY MONSTROMURK MENACE

Broadcast History
　　Premiere: December 1984
　　SYN/local station option (KTTV, Los Angeles, December 4 & 5,
　　　　1984, Tuesday & Wednesday 7:30-8:00 PM PST)

RAINBOW BRITE: THE MIGHTY MONSTROMURK MENACE. © 1983, Hallmark Cards, Inc. Couresty of SFM Entertainment and Hallmark Properties.

Sponsor: Mattel
SYN/Repeats: April 17 & 18, 1985 +
Executive Producers: Jean Chalopin, Andy Heyward
Producer: Tetsuo Katayama
Associate Producer: Rita Rokisky
Director: Bernard Deyries
Writer: Woody Kling
Music: Shuki Levy, Haim Saban
Company: A Hallmark Properties Presentation in association with DIC Enterprises/60 minutes, 2 parts
Distributor: SFM Entertainment/1984-
Home Video: Children's Video Library #1510 (Vestron)

Principal Characters and Voices

Rainbow Brite	Bettina Rush
Starlite/Spectran	Andre Stojka
Brian	Scott Menville
Murky Dismal	Peter Cullen
Lurky/Buddy Blue/Puppy Brite	Patrick Fraley
Twink/Shy Violet/Indigo/ La La Orange	Robbie Lee
Krys	David Mendenhall
Count Blogg	Jonathan Harris
Stormy	Marissa Mendenhall

| Princess/Moonglow/Tickled Pink Patty O'Green/Red Butler/Canary Yellow/Castle Creature | Ronda Aldrich |
| | Mona Marshall |

Rainbow Brite: The Mighty Monstromurk Menace introduced a new villain who threatened Rainbowland and its happy inhabitants. In Part I, Monstromurk, a laboratory creation of Murky Dismal, had an electromagnetic force so powerful that he could drain all color from the Earth, plunging it back into a colorless wasteland. Murky Dismal and Lurky did not want to release him until they could figure out a way to control him, but before Murky and Lurky could devise a plan, Monstromurk escaped from a bottle where he had been held prisoner for 700 years. Immediately, he set off to Rainbow Land, where he began to drain all the color. To protect themselves and their land, Rainbow and her friends created a giant wall made of Star Sprinkles, which stopped Monstromurk from further penetration. Finally, with the use of a shield, Monstromurk, Murky and Lurky broke down the wall and captured Rainbow Brite.

In Part II, the three villainous creatures encased Rainbow Brite in Monstromurk's bottle. Enroute back to "The Pits," the bottle slipped from their hands and plunged into the "No Return River." Assuming that Rainbow Brite was finally out of their way, Murky and Lurky devised a plan to regain control of Monstromurk. They told him he was King of Rainbow Land and crowned him with a headpiece that was activated with memoray, a substance that caused loss of memory. Finally, with everyone under control, they began to drain all the color from the land. However, with the help of her friends, Rainbow Brite escaped from her glass prison and the raging river to return in time to overcome their evil nemeses. Monstromurk was forced back into his bottle, and Murky and Lurky were prevented from depriving the world of its color.

REALLY ROSIE
(Starring the Nutshell Kids)

Broadcast History
    Premiere: February 19, 1973
    CBS/Wednesday 8:30-9:00 PM
    CBS/Repeat: MAURICE SENDAK'S REALLY ROSIE, June 8, 1976
    SYN/Repeats: 1983 +
Producer: Sheldon Riss
Director/Writer/Creator: Maurice Sendak
Music: Carole King
Lyrics: Lou Adler
Company: Sherriss Productions in association with D & R Productions
Distributor: LBS Communications ("LBS Children's Theatre")/1983-1985
Record Album: Ode 77024; Epic 34955 (reissue)
Home Video: CC Studios

REALLY ROSIE. © 1973, Sherriss Productions, Inc. Courtesy of
LBS Communications.

Principal Characters and Voices
Rosie   Carole King
Nutshell Kids

Other Voices
   Baille Gerstein, Mark Hampton, Alice Playten, Dale Soules

Vocalists
   Carole King, Louise Goffin, Sherry Goffin

Really Rosie incorporated characters from five of Maurice Sendak's
books, featuring the author-illustrator's popular youngster, Rosie.
It was the story about the imaginative and bossy little girl, fond of
dressing up in oversized clothes and acting like a star, whose big
ambition was to direct a movie of her life. Rosie insisted that her
neighborhood friends, the Nutshell Kids, cooperate in the making of
the pretend film, as well as helping her solve the mystery of their
missing chum, Chicken Soup. But first she decided to screen-test
the Nutshell Kids in make-believe try-outs. The auditions took the
form of whimsical fantasies, like an alphabet tune that had alligators
entertaining elephants and an ensemble salute to chicken noodle soup
with rice. Carole King wrote the score for the film, which captured
the feeling of a 1940s Hollywood musical, and her children supplied
the voices of Rosie's friends, who were based on characters in Sendak's "Nutshell Library."

RED BARON, THE

Broadcast History
    Premiere: December 9, 1972
    ABC/ABC SATURDAY SUPERSTAR MOVIE, Saturday 9:30-10:30
        AM
    ABC/Repeats: 1973-1974
    SYN/Repeats: 1976 +
Producers/Directors: Arthur Rankin, Jr., Jules Bass
Writer: Leonard Starr
Music: Maury Laws
Company: Rankin-Bass Productions/60 minutes
Distributor: Viacom Enterprises/1986-
Home Video: Prism

Voices
    Bradley Bolke, Robert McFadden, Rhoda Mann, Allen Swift

The Red Baron featured a dapper flying schnauzer summoned from
retirement to seek new glory in the skies over Pretzelheim. When
an evil cat named Putzi abducted Pretzelheim's Princess Sophie, that
meant war. Despite the sneers of Captain Von Zipper, the famed
flying-ace decided to take to the skies again, but first he had to
build a new airplane. Having accomplished this task, the daring dog
led his squadron to victory, defeating the cat people and their cunning Catahari.
    The film was originally telecast on the Saturday morning series
The ABC Saturday Superstar Movie (ABC, 1972-1974), described in
Children's Television, Part I (Scarecrow, 1983), pp. 5-7.

REMARKABLE ROCKET, THE

Broadcast History
    Premiere: c1974
    SYN/local station option
Executive Producer: Murray Shostak
Producer/Writer: Gerald Potterton
Directors: Gerald Potterton, Sebastian Grunstra
Music: Howard Blake
Company: A Reader's Digest Presentation in association with Potter-
    ton Productions, Montreal, Canada
Distributor: LBS Communications ("LBS Children's Theatre")/1983-
    1985
Home Video: Random House Home Video

Narrator: David Niven

Voices: Graham Stark

The Remarkable Rocket demonstrated Oscar Wilde's reputation as a master of English wit in this film adaptation of his story. Although the leading characters of Wilde's story were a group of fireworks preparing to be set off during a royal wedding celebration, the attitudes and foibles the fireworks displayed were all recognizable human. Foremost among them was the Remarkable Rocket himself, whose adventures were the subject of the tale. Graham Stark provided all the voices for the characters, from the pompous King to the explosive little fireworks.

RETURN OF BUNJEE, THE

Broadcast History
Premiere: April 6 & 13, 1985
   ABC/ABC WEEKEND SPECIALS, Saturday 12:00-12:30 PM
   ABC/Repeat: September 21 & 28, 1985
Executive Producer: Doug Paterson
Producers: Steve Lumley, Buzz Potamkin
Director: Chris Cuddington
Writer: Malcolm Marmorstein
Music: Bruce Rowland
Company: Hanna-Barbera Productions, Sydney, Australia (Southern Star Productions)/60 minutes, 2 parts

Narrator: Michael Rye

Principal Characters and Voices

Bunjee	Frank Welker
Karen Winsborrow	Nancy Cartwright
Andy Winsborrow	Robbie Lee
Mr. Winsborrow	Michael Rye
Mrs. Winsborrow	Linda Gary
Others	Peter Cullen
	Pat Musick

The Return of Bunjee, found the prehistoric creature from 100 million B.C. not too successful at playing Mom to the rambunctious babies he hatched in the first show. In Part I, their antics sent Bunjee scurrying to the twentieth-century with them in the time machine, loaned to him by the Winsborrow family. With the help of one of Mr. Winsborrow's new inventions, Bunjee prepared to set out to find a mate and mother for his offspring. An accidental flip of a switch, however, whisked Bunjee and his friends, Karen and Andy Winsborrow, off to the Middle Ages, where they encountered a ferocious three-headed dragon and an evil sorceress.

In Part II, Bunjee found his Bunjee bride, but finding acceptance by the youngsters was a different matter altogether. A sequel to The Amazing Bunjee Venture [q.v.], the characters were adapted from the book, The Bunjee Venture, by Stan McMurty.

THE RETURN OF THE KING. © 1980, Rankin/Bass Productions, Inc.
Courtesy of Rankin/Bass Productions and Lorimar Syndication.

RETURN OF THE KING, THE

Broadcast History
Premiere: May 11, 1980
ABC/Sunday 7:00-9:00 PM
ABC/Repeat: July 21, 1983
SYN/Repeats: 1986 +
Executive Producers/Producers/Directors: Arthur Rankin, Jr., Jules
Bass
Associate Producer: Musaki Iizuka
Writer: Romeo Muller
Music: Maury Laws
Lyrics: Jules Bass
Company: Rankin-Bass Productions in association with Toei Anima-
tion, Tokyo, Japan/120 minutes
Distributor: Lorimar Syndication ("Animated Holiday Specials")/1986–
Record Albums: Disneyland 3822 (with book); Disneyland 382 (single)

Narrator: John Huston

Principal Characters and Voices
Frodo	Orson Bean
Samwise	Roddy McDowall

Gandalf	John Huston
Aragorn	Theodore Bikel
Denethor	William Conrad
Minstrel	Glenn Yarbrough

Other Voices
Nellie Bellflower, Paul Frees, Casey Kasem, Sonny Melendrez, Don Messick, John Stephenson, Theodore

The Return of the King continued J. R. R. Tolkien's saga of the Hobbits, loosely based on the last book in the trilogy, The Lord of the Rings. "Hear you now a story of Good against Evil," rasped the sepulchral voice of John Huston, as the film erupted in fiery skies, jagged, impenetrable mountains, massive boulders and spindly towers. Terrible combat ensued between armored knights and skull-like cavalrymen riding winged horses who swooped out of the churning skies. Thus began a drama of Middle Earth with the wizard Gandalf and those intrepid Hobbits, Frodo, kin to the aged Bilbo Baggins, and his servant Samwise. The enduring Magic Ring, while still very powerful, had become the evil Ring of Doom, and with it Sauron, the ultimate Lord of Evil, could conquer Middle Earth. Frodo and Samwise set off to destroy the ring in the raging fires of Mr. Doom at a time when the free people of Middle Earth were in desperate straits with the monster armies of Sauron at their gates. The dreary monster Orcs (goblins) lamented they did not want to go to war while their master, the Lord of the Lash, cracked his whip over them. As wizards and warriors battled with demons of every imaginable size and shape, including the slimy Gollums, Frodo and Sam made their way to the depths of Middle Earth, risking their lives at every turn. During a perilous journey through Sauron's dread kingdom of Mordor, Frodo was captured and freed by Samwise, and together the two continued their terrible trek to throw the ring into Mt. Doom's fiery lava where it had been forged. Without it, Sauron was helpless and the noble ruler Aragorn was able to return to his kingdom and triumph over the Sauron's hideous realm. How Frodo lost a finger was the grisly climax of the tale. The third stage of Middle Earth completed, peace thrived across the land and the Hobbits ushered in the Age of Man. Legolas, the Elven prince, and Gimli, the Dwarf lord, two major characters in book, did not appear in film. Songs: "Frodo of the Nine Fingers," "It's So Easy Not to Try," "Bearer of the Ring," "Less Can Be More," "Roads," "Where There's a Whip," "Leave Tomorrow Till It Comes," "The Cracks of Doom," "Choice of Evils," "The Return of the King."

RETURN TO OZ
(A Return to the Mystical, Magical World of Oz)

Broadcast History
Premiere: February 9, 1964
NBC/Sunday 5:00-6:00 PM

NBC/Repeat: February 21, 1965
CTV/Repeat: December 25, 1973
SYN/Repeats: 1976 +
Producers: Arthur Rankin, Jr., Jules Bass
Directors: F. R. Crawley, Thomas Glynn, Larry Roemer
Writer: Romeo Muller
Music & Lyrics: Gene Farrell, Edward Thomas, James Polack, George
 Wilkins
Company: Rankin-Bass Productions in association with Videocraft
 International and Crawley Films, Ottawa, Canada/B&W, 60 minutes
Distributor: Viacom Enterprises/1986-
Home Video: Prism

Principal Characters and Voices

Dorothy	Susan Conway
Dandy Lion/Wizard	Carl Banas
Socrates (Strawman)	Alfie Scopp
Rusty (Tinman)	Larry Mann
Munchkins	Susan Morse
Glinda/Wicked Witch	Pegi Loder
Toto (Dorothy's dog)	

Return to Oz was a musical fantasy in which Dorothy returned to
the magic kingdom to again meet most of L. Frank Baum's original
cast. Invited back to the fabled Land of Oz, Dorothy and her dog
Toto searched out Socrates the Strawman, Dandy Lion and Rusty the
Tinman. But soon after Dorothy arrived she discovered they were
all in grave danger from her host, the Wicked Witch of the West,
who was still very much alive. Finding and setting out with her
friends to visit the Wizard of Oz in the Emerald City, they had run-
ins with the old crone's evil machinations, ranging from flying crocodiles to lightning bolts. Determined in their goal, Dorothy and her
friends braved the witch's wrath and freed the great wizard who was
held captive by the sorceress, as the wicked witch turned to stone.
The story was based on Baum's classic book, The Wonderful Wizard
of Oz. Songs: "I Wanna Go Back," "Moonbeam" (Dorothy), "We're
Munchkins, Naturally" (Dorothy, Munchkins), "You Can't Buy a Brain"
(Socrates), "Wickedest, Wicked Old Witch" (Witch), "I'm Heartless,
Through and Through" (Rusty), "Dan, Dan, Dandy Lion" (Dandy).
 This was the first special associated with filmmakers Arthur
Rankin, Jr. and Jules Bass, who became the most prolific producers
of animated special programs, usually featuring some star talent as
voices. The same companies also produced the 130-episode, 5-minute
animated series, Tales of the Wizard of Oz (SYN, 1961-), with new
stories featuring the same characters, recently redistributed by Viacom Enterprises.

RIKKI-TIKKI-TAVI

Broadcast History
 Premiere: January 9, 1975

CBS/Thursday 8:00-8:30 PM
CBS/Repeats: April 12, 1976; April 4, 1977; January 23, 1978;
    February 9, 1979
SYN/Repeats: 1983-1985 ("LBS Children's Theatre"), 1986 +
Producer/Director/Writer: Chuck Jones
Music: Dean Elliott
Company: Chuck Jones Enterprises
Distributor: Berle Adams/1986-
Home Video: Family Home Entertainment

Narrator: Orson Welles

Principal Characters and Voices
Rikki-tikki-tavi   Orson Welles
Nag/Chuchundra   Shepard Menken
Teddy   Michael LeClaire
Nagaina/Darzee's Wife/Mother   June Foray
Father   Les Tremayne
Darzee   Lennie Weinrib

Rikki-tikki-tavi told about one of the greatest fights in animal-story
literature, between a mongoose and a cobra. Named Rikki-tikki-tavi
from the sound it made, the mongoose was washed out of its burrow
by a flood and was saved from drowning by an Englishman and his
wife. Rikki became a house pet and brave defender of the family
in the Segowlee cantonment in India, particularly beloved by the
little son, Teddy. Poking around in the garden of the house, Rikki
met Darzee the Tailorbird and his wife and narrowly avoided death
from the big black cobra Nag and his wife, Nagaina. During his
nightly walks around the house, Rikki ran up against Chuchundra
the Muskrat and learned that the two king cobras planned to kill
the people in the bungalow. "So long as the bungalow is empty, we
are king and queen of the garden." Entering the house through a
sluice in the bathroom, Nag was soon dispatched through the efforts
of Rikki and the Englishman. Later, seeking revenge, Nagaina was
about to strike Teddy when Rikki rushed to the rescue, saving the
boy's life. The mongoose chased the snake into a rathole and emerged
victorious, returning to the grateful, loving care of Teddy and the
family. The film was adapted from The Jungle Books (1894) by Rudyard Kipling and captured suggestions of the Bombay-born author's
India through the artwork. Song/Theme: "Dawn Song."

ROBIN HOOD   see   LEGEND OF ROBIN HOOD, THE

ROBIN HOOD

Broadcast History
    Premiere: November 26, 1973

SYN/FESTIVAL OF FAMILY CLASSICS, WABC, New York, Sunday
7:00-7:30 PM
SYN/Repeats: 1973 +
Producers/Directors: Arthur Rankin, Jr., Jules Bass
Associate Producer: Mary Alice Dwyer
Writer: William Overgard
Music: Maury Laws, Jules Bass
Company: Rankin-Bass Productions
Distributor: Viacom Enterprises/1986-
Home Video: Prism

Robin Hood presented a new version of the classic tale, incorporating a boy, his sheepdog and a badger. Plotting to capture their
foe Robin Hood, friend of the downtrodden and brave leader of his
outlawed Merry Men, the Sheriff of Nottingham and his bowman,
William O'Leslie, imprisoned an innocent woodcutter as bait to lure
Robin to the castle. After the stratagem succeeded, the Sheriff
reneged on his word and jailed not only Robin, but the woodcutter
and his son in the dungeon. Seeking his master, the boy's sheepdog chased a badger burrowing through a tunnel, leading to Robin's
cell. When water from the moat flooded the tunnel, it provided a
fortuitious escape, foiling the Sheriff and his henchman. Robin and
the others were able to float to freedom on a raft made from a table
as the undermined castle collapsed.

ROBIN HOODNIK

Broadcast History
    Premiere: November 4, 1972
    ABC/ABC SATURDAY SUPERSTAR MOVIE, Saturday 9:30-10:30
        AM
    ABC/Repeats: 1973-1974
    SYN/Repeats: 1978 +
Executive Producers: William Hanna, Joseph Barbera
Music: Hoyt Curtin, Paul DeKorte
Company: Hanna-Barbera Productions/60 minutes
Distributor: Worldvision Enterprises/1979-

Principal Characters and Voices
Robin Hood/Alan Airedale/Whirlin'
    Merlin/Lord Scurvy/Friar
    Pork/Little John   Lennie Weinrib
Sheriff of Nottingham/
    Carbuncle   John Stephenson
Oxx   Joe E. Ross
Donkey/Town Crier/Buzzard   Hal Smith
Scrounger/Richard the
    Iron-Hearted   Daws Butler
Maid Marian/Widow Weed   Cynthia Adler

Robin Hoodnik spoofed the celebrated adventures of the famous hero
of Sherwood Forest in a fantasy tale with a collection of colorful
animals. After 239 attempts to capture a canine Robin and his pack
of jolly critters, the unscrupulous Sheriff of Nottingham and his
deputy, Oxx, devised an elaborate trap aided by their not-so-loyal
dog Scrounger. Chancing upon the pit, it reminded Robin to steal
some money for road repairs, and the merry band went off singing
as the evil Lord Scurvy toppled into the trap instead. After Oxx,
disguised as Robin, announced a new policy of stealing from the poor
and keeping it, which enraged the peasants, Robin rescued the Widow
Weed's cow from the Sheriff's jail, escaping thanks to Friar Pork's
rocket roller invention, to become again their hero. In a new scheme,
the Sheriff and Oxx enlisted Whirlin' Merlin the wizard, whose potion made Maid Marian fall in love with Lord Scurvy, who kidnapped
her and announced their forthcoming marriage, planning to entrap
Robin. Richard the Iron-Hearted arrived to oversee the wedding as
Scurvy, driven daffy by Marian's constant chatter and trying to end
the engagement, sent Robin a note with her location and loosened
her barred window. But the plan was foiled by diligent Oxx. When
the town crier announced the nuptials, Robin and his Merry Men
raced to the rescue to find Scurvy in tears, taking his vows. Fortunately, the potion wore off before "I Do," and Robin rescued Marian
with his U-turn boomerang bow and arrow. Safely back in Sherwood
Forest, Marian, longing to live in a castle instead of sitting in poison
ivy, bemoaned her plight, "Green is not my color."
  The special was originally aired on The ABC Saturday Superstar Movie (ABC, 1972-1974), described in Children's Television,
Part I (Scarecrow, 1983), pp. 5-7.

ROBINSON CRUSOE

Broadcast History
    Premiere: November 23, 1972
    CBS/FAMOUS CLASSIC TALES, Thursday 12:00-1:00 PM
    Sponsor: Kenner Products (Toy Group, General Mills)
    CBS/Repeat: October 8, 1973
    SYN/Repeats: 1974 +
Executive Producer: Walter J. Hucker
Director: Leif Gram
Writer: John Palmer
Music: Richard Bowden
Company: Air Programs International, Sydney, Australia/60 minutes
Distributor: D. L. Taffner ("Animated Classics for Children")/1983-
Home Video: Classics for Kids (MGM/UA)

Voices
    Alistair Duncan, Ron Haddrick, Mark Kelly, John Llewellyn, Owen
    Weingott

Robinson Crusoe was an hour-long literal version of Defoe's 1719 classic tale about shipwreck, solitude and survival on an isolated tropical island, with Crusoe resourcefully fashioning the necessities of life out of nature until the day he was rescued and returned to a new and different world.

ROBINSON CRUSOE

Broadcast History
    Premiere: February 18, 1973
    SYN/FESTIVAL OF FAMILY CLASSICS, WABC, New York, Sunday
        7:00-7:30 PM
    SYN/Repeats: 1973 +
Producers/Directors: Arthur Rankin, Jr., Jules Bass
Associate Producer: Mary Alice Dwyer
Writer: William Overgard
Music: Maury Laws, Jules Bass
Company: Rankin-Bass Productions
Distributor: Viacom Enterprises/1986-
Home Video: Prism

Robinson Crusoe was a half-hour version of Daniel Defoe's tale of a man shipwrecked and marooned on a deserted jungle island for 25 years. Walking the beach with his talkative parrot Poll, Crusoe found a human footprint in the sand. Searching for the person, he daringly rescued the man from savage cannibals and named him Friday. One day a strange ship entered the harbor with a mutinous crew. Learning that the Captain had been imprisoned aboard, Crusoe and Friday freed the man and together they defeated the mutineers. Grateful, the Captain give Crusoe and Friday passage back to civilization to enjoy freedom in a new world.

ROBOTMAN AND FRIENDS

Broadcast History
    Premiere: 1985
    SYN/local station option (KTLA, Los Angeles, October 27, 1985,
        Sunday 12:30-2:00 PM PST)
Executive Producers: Jean Chalopin, Andy Heyward, Tetsuo
    Katayama
Co-Executive Producer: Jay Poynor
Associate Producer: Carol Corwin
Director: Bernard Deyries
Writer: Woody Kling
Music: Peter Shelley
Company: DIC Enterprises in association with United Media/90 minutes
Distributor: LBS Communications/1985-
Home Video: Children's Video Library (Vestron)

Principal Characters and Voices

Robotman	Greg Berg
Roberon/Sound-Off	Frank Welker
Stellar	Katie Leigh
Uncle Thomas Cooper	Phil Proctor
Michael/Oops	Adam Carl
Lint (furry pet)	
Bleep (robot dog)	

Robotman and Friends pitted the evil robot Roberon and his magic flute against three micro-chip pals from Robotland; young Robotman, his young female counterpart, Stellar, and little Oops. Lint, all fur and shoes, was their pet. The youngsters wore beanies with propellers on top which enabled them to fly and were in constant need of love (hands on heart) which recharged their energy. In Part I, they were befriended on Earth by young Michael and his Uncle Thomas Cooper, an inventor of sorts. Seeking to program the robots to hate instead of love, Roberon, through various schemes, tried to entice the robots into the wood where he could capture them but was foiled by the music from Uncle Cooper's latest device, as music was something Roberon could not stand.

In Part II, Michael and Uncle Cooper's musical kite fell into the clutches of Roberon, and the robots again tried their music, this time to no avail. Sound-off, Roberon's lackey, had placed his hands over Roberon's ears, but a clap of eraser chalkdust finally made him cough up his magic flute. However, Sound-Off stole it back from Uncle Cooper's robot dog Bleep and used it to capture Stellar and Oops. Both Lint and Robotman tried to free them but were trapped as well. Michael reached his friends but was stunned and believed to be dead, leaving the rescue up to Bleep, who knocked Sound-Off away from Roberon and let the music through to chase him away.

In Part III, the robots took Michael to Robotland where he was revived by a special machine. Upon leaving for home with Uncle Cooper, Michael was given a magic box filled with music which would allow them to return. But Roberon's birds found the secret entrance and guided him to Robotland, whereupon he finally captured the robots, intending to take them to Shadowland to be filled with hate. Suspecting something was amiss, Michael and his Uncle returned to Robotland, where he used the musical box to drive Roberon away and free his friends.

Throughout the program, after the robots were involved in dangerous situations, safety tips were added before the commercial breaks, such as warning children not to climb into confined spaces like trunks or refrigerators. The special was based on the Robotman characters, a property of United Feature Syndicate. Songs: "I Want to be Your Robotman," "We Are the Robots," "Oops, He's Done It Again," "Strength From the Heart," "We'll Always Be There."

Based on the Kenner toy, Robotman was transferred to a comic strip in 1985 for the United Feature Syndicate by Jim Merrick, who also draws political cartoons for the Newspaper Enterprise Association;

both corporations are divisions of United Media, a Scripps Howard Company. A 1983 graduate of Washington University, St. Louis, Missouri, Merrick won the Chicago Tribune Student Cartoonist Contest for his strip, "Paperback Writer."

ROMANCE OF BETTY BOOP, THE

Broadcast History
Premiere: March 20, 1985
CBS/Wednesday 8:30-9:00 PM
Sponsors: Peter Paul Cadbury, Nabisco Brands
Executive Producer: Bruce L. Palsner
Producers: Lee Mendelson, Bill Melendez
Producer/King Features: Charles E. Shutt
Associate Producer/King Features: Beverly L. Smith
Director: Bill Melendez
Writer: Ron Friedman
Music & Lyrics: Ed Bogas, Desiree Goyette
Company: King Features Entertainment in association with Lee Mendelson-Bill Melendez Productions

Principal Characters and Voices
Betty Boop	Desiree Goyette
Freddie	Sean Allan
Waldo Van Lavish	Derek McGrath
Johnny Throat/Punchie	George R. Wendt
Beverly	Marsha Meyers
Mischa Bubbles	Sandy Kenyon
Parrot	Frank W. Buxton
Chuckles	Robert Towers
Ethnic Voices	Ron Friedman

Announcer: John Stephenson

Vocalists
Desiree Goyette, Sean Allan

The Romance of Betty Boop starred the cartoon vamp, who blithely satirized the screen sirens of the jazz-age in an adult-oriented special set in 1939 New York. A spunky lass with big eyes, a "10" body, brunette spit curls and a high, squeaky voice, Betty was on a determined quest for a successful career, personal happiness and romance. Still trying to hook a millionaire, she had a crush on Waldo Van Lavish, whose picture adorned the latest issue of Blab! magazine. Understandably, she was not impressed with the neighborhood iceman Freddie, who crooned, "I Only Have Ice for You," and relegated him to the deep freeze. A hard-working girl, living in a one-room walk-up flat in an ethnic polyglot neighborhood, Betty toiled as a shoe clerk by day and as a toe-tapping performer by night at the Club Bubble, where her life was brightened by the kindly, if hapless

owner, Mischa Bubbles. When everyone else quit, due to threats by the mobster Johnny Throat, she was forced to go on alone: "I've got three more shows to do and I'm too pooped to boop." She perked up after learning that Van Lavish was in the audience and wowed him with her signature song, "I Want to Be Loved by You." Waldo was a cad, of course, and her aspiring boyfriend Freddie was at hand to help save her from the slob and the mob, who were endangering her dreams of show business stardom. More fickle than grateful, in the final scene Betty was considering whether to accept an offer from Hollywood or to marry eveready Freddie. Musical melodies of the era were scattered throughout, including such tunes as "Bei Mir Bist du Schon," "I Only Have Eyes For You," "You're the Cause of It All," "I Can't Give You Anything But Love, Baby" and "I Want to Be Loved by You." Other songs: "I'm Betty Boop," "Boop-Oop-a-Doop" (Goyette).

The film carried special thanks to animator Grim Natwick, who first drew Betty Boop. It was the first TV special and new film starring the character since Yip Yip Yippy (August 11, 1939). A film compilation was released as the movie Hurray for Betty Boop (NTA-DKC, 1980). Originally created by Natwick as an unnamed canine character in Dizzy Dishes ("Talkartoon," August 9, 1930), produced by Max and Dave Fleischer, she made her first appearance as a girl in Any Rags ("Talkartoon," January 12, 1932), although another prototype had appeared with Rudy Vallee in Betty Coed ("Screen Song," August 1, 1931), from which she derived her first name. She first sang the eponymous song in Boop-Oop-a-Doop ("Talkartoon," January 16, 1932). Voiced mainly by Mae Questel, Betty Boop was then starred in 112 cartoons, beginning with Stop the Show (August 12, 1932), which were first syndicated in 1956, described in Children's Television, Part I (Scarecrow, 1983), pp. 44-46.

ROMIE-0 AND JULIE-8
(aka RUNAWAY ROBOTS)

Broadcast History
    Premiere: April 8, 1979
    CBC/Sunday 8:00-8:30 PM
    SYN/local station option (KNBC, Los Angeles, April 19, 1979,
        Thursday 7:30-8:00 PM PST)
    SYN/Repeats: 1980 +
Executive Producer: Gordon Arnold
Producers: Patrick Loubert, Michael Hirsh
Director: Clive Smith
Writers: Ken Sobol, Elaine Pope
Music/Songs & Lyrics: John Sebastian, Richard Manuel

Opposite: THE ROMANCE OF BETTY BOOP. © 1985, King Features Syndicate, Inc. Courtesy of King Features Entertainment.

Music: Patricia Cullen
Company: Nelvana Limited, Toronto, Canada, in association with CBC
Distributor: Viacom Enterprises/1979–
Home Video: Warner Home Video #4006 ("Nelvanamation")

Principal Characters and Voices

Romie-0	Greg Swanson
Julie-8	Donann Cavin
Mr. Thunderbottom	Max Ferguson
Ms. Fassbinder	Marie Aloma
Gizmo	Nick Nichols
Junk Monster	Bill Osler

Vocalists
   John Sebastian, Rory Block, Richard Manuel

Romie-0 and Julie-8 brought Shakespeare into the space age in a
musical adaptation of one of the world's greatest love stories. It
involved Romie-0 and Julie-8, two of the newest, greatest, most ver-
satile and best looking robots that ever came off the assembly line.
They fell in love despite the fact that they were produced by two
competing companies, Megastellar and Supersolar, which spared no
effort to keep them apart. Deciding to run away, the pair temporarily
wound up in the hands of the horrible Junk Monster. But love
triumphed, and Romie-0 and Julie-8 were finally allowed to clank
down the path of life together as Megastellar and Supersolar contem-
plated a merger. Songs: "Convention Song," "Living Space," "Junk
Song."

ROSE-PETAL PLACE

Broadcast History
   Premiere: May 1984
   SYN/local station option (KTLA, Los Angeles, May 23, 1984,
      Wednesday 7:30-8:00 PM PST)
   Sponsor: Kenner-Parker Products (Toy Group, General Mills)
   SYN/Repeats: October 12, 1984 +
Executive Producers: Joe Ruby, Ken Spears
Producer/Creator: David Kirschner
Director: Charles A. Nichols
Writer: Mal Marmorstein
Music/Songs & Lyrics: Greg Scelsa
Music: Dean Elliott, Paul DeKorte
Company: Ruby-Spears Enterprises in association with David Kir-
   schner Productions and Hallmark Properties
Distributor: SFM Entertainment/1984–
Home Video: Worldvision

Cast

Little Girl in the Garden	Nicole Eggert

ROSE-PETAL PLACE. © 1984, David Kirschner Productions, Inc.
Courtesy of SFM Entertainment and Hallmark Properties.

Principal Characters and Voices

Rose-Petal	Marie Osmond
Nastina	Marilyn Schreffler
Sunny Sunflower/Daffodil	Susan Blu
Orchid/Little Girl/Lily Fair	Renae Jacobs
Iris	Candy Ann Brown
P.D. Centipede/Seymour J.	
Snailsworth/Tumbles/	
Elmer/Horace Fly	Frank Welker
Pitterpat (Rose-Petal's Kitten)	

Rose-Petal Place was set in an untended garden of an abandoned Victorian mansion, a sunny world full of bright splashes of color. At one time the flowers had been the make-believe friends of a young girl who had lived there, but when her family had to move away and the heartbroken girl wept goodbye, her teardrops magically brought the flowers to life. Now the garden was Rose-Petal's Place, named for the aspiring young singer whose merry songs kept the flowers alive, to the habitual disgust of the evil spider Nastina and her henchman Horace Fly, who wanted every blooming thing in the garden destroyed. Nastina devised a nasty scheme to kidnap Rose-Petal so she could no longer sing, for it was through her voice that the flowers bloomed. Her five special friends were Sunny Sunflower, her best friend and an outspoken tomboy; Lily Fair the dancer; Iris, a shy artist; Daffodil, who owned a designer boutique; and Orchid, the fashion-conscious member of the group. They shared the garden with some unusual creatures: Tumbles, a happy-go-lucky hedgehog; Seymour J. Snailsworth, the resident intellectual and preppy who liked to give advice; and P.D. Centipede, the resident athlete who lived in an old football. After she was imprisoned in Nastina's dreadful castle, Rose-Petal's kitten Pitterpat and the others summoned up the courage to enter Nastina's frightful domain to rescue the flower sprite. Through her songs and the support of her friends, Rose-Petal continued to thwart the wicked Nastina and to maintain an enchanted world where dreams come true. Songs: "Friends," "Sing a Happy Song" (Osmond), "I Love to Hate" (Nastina).

ROSE-PETAL PLACE II: "REAL FRIENDS"

Broadcast History
    Premiere: April 1985
    SYN/local station option (KTLA, Los Angeles, April 28, 1985,
        Sunday 8:30-9:00 AM PST)
    Sponsor: Kenner-Parker Products (Toy Group, General Mills)
    SYN/Repeats: October 24, 1985 +
Executive Producers: Joseph Ruby, Ken Spears
Producer/Creator: David Kirschner
Associate Producer: Larry Huber
Director: Charles A. Nichols
Writer: Mal Marmorstein
Music/Songs & Lyrics: Greg Scelsa

Music: John Debney, Paul DeKorte
Company: Ruby-Spears Enterprises in association with David Kirschner Productions and Hallmark Properties
Distributor: SFM Entertainment/1985-
Home Video: Worldvision

Cast
Little Girl in the Garden   Nicole Eggert

Principal Characters and Voices
Rose-Petal	Marie Osmond
Sunny Sunflower/Canterbury Belle/Fuschia	Susan Blu
Elmer/Horace Fly/Seymour J. Snailsworth/P.D. Centipede/ Tumbles	Frank Welker
Nastina/Lily Fair/Marigold	Marilyn Schreffler
Sweet Violet/Cherry Blossom	Renae Jacobs
Ladybug	Stacy McLaughlin
Pitterpat (Rose-Petal's kitten)	

Rose-Petal Place II: "Real Friends" returned to the enchanted garden, home of the flower sprite and some new friends. Introduced in the special were Canterbury Belle, the official baker who created delicious treats; Fuschia, the garden socialite who loved to plan parties and entertain friends including Orchid, most of the time; Cherry Blossom, an interior decorator; Gladiola, a tap-dancer full of glad tidings who wanted to open a dancing school with Lily Fair, a ballerina; Marigold, a fashion designer and an accomplished seamstress; and Sweet Violet, a southern charmer who was dramatic even when she wasn't acting on stage. Readying for her debut at Carnation Hall, Sweet Violet was insecure, afraid everyone would laugh at her, but Rose-Petal persuaded her to go on. Jealous of Rose-Petal's popularity and constantly plotting to subvert the tranquil garden, Nastina the spider and Horace Fly hatched a plan to turn everyone against her and hid in the hall. Sweet Violet began her recitation from Shakespeare's Romeo and Juliet, but suddenly she heard laughter and began to stammer. As the laughter rose to crescendo, she was unable to finish and bolted off stage, humiliated, and accused Rose-Petal of ruining her career. The opportunistic Nastina and Horace Fly echoed the sentiments of the other flower maidens, who agreed Rose-Petal had pushed Sweet Violet too hard. They helped her write a letter to Rose-Petal saying that she was leaving the garden forever. Determined to bring Sweet Violet back, Rose-Petal asked her friends for support, and together they set off on a search for her. After they left, the spider decided it was time to take over and cast a dark shadow over Rose-Petal Place. After finding Sweet Violet and realizing they were victims of a plot, Rose-Petal returned for a victorious confrontation with Nastina, saved the beautiful garden and left her friends with another lesson about good triumphing over evil and believing in yourself and your friends in order to succeed. Songs: "Believe in Yourself," "Friends" (Osmond).

RUDOLPH AND FROSTY

Broadcast History
    Premiere: November 25, 1979
    ABC/Sunday 7:00-8:30 PM
    ABC/Repeats: December 20, 1981
Producers/Directors: Arthur Rankin, Jr., Jules Bass
Writer: Romeo Muller
Music/Songs & Lyrics: Johnny Marks
Music: Maury Laws, Michael Colicchio
Company: Rankin-Bass Productions/90 minutes
Distributor: Lorimar Syndication
Home Video: Lightning Video

Narrator
Santa Claus   Mickey Rooney

Principal Characters and Voices
Rudolph   Billie Richards
Frosty   Jackie Vernon
Crystal   Shelley Winters
Milton   Red Buttons
Lily   Ethel Merman
Scratcher   Alan Sues
Big Ben   Harold Peary

Other Voices
    Cynthia Adler, Nellie Bellflower, Steffi Calli, Darlene Conley,
    Shelby Flint, Paul Frees, Eric Hines, Robert McFadden, Don
    Messick, Howard Shapiro

Rudolph and Frosty pitted the Red-Nosed Reindeer Rudolph and
Frosty the Snowman against Winterbolt, an icy wizard who plotted
to make the North Pole his own evil domain by snuffing out Rudolph's
radiant nose, thereby defeating Santa's annual stormy-weather toy
deliveries and allowing Winterbolt to reign supreme. With his sidekick, the reindeer Scratcher, a wretched comical dropout from Santa's
team, Winterbolt plotted to trap Rudolph, Frosty, his wife Crystal
and their twins Millie and Chilly through an invitation by Milton, the
Flying Ice Cream Man, to help save a nearly bankrupt seaside circus
on the Fourth of July. There they met the owner, Lily Loraine, her
daughter Lanie and all the circus folk and animals. Rudolph, with
his shiny red nose, was the star attraction that night, but Winterbolt conned him into delivering the box office money to crook Sam
Spangles instead of the bank. In turn he then blackmailed Rudolph
and Frosty, promising to save Frosty and his family from melting if
Rudolph would turn off his nose for good, and promising Frosty to
restore Rudolph's radiant nose in exchange for his magical hat.
They agreed, but Frosty became a lifeless snowman, while Rudolph,
after helping rob the circus, could regain his lighted nose only by
doing a brave, good deed. Furious over Frosty's plight, Rudolph
leaped into the sky and bravely challenged Winterbolt, Scratcher and

the terrible snow-serpents which pulled their sleigh, and with the aid of the circus folk and animals eventually smashed Winterbolt's enchanted ice-scepter, which transformed the wizard into a gnarled tree trunk. His destruction signalled the end of the magic maintaining Frosty and his family; however, who melted into four puddles. Swiftly, they were refrozen back to life by Jack Frost, who was brought to the scene by Big Ben, Rudolph's clockwork-whale friend. Finally, Santa arrived to cart the Frostys home in his sleigh as part of a great Circus Parade in the Sky led by Rudolph and followed by all the circus animals, who were fed Santa's magic feed corn which made his reindeer fly. Originally titled "Rudolph and Frosty's Christmas in July," the 90-minute special was filmed using stop-motion animated puppets (Animagic). Songs: "Rudolph, the Red-Nosed Reindeer," "Everything I've Always Wanted," "Christmas in July," "Chicken Today and Feathers Tomorrow," "I See Rainbows," "Don't Let the Parade Pass You By," "I Heard the Bells on Christmas Day," "Rockin' Around the Christmas Tree," "No Bed of Roses," "Frosty the Snowman," "Now and Then," "We're a Couple of Misfits."

RUDOLPH, THE RED-NOSED REINDEER

Broadcast History
    Premiere: December 6, 1964
    NBC/FANTASY HOUR, Sunday 5:30-6:30 PM
    Sponsor: General Electric
    NBC/Repeats: December 5, 1965; December 4, 1966; December
        8, 1967; December 6, 1968; December 5, 1969; December 4,
        1970; December 6, 1971
    CBS/Repeats: December 8, 1972; December 7, 1973; December
        13, 1974; December 3, 1975; December 1, 1976; November 30,
        1977; December 6, 1978; December 6, 1979; December 3, 1980;
        December 14, 1981; December 1, 1982; December 3, 1983; De-
        cember 1, 1984; December 3, 1985; December 9, 1986
Producers/Directors: Arthur Rankin, Jr., Jules Bass
Director: Larry Roemer
Writer: Romeo Muller
Music/Songs & Lyrics: Johnny Marks
Music/Conductor: Maury Laws
Company: Rankin-Bass Productions/60 minutes
Distributor: Viacom Enterprises/1987-

Host/Narrator
Sam the Snowman   Burl Ives

Principal Characters and Voices
Rudolph   Billie Richards
Hermy the Elf   Paul Soles
Yukon Cornelius   Larry D. Mann
Santa Claus   Stan Francis
Clarice   Janet Orenstein

RUDOLPH, THE RED-NOSED REINDEER. © 1964, Rankin/Bass Productions, Inc. Courtesy of Rankin/Bass Productions and Viacom Enterprises.

Other Voices
Corinne Connely, Peg Dixon, Paul Kligman, Alfie Scopp

Rudolph, the Red-Nosed Reindeer, a Yuletide classic, told how a
shy young buck helped save Christmas for children everywhere.
Burl Ives donned the suit of Sam the Snowman to narrate this musical fantasy about the reindeer born with the glowing red nose in
Christmasville. An outcast because of his shiny snout, Rudolph, not
to be outdone by humans, developed a complex about his difference
that was heightened when other reindeer banned him from their social
gatherings. To escape the ridicule, he ran away and was joined by
the elf, Hermy. Pursued by the Abominable Snowmonster, they fled
to the Island of Misfit Toys in the Arctic wilderness. A bushy-
bearded prospector they met along the way, Yukon Cornelius, came
to their rescue. Returning to Christmasville, where Rudolf was reunited with his doe-friend, Clarice, Rudolph and Hermy learned that
a blizzard might prevent Santa Claus's sleigh from flying on Christmas Eve, causing Christmas to be cancelled. To assure the children
of the world their presents on Christmas morning, Rudolph volunteered to lead the way, his illuminated nose glowing brightly and
serving as a beacon, guiding the team of reindeer and Santa's toy-
laden sleigh through the dark, snowy skies. Filmed using stop-
motion animated puppets (Animagic), the special was based on the
original story by Robert L. May and was the basis of the hit title
song by Johnny Marks, who also wrote all the tunes for the score.
Songs: "Silver and Gold" (Ives), "A Holly Jolly Christmas," "Rudolph,
the Red-Nosed Reindeer" (Ives, Chorus), "There's Always Tomorrow"
(Orenstein), "Jingle, Jingle, Jingle" (Francis), "We Are Santa's
Elves" (Chorus), "We're a Couple of Misfits" (Richards, Soles).
 The longest consecutively aired animated special of all time
through 1986, the film was the first of three made-for-TV Christmas
specials built around the song and the Rudolph character. Robert
L. May wrote the "Rudolph" story in 1939 as a Christmas giveaway
for his employer, Montgomery Ward, and Johnny Marks adapted it
to music in 1949. In one of his biggest hit recordings, Gene Autry
popularized the tune. Prior to the Rankin-Bass production, the
first animated-cartoon version of Rudolph, the Red-Nosed Reindeer
(Jam Handy, 1944), produced by Max Fleischer, was also televised
sporadically.

RUDOLPH'S SHINY NEW YEAR

Broadcast History
 Premiere: December 10, 1976
 ABC/Friday 8:00-9:00 PM
 Sponsor: Parker Brothers
 ABC/Repeats: December 11, 1977; December 9, 1978; December
  16, 1979; December 14, 1980; December 10, 1981; December
  6, 1982
 SYN/Repeats: 1985 +

Producers/Directors: Arthur Rankin, Jr., Jules Bass
Writer: Romeo Muller
Music/Songs & Lyrics: Johnny Marks
Music: Maury Laws
Company: Rankin-Bass Productions/60 minutes
Distributor: Lorimar Syndication ("Animated Holiday Specials")/1985-
Home Video: Lightning Video

Narrator
Father Time   Red Skelton

Principal Characters and Voices
Rudolph   Billie Richards
Sir Tentwothree/Camel   Frank Gorshin
One Million B.C.   Morey Amsterdam
Santa Claus/Aeon   Paul Frees
Big Ben   Hal Peary

Rudolph's Shiny New Year posed another predicament for the Red-
Nosed Reindeer, to find Happy, the Baby New Year, who had run
away from Father Time. Embarking on the mission for Santa, Rudolph
ventured out in the midnight fog to locate the missing Happy, for if
he was not found there would be no New Year and December 31st
would last forever, jeopardizing future Christmases. Enroute to the
palace of Happy New Years, Rudolph met up with Aeon, a despicable
monster bird also searching for Happy, whose plan was to bring time
to a halt. Enlisting the aid of a caveman and a whale in his search,
Rudolph island-hopped the isles of time. But Aeon beat him to the
young New Year and absconded with Happy, who was living with three
bears. Rudolph soon caught up with the pair only to learn that
Happy, anything but happy, was self-concious and ashamed because
his ears were so big. Rudolph convinced him that if a reindeer could
sport a shiny nose, a baby could certainly show his floppy ears. Indeed, when Happy showed his ears to Aeon, the monster bird left
with a smile on his face. In the St. Nick of time, Santa arrived to
take Happy back in time to start the New Year. The special was
filmed using stop-motion animated puppets (Animagic). Songs:
"Rudolph, the Red-Nosed Reindeer," "Have a Happy," "Turn Back
the Years."

RUMPELSTILTSKIN

Broadcast History
    Premiere: December 12, 1985
    CTV/Thursday 7:30-8:00 PM
    CTV/Repeat: December 8, 1986
    HBO/Repeats: multiple option, February 11, 1986 +
    SYN/Repeats: 1986 +
Executive Producer: William H. Stevens, Jr.

RUMPELSTILTSKIN. © 1985, Animated Investments, Inc. Courtesy of Crawley Films, Limited.

Producer: Hugh Campbell
Associate Producer: Alison Clayton
Directors: Pino Van Lamsweerde, Sebastian Grunstra
Writers: Mary Crawford, Alan Templeton
Music/Song & Lyrics: Alan Templeton
Music: John Harris, Peter Chapin
Company: Atkinson Film-Arts, Ottawa, Canada, in association with Telefilm Canada and CTV
Distributor: Crawleys International ("Cartoon Classics")/1986-
Home Video: Family Home Entertainment

Narrator: Christopher Plummer

Principal Characters and Voices

Rumpelstiltskin	Robert Bockstael
Miller	Les Lye
Miller's Daughter/Queen	Charity Brown
King	Al Baldwin

Rumpelstiltskin had just the right touch of menacing danger for this spritely version of the Grimm Brothers fairy tale. A well transposed story, it was about a Miller who often stretched the truth and who told the King that his daughter could spin straw into gold. Imprisoned in the royal tower with loads of hay, the Miller's Daughter was ordered by the King to spin it into gold by sunrise or she would die. Learning of her plight, Rumpelstiltskin, a loathsome wizard, assisted her in the magical deed for a price--possession of her first-born child. After the King married the beautiful maiden and made her his Queen, they had a child. Deep in a forest full of ominous gnarled trees, Rumpelstiltskin crooned a deliciously wicked tune and set off to the castle in a spiral of silver dust to claim his debt. Only if the Queen could guess his true name would he renege, but even though she sent soldiers throughout the land in a desperate effort, she failed. All was lost until the Miller found the wizard's secret lair, overheard his name and Rumpelstiltskin's despicable plan was dashed. Song/Theme: "It's a Fine Night for Worms and Slugs" (Rumpelstiltskin).

RUNAWAY ROBOTS see ROMIE-0 AND JULIE-8

SANTA AND THE THREE BEARS

Broadcast History
    Premiere: 1970
    SYN/local station option
Producer/Director/Writer: Tony Benedict
Associate Producer: James Kernodle
Music/Songs & Lyrics: Joe Leahy; Joyce Taylor, Doug Goodwin
Company: Tony Benedict Productions in association with Key In-
    dustries, Vancouver, Canada/60 minutes
Distributor: Warner Bros.-Seven Arts (WB-TV)/1970–
Record Album: Pickwick/SPC 1501
Home Video: Prism

Cast
Grandfather   Hal Smith
Beth   Beth Goldfarb
Brian   Brian Hobbs

Principal Characters and Voices
Ranger   Hal Smith
Nana   Jean VanderPyl
Nikomi   Annette Ferra
Chinook   Bobby Riha

Santa and the Three Bears developed as a story related one Christ-mas Eve by their Grandfather to young Beth and Brian. It was a simple hour-long musical tale of three hibernating bears, Nana and her cubs Nikomi and Chinook, in Yellowstone National Park and how they discovered the magic and wonder of Christmas. Fascinated with the Yuletide preparations at the Ranger's cabin, the cubs begged him to tell them about the holiday, which they had never experienced due to their winter's sleep. After a brief explanation of the nativity, he told them of the tradition of gift-giving and about Santa Claus. Determined to stay up until Christmas Eve to see the jolly gent, the cubs awakened Nana to help them fell and drag a small tree to their cave. Donning his department-store Santa suit, the Ranger set out to bring presents to the cubs but had to seek shelter from a blizzard. Beset by her disappointed cubs, Nana informed them that it was really the Ranger who played Santa and later when he finally appeared Nikomi and Chinook passed it off as their friend. Early next morning, when the Ranger arrived, they realized the real Santa had paid them a visit and left their stocking-full of gifts, as his "Ho, Ho, Ho" echoed across the valley and his sleigh and reindeer were silhouetted against the moon. Songs: "It's Wintertime," "Children's Toys," "The Wonder of Christmastime," "Good Night, Little Ones."

SANTA CLAUS IS COMIN' TO TOWN

Broadcast History
    Premiere: December 14, 1970
    ABC/Sunday 7:00-8:00 PM

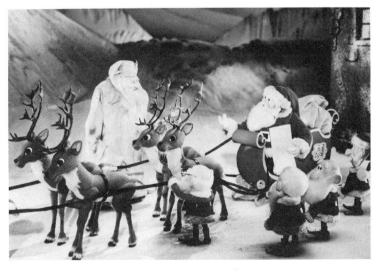

SANTA CLAUS IS COMIN' TO TOWN. © 1970, Rankin/Bass Productions, Inc. Courtesy of Rankin/Bass Productions and Viacom Enterprises.

ABC/Repeats: December 3, 1971; December 1, 1972; November
    30, 1973; December 5, 1974; December 9, 1975; December 12,
    1976; December 1, 1977; December 10, 1978; December 2, 1979;
    December 8, 1980; December 19, 1981
  SYN/Repeats: 1985 +
Producers/Directors: Arthur Rankin, Jr., Jules Bass
Writer: Romeo Muller
Music & Lyrics/Title Song: J. Fred Coots, Haven Gillespie
Music: Maury Laws
Lyrics: Jules Bass
Company: Rankin-Bass Productions/60 minutes
Distributor: Viacom Enterprises/1985-

Narrator
S. D. Kluger   Fred Astaire

Principal Characters and Voices
Kris Kringle   Mickey Rooney
Jessica   Robie Lester
Winter Warlock   Keenan Wynn
Tanta Kringle   Joan Gardner
Burgermeister   Paul Frees
Children   Dina Lynn/Greg Thomas

Santa Claus Is Comin' to Town delved into the mysteries and myths
of Kris Kringle, alias Santa Claus, narrated by Fred Astaire as the
town's mailman, S. D. Kluger. The musical tale began when Tanya
Kringle found an abandoned baby, named Kris Kringle, who grew up
in Rainbow River Valley and among the Kringle toymaker elves who
learned how to make toys, which were intended for the good children
of Sombertown. Afraid of the raging Winter Warlock, the elves were
unable to deliver their toys until an older, larger Kris braved passing his lair on the Mountain of the Whispering Winds. Along the way,
Kris met a penguin looking for the South Pole and after arriving in
Sombertown discovered that the tyrannical old Burgermeister hated
toys and had banished them. He declared Kris an outlaw. During
their hasty retreat, Kris and his penguin companion were captured
by the Warlock. Warming the reprobate's cold heart with kindness,
Kris became friends with the Warlock. With the aid of Jessica, a
schoolteacher he also befriended and later married, Kris began sneaking into Sombertown and delivering his toys via chimneys. Furious,
the Burgermeister imprisoned him in a dungeon, but again Kris and
his companions escaped, riding on reindeer that flew across the moon-
lit sky. To prevent further recrimination by the Burgermeister, Kris,
Jessica and the Kringle family moved to the North Pole and decided
to limit the toy deliveries to only one night a year, the most holy
night, Christmas Eve. The program addressed several of the legends
surrounding Santa Claus: why Santa had whiskers, wore a red suit,
came down chimneys, left presents in stockings, and why only on
Christmas Eve. The special was filmed using stop-motion animated
puppets (Animagic) and built around the eponymous song by Coots

and Gillespie. Songs: "Santa Claus Is Comin' to Town," "Santa's Song," "The Toymaker Song," "Put One Foot," "My World," "Christmas Carol."

SANTABEAR'S FIRST CHRISTMAS

Broadcast History
    Premiere: November 22, 1986
    ABC/ABC WEEKEND SPECIALS, Saturday 12:00-12:30 PM
Executive Producer: Christopher Campbell
Producer/Director: Mark Sottnick
Associate Producer: Mary Meehan
Writer: Tom Roberts
Music: Michael Hedges
Company: Rabbit Ears Productions
Record Album: Windham Hill

Narrator: Kelly McGillis

Santabear introduced a young snow bear who became separated from his family at the North Pole when he was swept away on an ice floe. Finding himself in a strange and frightening place, a friendly little girl explained that he had entered a forest and took him home to live with her and her grandfather, a woodcutter. There the furry white bear made some new friends and learned about new things such as Christmas and Santa Claus. One day, after the grandfather fell into an icy river and became ill and there was no firewood in the little cabin to keep him warm or to prepare food, the bear ventured into the forest to find kindling. Even with his new forest friends, however, he could not locate enough dry wood. Just as he was beginning his Christmas Eve deliveries, Santa and his reindeer happened by and the bear explained he would like some firewood for Christmas to help the old woodcutter and his granddaughter. Impressed with the little bear's unselfish request, after the firewood was gathered Santa asked the bear to be his helper every year, to deliver toys to the woodland animals and forever after to be known as Santabear.
    The special was based on a story by Barbara Reed and built around the Santabear character, a property developed and owned by the Dayton-Hudson Department Store company, and used illustrations by H. B. Lewis animated by camera movement.

SCHOOL ... WHO NEEDS IT?

Broadcast History
    Premiere: August-September 1971
    SYN/local station option
Producers: Art Clokey, Ruth Clokey
Directors: Art Clokey, Raymond Peck
Writer: Nancy Moore

SCHOOL ... WHO NEEDS IT? © 1975, Lutheran Church in America. Courtesy of the Department of Telecommunications, Lutheran Church in America.

Music: John Seely, Patricia Beck
Company: Clokey Productions for the Lutheran Church in America
Distributor: Department of Telecommunications, Lutheran Church in America/1985-

Principal Characters and Voices
Davey Hanson/Sally Hanson/
    Teacher   Norma McMillan/Nancy Wible
Goliath   Hal Smith

School ... Who Needs It? carried a message of mutual cooperation and friendship. It was back-to-school time, and Davey and his friends from the Jickets clubhouse decided to protest. "Down with School," "I Hate School" and "School--Who Needs It?" were some of the slogans on their signs as they marched on opening day. Through the patience of an understanding teacher, the enthusiasm of Doug, the new boy in their class, and an accidental fire that almost destroyed the class' safety parade float, Davey and his pals realized that school taught some valuable lessons after all and that their teacher was their friend. One of six special programs, each focusing on a basic lesson in Christian living, it featured the stop-motion animated puppets seen on Davey and Goliath (SYN, 1962-).

SCOOBY GOES HOLLYWOOD

Broadcast History
Premiere: December 23, 1979
ABC/Sunday 7:00-8:00 PM
ABC/Repeat: January 25, 1981
Executive Producers: William Hanna, Joseph Barbera
Producer: Don Jurwich
Director: Ray Patterson
Writers: Dick Robbins, Duane Poole
Music: Hoyt Curtin, Paul DeKorte
Company: Hanna-Barbera Productions/60 minutes
Distributor: Worldvision Enterprises
Home Video: Worldvision

Principal Characters and Voices

Scooby-Doo/Bulldog/Second Man	Don Messick
Shaggy/First Man/Pilot's Voice	Casey Kasem
Fred/Afghan/The Groove/Baby Scooby-Doo	Frank Welker
Velma/First Woman/Lucy Lane	Pat Stevens
Daphne/Treena/Mailgirl	Heather North Kenney
C.J.	Rip Taylor
Director/First V.P./Terrier	Stan Jones
Jesse Rotten/V.P./Jackie Carlson	Michael Bell
Cherie/Sis/Receptionist	Marilyn Schreffler
Lavonne/Second Woman/Waitress	Joan Gerber
Kerry/Girl Fan/Executive Secretary	Ginny McSwain
Brother/Guard/Announcer's Voice	Patrick Fraley

Scooby Goes Hollywood spotlighted the Great Dane star in his first prime-time musical special with his mystery-solving friends, Shaggy, Fred, Daphne and Velma. Deciding it was time to change his image, the Great Dane and Shaggy put together a TV pilot, "How Scooby Won the West," in which Scoob was featured as a shaky, scared sheriff, for presentation to C.J., the network president, who dismissed them with an deprecating laugh. But Scooby and Shaggy were serious and Scoob quit his own show to concentrate on his star qualities. And they made more pilots: Lavonne took time off from her own hit series to help Scoob prove he was a star on roller skates, but they wound up stuck in a revolving door; the pooch greased his hair, donned a leather jacket and smashed the jukebox in "Scooby Days"; in "Super Scooby" he botched an attempt to save Lucy Lane, who was strapped to a rocket; he fell over the hills in the title role of "Sound of Music"; he muffed his magician act with Cherie; he blew his role as a dynamic variety show host; and he forgot to untie the craft from the dock in "Love Ship." Wanting to get Scooby back on

SCOOBY GOES HOLLYWOOD. © 1979, Hanna-Barbera Productions, Inc. Courtesy of Hanna-Barbera Productions and TECO.

his own series, C.J., his V.P.'s and the gang staged a mock audition to find a new dog star--a ridiculous Afghan. Then they set Scooby for an interview on the "Jackie Carlson Show," where children learned for the first time that Scoob would no longer star on the Saturday morning program. Undeterred, Scooby's persistent agent Shaggy screened yet another pilot for C.J., "Scooby's Angels," in which the dog was still a washout. Suggesting again that Scooby return to his own show, where he was a star in his own right, C.J. opened the window, and thousands of children below began to chant and sing "Scooby-Doo! We love you! We need You!" Touched at the outpouring, Scooby finally agreed to return, as he put it, "ror the rids ... ror my rans!" Songs: "Scooby Opener," "Move Over" (Shaggy), "Roody Cool Buy" (The Groove, Scooby), "Gotta Have Time" (Scooby, Cherie), "Scooby, Come Back" (Shaggy).

The enduring canine has been a network fixture for 17 years on Saturday mornings since his debut on September 13, 1969 and has been seen in the various series of Scooby-Doo (CBS, 1969-1976/ABC, 1976-1986), described in Children's Television, Part I (Scarecrow, 1983), pp. 249-253. Scooby also starred in three two-hour, made-for-TV movies, Scooby and the Boo Brothers, Scooby-Doo and the Ghoul School and Scooby and the Reluctant Werewolf, optioned by the FOX network for 1987-1988.

SCRUFFY

Broadcast History
    Premiere: October 4, 11 & 18, 1980
    ABC/ABC WEEKEND SPECIALS, Saturday 12:00-12:30 PM
    ABC/Repeats: February 7, 14 & 21, 1981; February 13, 20 & 27
       1982; February 26, March 5 & 12, 1983
Executive Producers: Joseph Ruby, Ken Spears
Producer: Jerry Eisenberger
Director: Charles A. Nichols
Writer: Sheldon Stark
Music: Dean Elliott
Company: Ruby-Spears Enterprises/90 minutes, 3 parts
Distributor: Worldvision Enterprises
Home Video: Worldvision

Narrator: Alan Young

Principal Characters and Voices
Scruffy   Nancy McKeon
Tibbles   Hans Conreid
Butch   Michael Bell
Dutchess   June Foray

Other Voices
    Alan Dinehart, Walker Edmiston, Linda Gary, Michael Rye, Janet Waldo, Frank Welker

Scruffy told of a stray dog whose search for a home led her through
a maze of adventures with life-threatening escapes. In Part I, the
puppy was trapped in a burning abandoned house with her mother
Dutchess, rescued by a demolition worker and when old enough to
travel ventured with her mother seeking her owners. Mistaken for
sheep killers and shot at by two errant ranchers, Dutchess was killed
but the puppy escaped. Tired, cold and hungry, the pup wandered
into the city and met Joe Tibbles, a destitute Shakespearean street
actor who adopted her and named her Scruffy. After Tibbles taught
Scruffy some tricks and the pair made some money, they were threatened by two crooks who pursued them.

In Part II, Scruffy and Tibbles outwitted the crooks and returned to their home under a park bridge where Scruffy learned
some more tricks, but during a performance, Tibbles, overcome by
consumption, died enroute to the hospital. In pursuit of the ambulance, Scruffy was saved by Butch, another stray, when she fell off
a bridge and almost drowned. Scruffy accepted Butch's invitation
to join his stray friends, and even though they lived a sorrowful
life Butch proved a friendly companion. Still distraught over Tibbles,
Scruffy wandered off to the park bridge and into the deceiving hands
of the dastardly Catlin and his conniving canine, Caesar. Tracking
Scruffy to a grocery store where she was providing a diversion with
her tricks for Catlin, who was robbing the cash register, Butch
alerted the puppy and together they foiled the robbery and raced
off. Angrily, Catlin sent Caesar to get her back and after catching
up with the pair he viciously attacked Butch.

In Part III, although critically injured, Butch finally triumphed
and recovered, buoyed by Scruffy's prayers, to continue leading the
strays in their daily scrounging. Warned about some pursuing dog
catchers by the banished Caesar, the strays hid but soon scattered.
Cornered by the dog catchers, Butch and Scruffy were carted off
to the pound, where they learned that all their stray friends had
been caught too. Scheduled to be killed, the dogs were visited by
a reporter who featured them in a newspaper article with a picture
of Scruffy behind bars. The next day, just as Butch was dragged
off to die, dozens of people hoping to adopt the dogs descended on
the pound, and Scruffy, Butch and the other strays found permanent
happy homes--and Scruffy was tagged with the title "Dog of the
Year." The specials were based on the book by Jack Stoneley.

SECRET WORLD OF OG, THE

Broadcast History
　　Premiere: April 30, May 7 & 14, 1983
　　ABC/ABC WEEKEND SPECIALS, Saturday 12:00-12:30 PM
　　ABC/Repeats: December 3, 10 & 17, 1983; October 27, November
　　　10 & 17, 1984; March 15, 22 & 29, 1986; February 21 & 28,
　　　March 7, 1987
Producer: Doug Paterson
Associate Producer: Steve Lumley

Director: Geoff Collins
Writer: Mark Evanier
Music: Ian Mason
Company: Hanna-Barbera Productions, Sydney, Australia (Southern
   Star Productions)/90 minutes, 3 parts

Narrator: Michael Rye

Principal Characters and Voices

OG/Old Man/Glub/Villager	Fred Travalena
Penny	Noelle North
Pamela	Marissa Mendenhall
Patsy	Brittany Wilson
Peter	Josh Rodine
Pollywog/Green Lady/Woman's Voice	Julie McWhirter Dees
Mother/Old Lady	Janet Waldo
Yukon "Yukie" Pete (family dog)/Earless (Pollywog's cat)/Long John Silver	Peter Cullen
Flub/Blib/Little Green Man #2/Floog/Little OG's Boy	Dick Beals
Sheriff/Little Green Man #1/Butcher/Villager/Mushroom Harvester	Hamilton Camp
Teacher	Beth Clopton
Pirate #1/Mayor/Man's Voice	Dick Erdman
Worker/Cowboy #1/Green Deputy	Michael Rye
Victim #2/Green Man	Joe Medalis
Victim #1/Elder OG/OG Father	Andre Stojka
Snavely (Patsy's pet snake)	

The Secret World of OG swept five brothers and sisters into a strange
underground land of small green people who loved games of make-
believe. In Part I, one Saturday afternoon, Penny, 12; Pamela, 10;
Patsy, 8; Peter, 7; and their baby brother Pollywog, who habitually
frustrated their busy mother by escaping from his crib, were at home
in their playhouse when an elfin creature sawed his way up through
the floor to help himself to some comic books. Pamela, notorious for
fantasizing, spotted him but decided not to tell the others for fear
they wouldn't believe her. But when Pollywog and his pet cat Earless vanished from sight in the playhouse with the older children
present, Pamela told them he disappeared through the trapdoor.
Finding a secret downward passageway beneath it, the astonished
children and their dog Yukon Pete followed it to search for Pollywog.
The elf-like little creature secretly watched as they entered his colorful underground world of OG, with its own city of mushroom-shaped
buildings. There Penny was taken prisoner by the small green inhabitants, whose fanciful games were based on famous fictional characters they found in comic books and other works they had pilfered
from the children's home.

In Part II, jailed with her baby brother Pollywog, Penny suddenly discovered that the town sheriff could talk, but only in lingo learned from the children's Western comics. Meanwhile, Peter, Pamela and Patsy planned a daring rescue attempt, using a tube of paint to daub themselves green to resemble the OG people so they could slip into the mushroom town to rescue their brother and sister and the missing Earless. Since there was not enough paint for Patsy, she was left behind with her pet snake Snavely and the family dog, Yukie. After finding Earless, Peter and Pamela were chased by an angry OG mob, and Peter was forced into a duel with a little, green Long John Silver, who had been reading Pamela's lost library book, Treasure Island.

In Part III, failing in their rescue attempt, the children found themselves aboard a sinking ship and were recaptured by the people of OG. Then panic struck after a close encounter with Patsy and Snavely, when the OGians believed they were about to be attacked by "The Snake People." Striking a bargain with the children, the little people of OG agreed to help them find their way back home if they would destroy the dreaded enemies. The three-part special was adapted from the book by Pierre Berton.

SELFISH GIANT, THE

Broadcast History
  Premiere: March 28, 1973
  CBS/Wednesday 8:30-9:00 PM
  CBS/Repeats: March 25, 1974; April 6, 1976
  SYN/Repeats: c1978 +
Executive Producer: Murray Shostak
Producer: Peter Sander
Directors: Julian Szuchopa, Paul Sabella, Juan Pina, April Johnson
Writer: Peter Sander
Music: Ron Goodwin
Company: A Reader's Digest Presentation in association with Gerald Potterton Productions, Montreal, Canada
Distributor: LBS Communications ("LBS Children's Theatre")/1983-1985
Home Video: Random House Home Video

Narrator: David Niven (1973), Paul Hecht

The Selfish Giant was based on Oscar Wilde's enchanting fairy tale about a gruff and lonely ogre who refused to share his garden. When he discovered the children of a nearby village playing in his castle gardens, he built a mammoth wall to keep them out, an act that resulted in his grounds being plunged into permanent winter bereft of sunshine. The wall also kept out all the things that could bring joy and happiness to the giant's life, and it was not until he encountered a very special child in the garden that he came to understand and right what he had done.

The special was the first of five Reader's Digest presentations and was nominated for a Motion Picture Academy award (1972) as Best Animated Short Subject.

SHE'S A GOOD SKATE, CHARLIE BROWN

Broadcast History
Premiere: February 25, 1980
CBS/Monday 8:00-8:30 PM
Sponsor: Interstate Brands
CBS/Repeats: February 25, 1981; February 10, 1982
Executive Producer: Lee Mendelson
Producer: Bill Melendez
Director: Phil Roman
Writer/Creator: Charles M. Schulz
Company: Lee Mendelson-Bill Melendez Productions in association with Charles M. Schulz Creative Associates and United Feature Syndicate
Home Video: Snoopy's Home Video Library #335/Hi-Tops Video (nee Media Home Entertainment)

Principal Characters and Voices

Charlie Brown	Arrin Skelley
Marcie	Casey Carlson
Peppermint Patty	Patricia Patts
Coach/Announcer	Scott Beach
Teacher	Debbie Muller
Boy	Tim Hall
Snoopy	Bill Melendez
Woodstock	Jason Serinus (Whistling)

She's a Good Skate, Charlie Brown entered the world of Ice Skating competition with the Peanuts clan cheering on Peppermint Patty. Accused of falling asleep in class because of an uncorrected astigmatism, Patty explained: "I've been getting up every morning at 4:30 to practice skating." "That's crazy, Sir," said Marcie, "...Even the ice is asleep at 4:30!" But Patty's tempermental canine coach was not as punctual, liked his "Z's" and had to be rudely awakened in the morning. Under the beagle-eye of Snoopy, Patty went through vigorous practice sessions, polishing her routine for the upcoming figure-skating competition. When Marcie failed to come up with an appropriate skating dress, the beagle even turned seamstress and produced his own designer-label blue outfit. At the big event, Snoopy botched up the music tape, momentarily stranding an expectant, nervous Patty on the ice. Saving the day with some eleventh-hour heroics, the resourceful Woodstock whistled a lilting score while Patty performed to perfection, winning the skating competition. "Don't you have anything good to say?" Patty asked her grumbling coach at the close. Balancing on his toes, Snoopy leaned over and kissed her on the cheek.

Jason Serinus made his off-camera debut in this film, whistling Puccini's "O mio babbino caro" as Woodstock. Among the most engaging of the Peanuts specials, it was adapted from one of the longest series of Schulz's comic strips built around a single idea, which ran for five weeks. Film of skater Mary Ellen Kinsey was studied and rotoscoped to help create Patty's animated ice-skating scenes.

SILENT NIGHT

Broadcast History
    Premiere: c1977
    SYN/local station option (KTTV, Los Angeles, December 19, 1977, Tuesday 5:30-6:00 PM PST)
    SYN/Repeats: 1978 +
    SHO/Repeats: multiple option, 1985
Executive Producer: Milton Saltzberg
Distributor: National Telefilm Associates (Republic Pictures)/1977-
Home Video: Media Home Entertainment

Silent Night told how the famous carol was written by Austrian pastor Josef Mohr. Strolling through the snow-covered slopes above Oberndof before Christmas Eve, Mohr gazed at the scattered lights in the village below. The sight of the peaceful town, huddled warmly in the foothills, stirred his imagination. Surely, it was on such a clear and quiet night as this that hosts of angels sang out the glorious news that the Saviour had been born, he thought. As his mind filled with visions of the first Christmas, Mohr shaped them into the words of a poem. The new organ had broken down, but Franz Gruber, the organist, thought that music should be set to the words and softly strummed a melody that came to him. On Christmas Eve, 1818, in the small Austrian village, the Oberndof choir, accompanied only by a guitar, sang for the first time the enduring hymn, "Silent Night, Holy Night...."

SILVERHAWKS

Broadcast History
    Premiere: 1986
    SYN/local station option (KTTV, Los Angeles, January 24, 1986, Friday 4:00-5:00 PM PST)
Executive Producers: Arthur Rankin, Jr., Jules Bass
Producer: Lee Dannacher
Director/Pacific Animation: Masaki Iizuka
Writers: Peter Lawrence, Lee Schneider
Music: Bernard Hoffer
Company: Rankin-Bass Productions in association with Pacific Animation, Tokyo, Japan/60 minutes
Distributor: Lorimar Syndication/1986-
Home Video: Lorimar Home Video (nee Karl-Lorimar)

Principal Characters and Voices

Quicksilver	Peter Newman
Melodia/Steelheart	Maggie Jakobson
Windhammer	Doug Preis
Mon*Star/Stargazer	Earl Hammond
Poker-Face/BlueGrass/	
Time-Stopper	Larry Kenney
HardWare/Steelwill/Yes-Man/	
Mo-Lec-U-Lar	Robert McFadden
Hotwing	Adolf Caesar/Doug Preis
Buzz-Saw	(Flange)
Copper Kidd	(Vocorder)
Mumbo-Jumbo	(Flange & Harmonizer)
Tally-Hawk	(musical effect)
Skyrunner (Mon*Star's steed)	

Silverhawks was a space saga set in the Limbo Galaxy, arraying a volunteer android team sent by Earth to keep law and order against the most dangerous criminals in the universe. The Mob was led by Mon*Star, Intergalactic Public Enemy #1, who broke out of Limbo's Penal Planet during a Moon*Star burst which transformed him into an armored android monster. He rode about on Skyrunner, an armored space squid, and freed from prison a variety of miscreants: Yes-Man, Mon*Star's syncophantic sidekick; Mo-Lec-U-Lar, who could assume any disguise; Time-Stopper, who could freeze time temporarily; Buzz-Saw, a robot assassin; Poker-Face, a gambling boss; Mumbo-Jumbo, a strong-arm robot bull; Windhammer, who manipulated galactic storms; HardWare, a weapons specialist; and Melodia, who had musical super powers. Headquartered at Hawkhaven, the Earthian android Commander Stargazer called for help to combat The Mob and was sent five Earth volunteers, super androids known as the Silverhawks, who could glide through space using silver wings. Quicksilver was their leader; BlueGrass, a cowboy pilot of their spaceship Maraj and whose guitar fired lasers; Sergeants Steelheart and Steelwill, twin technologists; and the Copper Kidd, an acrobatically-inclined space creature from the Planet of the Mimes. They were aided by Tally-Hawk, an armored falcon controlled by Quicksilver, who could relay messages through space and record videotapes of crimes. After The Mob attacked Hawkhaven, the Silverhawks flew out for a series of one-on-one confrontations, forcing them to retreat to Brim*Star and winning their first big battle against Mon*Star's evil forces.

    The special was comprised of the first two episodes of the 65-episode half-hour weekday strip-series, Silverhawks (SYN, 1986-). Kenner Products released a line of action toys based on the characters.

SIMPLE GIFTS

Components

    THE CHRISTMAS BOY; DECEMBER 25TH, 1914; THE GREAT

FROST; LOST AND FOUND; A MEMORY OF CHRISTMAS; MY
CHRISTMAS; NO ROOM AT THE INN

Broadcast History
    Premiere: December 16, 1978
    PBS/Sunday 8:00-9:00 PM
    PBS/Repeats: December 12, 1979 +
Producer/Creator: R. O. Blechman
Directors/Animators/Artwork: Ed Smith, Bill Littlejohn, Seymour
    Chwast, Tisa David, C. B. Slackman, James McMullan
Writers: Maurice Sendak, Moss Hart, Fontaine Fox, Virginia Woolf,
    Theodore Roosevelt, R. O. Blechman
Company: R. O. Blechman for PBS/60 minutes

Narrators
    José Ferrer ("A Memory of Christmas")
    Hermione Gingold ("The Great Frost")

Simple Gifts consisted of an overture and six cartoon segments, each
about a holiday gift of one sort or another, by some of America's
most talented and acclaimed animators and artists. The Christmas
Boy, by Maurice Sendak, animated by Ed Smith, opened the program
with a colorful segment about a shoeless, ragged waif who transformed
himself into a richly glowing Christmas tree--illustrating the gift of
giving oneself for the sake of others. A Memory of Christmas, which
illustrated reminiscences of playwright Moss Hart's achingly impov-
erished childhood in a series of dramatic photographs, was adapted
from Hart's autobiography, Act One, narrated by José Ferrer. Lost
and Found, animated by Bill Littlejohn and based on the comic strip
Toonerville Trolley by Fontaine Fox (1884-1964), told the story of
the Smith baby who was accidentally thrown out of his house along
with all the wrappings left over from Christmas packages. The Great
Frost, based on an episode from Virginia Woolf's Orlando, narrated
by Hermione Gingold, was the love story of a simple young nobleman
and a mysterious Russian princess whose boat was ice-bound on the
frozen Thames River. Woolf's prose was captured in the artwork of
Seymour Chwast and in the animation of Tisa David. My Christmas
was an entry from young Theodore Roosevelt's diary on his eleventh
Christmas, celebrated in Rome, with artwork by C. B. Slackman.
December 25th, 1914 described an extraordinary, short-lived truce
that took place on a Christmas day during the First World War. The
episode, based on a letter from Captain Sir Edward Hulse to his
mother, was recalled in dreamlike sequences painted by James McMul-
lan. No Room at the Inn was an animated retelling of the traditional
Christmas story based on the eponymous book by R. O. Blechman,
animated by Ed Smith.

SLEEPING BEAUTY

Broadcast History
    Premiere: January 21, 1973

SYN/FESTIVAL OF FAMILY CLASSICS, WABC, New York, Sunday
    7:00-7:30 PM
SYN/Repeats: 1973 +
Producers/Directors: Arthur Rankin, Jr., Jules Bass
Associate Producer: Mary Alice Dwyer
Writer: Ken Donnelly
Music: Maury Laws, Jules Bass
Company: Rankin-Bass Productions
Distributor: Viacom Enterprises ("Family Classics")/1986-
Home Video: Prism

Sleeping Beauty blended some charm and humor in this retelling of
the fairy tale in which a kingdom took time out for a 100-year snooze.
It concerned a wicked witch who placed a curse on a beautiful young
princess--she would prick her finger and die. But a kind fairy godmother softened the malediction--the princess and her subjects would
sleep until she was wakened by love's first kiss. Even though all
the pins and needles in the kingdom were destroyed, the 20-year-
old princess accidently pricked her finger on the spindle of a spinning wheel and everyone fell into a trance. One hundred years
later, along came the handsome and courageous Prince Daring, who
kissed Beauty, and the entire kingdom was aroused from their sleep.
Adding to the merriment were a W. C. Fields-like towncrier, a Stan
Laurel-like prince's aide and an outlandish aggregation of royalty.

SMURF SPRINGTIME SPECIAL, THE

Broadcast History
    Premiere: April 8, 1982
    NBC/Thursday 8:00-8:30 PM
    Sponsor: Kellogg's
    NBC/Repeats: April 1, 1983; April 20, 1984
Executive Producers: William Hanna, Joseph Barbera
Producer/Director: Gerard Baldwin
Writers: Peyo, Yvan Delporte, Len Janson, Chuck Menville
Music: Hoyt Curtin, Paul DeKorte
Company: Hanna-Barbera Productions in association with SEPP In-
    ternational

Principal Characters and Voices

Gargamel	Paul Winchell
Papa Smurf/Azrael	Don Messick
Smurfette	Lucille Bliss
Mother Nature/Jokey	June Foray
Handy/Grouchy/Lazy	Michael Bell
Clumsy	Bill Callaway
Harmony	Hamilton Camp
Balthazar	Keene Curtis
Brainy/Tailor	Danny Goldman
Vanity	Alan Oppenheimer
Hefty/Poet/Duckling	Frank Welker

The Smurf Springtime Special posed another bizarre menace for the little blue folk at the hands of the evil wizard Gargamel. As Smurf village happily busied itself in preparations for Easter, and a newly hatched baby duck adopted an astonished Smurfette for its mother, Gargamel was depressed over the arrival of Spring because it made the Smurfs happy and he hated "happy." Since all his plans to catch the Smurfs had failed, he decided to seek help from his terrible godfather Balthazar, a horrible wizard who even struck fear into the nasty hide of Gargamel's henchcat Azrael. Claiming that the Smurfs were only a myth, Balthazar refused to help his loathsome godson, but Gargamel managed to slip away with the wizard's magic book containing a formula of how to boil six Smurfs with lead to make gold and evoked a spell to put Mother Nature to sleep and freeze the Smurfs out of their village. Sensing winter had returned, Papa Smurf prepared the village for a terrible storm and sought out Mother Nature to correct the problem. Entrapped by Gargamel, who captured six Smurfs, Papa managed to escape, organized a rescue party and freed the captives as Balthazar angrily arrived at Gargamel's castle to retrieve his book. Spotting the escaping Smurfs, Balthazar used his musket--"the magic wand of the future"--and stunned Papa and the duck which tried to rescue him. Enlisting the aid of woodland creatures, the Smurfs attacked the villains with snowballs while a huge grizzly bear broke and knocked the gun from Balthazar's hands. Awakened by Papa Smurf, Mother Nature entwined Gargamel and Azrael in a vine, burned the book and united Smurfette with her woozy duckling. Happiness again returned with Spring to the village, and Mother Nature and her woodland creatures joined the Smurfs in their Easter festival.

The program was one of six prime-time specials featuring the characters from the popular Saturday morning series, The Smurfs, (NBC, 1981-), which was an instant hit, had phenomenal ratings and led NBC's Saturday morning lineup to first place dominance. Created by Belgian cartoonist Pierre Culliford (Peyo) in 1958, the Smurfs had been a merchandising success for some time when Fred Silverman, who noticed his daughter playing with the little figures, commissioned Hanna-Barbera to make them TV stars. (As well, "Smurfs" has become a dubious part of English slang, denoting the little guys who run for dope dealers to various banks laundering money in denominations under $10,000; the practice is known as "Smurfing.") The off-network series, 1981 through 1984, were distributed to local stations as the Smurfs' Adventures (SYN, 1986-) by Television Program Enterprises. The elfin characters also were starred in the animated movie, The Smurfs and the Magic Flute (Atlantic, 1983).

SMURFIC GAMES, THE

Broadcast History
    Premiere: May 20, 1984
    NBC/Sunday 7:00-7:30 PM

Sponsors: McDonald's, Mattel
NBC/Repeat: May 11, 1985
Executive Producers: William Hanna, Joseph Barbera
Producer/Director: Gerard Baldwin
Associate Producer: Bob Hathcock
Writers: Peyo, Yvan Delporte, Patsy Cameron, Tedd Anasti
Music: Hoyt Curtin, Paul DeKorte
Company: Hanna-Barbera Productions in association with SEPP International

Principal Characters and Voices

Papa Smurf/Azrael	Don Messick
Baby Smurf	Julie McWhirter Dees
Smurfette	Lucille Bliss
Clumsy/Painter/Dragon	Bill Callaway
Grouchy/Handy/Lazy/Argus	Michael Bell
Greedy/Harmony	Hamilton Camp
Jokey	June Foray
Hefty/Frog/Bird/Poet	Frank Welker
Tailor	Kip King
Gargamel	Paul Winchell
Bigmouth	Lennie Weinrib
Vanity	Alan Oppenheimer

The Smurfic Games involved the little blue folk in their first athletic competition, sparked by a sneak attack by Gargamel's troublesome cat Azrael. Papa Smurf suggested they get into better shape, tone their bodies and sharpen their athletic abilities by inaugurating the "Smurfic Games," modeled after the ancient Greek competition. Smurf village was divided into halves, one team led by Hefty, the other by Handy. Unwanted, Clumsy was claimed by Smurfette for her own team. The events included smurfnastics, weightsmurfing, the smurfberry toss and the smurfathon. Brainy volunteered to judge the games, and after three events all three teams were tied. Meanwhile, Gargamel learned about the destructive powers of the Medallion of Poseidon, which his sickly but good cousin Argus had sent to Papa Smurf for safekeeping. Finding a book on how to activate its deadly powers, Gargamel plotted his own evil victory. As the games wound down to the final tie-breaking smurfathon, Handy's and Hefty's teams were fierce rivals, bitterly turned against each other. But they learned a lesson in good sportsmanship when Handy had to rely upon Hefty to save him from danger, allowing Clumsy to cross the finish line. As Smurfette and Clumsy were awarded the Medallion by Brainy, Gargamel activated it, creating a tremendous earthquake that destroyed Smurf Village. Reacting quickly, Papa Smurf kicked the Medallion into a fissure, halting the quake. Afterwards, he gave Clumsy a garland of victory and, since the games were so troublesome, decreed they would occur once every four years. Although the Smurfs were crestfallen over the loss of their village, they vowed to rebuild it, joining hands in an unbreakable bond of unity. The special aired a few months before the 1984 Los Angeles Olympic Games.

SMURFILY EVER AFTER

Broadcast History
    Premiere: February 13, 1985
    NBC/Wednesday 8:00-8:30 PM
    NBC/Repeat: March 30, 1986
Executive Producers: William Hanna, Joseph Barbera
Producer/Director: Gerard Baldwin
Associate Producer: Larry Latham
Director/Animation: Alan Zaslove
Writers: Patsy Cameron, Tedd Anasti
Music: Hoyt Curtin, Paul DeKorte
Company: Hanna-Barbera Productions in association with SEPP
    International

Principal Characters and Voices

Papa Smurf/Azrael	Don Messick
Smurfette	Lucille Bliss
Hefty/Monster	Frank Welker
Handy/Lazy/Grouchy	Michael Bell
Jokey	June Foray
Gargamel	Paul Winchell
Clumsy	Bill Callaway
Vanity	Alan Oppenheimer
Brainy	Danny Goldman
Greedy/Woody	Hamilton Camp
Tailor	Kip King
Farmer	Alan Young
Elderberry	Peggy Webber
Bramble	Robbie Lee
Pansy	Susan Blu
Lilac	Janet Waldo
Holly	Alexandra Stoddart
Acorn	Patti Parris

Smurfily Ever After celebrated the wedding of Laconia, the mute
wood elf, while failure to overlook imperfections doomed Smurfette's
dreams to find her "Mr. Right." Using sign language, Woody the
elf asked Laconia to marry him and they decided upon a simple service conducted by Papa Smurf. But an elated Smurfette began planning "the wedding of the century." An invitation fell into the hands
of Gargamel, who, in a foul plot to eliminate the Smurfs, delivered
his Ghouliope, a diabolized calliope, to the wedding site, Bluebell
Dell. Meanwhile, Smurfette fantasized about her own future with
Greedy, Hefty, Lazy and Clumsy, finding each one unacceptable.
All went well on the wedding day until the wedding march, when suddenly the Ghouliope, with Gargamel inside, emitted macabre music as
ghosts emerged from the pipes in a strange dancing frenzy which
engulfed everyone in the wedding party except for Laconia. Realizing the demonic happenings were caused by sound, she placed her
veil with its flower petal ear-coverings over a gyrating Smurfette,

who returned to normal. Together they filled Handy's new rice thrower with the wedding cake, lobbing globs into the organ's pipes just as the others, led by Papa Smurf, were about to drop from a gangway into a flaming cauldron. The sounds were reduced to muted pipings, and the Smurfs escaped into the woods as the organ exploded. Later, Papa Smurf conducted the simple ceremony desired by Woody and Laconia, their vows exchanged in sign language as they gazed lovingly at each other. Underscoring the moral, Papa Smurf explained to Smurfette that when you love someone, "the smurfy things about them make the unsmurfy things unimportant." Patsy Cameron provided the sign language for the program, which was initially telecast as a Valentine's Day special.

SMURFS, THE

THE SMURFS. © 1982 & 1983, Hanna-Barbera Productions, Inc. and SEPP International. Courtesy of Applause, Inc. for SEPP International; Hanna-Barbera Productions and TECO.

Broadcast History
Premiere: November 29, 1981
NBC/Sunday 7:00-8:00 PM
Executive Producers: William Hanna, Joseph Barbera
Producers: Gerard Baldwin, Kay Wright
Directors: Ray Patterson, George Gordon, Bob Hathcock, Carl Urbano, Rudy Zamora
Writers: Len Janson, Chuck Menville, Ray Parker
Music: Hoyt Curtin, Paul DeKorte
Company: Hanna-Barbera Productions in association with SEPP International/60 minutes

Principal Characters and Voices

Papa Smurf/Azrael	Don Messick
Gargamel	Paul Winchell
Brainy	Danny Goldman
Clumsy	Bill Callaway
Hefty	Frank Welker
Jokey	June Foray
Smurfette	Lucille Bliss
Vanity	Alan Oppenheimer
Greedy/Harmony	Hamilton Camp
Lazy/Handy/Grouchy	Michael Bell

The Smurfs presented three episodes from the 1981-1982 Saturday morning series, which introduced a colony of little blue people, three apples high, living in a mushroom village tucked away in a medieval world. Their idyllic existence was threatened by the wicked wizard Gargamel and his nasty henchcat Azrael. In "Supersmurf," Bigmouth stold the Smurfs' winter food supply and Brainy concocted one of Papa Smurf's magic strength potions to fight the greedy giant. When the superformula wore off, inopportunely, Papa Smurf worked a fast switch, replacing the food with rocks, and Bigmouth was none the wiser. "The Smurfette" introduced the only female member of Smurfland, when Gargamel created an enticing Smurfette to lure the little folk into his castle. Thoroughly entranced with the little Smurfs, however, Smurfette became one of them and together they caused Gargamel's evil scheme to backfire. In "The Baby Smurf," Gargamel transformed himself into a little infant which was adopted by Smurfette. As well as creating chaos, he plotted to blow up Smurf Village with a time bomb until Papa Smurf discovered the ruse and used the explosive to rocket the wizard back to his dismal castle.

SMURFS' CHRISTMAS SPECIAL, THE

Broadcast History
Premiere: December 13, 1982
NBC/Monday 8:00-8:30 PM
Sponsors: Mattel, M & M/Mars; McDonald's
NBC/Repeats: December 9, 1983, December 22, 1984; December 5, 1986

Executive Producers: William Hanna, Joseph Barbera
Producer/Director: Gerard Baldwin
Writers: Peyo, Gerard Baldwin, Yvan Delporte, Len Janson, Chuck
    Menville
Music: Hoyt Curtin, Paul DeKorte
Company: Hanna-Barbera Productions in association with SEPP Inter-
    national

Principal Characters and Voices

Papa Smurf/Azrael/Horse	Don Messick
Harmony/Greedy/Bailiff	Hamilton Camp
Jokey/Squirrel	June Foray
Gargamel	Paul Winchell
Smurfette	Lucille Bliss
Grouchy/Lazy/Handy	Michael Bell
Grandfather/Vanity/Servant	Alan Oppenheimer
Stranger	Rene Auberjonois
William	David Mendenhall
Gwenevere	Alexandra Stoddart
Brainy	Danny Goldman
Clumsy/Painter/Wolf #1	Bill Callaway
Tracker/Wolf Leader	Henry Polic
Hefty	Frank Welker

The Smurfs' Christmas Special wove a morality tale, of how love and
goodness conquered evil, into a holiday theme. Deep in the forest,
a pack of wolves sent by a mephistophelean character known as the
Stranger, frightened the horse upsetting a sleigh carrying young
William, Gwenevere and their Grandfather, enroute for the holidays
to their uncle's, a Bailiff who, concerned for their safety, was leading a search party to find them. As Grandfather lay unconscious
in the snow, the frightened children wandered off for help and encountered Gargamel, busy conjuring up evil spells to spoil Christmas
and capture the Smurfs, who turned the youngsters away. Striking
a pact with Gargamel, the Stranger offered him directions to Smurf
Village and a spell for their destruction in exchange for the children in order to settle an old score with their uncle. Luckily, the
Smurfs, searching for nuts, saved the lost children from a pack of
wolves but were later tricked by Gargamel, who grabbed the youngsters and gave them to the Stranger, then used his evil magic to
burn down empty Smurf Village. Taking Gargamel prisoner as well,
for an attempt to betray him, the Stranger took the children to an
outdoor amphitheater to prepare for "the final journey to a much
warmer home." As the Smurfs arrived, led by Tracker, the Stranger
caused a great ring of fire to envelop his captives. Recognizing the
terrible evil of the Stranger, Papa Smurf instructed his band to sing
with all the love they could muster and, joined by the children and
even Gargamel, goodness prevailed as the fire was extinguished and
the Stranger dissolved into the snow. After their uncle arrived and
left with the children, the Smurfs returned to their blackened village,
happy to be alive and together. When Harmony decided to cheer them

up with a tune on his trumpet, the sky radiated with light and their village was miraculously restored with its great decorated fir tree laden with tiny presents. Songs: "Smurfs Main Theme," "Goodness Makes the Badness Go Away" (Smurfs and children).

SMURF'S VALENTINE SPECIAL, THE   see   MY SMURFY VALENTINE

SNOOPY'S GETTING MARRIED, CHARLIE BROWN

Broadcast History
    Premiere: March 20, 1985
    CBS/Wednesday 8:00-8:30 PM
    Sponsors: Peter Paul Cadbury, Nabisco Brands
    CBS/Repeat: January 16, 1987
Producers: Lee Mendelson, Bill Melendez
Director: Bill Melendez
Writer/Creator: Charles M. Schulz
Music: Judy Munsen
Company: Lee Mendelson-Bill Melendez Productions in association
    with Charles M. Schulz Creative Associates and United Feature
    Syndicate
Home Video: Kartes Video Communications

Principal Characters and Voices

Charlie Brown	Brett Johnson
Lucy Van Pelt	Heather Stoneman
Schroeder	Danny Colby
Peppermint Patty	Gini Holtzman
Sally Brown	Stacy Ferguson
	Dawnn S. Leary (singing)
Marcie	Keri Houlihan
Linus Van Pelt	Jeremy Schoenberg
Pig Pen/Franklin	Carl Steven
Snoopy	Bill Melendez

Snoopy's Getting Married, Charlie Brown turned the Peanuts world topsy-turvy when they faced the prospect of losing their braggadocio bachelor beagle to the vows of matrimony. Standing watchdog duty at Peppermint Patty's house, with the eerie sounds of night ringing in his ears, Snoopy disappeared after two large eyes suddenly appeared in the darkness. Next morning, in a paw-written letter he asked Charlie Brown to mail to his brother Spike, Snoopy explained that the eyes he spied belonged to a beautiful French poodle, Jan-Viev. They had struck up a friendship, went canoeing by moonlight, saw Citizen Kane, the best movie ever, and ate dinner in a romantic French bistro. They were in love and had decided to wed. "Would Spike kindly be his best beagle?" the letter inquired. Unsettled, Charlie Brown worried that Snoopy did not understand the responsibility of having a wife and family. "Good Grief!" he wondered,

"Does this mean they'll all move in with him?" Spike, a genial desert rat living in Needles, California, made his television debut as he cheerfully set about earning money for the trip, unsuccessfully, eventually hitchhiking through heat and rain and sneaking a ride on a freight train. Chuck went shopping with Snoopy to select his top hat and tails while preparations began for the big event in his backyard: Woodstock and the birds repainted Snoopy's doghouse in pink and white, Linus drafted the marriage vows and Lucy worked on the menu, half to be served in dog dishes. Schroeder presided over Snoopy's bachelor party, a raucous affair with everyone swilling endless mugs of root beer. "To Snoopy, the bon vivant that was," they toasted, but the affair was tinged with sadness at the thought of losing the devilish dashing dog to puppy love. And Snoopy began to get cold paws and starting crying in his root beer. Then after a romantic tune by Sally, accompanied by Schroeder, and with Linus set to read the nuptial vows, the zinger occured when bridesmaid Lucy announced that Jan-Viev had run off with a golden retriever, leaving behind a still-single Snoopy. While Spike set out home via a slow freight, a relieved Snoopy dined with Woodstock atop his doghouse on the wedding feast. Song/Theme: "Oh Let Me Be the One" (Sally).

SNOW QUEEN, THE

Broadcast History
   Premiere: c1977
   SYN/local station option
Director/Writer (English): Fred Laderman
Music: Frank Skinner
Company: Greatest Tales
Distributor: LBS Communications ("LBS Children's Theatre")/1983-
   1985
Record Album: Decca DL 8977; Decca DL 78977 (stereo)

The Snow Queen retold Hans Christian Andersen's classic about two small children, Gerta and Kay, the love they had for each other and Gerta's search for her brother after he was kidnapped by the evil Snow Queen. Season after season, Gerta searched for Kay but he was nowhere to be found. After a harrowing encounter in the Northern Woods with thieves, Gerta told them of her quest for Kay. Sympathetic to her plight, they provided her a reindeer to take her to the Queen's ice palace in the North, warning her that one touch from the Snow Queen and she would turn to ice. However, the Queen's powers were harmless against one whose heart was pure, and through prayer and her love for Kay, Gerta succeeded in his rescue. The goodness and purity of heart that radiated from Gerta and Kay turned the Snow Queen into flame, destroying her forever. The half-hour foreign film was reedited and redubbed in English.

SNOW WHITE

Broadcast History
    Premiere: March 4, 1973
    SYN/FESTIVAL OF FAMILY CLASSICS, WABC, New York, Sunday
        7:00-7:30 PM
    SYN/Repeats: 1973 +
Producers/Directors: Arthur Rankin, Jr., Jules Bass
Associate Producer: Mary Alice Dwyer
Writer: Stu Hample
Music: Maury Laws, Jules Bass
Company: Rankin-Bass Productions
Distributor: Viacom Enterprises ("Family Classics")/1986-
Home Video: Prism

Snow White was a half-hour version of the Grimm Brothers fairytale
for children about the endearing rosy-lipped girl hated by her cruel
stepmother, the Queen, because she was the fairest in the land.
She was her own sweet self in this familiar tale, escaping from her
assassin-guard and fleeing to the woods where she was aided by the
animals and met the Seven Dwarfs. After she took a bite of poisoned
apple offered by her disguised stepmother, Snow White fell into a
deep sleep under an evil spell. Enter a handsome young prince, who
dislodged the piece of apple in her throat and awakened the girl.
They married and ruled the happiest kingdom in the world.

SNOW WHITE CHRISTMAS, A

Broadcast History
    Premiere: November 19, 1980
    CBS/Wednesday 8:00-9:00 PM
    CBS/Repeat: December 7, 1983
    SYN/Repeats: 1985 +
Executive Producers: Louis Scheimer, Norman Prescott
Producer: Don Christiansen
Director: Kay Wright
Art Directors: Carol Lundberg, Herb Hazelton
Writer: Marc Richards
Music/Songs & Lyrics: Yvette Blais, Jeff Michael, Dean Andre
Company: Filmation Studios/60 minutes
Distributor: Group W Productions/1985-
Home Video: Prism

Principal Characters and Voices

Snow White	Ericka Scheimer
Finicky/Corney/Tiny/Brawny/	
Hicker/Weeper/Villager	Arte Johnson
Wicked Queen/Hag	Melendy Britt
Queen	Diane Pershing
Grunyon	Charlie Bell

A SNOW WHITE CHRISTMAS. © 1980, Filmation Studios, Inc. Courtesy of Group W Productions.

Mirror	Larry Mann
Thinker	Clinton Sundberg

A Snow White Christmas borrowed some characters and the setting from the classic Grimm Brothers fairy tale and added a new story for this Yuletide fare. Snow White's daughter was the heroine in this musical special which teamed her with seven very unusual friends. Not dwarfs, but the giants Thinker, Finicky, Corney, Brawny, Tiny, Hicker and Weeper. The plot revolved around the evil Queen, who had returned to ruin Christmas with her magic mirror, and it was up to young Snow White and her Brobdingnagian pals to restore the joy and magic of the holiday season. Songs: "A Snow White Christmas" (Opening Theme), "It's Christmas," "A Darker Side," "She's Sleeping," "The Perfect Christmas," "Seven Friendly Giants," "A Christmas Merry" (Closing Theme).

SNOWMAN, THE

Broadcast History
    Premiere: December 26, 1983
    HBO/Friday 7:30-8:00 PM
    PBS/Repeats: December 2, 1985, December 25, 1986
Producer: John Coates
Directors: Jimmy Murakami, Diane Jackson
Writer: Raymond Briggs
Animators: Joanne Fryer, Stephen Weston, Robin White
Music: Howard Blake
Company: Snowman Enterprises in association with T. V. Cartoons,
    London, England
Distributor: Fremantle International
Home Video: Sony

Host: David Bowie (PBS)

The Snowman used only animation mime and music to tell about the
instant joys and sorrows of childhood. Based on the book by Raymond Briggs, it recounted how a country boy built a snowman which
came to life in a Christmas Eve dream. The boy invited his creation
into the house, where the naive Snowman quickly learned about fire-
places, gas stoves, false teeth and light switches. Enjoying a playful romp, the boy and his new friend tried on the clothes of the boy's
parents and even watched television. Outside, the Snowman took a
ride on a motorcycle, startling forest creatures in the headlight's
beam. Then the Snowman shared the wonders of his cold world with
the boy as they soared into the sky on a lyrical flight to Santa's
workshop at the North Pole, where they were greeted by a crowd of
snowmen revelers, toasting and making merry. As dawn broke, the
boy and the Snowman had to leave, but before they departed, Santa
gave the boy a special "snowman's" scarf. Surprise and disappoint-
ment awaited the boy the next morning; the scarf was wrapped around
his neck, but his special friend had disappeared. British Film and
Television Academy award (1982), Best Children's Film; British Design and Art Director's Award, Best Animation.
    Notable as a film of such length without dialogue, The Snowman
was also nominated for a U.S. Motion Picture Academy Award (1982)
as Best Animated Film.

SOLDIER'S TALE, THE

Broadcast History
    Premiere: March 19, 1981
    PBS/GREAT PERFORMANCES, Monday 9:00-10:00 PM
    PBS/Repeats: October 30, 1981 +
Producer/Director/Writer/Artist: R. O. Blechman
Music: Igor Stravinsky, Gerard Schwarz

THE SOLDIER'S TALE. © 1981, R. O. Blechman. Courtesy of the Public Broadcasting Service.

Company: R. O. Blechman Productions with WGBH, Boston, in association with PBS/60 minutes
Home Video: MGM/UA

Narrator: André Gregory

Principal Characters and Voices
Devil   Max Von Sydow
Princess   Galina Panova

A Soldier's Tale, set after the First World War, reflected that post-war period of wildly original and varied experiments in the arts. An animated version of the classic Russian children's fable about a simple soldier who sold his soul, as represented by his violin, to the Devil, it followed his subsequent struggle between spiritualism and materialism. Igor Stravinsky wrote L'Histoire du Soldat (1918), with a narrative contributed by Swiss poet C. F. Ramuz, as a theater piece. He incorporated many of the forms of the period, including jazz, tango, waltzes and marches, and scored it for an unconventional seven-piece ensemble of strings, woodwinds, brass and percussion. Its popularity led to other interpretations in mime, dance and puppetry. Award-winning New Yorker cartoonist R. O. Blechman decided to make it into the first animated production, a free-wheeling adaptation, "the way Stravinsky's composition is free-wheeling." For the film he used a variety of materials and techniques: paints, crayons, color pencils, cut-outs and collages. The music was performed by the Los Angeles Chamber Orchestra under the direction of Gerard Schwarz.

The program was a special presentation of the Great Performances Alliance: WNET/Thirteen, New York; KERA, Dallas-Ft. Worth;
KQED, San Francisco; SCETV, Columbia, South Carolina; and WTTW,
Chicago. Jac Venza was executive producer for Great Performances,
made possible by grants from Exxon, the Corporation for Public
Broadcasting and public television stations, with special funding for
the film provided by the National Endowment for the Arts.

SOMEDAY YOU'LL FIND HER, CHARLIE BROWN

Broadcast History
    Premiere: October 30, 1981
    CBS/Friday 8:00-8:30 PM
    CBS/Repeat: March 21, 1983
Executive Producer: Lee Mendelson
Producer: Bill Melendez
Director: Phil Roman
Writer/Creator: Charles M. Schulz
Music: Ed Bogas, Judy Munsen
Company: Lee Mendelson-Bill Melendez Productions in association
    with Charles M. Schulz Creative Associates and United Feature
    Syndicate
Home Video: Hi-Tops Video (nee Media Home Entertainment)

Principal Characters and Voices
Charlie Brown   Grant Wehr
Linus Van Pelt   Earl Reilly
Carita   Nicole Eggert
Little Girl (Mary Jo)   Jennifer Gaffin
Teenager   Melissa Strawmeyer
Snoopy   Bill Melendez
Woodstock
Brutus (Mary Jo's Bob Cat)

Vocalist: Becky Reardon

Someday You'll Find Her, Charlie Brown found the round-headed
little loser in love again with a comely girl he saw for just two sec-
onds in a TV "honey" shot while watching a football game. Instantly
infatuated, Charlie vowed to find her, enlisting Snoopy, Woodstock
and a reluctant Linus, who sarcastically reminded his friend that
"every week you fall in love." Playing detective, Charlie and Linus
located her stadium seat and a lead. Too embarassed to meet her
face-to-face, a tongue-tied Charlie convinced Linus to be his Cyrano.
After several false starts, they learned that the girl lived on the
Happy Valley Farm, way out in the country. "This might cost all of
50 cents to get there," said Linus. "The cost doesn't matter Linus,"
Charlie replied, "I must find her!" Finally, they did, after surviving a brush with her snarling pet Bob Cat, and Linus knocked on
her door while Charlie watched from afar. She answered, holding a

blanket. "I see you also have a blanket ... I love my blanket and hate to be separated from it," she said. Immediately smitten, Linus was invited inside for milk and cookies while an agonizing Charlie waited anxiously. Emerging, a happy Linus told his glowering friend, "We're going to spend the holidays together, Charlie Brown. I think you will like her when you meet her!" "You were suppose to tell the little girl about me! ...I saw her first!" wailed an incensed Charlie. "I'm madly in love with Mary Jo!" replied an ecstatic Linus. "Arghh!" cried frustrated Charlie, "Just when you think everything is perfect, life deals you a blow! ...I can't stand it!" Song/Theme: "Alone" (Reardon).

SORCERER'S APPRENTICE, THE

Broadcast History
    Premiere: October 1984
    SYN/local station option
Executive Producer: Bertram McMannis
Producer/Director/Writer: Peter Sander
Music: Hagood Hardy
Company: Gary Moscowitz with Astral Bellevue Pathé
Distributor: LBS Communications ("LBS Children's Theatre")/1983-
    1985
Home Video: Lorimar Home Video #111 (Kideo Video)

THE SORCERER'S APPRENTICE. © 1984, Gary Moscowitz and Astral Bellevue Pathé. Courtesy of LBS Communications and Lorimar Home Video.

Narrator: Vincent Price

The Sorcerer's Apprentice was drawn from the Jacob Grimm classic fairy tale about a poor young lad, Hans, who set out into the world to seek his fortune. In his travels the boy encountered the Sorcerer, who offered Hans a job as his apprentice. When he learned that the Sorcerer used all his amazing powers to perpetuate evil, Hans, asaisted by the beautiful servant girl Greta, decided to secretly study the villain's book of magic so that he might overcome the Sorcerer and end his devilish ways. Eventually discovering the boy's intrigue, the enraged Sorcerer endeavored to destroy Hans with every nasty trick at his disposal. In the fierce battle of magic that ensued between them, Hans finally prevailed and the Sorcerer was destroyed. Informing Greta that he had learned a valuable lesson from the wicked Sorcerer's example, Hans vowed to put all of his knowledge to work for the benefit of mankind.

SPECIAL MAGIC OF HERSELF THE ELF, THE

Broadcast History
    Premiere: Spring 1983
    SYN/local station option (KTLA, Los Angeles, April 22, 1983,
        Friday 7:00-7:30 PM PST)
    Sponsors: Mattel, American Greetings
    SYN/Repeats: 1983 +
Executive Producer: Jane Startz
Associate Executive Producer: Ray Peterson
Producers: Michael Hirsh, Patrick Loubert, Clive Smith
Associate Producer: Craig Virden
Directors: Gian Celestri, Raymond Jafelice
Writer: Dianne Dixon
Music/Songs & Lyrics: Judy Collins
Music: Jonathan Tunick, Lewis Hahn, Patricia Cullen
Company: Scholastic Productions in association with Those Char-
    acters From Cleveland and Nelvana Limited, Toronto, Canada
Distributor: Scholastic Productions/1983-
Home Video: Lorimar Home Video #207

Principal Characters and Voices

Herself the Elf	Priscilla Lopez
Creeping Ivy	Ellen Greene
King Thorn	Jerry Orbach
Willow Song	Georgia Engel
Meadow Morn	Denny Dillon
Snow Drop	Terri Hawkes
Wilfie	Jim Henshaw
Wood Pink	Susan Roman

Vocalist: Judy Collins

The Special Magic of Herself the Elf introduced a comely little sprite charged with watching over nature. Keeping the flowers blooming, the birds singing and the breezes blowing was Herself's responsibility. When nasty King Thorn and his scheming daughter Creeping Ivy stole Herself's magic wand in an attempt to take nature into their own evil hands and destroy all that was beautiful, it was up to Herself and her elfin friends Willow Song, Meadow Morn, Snow Drop, Wilfie and Wood Pink to use their collective wits and get the wand back. Featuring gentle elf characters, the special carried a pro-social theme of mutual cooperation and the importance of teamwork and featured animated characters created by Those Characters From Cleveland, an American Greetings company. Song/Theme: "The Special Magic of Herself the Elf" (Collins).

SPECIAL VALENTINE WITH THE FAMILY CIRCUS, A

Broadcast History
    Premiere: February 10, 1978
    NBC/Friday 8:00-8:30 PM
    NBC/Repeats: February 8, 1980; February 13, 1983
Producer: Edward F. Cullen
Associate Producer: Saul Kasden
Director: Al Kouzel
Writer: Joseph C. Cavella
Music/Songs & Lyrics: Sammy Fain, E. Y. (Yip) Harburg
Music: Tom McIntosh
Company: Cullen-Kasden Productions in association with the Register
    & Tribune Syndicate
Distributor: Fremantle International/1980-
Record Album: Affiliated Artists
Home Video: Family Home Entertainment

Principal Characters and Voices
Mommy   Anne Costello
Daddy   Bob Kaliban
Billy   Mark McDermott
Dolly   Missy Hope
Jeffy   Nathan Berg
P.J./Teacher   Suzanne Airey
Bus Driver   Sammy Fain
Barfy (pet dog)

A Special Valentine with the Family Circus involved the four children in Bil Keane's average American family in some minor shenanigans as they vied to make the best Valentine, or the biggest, to impress their parents. Their attempts to keep their creations private until the big day provided some diverting moments, such as when Dolly tried to hide hers in the bureau and their pet dog Barfy, a pointer, went straight to it. The three older children were of sufficient age for their artistic creations to be legible, but it was baby P.J.'s

scribbling that provided the plot peg. His writing could not be understood, and his pony-tailed sister Dolly and older brothers Billy and
Jeffy made fun of his card. Their later efforts to soothe his feelings
after laughing at his Valentine were a bust, failing to console the
heartbroken tot. It took Mommy to calmly make the children understand that it was P.J.'s thought that counted, not whether or not
he could read. Song/Theme: "If Every Day Were Valentine's Day."

The special marked the first of three animated films based on
Keane's popular daily-cartoon panel, The Family Circus, which de-
buted February 19, 1960, distributed by the Register & Tribune
Syndicate. Originally only three children appeared in the comic.
The third, baby P.J., was added in 1962.

SPIRIT OF '76, THE

Broadcast History
    Premiere: July 1984
    SYN/local station option
Producer: Marvin Grieve
Director: Marcia Kuyper Schneider
Music: Oscar Brand
Company: MG Films
Distributor: LBS Communications ("LBS Children's Theatre")/1983-
    1985

Narrator: Oscar Brand

The Spirit of '76, based on the eponymous stories for children about
the birth of the United States, related the historical events that led
to independence from England through live action, animation and
song. The half-hour special incorporated several of the 4-1/2 minute
films from the 104-episode 1975-1976 syndicated series sponsored by
General Foods.

SPORT GOOFY (I)

Broadcast History
    Premiere: May 21-June 12, 1983
    SYN/local station option (WXIA, Atlanta, Georgia, May 21, 1983,
    Saturday 5:30-6:00 PM)
Director: Jack Kinney
Writer: Dick Kinney
Music/Song & Lyrics: Dale Gonyea
Music: Oliver Wallace
Company: Walt Disney Television
Distributor: SFM Entertainment/1983-

Sport Goofy (I) starred the daffy Disney dog in laugh provoking scenes while demonstrating various athletic skills and participating in sporting events. Recycled from the Disney library, the cartoons demonstrated Goofy's pitching form in How To Play Baseball (1942) and diving and swimming techniques in How To Swim (1942). Tennis Racquet (1949) featured two Goofs competing in a wild match for a huge trophy. The film used wraparound highlights of Goofy performing fantastic sports feats set to the theme song, "You Can Always Be Number 1."

It was the first of a batch of such sport specials starring the cartoon canine, seven distributed in 1983-1984 and kindled by the 1984 Los Angeles Olympic Games, including Walt Disney Presents Sport Goofy's Olympic Games Special [q.v.] and several Walt Disney's Mickey, Donald and Sport Goofy Shows [q.v.]. An hour-long special was aired on NBC as An All New Adventure of Disney's Sport Goofy [q.v.].

SPORT GOOFY (II)

Broadcast History
    Premiere: August 21-September 24, 1983
    SYN/local station option (KVHP, Lake Charles, Louisiana, August
        21, 1983, Sunday 12:30-1:00 PM CST)
Director: Jack Kinney
Writers: Milt Schaffer, Dick Kinney
Music/Song & Lyrics: Dale Gonyea
Music: Paul J. Smith
Company: Walt Disney Television
Distributor: SFM Entertainment/1983-

Sport Goofy (II) was similar in format to the first special and starred the goofy canine in the Disney cartoons How To Play Football (1944), Goofy's Glider (1940) and Get Rich Quick (1951). Song/Theme: "You Can Always Be Number 1."

SPORT GOOFY (III)

Broadcast History
    Premiere: November 6-December 19, 1983
    SYN/local station option (WMGC, Binghamton, New York, November
        6, 1983, Sunday, 2:00-2:30 PM)
Directors: Jack Kinney, Jack Hannah
Writers: Bill Berg, Dick Kinney, Milt Banta
Music/Song & Lyrics: Dale Gonyea
Music: Paul J. Smith, Oliver Wallace
Company: Walt Disney Television
Distributor: SFM Entertainment/1983-

Sport Goofy (III) featured the Disney cartoons Hockey Homicide (1945), Double Dribble (1946) and The Art of Skiing (1941). Song/ Theme: "You Can Always Be Number 1."

STANLEY, THE UGLY DUCKLING

Broadcast History
    Premiere: May 1, 1982
    ABC/Saturday 8:30-9:00 PM
    ABC/Repeat: ABC WEEKEND SPECIALS, February 4, 1984
    NIK/Repeats: multiple option, July 20, 1986 +
Executive Producer: Steve Binder
Producer/Director: John Wilson
Associate Producer: Angela Wilson
Writers/Songs & Lyrics: Norman L. Martin, Lee Pockriss
Music: Norman L. Martin, Lee Pockriss, Artie Butler
Company: Fine Arts Productions in association with I Like Myself
    Productions
Home Video: IMA V-302

Principal Characters and Voices
Stanley   Susan Blu
Nathan   Jack DeLeon
Eagle One   Wolfman Jack

Other Voices
    Brian Cummings, Rick Dees, Julie McWhirter, Lee Thomas

Stanley, the Ugly Duckling introduced a little misfit whose mother
even thought him "different," a cute little duck who did not think
he was one in this musical fantasy. Since he couldn't swim or quack
and didn't even look like a duck, "Where do I belong? I've got to
find out." So Stanley tried to become a dog and joined a pack of
hounds chasing Nathan the Fox, whom Stanley rescued. Since the
duck had saved him, Nathan couldn't eat him, so he named him
Stanley from a sweethearts' carving on his treehouse, "Stan loves
Lee." After parting from Nathan, Stanley fell into trouble with the
moonshiners, Billy Bob and John Boy, a pair of turkeys who thought
him a revenuer. This time Nathan rescued Stanley. Still seeking
his true identity, the little duck joined the Hell's Eagles, a motorcycle gang led by Eagle One, who chased down Nathan and trussed
him to a spit. "What's cooking?" asked Stanley. "I will be, if you
don't get me out of here," said Nathan. Escaping to the beach,
Stanley met up with a John Wayne-talking old salt, a fiesty pelican
who rounded up his flying friends and engaged the Eagles in an
aerial showdown as Stanley again rescued Nathan. Pointing out that
Stanley had learned some self-confidence and that he had to learn to
like himself, in song, Nathan and his little pal strolled off together
down the road to some "travelin' music." Songs: "I'm Definitely
Not a Duck" (Stanley), "A Little Travelin' Music, Please" (Stanley,
Nathan), "Do Something Terrible" (Stanley & Hell's Eagles), "I Like
Myself!" (Stanley, Nathan).

STAR FAIRIES

Broadcast History
Premiere: 1985
SYN/local station option, (part of a 2-hour special, KCOP, Los
   Angeles, October 26, 1985, Saturday 2:00-4:00 PM PST)
Sponsor: Tonka Toys
Executive Producers: William Hanna, Joseph Barbera, Joe Taritero
Producer: Mitch Schauer
Writers: Mark Seidenberg, Richard Fogel
Music: Hoyt Curtin, Paul DeKorte
Company: Hanna-Barbera Productions
Distirbutor: Worldvision Enterprises/1985-
Home Video: Family Home Entertainment

Principal Characters and Voices

Spice	Didi Conn
True Love	Jean Kasem
Jazz	Susan Blu
Nightsong	Ta Tanisha
Whisper	Marianne Chinn
Sparkle/Michelle/Mother	B. J. Ward
Troll	Billy Barty
Giant	Michael Nouri
Dragon Head #1	Howard Morris
Dragon Head #2	Arte Johnson
Harvey	Shavar Ross
Benjamin	Matthew Gotlieb
Jennifer	Holly Berger
Puppy/Lavendar/Vanity	Frank Welker
Freddie/Frump/Spectre	Michael Bell
Giggleby	Jerry Houser
Blunderpuff/Elf	Don Messick
Wishing Well	Herschel Bernardi
Winthrop the Wizard	Jonathan Winters
Hillary	Drew Barrymore

Star Fairies introduced a special band of sprites, so named because
they were created from stars, striving to grant the wishes of every
child in the world. Since there were countless wishful children on
Earth, it was an enormous task but one which they carried out with
love. With spunk and intelligence, Princess Sparkle led her tiny
troop from her pink castle Wishstar in the Land of Wishcometrue,
where she could count on help from Winthrop the Wizard and her
magical Wishing Well. As well, Sparkle had the dedicated devotion
of Spice, the energy fairy; Nightsong, the dream fairy; Jazz, the
talent fairy; True Love, the love fairy; and Whisper, the secret
wish fairy. Through their varying talents, the Star Fairies were
able to acknowledge and grant wishes, often creatively. Though
their intentions were never faulted, sometimes they made miscues
since they were rather new to the job. Their task was not easy,

thanks to the interference of the troublesome elves led by Blunder-puff and his toadies, Frump and Giggleby. In the story, Blunder-puff stole Sparkle's magic wand and turned Wishcometrue into a bleak wasteland. At the end, the earth was disengrating and faults threatened to swallow up the evil elves, but through a return of her wand and the combined power of the other Star Fairies, the cataclys-mic destruction was halted and the land returned to its former beauty.

The film was part of a two-hour special package which included Pound Puppies [q.v.] and The Harlem Globetrotters Meet Snow White [q.v.].

STAR FOR JEREMY, A

Broadcast History
    Premiere: December 1984
    SYN/local station option
Executive Producer/Writer/Creator: Allan J. Howes
Producer: Terrence Carson
Company: TPC Communications
Distributor: LBS Communications ("LBS Children's Theatre")/1983-
    1985
Home Video: Lorimar Home Video #110 (Kideo Video)

Voices
    Leif Ancker, James Gleason, Charlotte Jarvis, Larry Kenny, Stacy
    Melodia, Christopher Potter, Tia Relbling

A Star for Jeremy featured a little boy who learned the symbolic meaning of the Christmas Star atop his tree one Christmas Eve in Victorian England. In a dream that night, Jeremy was transported to the Lord's garden, where God assigned places for all the respec-tive stars in the universe, except one. That star, named Stan, the tiniest of them all, had to remain behind for thousands of years until summoned to announce the birth of Jesus in the small town of Bethle-hem. On Christmas day Stan shined in all his glory and lighted the faces of Angels as they sang, announcing Christ's birth. Proudly shining more brightly than ever, Stan returned home, where God proclaimed that he would always be known as The Christmas Star, earning his place at the top of the tall Norway pine where he was seen every year at Christmas.

STINGIEST MAN IN TOWN, THE

Broadcast History
    Premiere: December 23, 1978
    NBC/Saturday 8:00-9:00 PM
    Sponsor: Alcoa
    NBC/Repeat: December 22, 1979

A STAR FOR JEREMY. © 1984, TPC Communications, Inc. Courtesy of LBS Communications and Lorimar Home Video.

SYN/Repeats: 1985 +
Producers/Directors: Arthur Rankin, Jr., Jules Bass
Writer: Romeo Muller
Music: Fred Spielman
Lyrics: Janice Torre
Music/Conductor: Bernard Hoffer
Company: Rankin-Bass Productions/60 minutes
Distributor: Lorimar Syndication ("Animated Holiday Specials")/1985-

Narrator
B.A.H. Humbug   Tom Bosley

Principal Characters and Voices
Ebenezer Scrooge   Walter Matthau
Ghost of Marley   Theodore Bikel
Young Scrooge   Robert Morse
Fred   Dennis Day
Tiny Tim   Robert Rolofson
Mrs. Crachit   Darlene Conley
Ghost of Christmas Past   Paul Frees
Martha   Debra Clinger
Belinda   Steffanie Calli
Peter   Eric Hines
Boy   Charles Matthau

Other Voices
   Shelby Flint, Diana Lee, Sonny Melendrez, Dee Stratton

The Stingiest Man in Town was a tuneful version of Charles Dickens'
A Christmas Carol, narrated by Tom Bosley as B.A.H. Humbug, a
new character who broke into song during the film, summing it all
up in his solo, "The Birthday Party of the King." It was the familiar
Christmas ghost tale of Ebenezer Scrooge, the sad, lonely miser, un-
doubtedly the stingiest old gentleman around, who kept his employees
Humbug and Bob Crachit working late in the office on the holiday
eve. That evening the Ghost of Jacob Marley, Scrooge's deceased
business partner, suddenly appeared. Marley warned Scrooge that
he would join three chained phantoms who would visit him later that
night. But should Scrooge repent and change his miserly ways, he
would live in happiness. The Ghosts of Christmas Past, Christmas
Present and Christmas Yet-to-Come frightened Scrooge so badly that
he did indeed change overnight. After performing other good deeds,
on Christmas day he bore gifts and a turkey to the Crachits, their
daughter Martha and crippled Tiny Tim, their young son. Tiny Tim
embraced the joyful Scrooge, who had learned to enjoy the wonders
of generosity and to know the love of his fellow man. Songs: "A
Christmas Carol," "Stingiest Man in Town" (Bosley & chorus), "An
Old Fashioned Christmas" (Day & chorus), "Humbug" (Matthau &
Day), "I Wear a Chain" (Bikel), "Golden Dreams," "It Might Have
Been" (Morse & Lee), "Christmas Spirit" (Matthau & chorus), "Yes,
There Is a Santa Claus" (Clinger), "Birthday Party of the King"

(Bosley), "One Little Boy" (Matthau & Frees), "Mankind Should Be My Business" (Matthau).

STORY OF BABAR, THE LITTLE ELEPHANT, THE

Broadcast History
    Premiere: October 21, 1968
    NBC/Monday 7:30-8:00 PM
    Sponsors: Viking Carpets; Burger Chef (1975-1976)
    NBC/Repeat: April 21, 1969
    SYN/Repeats: 1975 +
Producers: Lee Mendelson, Bill Melendez
Directors: Bill Melendez, Ed Levitt
Writer: Laurent de Brunhoff
Music: John Scott Trotter
Lyrics: Tom Adair
Company: Lee Mendelson-Bill Melendez Productions in association
    with Laurent de Brunoff and the cooperation of Random House
Distributor: Lee Mendelson Productions/1986-
Home Video: Children's Video Library (Vestron)

Narrator: Peter Ustinov

Vocalists: (The Celesteville Singers)
    B. J. Baker, Gene Merlino, Lulie Jean Norman, Sally Stevens,
    Bob Tebow

The Story of Babar, the Little Elephant introduced the King of Elephant Land, orphaned when his mother was cruelly killed by a wicked
hunter in the forest. Running away to Paris, there Babar met a rich
Old Lady, fond of elephants, who taught him parlor manners and
gave him money to buy fine clothes and a snappy red roadster. While
leading the life of a wealthy gentleman, Babar had a happy reunion
with his cousins Artur and Celeste, also runaways. But a bird
spotted them and informed the other elephants, searching for their
kin. When they arrived to fetch the errant youngsters, Babar decided to return to the jungle too, promising to return one day. Because he had become a world traveler, the elder elephant Cornelius
suggested that Babar become the new King of the elephants. After
accepting the post, Babar also announced his engagement to Celeste
and his plans to build a great city. He dispatched a dromedary,
along with Artur and Zephir the Monkey, to the city to get clothing
for his wedding and coronation and to bring his friend the Old Lady.
The bird was sent to invite all the other animals. The caravan returned safely, but along the way Artur and Zephir played some mean
pranks on the rhinos. Deciding to name his city Celesteville, Babar
proceeded with his plans, but, bent on revenge, the rhinos virtually
destroyed it. In a second attack, the herd was scared away by the
painted hindquarters of the elephants and Babar was victorious in
the War with the Rhinoceroses. After Celesteville was rebuilt, all

the animals celebrated the wedding and coronation of King Babar, dapper in his signature gold crown, white spats and a three-piece green suit, and Queen Celeste. Songs: "Long Live Babar," "The Babar Waltz," "This Is the Day of Days" ("Babar's Coronation Song"). "The Test of Time," "It's a Ding Dong Dilly of a Day," "A Job Well Done," "Oh! What a Lovely Live," "Long Live Happiness!"

Adapted by Laurent de Brunhoff, the special was based on the first three Babar children's books by his father, French artist, illustrator and author Jean de Brunhoff. Babar was actually dreamed up by Laurent's mother, Cecile Sabouraud, a pianist who invented a bedtime story about a family of elephants to entertain Laurent and his older brother Mathieu. Babar celebrated his 55th anniversary in 1986.

STORY OF THE FIRST CHRISTMAS SNOW, THE   see   FIRST CHRIST-
    MAS, THE

STRAWBERRY SHORTCAKE AND THE BABY WITHOUT A NAME

Broadcast History
    Premiere: Spring 1984
    SYN/local station option (KTLA, Los Angeles, March 30, 1984,
        Friday 7:30-8:00 PM PST)
    Sponsor: Kenner Products (Toy Group, General Mills)
    SYN/Repeats: October 26, 1984 +
Executive Producers: Bernard Loomis, Carole MacGillvray
Producers: Michael Hirsh, Patrick Loubert, Clive A. Smith
Associate Producer: Paul Pressler
Director: Arna Selznick
Director/Animation: Charlie Bonifacio
Writer: Peter Sauder
Music/Songs & Lyrics: Bob Chimbel, Merry Loomis
Music: Patricia Cullen, Ben Lazarone
Company: MAD Productions in association with Those Characters
    From Cleveland and Nelvana Limited, Toronto, Canada
Distributor: LBS Communications/1984-
Home Video: Family Home Entertainment F379

Narrator
Sun   Chris Wiggins

Principal Characters and Voices
Strawberry Shortcake   Russi Taylor
Purple Pieman   Bob Ridgely
Sour Grapes/Fig-Boot   Jeri Craden
Plum Puddin'   Laurie Waller
Lemon Meringue/Lime Chiffon   Melleny Brown
Peach Blush/Orange Blossom   Susan Roman
Lullaberry Pie   Monica Parker
Orange Blossom   Cree Summer Francks

Strawberry Shortcake and the Baby Without a Name began in Strawberry Land when Plum Puddin', Peach Blush and the Baby Without a Name arrived for Strawberry Shortcake's big summer camp-out. Little did the unsuspecting campers realize that a monster was lurking somewhere in the forest, and Purple Pieman and Sour Grapes were out to capture it for their own wicked ends. Later the first night, after some scary stories around the campfire, the Baby Without a Name crawled away to follow the monster's giant tracks into the forest and wound up becoming a friend of the big-footed, cuddly creature. Following out their nasty plan, the Peculiar Purple Pieman and the villainess imprisoned Strawberry Shortcake and friends and kidnapped Fig-Boot. Saving the day, Strawberry Shortcake and the others escaped opportunely and managed to save Fig-Boot from the clutches of the dastardly duo. Songs: "We're Going Camping," "Berry Scary Holiday," "Friend" (Taylor), "Monster Song" (Ridgely and Craden).

The special was one in a series of six programs featuring the Strawberry Shortcake characters created by American Greetings and first introduced to television in The World of Strawberry Shortcake [q.v.], sponsored by Kenner Products, whose toy lines included Strawberry Shortcake, Play-Doh and Star Wars dolls and novelties.

STRAWBERRY SHORTCAKE IN BIG APPLE CITY

Broadcast History
  Premiere: Spring 1981
  SYN/local station option (KTLA, Los Angeles, April 10, 1981,
    Friday 7:30-8:00 PM PST)
  Sponsor: Kenner Products (Toy Group, General Mills)
  SYN/Repeats: October 14, 1981 +
Executive Producer: Robert L. Rosen
Producer: Buzz Potamkin
Director: Hal Silvermintz
Director/Animation: Vincent J. Cafarelli
Writer/Lyrics: Romeo Muller
Music: Mark Volman, Howard Kaylan
Company: RLR Associates in association with Those Characters From
  Cleveland and Perpetual Motion Pictures
Distributor: Sunbow Productions/1987–
Record Album: Kids Stuff KSS 163
Home Video: Family Home Entertainment

Narrator
Sun   Romeo Muller

Principal Characters and Voices
Strawberry Shortcake   Russi Taylor
Purple Pieman   Bob Ridgely
Coco Nutwork   Bob Holt
Orange Blossom   Diane McCannon

STRAWBERRY SHORTCAKE IN BIG APPLE CITY. © 1981, American Greetings Corporation. Courtesy of RLR Associates and Those Characters From Cleveland.

Blueberry Muffin/Apple
    Dumplin'/Apricot   Joan Gerber

<u>Vocalists</u>: Flo and Eddie

<u>Strawberry Shortcake in Big Apple City</u> described the musical moppet's attempt to outwit the Peculiar Purple Pieman of Porcupine Peak in the Big Bake Off in which both were finalists. In his inimical style, the Pieman threw all kinds of obstacles in her path to prevent her from completing her speciality, a strawberry shortcake. His unethical efforts to gain first place honors for his own kohlrabi cookies brought into play Strawberry's many friends, who outmaneuvered the Pieman at every turn. Strawberry's new friends included Orange Blossom, a shy artistic girl; Guacamole, a mole recognized as the world's greatest digger; Lemon Meringue, a perpetually primping model who lived in Spinach Village, the artistic colony of Big Apple City; T. N. Honey, a scientist-inventor with a British accent, tweeds and sensible shoes; Apricot, a fun-loving toddler who used multi-syllable words; Hopsalot, Apricot's pet bunny; Horse Raddish, a swayback horse that pulled a hansom cab in Big Apple City; and a harried, bald television executive called Coco Nutwork. Their courage and consistency conquered all, and in the end the little heroine

won out against what seemed like discouraging odds. Songs: "What a Day," "Big Apple City," "New Friends," "Bake Off," "Strawberry Land."

STRAWBERRY SHORTCAKE MEETS THE BERRYKINS

Broadcast History
    Premiere: Spring 1985
    SYN/local station option
    Sponsor: Kenner Products (Toy Group, General Mills)
    SYN/Repeats: October 1985 +
Executive Producers: Carole MacGillvray, Paul Pressler
Producers: Michael Hirsh, Patrick Loubert, Clive A. Smith, Lenora
    Hume
Director: Laura Shepherd
Director/Animation: Ken Stephenson
Writer: Peter Sauder
Music/Songs & Lyrics: John Sebastian
Music: Patricia Cullen
Company: MAD Productions in association with Those Characters
    From Cleveland and Nelvana Limited, Toronto, Canada, with Hanho
    Heung-Up, Seoul, Korea
Distributor: LBS Communications/1985-
Home Video: Family Home Entertainment F396

Narrator
Sun   Chris Wiggins

Principal Characters and Voices
Strawberry Shortcake   Russi Taylor
Purple Pieman   Robert Ridgely
Sour Grapes   Jeri Craden
Banana Twirl/Banana Berrykin   Melleny Brown
Berry Princess/Peach Blush/
    Peach Berrykin   Susan Roman
Plum Puddin'/Plum Berrykin/
    Orange Blossom   Laurie Waller
Raspberry Tart/Blueberry Muffin   Susan Snooks
VO   Patrick Black

Vocalists
    Nadia Medusa, Ben Sebastian, John Sebastian, Russi Taylor,
    Nicole Wills

Strawberry Shortcake Meets the Berrykins again featured the familiar pastry clan from Strawberry Land, where calamity struck in the form of rain from a strange purple cloud. It arrived in the midst of Strawberry's garden party for her friends and was giving all their luscious fruit a terrible smell. And it was not the fault of the Berrykins, the wee little creatures who sprinkled scents on all the fruit.

Perplexed, the Berry Princess, who looked after the tiny Berrykins, hadn't a clue. But the Princess and some of her Berrykins figured out that the Peculiar Purple Pieman and his wacky villainess cohort Sour Grapes were causing the big stink with the escaping gases that rose from the kitchen where they had been whipping up the world's favorite perfume from a bizarre recipe. Solving the problem, Strawberry had the Berrykin's impart their flavorful essence to the vat. Songs: "The Berry Berry Best in Berryland" (Sebastian, Taylor, Medusa), "I Want to Look Like Who I Want to be When I Grow Up" (Black, Taylor, Sebastian, Medusa), "Sometimes Things Aren't What They Seem to Be" (Taylor, Sebastian, Medusa), "Keep Those Bright Eyes Bright" (Wills).

STRAWBERRY SHORTCAKE: PETS ON PARADE

Broadcast History
   Premiere: Spring 1982
   SYN/local station option (KTLA, Los Angeles, April 9, 1982, Friday 7:30-8:00 PM PST)
   Sponsor: Kenner Products (Toy Group, General Mills)
   SYN/Repeats: October 12, 1982 +
Executive Producer: Robert L. Rosen
Producers: Romeo Muller, Fred Wolf, Tomoh Fukumoto
Director: Fred Wolf
Director/Animation: Kohsei Ohtani
Writer/Lyrics: Romeo Muller
Music: Mark Volman, Howard Kaylan
Company: Muller-Rosen Productions in association with Those Characters From Cleveland and Murakami-Wolf-Swenson Films with Toei Doga, Tokyo, Japan
Distributor: Sunbow Productions/1987-
Record Album: Kid's Stuff KSS 5024
Home Video: Family Home Entertainment F-368

Narrator
Sun   Romeo Muller

Principal Characters and Voices
Strawberry Shortcake   Russi Taylor
Purple Pieman   Robert Ridgely
Blueberry Muffin/Apple Dumplin'   Joan Gerber
Huckleberry Pie   Julie McWhirter

Vocalists: Flo and Eddie

Strawberry Shortcake: Pets on Parade centered around the "Second Annual Grand Old Petable Pet Show and Pet Parade," to which all youngsters in Strawberry Land were invited. Again trying to win by hook or crook, the villain, the Peculiar Purple Pieman of Porcupine Peak, turned up with a new cohort in crime, the equally hissable

villainess Sour Grapes and her harmless pet snake Dregs. During
the course of the morality play, the two tried to discredit Strawberry
Shortcake and Custard, who were pet show judges, while the little
heroine shooed the blues in song, surmounted the hurdles and upset
their apple cart, thanks to the intercession of the sweet-smelling
skunk, Soufflé. Angel Cake, an overly polite little creature who
was perpetually dieting, was one of Strawberry's new friends. Other
characters and their pets included Lemon Meringue and Frappé the
Frog; Orange Blossom and Marmalade the Butterfly; Lime Chiffon
and Parfait the Parrot; Cherry Cuddler and Goosenberry the Goose;
Butter Cookie and Jelly the Bear; Raspberry Tart and Rhubarb the
Monkey; and Blueberry Muffin and Cheesecake the Mouse. Songs:
"Perfect Place to Be," "Lower Than You," "Pet Parade," "Ah Sweet
Strawberry," "Berry Blue," "I Love You," "March Back to Town."

STRAWBERRY SHORTCAKE'S HOUSEWARMING SURPRISE

Broadcast History
    Premiere: Spring 1983
    SYN/local station option (KTLA, Los Angeles, April 1, 1983,
        Thursday 7:00-7:30 PM PST)
    Sponsor: Kenner Products (Toy Group, General Mills)
    SYN/Repeats: October 24, 1983 +
Executive Producers: Bernard Loomis, Carole MacGillvray
Producers: Michael Hirsh, Patrick Loubert, Clive A. Smith
Director: Raymond Jafelice
Director/Animation: Gian Celestri
Writer: Peter Sauder
Music/Songs & Lyrics: John Sebastian
Music: Patricia Cullen
Company: MAD Productions in association with Those Characters
    From Cleveland and Nelvana Limited, Toronto, Canada
Distributor: LBS Communications/1983-
Home Video: Family Home Entertainment F348A

Narrator
Sun   Chris Wiggins

Principal Characters and Voices
Strawberry Shortcake   Russi Taylor
Purple Pieman   Robert Ridgely
Sour Grapes   Jeri Craden
Captain Cackle/VO   Jack Blum
Lime Chiffon   Melleny Brown
Huckleberry/Parfait/Lem   Jeanine Elias
Blueberry/Crepe Suzette/Ada Susan Roman

Vocalists
    Phil Gladston, Bill Keith, Sharon McQueen, Ben Sebastian, John
    Sebastian

Strawberry Shortcake's Housewarming Surprise was a musical story featuring the pastry cast in Strawberry Land. When Strawberry Shortcake moved to a big new house, all of her good friends gathered to give her a surprise housewarming party and brought their favorite recipes. There were the old chums like Raspberry Tart, Blueberry Muffin and Peach Blush, plus new ones from around the world like Almond Tea, Cafe Olé and Crepe Suzette. But alas, the surprise was on them when the Peculiar Purple Pieman hatched a maniacal master plot and showed up to gobble up the goodies and steal the recipes which Sour Grapes planned to publish as the world's greatest cookbook. Strawberry came up with a "berry" clever plan of her own to recover the stolen recipes using the mimicking Berry Birds. Unfortunately, the twins Lem and Ada were trapped in the recipe basket but were finally rescued when Strawberry mustered help from her friends and received an unexpected assist from Dregs, Sour Grape's pet snake. Songs: "Pack 'Em Up and Move 'Em Out," "Nothing Like a Recipe," "If You Want to Talk Berry," "We're Having a Party."

SWISS FAMILY ROBINSON, THE

Broadcast History
   Premiere: January 13, 1973
   SYN/FESTIVAL OF FAMILY CLASSICS, WABC, New York, Sunday
      7:00-7:30 PM
   SYN/Repeats: 1973 +
Producers/Directors: Arthur Rankin, Jr., Jules Bass
Associate Producer: Mary Alice Dwyer
Writer: William Overgard
Music: Maury Laws, Jules Bass
Company: Rankin-Bass Productions
Distributor: Viacom Enterprises ("Family Classics")/1986-
Home Video: Prism

The Swiss Family Robinson followed the nineteenth-century Johann Wyss tale of a self-reliant family that flourished despite misfortunes when shipwrecked and stranded on a deserted island. Young Fritz and Franz helped their father and mother make-do as they grew to manhood in the comfortable tree house the family had constructed. When a rescue ship finally arrived five years later, Fritz and Franz returned to civilization, taking with them a just discovered young girl who had been shipwrecked there also and leaving behind their parents on the island, which had become their real home.

SWISS FAMILY ROBINSON, THE

Broadcast History
   Premiere: October 28, 1973
   CBS/FAMOUS CLASSIC TALES, Sunday 5:00-6:00 PM

Sponsor: Kenner Products (Toy Group, General Mills)
CBS/Repeat: November 28, 1974
SYN/Repeats: 1975 +
Producer: Walter J. Hucker
Director: Leif Gram
Writer: John Palmer
Music: Richard Bowden
Company: Air Programs International, Sydney, Australia/60 minutes
Distributor: D. L. Taffner ("Animated Classics for Children")/1985-
Home Video: Classics for Kids (MGM/UA)

Voices
    Jeannie Drynan, Alistair Duncan, Barbara Frawley, Ron Haddrick,
    Brenda Senders

The Swiss Family Robinson detailed the survival of the shipwrecked
emigrant castaways on a deserted island, a tale of discovery, ingenuity and adventure in this hour-long film based on Johann Wyss's
eponymous book (1812-1813).

TAKE ME UP TO THE BALLGAME

Broadcast History
    Premiere: September 14, 1980
    CBC/Sunday 7:00-7:30 PM
    SYN/local station option, September 1980 +
Executive Producers: Robert Foster, Ted Kernaghan, Nigel Martin
Producers: Patrick Loubert, Michael Hirsh
Director: Ken Stephenson
Writer: Ken Sobol
Music: Rick Danko (The Band)
Lyrics: Julia Bourque, Rick Danko
Company: Nelvana Limited, Toronto, Canada, in association with CBC
Distributor: Viacom Enterprises/1986-
Home Video: Warner Home Video #30009, ("Nelvanamation II")

Principal Characters and Voices

Irwin	Phil Silvers
Beaver	Bobby Dermer
Eagle	Derek McGrath
Commissioner	Don Ferguson
Announcer	Paul Soles
Edna	Anna Bourque
Jake	Maurice LaMarche
Mole	Melleny Brown

Vocalist: Rick Danko

Take Me Up to the Ballgame combined baseball and science fiction
in a tuneful fantasy about an intergalactic playoff between the Earth's

TAKE ME UP TO THE BALLGAME. © 1980, Nelvana Limited. Courtesy of Nelvana Limited and Viacom Enterprises.

ragtag animal team and the unscrupulous champions of the universe. The Giants, a sandlot baseball team consisting of an Eagle, a Beaver, a Bear, a Kangaroo, a Cat and a Mole, were recruited by Irwin, an interplanetary promoter who hustled the team into celestial competition. They were "beamed up" to a spaceship and taken to an outer-space baseball stadium to play for the interstellar championship against the Outer-Space All Stars, an awesome team that had never lost a game or been scored upon, infamous as the biggest cheaters in the universe. The Interstellar Baseball Commissioner explained that this was how the game was played in outer space. Nonetheless, the Giants accepted the challenge with gusto, but after one full inning the score was 99 to 0. When some of the members of the Giants considered cheating too, Beaver, the team leader, reminded them that cheaters never prosper. Prophetically, the nasty tricks soon turned against the All Stars, who outsmarted themselves and fell into their own traps. Irwin, afraid of losing all the money he had bet against the Giants, turned up as a pinch hitter for the All Stars in the top of the ninth and hit a pitch high up and above the stadium. The Giants piled on top of each other's shoulders to catch it, but it bounced off the top glove, landing in the glove of the inattentive Cat, who had stopped in the middle of the field to smell a flower, his glove outstretched behind his back. Victorious, the Earth team ended up ahead by one run and honesty ruled the universe. Songs: "Baseball," "Trust Me," "Cheating."

TALE OF FOUR WISHES, A

Components
HUG ME, THE MAN WHO HAD NO DREAM, SILVER PONY, JANE WISHING

Broadcast History
Premiere: November 8, 1981
CBS/CBS LIBRARY SPECIALS, Sunday 5:00-6:00 PM
Sponsor: General Foods
CBS/Repeat: July 6, 1982
SYN/Repeats: 1985 +
Producer: Nick Bosustow
Director/Animation: Sam Weiss
Director/Live Action: Seth Pinsker
Writer: George Arthur Bloom
Music: Larry Wolff
Company: Bosustow Entertainment/60 minutes
Distributor: Coe Film Associates/1985–

Cast/Hosts
Jane	Tracey Gold
Skeeter	Rick Nelson

Supporting Cast
Grandmother	Bibi Osterwald
Mother	Judy Farrell
Father	Bob Ross
Margaret	Seeley Ann Thumann
Daniel	Chad Krentzman

A Tale of Four Wishes was a live-action and animated special about wish-making. The leading lady was Jane, a girl who wished a lot because nobody understood her and nothing ever went right for her. Then she met the gentle storyteller Skeeter, who spun animated tales about a lonely porcupine that yearned for someone to Hug Me, about The Man Who Had No Dream because there wasn't anything that he couldn't buy, and about the boy who dreamed of owning a flying Silver Pony. Finally, Skeeter told the story of Jane Wishing, which concerned Jane's dream of being a princess with red hair and sea-blue eyes. It was a tale that opened her eyes to the value of wishes-- and what she had to do to make them come true. The stories were selected from the annual lists of children's books recommended by the United States Library of Congress.

TALE OF TWO CITIES, A

Broadcast History
    Premiere: 1984
    SYN/local station option
    NIK/Repeats: multiple option, 1986
Executive Producers: Tom Stacey, George Stephenson
Producer: Eddy Graham
Director: Warwick Gilbert
Writer: Russell Thornton
Music: Mark Isaacs
Company: Burbank Films, Sydney, Australia/90 minutes
Distributor: Twentieth-Century Fox Television ("Charles Dickens
    Classics")/1984-
Home Video: Vestron Entertainment

Voices
    John Benton, John Everson, Phillip Hinton, Liz Horne, Moya
    O'Sullivan, Robin Stewart, John Stone, Henri Szeps, Ken Wayne

A Tale of Two Cities followed Charles Dickens' 1859 story set in London and Paris during the French Revolution, focusing on Sidney Carton, a dissolute English barrister who, by spiriting his lookalike out of the Bastille and taking his place, saved French aristocrat Charles Darnay, a nephew of the Marquis de St. Evremonde about to meet his death at the guillotine.

TALES OF WASHINGTON IRVING

Broadcast History
    Premiere: November 1, 1970
    CBS/FAMOUS CLASSIC TALES, Sunday 5:00-6:00 PM
    Sponsors: Kenner Products (Toy Group, General Mills), Parker
        Brothers
    CBS/Repeat: October 24, 1971
    SYN/Repeats: 1972 +
Executive Producer: Walter J. Hucker
Director: Zoran Janjic
Writer: Michael Robinson
Music: Richard Bowden
Company: Air Programs International, Sydney, Australia/60 minutes
Distributor: D. L. Taffner ("Animated Classics for Children")/1983-
Home Video: Classics for Kids (MGM/UA)

Voices
    Mel Blanc, George Firth, Joan Gerber, Byron Kane, Julie McWhirter, Don Messick, Ken Samson, Lennie Weinrib, Brian Zax, Larraine Zax

Tales of Washington Irving featured two of the author's most famous folktales, "The Legend of Sleepy Hollow" and "Rip Van Winkle," set in the Hudson River Valley settled by Dutch burghers. Adhering closely to Irving's short stories, they told about the lanky, scarecrowish schoolmaster, Icabod Crane, who was last seen one moonless autumn night fleeing from a headless spectre over a haunted wooden bridge near Tarrytown Old Dutch Graveyard, and the good natured, henpecked ne'er-do-well Rip Van Winkle, who, during a walk in the Catskills at twilight, joined a group of Dutch elves, took a sip from their keg and fell asleep for 20 years.

The film was the first of 15 specials, aired on CBS (1970-1982) and produced by API through Sive Associates for Kenner, which were acquired with four others and redistributed by D. L. Taffner under the title, "Animated Classics for Children" (SYN, 1983-).

TALKING PARCEL, THE

Broadcast History
    Premiere: 1983-1984
    SYN/local station option
Executive Producer: Sue Turner
Producers: Brian Cosgrove, Mark Hall
Director: Brian Cosgrove
Writer: Rosemary Anne Sisson
Music: David Rohl, Stuart J. Wolstenholme
Company: Cosgrove-Hall Productions, division of Thames Television, Manchester, England
Distributor: LBS Communications ("LBS Children's Theatre")/1983-1985
Home Video: Thorn

Principal Characters and Voices

Penelope	Lisa Norris
Parrot	Freddie Jones
Hortense, the Flying Train	Mollie Sugden
Ethelred	Roy Kinnear
H. H. Junketbury	Edward Kelsey
Chief Cockatrice	Windsor Davies
Oswald, the Sea Serpent	Sir Michael Hordern
Werewolf	Peter Woodthorpe
Duke Wensleydale	Harvey Ashby
Others	Raymond Mason
	Daphne Oxenford

The Talking Parcel resurrected some beasties from ancient mythology, brought brilliantly to life via animation. The tale opened when Penelope, played by 12-year-old Lisa Norris, found a talking parcel on the seashore, its voice that of a Parrot who had just arrived from Mythologia where the mythical beasts dwelled. While seated on the beach and chatting with the Parrot, she learned that the ruler, the Wizard H. H. Junketbury, had been imprisoned by the fearsome

THE TALKING PARCEL. © 1978, Cosgrove-Hall Productions, Ltd., division of Thames Television, Manchester, England. Courtesy of LBS Communications.

fire-breathing Cockatrices, huge monsters, half cockerel and half reptile. So Penelope and the Parrot journeyed by Hortense the Flying Train to the fabled Land of Mythologia to rescue the Wizard. Their adventures led to a meeting with Ethelred the Toad, who became their ally, and encounters with Oswald the Sea Serpent, a Werewolf, will-o'-the-wisps, dragons, unicorns, griffons and even the cowardly weasels, whose bite was reputedly fatal to the Cockatrice. They endured the perils of Werewolf Island, and in the finale the good animals stormed the castle where the Wizard was imprisoned, rescued him and defeated the evil Cockatrices.

Initially telecast on December 26, 1978 at 12 noon on Thames Television, London, the film was based on the children's fantasy by author and naturalist Gerald Durrell.

THANKSGIVING IN THE LAND OF OZ

Broadcast History

Premiere: November 25, 1980
CBS/Tuesday 8:30-9:00 PM
Sponsor: Mattel
CBS/Repeat: DOROTHY IN THE LAND OF OZ, December 10, 1981

THANKSGIVING IN THE LAND OF OZ. © 1980, RLR Associates, Inc. Courtesy of RLR Associates.

SHO/Repeats: multiple option, November 1985 & 1986
HBO/Repeats: DOROTHY IN THE LAND OF OZ, multiple option,
   1986-1987
SYN/Repeats: 1986 +
Executive Producer: Robert L. Rosen
Producers: Romeo Muller, Fred Wolf, Charles Swenson
Director: Charles Swenson
Writer/Lyrics: Romeo Muller
Music: Stephen Lawrence, David Campbell
Company: Muller-Rosen Productions in association with Murakami-
   Wolf-Swenson Films
Distributor: Sunbow Productions/1987–
Home Video: Family Home Entertainment

Narrator
Wizard of Oz   Sid Caesar

Principal Characters and Voices
Dorothy   Mischa Bond
Jack Pumpkinhead/Tyrone, the
   Terrible Toy Tinker   Robert Ridgely
Tik-Tok/Ozma, Queen of Oz   Joan Gerber
Hungry Tiger   Frank Nelson
U.N. Krust   Sid Caesar
Aunt Em   Lurene Tuttle
Uncle Henry   Charles Woolf
Toto (Dorothy's Dog)

Thanksgiving in the Land of Oz brought back the pigtailed little girl
who was carried away with her dog Toto in a hot-air balloon to the
imaginary land.   In her further adventures, she encountered some
new friends and had a showdown with a new villain, all backed by a
new musical score.   Since the Wicked Witch of the West had been
"liquidated," Tyrone, the Terrible Toy Tinker, in his megalomaniac
lust for power, created new evils for the spunky 9-year-old to overcome in his attempt to take control of Winkle Country, a community
in Oz.   Along with her friends the Lion (no longer a coward), the
Tin Man and the Scarecrow, she battled Tyrone, his toy-soldier bat-
talion and his hench-thing, the giant Green Gobbler, a balloon in
the shape of a turkey which Tyrone had brought to life.   During her
formidable task, several of the lesser known characters in L. Frank
Baum's works were woven into the story, including Jack Pumpkinhead; the Hungry Tiger; Tik-Tok, the wind-up mechanical man; Ozma,
the Queen of Oz; and another creation, U.N. Krust, a living, talking mince pie that used a different dialect every time he minced his
words.   Songs: "Oz Can Be," "Beans in Your Button," "Christmas
Toys and Oz."
   Only the CBS premiere was titled Thanksgiving in the Land of
Oz.   The musical special carried the recommendation of the National
Educational Association.

THANKSGIVING THAT ALMOST WASN'T, THE

<u>Broadcast History</u>
    Premiere: November 1972
    SYN/local station option
Executive Producers: William Hanna, Joseph Barbera
Associate Producer: Alex Lovy
Director: Charles A. Nichols
Writers: Ken Spears, Joe Ruby
Music: Hoyt Curtin, Paul DeKorte
Company: Hanna-Barbera Productions
Distributor: Worldvision Enterprises/1979-

<u>Principal Characters and Voices</u>

Johnny Cooke	Bobby Riha
Little Bear	Kevin Cooper
Janie/Mom/Mary Cooke	Marilyn Mayne
Jimmy/Son Squirrel/Mom	
Squirrel	June Foray
Jeremy Squirrel/Dad	Hal Smith
Dad Squirrel/Francis Cooke/	
Indian (Massasoit)	Vic Perrin
Wolf/Rabbit/Sparrow #1	Don Messick
Sparrow #2	John Stephenson

<u>The Thanksgiving That Almost Wasn't</u> relied upon Jeremy Squirrel to prevent disaster for the Pilgrims, who had endured a year of hardships and triumphs and planned to rejoice with their first Thanksgiving feast. Living in a tree above the settlement in Plymouth Colony, Jeremy scampered off into the woods to search for Johnny Cooke, a Pilgrim boy, and Little Bear, son of an Indian, discovered missing by their parents. He soon located the boys in a clearing, lost while playing hunter and chasing some imaginary wolves (which turned out to be chipmunks), arguing over which direction they should take out of the forest. Leaving them in the care of his small forest friends, Jeremy set out to look for the search party. Meanwhile, the rambunctious youngsters continued their game, unaware they were being stalked by a real timberwolf that soon pursued them ferociously up the side of a cliff. Alerted by a small sparrow that had been watching the boys and led by Jeremy, the search party set off to rescue the pair. Reaching the cornered lads, the Pilgrims were afraid to fire at the wolf for fear of hitting them, and Jeremy rushed to their rescue, biting the wolf's tail. The animal howled in pain and turned to attack Jeremy, who scrambled into a hollow log. Hot in pursuit, the wolf was tightly trapped in the log. Happily, the boys were reunited with their anxious families with Jeremy as guest of honor at their Thanksgiving feast, dining on his own roasted chestnut.

THAT GIRL IN WONDERLAND

Broadcast History
    Premiere: January 13, 1973
    ABC/ABC SATURDAY SUPERSTAR MOVIE, Saturday 9:30-10:30 AM
    ABC/Repeats: 1973-1974
    SYN/Repeats: 1975 +
Producers/Directors: Arthur Rankin, Jr., Jules Bass
Associate Producer: Basil Cox
Writer: Stu Hample
Music: Maury Laws, Jules Bass
Company: Rankin-Bass Productions/60 minutes
Distributor: Viacom Enterprises/1986-

Principal Character and Voice
Ann Marie   Marlo Thomas

Other Voices
    Patricia Bright, Dick Hehmeyer, Rhoda Mann, Ted Schwartz

That Girl in Wonderland featured the voice of Marlo Thomas, in a
spin-off of her prime-time series, That Girl (ABC, 1966-1971), here
portrayed as an editor for a children's book publisher. Daydreaming
while preparing a book of fairy tales, she imagined herself on a whirl
through lands of fantasy and make-believe as the various heroines
of "The Wizard of Oz," "Snow White," "Sleeping Beauty," "Cinderella"
and "Goldilocks." Although the stories became mixed up, the endings
were happy ones.
    The film was originally seen on The ABC Saturday Superstar
Movie (ABC, 1972-1974), described in Children's Television, Part I
(Scarecrow, 1983), pp. 5-7.

THERE'S NO TIME FOR LOVE, CHARLIE BROWN

Broadcast History
    Premiere: March 11, 1973
    CBS/Sunday 7:30-8:00 PM
    Sponsor: Dolly Madison, Coca-Cola
    CBS/Repeat: March 17, 1974
Producers: Lee Mendelson, Bill Melendez
Director: Bill Melendez
Writer/Creator: Charles M. Schulz
Music: Vince Guaraldi, John Scott Trotter
Company: Lee Mendelson-Bill Melendez Productions in association
    with Charles M. Schulz Creative Associates and United Feature
    Syndicate
Home Video: Kartes Video Communications

Principal Characters and Voices
Charlie Brown   Chad Webber

Peppermint Patty	Christopher DeFaria
Lucy Van Pelt	Robin Kohn
Marcie	Jimmy Ahrens
Sally Brown	Hillary Momberger
Franklin	Todd Barbee
Linus Van Pelt	Stephen Shea

There's No Time for Love, Charlie Brown revealed Peppermint Patty's
lingering crush on an unresponsive Charlie. The Peanuts clan was
whirling through a day of essay tests. Sally was uptight and Patty
was discouraged: "Tests to take, reports to write, all those dumb
things to do! There's no time for love, Chuck!" she said. When
the grades came out, Charlie got a "C" in everything. "I'm a
straight 'blah' student," he told Linus. After the teacher announced
a field trip to the art museum, Charlie said, "I have to get an 'A'
on my report or I'll fail the whole course." Marcie was scared to
death of field trips, and Sally was afraid she would get sick on the
bus. True to form, after they arrived, Marcie, Patty and Chuck
got lost, following Snoopy into the Ace Super Market, where they
mistook the displays of stacked cans for pop art. After Marcie accused Patty of being in love with Charlie, Patty falsely denied it:
"How could anyone be in love with boring, dull, wishy-washy Chuck!"
Overhearing the remark, Charlie Brown left dejected. Trying to make
amends, Patty invited him over to write his report, promising to help.
Later he realized, "I wrote a report about a trip to the grocery store.
I'm doomed!" But when the grades were passed out, Charlie had
the only "A" in the class. "Your analogy comparing the museum to
a supermarket was a stroke of genius," said Linus. Again Patty offered apologies for her remarks, but Charlie only expressed thoughts
of the Little Red-Haired Girl. "I can't stand you, Chuck!" Patty
yelled. "Well sir, you said the wrong thing again, didn't you?" said
Marcie.

THIS IS YOUR LIFE, DONALD DUCK

Broadcast History
    Premiere: March 11, 1960
    ABC/WALT DISNEY PRESENTS, Friday 7:30-8:30 PM
    NBC/Repeats: THE WONDERFUL WORLD OF DISNEY, February
        13, 1977; NBC SPECIAL PRESENTATION, February 22, 1980,
        Friday 8:00-9:00 PM
Producer: Walt Disney
Directors: Jack Hannah, C. August Nichols, Jack Kinney
Writers: Albert Bertino, Dave Detiege, Nick George
Music: Joseph S. Dubin
Company: Walt Disney Television/60 minutes

Host
Jiminy Cricket   Cliff Edwards

Principal Character and Voice
Donald Duck   Clarence Nash

This Is Your Life, Donald Duck followed the format of the popular
show created by Ralph Edwards, This Is Your Life (NBC, 1952-1961),
featuring a surprise guest of honor who was transported to the studio
where his life story was presented. In this instance, Donald's nephews Huey, Dewey and Louie overwhelmed their uncle and dragged
him off to sit onstage in the chair of honor. Host Jiminy Cricket
began Donald's life story at the beginning--with Donald coming out
of an egg squawking. In cartoon flashbacks, a young Donald played
hookey with his alter-ego, a devil-Donald, in Donald's Better Self
(1938); pedaled his new bicycle into trouble as a delivery boy in
Donald's Lucky Day (1938); and created chaos as an Army recruit
and paratrooper, falling into the General's headquarters, in Donald
Gets Drafted (1942) and Sky Trooper (1942). Donald relived his
first civilian job, coping with the chipmunks and the elephant Dolores
at the zoo in Working For Peanuts (1953), and had a humiliating in-
troduction to show business reciting a poem in Mickey's Amateurs
(1937). Signed to a Disney contract, Donald made his first appearance in a "Bee" picture, noted Jiminy, battling with his co-star in
Bee at the Beach (1950). Lastly, Jiminy asked why Donald had never
married, and Daisy produced a book explaining the whole story,
from Donald's Diary (1954). At the close, Donald's cartoon friends
joined him onstage, singing, "For He's a Jolly Good Fellow."
      Aired as a NBC special in 1980, This Is Your Life, Donald
Duck was originally an episode of the prime-time series of Walt Disney, described in Children's Television, Part II (Scarecrow, 1985),
pp. 542-547.

THREE MUSKETEERS, THE

Broadcast History
    Premiere: November 23, 1973
    CBS/FAMOUS CLASSIC TALES, Friday 4:30-5:30 PM
    Sponsor: Kenner Products (Toy Group, General Mills)
    CBS/Repeats: November 28, 1974; November 22, 1979
    SYN/Repeats: 1975 +
Producers: William Hanna, Joseph Barbera
Associate Producer: Zoran Janjic
Director: Peter Luschwitz
Writer: Draper Lewis
Music: Bob Young, Hoyt Curtin
Company: Hanna-Barbera Productions, Sydney, Australia/60 minutes
Distributor: Worldvision Enterprises/1979-
Home Video: Worldvision

Voices
    James Condon, Neil Fitzpatrick, Barbara Frawley, Ron Haddrick,
    Jane Harders, John Martin, Richard Meikle

The Three Musketeers was based on the best known historical novel
(1844) by Alexandre Dumas, père, describing the exploits of Athos,
Porthos, Aramis and their protégé d'Artagnan of Monsieur de Tré-
ville's regiment. Set in France in 1625 against the rich background
of the reign of Louis XIII, it centered around the antagonism between
the deceitful and ruthless Cardinal de Richelieu and Queen Anne
d'Autriche. The loyal protectors of King Louis and Queen Anne,
the Musketeers foiled the Cardinal's plan to divide the royal powers
through his plot to prove to Louis XIII that Queen Ann was conspir-
ing against his throne with the English, specifically the Duke of
Buckingham, culminated by their recovery of the queen's diamonds
in time for the royal costume ball.

THUNDERCATS

Broadcast History
    Premiere: 1985
    SYN/local station option (WTAF, Philadelphia, January 27, 1985,
        Sunday 8:00-9:00 PM; WNEW, New York, February 1, 1985, Fri-
        day 5:00-6:00 PM)
Executive Producers: Arthur Rankin, Jr., Jules Bass
Producer: Lee Dannacher
Director/Pacific Animation: Masaki Iizuka
Writer: Leonard Starr
Music: Bernard Hoffer
Company: Rankin-Bass Productions in association with Pacific Anima-
    tion, Tokyo, Japan/60 minutes
Distributor: Lorimar Syndication/1985–

Principal Characters and Voices
Lion-O/Jackalman	Larry Kenney
Snarf/S-S-Slithe	Robert McFadden
Cheetara/Wilykit	Lynne Lipton
Panthro	Earle Hyman
Wilykat/Monkian/Tygra	Peter Newman
Mumm-Ra/Vultureman/Jaga	Earl Hammond

ThunderCats took place in the distant future when mankind was extinct and a band of feline-like humanoids landed on Third Earth,
bringing with them the laws and ideals of their doomed planet Thun-
DERa, located far beyond any known galaxy. They were Jaga, the
wise; Tygra, the invisible; Cheetara, the quick; Wilykat and Wilykit,
a cunning junior duo; Panthro, the deadly; and Snarf. All were
sworn to serve their young Lord Lion-O and to instruct him in the
secrets of the "Eye of ThunDERa" imbedded in the hilt of the Sword
of Omens, the source of the ThunderCats power. When he raised
the sword with the incantation, "Thunder-Thunder-Thunder Thunder-
Cats Ho!" a beam of light streaked from the hilt and projected the
ThunderCat logo in the sky. Using the weapon, which grew in
length and strength, in his first encounter Lion-O defeated Mumm-Ra

THUNDERCATS. © 1984, Telepictures Corporation and Rankin/Bass Productions, Inc. Courtesy of Rankin/Bass Productions.

("Where evil exists, Mumm-Ra lives"), who had transformed himself into a fearsome warrior from another age. An ageless devil-priest, Mumm-Ra formed an unholy alliance with the hideous Mutants, who pursued the ThunderCats to Third Earth, determined to possess the "Eye" for their own evil purposes. From the planet Plun-Darr, led by the reptilian S-S-Slithe, the Mutants resembled frogmen, jackal-men, monkeymen and vulturemen.

The special was telecast prior to the distribution of the half-hour, 65-episode weekday strip-series, ThunderCats (SYN, 1985-   ) and based on characters created by Ted Wolf.

THUNDERCATS HO!

Broadcast History
    Premiere: 1986

SYN/local station option (KTTV, Los Angeles, October 4, 1986, Saturday 2:00-4:00 PM PST)
Executive Producers: Arthur Rankin, Jr., Jules Bass
Producer: Lee Dannacher
Director/Pacific Animation: Masaki Iizuka
Writer: Leonard Starr
Music: Bernard Hoffer
Company: Rankin-Bass Productions in association with Pacific Animation, Tokyo, Japan/120 minutes
Distributor: Lorimar Syndication/1986-

Principal Characters and Voices

Lion-O/Jackalman	Larry Kenney
Lynx-O/Snarf/S-S-Slithe	Robert McFadden
Cheetara/Wilykit	Lynne Lipton
Panthro	Earle Hyman
Wilykat/Monkian/Ben-Gali/Tygra	Peter Newman
Mumm-Ra/Vultureman/Jaga	Earl Hammond
Pumyra	Gerrianne Raphael

ThunderCats Ho! featured the heroic feline characters who once again squared off with their archenemy Mumm-Ra. In this special two-hour made-for-TV movie, which inaugurated a second season of the episodic series, the ThunderCats discovered via Cheetara's trance that other ThunDERians were saved from their erupting planet, including Pumyra, Lynx-O (who overcame his blindness by developing special powers) and Ben-Gali. Meantime, Mumm-Ra employed the evil Ma-Mut to search out and destroy the new ThunDERians and made a deal with a roving band of troublemakers, led by Hammerhand, called the Berserkers, who had a powerful weapon in their Skull-Head Rays. When the ThunDERians were captured by Mumm-Ra, Lion-O and his friends rescued their colleagues after a series of conflicts with Mumm-Ra's various formidable henchmen, including S-S-Slithe in his Sky-Cutter, using two new vehicles, the Thunder Claw and HoverCat. At the close, Lynx-O, Pumyra and Ben-Gali were inducted into the official family of ThunderCats.

Following its telecast, the film was edited into a five-part half-hour miniseries, later added to the existing 65-episode series, ThunderCats (SYN, 1985-).

TIN SOLDIER, THE

Broadcast History
    Premiere: December 13, 1986
    CTV/Saturday 7:30-8:00 PM
    SYN/Repeats: 1987 +
Executive Producers: Alison Clayton, David Grimes
Producer: William H. Stevens, Jr.
Director: Rick Morrison
Writers: Alan Templeton, Mary Crawford

Music: Gary Morton
Company: Atkinson Film-Arts, Ottawa, Canada, in association with Telefilm Canada and CTV
Distributor: Crawley's International ("Cartoon Classics")/1986-
Home Video: Hi-Tops Video (nee Media Home Entertainment)

Narrator: Christopher Plummer

Principal Characters and Voices

Fred	Terrence Scammell
Sam	Pier Kohl
Boy	Adam Hodgins
Lefty/Rat #1/Rat #3	Rick Jones
King Rat/Rat #2/Rat #4	Robert Bockstael

The Tin Soldier was based on Hans Christian Andersen's story of the one-legged Tin Soldier and the Music Box Ballerina. This updated version featured Fred and Sam, two charming little mice who befriended the Tin Soldier. The film was one of several in a new series of "Cartoon Classics" produced by Atkinson Film-Arts.

TINY TREE, THE

Broadcast History
    Premiere: December 14, 1975
    NBC/BELL SYSTEM FAMILY THEATRE, Sunday 7:30-8:00 PM
    Sponsor: Bell Telephone System
    NBC/Repeat: December 12, 1976
    ABC/Repeat: December 18, 1977
    CBS/Repeats: December 16, 1978; December 19, 1979
    SYN/Repeats: 1980 +
Executive Producers: David H. DePatie, Friz Freleng
Producer/Director: Chuck Couch
Writers: Chuck Couch, Bob Ogle, Lewis Marshall
Music/Songs & Lyrics: Johnny Marks
Music: Dean Elliott
Company: DePatie-Freleng Enterprises
Distributor: Fremantle International/1980-

Narrator

Squire Badger	Buddy Ebsen

Principal Characters and Voices

Hawk	Allan Melvin
Turtle	Paul Winchell
Lady Bird/Little Girl	Janet Waldo
Boy Bunny/Girl Raccoon	Stephen Manley
Groundhog/Father Bird/Beaver/ Mole	Frank Welker

Vocalist, Roberta Flack

The Tiny Tree was related by Buddy Ebsen as Squire Badger to two young bunnies. A tale of love and sharing all year around, it was about a small Whispering Pine in a meadow and its circle of animals who befriended a lonely little farm-girl in a wheelchair. Cheered and loved by the animals, the crippled child enjoyed their friendship as the seasons passed into winter. Then in a snowstorm, while trying to save the mole from the hunger-crazed hawk, the kindly girl fell out of her wheelchair but was rescued by the animals who tucked her in bed. The blizzard threatened to prevent her father's return with a tree and her presents in time for Christmas. To ensure the despondent girl's holiday was a happy one, the young sapling that woodsmen said was only good enough to be a Christmas tree decided to be one. Led by the mole, the animals moved the tiny tree opposite her window on Christmas Eve. As the Christmas Star illuminated the decorated tree, the girl left her bed, limped hesitantly to the window and smiled. Songs: "The Tiny Tree," "To Love and Be Loved," "When Autumn Comes" (Flack), "Tell It to a Turtle" (Winchell), "A Caroling We Go" (Animals).

Featuring a top-notch score, this exceptionally fine heart-tugging film, created by Chuck Couch with characters developed by Louis Schmitt, was the first of only two animated specials aired on all three networks. The other was Winnie the Pooh and Tigger Too [q.v.].

TO THE RESCUE

Broadcast History
  Premiere: 1975
  SYN/local station option
Producers: Art Clokey, Ruth Clokey
Directors: Art Clokey, Raymond Peck
Writer: Nancy Moore
Music: John Seely, Patricia Beck
Company: Clokey Productions for the Lutheran Church in America
Distributor: Department of Telecommunications, Lutheran Church
  in America/1985-

Principal Characters and Voices
Davey Hanson/Sally Hanson/	
Mary Hanson	Norma McMillan/Nancy Wible
Goliath/John Hanson	Hal Smith

To The Rescue, set during summer vacation at Roaring River Camp, galvanized a group of discordant youngsters into a coordinated rescue squad during an emergency. Davey, his dog Goliath and his friends set off on a hike through dense forest to rescue a man and his daughter from the wreckage of a light airplane. The grateful pilot called them "quite a team" as they produced medical supplies, tended to the injured pair, improvised a stretcher and moved them to the nearest road and a waiting ambulance. Meanwhile, the young friends, who were often at odds during earlier camp experiences, learned a basic lesson about interdependence. One of six specials featuring Davey and Goliath, a large brown canine that talked, the stop-motion animated puppet films focused on demonstrations of Christian living.

TOM SAWYER

Broadcast History
    Premiere: February 25, 1973
    SYN/FESTIVAL OF FAMILY CLASSICS, WABC, New York, Sunday
        7:00-7:30 PM
    SYN/Repeats: 1973 +
Producers/Directors: Arthur Rankin, Jr., Jules Bass
Associate Producer: Mary Alice Dwyer
Writer: Bob Littell
Music: Maury Laws, Jules Bass
Company: Rankin-Bass Productions
Distributor: Viacom Enterprises ("Family Classics")/1986-
Home Video: Prism

Tom Sawyer captured the fun and excitement of growing up along the Mississippi River in pre-Civil War days. Narrated by Mark Twain as an animated character, the film related Tom's famous fence-painting episode and his adventures with Becky Sharpe while exploring a cave, where they came upon the desperado Injun Joe and his treasure chest of gold coins. Believing the pair lost forever, Aunt Polly, Huckleberry Finn and the other townsfolk were gathered at the church to pay their last respects. Escaping through a secret tunnel, the youngsters returned in time to attend their own funeral. Later, Tom and Huck retrieved the treasure and the newly-rich pair became "country gentlemen."

TRAVELS OF MARCO POLO, THE see MARCO POLO

TREASURE ISLAND

Broadcast History
    Premiere: November 28, 1971
    CBS/FAMOUS CLASSIC TALES, Sunday 5:00-6:00 PM
    Sponsor: Kenner Products (Toy Group, General Mills)
    CBS/Repeats: October 29, 1972; December 1, 1973
    SYN/Repeats: 1974 +
Executive Producer: Walter J. Hucker
Director: Zoran Janjic
Writer: Michael Robinson
Music: John Sangster
Company: Air Programs International, Sydney, Australia/60 minutes

Distributor: D. L. Taffner ("Animated Classics for Children")/1985-
Home Video: Classics for Kids (MGM/UA)

Voices
  Ron Haddrick, John Kingley, John Llewellyn, Bruce Montague,
  Brenda Senders, Colin Tilley

Treasure Island was an hour-long straightforward adaptation of the
1883 childhood tale by Robert Louis Stevenson. It concerned Captain
Flint's treasure map, discovered in the papers of Captain Bones at
the Admiral Benbow Inn by young Jim Hawkins. Jim outwitted Bones'
former confederates, who were seeking the map, and gave it to
Squire Trelawney. In search of the booty, Jim sailed as cabinboy
with Trelawney and Doctor Livesay aboard the Hispaniola, commanded
by Captain Smollett, with the majority of the crew, old buccanneers,
recruited by the one-legged pirate Long John Silver, the ship's cook.
The crew's plan to seize the ship and kill the Squire's party was
overheard by Jim, and after a series of fierce fights, harrowing escapes and adventures it was completely thwarted. After the Squire
secured the treasure with the help of Jim's friend Ben Gunn, a
marooned pirate who had long before looted the cache, and heeded
Jim's plea for Silver's life, they set sail to the West Indies, where
Silver escaped, and eventually returned to England with the treasure.

TREASURE ISLAND

Broadcast History
    Premiere: April 29, 1980
    NBC/NBC SPECIAL TREAT, Tuesday 4:00-5:00 PM
    NBC/Repeat: January 31, 1981
    SYN/Repeats: 1982 +
Executive Producer: Jacqueline Smith
Producers: Louis Scheimer, Norman Prescott
Director: Hal Sutherland
Music: George Blais
Company: Flimation in association with Warner Bros. Television/60
    minutes
Distributor: Warner Bros. Television Distribution/1986-

Hostess: Melissa Sue Anderson

Principal Characters and Voices

Long John Silver	Richard Dawson
Captain Flint	Larry Storch
Jim Hawkins	Davy Jones
Squire Trelawney	Larry D. Mann
Mother	Jane Webb
Parrot	Dal McKennon
Hiccup the Mouse	

TREASURE ISLAND. © 1974, Warner Bros., Inc. Courtesy of Warner Bros. Television.

Treasure Island added some new characterizations to the familiar cast in this musical version of the 1883 children's tale by Robert Louis Stevenson. Young Jim Hawkins was paired with Hiccup the Mouse, who first tried to obtain the treasure map for himself and, running for his life, was saved by Jim. Aboard the Hispaniola, Hiccup led Jim to his hiding place in the apple barrel, and on the island he saved Jim's life. There were also some unusual members of the pirate crew; Eins, Zwei and Drei, who moved and talked in unison; Musica, who talked through a swallowed harmonica; and Big Ben, who dangled a bell from his earlobe. And salty old seaman Ben Gunn, who lived in the island cave with the retrieved treasure of Captain Flint, always talked backwards. Songs: "Fifteen Men on a Dead Man's Chest," "Find the Boy/Find the Mouse and We Find the Map," "Proper Punishment."

Briefly released as a 75-minute movie in November 1972 by Warner Bros., the film was reedited for television.

TREASURE ISLAND REVISITED

Broadcast History
    Premiere: 1972

SYN/local station option (WGN, Chicago, February 20, 1972, Sunday 5:30-6:30 PM CST)
SYN/Repeats: 1973 +
Producer: Hiroshi Okawa
Director: Yasuo Mori
Writer: Hirosha Ikeda
Company: American International Television in association with Toei Animation, Tokyo, Japan, and Titan Productions/60 minutes
Home Video: Congress Video

Treasure Island Revisited was an anthropomorphic version of the tale by Robert Louis Stevenson with cast members depicted as various creatures. For instance, Long John Silver was a pig, and young Jim Hawkins had a bespectacled rat as a companion. It also paired a young boy and girl competing with the pirates to locate the hidden treasure.
    Made for Japanese audiences, the film was acquired by AIP, reedited and dubbed into English by Titan Productions.

TROLLS AND THE CHRISTMAS EXPRESS, THE

Broadcast History
    Premiere: December 9, 1981
    HBO/Wednesday 5:30-6:00 PM
    HBO/Repeats: multiple option, 1981-1990
Executive Producer: Sheldon Sachs
Producers: Beryl Friesen, William H. Stevens, Jr.
Associate Producer: John Nyhuus
Directors: Vic Atkinson, John R. Gaug
Writers: Mel Waskin, J. William Walker
Music: Hagood Hardy
Lyrics: Beryl Friesen
Company: Titlecraft with Atkinson Film-Arts, Ottawa, Canada
Distributor: Crawleys International ("Cartoon Classics")/1986-
Home Video: Paramount

Narrator: Roger Miller

Principal Character and Voice
Troglo   Hans Conreid

Other Voices
    Carl Banas, Len Carlson, Paul Soles, Billie Mae Richards

The Trolls and the Christmas Express hinged on several plots to ruin Christmas that were foiled by Santa's elves. Six roguish Trolls, led by Troglo, infiltrated Santa's village disguised as elves to stop the delivery of toys on Christmas day. They joined the assembly line and created havoc, magically making dogs "meow," dolls "bark," cats say "mama," and building doll houses upside down and equipping bicycles with square wheels. Oblivious to the sabotage, the hard-working elves doggedly corrected all the mistakes, frustrating the Trolls' goal. So Troglo came up with another devious scheme to keep the reindeer up all night swaying and stomping in a country-music romp. The next morning the reindeer were too exhausted to pull Santa's sleigh. Christmas seemed ruined as the gloating Trolls began slipping out of the village, ecstactic about their success. Meldin, the chief elf, momentarily saved the day when he suggested rerouting the village train to connect the North Pole with all the railroads in the world. But as the elves were laying track, the Trolls diverted it in a circle. Santa spotted the imposters, exposed them and learned that they had decided to mess up Christmas because they sought revenge, "Because nobody likes Trolls. Everybody hates us!" The Trolls exhibited a change of heart, however, after Melkin sang the opening verse of "Deck the Halls," bringing to their attention the line, "troll the ancient Yuletide Carol." Convinced they should be part of Christmas again, the Trolls, elves and Santa joined together on the Christmas Express to bring joy to children around the world. The original concept was developed by Coronet Films, a division of Esquire magazine. Songs: "Trolls Song," "Deck the Halls," "Christmas Express" (Miller).

TROUBLE WITH MISS SWITCH, THE

Broadcast History
  Premiere: February 16 & 23, 1980
  ABC/ABC WEEKEND SPECIALS, Saturday 12:00-12:30 PM
  ABC/Repeats: May 31 & June 7, 1980; September 13 & 20, 1980;
    April 18 & 25, 1981; July 3 & 10, 1982; January 22 & 29, 1983;
    May 25 & June 1, 1985
Executive Producers: Joe Ruby, Ken Spears
Producer: Jerry Eisenberger
Director: Charles A. Nichols
Writer: Sheldon Stark
Music: Dean Elliott
Company: Ruby-Spears Enterprises/60 minutes, 2 parts

Principal Characters and Voices

Miss Switch	Janet Waldo
Rupert P. Brown III ("Rupe")	Eric Taslitz
Amelia Matilda Daley	Nancy McKeon
Bathsheba/Saturna	June Foray

Other Voices
  Alan Dinehart, Phillip Tanzini, Frank Welker

The Trouble With Miss Switch was a tale of magic and adventure. In Part I, noticing that Miss Switch, his new teacher, cleared an entire blackboard with one swoop of the eraser and seemed to have other mystical powers, Rupert, a 10-year-old whose passion for science did not allow for mysteries, decided to return to his classroom one evening to search for clues to her magic. There he met Amelia, a snoopy 10-year-old girl, and together they spotted Miss Switch dressed as a witch in a black gown and tall, pointed hat. She had been waiting for them as she needed their help. Miss Switch explained that she was a good witch who faced banishment to the Dead Forest by the bad head-witch Saturna because her witchcraft was out of date. She had to come up with a new idea in 24 hours. Rupe suggested she could help their school, Pepperdine, win its first football game against their arch rival, Dinwiddie, but Saturna fixed her spell so it wouldn't work. Against her best judgment, Rupe then convinced Miss Switch to take them to Witch Mountain to present their case before Saturna and the comput-o-witch.

In Part II, Saturna sent her bats to intercept Miss Switch and the children to keep them from reaching Witch Mountain. While enroute through the Dead Forest, Miss Switch's broomstick was broken by the bats, who finally succeeded in seizing and imprisoning her cat Bathsheba and the children in an abandoned well. They carted Miss Switch off to the Witches' Council to stand adjudged by the comput-o-witch. Escaping from the well, the children and Bathsheba mended Miss Switch's broomstick, which carried them to the meeting. There Rupert presented his argument that Miss Switch was a good and fair teacher who had practiced some remarkably innovative witchcraft by motivating the children's interest in going to school, where she had made learning fun, which no one else had done as well before. After delivering a "not guilty" verdict, the comput-o-witch blew up. Briefly returning to school, Miss Switch finally decided to leave for Witch Mountain; Saturna had been banished, and the Council had made her head witch. The specials were based on the eponymous book (Abingdon, 1971) by Barbara Brooks Wallace and prompted a sequel, Miss Switch to the Rescue [q.v.].

TUKIKI AND HIS SEARCH FOR A MERRY CHRISTMAS

Broadcast History
    Premiere: December 24, 1979
    CBC/Monday 7:30-8:00 PM
    SYN/Repeats: 1980 +
Producers: Beryl Friesen, William H. Stevens, Jr.
Associate Producer: John Nyhuus
Directors: Vic Atkinson, Pino Van Lamsweerde
Writer: Christine Atkinson
Music: Hagood Hardy
Lyrics: Beryl Friesen
Company: Titlecraft with Atkinson Film-Arts, Ottawa, Canada, in
    association with CBC
Distributor: Crawleys International ("Cartoon Classics")/1980-
Home Video: Congress Video

Principal Characters and Voices
Tukiki   Adam Rich
Northwind   Sterling Holloway

Other Voices
  Sharon Burke, Bob Dermer, Fred Little, Bill Luxton, Bernard
  McManus, Richard Perigrine, Lee St. Louis, Noreen Young

Vocalist: Stephanie Taylor

Tukiki and His Search for a Merry Christmas related the Christmas
Eve fantasy of an Eskimo boy who traveled to celebrations around
the world with his friend Northwind to discover the meaning of "Merry
Christmas." Intrigued by the cheerful greeting on a Christmas card
blown in on the wind, Tukiki first asked his Arctic friends Walrus,
Polar Bear, Caribou and Muskox if they knew the meaning, but they
were too busy with their own selfish problems to help him. Muskox,
however, suggested that Tukiki seek advice from the Northwind.
Tukiki was given a rhyming riddle to solve and was carried on Northwind's back to countries with varying cultures and customs: together
they tumbled down the chimney in a Dutch house where the toys came
alive; befriended a lively animated flute in Africa; encountered a trio
of fast-talking Tomtars in Sweden; and with the aid of a shy, ever-
changing old chameleon, participated with other Mexican children in
the joy of Navidad. After flying over North America, past churches,
ships and towns twinkling with the lights of Christmas, home again,
Tukiki found nothing had changed until he gave his friends the gifts
he brought back. Through Tukiki's thoughtfulness and act of love,
gone was the selfishness, sadness and discord and harmony reigned.
Seeking Northwind to thank him, Tukiki discovered only his coat
and hat, but from a far off star a distant voice asked if he found
the meaning of Christmas. Declaring he knew the answer to the
riddle, Tukiki responded and the sky exploded into a brilliant display of Northern Lights. Song: "Tukiki" (Taylor). Animation award
(1980), Children's Broadcast Institute, Canada.

TURKEY CAPER, THE

Broadcast History
  Premiere: 1985
  SYN/local station option (KCBS, Los Angeles, November 28, 1985,
    Thursday 7:30-8:00 PM PST)
  Sponsor: Tonka Toys
  SYN/Repeats: 1986 +
Producers/Directors: Bill Hutten, Tony Love
Writer: John Bates
Music: Larry Fotine
Company: Encore Enterprises
Distributor: Muller Media/1985-

Principal Characters and Voices

Rusty/Rosie	Kathy Ritter
Buttons	Barbara Goodson
Ranger Jones	Bill Boyett
Abner	Alvy Moore
George	Bill Ratner
Bridgett	Morgan Lofting

The Turkey Caper began in a flashback covering the traditions of Thanksgiving as Ranger Jones read a story about the first Thanksgiving to the bear cub Buttons and young fox Rusty. Later, in the forest, Buttons and Rusty encountered Priscilla and Marty, two young turkeys, and learned that all the wild turkeys in the forest had been captured. Deciding to help, the youngsters rescued the gobblers and concealed them in new storage sheds built by Button's father, Abner. Panic and bedlam ensued when a surprised Abner discovered all the wild turkeys in his cave, and it was up to the reliable Ranger Jones to resolve the problem. Of course the turkeys were saved to spend their days in the forest as Buttons, Rusty, their parents and Jones joined in a thankful celebration. Song/Theme: "Togetherness."

The film was the third of the Rusty and Buttons specials following their debut in The Christmas Tree Train [q.v.].

'TWAS THE NIGHT BEFORE CHRISTMAS

Broadcast History
Premiere: December 8, 1974
CBS/Sunday 8:00-8:30 PM
Sponsor: McDonald's (1985, 1986)
CBS/Repeats: December 9, 1975; December 17, 1976; December 12, 1977; December 18, 1978; December 8, 1979; December 13, 1980; December 16, 1981; December 18, 1982; December 14, 1983; December 11, 1984; December 4, 1985; December 17, 1986
Producers/Directors: Arthur Rankin, Jr., Jules Bass
Writer: Jerome Coopersmith
Music: Maury Laws
Lyrics: Jules Bass
Company: Rankin-Bass Productions with animation by Toru Hara and Tsuquyuki Kubo

Narrator

Joshua Trundel, the Clock-maker	Joel Grey

Principal Characters and Voices

Albert Mouse	Tammy Grimes
Mayor of Junctionville	John McGiver
Father Mouse	George Gobel

'TWAS THE NIGHT BEFORE CHRISTMAS. © 1974, Rankin/Bass Productions, Inc. Courtesy of Rankin/Bass Productions.

Other Voices
   Patricia Bright, Scott Firestone, Robert McFadden, Allen Swift, Christine Winter

Vocalists: The Wee Winter Singers

'Twas the Night Before Christmas, a sort of "Upstairs/Downstairs" look at events culminating on that night, zeroed in on the Trundle family, living above their clockshop, and the Mouse family, living below. "Not a creature was stirring, not even a mouse," but both Joshua Trundle and Father Mouse were unable to sleep, for there was big trouble this Christmas in Junctionville. In a flashback, Father Mouse's children were confused and disappointed when their letters to Santa Claus were returned marked, "Not Accepted by Addressee!" Indeed, the letters from every child in the village were returned, and they wanted to know why Santa cancelled his annual visit. Phoning Santa's company, Father Mouse reached a mouse-secretary who informed him that Santa was upset over an unsigned letter in the Junctionville Register, calling the old gent a phony myth. After some thought Father Mouse found the culprit, Albert Mouse, his college-age son, who rattled off his scientific reasons. Meantime, Mr. Trundel presented the Mayor with a model clock that played a song to welcome Santa, believing it would reaffirm their true affection for him. The Mayor authorized construction of the clock, but once completed it failed to work due to Albert Mouse, who had climbed into the mechanism. Repentant and making amends, Albert set about repairing the clock while Father Mouse informed Mr. Trundel what had happened. In the St. Nick of time, as the clock struck twelve on Christmas Eve, the chimes rang out the tune. Suddenly, "out on the lawn there arose such a clatter," as the townfolk and town-mice esctatically celebrated the arrival of Santa, lyrically described by the remainder of the ballad. The fifth Yuletide classic following Frosty the Snowman [q.v.], the film was loosely based on Clement Moore's Christmas poem. Songs: "Even a Miracle Needs a Hand," "Silent Night," "Christmas Chimes," "Give Your Heart a Try," " 'Twas the Night Before Christmas."

20,000 LEAGUES UNDER THE SEA

Broadcast History
      Premiere: October 1 & 8, 1972
      SYN/FESTIVAL OF FAMILY CLASSICS, WABC, New York, Sunday
          7:00-7:30 PM
      SYN/Repeats: 1973 +
Producers/Directors: Arthur Rankin, Jr., Jules Bass
Associate Producer: Mary Alice Dwyer
Writer: Richard Neubert
Music: Maury Laws, Jules Bass
Company: Rankin-Bass Productions/60 minutes, 2 parts
Distributor: Viacom Enterprises ("Family Classics")/1986-
Home Video: Prism 1209

20,000 Leagues Under the Sea, adapted from the classic Jules Verne novel, related the adventures of scientific journalist Pierre Arronax, his 16-year-old assistant Conrad and harpooner Ned Land aboard the Nautilus, which had rammed and seriously damaged their pursuing warship. As "guests" of Captain Nemo, the embittered inventor of the mysterious craft, the trio, along with a friendly dolphin, Fifi, embarked on a fantastic undersea journey to the fabled lost continent of Atlantis and explored the underwater jungle of the Sargasso Sea. In one suspenseful episode, a giant octopus threatened to crush the steel shell of their craft, forcing it to surface so the crewmen and passengers could cut away the enveloping tenacles that endangered the sub and their lives.

20,000 LEAGUES UNDER THE SEA

Broadcast History
      Premiere: November 22, 1973
      CBS/FAMOUS CLASSIC TALES, Thursday 3:30-4:30 PM
      Sponsor: Kenner Products (Toy Group, General Mills)
      CBS/Repeat: November 16, 1974

20,000 LEAGUES UNDER THE SEA. © 1973, Hanna-Barbera Productions, Inc. Courtesy of Hanna-Barbera Productions and TECO.

SYN/Repeats: 1975 +
HBO/Repeats: multiple option, 1986-
Producers/Directors: William Hanna, Joseph Barbera
Associate Producer: Zoran Janjic
Director: Peter Luschwitz
Writer: Draper Lewis
Music: Hoyt Curtin, Paul DeKorte
Company: Hanna-Barbera Productions, Sydney, Australia/60 minutes
Distributor: Worldvision Enterprises/1979-
Home Video: Worldvision

Voices
Tim Elliott, Ron Haddrick, Don Pascoe, John Stephenson

20,000 Leagues Under the Sea added a new ecology theme in this version based on the 1869 novel by Jules Verne, which introduced the submarine in fantasy literature. It began in the harbors along the New England coast in 1866, where a giant sea monster, rumored to be a mammoth artic narwhal with a twisted tusk like a unicorn, was roaming the oceans, sinking whalers and fishing trawlers. The Abraham Lincoln, a U.S. Navy frigate commanded by Captain Farragut, was sent to find the marauder by the President of the United States, who enlisted the help of a marine research authority, Professor Pierre Aronnax. Also aboard was famous harpooner Ned Land. After a year of searching, one foggy night the monster with huge glowing eyes approached the ship. Land's harpoon bent and bounced off its back. Turning about, the creature hit the ship, throwing Land and Aronnax into the sea. Dragged unconscious under the water, they awoke in an iron ship, the submarine Nautilus, commanded by Captain Nemo, to learn there was no giant maurauding narwhal, only the incredible sub which could travel at great speed beneath the sea. A genius with a grievance against the destroyers, the polluters, and the wasteful netters, Nemo had dedicated his life to sinking the whaling ships and trawlers that were decimating the schools of whales and fish, never meant to be harvested and thrown back dead and rotting into the oceans.

2000 YEAR OLD MAN, THE

Broadcast History
Premiere: January 11, 1975
CBS/Saturday 8:30-9:00 PM
CBS/Repeat: April 11, 1975
SYN/Repeats: 1980 +
Producer: Leo Salkin
Director: Dale Case
Writers: Carl Reiner, Mel Brooks
Company: Crossbow Productions and Acre Enterprises in association with Leo Salkin Films
Distributor: Wrightwood Entertainment/1980-

THE 2000 YEAR OLD MAN. © 1974, Leo Salkin Films, Inc. Courtesy of Wrightwood Entertainment, Ltd., as distributor for Brooksfilms Limited.

Record Album: RCA
Home Video: Hi-Tops Video (nee Media Home Entertainment #M711)

Principal Characters and Voices
Commentator   Carl Reiner
2000 Year Old Man   Mel Brooks

The 2000 Year Old Man was developed from the hilarious routines and recording by Carl Reiner and Mel Brooks. Reiner was a commentator and Brooks a 2,000-year-old man from somewhere in the Middle East. Their conversation ranged from the patriarch's notes on the discovery of women and the truth about Robin Hood ("He stole from everybody and kept everything--he just had a good press agent") to the first song and the first language ("Basic rock--about 200 years before Hebrew"). Delivering a barrage of one-liners in a funny, fast-paced cartoon, the ancient sage had advice about living long ("Never run for a bus"); moaned about his 42,000 children ("Not one comes to visit me"); told how he first learned to speak basic Rock ("Hey, don't throw that rock at me! Put that rock down! That was Rock"); knew Joan of Arc ("Ah! What a cutie!"); revealed the greatest thing man has devised in 2,000 years ("Saran Wrap--it clings and it's great. You can look right through it"); and had a farewell address ("Hello dere! ... Keep a smile on your face and stay out of a Ferrari or any small Italian car ... and eat a nectarine. It's the best fruit ever made."). A cartoon special for adults, it was one of the funniest improvisional schticks aired on television up to its time. Using cartoon illustrations, The 2000 Year Old Man (Warner, 1981) was also released as a book.

UNCLE SAM MAGOO

Broadcast History
    Premiere: February 15, 1970
    NBC/Sunday 6:30-7:30 PM
    Sponsor: General Foods
    SYN/Repeats: 1971 +
Executive Producer: Henry G. Saperstein
Producer: Lee Orgel
Director: Abe Levitow
Writer: Larry Markes
Music: Walter Scharf, Eliot Daniel (Chorale)
Company: UPA Pictures/60 minutes
Distributor: UPA Productions of America/1971-
Home Video: Paramount

Principal Characters and Voices

Mr. Magoo	Jim Backus
Uncle Sam/John Alden/Miles Standish/Paul Revere/ Davy Crockett/James Marshall/Johnny Appleseed/ Captain John Parker/Robert E. Lee/Daniel Webster/John F. Kennedy	Lennie Weinrib
Mark Twain/John Sutter/President/Daniel Boone/Patrick Henry/U.S. Grant/Martin Luther King/Abraham Lincoln	Barney Phillips
Indian Chief (American)/Indian Chief (Tropical)/John Smith/ Powhattan/Massasoit/Francis Scott Key/Kit Carson/Paul Bunyan/F. D. Roosevelt/ Harry Truman/Wendell Willkie	Bob Holt
Leif Ericsson/Columbus/Elder Brewster/Tom Paine/Thomas Jefferson/Woodrow Wilson	Dave Shelley
Priscilla/Betsy Ross/Tom Sawyer/Amelia Earhart/Eleanor Roosevelt/Susan B. Anthony	Patti Gilbert
George Washington/Walt Whitman/Oliver Wendell Holmes	John Himes

Dwight D. Eisenhower/Herbert Hoover/Carl Sandburg	Bill Clayton
Benjamin Franklin/Thomas Wolfe/George Washington Carver	Sid Grossfield
Others	Sam Rosen

<u>Uncle Sam Magoo</u> traced the history of the United States through vignettes of great events and men, America's golden legends and heroes, from the landing of the Pilgrims to the landing on the moon. Quincy Magoo found himself in a costume shop dressed as Uncle Sam and rambled along as a roving raconteur, reviewing the founding of America: Ericsson and the Norsemen, Columbus, Paul Revere, and that rocket-filled night in 1812 at Fort McHenry. Magoo was there at the Pilgrims' first Thanksgiving, charging up the hill at San Juan with Teddy Roosevelt, joining the Gold Rush in California, during the building of the transcontinental railroad and fighting wars at home and abroad. Visiting with such illustrious figures as Washington, Ben Franklin, Lincoln, Davy Crockett, Mark Twain, Carl Sandburg, Woodrow Wilson, John F. Kennedy and Martin Luther King, Magoo heard excerpted remarks attributed to them and some fiction about folk heroes Johnny Appleseed and Paul Bunyan. Imaginative graphic styles and a thumping good musical score conveyed an appropriate background to the varied historical epochs. The credits paid special thanks to the Sierra Club, Charles H. Belding and the Country Beautiful Foundation for their help on the "America the Beautiful" sequence.

VELVETEEN RABBIT, THE

Broadcast History
    Premiere: March 9–24, 1985
    PBS/local station option
    PBS/Repeats: 1985 +
Executive Producer: Clay V. Stites
Producer/Director: Mark Sottnick
Associate Producer: Joel Tuber
Writer: Mark Sottnick
Music: George Winston
Company: Rabbit Ears Productions in association with Random House Home Video
Home Video: Random House

Narrator: Meryl Streep

<u>The Velveteen Rabbit</u> used drawings by illustrator David Jorgensen animated by camera movement in this PBS version of the 1922 classic tale written by Margery Williams (Bianco). Narrated by Academy Award-winning actress Meryl Streep with a homey quality, as if a parent were reading the tale to a child, it concerned a velveteen toy

bunny given to a small boy one Christmas and made "real" by love. According to producer Mark Sottnick, "The rabbit grows not by any extraordinary heroic deed--he doesn't put his finger in a wall to save a city, or slay any dragons--but because of the love and attention he freely gives to the boy." And in order to experience the human emotions of happiness and love, the rabbit found he must experience some sadness as well during the stages of his inseparable companionship, abandonment and final independence. One of three animated adaptations of the book, the film was shown during public television's "Festival '85" fund-raising weeks in March 1985.

VELVETEEN RABBIT, THE (or How Toys Become Real)

Broadcast History
    Premiere: April 2, 1985
    CTV/Tuesday 7:30-8:00 PM
    CTV/Repeat: December 10, 1986
    SYN/Repeats: 1985 +
Executive Producer: William H. Stevens, Jr.
Producer: Hugh Campbell
Associate Producer: Alison Clayton
Directors: Pino Van Lamsweerde, Sebastian Grunstra
Writers: Mary Crawford, Alan Templeton
Music/Songs & Lyrics: Alan Templeton
Music: John Harris
Company: Atkinson Film-Arts, Ottawa, Canada, in association with
    Telefilm Canada and CTV
Distributor: Crawleys International ("Cartoon Classics")/ 1985-
Home Video: Family Home Entertainment

Narrator: Christopher Plummer

Principal Characters and Voices
Jones   Don Westwood
Tin Soldier   Jim Bradford
Rabbit #1/Rabbit #2   Rick Jones
Skin Horse   Bernard McManus
Doctor   Eddie Nunn
Fairy Queen   Charity Brown

The Velveteen Rabbit or "How Toys Become Real" was a musical version of Margery Williams Bianco's charming tale about love, committment and childhood. It was about a stuffed rabbit, given to a little boy for Christmas, that soon was relegated to the cupboard with the other toys, most of them of the windup variety. A velveteen toy with a brown-and-white coat and pink satin-lined ears, the rabbit was befriended by a wise old rocking horse who instructed him that he could become real if a child loved him. After being selected by a nanny to be the boy's new playmate, the velveteen rabbit's obstacles on the way to his transformation were the basis for the rest

THE VELVETEEN RABBIT. © 1985, Hanna-Barbera Productions, Inc. Courtesy of Hanna-Barbera Productions, Sydney, Australia, and TECO.

of the sweet classic story.   Songs: "Soldier's Song," "Fairy's Song," "Being Real."

VELVETEEN RABBIT, THE

Broadcast History
    Premiere: April 20, 1985
    ABC/ABC WEEKEND SPECIALS, Saturday 12:00-12:30 PM
    ABC/Repeats: October 19, 1985; December 20, 1986
Producers: Steve Lumley, Buzz Potamkin
Director: Chris Cuddington
Writer: Malcolm Marmorstein
Music: Dean Elliott, Paul DeKorte
Company: Hanna-Barbera Productions, Sydney, Australia (Southern
    Star Productions)

Principal Characters and Voices

Velvee	Chub Bailey
Robert	Josh Rodine
Skin Horse/Nana	Marilyn Lightstone
Father	Peter Cullen
Tug	Bill Scott
Scungilli	Barry Dennen
Spinner	Hal Smith
Mouse	Frank Welker
Brenda	Jodi Carlisle
Harry	Brian Cummings
Mother/Nursery Fairy	Beth Clopton

The Velveteen Rabbit traced the life of a spanking new stuffed toy given to little Robert one Christmas morning. Soon Velvee came to know the other toys in Robert's room, old and new, along with their distinctive personality quirks and little jealousies, all competing for their young owner's love. As the months flew by, Velvee learned to know and love little Robert and, to his utter happiness, became the little boy's favorite plaything. When Robert became seriously ill, Velvee, his eyes no longer shiny and his fur discolored, was threatened with destruction as a discarded outcast. Learning an important and touching lesson in love when he shed a tear, a real tear, he was rescued by the Nursery Fairy, who appeared and transformed him into a real rabbit. The special was based on the book by Margery Williams (Bianco).

VERY MERRY CRICKET, A

Broadcast History
    Premiere: December 14, 1973
    ABC/Friday 8:00-8:30 PM

ABC/Repeats: November 28, 1974; December 5, 1975
SYN/Repeats: c1978 +
Producer/Director/Writer: Chuck Jones
Associate Producers: Joseph Aidlin, John Allen
Music: Dean Elliott
Lyrics: Marian Dern
Music/Violinist: Israel Baker
Company: Chuck Jones Enterprises
Distributor: Berle Adams/1986-
Home Video: Family Home Entertainment VHS 710528

Principal Characters and Voices

Chester C. Cricket/Harry the Cat	Les Tremayne
Tucker the Mouse/Alley Cat	Mel Blanc

A Very Merry Cricket brightened the Big Apple Yuletide when the
Connecticut chirper returned to spread the spirit of Christmas in
this sequel to The Cricket in Times Square [q.v.]. Disturbed and
dismayed over the tide of rude humanity trying desperately to get
through, rather than to, Christmas, Tucker the Mouse and Harry
the Cat remembered that their friend Chester with his musical wings
had been able to bring a little joy to the metropolis on an earlier occasion, so why not again? Hopping a train to Connecticut, the two
denizens of an abandoned sewer pipe picked up Chester, and after
a hazardous and humorous trip arrived in New York prepared to
convert the citizenry to joy and good will. As the scurrying masses
of shoppers pushed and shoved their way through slushy streets
and crowded stores, Chester fiddled away but was completely ignored.
Then the streets went suddenly dark and traffic stopped as New
York experienced a blackout. Confused and frightened, the crowds
soon quieted and listened to the soothing tones of Chester's music.
As they marveled at the cricket virtuoso in the peaceful stillness,
people actually felt the spirit of the holiday. And, for a short time,
the city became a huge Christmas Wonderland where good cheer and
fellowship prevailed. Songs: "Christmas in New York," "What If
Humans Were More Like Mice?"

VISIT FROM ST. NICHOLAS, A see NIGHT BEFORE CHRISTMAS,
THE

WALT DISNEY PRESENTS SPORT GOOFY'S OLYMPIC GAMES SPECIAL

Broadcast History
Premiere: June 2-17, 1984
SYN/local station option (WKBW, Buffalo, New York, June 2, 1984,
Saturday 1:30-2:00 PM)
Director: Jack Kinney
Writers: Dick Kinney, Milt Schaffer, Bill Berg, Milt Banta

Music/Song & Lyrics: Dale Gonyea
Music: Oliver Wallace, Paul J. Smith
Company: Walt Disney Television
Distributor: SFM Entertainment/1984-

Walt Disney Presents Sport Goofy's Olympic Games Special, like the specials entitled Sport Goofy [q.v.], was a compilation of cartoons from the studio's library. Included were Olympic Champ (1942), Goofy Gymnastics (1949), How to Swim (1942) and Art of Self-Defense (1941). Song/Theme: "You Can Always Be Number 1."

WALT DISNEY'S MICKEY, DONALD AND SPORT GOOFY SHOW:
"GETTING WET"

Broadcast History
    Premiere: September 7-23, 1984
    SYN/local station option (WPMT, York, Pennsylvania, September
        7, 1984, Friday 3:00-3:30 PM)
Director: Jack Kinney
Writers: Dick Kinney, Milt Schaffer, Bill Berg, Milt Banta
Music/Song & Lyrics: Dale Gonyea
Music: Oliver Wallace, Paul J. Smith
Company: Walt Disney Television
Distributor: SFM Entertainment/1984-

Walt Disney's Mickey, Donald and Sport Goofy Show: "Getting Wet" featured the Disney characters in the cartoons The Simple Things (1953), Chips Ahoy (1956) and Aquamania (1961). Song/Theme: "You Can Always Be Number 1."

WALT DISNEY'S MICKEY, DONALD AND SPORT GOOFY SHOW:
"HAPPY HOLIDAYS"

Broadcast History
    Premiere: December 1-23, 1984
    SYN/local station option (KYW, Philadelphia, Pennsylvania, Decem-
        ber 1, 1984, Saturday 2:00-2:30 PM)
Director: Jack Kinney
Writers: Dick Kinney, Milt Schaffer, Bill Berg, Milt Banta
Music/Song & Lyrics: Dale Gonyea
Music: Oliver Wallace, Paul J. Smith
Company: Walt Disney Television
Distributor: SFM Entertainment/1984-

Walt Disney's Mickey, Donald and Sport Goofy Show: "Happy Holi-days" included the cartoons Pluto's Christmas Tree (1952), The Clock Watcher (1945) and "How To Ride a Horse" from The Reluctant Dra-gon (1941). Song/Theme: "You Can Always Be Number 1."

WALT DISNEY'S MICKEY, DONALD AND SPORT GOOFY SHOW:
"SNOWTIME"

Broadcast History
    Premiere: November 17-December 23, 1984
    SYN/local station option (KOKI, Tulsa, Oklahoma, November 17,
       1984, Saturday 3:00-3:30 PM CST)
Director: Jack Kinney
Writers: Dick Kinney, Milt Schaffer, Bill Berg, Milt Banta
Music/Song & Lyrics: Dale Gonyea
Music: Oliver Wallace, Paul J. Smith
Company: Walt Disney Television
Distributor: SFM Entertainment/1984-

Walt Disney's Mickey, Donald and Sport Goofy Show: "Snowtime"
presented the cartoons Lend a Paw (1941), Chip 'n' Dale (1947) and
How To Fish (1942). Song/Theme: "You Can Always Be Number 1."

WEEP NO MORE, MY LADY

Broadcast History
    Premiere: February 10, 1979
    ABC/ABC WEEKEND SPECIALS, Saturday 12:00-12:30 PM
    ABC/Repeats: May 19, 1979; September 8, 1979; July 19, 1980;
       May 30, 1981; September 5, 1981; April 9, 1983; June 2, 1984
Executive Producers: Joseph Ruby, Ken Spears
Producer: Jerry Eisenberger
Directors: Rudy Larriva, Manny Perez
Writer: Sheldon Stark
Music: Dean Elliott
Company: Ruby-Spears Enterprises

Principal Characters and Voices
My Lady (African Basenji)   (non-speaking)
Skeeter   Jeremy Lawrence
Uncle Jess   Alan Oppenheimer
Alligator Ike   Larry D. Mann
Mr. Rackman   Michael Rye
Tiger (Ike's Dog)
Crooktail (crocodile)

Weep No More, My Lady told of the relationship of two very dissimilar
characters: a 13-year-old backwoods Mississippian, Skeeter, and the
strange-looking dog he found in the swamps. Leading a Huck Finn
life in the bayou country, Skeeter adopted the stray, which he named
My Lady, and brought her home to the cabin he shared with his
Uncle Jess. Convinced My Lady could be a very good bird-dog,
Skeeter accepted a challenge by Alligator Ike, the nastiest man around,
to pit her against his equally nasty dog, Tiger, the best bird-dog
in the bayou. Skeeter trained My Lady to become a top-notch pointer,

and she went on to win the contest, angering Ike, who vowed revenge. Then Mr. Rackman appeared, informing Jess that he believed My Lady was a runaway champion Basenji, an extremely valuable hunting dog. Overhearing the conversation and instead of giving up the dog, Skeeter took My Lady and ran away in his boat, which was wrecked by Crooktail, a vicious crocodile. After swimming ashore, they were captured by Ike, bound and carted to his cabin. As Ike slept, My Lady freed Skeeter's hands and the pair escaped, pursued by Ike and Tiger, whom they managed to elude by loosening a log bridge and dumping the villains into a stream. My Lady guided them safely home, where Skeeter faced the difficult and sad decision to return the dog to her rightful owner--a poignant lesson in "growing up." Heartbroken, but knowing it was only right, Skeeter watched as Rackman drove off with My Lady. To his surprise and great joy, Rackman returned a few weeks later and presented the boy with one of My Lady's pups. The special was based on the short story by James Street.

WEIRD HAROLD

Broadcast History
    Premiere: May 4, 1973
    NBC/Friday 8:30-9:00 PM
    NBC/Repeat: September 7, 1973
Executive Producer: William H. Cosby, Jr.
Producers: Louis Scheimer, Norman Prescott
Director: Hal Sutherland
Writers: Jim Ryan, Bill Danch
Company: Filmation in association with Bill Cosby Productions

Principal Characters and Voices
Fat Albert/Mushmouth/Young Bill/
    Father   Bill Cosby
Weird Harold   Gerald Edwards
Judge   Henry Silva

Weird Harold focused on one of Bill Cosby's favorite characters created from recollections of his childhood chums in a North Philadelphia neighborhood. Harold would do anything on a dare: walk ledges, eat worms, wear his clothes inside out, even hide behind the classroom door all day. But when his pranks backfired, he always yelled for Fat Albert to bail him out. And while Fat Albert did not approve of Harold's "Hairbreadth Harry" antics, when Albert needed someone to lend a hand, Weird Harold was the one who got the call. So it was in this original comedy by Cosby in which the Great Go-Cart Race was at stake with Harold, Fat Albert, Young Bill and the others competing. More like a demolition derby than an organized event, their make-do soap-box buggies careened and collided down dangerous Deadman's Hill, resulting in Cosby and his friends being arrested by police for their recklessness. Of course, all turned right in the tag, with a nice little moral about safety, responsibility and winning. The second special featuring the Cosby characters after their debut in Hey, Hey, Hey, It's Fat Albert [q.v.], the film was followed by three holiday specials starring Fat Albert [q.v.].

WHAT A NIGHTMARE, CHARLIE BROWN

Broadcast History
　　Premiere: February 23, 1978
　　CBS/Thursday 8:00-8:30 PM
　　Sponsors: Interstate Brands, McDonald's; Cadbury, Nabisco
　　　　Brands
　　CBS/Repeat: April 13, 1987
Executive Producer: Lee Mendelson
Producer: Bill Melendez
Directors: Phil Roman, Bill Melendez
Writer/Creator: Charles M. Schulz
Music: Vince Guaraldi, Ed Bogas
Company: Lee Mendelson-Bill Melendez Productions in association
　　with Charles M. Schulz Creative Associates and United Feature
　　Syndicate
Home Video: Snoopy's Home Video Library #339/Hi-Tops Video (nee
　　Media Home Entertainment)

Principal Characters and Voices
Charlie Brown　　　　　　　　　Liam Martin
Snoopy　　　　　　　　　　　　Bill Melendez

Vocalist: Larry Finlayson

What a Nightmare, Charlie Brown departed from the usual Peanuts-special format, devoting most of the half hour to the animated pantomime fantasies of Snoopy, something that had not been done extensively in prime time before. Charlie Brown started the whole thing by suggesting that Snoopy play Eskimo husky to his sled, but to Snoopy mush was a breakfast and not a command. After a snowstorm, Charlie tried to make a sled dog of the pampered beagle anyway, but Snoopy conned him into demonstrating how to pull a sled and cracked the whip over Charlie all the way home. Later, when he retired after overindulging in too many pizzas, Snoopy had a nightmare about being harnessed to a team of sled dogs in the Arctic, driven across the tundra, mistreated and denied food. Humbled and bullied, he found "civilization" in a root-beer saloon and showed off by playing poker and the piano, and worked up his courage to put down those pesky huskies. Finally deciding to become a "real" dog, he challenged the lead dog to a fight. Replacing him, Snoopy soon found himself in a worse predicament when the team fell through the ice. Awakened and trembling when he fell from his snow-covered doghouse, Snoopy rushed inside to Charlie Brown's bed for a warm, comforting snooze. Song/Theme: "Over Civilized" (Finlayson).

After reading an article about husky dogs, Schulz wondered what might happen if a sophisticated, civilized dog like Snoopy was suddenly forced to survive as a member of an Arctic sled team, and the idea for the program took shape. This was the 16th and last Charlie Brown thematic special scored with the original music of the late Vince Guaraldi, whom Schulz credited for much of the success of the television specials. Guaraldi's original soundtrack jazz impressions, A Boy Named Charlie Brown, was released on Fantasy Records in 1977.

WHAT HAVE WE LEARNED, CHARLIE BROWN?

Broadcast History
    Premiere: May 30, 1983
    CBS/Monday 8:00-8:30 PM
    Sponsor: Kraft Foods, McDonald's
    CBS/Repeats: May 26, 1984
Producers: Lee Mendelson, Bill Melendez
Director: Bill Melendez
Writer/Creator: Charles M. Schulz
Music: Judy Munsen, Dawn Atkinson
Company: Lee Mendelson-Bill Melendez Productions in association
    with Charles M. Schulz Creative Associates and United Media
Home Video: Kartes Video Communications

Principal Characters and Voices

Charlie Brown	Brad Kesten
Peppermint Patty	Victoria Vargas
Sally Brown	Stacy Heather Tolkin
Linus Van Pelt	Jeremy Schoenberg
Marcie	Michael Dockery
French Woman	Monica Parker
Snoopy	Bill Melendez

What Have We Learned, Charlie Brown? was a thought-provoking, bittersweet Memorial Day tribute, through a flashback to Charlie's vivid memories of his trip to France as an exchange student with some of his Peanuts peers. Bumbling their way through mini-disasters over country roads in a dilapidated crank-motered rental car, Snoopy as chauffeur-mechanic headed toward the Normandy coast with Marcie as interpreter and Peppermint Patty calling out the wrong phrases from her guidebook. On a bluff near the sea, where the clan set up camp for the night, the sensitive and perceptive Linus was wakeful. At dawn he walked to the beach and in the silence, broken by the gentle sounds of the water and wind, visualized Omaha Beach as it was on V-Day, June 6, 1944 and witnessed a ghostly reenactment of the Allied landing. Later, gazing over the rows of crosses at the American Cemetery, he recalled General Eisenhower's words about that day, as Ike's actual voice-recording spoke of the preservation of freedom, the heartbreaking sacrifices of war and the hope

WHAT HAVE WE LEARNED, CHARLIE BROWN? © 1983 United Feature Syndicate, Inc. Courtesy of Charles M. Schulz Creative Associates and United Media.

that humanity had learned from it all. The clan moved further along the coast, past Belgian trenches, German bunkers, a mine crater and to the place where Lt. Col. J. M. McRae wrote the poem, In Flanders Field, the first verse of which Linus solemnly recited. In the quiet that ensued, Linus turned to Charlie and asked, "What have we learned, Charlie Brown?" George Foster Peabody award (1983).

The special was based on some of the personal experiences of Schulz during the Second World War. The rotoscope technique, used to trace live-action footage onto animation cels which are later colored, was incorporated for some of the location scenes.

WHICH WITCH IS WHICH?

Broadcast History
Premiere: 1984
SYN/local station option (KCBS, Los Angeles, October 26, 1984, Friday 7:30-8:00 PM PST)
SYN/Repeats: 1985 +
Producers/Directors: Bill Hutten, Tony Love
Writer: John Bradford
Music: Larry Fotine
Company: Encore Enterprises
Distributor: Muller Media/1984-

Principal Characters and Voices

Rusty/Rosie	Kathy Ritter
Buttons/Christie	Barbara Goodson
Abner	Alvy Moore
George	Bill Ratner
Bridgett	Morgan Lofting
Ranger Jones	Bill Boyett
Rocky (children's dog)	

Which Witch Is Which? offered some sage advice about trick-or-treating through the misadventures of the bear cub Buttons and the young fox Rusty. Since it was Buttons' and Rusty's first Halloween, it was up to Ranger Jones to tell them about how folks dress up, bob for apples and go door-to-door seeking treats. Their first experience was at the home of Mabel Thorn, a witch, which scared the dickens out of the pair, who wound up in more trouble than you could shake a broomstick at. While Ranger Jones was giving a Halloween party for the children at the trailer park, two shady characters, Lenny and Lulu Spratt, costumed as a bear and a fox, engaged in some trick-or-treating of their own, pilfering Mabel's house. When Abner Bear and George Fox went looking for their fun-loving offspring, they spotted the Spratts and, believing they were Buttons and Rusty, chased after them. Thinking they had found two new friends with whom to go trick-or-treating, the cubs approached the Spratts as they were sneaking out of a trailer with a pillowcase crammed full of goodies. But when it dawned on the Spratts that they were real animals, they dropped their loot and headed for the hills, where they were eventually rounded up by Ranger Jones and his animal friends. Song/Theme: "Which Witch Is Which?"

The film was the second of the Rusty and Buttons specials, following their debut in The Christmas Tree Train [q.v.].

WHITE SEAL, THE

Broadcast History
    Premiere: March 24, 1975
    CBS/Monday 8:00-8:30 PM
    CBS/Repeats: October 17, 1975; May 13, 1977; September 9, 1981
    SYN/Repeats: 1983-1985 ("LBS Children's Theatre"); 1986 +
Producer/Director/Writer: Chuck Jones
Music: Dean Elliott
Company: Chuck Jones Enterprises
Distributor: Berle Adams/1986-
Home Video: Family Home Entertainment

THE WHITE SEAL. © 1975, Chuck Jones Enterprises. Courtesy of LBS Communications.

Narrator: Roddy McDowall

Principal Characters and Voices
Kotick/Sea Catch/Sea Cow/
    Killer Whale/Walrus   Roddy McDowall
Matkah   June Foray

The White Seal followed the life of Kotick, who grew from just a
sprout, defeated the older bulls and became the leader of his flock.
The only snow-white pup born on Novastoshnah on the Island of St.
Paul in the Bering Sea, Kotick was the son of a huge gray fur-seal,
Sea Catch, a 15-year-old bull, and Matkah, his soft, sleek, gentle-
eyed wife. Kotick enjoyed the delights of sea and land and soon
learned that all creatures were not his friends. During the annual
ravages of his colony, the horrified white seal was the only one to
rebel against the seal hunters' savage slaughter. He vowed to find
a place where his fellow seals could live in peace without fear or
man. In his search he eluded a killer whale and followed the Sea
Cows to a safe island, a tranquil place where he moved the colony.
The special was the last in the trilogy adapted by Chuck Jones from
Rudyard Kipling's The Jungle Book (1894).

WILLIE MAYS AND THE SAY-HEY KID

Broadcast History
    Premiere: October 14, 1972
    ABC/ABC SATURDAY SUPERSTAR MOVIE, Saturday 9:30-10:30
        AM
    ABC/Repeats: 1973-1974
    SYN/Repeats: 1975 +
Producers/Directors: Arthur Rankin, Jr., Jules Bass
Writer: Romeo Muller
Music: Maury Laws
Company: Rankin-Bass Productions/60 minutes
Distributor: Viacom Enterprises/1986-

Principal Characters and Voices
Willie Mays   Willie Mays
Veronica   Tina Andrews
Iguana   Paul Frees
Veronica's Aunt   Ernestine Wade

Willie Mays and the Say-Hey Kid was a story about an eccentric angel
who granted the baseball great's wish--to make an almost impossible
catch of a fly ball and clinch the National League Pennant. Of
course, there was a catch. Willie had to provide a loving home for
lonely, mischievous Veronica, an orphan who had been named as his
godchild without his knowledge. With her talking pet Iguana, Veronica
continually upset Willie's lifestyle, but his deeper feelings surfaced
when her relatives, hearing that she had inherited a fortune, showed
up to claim her.

The film was first seen on The ABC Saturday Superstar Movie (ABC, 1972-1974), described in Children's Television, Part I (Scarecrow, 1983), pp. 5-7.

WIND IN THE WILLOWS, THE

<u>Broadcast History</u>
 Premiere: July 5, 1987
 ABC/AN ABC MOVIE PRESENTATION, Sunday 7:00-9:00 PM
 ABC/Repeat: September 12, 1987, Saturday 8:00-10:00 AM
Producers/Directors: Arthur Rankin, Jr., Jules Bass
Associate Producer: Lee Dannacher
Director/Animation: Masaki Iizuka
Writer: Romeo Muller
Music: Maury Laws
Lyrics: Jules Bass
Company: Rankin-Bass Productions in association with Cuckoos (aka CooKoos) Nest Animation, Taipei, Taiwan/120 minutes
Home Video: Family Home Entertainment

THE WIND IN THE WILLOWS. © 1985, Rankin/Bass Productions, Inc. Courtesy of Rankin/Bass Productions.

Principal Characters and Voices

Mr. Toad	Charles Nelson Reilly
Ratty	Roddy McDowall
Badger	José Ferrer
Moley	Eddie Bracken
Wayfarer	Paul Frees
Magistrate	Robert McFadden

Other Voices
  Jeryl Jagoda, Ron Marshall, Gerry Matthews, Ray Owens, Alice
  Tweedie

Vocalist: Judy Collins

The Wind in the Willows, a musical adaptation of the 1908 Kenneth
Grahame children's tale, opened on Toad Hall, a dignified old house
with well-kept lawns reaching to rivers' edge, the home of Mr. Toad.
Fancying himself a great sea captain, Mr. Toad rushed out and
boarded his tiny steamboat, S.S. Toad, and as he putt-putted down
stream succeeded in destroying half the dock and nearly drown most
of his animal friends, a poetic rat, shy mole and cranky badger. Although Badger ran away, Mr. Toad flooded Moley out of his hole
and capsized Ratty's rowboat. Bored with boating, Mr. Toad planned
a new adventure in a gypsy caravan wagon he bought and persuaded
Ratty and Moley to join him. After they were forced off the road
by a fancy automobile the next day, the rich and hauty Mr. Toad
had an all-consuming passion for motoring, bought a Rolls Royce
and behind the wheel enjoyed careening through the countryside,
throwing up billowing clouds of dust. His foolish escapades in the
menacing Wild Wood and continued mischief-making finally raised the
hackles of his forest neighbors, who had struggled to keep the boastful Mr. Toad from danger, and they vowed to make him repent for
his follies. However, Mr. Toad continued his devilment--even crashed
a stolen car--until the law caught up with him and put him behind
bars. Meantime, making matters worse were a band of wicked Weasels,
Ferrets and Stoats who overran, occupied and trashed Mr. Toad's
mansion. Following his short-lived performance as a penitent, his
audacious escape from prison and his frantic bid for freedom aboard
a speeding old steam engine, hotly pursued by another bristling with
police, Mr. Toad returned to recapture Toad Hall with the help of
his friends. Songs: "Messin' Around in Boats" (McDowall), "We
Don't Have Any Pâté De Foie Gras" (McDowall & Bracken), "I Hate
Company" (Ferrer), "Benefit of the Doubt," "A Party That Never
Ceases" (chorus), "The Wind in the Willows" (Collins).
    Although there have been at least two notable screen versions
of Grahame's classic, The Adventures of Ichabod and Mr. Toad (Disney, 1949), which left out some of the book and re-wrote most the
rest, and the 90-minute animated-puppet feature, The Wind in the
Willows (Cosgrove-Hall, 1983), the Rankin-Bass two-hour movie was
the first to present the story in its entirety in full animation. The
special had no connection with their Saturday morning series, The

Reluctant Dragon and Mr. Toad (ABC, 1970-1972), described in Children's Television, Part I (Scarecrow, 1983), pp. 234-235.

WINNIE THE POOH AND A DAY FOR EEYORE

Broadcast History
    Premiere: May 6, 1986
    DIS/Sunday 4:30-5:00 PM
    DIS/Repeats: 1986 +
Producer/Director: Rick Reinert
Writers: Peter Young, Steve Hulett, Ron Clements, Tony L. Marino
Music & Lyrics/Title Song: Richard M. Sherman, Robert B. Sherman
Music: Steve Zuckerman
Company: Walt Disney Television
Home Video: Walt Disney Home Video #226

Principal Characters and Voices

Winnie the Pooh	Hal Smith
Eeyore	Ralph Wright
Piglet	John Fiedler
Rabbit	Will Ryan
Christopher Robin	Kim Christianson
Roo	Dick Billingsley
Kanga	Julie McWhirter Dees
Tigger	Paul Winchell

Winnie the Pooh and a Day for Eeyore related another tale about
Pooh Bear and his friends on a bright autumn day in the Hundred
Acre Wood. With Rabbit, Piglet and Roo, Pooh was involved in a
game he called "Pooh Sticks," dropping sticks into the stream and
waiting to see whose stick was first to drift out from beneath the
bridge. But instead of a stick, Eeyore, the doleful donkey, drifted
into view first, bounced into the stream by Tigger. Emerging a
sodden mess, Eeyore trudged away more deeply depressed than usual.
Joining Eeyore, Pooh learned that everyone had forgotten the donkey's birthday. To remedy the problem, Pooh set off to fetch Eeyore
a present, along the way telling Piglet and Owl, who flew off to tell
the others. Proceeding to Eeyore's home, Pooh had a "rumbly in
his tumbly" and ate all the honey he had planned to give the donkey.
Meanwhile, Piglet's red balloon burst but he gave it to his friend
anyway. Moments later, Pooh presented him with the empty jar, "a
useful pot to put things in." Eeyore put the balloon into it, and
both giftgivers were delighted that he had found a use for their presents. When Christopher Robin and the other animals arrived, they
brought a birthday cake, and even Tigger's appearance did not mar
the festivities. Finally happy, Eeyore invited Tigger to the bridge
to teach him "Pooh Sticks." A pleased Pooh noted that there was
good in everyone and Christopher agreed. Song/Theme: "Winnie
the Pooh."
    Based on a story by A. A. Milne, creator of the children's

tales, it was the first animated cartoon film starring the Pooh characters produced in 12 years since Winnie the Pooh and Tigger Too
[q.v.].

WINNIE THE POOH AND THE BLUSTERY DAY

Broadcast History
    Premiere: November 30, 1970
    NBC/Monday 7:30-8:00 PM
    Sponsor: Sears
    NBC/Repeats: December 1, 1971; November 29, 1972; November
       28, 1973; November 26, 1974; December 1, 1978
Executive Producer: Ron Miller
Director: Wolfgang Reitherman
Writers: Larry Clemmons, Julius Svendsen, Ralph Wright, Vance
    Gerry
Music/Songs & Lyrics: Richard M. Sherman, Robert B. Sherman
Music: Buddy Baker
Motion Picture Academy Oscar Award: 1968, Best Animated Film
Company: Walt Disney Television (BV, 1968)
Record Album: Disneyland 1317, 3953 (with book); 327 (single with
    book), 621 (single)
Home Video: Walt Disney Home Video #25

Narrator: Sebastian Cabot

Principal Characters and Voices

Winnie the Pooh	Sterling Holloway
Eeyore	Ralph Wright
Owl	Hal Smith
Christopher Robin	Jon Walmsley
Kanga	Barbara Luddy
Roo	Clint Howard
Rabbit	Junius Matthews
Gopher	Howard Morris
Tigger	Paul Winchell
Piglet	John Fiedler

Winnie the Pooh and the Blustery Day engulfed the Hundred Acre
Wood in a gathering storm as Pooh started out to wish Piglet a "happy
windsday." But Piglet was swept up into the air as Pooh clung to
his unraveling muffler. As Piglet flew kitelike above Pooh, the bear
was dragged past Kanga and little Roo's home and the doleful donkey
Eeyore's house of sticks and through Rabbit's carrot garden, harvesting the crop. Then a gust blew Pooh skyward, and with Piglet
he drifted into the Owl's treehouse which, in a sudden jolt, toppled
and was demolished. Surveying the damage, Christopher Robin and
the animals decided Owl needed a new home. That night, Pooh was
unnerved by the wind and a visit from Tigger, who warned him
about the honey-raiders, the elephant-shaped "heffalumps" and weasel-
like "woozles," which later appeared in Pooh's frightful nightmare.

He awoke to find his house flooded by the storm, which destroyed the homes of the animals, who took shelter on high ground. But Pooh was washed away and Piglet too. Carried over a waterfall, Pooh popped up and Piglet was discovered safe in Pooh's honey pot. Considered a hero by Christopher, Pooh was honored at a "hero party," which turned into a "two hero" celebration because of Piglet's noble deed, offering to share his home with Owl. The film was the second based on the A. A. Milne stories. Songs: "Winnie the Pooh," "The Wonderful Thing About Tiggers," "A Rather Blustery Day," "The Rain Rain Rain Came Down Down Down," "Hip Hip Pooh Ray."

WINNIE THE POOH AND THE HONEY TREE

Broadcast History
    Premiere: March 10, 1970
    NBC/Tuesday 7:30-8:00 PM
    Sponsor: Sears
    NBC/Repeats: March 22, 1971; March 14, 1972; April 4, 1973;
       March 26, 1974; November 25, 1977
Executive Producer: Walt Disney
Director: Wolfgang Reitherman
Writers: Larry Clemmons, Xavier Atencio, Vance Gerry, Ralph
    Wright, Ken Anderson, Dick Lucas
Music/Songs & Lyrics: Richard M. Sherman, Robert B. Sherman
Music: Buddy Baker
Company: Walt Disney Television (BV, 1965)
Record Album: Disneyland 1277, 3928 (with book); 313 (single with
    book), 618 (single)
Home Video: Walt Disney Home Video #25

Narrator: Sebastian Cabot

Principal Characters and Voices

Winnie the Pooh	Sterling Holloway
Eeyore	Ralph Wright
Owl	Hal Smith
Christopher Robin	Bruce Reitherman
Kanga	Barbara Luddy
Roo	Clint Howard
Rabbit	Junius Matthews
Gopher	Howard Morris

Winnie the Pooh and the Honey Tree found a hungry Pooh trying to steal a bee tree's cache when the limb broke. Underterred, Pooh borrowed a balloon from Christopher Robin and, disguised as a small black rain cloud, floated up beside the tree, angering the bees, which pursued him. Hanging on to his deflating balloon, Pooh finally dropped onto Christopher below. Taking refuge in a mud puddle, they shielded themselves from the bees with Christopher's umbrella. Hungrier than ever, Pooh called on Rabbit and consumed all his honey,

growing so stout that the bear became hopelessly wedged in the door-
way. After Rabbit ran for help, the Gopher ("I'm not in the book")
appeared outside and unsuccessfully dickered with Owl on a price
for extricating Pooh. Making the best of the situation until Pooh
lost weight, Rabbit decorated Pooh's rear inside the hutch, but the
posterior plan collapsed when the bear sneezed. Meantime, Christopher and the animals entertained Pooh's outside half as the bear
groaned with hunger. Thoughtless Gopher, on the swing shift,
wolfed down a meal right under Pooh's nose. Next morning, while
Christopher and his friends tugged outside, Rabbit ran like a batter-
ing ram at Pooh. Unstuck, Pooh was shot through the air, landing
in the bee tree, his head in the honey hole, where he ecstatically
lapped up the gooey syrup. Songs: "Winnie the Pooh," "Up, Down
and Touch the Ground," "Rumbly in My Tumbly," "Little Black Rain
Cloud," "Mind Over Matter."

The special was the first of three Pooh films originally released
theatrically and based on A. A. Milne's stories and Ernest H. Shepard's illustrations.

WINNIE THE POOH AND TIGGER TOO

Broadcast History
    Premiere: November 28, 1975
    NBC/NBC HOLIDAY SPECIALS, Friday 8:00-8:30 PM
    Sponsor: Sears
    ABC/Repeat: November 25, 1976
    CBS/Repeats: December 11, 1982, August 30, 1983
Executive Producer: Ron Miller
Producer: Wolfgang Reitherman
Director: John Lounsbery
Writers: Larry Clemmons, Ted Berman, Eric Cleworth
Music/Songs & Lyrics: Richard M. Sherman, Robert B. Sherman
Music: Buddy Baker
Company: Walt Disney Television (BV, 1974)
Record Album: Disneyland 3813 (with book); 333 (single), 336
    (single with book)
Home Video: Walt Disney Home Video #25

Narrator: Sebastian Cabot

Principal Characters and Voices

Winnie the Pooh	Sterling Holloway
Tigger	Paul Winchell
Rabbit	Junius Matthews
Piglet	John Fiedler
Kanga	Barbara Luddy
Roo	Dori Whitaker
Christopher Robin	Timothy Turner

Winnie the Pooh and Tigger Too took another trip to the Hundred

Acre Wood, where the animals were trying to "unbounce" the lively
Tigger, whose overly enthusiastic greetings usually knocked his
hapless friends flat on their backs. Rabbit, thoroughly irritated,
called a protest meeting and suggested a cure: losing Tigger temporarily in the Wood. Next morning, when Tigger bounced ahead,
Rabbit led Pooh and Piglet into hiding and became hopelessly lost.
Setting out on his own, Rabbit spent an eerie night alone, as trees
and frogs became frightening monsters, until he crashed through
the foliage into daylight and was immediately "bounced" by Tigger.
That winter, Roo and Tigger became stranded when they bounced
into a tree, unable to bounce or climb down. Pooh and Piglet had
been tracking a creature's footprints nearby when they heard the
calls for help. Christopher Robin and Rabbit joined in the rescue
but were unable to offer a solution. Tigger promised he would never
bounce again if the narrator of the story would help. By tilting
the book, Tigger was brought safely down and sadly started to
leave. Only Rabbit was adamant about the agreement, but under
pressure from the others he finally relented, admitting he liked the
old bouncy Tigger best, and the jubilant jumper started bouncing
again and taught the others to do the same. Songs: "Winnie the
Pooh," "The Wonderful Thing About Tiggers."

The film was one of only two animated specials, the other The
Tiny Tree [q.v.], aired in prime time on all three commercial networks.

WITCH'S NIGHT OUT

Broadcast History
    Premiere: October 27, 1978
    NBC/Friday 8:00-8:30 PM
    NBC/Repeat: October 30, 1979
    SYN/Repeats: 1985 +
Producer/Director: John Leach
Writers: John Leach, Jean Rankin
Music: Peter Rochon
Company: Leach-Rankin Productions, Toronto, Canada, in associa-
    tion with Rankin-Bass Productions
Distributor: Lorimar Syndication ("Animated Holiday Specials")/1985-
Home Video: Family Home Entertainment

Principal Characters and Voices

Witch ("The Godmother")	Gilda Radner
Rotten	Bob Church
Goody	John Leach
Tender	Naomi Leach
Small	Tony Molesworth
Malicious	Catherine O'Hara
Mincely	Fiona Reid
Bazooey	Gerry Salsberg

Witch's Night Out involved a hapless, has-been sorceress who sorrow-
fully found herself unemployed on Halloween afternoon. Needless to
say, she was down in the dumps. Her dreams were buoyed, however, when the townspeople decided to have their Halloween party
in her haunted mansion. Moreover, she really felt needed again
when she answered the call of two children and their babysitter who
longed to be scary monsters for the party that evening. With a
wave of her wand, their wish came true; in fact they performed so
well in their new roles that the guests stampeded out of the mansion
in terror. In the crush, the witch's wand disappeared, creating a
predicament: if it was not found, the children would stay monsters
forever. Of course, finally, the witch retrieved her wand, and much
to her joy the whole town embraced the spirit of Halloween. Song/
Theme: "Halloween."

WORLD OF SECRET SQUIRREL AND ATOM ANT, THE

Broadcast History
    Premiere: September 12, 1965
    NBC/Sunday 6:30-7:30 PM
Producers/Directors: William Hanna, Joseph Barbera
Music: Ted Nichols
Company: Hanna-Barbera Productions/60 minutes

Principal Characters and Voices
Secret Squirrel   Mel Blanc
Morocco Mole   Paul Frees
Atom Ant   Howard Morris
Mr. Moto/Others   Don Messick

The World of Secret Squirrel and Atom Ant was an hour-long special
preview of the two Saturday morning series which debuted on the
network, October 2, 1965. Clad in a traditional trenchcoat and
fedora, Secret Squirrel was the animal kingdom's James Bond, an
intrepid secret agent paired with a puerile partner, Morocco Mole,
working undercover for his boss Double Q. In his segments he dis-
closed the methods he used to battle Yellow Pinkie, his archenemy.
Endowed with superpower, Atom Ant was the smallest but mightiest
defender of law and order, battling crime everywhere and mocking
Mighty Mouse (CBS, 1955-1966/1979-1982). In his films, Atom Ant
revealed his remarkable strength and introduced his friends and foes,
including the wily Mr. Moto.
    Aired during NBC Week, it was the first cartoon preview aired
in prime time, an idea that would proliferate to eventually cover the
entire new Saturday morning network schedules through the 1970s
and 1980s. It was unique in that it focused on just one block of
programs, was the vanguard of the Saturday-morning packaged program concept and predated The King Kong Show [q.v.], the initial
prime-time preview of a single cartoon series on ABC. The Saturday

series each had two components featuring different cartoon characters
and were initially televised separately but back-to-back as described
in Children's Television, Part I (Scarecrow, 1983), pp. 27-29.

WORLD OF STRAWBERRY SHORTCAKE, THE

Broadcast History
    Premiere: March-April 1980
    SYN/local station option (KTLA, Los Angeles, March 28, 1980,
        Friday 7:30-8:00 PM PST)
    Sponsor: Kenner Products (Toy Group, General Mills)
    SYN/Repeats: September 4, 1980 +
Executive Producer: Robert L. Rosen
Producers: Romeo Muller, Charles Swenson, Fred Wolf
Director: Charles Swenson
Writers: Romeo Muller, Robert L. Rosen
Music: Mark Volman, Howard Kaylan
Lyrics: Romeo Muller
Company: RLR Associates in association with Those Characters
    From Cleveland and Murakami-Wolf-Swenson Films
Distributor: The Television Program Source/1986-
Record Album: Kid's Stuff 165
Home Video: Family Home Entertainment

Narrator
Sun   Romeo Muller

Principal Characters and Voices
Strawberry Shortcake   Russi Taylor
Purple Pieman   Robert Ridgely
Huckleberry Pie   Julie McWhirter
Blueberry Muffin/Apple Dumplin'   Joan Gerber
Raspberry Tart   Pamela Anderson
Ben Bean/Escargot   Bob Holt

Vocalists: Flo and Eddy

The World of Strawberry Shortcake depicted a day's activities in
Strawberry Land, a fantasy world where ice-cream mountains looked
down on soda-pop streams. There lived Strawberry Shortcake,
dressed in a cute little frock in strawberry red covered with a
frilly white apron trimmed with strawberries. On her flopsie-mopsie
head was a granny cap garnished with ... need one guess? Together
with her friends Huckleberry Pie, Blueberry Muffin, Apple Dumplin'
and Raspberry Tart, Strawberry Shortcake frolicked and worked to
overcome minor setbacks and major obstacles, always with a sunny
disposition and often breaking into song. The ridiculous villain was
the Peculiar Purple Pieman of Porcupine Peak, who performed a
little jig when he spoke and enlivened things with his army of Berry
Birds, who were pitted against a forest of Tall Trees friendly to the

little girl. In the end, the Pieman turned over a new pastry leaf in this fairyland morality play for tots which emphasized how friendship, sharing and working together could enrich one's life. Songs: "Strawberry Shortcake Theme," "Smile a Sunny Morning," "Sunflower Market," "Monster Trees," "Berry Talk."

The Easter program was seen in more than 95 markets and was the first of six specials starring Strawberry Shortcake [q.v.]. Originally created by Those Characters From Cleveland, an American Greetings company, the characters were featured in novelty cards. The films were sponsored partly by Kenner Products, which released a doll and toy line modelled on the characters; some of the dolls were scented to match their names. More than 66 companies have cranked out hundreds of Strawberry Shortcake products and novelties.

YABBA DABBA DOO 2

Broadcast History
    Premiere: October 12, 1979
    CBS/Friday 8:00-9:00 PM
    CBS/Repeat: June 1, 1982
Executive Producers: William Hanna, Joseph Barbera
Producer/Director: Robert Guenette
Writer: Len Janson
Music: Hoyt Curtin, Paul DeKorte
Company: Hanna-Barbera Productions in association with Robert
    Guenette Productions/60 minutes

Host: Bill Bixby

Yabba Dabba Doo 2 was a live-action and animated salute to William Hanna and Joseph Barbera, a retrospective on their cartoon stars that made them one of the world's most prolific producers of filmed animation. Presenting scenes of many of their cartoon "underdogs," the program recalled their earlier success, MGM's superstars Tom and Jerry, the first cartoon characters they created as a team. Actually an undermouse, Jerry has outwitted, outfought, outsmarted and outconned Tom the cat in theaters and on television since their debut in Puss Gets the Boot (February 10, 1940). Other scenes included that favorite underbear, Yogi Bear, who waged a constant and often losing battle against autocratic authority; Quick Draw McGraw the underhorse, the put-upon sheriff who was always bested by the quicker-drawing varmints; Huckleberry Hound, the quietly persevering underhound in constant jeopardy of impending failure; Ruff, an undercat whose quick wit saved him from the disasters perpetrated by the dullard dog, Reddy; and Scooby-Doo, a chicken-hearted underdog who lived his life in constant fear of being challenged by apparitions and bullies. The principal focus was on The Flintstones, the first animated situation comedy, which ran in prime time for six years and for many additional years on Saturday mornings. The entire Bedrock cast returned for a visit (in clips) of their cave-age environment and their resourceful facsimiles of household items reflective of modern suburbia. Supporting characters were also spotlighted, such as Perry Masonry, Bedrock's most successful lawyer; Ed Sullystone, a popular TV host; and Ann Margrock, a perky teenager. "Yabba Dabba Doo!" was the exuberant catch-cry of Fred Flintstone.

YANKEE DOODLE

Broadcast History
    Premiere: 1972-1973
    SYN/FESTIVAL OF FAMILY CLASSICS, (WABC, New York, Sunday 7:30-8:00 PM)
    SYN/Repeats: 1973 +
Producers/Directors: Arthur Rankin, Jr., Jules Bass
Associate Producer: Mary Alice Dwyer
Writer: Fred Halliday
Music: Maury Laws, Jules Bass
Company: Rankin-Bass Productions
Distributor: Viacom Enterprises ("Family Classics")/1986-
Home Video: Prism (with JACK O'LANTERN)

Yankee Doodle recreated some Revolutionary War days as seen through the eyes of 12-year-old Danny and his Midnight Militia friends Freddy and Timmy. Forced to dismount when his horse lost a shoe, Paul Revere resumed his gallant ride to warn the Colonials after Danny reshoed his horse. For this deed Danny was arrested, but released by Spotless Harry, the British General. Undeterred, Danny and his friends continued their mischief to harass the British. Captured again, he was put to work in Spotless Harry's laundry where he managed to mangle the soldiers' uniforms, making it impossible for Harry's troops to march or fight.

YANKEE DOODLE CRICKET

Broadcast History
    Premiere: January 16, 1975
    ABC/Thursday 8:00-8:30 PM
    ABC/Repeat: June 28, 1976
    SYN/Repeats: 1979 +
Producer/Director/Writer: Chuck Jones
Associate Producers: Joseph Aidlin, John Allen
Music: Dean Elliott
Music/Violinist: Israel Baker
Company: Chuck Jones Enterprises
Distributor: Berle Adams/1986-
Home Video: Family Home Entertainment

Principal Characters and Voices

Chester C. Cricket/Harry the Cat	Les Tremayne
Tucker the Mouse	Mel Blanc

Yankee Doodle Cricket revealed how Chester, a music-making cricket, and his friends Harry the Cat and Tucker the Mouse each played an important role in America's War for Independence. With apologies to American history, the Connecticut cricket, daring mouse and clever cat took a step back in time to re-live the colonial adventures of their forefathers. Tucker's ancestor was inspired by Patrick Henry to write a Declaration of Equality between cats and mice; Harry's colonial relative let his master, Thomas Jefferson, adapt the declaration for the cause of freedom; and Chester's great-grandfather wrote the stirring revolutionary anthem, "Yankee Doodle." The three patriots united their countrymen with the song as they marched to Boston. There they helped send the signal that the British were coming and poked a stubborn horse into action for Paul Revere's famous ride. There were also whimsical notes on the origin of "Don't Tread on Me" and the significance of the American Bald Eagle in this Bicentennial fantasy. The characters were created by George Selden for his book The Cricket in Times Square (Farrar, Straus, 1960) and introduced in the eponymous special [q.v.].

YEAR WITHOUT A SANTA CLAUS

Broadcast History
    Premiere: December 10, 1974
    ABC/Tuesday 8:00-9:00 PM
    ABC/Repeats: December 10, 1975; December 14, 1976;
        December 9, 1977; December 10, 1978; December 9, 1979;
        December 21, 1980
    SYN/Repeats: 1985 +
Producers/Directors: Arthur Rankin, Jr., Jules Bass
Writer: William Keenan
Music: Jules Bass
Lyrics: Maury Laws
Company: Rankin-Bass Productions/60 minutes
Distributor: Lorimar Syndication ("Animated Holiday Specials")/1985-
Home Video: Lightning Video

Narrator

Mrs. Santa Claus	Shirley Booth

Principal Characters and Voices

Santa Claus	Mickey Rooney
Snowmiser	Dick Shawn
Heatmiser	George S. Irving
Jingle Bells	Robert McFadden
Jangle Bells	Bradley Bolke
Mother Nature	Rhoda Mann

YEAR WITHOUT A SANTA CLAUS. © 1974, Rankin/Bass Productions, Inc. Courtesy of Rankin/Bass Productions and Lorimar Syndication.

Mr. Thistlewhite	Ron Marshall
Ignatius Thistlewhite	Colin Duffy
Blue Christmas Girl	Christine Winter

Vocalists: The Wee Winter Singers

Year Without a Santa Claus was narrated by Shirley Booth as Mrs. Claus, who told about the time that her husband decided not to deliver presents because he was disenchanted with the lack of holiday spirit in the land. In bed with an awful cold, feeling forgotten and tired, Santa thought nobody cared about him anymore. On the day before Christmas, Mrs. Claus herself donned the famous red suit to do the job, but the elves first wanted to demonstrate to their boss that he was indeed appreciated by all. Finally getting out of his bed, Santa went down to check out what his brood was up to and looked in upon children preparing for his annual visit. When the elves gave him presents from the youngsters, all gifts for Santa, the jolly man in the red suit decided to make his traditional Christmas Eve sleigh ride after all. The special was based on Pulitzer Prize-winner Phyllis McGinley's children's book and filmed using stop-motion animated puppets (Animagic). Songs: "Year Without a Santa Claus," "Here Comes Santa Claus," "Blue Christmas," "Sleigh Ride."

YES, VIRGINIA, THERE IS A SANTA CLAUS

Broadcast History
    Premiere: December 6, 1974
    ABC/Friday 8:00-8:30 PM
    Sponsor: Timex
    ABC/Repeat: December 5, 1975
    SYN/Repeats: 1976 +
Executive Producer: Burt Rosen
Producers: Bill Melendez, Mort Green
Director: Bill Melendez
Writer: Mort Green
Music: Jerry Styner

YES, VIRGINIA, THERE IS A SANTA CLAUS. © 1974, Burt Rosen Company. Courtesy of Bill Melendez Productions.

Company: Burt Rosen Company in association with Wolper Productions and Bill Melendez Productions
Distributor: ABR Entertainment/1986-
Home Video: Paramount

Narrator: Jim Backus

Principal Characters and Voices

Miss Taylor	Susan Silo
Virginia O'Hanlon	Courtney Lemmon
Billie	Billie Green
Specs	Sean Manning
Mary Lou	Tracy Belland
Arthur	Christopher Wong
Amy	Vickey Ricketts
Peewee	Jennifer Green
Officer Riley	Herb Armstrong
Sergeant Muldoon	Arnold Ross

Vocalist: Jimmy Osmond

Yes, Virginia, There Is a Santa Claus was based on 8-year-old Virginia O'Hanlon's letter to the editor of the New York Sun to find out if Santa really existed. In 1897 young Virginia found herself alone among her very skeptical friends in believing in Santa Claus. Her faith shaken, to confirm her belief Virginia wrote a plaintive letter to the editor of the New York Sun, confident that a newspaper promising, "If you see it in the Sun, It's so," would give her a straight answer. Virginia's confidence was well-placed, and this film retold her story, including the famous editorial reply written by Francis Church. Virginia's voice was supplied by Courtney Lemmon, then the 8-year-old daughter of Jack Lemmon. Television Academy Emmy award (1974-1975), Outstanding Children's Special.

YOGI BEAR'S ALL-STAR COMEDY CHRISTMAS CAPER

Broadcast History
    Premiere: December 21, 1982
    CBS/Tuesday 8:30-9:00 PM
    CBS/Repeat: December 18, 1984
Executive Producers: William Hanna, Joseph Barbera
Producer: Art Scott
Director: Mark Lumley
Writer: Mark Evanier
Music: Hoyt Curtin, Paul DeKorte
Company: Hanna-Barbera Productions
Distributor: Worldvision Enterprises

Principal Characters and Voices
Yogi Bear/Quick Draw McGraw/
    Huckleberry Hound/Snagglepuss/

Hokey Wolf/Snooper/Blabber/ Augie Doggie/Mr. Jinks/ Dixie/Wally Gator	Daws Butler
Boo Boo/Ranger Smith/Pixie	Don Messick
Judy Jones	Georgi Irene
Doggie Daddy/Butler/Announcer	John Stephenson
Mr. Jones/Zookeeper #1/Sergeant	Hal Smith
Mrs. Jones/P.A. Voice/Lady in the Street	Janet Waldo
Yakky Doodle/Zookeeper #2	Jimmy Weldon
Magilla Gorilla/Chief Blakc/Murray	Allan Melvin
Fred Flintstone/Policeman/ Security Guard #1	Henry Corden
Barney Rubble/Bulldog/Security Guard #2	Mel Blanc

Yogi Bear's All-Star Comedy Christmas Caper involved a busload of Hanna-Barbera characters, among them Huckleberry Hound, Quick Draw McGraw and Snagglepuss, who arrived in Jellystone Park for a celebration with their friends Yogi Bear and Boo Boo. Discovering that the bears had stowed away in a tourist bus to join them in the city, and slipped past the local zookeepers alerted by Ranger Smith, the friends turned back to help in the search. To avoid capture, Yogi and Boo Boo had joined the ranks of some department-store Santas. Meanwhile, a lonely little rich girl, Judy, sent to shop alone because her millionaire father, Mr. Jones, was too busy to spend Christmas with her, encountered the disguised Yogi, who promised her a fun Christmas. Growing impatient, Mr. Jones ordered store security to find his daughter, and the chase was on as the bears and Judy headed for the nearest park in a runaway snow-mobile. Locating the bears, Yogi's friends realized the little girl had to be taken home and scurried off to find every Jones listed in the phone book, along the way running into more characters, such as Yakky Doodle, Wally Gator, Fred Flintstone and Barney Rubble. Remorseful over his lack of attention to his lost child, Mr. Jones called the police, who issued an all-points bulletin for the three. Soon everyone converged on the park, and Yogi was nearly carted off in a paddywagon before a guilt-ridden Mr. Jones forgave the bears and was happily reunited with Judy and the cast celebrated together singing Christmas carols.

YOGI'S FIRST CHRISTMAS

Broadcast History
Premiere: November 22, 1980
SYN/OPERATION PRIME TIME (KCOP, Los Angeles, Saturday 6:00–8:00 PM PST)
SYN/Repeats: 1981 +
Executive Producers: William Hanna, Joseph Barbera
Producer: Lew Marshall

YOGI'S FIRST CHRISTMAS. © 1980, Hanna-Barbera Productions, Inc.
Courtesy of Worldvision Enterprises.

Director: Ray Patterson
Writer: Willie Gilbert
Music: Hoyt Curtin, Paul DeKorte
Company: Hanna-Barbera Productions/120 minutes
Distributor: Worldvision Enterprises/1985-
Home Video: Worldvision

Narrator: John Stephenson

Principal Characters and Voices

Yogi Bear/Huckleberry Hound/ Augie Doggie/Snagglepuss	Daws Butler
Boo Boo/Ranger Smith/Herman the Hermit	Don Messick
Doggie Daddy/Mr. Dingwell	John Stephenson
Cindy Bear/Mrs. Throckmorton	Janet Waldo
Otto the Chef/Santa Claus	Hal Smith
Snively	Marilyn Schreffler

Yogi's First Christmas related how the genial panhandler and his sidekick Boo Boo were awakened from hibernation to celebrate their first Yuletide and help save Jellystone Lodge. Huckleberry Hound, Snagglepuss, Augie Doggie and Doggie Daddy arrived at the lodge for another holiday of fun only to learn from the manager, Mr. Dingwell, and Chef Otto that the lodge might be sold by the owner, Mrs. Throckmorton, because of a rash of strange occurences last year and a dwindling guest list. Dingwell and Otto determined to change her mind and show her a great time, and their merriment aroused Yogi and Boo Boo from their sleep. While Yogi's friends were happy to see him, Ranger Smith vowed to chase him back to his cave so as not to disturb Mrs. Throckmorton. Boo Boo awakened Cindy Bear so she could enjoy the winter fun; later she added her voice to the harmony of the caroling. By saving Mrs. Throckmorton's car from an avalanche and winning her favor, Yogi and his little friend were made bellhops and exasperated their foes Herman the Hermit, who hated happiness and was responsible for the pranks, and his partner-in-mischief Snively, the owner's conniving nephew. Yogi was promoted successively to ski instructor, chief of security and lodge manager after he foiled Herman's plot to salt the ice rink, out-skated and out-skied nasty little Snively, chased away Herman disguised as an abominable snowman and unmasked the pair posing as Santa and his helper out to ruin the holiday. Yogi brought a tractor-load of foundlings to the lodge for the festivities, and Mrs. Throckmorton announced that she had donated it to the Jellystone Foundation, a year-round vacation place for orphans. Yogi and Boo Boo impersonated Santa and his helper and invited a repentant Herman and Snively to join in the fun. Receiving a big kiss from Yogi Claus, Cindy was presented with a ribbon and crown as "Miss Jellystone Park." Suddenly, the real Santa plummeted down the chimney, thanked an embarrassed Yogi and Boo Boo for their help and distributed gifts. Alas, Yogi fell asleep and with Boo Boo was returned to his cave in a torchlight procession on skis, to slumber peacefully with some great memories awaiting him in spring.

A two-hour made-for-TV animated movie, the film featured characters from some of Hanna-Barbera's series, such as Yogi's Gang (ABC, 1973-1975), described in Children's Television, Part I (Scarecrow, 1983), pp. 315-319. One of the few made-for-TV cartoon superstars, Yogi was starred in the animated feature, Hey There, It's Yogi Bear (COL, 1964/ClubHouse 1986). Three more two-hour, made-for-TV movies also star the popular character, Yogi's Great Escape, Yogi and the Invasion of the Space Bears and Yogi and the Magical Flight of the Spruce Goose, optioned by the FOX network for 1987-1988.

YOU'RE A GOOD MAN, CHARLIE BROWN

Broadcast History
    Premiere: November 6, 1985
    CBS/Wednesday 8:00-9:00 PM

Sponsors: Mars, McDonald's
Producers: Lee Mendelson, Bill Melendez
Associate Producer: Desiree Goyette
Director: Sam Jaimes
Writer/Music & Lyrics: Clark Gesner
Music: Ed Bogas, Desiree Goyette
Company: Lee Mendelson-Bill Melendez Productions in association
   with Charles M. Schulz Creative Associates and United Media/
   60 minutes

Principal Characters and Voices

Charlie Brown	Brad Kesten
	Kevin Brando (singing)
Lucy Van Pelt	Jessie Lee Smith
Linus Van Pelt	David Wagner
Marcie	Michael Dockery (dialogue only)
Schroeder	Jeremy Reinbolt
Sally Brown	Tiffany Reinbolt
Snoopy	Robert Towers

You're a Good Man, Charlie Brown was a cartoon adaptation of Clark
Gesner's 1967 off-Broadway musical based on the Peanuts comic strip,
spotlighting the triumphs and failures of the hapless round-headed
tyke and his Peanutland pals. In spite of their vicissitudes and occasional squabbles, the clan opened their vulnerable little hearts by
telling, in song, what "Happiness" is to each of them. The story
was a veritable celebration of Charlie Brown, whose hopes were
dashed as often as his kite was mangled in that "kite-eating tree,"
life a constant source of frustration and "Good Grief!" his rallying
cry. When his popularity was put on the line in his team's big baseball game, it was no surprise that disaster struck the mound. Losing by one run perhaps the only game the Peanuts ever had a chance
of winning, and believing that everyone disliked him, Charlie's dis-
couragement was tempered when he realized that he was a good man
after all. Lucy softened only briefly, however, and was mainly true
to form, hurling pompous verbal punches indiscriminately at everyone
except Schroeder, whose music-oriented heart she was determined
to win but instead learning a valuable lesson: "Never try to discuss
marriage with a musician." After dancing up a storm in the rousing
"Suppertime," Snoopy also shared his dreams and alternating moods,
from being content with a dog's life that's "not bad, not bad at all"
to feeling now and then that he had "gotta fight someone."
   The Peanuts, each with his or her unique obsessions and in-
securities, formed a reflection of human nature that was both funny
and insightful. Their individual personalities were distinctly drawn
as they approached a homework assignment--a book report on Peter
Rabbit. Schroeder did his on a home computer; Lucy counted every
word as she scribbled her essay, realizing at one point that she had
83 words to go; Linus gave it his philosophical approach, zeroing in
on Peter Rabbit's "sociological pressures"; while Charlie procrastinated
worrying the whole time about "the pressure" it was putting on him.

Songs: "You're a Good Man, Charlie Brown," "Moonlight Sonata," "The Kite," "Snoopy," "The Book Report," "Little Known Facts," "The Baseball Game," "Queen Lucy," "Glee Club Rehearsal," "Suppertime," "Happiness."

Snoopy, the intrepid beagle voiced by Robert Towers, an original member of the Los Angeles production in 1967, talked and sang for the first time on television. Otherwise only juvenile voices were heard in the special, unlike the stage presentations, which used adult actors. Since the original production by Arthur Whitelaw and Gene Persson, with book and music by Clark Gesner and Gary Burghoff as Charlie Brown, it has become one of the most produced musicals of all time with more than 1,800 productions each year in the U.S. alone. The hit song "Happiness" inspired the small book, Happiness Is a Warm Puppy, (Determined Productions, 1962), which became a number one bestseller. In New York City, one evening on December 7, 1969, Charlie Brown simultaneously played before a sellout crowd for the stage show; a sellout audience for the first feature, A Boy Named Charlie Brown (CCF, 1969), at the Radio City Music Hall; and a repeat network TV special, A Charlie Brown Christmas, seen by 55 million other Americans across the country. According to producer Lee Mendelson, "No performer in the history of show business can make that statement." As a Hallmark Hall of Fame presentation, the musical was seen as a 90-minute TV adaptation on NBC (February 9, 1973) with Wendell Burton in the title role. You're a Good Man, Charlie Brown is considered by Charles Schulz as his favorite adaptation of his famed comic strip characters.

YOU'RE A GOOD SPORT, CHARLIE BROWN

Broadcast History
    Premiere: October 28, 1975
    CBS/Tuesday 8:00-8:30 PM
    Sponsors: Peter Paul, Kellogg's
    CBS/Repeat: January 23, 1978
Executive Producer: Lee Mendelson
Producer: Bill Melendez
Director: Phil Roman
Writer/Creator: Charles M. Schulz
Music: Vince Guaraldi, John Scott Trotter
Company: Lee Mendelson-Bill Melendez Productions in association
    with Charles M. Schulz Creative Associates and United Feature
    Syndicate
Record Albums: Disneyland 408 (single); Western Publishing
Home Video: Kartes Video Communications

Principal Characters and Voices

Charlie Brown	Duncan Watson
Linus Van Pelt	Liam Martin
Peppermint Patty	Stuart Brotman
Sally Brown	Gail M. Davis

YOU'RE A GOOD SPORT, CHARLIE BROWN. © 1975, United Feature
Syndicate, Inc. Courtesy of Charles M. Schulz Creative Associates
and United Media.

Marcie   Jimmy Ahrens
Lucy Van Pelt   Melanie Kohn

You're a Good Sport, Charlie Brown showcased Snoopy on the tennis
court, displaying good form, teeth-gritting concentration and very
poor sportsmanship as he trashed his racquet after losing to his opponent, Woodstock. The defeat elicited a squeak or two from the
beagle, even a yip: Snoopy barked for the first time. However,
after Lucy pulled the old football placekick trick, the emphasis was
on a Moto-Cross race. Following an irregular course of obstacles
including jumps, sandbars, rocks, dry riverbeds, mud pits and
whoop-de-dos, the motorcycle competition had Peppermint Patty on
bike #7, Charlie Brown on #13, and the favorite, Snoopy as the
Masked Marvel, on #1. Their pit crews were Franklin, Linus and
Woodstock, respectively. When a wipeout put Charlie and the Masked
Marvel in an ambulance, a foul-up found Snoopy in the hospital reading "Playdog" and Charlie at the vets', temporarily. Rejoining the

event, the Masked Marvel and Charlie were soon back in the race.
At the flag, "Ol' Charlie Brown is first!" Lucy exclaimed, "I think
the world is coming to an end!" Awarded a prize of five haircuts,
Charlie was crushed. "Haircuts? My dad is a barber. And besides,
I don't have much hair to cut!" he muttered. But buoyed by Linus
and winning his first race, Charlie felt he had the winning spirit
at last. Back on the diamond again he proved his real mettle. His
first pitch produced a line drive that knocked him off the mound
and resulted in another in a string of 980 defeats. Television Academy
emy Emmy award (1975-1976), Outstanding Evening Children's Special.

The inspiration for the Moto-Cross sequences came from Charles
Schulz's son Craig, who was into motorcycling at the time.

YOU'RE IN LOVE, CHARLIE BROWN

Broadcast History
Premiere: June 12, 1967
CBS/Monday 8:30-9:00 PM
Sponsor: Coca-Cola
CBS/Repeats: June 10, 1968; June 11, 1969; June 10, 1970; June
7, 1971; June 3, 1972
Producers: Lee Mendelson, Bill Melendez
Director: Bill Melendez
Writer/Creator: Charles M. Schulz
Music: Vince Guaraldi
Company: Lee Mendelson-Bill Melendez Productions in association
with Charles M. Schulz Creative Associates and United Feature
Syndicate
Record Albums: Disneyland 3705 (with book); Disneyland 405
(single); Western Publishing
Home Video: Kartes Video Communications

Principal Characters and Voices
Charlie Brown	Peter Robbins
Linus Van Pelt	Christopher Shea
Lucy Van Pelt	Sally Dryer
Peppermint Patty	Gail DeFaria
Sally Brown	Kathy Steinberg
Schroeder	Glenn Mendelson

You're In Love, Charlie Brown had that old adage, "All the world
loves a lover," going for it, in this case the romantic capers of
lovable loser Charlie Brown. Linus listened to him tell how strange
he had been feeling lately and noted Charlie had a funny look on his
face after watching the cute Little Red-Haired Girl in their class.
Only two school days remained until summer vacation, but Charlie
was miserable. "I know what your trouble is," said Linus, "You're
in love, Charlie Brown!" While Charlie tried the old flower method,
plucking each petal while reciting, "She loves me, she loves me not,"
Linus broke in with another statement that deflated the whole business:

"It is difficult for me to believe that a flower should have the gift
of prophecy!" Too shy to speak to her, in a panic, Charlie tried
note-writing, the John Alden gambit and even psychoanalysis.
"There's nothing like unrequited love to ruin the taste of a peanut
butter sandwich," Chuck said profoundly. Gravel-voiced and tom-
boyish Peppermint Patty, girl baseball player extraordinaire, made
her debut when she tried to solve Chuck's baseball problems and
what she thought was "an affair d'amour" between Charlie and Lucy.
On the last day of school, at the school bus stop, as his classmates
stampeded past him to board, someone tucked a note in his hand:
"I like you, Charlie Brown, signed, Little Red Haired Girl." Charlie
shouted, jumped up, clicked his heels together and jogged in joy
up the hill towards home.

YOU'RE NOT ELECTED, CHARLIE BROWN

Broadcast History
    Premiere: October 29, 1972
    CBS/Sunday 7:30-8:00 PM
    Sponsor: Interstate Brands
    CBS/Repeats: October 15, 1973; September 23, 1976
Producers: Lee Mendelson, Bill Melendez
Director: Bill Melendez
Writer/Creator: Charles M. Schulz
Music: Vince Guaraldi, John Scott Trotter
Company: Lee Mendelson-Bill Melendez Productions in association
    with Charles M. Schulz Creative Associates and United Feature
    Syndicate
Home Video: Hi-Tops Video (nee Media Home Entertainment)

Principal Characters and Voices

Charlie Brown	Chad Webber
Linus Van Pelt	Stephen Shea
Lucy Van Pelt	Robin Kohn
Russell Anderson	Todd Barbee
Sally Brown	Hilary Momberger
Violet	Linda Ercoli
Schroeder	Brian Kazanjian

You're Not Elected, Charlie Brown involved the Peanuts clan in some
polite politics. Mad because her school locker wouldn't open, Sally
inveigled her brother's help--not with the pesky lock as he thought,
but for a "Show and Tell" project in front of her class. "I am showing you my big brother," said Sally, who whispered to Charlie,
"Stand up straight ... don't goof it for me!" After the ordeal,
Charlie muttered to himself, "That has to be the most embarrassing
thing that's ever happened to me in my whole life!" Then Linus
collared him in the hall, announcing to his friends that Charlie Brown
would make a good candidate for president in the forthcoming elections. "No," Lucy said, "I've already taken a poll ... Charlie Brown

could never be elected." The gang's next choice was Linus. So the big campaign was on: Linus Van Pelt running against Russell Anderson, with Linus's platform advocating better lockers, lower drinking fountains and fourth-grade dancing parties. Snoopy and Woodstock made posters, and Lucy booked Linus on a talk show--and did most of the talking herself. At the final assembly, Linus blew it when his mention of the Great Pumpkin was greeted by howls of laughter. "You blockhead!" said Lucy, "... we'll be lucky to get half the votes." And she was right. The final balloting gave each candidate 83 votes--with only Russell remaining to cast a ballot, which he did, for Linus. "I think he would make a better president," Russell explained. But after a meeting with the principal, Linus explained to Sally that he wouldn't be able to do as much as he thought: "The principal still runs the school." "You sold out!" Sally shrieked, "Next time ... we might just as well vote for Charlie Brown!!" Song/ Theme: "Joe Cool" (Guaraldi).

YOU'RE THE GREATEST, CHARLIE BROWN

Broadcast History
    Premiere: March 19, 1979
    CBS/Monday 8:00-8:30 PM
    Sponsors: Interstate Brands, McDonald's
    CBS/Repeats: May 5, 1980; March 20, 1981
Executive Producer: Lee Mendelson
Producer: Bill Melendez
Director: Phil Roman
Writer/Creator: Charles M. Schulz
Music: Ed Bogas, Judy Munsen
Company: Lee Mendelson-Bill Melendez Productions in association
    with Charles M. Schulz Creative Associates and United Feature
    Syndicate
Record Albums: Disneyland 411 (single); Western Publishing
Home Video: Hi-Tops Video (nee Media Home Entertainment)

Principal Characters and Voices

Charlie Brown	Arrin Skelley
Peppermint Patty	Patricia Patts
Marcie	Casey Carlson
Lucy Van Pelt	Michelle Muller
Freddie	Tim Hall
Linus Van Pelt	Daniel Anderson
Snoopy	Bill Melendez

You're the Greatest, Charlie Brown found the little loser dreaming of glory, fantasizing about becoming an athlete like Bruce Jenner, who served as consultant on the production. A member of his school's team in the Junior Olympics and entered in the most gruelling 10-event decathlon, Charlie trained rigorously under the watchful eye of his coach, Peppermint Patty, in hopes of helping his school win the meet. It was a good thing, too, for the games would feature strong competition from Freddie Fabulous, last year's cocky winner; Charlie's own teammate Marcie, a last-minute backup in case he botched it; and the Masked Marvel, a mysterious beagle representing the Ace Obedience School. In the first few events, a dejected Charlie came in last. But then he started to do better and actually won the seventh event. His chances looked good for winning the entire decathlon and hinged on the last event, the 1,500-meter race. "If you win your event," Lucy told him encouragingly, "our school has a good chance of winning the track meet. So don't blow it!" True to form, Charlie did not watch where he was running, ran off the track and lost the race.

ZIGGY'S GIFT

Broadcast History
    Premiere: December 1, 1982
    ABC/Wednesday 8:00-8:30 PM
    ABC/Repeat: December 8, 1983
Executive Producer: Lena Tabori
Producers: Tom Wilson, Richard Williams, Lena Tabori
Director: Richard Williams
Director/Animation: Eric Goldberg
Writer/Creator: Tom Wilson
Music & Lyrics: Harry Nilsson
Music: Perry Botkin
Company: Welcome Productions in association with the Universal
    Press Syndicate
Home Video: Vestron

Principal Characters and Voices
Ziggy   (non-speaking)
Crooked Santa   Richard Williams
Officer O'Connor   Tom McGreevey
Butcher   Tony Giorgio
Fuzz (Ziggy's dog)

Other Voices
    David Arias, Perry Botkin, Katrina Fried, Natasha Fried, John
    Gibbons, Jack Hanrahan, Linda Harmon, Anna Ostblom, Latoya
    Prescod, Gloria Gale Prosper, Andy Raub, Terry Stillwell-Harriton,
    Lena Tabori, Holly Williams, Tim Williams, Tom Wilson, Tom Wilson,
    Jr.

Vocalist: Harry Nilsson

Announcer: John Gibbons

Ziggy's Gift starred an unlucky and bland little guy, completely bald, neck-less and speechless, who only whistled, yawned or called his

ZIGGY'S GIFT. © 1982, Universal Press Syndicate. Courtesy of
Welcome Enterprises, Tom Wilson and Universal Licensing.

dog Fuzz with a kissy whistle. Accompanied by Fuzz, he applied
for work as a streetcorner Santa to collect money for the needy.
An innocent in a commercialized world, overweight and underwhelmed,
Ziggy unsuspectingly went to work for a money-grubbing con artist
operating a fraudulent ring of sidewalk Santas. Soon exposed by
the police, every fake Santa was rounded up except Ziggy, who was
fair game but somehow led a charmed life and was totally oblivious
that he was suspect. Not only was he pursued by a dogged cop
determined to nail "the little guy," but also he was trailed by a
malevolent pickpocket who wanted to pilfer the cash in Ziggy's kettle.
Going about his business doing the good deeds that came naturally
to him, Ziggy liberated a slew of turkeys destined for Christmas-
dinner tables, befriended a stray kitten, saved a scrawny Christmas
tree from destruction and brought holiday cheer to an orphanage.
His showdown with the cop and pickpocket finally took place at the
foster home, where the full meaning of Christmas happily unfolded.
Television Academy Emmy award (1982-1983), Outstanding Animated
Program.

In an ABC-sponsored popularity contest between 100 cartoon
characters, Ziggy reportedly came in fifth, the only one ranking so
high who had not appeared on TV; this result was said to have
prompted the program. Actually, the special was written in the early
1970s and was finally produced when creator Tom Wilson teamed up
with Lena Tabori to form Welcome Enterprises. Ziggy first appeared

in the little book, <u>When You're Not Around</u> (American Greetings, 1968), and by 1970 was established as a daily comic panel distributed by Universal Press Syndicate, seen in more than 300 newspapers and in numerous books.

MOST FREQUENTLY AIRED/LONGEST RUNNING
NETWORK ANIMATED TV SPECIALS
(Through The 1986–1987 Season)

Rudolph, the Red-Nosed Reindeer (22)	NBC 1964-1971
	CBS 1972-
A Charlie Brown Christmas (21)	CBS 1965-
Dr. Seuss' How the Grinch Stole Christmas (20)	CBS 1966-
Frosty the Snowman (18)	CBS 1969-
It's the Great Pumpkin, Charlie Brown (17)	CBS 1966-1971/ 1974/1976/ 1978
'Twas the Night Before Christmas (13)	CBS 1974-
A Christmas Carol (13)	CBS 1970-1983
A Charlie Brown Thanksgiving (12)	CBS 1973-1981/ 1984
Santa Claus Is Comin' to Town (12)	ABC 1970-1981
Dr. Seuss' Horton Hears a Who (9)	CBS 1970-1978
How Bugs Bunny Won the West (9)	CBS 1978-1980/ 1983/ 1984 (2)/ 1985 (2)/ 1987
Here Comes Peter Cottontail (8)	ABC 1971-1972
	CBS 1976-1981

The Little Drummer Boy (8)   NBC 1968-1975

Weep No More, My Lady (8)   ABC 1979 (3)/
                                                1980/
                                                1981 (2)/
                                                1983/1984

Dr. Seuss' The Cat in the Hat (7)   CBS 1971-1976/
                                                1979

Year Without a Santa Claus (7)   ABC 1974-1980

It's the Easter Beagle, Charlie
   Brown (7)   CBS 1974-1979/
                                                1986

Bugs Bunny: All-American Hero (7)   CBS 1981-

TV SPECIALS UTILIZING STOP-MOTION ANIMATED PUPPETS
(23 Programs Through The 1986-1987 Season)

Ballad of Smokey the Bear, The

Christmas Lost and Found

Easter Bunny Is Comin' to Town, The

Emperor's New Clothes, The

First Christmas, The

Halloween Who-Dun-It?

Happy Easter

Here Comes Peter Cottontail

Jack Frost

Leprechaun's Christmas Gold, The

Life and Adventures of Santa Claus, The

Little Drummer Boy, The

Little Drummer Boy, Book II, The

Nestor, the Long-Eared Christmas Donkey

New Year Promise

Pinocchio's Christmas

Rudolph and Frosty

Rudolph, the Red-Nosed Reindeer

Rudolph's Shiny New Year

Santa Claus Is Comin' to Town

School ... Who Needs It?

To the Rescue

Year Without a Santa Claus

HOLIDAY AND TOPICAL ANIMATED TV SPECIALS

HOLIDAY SPECIALS

Arbor Day

It's Arbor Day, Charlie Brown

Christmas

B.C.: A Special Christmas
Babar and Father Christmas
Bear Who Slept Through Christmas, The
Berenstain Bears' Christmas Tree, The
Bugs Bunny's Looney Christmas Tales
Cabbage Patch Kids' First Christmas, The
Casper's First Christmas
Charlie Brown Christmas, A
Chipmunk Christmas, A
Christmas Carol, A (3 versions)
Christmas Comes to Pac-Land
Christmas Every Day
Christmas Is
Christmas Lost and Found
Christmas Messenger, The
Christmas Raccoons, The
Christmas Story, A
Christmas Tree, A
Christmas Tree Train, The
City That Forgot About Christmas, The
Cosmic Christmas, A
Cricket on the Hearth, The
Deck the Halls with Wacky Walls
Disney Christmas Gift, A
Dr. Seuss' How the Grinch Stole Christmas
Family Circus Christmas, A
Fat Albert Christmas Special, The

Christmas (cont.)

First Christmas, The
Flintstone Christmas, A
For Better or For Worse: The Bestest Present
Fourth King, The
Frosty the Snowman
Frosty's Winter Wonderland
GLO Friends Save Christmas, The
Great Christmas Race, The
He-Man and She-Ra--A Christmas Special
Leprechaun's Christmas Gold, The
Life and Adventures of Santa Claus, The
Little Brown Burro, The
Little Drummer Boy, The
Little Drummer Boy, Book II, The
Little Rascals Christmas Special, The
Merry Mirthworm Christmas, A
Mickey's Christmas Carol
Mr. Magoo's Christmas Carol
Nestor, the Long-Eared Christmas Donkey
Night Before Christmas, The
Night the Animals Talked, The
Nutcracker, The
Pink Panther in "A Pink Christmas"
Pinocchio's Christmas
Raggedy Ann and Andy in "The Great Santa Claus Caper"
Rudolph and Frosty
Rudolph, the Red-Nosed Reindeer
Santa and the Three Bears
Santa Claus Is Comin' to Town
SantaBear's First Christmas
Silent Night
Simple Gifts, The
Smurfs' Christmas Special, The
Snow White Christmas, A
Snowman, The
Star for Jeremy, A
Stingiest Man in Town, The
Tin Soldier, The
Tiny Tree, The
Trolls and the Christmas Express, The
Tukiki and His Search for a Merry Christmas
'Twas the Night Before Christmas
Velveteen Rabbit, The (3 versions)
Very Merry Cricket, A
Year Without a Santa Claus
Yes, Virginia, There Is a Santa Claus
Yogi Bear's All-Star Comedy Christmas Caper
Yogi's First Christmas
Ziggy's Gift

Easter

Berenstain Bears' Easter Surprise, The
Bugs Bunny Easter Special, The
Chucklewood Easter, A
Daffy Duck's Easter Show
Easter Bunny Is Comin' to Town, The
Easter Fever
Easter Is
Family Circus Easter, A
Fat Albert Easter Special, The
First Easter Rabbit, The
Happy Easter
Here Comes Peter Cottontail
It's a Brand New World
It's the Easter Beagle, Charlie Brown
Peter and the Magic Egg

Fourth of July

Freedom Is
Liberty and the Littles
Spirit of '76, The
Uncle Sam Magoo
Yankee Doodle
Yankee Doodle Cricket

Halloween

Adventures of the Scrabble People in "A Pumpkin Full of Nonsense,"
    The
Bugs Bunny Howl-O-Ween Special, The
Casper's Halloween
Disney's Halloween Treat
Dr. Seuss' Halloween Is Grinch Night
Garfield's Halloween Adventure
Great Bear Scare, The
Halloween Who-Dun-It?
It's the Great Pumpkin, Charlie Brown
Jack O'Lantern
New Misadventures of Ichabod Crane, The
Pac-Man Halloween Special, The
Raggedy Ann and Andy in "The Pumpkin Who Couldn't Smile"
Which Witch Is Which?
Witch's Night Out

Memorial Day

What Have We Learned, Charlie Brown?

Mother's Day

Bugs Bunny Mother's Day Special, The
Dennis the Menace: Mayday for Mother
Disney's All-Star Mother's Day Album

New Year's

Happy New Year, Charlie Brown
New Year Promise
Rudolph's Shiny New Year

Thanksgiving

B.C.: The First Thanksgiving
Bugs Bunny Thanksgiving Diet, The
Charlie Brown Thanksgiving, A
Daffy Duck's Thanks-for-giving Special
Intergalactic Thanksgiving
Mouse on the Mayflower, The
Thanksgiving in the Land of Oz (aka Dorothy in the Land of Oz)
Thanksgiving That Almost Wasn't, The
Turkey Caper, The

Valentine's Day

Be My Valentine, Charlie Brown
Berenstain Bears' Valentine Special, The
Bugs Bunny's Valentine Special
Disney's All-Star Valentine Party
Disney's D-TV "Doggone" Valentine
Disney's D-TV Valentine
I Love the Chipmunks, Valentine Special
My Smurfy Valentine
Pink Panther in "Pink at First Sight"
Popeye Valentine Special, The
Romie-0 and Julie-8
Special Valentine with the Family Circus, A

TOPICAL SPECIALS

Anniversaries

Bugs Bunny/Looney Tunes All-Star 50th Anniversary Special (aka
    The Bugs Bunny/Looney Tunes Jubilee)
Donald Duck's 50th Birthday

Anniversaries (cont.)

Flintstones' 25th Anniversary Celebration, The
Happy Anniversary, Charlie Brown
Happy Birthday, Charlie Brown
Happy Birthday, Donald Duck
It's Your 20th Television Anniversary, Charlie Brown
This Is Your Life, Donald Duck

Anthologies

Charlie Brown Celebration, A
Fabulous Shorts, The
It's An Adventure, Charlie Brown
Jean Marsh Cartoon Special, The
Simple Gifts, The

Baseball

Berenstain Bears' Littlest Leaguer, The
Charlie Brown's All-Stars
Flintstones' Little Big League, The
Flintstones: Windup Wilma, The
Horse That Played Centerfield, The
Take Me Up to the Ballgame
Willie Mays and the Say-Hey Kid

Biblical

It's a Brand New World
Kingdom Chums: Little David's Adventure, The
Noah's Animals

Biology/Human Development

All About Me
Everybody Rides the Carousel
Incredible, Indelible, Magical, Physical Mystery Trip, The
Magical Mystery Trip Through Little Red's Head, The

Olympic Games

Animalympics: Winter Games
Pink Panther in "Olympinks"
Smurfic Games, The
Walt Disney Presents Sport Goofy's Olympic Games Special

Springtime

Bugs Bunny's Bustin' Out All Over
Smurf Springtime Special, The

Wildlife Preservation

Bollo Caper, The
Last of the Curlews
No Man's Valley
White Seal, The

Women's Rights

Blondie & Dagwood
Cathy
Flintstones: Windup Wilma, The
Romance of Betty Boop, The

ANIMATED TV SPECIALS SERIES
(Original Air Date or Year)

ABC AFTERSCHOOL SPECIALS

Last of the Curlews	10/4/72
The Incredible, Indelible, Magical,	
Physical Mystery Trip	2/7/73
Cyrano	3/6/74
The Magical Mystery Trip	
Through Little Red's Head	5/15/74

ABC WEEKEND SPECIALS

The Incredible, Indelible, Magical,	
Physical Mystery Trip (repeat)	3/4/78
The Magical Mystery Trip	
Through Little Red's Head	
(repeat)	4/29/78
The Puppy Who Wanted a Boy	5/6/78
The Puppy's Great Adventure	2/3/79
Weep No More, My Lady	2/10/79
The Horse That Played Center-	
field	2/24 & 3/3/79
The Incredible Detectives	11/7/79
The Puppy's Amazing Rescue	1/26/80
The Trouble With Miss Switch	2/16 & 2/23/80
Scruffy	10/4, 10/11 & 10/18/80
The Puppy Saves the Circus	9/12/81
Miss Switch to the Rescue	1/16 & 1/23/82
Stanley, the Ugly Duckling	
(repeat)	5/1/82
The Secret World of OG	4/30, 5/7 & 5/14/83
The Amazing Bunjee Venture	3/24 & 3/31/84
Bad Cat	4/14/84
The Bollo Caper	2/2/85
The Return of Bunjee	4/6 & 4/13/85
The Velveteen Rabbit	4/20/85

Liberty and the Littles   10/18 & 10/25, 11/1/86
SantaBear's First Christmas   11/22/86

THE ARCHIES (CBS)

Archie and His New Friends   9/14/69
The Archie, Sugar Sugar, Jingle
    Jangle Show   3/22/70

B.C.

B.C.:   A Special Christmas   SYN c1971
B.C.:   The First Thanksgiving   NBC 11/19/73

BABAR

The Story of Babar, the Little
    Elephant   NBC 10/21/68
Babar Comes to America   NBC 9/7/71
Babar and Father Christmas   HBO 12/5/86

BENJI AND WALDO (International
    Lutheran Layman's League)

Christmas Is   SYN 11/7/70
Easter Is   SYN 1974
The City That Forgot About
    Christmas   SYN 1974
Freedom Is   SYN 1976

BERENSTAIN BEARS (NBC)

The Berenstain Bears' Christmas
    Tree   12/3/79
The Berenstain Bears Meet
    Pig Paw   11/20/80
The Berenstain Bears' Easter
    Surprise   4/14/81
The Berenstain Bears' Valentine
    Special   2/13/82
The Berenstain Bears' Littlest
    Leaguer   5/6/83

THE BLINKINS (SYN)

The Blinkins   Spring 1986

The Blinkins and the Bear .... September 1986
The Blinkins and the Blizzard .... Christmas 1986

BUGS BUNNY (CBS)

Carnival of the Animals 11/22/76
The Bugs Bunny Easter Special 4/7/77
Bugs Bunny in Space 9/6/77
The Bugs Bunny Howl-O-Ween
   Special 10/26/77
A Connecticut Rabbit in King
   Arthur's Court 2/23/78
How Bugs Bunny Won the West 11/15/78
The Bugs Bunny Valentine Special 2/14/79
The Bugs Bunny Mother's Day
   Special 5/12/79
Bugs Bunny's Thanksgiving Diet 11/15/79
Bugs Bunny's Looney Christmas
   Tales 11/27/79
Bugs Bunny's Bustin' Out All
   Over 5/21/80
The Bugs Bunny Mystery Special 10/15/80
Bugs Bunny: All-American Hero 5/4/81
Bugs Bunny's Mad World of TV 1/11/81
Bugs Bunny/Looney Tunes All-
   Star 50th Anniversary
   Special 1/14/86

BUNJEE (ABC Weekend Specials)

The Amazing Bunjee Venture .... 3/24 & 3/31/84
The Return of Bunjee .... 4/6 & 4/13/85

CBS LIBRARY SPECIALS

The Incredible Book Escape 6/3/80
Misunderstood Monsters 4/7/81
A Tale of Four Wishes 11/8/81

CAP'N O. G. READMORE (ABC
Weekend Specials)

Cap'n O. G. Readmore's Jack and
   the Beanstalk 10/12/85
Cap'n O. G. Readmore's Dr.
   Jekyll and Mr. Hyde 9/13/86

CARE BEARS (SYN)

The Care Bears in the Land Without Feelings	Spring 1983
The Care Bears Battle the Freeze Machine	Spring 1984

CASPER, THE FRIENDLY GHOST (NBC)

Casper's Halloween	10/30/79
Casper's First Christmas	12/18/79

CHARLES DICKENS CLASSICS (SYN)

A Christmas Carol	SYN 1984
David Copperfield	SYN 1984
Great Expectations	SYN 1984
Nicholas Nickleby	SYN 1984
The Old Curiosity Shop	SYN 1984
Oliver Twist	SYN 1984
A Tale of Two Cities	SYN 1984

CHARLIE BROWN/PEANUTS (CBS)

A Charlie Brown Christmas	12/9/65
Charlie Brown's All Stars	6/8/66
It's the Great Pumpkin, Charlie Brown	10/27/66
He's Your Dog, Charlie Brown	2/14/68
It Was a Short Summer, Charlie Brown	9/27/69
Play It Again, Charlie Brown	3/28/71
You're Not Elected, Charlie Brown	10/29/72
There's No Time for Love, Charlie Brown	3/11/73
A Charlie Brown Thanksgiving	11/20/73
It's a Mystery, Charlie Brown	2/1/74
It's the Easter Beagle, Charlie Brown	4/9/74
Be My Valentine, Charlie Brown	1/28/75
You're a Good Sport, Charlie Brown	10/28/75
Happy Anniversary, Charlie Brown	1/9/76
It's Arbor Day, Charlie Brown	3/16/76

It's Your First Kiss, Charlie Brown	10/24/77
What a Nightmare, Charlie Brown	2/23/78
Happy Birthday, Charlie Brown	1/5/79
You're the Greatest, Charlie Brown	3/19/79
She's a Good Skate, Charlie Brown	2/25/80
Life Is a Circus, Charlie Brown	10/24/80
It's Magic, Charlie Brown	4/28/81
Someday You'll Find Her, Charlie Brown	10/30/81
A Charlie Brown Celebration	5/24/82
Is This Goodbye, Charlie Brown?	2/21/83
It's an Adventure, Charlie Brown	5/16/83
What Have We Learned, Charlie Brown?	5/30/83
It's Flashbeagle, Charlie Brown	4/16/84
Snoopy's Getting Married, Charlie Brown	3/20/85
It's Your 20th Television Anniversary, Charlie Brown	5/14/85
You're a Good Man, Charlie Brown	11/6/85
Happy New Year, Charlie Brown	1/1/86

CHIPMUNKS (NBC)

A Chipmunk Christmas	12/14/81
I Love the Chipmunks, Valentine Special	2/12/84
A Chipmunk Reunion	4/13/85

CHESTER CRICKET (ABC)

The Cricket in Times Square	4/24/73
A Very Merry Cricket	12/14/73
Yankee Doodle Cricket	1/16/75

DAFFY DUCK (NBC)

Daffy Duck's Easter Show	4/1/80
Daffy Duck's Thanks-for-giving Special	11/20/80

DAVEY AND GOLIATH (SYN)
(Lutheran Church in America)

Christmas Lost and Found	SYN 1965

Happy Easter	SYN 1967
New Year Promise	SYN 1967
School ... Who Needs It?	SYN 1971
To The Rescue	SYN 1975
Halloween Who-Dun-It?	SYN 1977

DISNEY HOLIDAY SPECIALS

One Hour in Wonderland (Intro- duction)	NBC 12/25/50
The Walt Disney Christmas Show (Introduction)	CBS 12/25/51
Disney's Halloween Treat	CBS 10/30/82
A Disney Christmas Gift	CBS 12/20/83
Disney's All-Star Valentine's Party	CBS 2/14/84
Disney's All-Star Mother's Day Album	CBS 5/9/84
Mickey's Christmas Carol	NBC 12/10/84
Disney's DTV Valentine	NBC 2/14/86
Disney's DTV "Doggone" Valentine	NBC 2/13/87

DR. SEUSS

Dr. Seuss' How the Grinch Stole Christmas	CBS 12/18/66
Dr. Seuss' Horton Hears a Who	CBS 3/19/70
Dr. Seuss' The Cat in the Hat	CBS 3/10/71
Dr. Seuss' The Lorax	CBS 2/14/72
Dr. Seuss On The Loose	CBS 10/15/73
Dr. Seuss' The Hoober-Bloob Highway	CBS 2/19/75
Dr. Seuss' Halloween Is Grinch Night	ABC 10/29/77
Dr. Seuss' Pontoffel Pock, Where Are You?	ABC 5/2/80
Dr. Seuss' The Grinch Grinches the Cat in the Hat	ABC 5/20/82

DONALD DUCK

Happy Birthday, Donald Duck	NBC 4/4/79
This Is Your Life, Donald Duck	NBC 2/22/80
Donald Duck's 50th Birthday	CBS 11/13/84
Down and Out With Donald Duck	NBC 3/25/87

FAMILY CIRCUS (NBC)

A Special Valentine with the Family Circus	2/10/78
A Family Circus Christmas	12/18/79
A Family Circus Easter	4/8/82

FAMILY CLASSICS (SYN)

Alice in Wonderland	SYN 1972
The Arabian Nights	SYN 1972
Around the World in 80 Days	SYN 1972
The Ballad of Paul Bunyan	SYN 1972
A Christmas Tree	SYN 1972
Cinderella	SYN 1972
Hiawatha	SYN 1972
Jack O'Lantern	SYN 1972
Johnny Appleseed	SYN 1972
Puss-In-Boots	SYN 1972
Robin Hood	SYN 1972
Robinson Crusoe	SYN 1972
Sleeping Beauty	SYN 1972
Snow White	SYN 1972
The Swiss Family Robinson	SYN 1972
Tom Sawyer	SYN 1972
20,000 Leagues Under the Sea	SYN 1972
Yankee Doodle	SYN 1972

FAMOUS CLASSIC TALES (CBS)
ANIMATED CLASSICS FOR
CHILDREN (SYN, 1983)

Tales of Washington Irving	11/1/70
A Connecticut Yankee in King Arthur's Court	11/26/70
A Christmas Carol	12/13/70
The Legend of Robin Hood	11/14/71
Treasure Island	11/28/71
Robinson Crusoe	11/23/72
The Prince and the Pauper	11/26/72
The Count of Monte Cristo	9/23/73
Kidnapped	10/22/73
The Swiss Family Robinson	10/28/73
20,000 Leagues Under the Sea	11/22/73
The Three Musketeers	11/23/73
The Black Arrow	12/2/73
Mysterious Island	11/15/75
Ivanhoe	11/27/75
The Last of the Mohicans	11/27/75

Master of the World	10/23/76
Davy Crockett on the Mississippi	11/20/76
Journey to the Center of the Earth	11/13/77
Five Weeks in a Balloon	11/24/77
Black Beauty	10/28/78
Gulliver's Travels	11/18/79
The Adventures of Sinbad	11/23/79
Daniel Boone	11/27/81

FAMOUS CLASSIC TALES (SYN)
ANIMATED CLASSICS FOR
CHILDREN (SYN , 1983)

Marco Polo (aka The Travels of Marco Polo)	SYN 1972
Moby Dick	SYN c1975
From the Earth to the Moon	SYN c1976
Off On a Comet	SYN c1976

FAT ALBERT

Hey, Hey, Hey, It's Fat Albert	NBC 11/12/69
Weird Harold	NBC 5/4/73
The Fat Albert Halloween Special	CBS 10/24/77
The Fat Albert Christmas Special	CBS 12/18/77
The Fat Albert Easter Special	CBS 4/3/82

THE FLINTSTONES (NBC)

A Flintstone Christmas	12/7/77
The Flintstones' Little Big League	4/6/78
The Flintstones' New Neighbors	9/25/80
The Flintstones Meet Rockula and Frankenstone	10/3/80
The Flintstones: Windup Wilma	10/4/81
The Flintstones: Jogging Fever	10/11/81
The Flintstones: Fred's Final Fling	10/18/81
The Flintstones' 25th Anniversary Celebration	5/20/86

FLIP WILSON (NBC)

Clerow Wilson and the Miracle of P.S. 14	11/12/72
Clerow Wilson's Great Escape	4/3/74

FROSTY THE SNOWMAN

Frosty the Snowman	CBS 12/7/69
Frosty's Winter Wonderland	ABC 12/2/76
Rudolph and Frosty	ABC 11/25/79

GARFIELD (CBS)

Here Comes Garfield	10/25/82
Garfield on the Town	10/28/83
Garfield in the Rough	10/26/84
Garfield's Halloween Adventure	10/30/85
Garfield in Paradise	5/27/86
Garfield Goes Hollywood	5/8/87

THE HOBBIT

The Hobbit	NBC 11/27/77
The Return of the King	ABC 5/11/80

THE JUNGLE BOOK (CBS)

Rikki-tiki-tavi	1/9/75
Mowgli's Brothers	2/11/75
The White Seal	3/24/75

KENNER FAMILY CLASSICS (CBS)

Black Beauty (repeat)	11/6/83
The Legend of Hiawatha	11/24/83
Beauty and the Beast	11/25/83
The Adventures of Huckleberry Finn	11/23/84

KISSYFUR (NBC)

Kissyfur: Bear Roots	12/22/85
Kissyfur: The Birds and the Bees	3/30/86
Kissyfur: The Lady Is a Chump	6/1/86
Kissyfur: We Are the Swamps	7/6/86

LBS CHILDREN"S THEATRE (SYN)

The Adventures of Energy	SYN 1973-1975

Alice in Wonderland	SYN 1973-1975
B.C.: The First Thanksgiving	SYN 1973-1975
The Christmas Messenger	SYN 1973-1975
Curious George	SYN 1973-1975
The Happy Prince	SYN 1973-1975
The Little Mermaid	SYN 1973-1975
Mowgli's Brothers	SYN 1973-1975
The Notorious Jumping Frog of Calaveras County	SYN 1973-1975
The Nutcracker	SYN 1973-1975
Really Rosie	SYN 1973-1975
The Remarkable Rocket	SYN 1973-1975
Rikki-tikki-tavi	SYN 1973-1975
The Selfish Giant	SYN 1973-1975
The Snow Queen	SYN 1973-1975
The Sorcerer's Apprentice	SYN 1973-1975
The Spirit of '76	SYN 1973-1975
A Star for Jeremy	SYN 1973-1975
The Talking Parcel	SYN 1973-1975
The White Seal	SYN 1973-1975

THE LITTLE DRUMMER BOY (NBC)

The Little Drummer Boy	12/19/68
The Little Drummer Boy, Book II	12/13/76

THE LOLLIPOP DRAGON (SYN)

The Great Christmas Race	SYN 1986
The Magic Lollipop Adventure	SYN 1986

MICKEY MOUSE (NBC)

On Vacation with Mickey Mouse and Friends	4/11/79
Mickey's Christmas Carol	12/10/84

THE MIRTHWORMS

A Merry Mirthworm Christmas	SHO 1984
A Mirthworm Masquerade	SYN 1987

MISS SWITCH (ABC Weekend Specials)

The Trouble With Miss Switch	2/16 & 2/23/80
Miss Switch to the Rescue	1/16 & 1/23/82

MR. MAGOO

Mr. Magoo's Christmas Carol	NBC 12/18/62
Mr. Magoo's Treasure Island	CBS 10/12/67
Uncle Sam Magoo	NBC 2/15/70
Mr. Magoo's Storybook Snow White	CBS 11/26/70

MY LITTLE PONY (SYN)

My Little Pony	SYN 4/84
My Little Pony II--Escape from Catrina	SYN 4/85

NBC SPECIAL TREAT

It's A Brand New World	3/8/77
Treasure Island	4/29/80
Oliver Twist	4/14/81
The Legend of Hiawatha (repeat)	12/4/84

NOAH'S ANIMALS

Noah's Animals	ABC 4/5/76
King of the Beasts	NBC 4/9/77
The Last of the Red-Hot Dragons	NBC 4/1/80

PAC-MAN (ABC)

The Pac-Man Halloween Special	10/30/82
Christmas Comes to Pac-Land	12/16/82

PEANUTS see CHARLIE BROWN/PEANUTS

PINK PANTHER (ABC)

A Pink Panther Christmas	12/7/78
Pink Panther in "Olympinks"	2/22/80
Pink Panther in "Pink at First Sight"	5/10/81

POPEYE (CBS)

The Popeye Show	9/13/78
The Popeye Valentine Special	2/14/79

PUFF, THE MAGIC DRAGON (CBS)

Puff, the Magic Dragon	10/30/78
Puff, the Magic Dragon in "The Land of Living Lies"	11/17/79
Puff and the Incredible Mr. Nobody	5/17/82

THE PUPPY (ABC Weekend Specials)

The Puppy Who Wanted a Boy	5/6/78
The Puppy's Great Adventure	2/3/79
The Puppy's Amazing Rescue	1/26/80
The Puppy Saves the Circus	9/12/81

THE RACCOONS

The Christmas Raccoons	SYN 12/3/80
The Raccoons on Ice	CBC 12/20/81
The Raccoons and the Lost Star	SYN 12/1/83

RAGGEDY ANN AND ANDY (CBS)

Raggedy Ann and Andy in "The Great Santa Claus Caper"	CBS 11/30/78
Raggedy Ann and Andy in "The Pumpkin Who Couldn't Smile"	CBS 10/31/79

RAINBOW BRITE (SYN)

Rainbow Brite: Peril in the Pits	SYN 6/84
Rainbow Brite: The Mighty Monstromurk Menace	SYN 12/84
Rainbow Brite: The Beginning of Rainbow Land	SYN 4/85

THE READER'S DIGEST PRESENTATIONS

The Selfish Giant	CBS 3/28/73
The Little Mermaid	CBS 2/4/74
The Remarkable Rocket	SYN 1974
The Christmas Messenger	SYN 1975
The Happy Prince	SYN 1975

ROSE-PETAL PLACE (SYN)

Rose-Petal Place	SYN 5/84
Rose-Petal Place II: "Real Friends"	SYN 4/85

RUDOLPH, THE RED-NOSED REINDEER

Rudolph, the Red-Nosed Reindeer	NBC 12/6/64
Rudolph's Shiny New Year	ABC 12/10/76
Rudolph and Frosty	ABC 11/25/79

RUSTY AND BUTTONS (SYN)

The Christmas Tree Train	SYN 1983
Which Witch Is Which?	SYN 1984
The Turkey Caper	SYN 1985
A Chucklewood Easter	SYN 1987

THE SMURFS (NBC)

The Smurfs	11/29/81
The Smurf Springtime Special	4/8/82
The Smurfs' Christmas Special	12/13/82
My Smurfy Valentine	2/13/83
The Smurfic Games	5/20/84
Smurfily Ever After	2/13/85

SPORT GOOFY

Sport Goofy (I)	SYN 5/21/83
Sport Goofy (II)	SYN 8/21/83
Sport Goofy (III)	SYN 11/6/83
Walt Disney Presents Sport Goofy's Olympic Games Special	SYN 6/2/84
Walt Disney's Mickey, Donald and Sport Goofy Show: "Getting Wet"	SYN 9/7/84
Walt Disney's Mickey, Donald and Sport Goofy Show: "Snowtime"	SYN 11/17/84
Walt Disney's Mickey, Donald and Sport Goofy Show: "Happy Holidays"	SYN 12/1/84
An All New Adventure of Disney's Sport Goofy,	NBC 5/27/87

STRAWBERRY SHORTCAKE (SYN)

The World of Strawberry Shortcake	SYN 3/80
Strawberry Shortcake in Big Apple City	SYN 4/81
Strawberry Shortcake: Pets on Parade	SYN 4/82
Strawberry Shortcake's House-warming Surprise	SYN 4/83
Strawberry Shortcake and the Baby Without a Name	SYN 3/84
Strawberry Shortcake Meets the Berrykins	SYN 4/85

TED E. BEAR

The Bear Who Slept Through Christmas	NBC 12/17/73
The Great Bear Scare	SYN 10/82

TELEPICTURES ANIMATED HOLIDAY SPECIALS (SYN)

The Coneheads	SYN 1985-1987
The Easter Bunny Is Comin' to Town	SYN 1985-1987
The First Christmas	SYN 1985-1987
The First Easter Rabbit	SYN 1985-1987
Frosty's Winter Wonderland	SYN 1985-1987
The Hobbit	SYN 1985-1987
Jack Frost	SYN 1985-1987
King of the Beasts	SYN 1985-1987
The Last of the Red-Hot Dragons	SYN 1985-1987
The Leprechaun's Christmas Gold	SYN 1985-1987
The Little Drummer Boy, Book II	SYN 1985-1987
Nestor, the Long-Eared Christmas Donkey	SYN 1985-1987
Noah's Animals	SYN 1985-1987
Pinocchio's Christmas	SYN 1985-1987
The Return of the King	SYN 1985-1987
Rudolph's Shiny New Year	SYN 1985-1987
The Stingiest Man in Town	SYN 1985-1987
Witch's Night Out	SYN 1985-1987
Year Without a Santa Claus	SYN 1985-1987

WINNIE THE POOH

Winnie the Pooh and the Honey Tree	NBC 3/10/70

Winnie the Pooh and the Blustery Day	NBC 11/30/70
Winnie the Pooh and Tigger Too	NBC 11/28/75
Winnie the Pooh and a Day for Eeyore	DIS 5/6/86

YOGI BEAR

Yogi's First Christmas	SYN 11/22/80
Yogi Bear's All-Star Comedy Christmas Caper	CBS 12/21/82

(1) PRODUCERS, DIRECTORS, FILMMAKERS

* = Live Action
# = Stage/Other

508

NAME INDEX

(3) MUSICIANS AND LYRICISTS

* = Musical Group/Soloist
\# = Vocalists/Singers

Gleeson, Patrick 179
Glombecki, Gerry 140
Goffin, Louise #334
Goffin, Sherry #334
Gonyea, Dale 11, 390, 391, 441, 442
Goodman, Tommy 73, 174, 279, 282
Goodwin, Doug 28, 176, 301, 303, 358
Goodwin, Ron 190, 257, 368
Gouldman, Graham 14
Goyette, Desiree 167, #167, 168, #168, 169, #169, 170, #170, #171, 172, 189, 193, #194, 212, 215, #215, #216, 221, 289, #290, 345, #345, 468
Gregor, Wiley 232, 241, 290
Griffith, Andy #166
Gruber, Franz 370, *370
Guaraldi, Vince xvii, 27, 68, 70, 72, 185, 196, 210, 211, 214, 217, 219, 221, 222, 306, 414, 444, 445, 469, 471, 472, 473, *473

Hague, Albert 121
Hahn, Lewis 388
Hall, John see John Hall Band
Hamner, Earl 7
Hancock, Herbie 197
Hanna, William 98
Harburg, E. Y. (Yip) 389
Hardy, Hagood 58, 387, 425, 427
Harman, Barry 73, 174, 279, 282
Harris, Hilda #211
Harris, John 357, 437
Hart, Bobby 35, 37, 38
Haskell, Jimmy 65, 81, 89, 134, 163
Hayton, Lenny 223
Hedges, Michael 361
Hemric, Guy 134
Herb Alpert and the Tijuana Brass *137
Himmel, Roger 178, 262
Hinchey, Don 163
Hoffer, Bernard 93, 131, 248, 370, 396, 417, 419
Holmes, Rupert #84
Holtzman, Gini #215
Houston, John #200
Houston, Whitney #117
Hubley, Faith 112
Hubley, John 112
Huey Lewis & The News *117
Huge, Thom #167, #168, #169, #170

Iceberg, Michael *93

Isaacs, Mark 408
Ives, Burl #416, #355, #385

Jermyn, Peter 5
John, Elton #117
John Hall Band *208
Jones, Quincy 112
Jones, Ron 159

Kaff, T. #76
Kaye, Danny #135, #196
Kaylan, Howard 299, 399, 402, 458
Keith, Bill #403
Kelly, Gene #224
Kelly, Walt 307
Kemner, Randy #85
Kern, Jerome 328
Kesten, Brad #215
Kinder, Ford 279
King, Carole 333, 334, #334
Kostal, Irwin 266
Kuramoto, Don 92

Lava, Bill 42, 43, 47, 49, 50, 202
Lawrence, Amy 108
Lawrence, Elliot 29, 30, 31, 32, 33, 108, 162
Lawrence, Stephen 412
Laws, Maury 9, 15, 17, 23, 86, 89, 101, 131, 135, 145, 146, 150, 164, 165, 194, 198, 199, 225, 226, 228, 231, 244, 255, 260, 276, 284, 305, 323, 335, 337, 341, 343, 352, 353, 356, 360, 373, 382, 404, 414, 422, 429, 431, 449, 450, 460, 461
Lazarone, Ben 398
Leahy, Joe 358
Leary, Dawnn S. #380
Lee, Bill #21
Lee, Diana #288, #396
Leonhart, Helen #73
Levinson, Phyllis 175
Levy, Shuki 192, 235, 236, 237, 245, 309, 329, 330, 332
Lewis, Huey (see also Huey Lewis & The News) *116, #116
Lewis, Michael J. 252
Liebhart, Janis 227
Lipton, Leonard 318
Livingston, Jay 139
Lobos, Ada 6
Loomis, Merry 398

(4) VOICES

* = Narrator/Announcer
# = Host-Hostess/Guest Star/Cast/Other

519

SELECTED SUBJECT INDEX

(1) STUDIOS AND PRODUCTION COMPANIES

* = Creative/R&D Company
\# = Associate

534